LABOR MIGRATION
IN THE
ATLANTIC
ECONOMIES

Recent Titles in
Contributions in Labor History

LABOR MIGRATION IN THE ATLANTIC ECONOMIES

The European and
North American Working
Classes During the
Period of Industrialization

Edited by DIRK HOERDER

Contributions in Labor History, Number 16

Greenwood Press
Westport, Connecticut • London, England

Library of Congress Cataloging in Publication Data

Main entry under title:

Labor migration in the Atlantic economies.

(Contributions in labor history, ISSN 0146-3608 ; no. 16)
Bibliography: p.
Includes index.
1. Labor and laboring classes—Europe—History—19th
century.   2. Migration, Internal—Europe—History—
19th century.   3. Alien labor—United States—History
—19th century.   4. Labor and laboring classes—
United States—History—19th century.   I. Hoerder, Dirk.   II. Series.
HD8375.L33 1985   331.12'7   85-7975
ISBN 0-313-24637-8 (lib. bdg. : alk. paper)

Library of Congress Catalog Card Number: 85-7975
ISBN: 0-313-24637-8
ISSN: 0146-3608

First published in 1985

Greenwood Press
A division of Congressional Information Service, Inc.
88 Post Road West
Westport, Connecticut 06881

Printed in the United States of America

10 9 8 7 6 5 4 3 2 1

CONTENTS

Part II

Part III

FIGURES AND TABLES

FIGURES

TABLES

PREFACE

"To Bread!" was the cry of Polish migrants. Money wages, jobs, land, reunions with relatives—manifold were the goals of other newcomers. Propagandists summarized their numerous motivations by transforming them into one geographic move: "to America." For decades most historians and governmental commissions have followed this extreme simplification and talked about one single phenomenon: "immigration." Old and new immigrants were easily identified by their "race," according to the Dillingham Commission. All of this is wrong as we have learnt in the last two decades from the revival of ethnicity and a large body of sophisticated scholarship. Now it is time to consolidate the specialized studies into a survey of migratory movements and a new frame of reference.

This anthology is a step in that direction, but more remains to be done. The task is easily outlined: The migrations of the century between the end of the Napoleonic Wars and the beginning of World War I have to be related to earlier and subsequent movements of people. Migration of settlers has to be analytically differentiated from that of workers. The geographical complexity of the movements has to be taken into account, especially in the case of intra-European migration, which was much larger than the trans-Atlantic movement. In addition to this the high rate of return migration to the cultures of origin must be considered. Economically speaking, the nation states and empires of the regions from Finland to the Caspian Sea in the East to the Pacific Coast of North America in the West have to be considered as a mosaic of labor markets and labor force reservoirs, sections of which had been internationalized. Within the Atlantic economies—their specific towns, agricultures, and industries—a constant process of acculturation of labor migrants took place. Only a comparative study of this process will offer meaningful interpretations. Radical Swedish workers migrated to the ironworks of Worcester, Mass., and turned quiescent; radical Finnish workers of similar demographic and social characteristics migrated to the mines of the Mesabi range and established one of the most persistent radical traditions in North America. Only detailed comparisons can provide answers. The task is hard to fulfill.

The authors of the essays presented here offer surveys of the European migrations with reference to those across the Atlantic (Part I), they analyze ac-

culturation processes on the old continent and the new (Part II), and they deal
with the much neglected question of return migration (Part III). They do not yet
provide a labor market analysis on a hemispheric scale. Most of the essays have
been written specifically for this volume by experts in the field. No common
approach has been imposed on them nor has the selection of authors been guided
by a comprehensive theory of migration. The concept or rather ideology of a
"chosen country" has not been replaced by one of an international working
class. Signs that such a class existed are sometimes tantalizingly close but the
state of research does not permit this hypothesis of some scholars to be elevated
to the rank of a historiographical paradigm. No restrictions were placed on authors
concerning the subject matter: governmental regulation of migration and individual decisions, acculturation or return, seasonal and permanent migration have
to be fitted together in the laborious task of replacing the fairy tale of immigration
by a sound picture of international migrations. Readers may consider the result
as mixed fare or an approximation of scholarly pluralism. We consider it a
stepping stone toward a new synthesis.

Many debts have been incurred during the preparation of this volume. Without
a grant from the Stiftung Volkswagenwerk this collective work, based on international cooperation, would never have seen the light of day. Andrew Winter
has translated the essays by L. Elsner, H. Fassmann, M. Glettler, C. Kleßmann,
and C. H. Riegler. Both the authors and editor are grateful for his work. The
essays by K. J. Bade, E. J. Hobsbawm, and J. D. Sarna have been published
before; those by L. A. Cohen, W. Sewell, Jr., and L.-G. Tedebrand have been
revised from earlier published versions. We gratefully acknowledge the authors'
and publishers' permission to reprint and revise these essays. Christiane Harzig,
the editorial assistant, has carefully read the manuscripts and diligently retouched
many of them. Credit for numerous improvements is due to her. Monique Dun-
kake, Ursula Schnaars, Karen Schniedewind, and Thomas Weber helped with
bibliographic research, typing, and proofreading. Colleagues in Eastern and
Western Europe, the United States, and Canada have helped with advice and
suggestions for authors and topics. Milton Cantor and Bruce Laurie have commented on most of the essays. Only with this help and support was it possible
to produce this volume.

Dirk Hoerder

LABOR MIGRATION
IN THE
ATLANTIC
ECONOMIES

AN INTRODUCTION TO LABOR MIGRATION IN THE ATLANTIC ECONOMIES, 1815–1914

Dirk Hoerder

This introduction is intended to provide (1) background information on pre-nineteenth century migratory traditions, (2) a critique of the overwhelming emphasis on immigration to North America and of the basic assumptions of the "immigration" school of historians, and (3) a survey of labor migration in Europe. Because of its magnitude, the cross-Atlantic flow deeply impressed contemporaries. The main beneficiary, the United States, skillfully developed a cultural mystique of unlimited opportunities and success, freedom and equality, and absence of discrimination.[1] While historians have severely criticized this ideology by pointing to the limits of upward mobility, by showing the stratification of society in both North American nations, and by dealing with nativism and race prejudices, few of them have placed immigration in its larger context, an Atlantic economy with segmented labor markets, some segments of which had been internationalized.

Though labor migration—as industrialization in general—is not usually influenced decisively by political events, two wars mark its chronological limits. Labor migration in Europe as well as emigration to North America almost came to a standstill during the Napoleonic Wars. It resumed only after the Congress of Vienna had reapportioned Europe to a number of greater and lesser monarchs and sovereigns. A century later it came to a sudden halt when Germany and Austria began what was to become the First World War. Labor migration resumed after 1919. But because of the U.S. immigration restrictions of 1917 and 1924–1929 and then the Great Depression, it never again reached the volume of previous decades. Migration to rapidly industrializing countries, particularly to the two latecomer nations, the United States and Germany, from the 1880s to the 1910s represents a quantitatively and qualitatively new phase in the history of the displacement of labor toward capital.[2] But it draws on older traditions in Europe and was preceded by labor import and mobilization in North America.

THE ANTECEDENTS OF INDUSTRIAL LABOR MIGRATION

In the European context the migration of skilled labor dates back to the development of the urban centers with their craft guilds in the late Middle Ages and early modern period. Secondly, a mobilizing factor that established traditions of migration but not usually labor migration was the shifting of borders between the four central and east European empires. Thirdly, the policy of mercantilist states in central and western Europe prohibited emigration of skilled craftsmen— at least of some trades—while it encouraged immigration in order to increase the productive capacity of the state and, in consequence, court revenues. Fourthly, and more important, many crafts had a guild-regulated system of migration for skilled journeymen after they had completed their apprenticeship. Fifthly, the migration of unskilled laborers and domestics is connected with the population pressures in agrarian areas and the abolition of serfdom in the nineteenth century. In many instances the early migrations involved some type of formal coercion through guild rules on the expulsion of certain religious groups. This distinguishes them from the transfer of skilled and unskilled labor beginning in the first half of the nineteenth century, which assumed increasingly large dimensions from the 1840s onward.

For the early modern migration toward urban centers, two examples will illustrate the trend. Frankfurt on the Main had about 20,000 inhabitants in 1600, of whom several thousands were migrating skilled journeymen. In addition, almost 3,000 middle-class Protestant Netherlanders settled there, who had been expelled or had fled Spanish domination. Two thousand five hundred Jews were segregated into a ghetto and periodically persecuted and driven out. Thus about 40 percent of the population were not natives.[3] The pre-industrial migrations involved a considerable middle-class element. In seventeenth century Nördlingen, Germany, between 10 and 20 percent of the population were in-migrants. This was not a reflection of the relations of a growing city with its hinterland. Rather "to a large extent emigration and immigration reflected a pattern of circulation among cities, or to put it differently, the transfer of young people between distant cities." This involved middle-class men and women acquiring citizenship (permanent migrants) whose amount of property was similar to that of the native residents.[4] The situation in other towns in Europe was similar.

Rivalries between the European empires originally had little relation to later migration other than a mobilizing impact. The warfare between the Ottoman, the Austrian, and the Russian empires influenced population shifts and thus transfer of manpower in the southeastern parts of Europe and Asia Minor. The partition of Poland by Austria, Russia, and Prussia in 1772 led to displacement of parts of the population there. This means that the whole area from the southern shore of the Baltic Sea to the northern shores of the Adriatic and Aegean seas and the eastern shore of the Black Sea witnessed large-scale migrations—partly voluntary, mainly forced—of whole ethnic groups. In the nineteenth century, the power struggles of the empires became entwined with nationalist movements. Some of these were deliberately encouraged by the central and western European powers to weaken the Ottoman Empire (cliché: "the sick man of Europe") in order to further "the spread of capitalism to Eastern Europe and the rise of a bourgeois class."[5] The slow pace of industrialization of the eastern countries and the resulting scarcity of job opportunities pushed out an agrarian surplus population, causing migratory movements that became part of the "proletarian mass migration." Sometimes these migratory movements were encouraged by imperial authorities in order to weaken nationalist movements of subjugated peoples by means of population drain.[6]

A third type of early migration was the expulsion of religious minorities from some states. For example, about 500,000 Huguenots were expelled from France after 1685, and Lutherans were ejected from the Salzburg area of Austria in 1732. Mercantilist-oriented governments of neighboring states turned this flow of "human capital" to their own economic advantage by settling the refugees in urban or to a lesser degree rural colonies and by encouraging their skills through bounties or tax abatements.[7] When such "reserve armies of skills" were not available, states sent out recruiting agents. Thus Dutch people with experience in draining low-lying lands were attracted for German colonization schemes, and as a result of the modernizing efforts of Peter the Great (1689-1725), Russia began to attract artisans and entrepreneurs from all over western and northern Europe. Sweden is another example of a country that encouraged immigration. When it became an imperial power in the sixteenth and seventeenth centuries, impressive castles and parks were constructed to demonstrate the power of the ruling dynasty and the country. Soon the wealthy middle classes joined the building boom. As a result Sweden attracted master and journeymen masons, stonecutters, and other construction workers as well as gardeners from all over Europe. On the other hand, some mercantilist states prohibited emigration of skilled personnel. British ironworkers and loom builders could have taken their trade secrets, not yet the public knowledge of engineers, with them. Samuel Slater did so when he memorized the construction of the Arkwright frame and left for Rhode Island and founded a competing cotton industry center there.

More important in the context of labor migration was a fourth mobilizing factor, that of craft migration ("Gesellenwanderung," "Tour de France"). According to the customs and rules of their guilds established in the late Middle Ages, skilled craftsmen were forced to leave their hometowns after completing an apprenticeship lasting from one to ten years. Originally the purposes of this migration were additional training and technology transfer. This motivation continued long after the guilds had been abolished, and skilled workers as well as members of the emerging profession of engineers continued to migrate to technologically advanced countries to improve their skills and knowledge and to obtain better positions after their return home.[8] Migration was also necessary to balance labor supply and demand. Periods of economic boom, disasters like floods and fires, reconstruction after wars, and recessions demanded constant shifts of manpower including entrepreneurial talent.[9] In this framework of economic life, the migrations were to the benefit of journeymen, masters, and the local and regional economies as a whole. Therefore a system of craft-based social security, to use a modern term, supported the journeymen. If a journeyman applied for work but none was available, the master approached had to give him a small travel allowance that would support the applicant until he reached the next workshop. The journeymen of some crafts also established mutual benefit societies just as immigrants did in North America and elsewhere. In the seventeenth and eighteenth centuries the character of craft migration changed. The custom was rigidly enforced for the protection of established masters from competition by skilled journeymen. A system that had once served a variety of interests now ensured the power and profit of one group. These restrictive features were among the reasons that led to the abolition of the guild system by governmental decrees.[10]

Besides guild-regulated craft migration, special expertise also furthered migration all over Europe. German cabinetmakers had a reputation that secured jobs for them in France. Swiss dairy cattle laborers and the sons of farmers migrated to German farms in such numbers that the overseer of the dairy production was customarily called a "Schweizer," a man from Switzerland. While the Dutch were famous for their production of tiles, Italian skilled craftsmen did the tile-laying all over Europe (a migration that continues to the present).

The fifth and most important precipitating factor for labor migration was the division of the Atlantic economies and of their dependent colonial areas into industrializing or industrialized areas on the one hand and rural areas on the other with a resulting worldwide division of labor. In the less developed areas a relative and in some cases absolute surplus population could not find employment or be nourished. In the whole of Europe with the exception of France, population increase was not matched by an increase in jobs, nor did job-seeking surplus population and labor-seeking invested surplus capital match geographically. There began an out-migration by a landless proletariat, whether agricultural laborers, farmers' sons, or small farmers and their families, to far-off industrializing areas where unskilled labor was in demand.[11] This was frequently met by a numerically smaller countermovement of skilled workers into the slowly developing areas to provide the qualified labor for an industrial takeoff and to train local workers.

This migration of skilled workers to skilled jobs elsewhere because of relatively higher wages and of an unskilled un- or underemployed surplus population to areas with job opportunities assumed massive proportions in the 1880s and was identified as "proletarian mass migration."[12] Though basically adequate, the term needs some qualification: the migrants generally became industrial workers upon arrival, but at the time of departure many were skilled artisans or members of peasant societies. Some migrated to conserve traditional life-styles. Skilled German craftsmen, rather than enter a factory in Germany, migrated to the United States where their skills were still in demand. Their children, however, usually ended up in factories in the new culture.[13] Peasants from Norway to Italy sent members of their families to work abroad in order to accumulate the funds necessary to preserve a precarious rural existence and perhaps to increase meager landholdings.[14] Within Europe the large-scale movement from the countryside to the towns accelerated after the middle of the nineteenth century. To a differing degree according to country, region, and town, many industrializing areas failed to absorb the total influx of laborers. This led to the second migration, often a cross-Atlantic one, a migration in stages. This is reflected in the fact that even when the majority of migrants to North America came from rural areas, the proportion of urban emigrants in relation to the rural-urban distribution of population in the country of origin was larger than that from agricultural regions.[15]

In the North American context, particularly in the United States, the proletarian mass migration was part of the transfer and mobilization of manpower. First came the forced transfer of about 15 million enslaved black workers from Africa to the Americas.[16] The time lag between the legal end of the slave trade (1808) and the onset of the second transfer, migration from Ireland, which assumed large proportions in the 1840s, had been bridged by the mobilization of white female labor during the manufactory stage of industrialization in the northeastern section of the United States and by slave breeding and industrial slavery in the South.[17] "Free" migration from Europe, dependent on personal decisions within a framework of economic constraints and social and political barriers, marked the breakthrough of the laissez-faire ideology: the social costs of unemployment, old age, and so forth were shifted from the owners of laborers (slaveholders) or from paternalistic employers to the individual worker (and later to society at large represented by the state). Ideological moments gained the upper hand when fears mounted that South and East European immigrants might endanger the quality of the "racial stock" and that they might tend to espouse radical political and socio-economic ideologies. Then their migration was halted (1917–1929).[18] In a further transfer of labor, free blacks from the South were now encouraged to migrate to industrial centers. They were considered more docile, they could be segregated more easily, and they had no country to return to.[19] Also, because of the changes in the character of work, especially the increase in clerical jobs, women could be brought into the labor force once again in larger numbers.

Finally, the proletarian mass migration is usually regarded as a voluntary migration as opposed to migrations forced by, for example, religious intolerance. It took place, however, in a world system with a lack of jobs in some areas or countries and high rates of industrialization elsewhere. The migrants were not subject to government pressures, but poverty, un- and underemployment, and other forms of coercion through economic conditions played important roles. When economic coercion or—viewed from the other end—economic incentives like jobs and wages were insufficient to assure a supply of labor, capitalists used governmental means including wars to "capture" workers. The First World War, which coincidentally ended the period of voluntary migration, was fought— from the point of view of sections of German industry—to dominate population reservoirs in the east whose labor potential could be exploited by brute force.[20]

OLD INTERPRETATIONS—NEW INSIGHTS

The history of immigration to the United States has been refined considerably in recent years, but it still suffers from many shortcomings. A thorough reas-

sessment is needed. In Europe "migration history" has been a relatively neglected part of demography, and has often suffered from a disregard for economic
conceptualizations, particularly for labor market theories. In the United States
and Canada "immigration history"—note the difference in terminology—was
basically bound to an ideology exemplified in Emma Lazarus's poem about the
"poor huddled masses" receiving shelter from oppression and hunger.[21] A meth-
odology based on concepts like "the uprooted" and "the melting pot" has
obscured rather than clarified the migrants' experience.[22] The last two decades
have witnessed in Europe—Eastern and Western—and North America publication of a number of highly sophisticated studies of migration and acculturation
that warrant an attempt to outline a new frame of reference including a comparative approach.

The first fallacy of the old interpretation is the indiscriminate usage of the
term "immigration" to define population movements throughout United States
and Canadian history.[23] Only the direction of movement was similar for all
comers but neither the economic reasons, nor for that matter, the psychological
ones, which are in any case more difficult to assess, were constant. Immigration
of settlers and migration of workers are two distinct economic and social processes. The indiscriminate lumping together of both in the case of North America
has contributed to the confusion about the size of the migration, to the myth of
unequalled opportunities, and to the unwarranted thesis of American, that is,
United States exceptionalism.

Migration in order to settle on the relatively cheap and plentiful farmland in
the American West has to be compared with the chronologically parallel but
quantitatively smaller movement East to settlement of the southern plains of
European Russia, and later to Siberian territories. From 1763 onward, settlement
in "New Russia" was encouraged by a policy of low land prices and privileges
for immigrants. In the second half of the nineteenth century, Russia was fur-
thering a grain export economy. Under Catherine II, it was peopled by settlers
from Germany, Russian settlers from other parts of the empire, and later by
Slavic peoples. The coming of the latter reflected a shift in policy: Western
European settlers were considered difficult to assimilate, therefore Slavic peoples
became preferred immigrants. Figures of this migration of settlers vary widely—
Treadgold suggests 10 million migrants from 1815 to 1921, a period that includes
only about two decades of the operation of the first transcontinental railroad, the
Trans-Siberian, which was built between 1891 and 1904.[24] This process of
expansion of the European peoples through the Northern Hemisphere and into
parts of the Southern has been depicted impressively by Dollot and Scott.[25]

The labor migrations to the North American continent on the other hand do
not constitute an expansion, nor necessarily an *im*migration, but form part of
the transfer of labor toward capital (investment) in the Atlantic economies. This
distinction is not at all adequately described by the difference between "old"
and "new immigration," a term first used by the Dillingham Commission with
distinctly racist overtones. The "new immigration" as a labor migration began

with the arrival of poor people dependent on their daily labor in the United States during the 1820s and 1830s.[26] Numerous contemporary accounts describe their wretched condition, and historians have known for long that they had to remain in the cities of the East Coast. Labor migration assumed considerable proportions in the 1840s with the coming of the famine-stricken Irish. In the 1880s, the South and Eastern European peoples did send relatively more migrants than the Western European countries, but these continued to send migrants, and they came as workers, not as settlers. It took from 1820 to 1879 for 2.9 million Germans to come, but only another 15 years, 1880–1895, for a further two million to arrive.[27] The latter were mainly craftsmen and unskilled agricultural laborers from the Eastern provinces.[28] (In the areas of departure the farm workers were being replaced by Polish labor migrants.) Irish people continued to migrate by the tens of thousands annually,[29] and Scandinavian migrants, many of them workers, came in larger absolute numbers than ever before.[30]

Frequently the migration of laborers was not an immigration. According to the most recent research, about one-third returned from the United States to their countries of origin in the years from 1899 to 1924.[31] Among the incoming migrants there were seasonal and temporary ones, there were those who came for their working lives but returned after retirement, and the involuntarily permanent ones, who for whatever reasons never intended to immigrate, but postponed their decision to return until they were no longer able to do so.[32] Only those who from the beginning or early after their arrival decided to remain permanently in the United States and Canada or in a European labor-importing country are immigrants in any meaningful sense of the term. For each of these groups, the process of acculturation was different. Immigrants were probably more ready to accept new customs than temporary or merely seasonal migrants. But on the other hand, temporary migrants might try to make the most of their relatively short stay while permanent migrants knew that they could take their time.[33]

While hardly any serious historian continues to use the once widely held and officially propagated cliché of unlimited opportunities, a few remarks on comparative scope of the opportunities are in order. The chance to acquire cheap land did not make the United States or Canada a special case. Similar opportunities existed in Southern and Asiatic Russia, and Italian peasants are known to have taken up residence in deserted French villages for the same reason.[34] As to labor migrants, in the fifteen years from 1900 to 1914, their "starting capital" upon arrival in the United States amounted to:[35]

Germans:	$41.00	Slovaks:	$15.00
Czechs:	$28.00	Russians:	$14.00
Italians:	$26.50	Poles:	$12.80

Basically this leaves no opportunity but demonstrates a dire necessity to find a job as fast as possible.

Nevertheless a *relative* level of better opportunities did exist for migrants from the lesser developed European countries: in the United States and Canada, they could get a job, which they could not at home. Also, they could get money wages rather than wages in kind. European areas of similar industrialization offered similar opportunities. Accordingly migrants from certain European areas did not go to North America but to the next European centers of employment. Patterns of migration, however, varied. In Denmark, according to Hvidt, people living close to the towns migrated there (with the possibility of later going abroad), while those from the more distant parts of the country emigrated.[36] But such patterns differed from region to region, and much more research is necessary to establish the reasons for these patterns.

Upon arrival in North America, the migrants came into an "open society" with high rates of upward mobility—this notion is still current in the popular version that "Everyman" can make his own fortune. But social mobility means both upward mobility and downward mobility. Furthermore, horizontal (geographical) mobility does not necessarily have any connection with vertical (social) mobility. Studies of social mobility in the United States and Canada are now being supplemented by comparable studies for British, Danish, Dutch, French, German, and Swedish towns. H. Kaelble has attempted to overcome the difficulties raised by the different methods, time spans, definitions, and so forth, employed in these studies of growing and industrializing towns in the Atlantic economies.[37] He found that mobility may have been somewhat higher in North America according to the data, but that the data base biases the findings in favor of the United States. He argued that no clear North "American pattern of the overall rate of social mobility" between the four classes of un- or semi-skilled workers, skilled workers, the lower middle class, and the middle class emerges. Rather, "if there are any spectacular contrasts among nineteenth-century cities, the dividing lines running across America and perhaps also across Europe were as important as the contrast between America and Europe." Distinguishing between inter-generational and intra-generational (career) mobility, Kaelble noted for the former that there was no indication "that the proportion of inhabitants who left the social class of their fathers was larger in America than in Europe." Only downward mobility from a white-collar background to the working class was more frequent in Europe. Secondly, intra-generational mobility in the United States was somewhat higher than in Europe, particularly for unskilled workers. Within a period of ten years less than 10 percent of the workers achieved lower middle-class status in Europe, while the American figure was above 10 percent.[38] Kaelble concluded that

while industrialization in Western Europe as well as in the USA did lead to enormous geographical mobility, it produced far less social mobility and remarkably little upward mobility. . . . Above all, recent works on the USA and West European countries . . . confirm a slight increase in social mobility rates which has not, however, removed the high degree of inequality of opportunities.[39]

In the United States and Canada the percentage of foreigners in the total population was higher than in European towns. In 1920 it stood at 12.9 percent, in 1930 at 11.3 percent, dropping in 1940 to 8.7 percent (U.S. figures). In France it moved from 1 percent in 1852 to 2 percent in 1872 and 2.8 percent in 1911 but climbed to 7 percent in 1930. Rates for Germany and Belgium at the turn of the century oscillated between 2 and 4 percent.[40] (Note that the European figures do not include the multi-ethnic or multi-national character of many European states, a heterogeneity that continues to the present. It would be highly rewarding to compare the multi-culturalism of societies like those of Yugoslavia or Russia with the ethnic pluralism of the United States or Canada.)

Comparisons of the foreign element in a given population do not yield a picture of total in-migration. If all migrants are included in the statistics, whatever their national and ethnic origin, European industrial centers are remarkably similar to North American ones. To give only two examples, in 1907 47 percent of the German population (54 percent of the urban population) were internal migrants, to which the number of foreigners has to be added. Of almost 1.7 million inhabitants of Vienna in 1900, only 46.4 percent had been born there. More than a third of the population came from Bohemia, Moravia, Silesia, Hungary, Bosnia, Galicia, and Bukovina.[41] As in North America, a constant inflow of rural population had to be made to accept industrial discipline and notions of time. Organizing labor into unions was no less difficult a task in Europe than it was in America in view of geographical mobility.

This classification of migrations as internal or international and of ethnic groups as nations is an *ex post facto* point of view unavoidable for historians. German immigrants in the nineteenth-century United States considered themselves first and foremost Swabians or Bavarians. Migrants from the French provinces to Paris established mutual aid societies and other associations based on regional origin. What do political boundaries mean?

When the Poles were migrating from the Polish lands under Austrian and Russian rule to those under Prussian rule, then from the formal point of view these were migrations from two foreign states to a third; while from the Polish point of view they were migrations within a national area. On the other hand, when Poles were emigrating from Polish lands under Prussian rule up-country to Germany (or from central Poland—up country to Russia), then for these states they were domestic migrations, while from the Polish point of view they were migrations outside the national territory.[42]

... the Belgians, who in this period left for France to settle there permanently, did they consider themselves "emigrants?" One does not have to know much about the cultural affinities between France and Belgium to believe that for some this may have been the case. For the vast majority, however, the border between the two countries had hardly more psychological meaning than provincial borders. There were only a few more customs agents. Someone from Liège who left for Brussels or for Ghent would probably be more likely to consider himself an emigrant than in the case of moving to France.[43]

Migration was not only a factor to be reckoned with in the organizing activities of labor but also a form of competition in the labor market and a possible cause for anti-alien, anti-immigrant biases, discrimination, and violence. While there are instances of opposition to labor migration in the records of most European and North American labor unions, while riots against Italians occurred in the United States and France, and while Poles were considered inferior in Germany and in the United States, what is remarkable, given the extent of migration, is that so little direct action did occur. This becomes even more remarkable in view of the fact that employers in all Atlantic economies systematically imported labor from far-away regions to break strikes. Some of the workers thus duped by their prospective employers did turn back after discussion with and financial aid from the striking workers. But a considerable amount of strike-breaking did occur. Sophisticated labor market theories, which do not only assume a dual labor market but a highly segmented one, may explain part of the "détente." In a considerable number of segments, competition did not occur. The unskilled workers, especially in canal, road, and railroad construction, did not usually replace local labor—the local workers considered the working conditions too hard and the wages too low. The same goes for agricultural work. On the other hand skilled labor poured into areas where industrialization was just beginning and no trained local labor force was available.[44] Nevertheless, in many fields there was competition, and the numerous notices in European labor weeklies announcing strikes and warning potential migrants not to go there demonstrate the migratory potential, as well as the dangers of competition and lack of class or craft solidarity.[45]

Acculturation in the Atlantic economies proceeded along basically similar lines with considerable national differences. In the United States the melting pot idea was propagated; in France acculturation worked without such an ideology; in Britain middle-class Irish migrants integrated, and lower-class Irish formed a subculture; and in Germany acculturation was prevented by forcing at least part of the migrants from abroad to leave the country during the winter months. Cities and towns in Europe and America had ethnic neighborhoods, but usually not segregated ghettos. The settlement pattern was rather a concentration of in-migrants in certain (usually cheap) quarters, but within these areas and within each street a mixing with other ethnic groups and natives took place.[46] This facilitated acculturation as a two-way process—the acceptance of parts of the hegemonical culture but also the contribution of customs from the culture of origin to re-form the new society.[47]

Many migrants chose to limit their acculturation (or felt unable to withstand its pressures) and returned to their culture of origin. Return migration in Europe was (and is) higher than from North America since transportation is easier and usually cheaper. High return migration rates from receiving culture to culture of origin testify to the temporary character of labor migration. Several quantitatively less important return movements deserve attention because they reveal much about migrants' attitudes. Jewish migrants from pogrom-ridden Russia returned there because their old ways of life and the ghettos there still seemed more acceptable than New York or London tenements.[48] German and British (labor) migrants returned in larger numbers than conventional beliefs assume.[49] Russian-Germans—to take one rural example—moved to America in considerable numbers when later Czarist governments revoked some of their privileges; Finnish-Americans moved to Soviet Karelia in the 1930s when work conditions and political system proved to be exploitive and oppressive.[50] Neither did German migrants find the unlimited opportunities in the United States and Canada in which, at least some of them, had believed, nor did Czech migrants, who moved to the splendor of the imperial capital of Vienna, find unrestricted freedom from want and discrimination. Immigrant letters usually drew a relatively sobering picture of hard work and deprivation.

What migrants did have were certain expectations and hopes, and these do not equate with what historians and social scientists have called opportunities. The hope for a cash-paying job as opposed to unsteady agricultural work might demand adjustment from a cottage to a tenement block, a clear case of downward mobility as far as housing is concerned. Historians will have to understand migrants on their own terms. In one language the word "migration" has a second meaning—"sorrow."[51] The consequences for a family, including the departure from home, from a network of social relations and cultural habits, can be more important than the prospects for a bright future. Running water in one's apartment (or in the case of the tenement block, in the dirty courtyard below) might be meaningless to someone who is used to walking a mile to the nearest spring each morning.[52] Nevertheless, many wanted to migrate or had to, given economic conditions. In the following paragraphs some of the main migratory flows within Europe will be outlined, while the well-known movements across the Atlantic will receive only cursory attention.

A SURVEY OF EUROPEAN LABOR MIGRATION

Mobilization of labor in the nineteenth century passed through two stages before becoming a primarily industrial movement.[53] First there was a regional seasonal agrarian migration, frequently of the population of hilly and mountainous regions to fertile lowlands, more generally from naturally unproductive regions to naturally productive regions. Sometimes such migration was a two-way affair when crops in neighboring regions differed so that high demand for labor at harvest time occurred consecutively.[54] (See Figure 1.1.)

The second stage, an intensification of mobilization, was reached with railroad building. (We are concerned here with the process of construction, not the well-researched facilitation of migration.) Construction meant a temporary high demand for manpower in what were sometimes remote areas. The groundwork did not require any particular skills, wages were in money and not in kind. This attracted all available local labor, including many of those who had participated in the seasonal agrarian migrations. Additionally, foreign labor, particularly Italian workers in the case of Germany, were brought in.[55]

It would be a gross simplification to construe a single third stage when (1)

Figure 1.1 Destinations of Migrant Harvest Laborers in Central Europe, 1860s–1870s

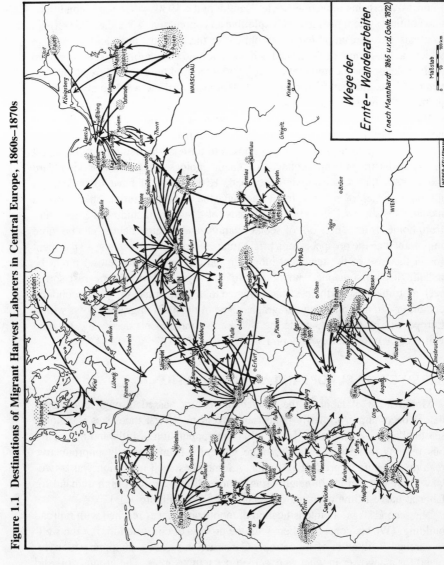

Source: Ingeborg Weber-Kellermann, Erntebrauch in der ländlichen Arbeitswelt des 19. Jahrhunderts auf Grund der Mannhardtbefragung in Deutschland von 1865 (Marburg, 1965), Map 3. Used with permission.

agricultural and construction workers turned to industry and (2) local and regional migrations became international. While migration was increasingly directed toward urban and industrial centers, agricultural workers and marginal farmers as well as the sons and daughters of small farmers continued to migrate for harvest work. Furthermore, small landowners migrated to industrial centers for a few years, planning to return and to invest their savings in more land. The move into industry was aimed at extending a precarious existence in agriculture: a temporary, voluntary proletarianization to avoid a permanent one. Skilled artisans and workers whose existence was threatened by mechanization moved to areas/ countries where their skills were still in demand to avoid descent into the class of unskilled workers. Skilled workers from eastern industrial areas, for example, the industries and mines of Silesia, migrated west to Berlin and the Ruhr district, others migrated east from Austria to Budapest. These migrations were a highly complex network of movements and countermovements of members of various social groups, which often changed or even reversed direction.

Any classification of labor-exporting (emigration) and labor-importing (immigration) countries is difficult to sustain. In the nineteenth century Europe became divided into an industrialized western part and a predominantly rural eastern and southern part. Most nations or areas within the European empires exported mainly unskilled labor, usually coming from agricultural areas and going to urban occupations, while at the same time importing skilled craftsmen and professional or entrepreneurial members of the middle classes. For reasons of convenience we will nevertheless employ the common terminology. Within Europe, England, Germany, France, and Switzerland were the main labor-importing countries. England and Germany exported labor to North America at the same time, while emigration from France was low. England drew workers mainly from its Irish colony, Switzerland from Italy, Germany from Poland and Italy, and France from most of its neighboring countries and Poland. Germany relied on a rotating labor force, while France was an immigration country.

Belgium and the industrializing sections of Austria, particularly the Vienna area, attracted considerable numbers of migrants but experienced heavy outmigration at the same time. The Scandinavian countries and Southeastern Europe exported labor to other European countries and North America but attracted skilled workers whenever demand exceeded supply in certain occupations. By the 1930s Sweden had become a labor-importing country. Southeastern Europe continued to export labor, high rates of return migration notwithstanding.

Poland, Ireland, and Italy have been labor-exporting countries throughout their history. Labor migration in the ethnically heterogeneous Russian territories has to be considered separately because internal migration remained dominant throughout the period from the emancipation of the serfs in 1861 to the Revolution of 1917. Southeastern Europe exported unskilled labor in large numbers while attracting skilled labor, entrepreneurs, and professionals. There was little migration from Spain and Portugal to other European countries before World War I with the exception of seasonal sojourns in France for grape-picking.

The labor exporting countries were characterized by a relative surplus population, a population that might be fed under ideal circumstances, but large parts of which were chronically or permanently underemployed. Beyond this generalization the particular economic and political circumstances of each country or area need investigation: The abolition of serfdom; the existence of large landed estates; the colonial subjugation of Ireland; the territorial, political, and cultural subjugation of Poland; and the orientation of Spain and Portugal toward South America all require more detailed examination.

Labor Migration into and out of the Smaller Countries

Of the countries that both exported and imported labor, Belgium had a negative migration balance from 1847 to 1900 and from 1911 to 1920, whereas in the other census periods more laborers entered than left the country. Nevertheless, the number of foreigners residing in Belgium increased from about 95,000 in the 1850s to a quarter of a million (3.5 percent of the population) in 1910. This was a result of spontaneous individual migration. Organized efforts to attract labor began after World War I. They came under state control in 1931. Settlement patterns in the towns showed dispersion of in-migrants. Ghettoization of residential concentration began only after World War I with the "new immigration" of Poles and Italians. Of the Netherlanders and Germans, about half of the men were industrial workers, while 30 to 50 percent of the women were in domestic service. The percentages were lower for the French. At the same time Belgian workers left in considerable numbers for France, especially for the Département du Nord and Paris. In the 1880s almost half a million migrated seasonally or for a few years at a time. Most went harvesting ("Franschmans"), but a considerable number took on road, rail, or canal construction work ("terrasiers"), which French laborers considered too hard and too dirty. Flemish labor migrants usually came from rural backgrounds. They were ready to accept new jobs because of the necessity to improve their living conditions. Workers from Hainault (often miners from the Borinage) stayed in their occupation looking only for better wages. Finally, there was considerable internal migration from Flanders to the Walloon area, that is, from the predominantly rural to the industrial section of the country.[56]

Detailed demographic studies of the Scandinavian countries have demonstrated that internal labor migration was quantitatively more important than emigration. It was one of the factors determining the area of origin of transatlantic migration. Rural areas close to industrializing centers were drawn into their orbit, and out-migration was toward them. There was the option of further migration when these centers could not provide the work and income sought. Migrants from more remote areas left directly for foreign, usually overseas industrial centers. Interregional, internal migration patterns developed with the onset of industrialization; for example, from "Central Sweden's agricultural and forest districts to the sawmill areas in southern and central Norrland." Among the Scandinavian countries labor intensive agriculture in some areas of Denmark attracted laborers, mostly girls, from southern Sweden (and later Poland). These areas experienced high overseas migration at the same time because local workers considered the wages too low. Finns migrated to Sweden and northern Norway in small numbers as well as to Russia in tens of thousands. Here, too, patterns can be discerned: from certain areas most migrants went to North America, from others to the Finnish industrial centers and to St. Petersburg. "We have found that beginning at least in the mid-1800s labor markets were in existence which encompassed major regions consisting of several countries and which had some degree of inter-Scandinavian character" (Åkerman, Uppsala Migration Research Project). From the 1880s onward most of the emigration was in search of labor and not of farms. The vast majority of overseas emigrants from the four Scandinavian countries and Iceland went to North America (Swedes, 98 percent; Norwegians, 96 percent; Danes, 89 percent; Finns, 83 percent).[57] By racial classification they belonged to the "old migration"; in economic reality mostly to the "new." K. Hvidt has established that 68.8 percent of Danish (1868–1900) and 55.1 percent of Swedish (1871-1900) emigrants were unskilled laborers, 18.5 percent and 16.3 percent, respectively, were skilled workers, while only 4.2 percent and 25.4 percent, respectively, were landowners. Swedish men in North America worked in construction, as tailors, blacksmiths, and joiners; Finns, as miners and lumberjacks. Swedish women frequently worked as maids in private households, a job opportunity that Italian migrants considered too restrictive for their personal autonomy. While Finland continued to export labor after World War I, Sweden had become a labor importing country by 1930 and has continued to be so up to the present.[58]

Southeastern Europe was divided between the Austro-Hungarian and Ottoman Empires, with Serbia, Romania, Bulgaria, and Greece as independent states. Compared with Western Europe, migration began later because in most areas abolition of serfdom and industrialization came later.[59] Here, too, regional labor migration preceded overseas emigration. Up to the beginning of the twentieth century, more than half of the Czech migrants went to Vienna, whilst in the years before World War I an increasing number went to Germany. Those going overseas—mostly to the United States—continued to follow the rural-urban migration pattern.[60] From 1899 to 1913, 68 percent of the Hungarian migrants to the United States came from agrarian society, but nine-tenths of them went into industry and mining. Hungary itself lacked skilled workers and experienced an in-migration from Bohemia, Moravia, and Austria. In 1875, 25 percent of the factory workers—35 percent in the iron and mechanical engineering works—of Budapest were foreigners. These emigrants trained the local labor force but upward mobility remained low.

Indeed, it seldom happened, that a start from farming, followed by urban day-labour, then work as a navvy or bricklayer should have finally led to a man rising to the rank of skilled labour. In the majority of cases have-nots got stuck somewhere between agriculture and industry; what is more, when the first powerful strides in the building of infrastructure lost their initial impetus considerable masses were compelled to resume agrarian labour. Subsequently many of them emigrated to America.[61]

From the South Slavic areas three kinds of migrations developed: seasonal toward the neighboring Eastern countries and their centers of economic life (e.g., Constantinople); temporary toward Western Europe, especially Austria, Germany, France, Belgium, and Sweden; permanent (except for the return migration) toward overseas destinations, mainly to North America. A special case of limited impact was the migration of unskilled construction workers to Russia when the Trans-Siberian Railway was built (1891-1904). At the turn of the century German and Swedish firms sent private agents and foremen to recruit labor to the South Slavic (Yugoslav) areas. With industrialization—the building of railways and exploitation of natural resources—foreign labor and experts were imported. Most of the investments necessary for development came from abroad, and one push factor that as yet has to be explored is the role of foreign capital in "colonial" or peripheral economies. Would societally responsible rather than merely economically profitable investments have slowed down the process of out-migration? Or did the foreign investments create a demand for labor that prevented sections of the local population from emigrating?[62] In parts of the South Slavic territories the in-migrating industrial workers formed the first labor organizations of Southeastern Europe. Out-migrating workers came under the influence of the strong social-democratic movements in Western Europe and upon return brought back this increased political awareness.[63]

The Austrian and Russian Empires

Austria experienced high out-migration toward North America and considerable internal flows of manpower at the same time. Especially Czechs and Hungarians migrated toward Vienna and the surrounding area of lower Austria. Jewish migrants mainly from Galicia and the Bukovina also came to Vienna, while Polish agricultural workers from Russia migrated to Galicia.

In Russia internal labor migration was slow to develop. As in the case of North America, it was preceded by a migration of settlers. The surplus population could leave local estates only after the abolition of serfdom in 1861. The 1860s witnessed a boom in railroad construction. But the new lines (only about 22,000 km [13,700 miles] by 1881—compared with 166,000 km [103,100 miles] in the United States) were for grain export rather than migration of laborers. In fact, long-distance express trains did not include third class cars. As elsewhere, railroad construction served as a mobilizing factor for the local peasant population, but railroad transport did not contribute to their mobility until the 1880s. Only then were low fares introduced to attract the migrants, who, in the intervening two decades, had customarily walked the roads or used river transportation. These were "worker-peasants" who returned to their villages only for the harvest—frequently over distances of several hundred kilometers. By the turn of the century the industrial centers of St. Petersburg and Moscow attracted a considerable number of workers. On the whole, most labor migration in Russia remained internal migration, yet a diverse ethnic and linguistic population were involved. Up to the nineteenth century limited numbers of foreign craftsmen, experts, merchants, and settlers were attracted. After the end of the nineteenth century emigration to Western Europe and, more importantly, to North America occurred. The anti-Semitic pogroms, especially from the 1880s onward, forced large parts of the Jewish population to leave.[64]

Each industrializing center created an orbit of dependent areas from which it drained manpower. Unfulfilled expectations in these metropolitan or sub-centers as well as a relative (occasionally absolute) surplus in population in the peripheral, rural areas that could not be absorbed within the country, empire, or within Europe, propelled about 14 million Europeans to the industrializing areas of North America from the 1850s to 1914. But the individual decision whether to leave for the next town, the next industrial center, the next country, or the next continent depended not simply on push and pull factors but also on cultural traditions and on migration patterns. It varied from region to region as Fassmann's typology of Austrian emigration areas and L. Hollen Lees's description of Irish farming patterns demonstrate.[65]

The Labor-Exporting Countries

Emigration from Italy, Poland, and Ireland may to some degree be considered as part of the nineteenth-century urbanization process during the industrial take-off.[66] England was the first country to attract foreign labor, and it could draw on its colony, Ireland.[67] Migration from Ireland came from the eastern modernizing areas where commercialization of agriculture was accompanied by growing unemployment. Collapse of the domestic textile industry, which had provided supplementary income, and the introduction of agricultural "machinery" as simple as the plow forced parts of the population below subsistence levels. The penetration of the cash economy into subsistence farming areas and tax collection in cash forced parts of the population into wage labor. The more traditional areas of noncommercial farming resisted the pull of British jobs at least in the first decades of the nineteenth century. Migration to Great Britain was usually seasonal at the beginning, while migration to North America was permanent. Where one chose to migrate was determined by financial standing—the fare to Britain was cheaper—and by agricultural standing—areas of family farming with only a limited surplus of labor provided seasonal laborers for Britain. The Irish replaced the migrant Welsh and Scottish agricultural laborers in the eighteenth century and had begun to settle in Liverpool, London, and other industrial centers by the end of the Napoleonic Wars. By 1851—after the Potato Famine—about 500,000 Irish people had settled in Britain. A decade later more than 180,000 first and second generation Irish lived in London alone.[68] But from the 1830s onward remittances from North America combined with cheap substandard shipping led to an increase in transoceanic migration. Between 1876 and 1921 only

8 percent of the migrants from the countries that became the Irish republic in 1922 sailed to Great Britain, while 84 percent went to the United States. In these years Irish migration to North America declined in proportion to the total in-migration but remained large in absolute numbers. While the Irish in Britain suffered as much from labelling by the dominant "race" as in the United States, their acculturation was comparatively easy—at least for those who spoke English rather than Gaelic. Still, an Irish sub-culture remained part of British society.[69]

Italian labor migration increased with the unification of Italy between 1860 and 1870, its economic stagnation and relative overpopulation, the industrial expansion in Switzerland, France, and Germany, and European penetration into other parts of the world. The statistics show that of 14 million emigrants (gross figures) from 1876 to 1915, 44 percent went to European countries, 29.5 percent to the United States, and 27 percent to other overseas countries (Canada 1 percent, South America 23.5 percent, Africa 1.5 percent).[70] Migration to South America included the oft-cited agricultural workers who worked in Italy from spring through the fall grape-picking season and in the Argentinian harvest in December and January. German plans to replace the politically undesirable Polish agricultural workers with Italian ones aborted when the latter considered the extremely low wages paid by the East-Elbian Junkers unacceptable and when sea transportation from Genoa to Buenos Aires proved cheaper than rail transportation to the eastern provinces of Germany. While migration to Germany was seasonal, to France, Austria, and Switzerland it could be seasonal, temporary, or permanent. During the 1905–1915 decade, 1.3 million Italians returned from the United States. Within Europe smaller numbers of migrants went to almost every state in addition to the four major receivers. In the 1890s the vast majority of the emigrants were agricultural laborers or small farmers and their sons; about one-fifth were in the building trades, including stonecutting; a tenth were artisans and factory workers. About two-thirds of the annual migrants left Italy during the three months from February to April, reflecting both the seasonal character of the migration and the expectation that spring offered the best job opportunities in the Northern Hemisphere. Migration as a whole seems to have reacted to long-term economic swings and to short-term recessions and depressions. Viewed in a micro-perspective, it followed well-established routes from one village or valley to a certain town or area abroad. To take only two examples, of the 2,200 inhabitants of Misocco about one thousand annually went to Paris as painters and plasterers; those from the Calanca valley went to Alsace and Lorraine as masons, painters, and glaziers. While the origin remained agricultural, the destination became increasingly industrial. From 1895 to 1901 industrial employment of Italian migrant workers in Switzerland increased by 173.8 percent, and they were found in all but 20 of the country's 157 industries.[71] After the end of World War I, Italian emigration continued on a reduced scale and was influenced by world economic conditions, emigration restrictions, and Italian fascist emigration policy. It increased after World War II and has continued to do so, particularly since the 1960s, toward Common Market countries and Switzerland.

The Polish situation was characterized by the country's division among Prussia, Austria and Russia with the Russian section temporarily semi-autonomous (1815–1831), by a large number of less than subsistence landholdings on the one hand and large estates on the other, and by a population increase of 105 percent (as compared with 70 percent for all of Europe). The closing of the border between the Russian and Prussian parts brought about a move of approximately 50,000 Prussian Poles, mainly tradesmen and manufacturers, into Congress Poland. In the second half of the nineteenth century, the outward movement increased rapidly. Although the Prussian authorities had expelled Poles for cultural reasons in 1885, Prussia had to open its borders to seasonal migration in 1890. Pressure came from large landowners in the Eastern provinces as well as Brandenburg and Hanover and from industrialists in Silesia and the Ruhr district. In part, factory workers from Upper Silesia were among the migrants.[72] The East Prussian agricultural territories had witnessed a flight ("Ostflucht") of agricultural laborers to the Berlin and Ruhr industrialized areas and to the United States (third wave of German emigration 1879–1895). In Russian Poland the movement in search of cash (or "bread") had increased after 1865. Only a few peasants, however, participated in the settlement of Siberia.[73] Unskilled workers made up only about one-third of the migration to Russia. The others were clerks, manufacturers, mechanics, skilled workers, and members of the professions. These groups were assimilated relatively easily. From Galicia (the Austrian section of Poland) migration into other parts of Austria was diverse.

During World War I and again during World War II a large number of Poles were forced to work in Germany under prison-camp conditions, some being prevented from returning at the end of their pre-war labor contracts, others being forcibly deported. Polish migration in the inter-war years was directed toward France, Belgium, and Denmark.[74]

The Labor-Importing Countries

In Switzerland the beginning of railroad construction and later the building of tunnels through the Alps created a demand for manpower from the middle of the nineteenth century onward that had brought between 80,000 and 150,000 seasonal Italian workers into the country by the beginning of the twentieth century.[75] To these have to be added the permanent migrants employed in industry. Of the total industrial labor force, 12.7 percent was foreigners in 1895, 16.5 percent in 1901, and 22.3 percent in 1911. Migrants came from Germany, Italy, France, and Austria, with Germans in the leading position in 1895, while after 1911 Italians made up the largest number. Italian women frequently worked in the Swiss textile industry. From 1860 to 1910 the foreign population as a percentage of the native population increased from 4.5 to 15.2, reaching almost North American proportions. Special schools financed by the Italian government or special classes for Italian children within the normal Swiss schools led to the acculturation of the second generation. (In Ticino, the Italian-speaking canton of Switzerland, there were, of course, few problems anyway. Fears that a separatist movement demanding annexation by Italy might develop in the canton proved unfounded.)[76] After the First World War labor migration came under government control and has remained there to the present.

Britain was the leading European country of emigration to North America. Its internal migration and immigration need brief elaboration. Migration of agricultural laborers from Wales and Scotland to England took place in the eighteenth and early nineteenth centuries. Then Irish migrants began to replace them. At this time there was also labor migration from Germany to England. While the Irish continued to send the largest number of workers, Italians, Lithuanians, and people from other nations came in small numbers. By the end of the century Eastern Jews also began to arrive in large numbers, as they did in Paris and New York. Migration because of relative technological superiority was first from Britain to German universities, but after the middle of the century from many countries to the then leading Britain. While the British government viewed migration to Britain with concern, it encouraged contract migration of Chinese workers to British-owned South African quarries.[77] British labor organizations remained in close contact with the country's American emigrants or migrant workers and established locals there. Charlotte Erickson and Rowland T. Berthoff have pointed out that return migration was an integral part of British labor migration. In fact, in some trades workers shuttled back and forth in complex patterns: "British house decorators were said to have three seasons: America each spring; Scotland during the summer, when the upper classes were in London; and London in autumn, when owners of townhouses went to shoot in Scotland."[78]

Germany began to import labor in large numbers from the 1880s onward in a sharp turnaround of its nationalist policies. In order to Germanize the Polish territories under Prussian control, Polish immigration had been prohibited and Polish-speaking persons had been subjected to a number of restrictions and harassments. But the extremely low wages paid to German agricultural workers on the large estates in the Eastern provinces resulted in high out-migration. This, as well as the demand for manpower in the mines of the Ruhr district, matched the availability of unskilled labor in agricultural Poland and of skilled labor in the Silesian districts. A reversal of the exclusion policy resulted from pressure from an alliance of Junkers and "industrial barons." Polish laborers were forced, however, to leave Germany in winter. It was not only cheaper for their agrarian employers, it was intended to prevent acculturation and permanent settlement. The governmental policy was to rotate jobs among temporary migrants in order to prevent immigration. This rule, too, could not be fully enforced—it was suspended for workers in mining and industry because of pressure from industry.

In addition, Italian workers came in large numbers. Their migration was "naturally" seasonal since most of them found jobs in construction, a sector that discharges most workers during the winter months. As did other labor importing countries, Germany also had workers coming in from other states. Ethnically heterogeneous workers arrived from the Austro-Hungarian Empire, and Swedish workers migrated to Germany. The effort to redirect the flow of Flemish agricultural workers to Germany (from their customary destination of France) failed.[79]

Europe's immigration country par excellence was France, where the number of foreigners increased from 381,000 in 1851 to 1,160,000 in 1911. Even larger was the internal migration. From a population that ranged between 35 and 40 million, migration was a way of life for up to one-fifth of families. Common laborers, construction workers, "terrassiers," and domestic servants migrated from everywhere. Some regions were known as recruiting areas for special trades. Lumbermen and charcoal burners came from the Auvergne, vineyard laborers from the Cévennes and many others. Most men from the Creuse became masons. The in-migration from abroad was just as mixed: in 1911 more than 400,000 Italians, 287,000 Belgians, 117,000 Germans and Austro-Hungarians, 110,000 Spanish and Portuguese, as well as Swiss, Russian (Jewish), Dutch, and other workers resided in France, while migration from the North African colonies was negligible. Distribution of foreign workers in 1920 was 29.6 percent in agriculture, 18.6 percent in common labor, 18.2 percent in building and digging, 12.6 percent in mining, 5.7 percent in metal-working trades, and 15.3 percent in miscellaneous trades.[80] France, like Britain and Germany, also witnessed the rise of some of the immigrants into the ranks of skilled workers and of a small segment into the lower middle classes as shopkeepers, tavern owners, and in similar trades that served mainly their immigrant countrymen. Migration to France continued after World War I and is still continuing at present.

Two forms of migration have to be mentioned separately. The temporary migration of skilled workers and technicians in order to improve their training (personal goals) and to further technology transfer (governmental aim of sending countries) was small compared with labor migration in the strict sense. But it was much larger than the enrollment of a few students in the natural sciences and engineering at institutions of higher learning suggests. In fact, it was not a migration to educational institutions but a migration of many thousands to jobs that promised further training.[81]

The other form is forced labor migration. After declaring war in 1914, Germany refused to permit voluntary migrant workers to return home. It also began a program of recruitment of labor in the western and eastern occupied territories that was designated "voluntary" but took place under military auspices. In the east the character of forced recruitment was soon openly admitted. Many of these workers (as well as prisoners of war) were worked to exhaustion and death. The project to force "racially inferior" workers to labor and die for the "Aryan master race" was repeated on a much larger scale during World War II. Whenever voluntary labor migration did not meet the demands of the receiving country, force was used.[82] Thus, France imported laborers during the war from its colonies and treated them like prisoners. Recruitment from European countries remained voluntary but once in France, these workers were kept under strict control.[83]

OUTLOOK AND CONCLUSION

During the inter-war years labor migration continued. While the United States sharply restricted migration, the European importing countries of France, Switzerland, and Germany subjected labor migration to a system of state controls that ensured both the selection of—from their point of view—economically desirable workers and their distribution into specific places and jobs. Poland and Italy remained the main sending countries, with Spain and Portugal being slowly integrated as suppliers of labor. Since World War II, especially during the boom period of the sixties, another mass migration of workers has taken place mainly from Southern and Southeastern Europe to Western and Northern Europe. It was abruptly stopped for workers outside of the European Community in 1973 when the current depression began. Migration also took place in more limited dimensions within socialist countries. This present-day migration is strictly state controlled.[84]

While many similarities exist between the migrations of the turn of the century and those of the last two decades and of the inter-war years, few studies have attempted to deal with them comparatively.[85]

The years after World War I were a period of considerable return migration, not only because of post-war economic problems in the receiving countries but, particularly in the case of the East European countries, because of the liberation of homelands from imperial subjugation, whether Russian, German, or Austro-Hungarian. Since these countries, too, suffered from the economic dislocations and devastations of the war, many return migrants did not find the economic security they were seeking. Only some political aspirations were fulfilled. The return movement has been investigated by scholars in East European countries, but their research has received little attention in the West.[86]

Return migration from North America to Europe, intra-European migration and some of its connections with cross-Atlantic migration, and a comparison of acculturation processes on both sides of the Atlantic form the three parts of this volume. These topics have received attention from specialized scholars, but a broad comparative perspective is still lacking.[87] Accordingly, this collection of essays intends to provide an introduction and to stimulate further research on a comparative basis. Many separate migratory movements can be and have been described and explained but most of these single-issue explanations do not fit together to yield an understanding of the complex total migratory movements. While an overall synthesis cannot be provided here, we hope to offer a first step in this direction.

NOTES

1. This volume deals with intra-European labor migration and with that toward North or Anglo-America. Migration to South or Latin America is excluded because it was primarily a movement of settlers. The authors deal with both the United States and Canada. Though the term "America" refers to the whole continent and its appropriation by the United States is resented as cultural imperialism by the other nations on the continent, it has not always been possible to avoid the term, since the contemporary immigrant expression was "to go to America" rather than "to go to the United States."

2. A large number of studies deal with the relationship of capital concentration and investment and the migration of labor: for example, William B. Harrison and Jang H. Yoo, "Labor Immigration in 1890–1914: Wage Retardation Vs. Growth–Conducive Hypothesis," *Social Science Journal* 18, no. 27 (April 1981), 1–12; and Ekkehart Krippendorff, "Migrationsbewegungen und die Herausbildung des kapitalistischen Weltmarkts," *Dritte Welt* 6, no. 1 (1978), 74-106.

3. Friedrich Bothe, *Geschichte der Stadt Frankfurt am Main* (Frankfurt, 1966).

4. Christopher R. Friedrichs, *Urban Society in an Age of War: Nördlingen, 1580-1720* (Princeton, N.J., 1979). The quotation is from an unpublished paper by the same author: "Immigration and Urban Society: Seventeenth-Century Nördlingen," 1982.

5. *Les migrations internationales de la fin du XVIIIe siècle à nos jours* (Paris, 1980), pp. 616, 620.

6. Poles were expelled from the Prussian part of the divided state in an attempt to Germanize the area. On the encouragement of Croatian emigration by the Austro-Hungarian authorities, see the essay by F. Kraljic in this volume.

7. The term "ghetto" was not yet used. To achieve the desired effects of high productivity and to facilitate acculturation of a slow but deliberate pace, model settlements were built rather than crowding the immigrants into slums.

8. For an example of migration of skilled artisans and workers as well as engineers in the late nineteenth and early twentieth centuries, see the essay by C. Riegler in this volume.

9. See, for the example of Sweden and the other Scandinavian countries, the essay by Hans Norman and Harald Runblom in this volume. For France the monumental study by Abel Chatelain gives a detailed description and analysis of the multitude of pre-industrial labor migrations: *Les migrants temporaires en France de 1800 à 1914*, 2 vols. (Lille, 1976).

10. For migration of skilled craftsmen in Germany, see Klaus J. Bade, "Altes Handwerk, Wanderzwang und Gute Policey: Gesellenwanderung zwischen Zunftökonomie und Gewerbereform," *Vierteljahresschrift für Sozial- und Wirtschaftsgeschichte* 69 (1982), 1–37.

11. In the preceding centuries there was also a countermovement of capital toward labor. The whole system of putting out work to rural households occurred at a time when the agrarian population did not want to move, the towns could not absorb them, and the entrepreneurs were content with seasonal work, provided it was cheap. This production system, however, belongs to the proto-industrial period.

12. The term was first used by the two statisticians who compiled the first survey of labor migration in the Atlantic economies: Walter F. Willcox and Imre Ferenczi, eds., *International Migrations*, 2 vols. (New York, 1929, 1931).

13. This has been demonstrated for German immigrants to Poughkeepsie, N.Y.: Clyde Griffen and Sally Griffen, *Natives and Newcomers. The Ordering of Opportunity in Mid-Nineteenth Century Poughkeepsie* (Cambridge, Mass., 1978).

14. Ingrid Semmingsen, *Veien mot Vest. Utvandringen fra Norge til Amerika, 1865–1915* [The Way West. Emigration from Norway to America, 1865–1915], 2 vols. (Oslo, 1941, 1950), vol. 2, pp. 460ff. For Italy see George R. Gilkey, "The United States and Italy: Migration and Repatriation," *Journal of Developing Areas*, 2 (1967), 23-35; Francesco P. Cerase, *L'emigrazione di ritorno: innovazione o reazione?* (Roma, 1971), based on the author's Ph.D dissertation, "From Italy to the United States and Back: Returned Migrants, Conservative or Innovative?" (Columbia University, 1971). See also Cerase, "A Study of Italian Migrants Returning from the U.S.A.," *Int. Migration Rev.* 1 (1967), 67-74, and "Expectations and Reality: A Case Study of Return Migration from the United States to Southern Italy," *ibid.*, 8 (1974), 245-262; Betty Boyd Caroli, *Italian Repatriation from the United States, 1900-1914* (New York, 1973).

15. Cf. the essays by K. Hvidt and S. Carlsson in *Les migrations internationales*, pp. 332, 353.

16. Philip D. Curtin, *The Atlantic Slave Trade. A Census* (Madison, Wis., 1969); Nathan I. Huggins, *Black Odyssey: The Afro-American Ordeal in Slavery* (New York, 1979). With a transport survival rate variously estimated as four in five or one in three, a total of 20 to 45 million Africans were enslaved. The attempt to proletarianize the original American Indian population led to near genocide. While in the northern part of the continent the attempt was unsuccessful and was therefore replaced by wars of expulsion and extermination, in Spanish America 75 to 95 percent of the original population (estimated variously at 2 to 25 million people) died as plantation or mining laborers or of imported diseases.

17. For example, on women, see Thomas Dublin, *Women at Work. The Work and Community in Lowell, Massachusetts, 1826–1869* (New York, 1979); or industry, Robert S. Starobin, *Industrial Slavery in the South* (New York, 1970); on breeding, see Herbert G. Gutman, *Slavery and the Numbers Game. A Critique of "Time on the Cross"* (Urbana, Ill., 1975), pp. 96–102.

18. Roy L. Garis, *Immigration Restriction* (New York, 1927); E. P. Hutchinson, *Legislative History of American Immigration Policy, 1798–1965* (Philadelphia, 1981); William Preston, Jr., *Aliens and Dissenters. Federal Suppression of Radicals, 1903–1933* (Cambridge, Mass., 1963) and the several books on the so-called Red Scare; Donald Avery, *'Dangerous Foreigners': European Immigrant Workers and Labour Radicalism in Canada, 1896–1932* (Toronto, 1979).

19. See, for example, Sterling D. Spero and Abram L. Harris, *The Black Worker* (New York, 1931). Demand for black labor also increased because of the war manpower requirements.

20. See the essay by Lothar Elsner in this volume. The debate about the connections between voluntary and forced labor migration will be briefly summarized in the Introduction to Part I.

21. Emma Lazarus, "The New Colossus" (1883), *The Poems of Emma Lazarus*, 2 vols. (Boston, 1889), vol. 1, pp. 202–203.

22. Rudolph J. Vecoli, "The Contadini in Chicago: A Critique of *The Uprooted*," *Journal of American History* 51 (1964–1965), 404–17.

23. Adherents of the "new criticism" in the study of literature realize that their method has numerous built-in shortcomings that distort both what the author wanted to express

and what the readers perceived. "*Im*migration" history is in a similar situation. Its assumptions prevent an adequate description and analysis of what happened and how it was perceived by the historical actors.

24. After the United States, Asian Russia ranked second in number of migrants received (10 million to 1921). A. M. Carr-Saunders, *World Population* (Oxford, 1936), p. 49; *Les migrations internationales*, p. 557; Donald W. Treadgold, *The Great Siberian Migration. Government and Peasant in the Resettlement from Emancipation to the First World War* (Princeton, N.J., 1957).

25. Louis Dollot, *Les migrations humaines* (Paris, 1965); Franklin D. Scott, ed., *World Migration in Modern Times* (Englewood Cliffs, N.J., 1968).

26. For contemporary news items, see, for example, *Niles' Register*. The recent community studies on the formation of the United States working class pay relatively little attention to the newcomers.

27. *Historical Statistics of the United States*, vol. 1, series C, pp. 89–101. The largest of three waves of German migration took place from 1879 to 1895.

28. For the acculturation of these labor migrants, see the publications of a research project directed by Hartmut Keil and John Jentz at the University of Munich.

29. Following the famine-induced migrations, an average of 44,000 Irish arrived annually from 1855 to 1914.

30. In 1882 a total of 103,000 Scandinavian immigrants arrived, two and a half times as many as the highest pre-1880 total. Several authors in this volume point to the inadequacy of the distinction between "old" and "new" immigration in the context of United States history. Note that the same distinction is used—with different connotations—for France and Belgium. For Belgium "new" immigration means the post-World War I migration, for France, the post-1945 migration.

31. *Harvard Encyclopedia of American Ethnic Groups*, Stephan Thernstrom and Ann Orlov, eds. (Cambridge, Mass., 1980), pp. 1036–37. The rate of return migration increased during the depression years but fell rapidly after World War II. By then, however, the character of the migration had totally changed to one of "displaced persons" and political refugees.

32. Even in the 1970s Polish migrants returned to Poland after a working life in the United States to spend the rest of their lives "at home" (and to take advantage of the currency exchange rate).

33. For a model of acculturation applicable both to the labor migration of the turn of the century and the present-day, see Dirk Hoerder, "Migration in the European and American Economies: Comparative Perspectives on Its Impact on Working-Class Consciousness." Paper read at the symposium, Emigration from Northern, Central and Southern Europe—Theoretical and Methodological Principles of Research, Kraków, 1984. Revised German translation in Klaus J. Bade, ed., *Auswanderung-Wanderarbeiter-Gastarbeiter: Bevölkerung, Arbeitsmarkt und Wanderung in Deutschland seit der Mitte des 19. Jahrhunderts* (Ostfildern, 1984).

34. G. Marcel-Rémond, *L'immigration italienne dans le Sud-Ouest de la France* (Paris, 1928), pp. 21–31. At present refugees from Vietnam are settling entire deserted French villages or are trying to concentrate in underpopulated ones.

35. Compiled from U.S. Commissioner of Immigration, *Annual Reports* (Washington, D.C., 1900–1914) by Josip Lakatoš, cited in Frances Kraljic, *Croatian Migration to and from the United States, 1900–1914* (Palo Alto, Calif., 1978), p. 22.

36. K. Hvidt in *Les migrations internationales*, p. 333; for Finland cf. ibid., p. 393.

37. Hartmut Kaelble, *Historical Research on Social Mobility. Western Europe and the USA in the Nineteenth and Twentieth Centuries* (New York, 1981), and his "Social Mobility in America and Europe: A Comparison of Nineteenth-Century Cities," *Urban History Yearbook, 1981* (Leicester, 1981), pp. 24–38.

38. Kaelble, "Social Mobility," pp. 25, 27, 29, 31.

39. Kaelble, *Historical Research*, p. 33.

40. *Statistical Abstract of the United States* (Washington, 1973), p. 34; Maurice Didion, *Les salariés étrangers en France* (Paris, 1911), p. 7; André Armengaud, *La population française au XXe siècle* (Paris, 1970), p. 43.

41. Wolfgang Köllmann, "Industrialisierung, Binnenwanderung und 'Sociale Frage'," in his *Bevölkerung in der industriellen Revolution* (Göttingen, 1974), p. 117; Reinhard E. Petermann, *Wien im Zeitalter Franz Josephs I.* (Vienna, 1908), pp. 143–44.

42. Quoted from Celina Bobińska and Adam Galos, "Poland: Land of Mass Migration (19th and 20th Centuries)," in *Poland at the 14th International Congress of Historical Sciences in San Francisco, 1975* (Wrocław, 1975), p. 170.

43. Quoted from Jean Stengers, "Les mouvements migratoires en Belgique aux XIXe et XXe siècles," in *Les migrations internationales*, p. 292 (translated by D.H.).

44. For examples, see this introduction that follows and other essays in this volume. Edna Bonacich, "A Theory of Ethnic Antagonism: The Split Labor Market," *American Sociological Review* 37 (1972), pp. 547–59. More recent works, for example, David M. Gordon, Richard Edwards, Michael Reich, *Segmented Work, Divided Workers. The Historical Transformation of Labor in the United States* (Cambridge 1982), do not pay sufficient attention to the many small labor markets.

45. For example, *Correspondenzblatt* of the German federated trade unions from the 1890s onward.

46. See the essay on Czechs in Vienna in this volume. The study by Hartmut Keil and others on Germans in Chicago demonstrates similar settlement patterns.

47. Cf. the concept of rural-urban acculturation, "urban villagers," developed by Oscar Lewis and Herbert J. Gans. Oscar Lewis, "The Folk-Urban Ideal Type," in Philip M. Hauser and L. Schnore, eds., *The Study of Urbanization* (New York, 1965), pp. 491–500; H. J. Gans, *The Urban Villagers: Group and Class in the Life of Italian-Americans* (New York, 1962).

48. Jonathan D. Sarna, "The Myth of No Return: Jewish Return Migration to Eastern Europe, 1881–1914," *American Jewish History* 71 (1981–82), 256–68, reprinted as chapter 17 in this volume.

49. *Harvard Encyclopedia of American Ethnic Groups*, pp. 1036–37.

50. Reino Kero, "Emigration of Finns from North America to Soviet Karelia in the Early 1930s," in Michael G. Karni, ed., *The Finnish Experience in the Western Great Lakes Region: New Perspectives* (Vammala, 1975), pp. 212–21.

51. This second meaning is in the Macedonian language. See Milorad Ekmecic, "The International and Intercontinental Migrational Movements from the Yugoslav Lands from the End of the XVIIIth Century till 1941," in *Les migrations internationales*, p. 581.

52. A second-generation Irish immigrant from Minnesota visiting his relatives in Ireland offered to pay for an electric power connection and a water pipe to their cottage. After considerable deliberation the family decided to accept electricity, but felt that the expense for the water pipe was unwarranted since the spring was only a mile off. T. E. O'Brien to author, interview 1973.

53. Notes and citations in this section have been kept to a minimum since a bibliographic essay at the end of this volume provides extensive annotation.

54. Ingeborg Weber-Kellermann, *Erntebrauch in der ländlichen Arbeitswelt des 19. Jahrhunderts* (Marburg, 1965), esp. pp. 287–308; Abel Chatelain, *Les migrants temporaires en France de 1800 à 1914*, 2 vols. (Lille, 1976); and numerous other studies for different countries.

55. Terry Coleman, *The Railway Navvies* (London, 1965); James E. Handley, *The Navvy in Scotland* (Cork, 1970); Runo B. A. Nilsson, "Rallareliv" [The life of railway construction workers] Ph.D. diss., Uppsala, 1982.

56. Jean Stengers, "Les mouvements migratoires en Belgique aux XIXᵉ et XXᵉ siècles," in *Les migrations internationales*, pp. 283–317.

57. *Les migrations internationales*, pp. 335–36, 352, 384–85, 392–93.

58. Ibid., pp. 334, 352, 383 (citation Åkerman) 599.

59. In periods of economic depression other occupational groups also migrated. Thus drapers and weavers from Bohemia and Moravia left for the Russian part of Poland and Western Europe after 1815. Because of foreign domination, Bulgarian merchants left for Vienna at the end of the eighteenth century.

60. Jiří Kořalka and Květa Kořalkova, "Basic Features of Mass Emigration from the Czech Lands during the Capitalist Era," in *Les migrations internationales*, pp. 503–25.

61. Julianna Puskás, "Emigration from Hungary to the United States before 1914," ibid., pp. 527–39, citation from p. 535. See also for more details, Julianna Puskás, *From Hungary to the United States (1880–1914)* (Budapest, 1982).

62. Milorad Ekmecic, "The International and Intercontinental Migrational Movements from the Yugoslav Lands from the End of the XVIIIth Century till 1941," in *Les migrations internationales*, pp. 565–94; the surveys of migration from Rumania, in ibid., pp. 541–53; and from Bulgaria, in ibid., pp. 555–63.

63. Ibid., pp. 579, 580.

64. Barbara A. Anderson, *Internal Migration during Modernization in Late Nineteenth-Century Russia* (Princeton, N.J., 1980); Robert E. Johnson, *Peasant and Proletarian: The Working Class of Moscow in the Late Nineteenth Century* (New Brunswick, N.J., 1979).

65. See the essay by H. Fassmann in this volume. Lynn Hollen Lees (cf. note 69 below), pp. 22–42. Cf. also J. Ehmer and H. Fassmann, "Zur Sozialstruktur von Zuwanderern in mitteleuropäische Städte des 19. Jahrhunderts," paper read at the symposium on Immigration and Urban Society in Europe, 1600 to 1900, Göttingen, Vienna, 1982, examining migration to Vienna, Rome, Fribourg, Zürich, and Zagreb.

66. Ehmer and Fassmann (note 65) emphasize that migration was not only to industrial centers but to towns in general.

67. In 1841 almost 60,000 Irish came to Britain for seasonal work especially to the market gardening areas around London, to the hop growing areas in Kent, as well as to Lincolnshire and elsewhere.

68. Most of the migrants were laborers from a rural background, but a limited number of skilled workers and a small number of middle-class Irish seeking the professional and educational opportunities of London also came.

69. For the Irish migration I have relied on Lynn Hollen Lees's excellent study, *Exiles of Erin. Irish Migrants in Victorian London* (Ithaca, N.Y., and Manchester, 1979).

70. Luigi Favero and Graziano Tassello, "Cent'anni di emigrazione italiana (1876–

1976), "in Gianfausto Rosoli, ed., *Un secolo di emigrazione italiana 1876–1976* (Rome, 1978), p. 19.

71. A. Sartorius Freiherr von Waltershausen, *Die italienischen Wanderarbeiter* (Leipzig, 1903), pp. 13, 20, 22, 27.

72. Bobińska and Galos, "Poland: Land of Mass Migration," pp. 169–209, esp. pp. 171, 174.

73. Cf. Vladimir Djakǒv, "Ob učastii Poljakov v izučenii i osvoenii Sibiri (XIX v.)" [On the role of Poles in the study of Siberia and its management, 19th Cent.], *Report at the Colloque de la Commission Internationale des Etudes Slaves* (Cracow, 1973).

74. Cf. Włodzimierz Jastrzębski, *Hitlerowkie wysiedlenia z ziem polskich wcielonych do Rzeszy w latach 1939–1945* [Expulsion of Poles from the areas annexed to the Reich, 1939–1945, by the Nazis] (Posnan, 1960); Ludwik Landau, *Wychodźstwo sezonowe na Łotwę i do Niemiec w 1937 r.* [Seasonal emigration to Latvia and Germany, 1937] (Warsaw, 1966); A. Zarychta, *Emigracja polska 1918–1931 i jej znaczenie dla państwa* [Polish emigration 1918–1931 and its significance for the state] (Warsaw, 1933).

75. From 1800 to 1914 Swiss emigration amounted to 510,000 persons.

76. Lucio Boscardin, *Die italienische Einwanderung in die Schweiz* (Basle, 1962), pp. 9–25; Erich Gruner, "Immigration et marché du travail en Suisse au XIXème siècle," in *Les migrations internationales*, pp. 175–94; Hermann-Michel Hymann, *Les travailleurs étrangers. Chance et tourment de la Suisse* (Lausanne, 1966), pp. 23–50.

77. For Irish migration, see notes 67–69. On German migration in the 1820s, see a note in Rudolf Engelsing, *Bremen als Auswandererhafen* (Bremen, 1961), p. 109. Lloyd P. Gartner, *The Jewish Immigrant to England, 1870–1914*, 2d ed. London, 1973). Harry Snell, *The Foreigner in England* (London, 1904).

78. Charlotte Erickson, *American Industry and the European Immigrant* (Cambridge, 1957), pp. 49, 56 passim, and *Invisible Immigrants. The Adaptation of English and Scottish Immigrants in Nineteenth-Century America* (Coral Gables, Fla., 1972), pp. 61–62, 214 passim; Rowland Tappan Berthoff, *British Immigrants in Industrial America, 1790–1950* (Cambridge, Mass., 1953), pp. 9–10, 52, 80–84, quotation from p. 82.

79. See the essay by K. Bade in this volume and the bibliographic essay.

80. See the essay by N. Green in this volume. Abel Chatelain, *Les migrants temporaires* (cf. note 54); Willcox and Ferenczi, eds., *International Migrations*, vol. 2, pp. 201–36.

81. See the essay by C. Riegler in this volume. On the other hand we do not deal separately with the transfer of specific forms of working-class consciousness. One reason is that much more research is needed in this field, the other that the most highly visible emigration of politically prosecuted workers and labor leaders under the anti-Socialist Law in Germany from 1878 to 1890 resulted in less than a thousand departures to the United States.

82. See the essay by L. Elsner in this volume and the series edited by his institute at Rostock University, *Fremdarbeiterpolitik des Imperialismus* (1975 onward).

83. Gary S. Cross, "Toward Social Peace and Prosperity: The Politics of Immigration in France during the Era of World War I," *French Historical Studies* 11 (1979–1980), 610–32.

84. Many studies of present-day migration pay considerably more attention to the connections between the movements of capital and the migration of labor, an aspect that most historians of the turn-of-the century migration neglect totally. This approach is

common both among Marxists and economists of the European community. See the numerous studies researched for and published by the Organization for Economic Co-operation and Development (OECD.) See also Stephen Castles and Godula Kosack, *Immigrant Workers in Western Europe* (London, 1973) and many others.

85. One methodologically important research effort was the UNESCO-sponsored sociological study of Italian and Polish labor migrants in Belgium and France. It combined quantitative studies with oral history (interviews), took patterns of employment and of housing (productive and reproductive spheres) into account, and compared "old" (pre-war) and partly acculturated migrants with "new" (Post-World War II) insecure and alienated ones. See the studies by René Clemens et al. for Belgium, by Alain Girard and Jean-François Stoetzel for France as well as W. D. Borrie, *The Cultural Integration of Immigrants* (Paris, 1952).

86. See for example the essays by Adam Walaszek of the Polonia Research Institute, Cracow, in *Przeglad Polonijny* 4, no. 4 (1978), 37–50; 5, no. 3 (1979), 21–39; 6, no. 1 (1980), 5–17; *Studia Historyzne* 23, no. 3 (1980), 471–79.

87. *Les migrations internationales*, based on several conferences, has attempted to research a broad approach by adding reports from many countries to form an overview. However some countries are not represented, some essays are of very poor quality, others are not primarily concerned with labor migration. Because of several high quality contributions the collection is indispensable, however.

LABOR ON THE MOVE: MIGRATION IN EUROPE BEFORE WORLD WAR I

The migratory movements of skilled and unskilled laborers resulting from the internationalization of segments of the labor market first in the European then in the Atlantic economies form the theme of Part I. In the first essay two scholars of the highly renowned Uppsala Migration Research Project, now engaged in preparing a handbook of Scandinavian migration, outline theories of migration, the comparatively advanced state of research, and the development from pre-industrial and internal to industrial and transoceanic migration in Scandinavia. They outline the continuity of migration over the centuries to the present. Heinz Fassmann, in the second essay, is concerned in part with methodological questions. His examples are migratory flows in imperial Austria toward Vienna and the patterns that develop. The acculturation of some of these migrants will be taken up in Part II by Monika Glettler. From an empire with high internal migration and considerable international labor migration, the perspective turns to the classic labor exporting country, Italy. The British colony of Ireland—see the afterword—provided migrants earlier than Italy and Poland did so, too (See Part II). But in no other country has labor migration abroad been so large *and* continuous a phenomenon as in Italy. It is still part of the life of many Italian workers today.

Germany and France, the subjects of the next two studies, received millions of migrants from Italy and elsewhere. Up to 1895 and to a lesser degree after that, Germany also witnessed large emigration and labor migration to North America. Outflow from France was low, and the country squarely faced the need for immigration, occasional anti-alien sentiments and violence notwithstanding. Germany, on the other hand, never established laws and regulations that made labor migration easy for the migrants. The only clear-cut policy since the 1890s was that foreign labor was needed permanently in peacetime or wartime. Though Poles were not regarded as desirable aliens and the government reduced their numbers in the Prussian-occupied Polish territories, agricultural and industrial interests won out and temporary in-migration of Polish agricultural and, to a lesser degree, industrial workers was permitted. They had to leave Germany each winter to prevent acculturation and permanent settlement. However, those in Germany at the outbreak of World War I were detained for forced labor.

Labor migration resumed during the post-World-War-II boom. Again the government was ready to import labor but not to accord the workers and their families immigrant status. As more migrants decided to stay permanently, the present government has increased harassment, such as separation of families (even close relatives may not follow the labor migrants) or deportation of outspoken migrants.

C. Riegler shows that even highly qualified immigrants from "racially" similar countries—as public and government opinion termed it—like the skilled and professional migrants from Sweden, faced discrimination. These immigrants attempted to organize after World War I to resist pressures to oust them. Organizing was denied to the forced laborers during the war. L. Elsner proves that industry, agriculture, and government considered a migrant labor supply vital for the war economy and for the expected expansion after the war. His thesis is that labor-importing policies show a continuity from the development of German industrialization and imperialism to present-day capitalist West Germany. West German historians prefer to interpret the recruitment of forced labor during the two wars as temporary aberrations. This it was, certainly, considering its formal aspect: forced rather than voluntary recruitment. But the documents quoted by Elsner do show a continuity of German intentions: assurance of a foreign labor supply as cheap and submissive as possible ("billig und willig") by whatever means possible. After the war, governments began to encourage in-migration of labor in Germany, France, Belgium, and elsewhere but tried to control it with the aid of semi-official recruiting agencies in the countries of origin. This selection process also ensured that only healthy and strong or qualified workers came. In other words, the selection further increased the advantage of the industrialized receiving country over the sending country.

2

MIGRATION PATTERNS IN THE NORDIC COUNTRIES

Hans Norman and Harald Runblom

MIGRATION RESEARCH IN THE NORDIC COUNTRIES

The population of the Nordic countries has been very mobile for centuries. Research during the last few decades has revealed an unexpectedly high rate of mobility even during the old agrarian society, thereby contesting common perceptions of static conditions during earlier ages. The main forms of movement were over short distances within limited regions, and in addition there were currents of seasonal labor both within and outside these countries. A new mobility arose with the transformation of the agrarian society during the nineteenth century, which also linked the Nordic countries more closely to the Atlantic economy and strongly involved them in overseas migrations. Compared to the rest of Europe, Scandinavia experienced an emigration that was large in proportion to its relatively small population.

For many years the study of population mobility in the Nordic countries was the speciality of cultural geographers, but since the 1960s historically oriented migration studies have been legion. Thus, social history in Scandinavia, aiming to write the history of the "many" and seeking explanations for migration movements with the aid of theories developed from the social sciences, is comparatively young. Until 1960 Nordic historians, with the exception of Norway's Ingrid Semmingsen, disregarded the great wave of transatlantic migration from 1825 to 1930.[1] The corresponding research in the recipient nations, on the other hand, started significantly earlier. In the 1920s scholars as important as Theodore Blegen and George Stephenson worked in the field.[2] The Finnish immigration to America, which was of a later date, was similarly treated by American historians before Finnish scholars began their work.[3] As far as Icelandic migration is concerned, there has been significantly greater interest in Canada than in the country of origin. The Icelandic Department at the University of Manitoba has functioned as an important research center.

Migration has become an object of multi-disciplinary study. The Swedish geographer Helge Nelson and the ethnographer Albin Widén have paved the way.[4] Furthermore, since the 1930s the so-called Stockholm school of economists under the leadership of Gunnar Myrdal has developed an interest in Swedish internal migration, not least of all as a measure for other social phenomena. The greatest contribution of this approach was by the American sociologist and economist Dorothy Swaine Thomas, who studied the movements of the Swedish population from a classification of parishes according to the degree of industrialization.[5] Since the 1960s historians have concentrated on migration to the United States, but other receiving areas have also been taken into consideration.[6]

During the years 1965–1975 emigration research was particularly lively at Uppsala University where a foundation-funded group of researchers under the direction of Sten Carlsson and Sune Åkerman worked in the project "Sweden and America after 1860: Emigration, Re-migration, Social and Political Debate."[7] In Norway and Denmark emigration research was less characterized by large projects. In Finland, where the post-war emigration, primarily to Sweden, aroused the attention of the authorities, interest and support for migration research has resulted in the founding of the Institute for Migration in Turku. Important centers for documentation of overseas migration are to be found in Växjö, Sweden; Aalborg, Denmark; and Stavanger, Norway.

Contacts between Scandinavian emigration researchers have been lively, and a Nordic emigration atlas as well as comparative local studies are some of the tangible results of this cooperation.[8] Migration to Australia and New Zealand has also been the subject of inter-Nordic cooperative research.[9] However, contacts with American scholars have come primarily from individual Scandinavian countries.[10] Since the end of the 1970s migration scholars from both Eastern and Western Europe have established means of international cooperation and have made fundamental contributions toward sketching the history of transatlantic migration.[11]

Research in emigration history in Scandinavia has been much influenced by the social sciences. Birgitta Odén in 1962 appealed for an analysis with industrialization and urbanization at its center and a close alliance with economic research. She went even further in 1971, when she advocated a close connection with American econometric research in order to analyze the people on the move as well as those not moving.[12] Several Uppsala historians have applied Brinley Thomas's theories on capital movements in the Atlantic region, and sociological and geographic explanatory models have influenced a number of investigations.[13] The extraordinarily advantageous source material that the population statistics provide has prompted much quantitative research. Especially in Sweden and Finland, one can follow individuals through a series of movements on the basis of parish records. In recent years, however, a tendency for a stronger orientation toward literary and ethnological data has occurred. Since for many people emigration occurred step by step, the investigations of mass migration led to a renewed interest in internal migration. A strong connection existed between long-distance (transatlantic) and short-distance movements.

NORDIC PRE-INDUSTRIAL MIGRATION

Nordic Population Exchange with Other Countries in the Sixteenth and Seventeenth Centuries

The discoveries of the sixteenth century and the subsequent colonization of non-European parts of the world entailed a comprehensive transoceanic movement of people, which in many respects represented a new order for Europe. The movement over the Atlantic started from the Iberian Peninsula. The rise of the Dutch, French, and British empires followed, but the consequent temporary or permanent transoceanic migration for purposes of trade or to exploit natural resources and indigenous labor remained limited. Only settlers' colonies received a steady inflow. Scandinavia was more indirectly affected by these changes. Its sparsely populated countries took only a marginal interest in colonial ventures, and their outposts remained small. Emigration, as a rule, was strictly regulated, but the administrative loopholes were many and the possibilities for control very limited.

European expansion and colonization went in various directions and took different forms. In Scandinavia settlement stretched northward. In Tsarist Russia an increasingly organized colonization and settlement occurred in the eastern areas. To the southeast, where the Turks had extended their rule, there was neither the space nor the motivation for expansion in the sixteenth and seventeenth centuries.

In western Europe the growth of centers of trade and finance, such as London and Amsterdam, proved attractive to the Nordic countries, and in the seventeenth century certain Dutch cities had an influx of Scandinavians, who not merely visited but also settled there. It must be assumed that Hamburg has played a similar role since the late Middle Ages.[14]

The migration from Norway during the second half of the seventeenth century followed two main paths. One led to Copenhagen, which after 1536 was also the Norwegian capital, the other to the great maritime powers. While immigrants to the Netherlands were for the most part seafarers who voluntarily made their way there, those who went to the British Isles were often fleeing military service.[15] In 1617 and 1620 the Swedish government, which was anxious to keep labor and soldiers within the country, found that extensive southward migration mainly of maids, farmhands, and workers from the Finnish areas had occurred not only to Denmark, but also to Germany, Prussia, and Poland. Migrants came for the most part from the Swedish provinces bordering Denmark, and they often had Copenhagen, Lübeck, and Danzig as their goals. A special type of migration consisted of soldiers who fled from Swedish regiments on the continent, as well as of men who wished to escape impending conscription.[16] There was also extensive wanderings of journeymen from the Nordic countries to the European continent, which in all likelihood led to the settlement of both individuals and small groups, particularly in German areas.

Of greater importance than out-migration was the in-migration to Scandinavia from the continent during the seventeenth century. A number of immigrants came to Norway from the countries surrounding the North Sea, and many of these, especially from the higher social strata, settled in the cities. Four different groups may be pointed out here: officials, often from Denmark; officers, frequently of German origin (German long remained the language of command in the Danish-Norwegian army); miners, many of whom came from Saxony; and merchants and craftsmen of varying extraction. To give only one example, 51 percent of the burghers of the city of Bergen in the period between 1621 and 1630 were born outside of Norway.[17]

Sweden as a rising power had a great demand for foreign expertise in the military, organizational, financial, and technical fields. The inclusion of the Baltic areas within the Swedish realm led to an influx from there: Baltic noble families were admitted to the House of Nobility (*Riddarhuset*) during the seventeenth century, and the Swedish armed services and state administration made use of Balts as officers and civilian officials. Germans played an important role in the internationalization of Swedish rule during the Age of Greatness (1560–1721). The German settlement in Sweden had its origin in the Middle Ages, and the merchants and miners of which it was made up had a permanent influence on Swedish society. In the sixteenth century Germans were recruited for the army and the civil service, and some Germans even became Councilors (*riksråd*). The strong German position in the Swedish cities led to fear of and contempt for foreigners. But cultural and economic life were also greatly influenced by them, and the fact that five Swedish cities had German church congregations bears witness to their great number.[18]

The political and economic expansion of the growing Swedish realm did not just attract immigrants from the other side of the Baltic. Influential groups also came from the Low Countries and Scotland. The Walloons were of great importance for the development of the Swedish iron industry from 1620 to 1660. Led by the merchant and financier Louis De Greer, they transformed some areas into thriving mining and metal-working centers. The Scots contributed soldiers, especially during the 1560s, and Dutch engineers played a part in the founding of Gothenburg. In its appearance the city has much in common with Amsterdam.[19]

Inter-Nordic Migration Patterns and Seasonal Labor Migration

Considerable territorial changes occurred in Scandinavia at the beginning of the nineteenth century. As a result of the Russian attack on Finland in 1808 and the Swedish-Russian Peace Treaty in 1809, Finland, since the Middle Ages a part of the Swedish kingdom, became a Grand Duchy under the Russian tsar and remained so until 1918. Norway was separated from Denmark by the Treaty of Kiel in 1814 and was combined with Sweden in a personal union under the Swedish monarch until 1905. During the nineteenth century, however, Norway had a relatively autonomous position in relation to Sweden as had Finland to Russia.

A few general characteristics will be considered before taking a closer look at the movements and labor migrations within the individual countries. An investigation of selected rural parishes and towns in Sweden has revealed a migration intensity during the seventeenth century that can be compared with that of the nineteenth century. Migration to and from rural areas often involved short distances, but migration to urban areas spread over great parts of the country as well as to Finland, Livonia, and Königsberg. The four cities studied (Nyköping,

Norrköping, Västerås, and Arboga) had an average rate of in-migration that exceeded 8 percent of the total population.[20]

The major movements in Sweden during the 1600s appear to have have been toward the iron-producing centers of the region of Bergslagen, but also to cities, which grew rapidly at that time in spite of the high rate of mortality. From 1620 to 1670 Stockholm quadrupled its population from approximately 10,000 to about 40,000. Similar patterns may be observed in Norway.[21]

Figure 2.1
The Nordic Countries (with Swedish County Boundaries)

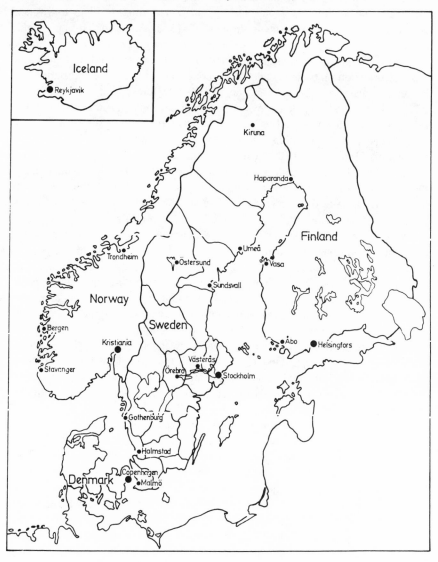

Industrialization reached Denmark and Norway earlier than Sweden. In Finland these changes came even later and were less radical. The period 1850–1900 was dominated by migration from the less industrialized Swedish-speaking regions of Finland to Norrland and to the Stockholm area; from southern Sweden to Denmark; and from western Sweden to Norway. The dominant element was the movement to the early industrialized and expanding regions of Copenhagen and Christiania (Oslo). Until the 1880s St. Petersburg, Russia, attracted an ever-increasing number of migrants from Finland.[22]

The migration between Finland and Sweden reflects the shifts in political power around the Baltic. These movements have occurred from the Middle Ages till today, only with varying intensity. Organized recruiting of Finns to Sweden began during the time of Gustavus Vasa (1521–1560). Some settled as peasants, others were employed in the rural iron industries and mines. In the 1570s many Finns from Savolax settled in the forested areas of central Sweden. This led to a new cultivation on a large scale. They broke land using slash and burn techniques for nearly a hundred years, laying waste to forests that were needed as fuel for the iron industry. In spite of wide distribution and lack of concentrations, the Finnish language as well as elements of material culture survived in these settlements up to the beginning of the twentieth century. Stockholm, which was the capital of Finland until 1809, exerted a constant pull, leading to the formation of a Finnish colony with both permanent and temporary members. Among them the proportion of laborers was especially high, and certain job categories, such as timbermen, were over-represented. The shipyards in Stockholm, as well as in Karlskrona and Kalmar, have long recruited Finnish labor.[23]

From the migration between the Nordic countries Norway made the largest net gains during the years from 1825 to 1865. It also had one of the highest rates of natural population growth. By far the largest group of immigrants was the Swedes who sought employment in forestry, agriculture, and construction work.[24] The migration contacts between both countries were primarily along the border, and the population streams were not greatly influenced by political ties. Only in exceptional cases did the political union lead to the migration of officials. Despite some marriages of Swedish and Norwegian aristocrats, the cultural contacts can scarcely be said to have been lively. Investors in the lumber industry were a small but important group emigrating from Norway to Sweden during the middle of the nineteenth century. This industry also attracted entrepreneurs from other countries.[25]

For Swedes and Danes it was natural to move back and forth across the border, especially since the present Swedish provinces of Skåne, Halland, and Blekinge belonged to Denmark before 1658. From the province of Kronoberg in southern Sweden emigration to Denmark and Germany was larger than to America during the 1850s. Such migration, however, has not created as much interest, since it was less dramatic than migration to America. As a rule, those who returned from Denmark's cities or the estates in Holstein did not display great wealth. They usually remained in the lower strata of society.[26] For Denmark southern Sweden represented a source of cheap male and female labor. Many Swedish women found employment in the large estates or in the sugarbeet-producing areas of Lolland and Falster. Their living conditions in barracks were often miserable. This emigration culminated during the first half of the 1800s, but waned after the turn of the century because Sweden had become increasingly industrialized.[27]

Seasonal labor migrations can be traced back several centuries. They increased during the nineteenth century and reached their peak before the emigration to America and the industrial takeoff had gained momentum.[28] As a rule, seasonal migrants went to naturally productive regions. They were normally recruited from among the poorer rural population, tenants, cottars, and so-called free laborers. These groups had increased sharply in connection with the rapid population growth of the early part of the nineteenth century.

It is sometimes difficult to differentiate between seasonal and permanent labor migration, since the former was often the preliminary stage of a definitive move to a new location. An example is the seasonal workers in the sawmill districts along the coast of Swedish Norrland, many of whom afterwards found steady work and settled there permanently.[29]

Four major directions can be distinguished in the seasonal migrations from Finland during the nineteenth century. One was internal and led to construction and building works in the cities of Helsinki and Turku. This migration, which came from many areas in Finland, increasingly resulted in permanent settlement. The second was toward the fishing districts along the Norwegian and Russian arctic coasts, where thousands took work from late winter to mid-summer. A third stream of laborers, mostly recruited from southern Finland, went to the St. Petersburg area. During the latter half of the nineteenth century, finally, a significant number sought work in the lumber industry, on the log drives, and in the sawmills along the Swedish coast of the Gulf of Bothnia.[30]

In Norway the majority of seasonal workers came from mountain communities and made their way to valleys, coastal plains, or fishing districts. Their primary goal outside of Norway was the large agricultural estates of Denmark. Many migrants from eastern Norway were also attracted by the building of the Swedish railways and by the lumber industry.

In Denmark seasonal migration was mainly from Jutland to the grazing districts in other parts of the country and to the large estates in northern Germany and Holland. Before 1914 many Swedish and Polish seasonal laborers were also attracted to Denmark.

In Sweden the provinces of Dalarna, Värmland, and Dalsland, as well as parts of Västergötland, Småland, and northern Skåne, had extensive seasonal labor migrations because of partitioning of land holdings coupled with a comparatively steep rise in population. Laborers migrated primarily to the large estates of the Lake Mälaren Valley and to the cities, especially Stockholm. In Dalarna a rich folk tradition about these wanderings has developed. Many western Swedes made their way to the Gothenburg area. From the southern provinces migrants went to the large labor-intensive farms of Denmark and northern Germany. Others sought work in Copenhagen and Hamburg. During the end of the eighteenth century, when herring fishing was flourishing on the Swedish west coast, about 12,000 seasonal laborers were employed in fishing, transporting, and preparing the catch. The majority of these came from Västergötland, Dalsland, and Värmland. Special foremen recruited teams of workers from the individual villages. When the herring fishing began to decline in about 1810, the seasonal laborers from the western part of the country began to search for opportunities in Norway, both in Östlandet, Christiania (Oslo), and in the Trondheim area. After the middle of the nineteenth century the lumber industry became an attractive new goal for itinerant laborers from the entire country, but especially for those from Värmland. Others went from northern Sweden over the Norwegian border to the Lofoten Islands and from the Torne Valley to northern Norway to fish in Arctic waters and work in the mines. (See Figure 2.2.)

Figure 2.2
The Directions of Seasonal Migration in Sweden c. 1750 and c. 1875

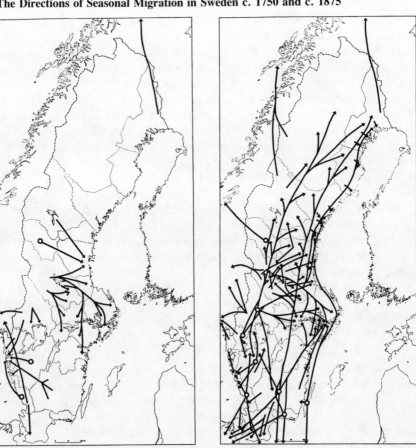

Source: G. Rosander, *Herrarbete* (Uppsala, 1967), pp. 309, 319.
Note: A circle means that nearly the whole province took part in the migrations.

THE ERA OF TRANSOCEANIC MIGRATION IN THE NORDIC COUNTRIES

Until about 1800 the Nordic countries carried out a population policy that is commonly labeled as mercantilistic. The fundamental goal was to maintain and, if possible, increase the size of the population, which, in turn, would contribute to the nation's economic, political, and military strength. Thus, emigration to other countries was considered an abomination, and a ban on emigration was one of several means of hindering the drain on the population potential. During the eighteenth century there were rigid regulations in Denmark that even prohibited movement within the kingdom for certain categories of workers. The *stavnsbaandet*, introduced in 1733 and abolished a century later, forbade men between the ages of fourteen and thirty-six to leave their employment on estates without the consent of the owners.

Chronology, Diffusion, and Interplay of Migrations

Apart from the state-supported Swedish colonization scheme of the mouth of the Delaware River (1638–1655), during the "Age of Greatness" only individual emigrants made their way from Scandinavia to North America. Transoceanic migration for the purpose of settlement was a nineteenth-century phenomenon. Beginning in the 1820s Norway was the first Scandinavian country with large-scale emigration. One can already speak of a mass migration during the 1850s. In Sweden the outflow gained momentum a decade later, while in Finland it began during the latter half of the 1880s. Emigration from Denmark, which never reached the intensity of that from its neighbors, had its first great upswing at the end of the 1860s. Iceland was a Danish territory with Copenhagen as its capital. Its emigration started abruptly when the Inman line announced the possibility of transport to America in 1873. In this year about one thousand persons, that is, no less than 1.4 percent of the island's population, signed emigration contracts. Climatic changes, a sheep disease, and the eruption of a volcano contributed to a short but intensive period of emigration.[31]

The development of emigration from the Nordic countries is shown in Figure 2.3 and in Table 2.1. In all countries except Finland the emigration culminated during the period 1880–1900. Thus, the mass emigration coincided with that of the rest of northwestern Europe. The table permits a comparison of the rate of emigration from the Nordic countries and from other selected European nations. Ireland was hardest hit, with more than four million emigrants and the highest emigration rate during all of the decades investigated.[32] Norway ranked next. During the period 1851–1930 the emigration from Norway totaled .8 million persons, from Denmark .4 million, from Sweden 1.2 million, and from Finland .4 million. The figure for Iceland, due to its small population, reached only 14,000.

To describe the outflow of people country by country is scarcely satisfying, as the regional differences within the countries were striking. Local emigration

Figure 2.3
Annual Emigration from the Nordic Countries to North America, 1851–1930
(Total number of emigrants per thousand inhabitants)

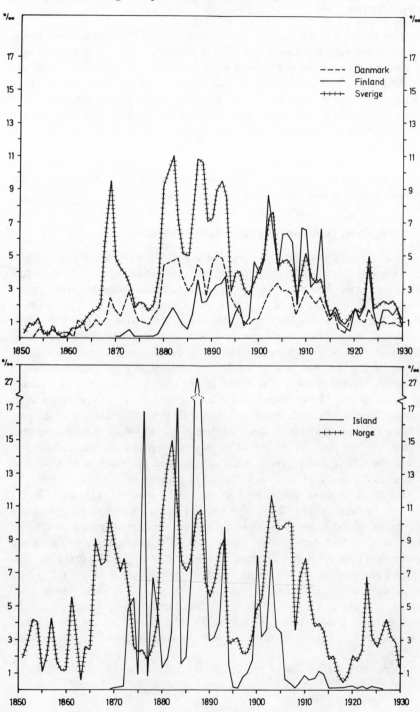

Source: Official Statistics of the Respective Countries.

has therefore been traced and divided into five-year periods between 1865 and 1914.[33] Two of the resulting maps, for the years 1865–69 and 1885–89, serve to illustrate the regional variations. (See Figure 2.4.) Relatively intense migration from many Norwegian areas is apparent during the second half of the 1860s, while the beginning of mass emigration in Sweden was very unevenly distributed. Emigration from Finland was still insignificant, but at the end of the century it gained momentum. The map for 1890–1894 discloses that emigration was strongest from the northern and western Swedish-speaking parts of Finland. Swedish emigration, at its beginning, was most intensive in the south, with the process not reaching the more northerly areas until later. In Denmark the areas with strong emigration remained identical, even if the emigration was more intensive during the 1890s.

Nordic historians have stressed that the early emigrants often determined the course of the rest of the emigration. The American travellers who left the harbor of Stavanger on 4 July 1825 aboard the sloop "Restaurationen" became a symbol of the Norwegian departure for the New World. With few exceptions, they came from a single location, Tysvaer, and many of them were related to each other. It is clear that they did not come from the poorest part of the population, as they had purchased the ship, a fact that also illustrates the group character of this enterprise. Many of those on board were Quaker sympathizers who joined this religious group in the United States.[34] A Swedish group was led by the farmer

Table 2.1

Transoceanic Emigration from the Nordic Countries and from Some Other European Countries (Mean annual emigration in per mille of the population 1851–1910)

	1851– 60	1861– 70	1871– 80	1881– 90	1891– 00	1901– 10
Denmark	0.3	1.0	2.1	3.9	2.2	2.8
Finland			0.2	1.2	2.4	5.5
Norway	2.4	5.8	4.7	9.6	4.5	8.3
Sweden	0.4	2.3	2.3	7.0	4.2	4.2
Iceland			4.2	8.8	3.0	2.3
Ireland		14.7	10.2	14.9	10.1	11.1*
England		2.8	4.0	5.7	3.6	5.8
German Reich	2.6	1.7	1.5	2.9	1.0	0.5*
France	0.3	0.2	0.2	0.3	0.2	0.1
Italy			1.0	3.2	4.9	10.8

Sources: Emigrationsutredningen. Betänkande och bilagor [Commission on emigration. Reports and supplements], 20 vols. (Stockholm, 1908–1913), bil. IV, tab. 26; W. F. Willcox and I. Ferenczi, *International Migrations*, 2 vols. (New York, 1929, 1931), vol. 2, tab. 9; Officiell statistik för de nordiska länderna [Official statistics of the Nordic countries].

*Related only to the years 1901–1908.

and carpenter Peter Cassel in the mid-1840s. Its members had practical training and founded a thriving settlement in New Sweden, Iowa.[35] A large group from the Swedish mining district near Karlskoga settled Stockholm, Wisconsin, in 1853–1854. Many of these emigrants were *bergsmän* (farmers with mining rights) who sold their farms in order to invest in better land in America.[36]

From Finland the emigration of groups was not as common. There the impulse to emigrate came from two directions. One was the contact that the Swedish-

Figure 2.4
Migration Overseas from the Nordic Countries, 1865–1894
(In per mille of the average population)

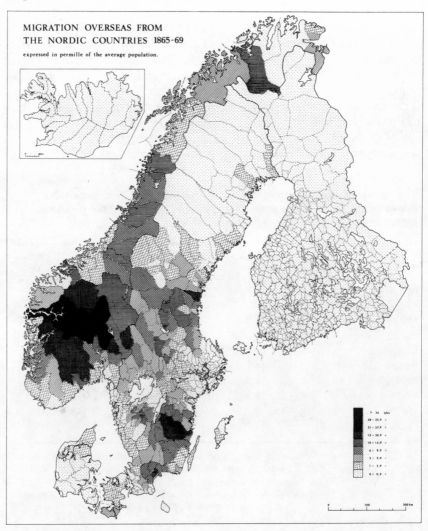

MIGRATION OVERSEAS FROM
THE NORDIC COUNTRIES 1865-69

expressed in permille of the average population.

speaking residents of the province of Vasa in western Finland had with the population on the Swedish side of the Gulf of Bothnia. The other was from the Finns who went to the mines and fishing districts of northern Norway. Emigration of miners and fishermen from there was common as early as the 1860s.[37]

There were several factors common to the early emigrants. They came from geographically limited areas, moved in large groups—often with an experienced guide—and were recruited as families. It is clear that religion was one element

Figure 2.4—*Continued*

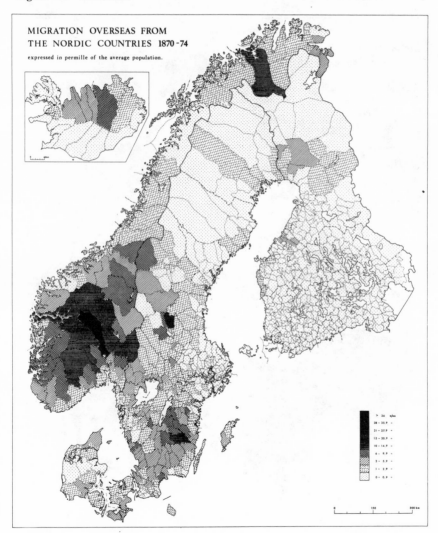

MIGRATION OVERSEAS FROM
THE NORDIC COUNTRIES 1870-74
expressed in permille of the average population.

in the decision to migrate, though persecution was not common. Other important reasons for the journey to America were, of course, the hope of attaining cheap land and better opportunities for employment. Low rates of emigration from the areas around expanding cities were a general pattern. Examples of such internal labor reservoirs were the regions surrounding Christiania (Oslo), Stockholm, and, to a certain extent, Copenhagen. In Finland migration from the southern and southeastern parts of the country went primarily to the growing cities,

Figure 2.4—_Continued_

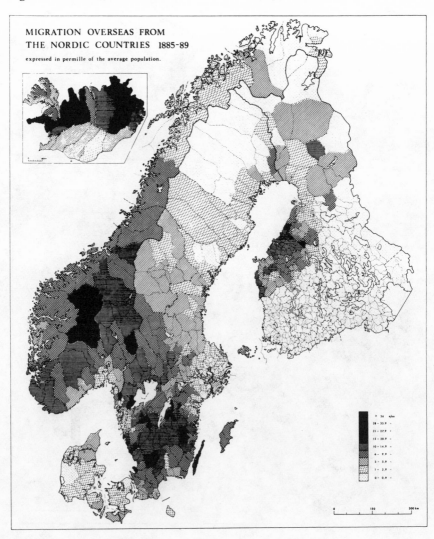

MIGRATION OVERSEAS FROM
THE NORDIC COUNTRIES 1885-89
expressed in permille of the average population.

especially Helsinki, and across the border to St. Petersburg.[38] Migration traditions led to the so-called stock effect, continuous overseas migration throughout the entire period, especially if the area was located far from the cities that were undergoing strong economic expansion.

This emigration must be viewed as one integral part of the total population movement, but not even during the greatest exodus was it the dominant form of movement.[39] Emigration and internal movements were aspects of the same

Figure 2.4—Continued

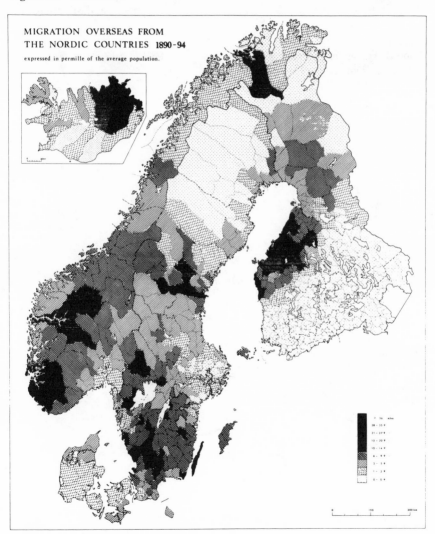

MIGRATION OVERSEAS FROM
THE NORDIC COUNTRIES 1890-94

expressed in permille of the average population.

phenomenon, a rupture with the older agricultural society. This is also demonstrated by the fact that areas with a high rate of emigration had low internal migration and vice versa. In the Swedish counties of Västernorrland and Örebro, emigration formed a significantly smaller portion of the total movement than internal migration.[40] In Finnish Österbotten, on the other hand, overseas migration was responsible for approximately half the total movement from that province. In Denmark, with its lower rate of emigration, this outflow comprised a substantially smaller proportion of the total migration. Periodically, the net in-migration to the city of Copenhagen reached a level equal to that of the country's emigration.[41]

Figure 2.5 illustrates the movements out of the Swedish parish of Gräsmark, located in the province of Värmland. There were four important destinations for

Figure 2.5
Major Directions of the Migration from Gräsmark Parish (Värmland County) to Destinations Outside the County

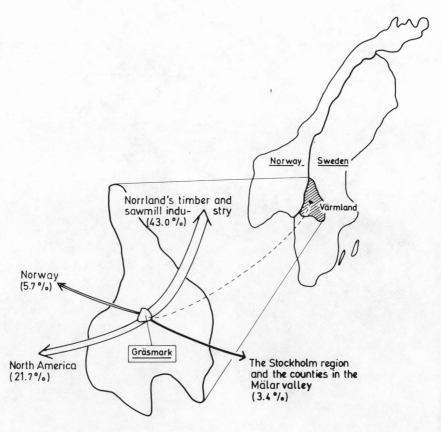

Source: A. Norberg, *Sågarnas ö* (Uppsala 1980), p. 46.

migrants. They went most frequently to the centers of the lumbering and timber industry in Norrland (43 percent), but a large part also made their way over the Atlantic to North America (21.7 percent). Gräsmark's location in western Sweden also meant that movements over the border to Norway were greater than to Stockholm and the Lake Mälaren Valley.[42]

The so-called step-by-step migration makes the connection between movements within and outside the country apparent. Cities had a higher emigration intensity than rural areas. But a considerable number of the emigrants from urban areas were people who had earlier moved in from the country. A Norwegian study has shown that more than half of those who left the country via Bergen had earlier moved into that city from the countryside. In Christiania (Oslo), the same was true of more than two-thirds who left during the years 1870–1900. Similar circumstances have been observed in Stockholm and Copenhagen, where approximately half the emigrants had resided in the city for five years or less.[43] This pattern applied particularly to women, who as a rule had a higher rate of migration to the cities than men because of the demand for household employees. At the same time more women than men emigrated from the cities; during the years 1881–1910, 114 women left for every 100 men. While men mostly departed for America directly from rural areas, women who made the same move frequently did so after spending some time in a city milieu in their native country.[44]

The Economic and Demographic Background and the Social Composition of the Emigration

The nineteenth century brought great economic changes within the Nordic countries. Commercialization and rationalization of agriculture occurred and by 1900 industrialization had made its breakthrough. Thus a number of employment opportunities came into being simultaneously with the massive emigration. Why then did this outflow reach such proportions? One fundamental reason was the rapid population increase. Because of this the authorities abandoned their earlier restrictive stands regarding emigration. Secondly, there were certain parallels between transatlantic flows of capital and labor. European export of capital promoted the development of transportation facilities and, in turn, increased the capacity for conveying large numbers of emigrants.

The yearly fluctuations in emigration generally followed the same pattern in all countries, even if the size of the outflow varied considerably. Since the business cycles in Europe and the United States did not often coincide, the question of whether push or pull factors were primarily responsible for the great fluctuations in the flow of people has been raised.

Much speaks for the developments in America as the determining factors. Push factors in the form of a population surplus, unemployment, and proletarization remained constant. Close contacts between earlier emigrants and potential migrants in the areas of origin conveyed information on the business cycles and the labor market to relatives and friends. Letters from America and tales of return migrants served as catalysts for emigration, especially when prepaid tickets and concrete information on the possibilities of employment and on travel modes and costs were provided. That the intensity of departures fluctuated so greatly both over time and between various regions can be explained to a great extent by these self-generating effects, which comprised an essential component of the emigration tradition discussed earlier. The network of emigrant agents, created by transatlantic steamship companies at the end of the 1860s when they came to dominate the business, had less effect than expected on both the total volume and the yearly fluctuations.[45]

The emigrants came from all social strata, and most of them were unmarried males and females, often under the age of twenty-five. The majority were the sons and daughters of farmers, tenants, or other groups of the lower strata within agricultural society. Later the number of industrial workers increased. During the years following 1900 the number of trained and educated emigrants grew. Finnish emigration had a particularly agrarian character. Nearly 90 percent of all those who left came from the countryside. This migration was also highly male-dominated, with men making up two-thirds of the total. In the other Nordic countries the emigrants were more evenly divided between men and women.[46] However, the continuing importance of the family must not be underestimated, since many of these single emigrants traveled within the framework of the movement of a family. For a family such moves might have occurred at different times and from different places. Many young emigrants with departure certificates from cities traveled westward to North America, joining family members who had settled there. When this "gradual family emigration" is taken into consideration, the bonds of family and kin stand out as important throughout the entire emigration period.

From 1880 to 1900 the character of migration changed from a settler migration to the Midwest, to a labor migration to the industrial centers along the East Coast, to the Chicago area, and to the lumber districts along the Pacific Coast. While the Swedish labor movement regarded emigration as a sign that the class society at home could not take care of sections of its population, some labor activists and strikers did migrate, and the newspaper *Socialdemokraten*, which was first published in 1886, regularly reported on conditions in the United States. During strikes, in the aftermath of lost strikes, and in consequence of the black-listing of strikers, strike leaders, and union activists, workers left their home areas, or to phrase it more cautiously, their workplaces and the communities they lived in, to which they had often migrated only a short time before. Part of this movement remained internal or Nordic migration, other workers went to the United States. They knew, however, this only meant going to another capitalist society. "The old 'liberal' picture of America as the land of political liberty, justice, and religious tolerance faded under the influence of developments that took place in the United States and Sweden."[47] Workers' decisions to migrate were based on a well-informed evaluation of job opportunities and labor market developments. The information came from returnees (19 percent of emigration), "America letters" (perhaps as many as two million a year), and from newspaper reports. While it has been argued that the Norwegian returnees, disappointed with North American conditions, had a radicalizing influence on the labor movement in the 1920s, no such argument is valid for Sweden.

From newspapers Swedish workers knew about low wages and very limited job opportunities in the late 1880s. Strikes were reported by *Socialdemokraten* as signs of the stirring of American workers. After a brief lull in reports about unemployment in 1890, the situation took a turn for the worse in 1891, culminating in reports of the Homestead strike of 1892. The picture presented, as well as Swedish emigration, reached a low in 1894. When Swedish workers migrated, they did so not because they had illusions about opportunities but because they considered the labor market situation—and in some cases employer pressure—in Sweden to be worse than conditions in America. According to Lars-Göran Tedebrand's study "In a situation where a strike or socialist activity led to blacklisting, and a feeling of expulsion from the community existed among workers, emigration to America could be an attractive alternative."[48]

Once in the United States, some labor militants remained active, but other workers did not get involved in further organizational or strike efforts. The case of Swedish workers in Worcester, Mass., is an example. Two migration chains converged there. In 1869 two potters from Höganäs went to the Norton pottery works and unleashed a stream of migrants that reached its high point in the two decades after 1900. A study trip to Sweden by a Worcester ironworks entrepreneur, which included some casual recruiting of iron mill laborers from Bergslagen, induced a second stream. By the middle of the 1890s Swedish in-migrants constituted about one-tenth of Worcester's population of 100,000. The vast majority of them belonged to the working class. In 1880 only 3 percent of the migrants was comprised of landowners, farmers, entrepreneurs, officials, master artisans, shopkeepers, teachers, and foremen. Farm workers and domestic servants comprised another 15.8 percent, while 81.2 percent were craftsmen, artisans (below the rank of master), skilled workers, and unskilled workers in industry and commerce. The last group had slightly increased to 85.3 percent by 1907. The farm workers and domestic servants, however, had become a negligible quantity (0.3 percent), while an emerging middle class from the level of shopkeeper upward comprised 14.4 percent of the Swedish-American population.[49] The shift from agriculture to industry had been completed among the working-class section of the town's population, while the process of community-building had gained momentum. It was to these activities that the Swedish migrants turned their attention. They "were busy reshaping their social and cultural neighborhood and not just accepting the limitations of the established host society." Under these new conditions even experienced immigrant labor activists lost their political stamina. Worcester employers reacted to unionization with primitive repression as well as sophisticated paternalism. There was a constant danger of being fired. As a result, savings in good years were used to establish supportive clubs and lodges as well as for other social activities. Politically the Swedish migrants could not develop any clout. By 1904 only 2,000 of them could vote. Many did not even bother to obtain the first papers that would begin the process to become citizens. They wanted to return because they felt the existing political system to be unresponsive. It might be noted that their working-class predecessors, the Irish, had established a political position that did give them considerable influence via the Democratic Party. For Swedes this development came later.[50] Thus, on the eve of World War I, the Swedish immigrants were far removed from the agrarian movement in the Midwest. This development has not received sufficient attention from historians.

Reactions to Emigration in the Countries of Origin

The transition from a mercantilistic population policy to one that may be designated liberal occurred as a consequence of radical economic changes and a substantial population increase. This population rise without a corresponding increase in employment opportunities led to an increase in the number of people living at the poverty level, which was especially noticeable from the beginning of the nineteenth century. The poor strata of the population became a reserve of labor, whose usefulness from the point of view of the employer increased if people had the freedom to move. With an economy that was more liberal in other respects, and in which market forces were given more freedom, it was also consistent to permit inhabitants to leave the kingdom. In Sweden this right became law in 1840, and a further relaxation was the removal of the compulsory passport in 1860. In Denmark the right to emigrate was not codified, but was implicit within other regulations. In Norway, where the increase in population was greater than in other Nordic countries during the years 1750–1850, the incipient emigration was greeted by the authorities with a sigh of relief. The massive departures of the 1850s and 1860s were seen as a safety valve. In Denmark deportation, which was common in Great Britain, was also practiced. Without awakening noteworthy reactions the Danish authorities forced both criminals and leaders of the labor movement to leave the country and embark for America. Those expelled received pecuniary support from the state.

The indifference to emigration is evident over a long period of time. It was not the subject of political debate until the end of the century. From the 1880s onward, the governments began to investigate and regulate the transportation of migrants. Laws were passed regulating the transoceanic voyage and the activities of profit-hungry shipowners and agents. In 1882 the Swedish county governors (*landshövdingar*) were ordered to investigate the extent of and motivation for emigration in each county. New insights were gained but, with the exception of restrictions on the emigration of those of draft age, no measures were taken as a result.

In several western European countries a change occurred during the first decade of the twentieth century in the official attitude toward emigration. In Sweden the question was considered in the *Riksdag* in 1903 and 1904. Among the reasons for this revised attitude was uneasiness about negative consequences for the nation's military forces. Also, those who employed agrarian laborers feared a labor shortage, while radicals saw the exodus as an expression of dissatisfaction with social conditions. The most noteworthy result was a comprehensive investigation, published in twenty-one volumes between 1908 and 1913. While the question of new legal restrictions was raised, certain social and political reforms were undertaken. Acquisition of smaller plots of land was facilitated by the "own your own home" (*egnahem*) movement subsidies that were introduced in 1904 and increased thereafter. In order to counterbalance the flight from the country, the National Association against Emigration (*Nationalföreningen mot Emigrationen*), formed in 1907, used primarily propagandistic means. Its effect on the formation of opinion was far from insignificant, but its influence upon the rate of emigration was probably no more than marginal.

Norwegian officials were concerned about emigration, and a cabinet-level committee published "Basic Tendencies in the History of Norwegian Emigration" (*Grundlinjer i norsk utvandrings historie*) in 1915. The Society for the Limitation of Emigration (*Selskapet til Emigrationens Indskraenking*) was established in Norway in 1908. Its magazine was both anti-American and super-patriotic, but the decrease in the rate of emigration cannot be attributed to this organization.[51] In Finland an organization was also founded to stem the outflow. There was no comparable reaction in Denmark, probably because of the low rate of emigration from that country.[52]

Destination Areas and Settlement Patterns

During the early period, 1840–1890, the greater part of the Nordic immigrants to the United States settled in the Middle West.[53] Later many immigrants made their way to the expanding industrial areas of the East and to the states on the Pacific Coast. After 1890 many worked in the lumbering districts along the Pacific Coast of the United States and Canada, and an increasing number settled in the prairie provinces of Canada. This parallel movement of settlers and workers is characteristic of Scandinavian migration.

A comparison of the immigrants from the various Nordic countries (see Figure 2.6) shows that the Norwegians, who to a greater extent than any other immigrant group became farmers, had the strongest concentration in the Midwest. In 1910, no less than 65 percent of the Norwegian immigrants lived in the states of Minnesota, Wisconsin, North Dakota, and Iowa. The corresponding figure for Swedes was 45 percent, for Danes 40 percent. Nearly half of all immigrants from Finland settled in Michigan and Minnesota. Scandinavian migrants also concentrated in the cities. Every tenth Swedish-American at the turn of the century lived in Chicago. At that time only Stockholm had a larger Swedish urban population.[54]

Figure 2.6
Distribution of Danish-, Finnish-, Norwegian-, and Swedish-Born Population in the United States, 1910

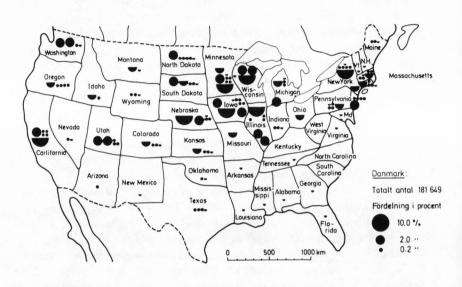

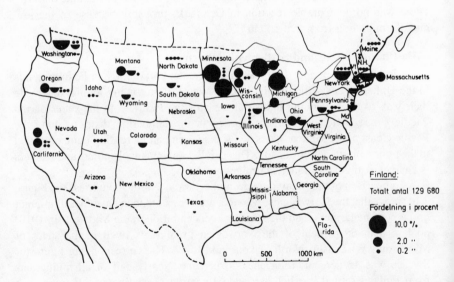

Source: U.S. Population Census, 1910.

Figure 2.6—_Continued_

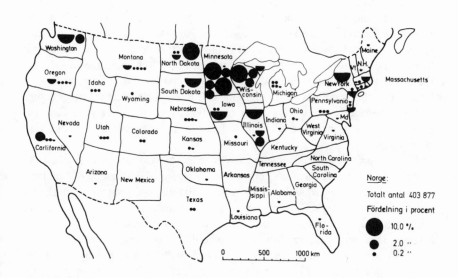

Norge:

Totalt antal 403 877

Fördelning i procent

- 10.0 %
- 2.0 ··
- 0.2 ··

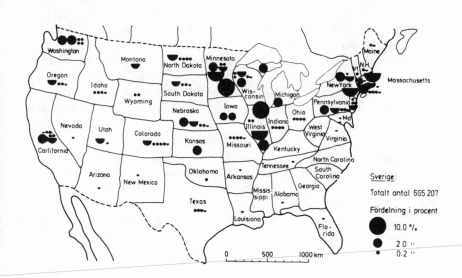

Sverige:

Totalt antal 665 207

Fördelning i procent

- 10.0 %
- 2.0 ··
- 0.2 ··

When Canada received the status of a dominion within the British Commonwealth in 1867, it began to plan the colonization of the prairie provinces, and immigrants were recruited from the Nordic countries. A substantial number of Icelanders came via Wisconsin to Gimli, Manitoba. Their ethnic solidarity has been remarkable, and they have preserved their Icelandic traditions and language.[55] Furthermore, second-generation immigrants to the Midwest area of the United States were enticed by land companies to move to Canada. Finns, Norwegians, and Swedes also found work in the construction of railways. In British Columbia they worked in the forests and mines. Many were employed for shorter periods of time and later returned to their native countries with their savings. A large part of the Scandinavian immigration to Canada during the twentieth century had the character of temporary labor migration. Toronto, Winnipeg, Calgary, Edmonton, and Vancouver all have had significant elements of Scandinavian population.

A small part of the movement from Sweden to America also reached the southern half of the hemisphere, otherwise the preferred destination of Southern European immigrants. With the support of the Brazilian government, emigration agents distributed highly misleading propaganda materials in Scandinavia and occasionally offered free passage or generous travel allowances. In the case of Sweden, they attracted large families who could not otherwise have afforded to leave. Concentrated Danish settlements were founded in some areas of the Argentinian provinces of Buenos Aires and Mendoza. A large group of primarily Swedish-speaking Finnish intellectuals established the "Colonía Finlandesa" in Misiones, Southern Argentina. This Finnish emigration may be seen as an expression of discontent directed toward the Russian regime and the russification that was promoted during the 1890s in the Grand Duchy of Finland. The Swedish emigration was primarily directed toward Brazil and took place during the famine years of 1868–1869, the winter of 1890–1891, and 1909–1911. Discontent among various labor groups was an important element. The emigration from Sundsvall during 1890–1891 was preceded by the so-called Brazil meetings, which were directed against sawmill employers. The emigration from Kiruna, 1909–1911, had a clear connection with the country-wide general strike of 1909.[56] In Brazil and Argentina the majority of the Scandinavian immigrants ended up destitute. The evacuation and transportation home of hundreds of Swedes in 1912 under the direction of the Swedish government can be seen as proof of the difficulties faced by these people.

Only very few Scandinavians emigrated to Australia. Approximately 5,000 are calculated to have arrived during the 1850s and 1860s, with the gold fields of Victoria as their main goal. Some returned to their native countries, while others participated in the "from mines to soil" movement and found a livelihood in agriculture. A larger wave of Scandinavian emigration occurred from 1870 to 1914, periodically stimulated by "assisted passages" from the Australian authorities. This wave was male dominated and included many former seamen.

The Finnish and Swedish immigration continued at a high rate after the First World War.[57]

Ethnic, Cultural, and Political Aspects

Scandinavians promptly established religious congregations and other ethnic associations upon their arrival in America. Because of their small numbers Danes, Norwegians, and Swedes often organized jointly, for example, in the Scandinavian Association in New York, founded in 1844. As a rule they were eager to form their own religious organizations independent of those of Americans and Germans. Increased immigration figures, however, meant decreasing cooperation. It is significant that the Augustana Synod, founded in 1860 by Swedes and Norwegians, was partitioned into a Swedish and a Norwegian synod in 1870. Finnish churches and organizations long kept noticeably isolated from the activities of other immigrant and native American groups. The Swedish-speaking Finns, however, were more open than those who spoke only Finnish. Language was an important factor affecting possibilities for contact, and Finnish-speaking immigrants thus experienced the greatest difficulties.[58]

Especially in the cities, secular organizations were founded: temperance lodges, singing societies, fraternal orders, athletic clubs, theater groups, associations of engineers, sewing circles, and women's organizations among others.[59] In the larger cities a dualism within the ethnic group frequently developed between those following religious interests and those preferring secular ones. Basic social differences also played a role, as may be observed in the Swedish immigrant group in Chicago. The ordinary, poor immigrants lacked both the time and the money to participate in the activities of the fraternal orders and societies. These organizations were looked upon as an extension of Swedish bourgeois exclusiveness to the American scene. For many, meetings, instruction, aid societies, and other activities of the Lutheran Augustana congregations had to suffice. Better off immigrants with a more liberal outlook sought a wider range of activities. They were often more positively disposed toward their own assimilation and less apt to try to safeguard Swedish customs and language. This dualism, so difficult to describe in a few words, can also be traced in the positions of the leading Swedish newspapers.[60]

The political activity of the immigrants depended on a number of factors, such as the size of the group, its geographical distribution, the time of the settlement, and the character of the cultural and political heritage from the home country. On the other hand, no automatic correlation can be found between the total number of immigrants from a particular country and their political role. The Icelanders have, because of their concentration, been able to maintain a solidarity and achieve a political representation out of proportion to their total number. The Norwegian and Finnish concentration within a few states also made possible a high degree of political participation. The Danes, on the other hand, spread out over the entire American continent, have not been able to hold together, and thus have a reduced political potential.[61]

The Swedes, Norwegians, and Danes came from countries with a highly developed system of local self-government, something that has generally contributed to their ability to advance politically in America. The ability to read and write was also important, but in this regard Scandinavians hardly differed from Germans. The Norwegian immigrants received strong inspiration from their homeland; sympathy for the labor movement and leftist movements was great among them. Norwegian-American voters were radical without being revolutionary. There was a widespread opposition to "big money" in the form of banks, industrial conglomerates, and trusts. In the Midwest they organized Viking Leagues and Republican Leagues in order to repudiate the social Darwinism of which big business was one expression. The connection with the Populist movement was apparent. In Wisconsin La Follette and the Progressive movement received strong support from Norwegian voters.[62]

Swedes, at the turn of the century, broke away from the established parties to give their support to Populist-oriented groups, as, for example, the Farm Labor Party in Minnesota. Swedish-American socialist organizations were to be found in several American cities, and they exerted great influence in Rockford, Illinois.[63] A study of the Scandinavian radical press reveals that, like in the other social movements, a trend toward cooperation between Danish, Norwegian, and Swedish immigrants is discernible. About two-fifths of some ninety labor periodicals published by these immigrants in the United States and Canada were addressed to two or more groups. The radical Finns established another sixty newspapers and periodicals to advocate anything from reform to violent overthrow of the existing government. In many cases this type of activity followed upon a period of community-building. The first of the Scandinavian periodicals was published in Chicago in 1877. Like many others, it was very short-lived. By the 1900s, however, dozens of left-wing and labor organizations existed and had their own newspapers and bulletins. Some of the Finnish-American ones have continued to the present day. In the 1910s and later the Worcester Swedes, too, tried to establish labor periodicals. Of the many ethnic groups that came to America, the Norwegians and Swedes were among those who over limited periods of time achieved a relatively high degree of interethnic cooperation and who boasted a labor press long before the quintessential proletarian mass migrants from Southern and Eastern Europe began to come and to organize.[64]

Among the Finnish-American voters, socialist sympathies were widespread, and the Finns were among the most radical ethnic groups in the United States. A special characteristic of the Finnish settlements was the formation of consumer cooperatives. Finnish-American labor radicalism, which was strongest in the mining districts of northern Minnesota and northern Michigan, was weakened by internal dissension and never achieved power at the state level. During the 1930s many disappointed and disillusioned members left the United States to seek a better society in the Soviet Union. Nearly 10,000 Finnish-Americans are estimated to have settled in Soviet Karelia, where many soon lost their illusions and packed their bags for a further move.[65]

SCANDINAVIA'S ROLE IN INTERNATIONAL MIGRATION, 1919–1945

The Scandinavian emigration to the United States and Canada dwindled during the First World War. In the post-war era U.S. politics was characterized by isolationism, and immigration became less attractive. The Swedish immigrants did not even fill their quotas during the 1920s. In addition, the gap in economic development between the United States and the Nordic countries decreased. Wage differences became smaller, differences in the per capita gross national product diminished, opportunities for industrial employment at home increased. The fluctuations of the business cycles in the United States during the 1920s may have also decreased its attractiveness.

Noneconomic factors presumably also contributed to the latter. Propaganda against migration had only a marginal effect. American participation in World War I reduced the desire of young men to emigrate. The knowledge that earlier emigrants, who had made their way to the United States and Canada in order to avoid military service, had been recruited into the army was not encouraging. Following the general European pattern, Scandinavian emigration leveled off after a last rise in 1923–1924. With the depression figures became insignificant, and for the Nordic countries the 1930s were a period of net immigration from North America.[66]

Sweden implemented a restrictive immigration policy at the beginning of the century. During the First World War it introduced passport controls; during the 1920s immigration to Sweden from Finland, Russia, the Baltic area, eastern Europe, and Germany was made more difficult since immigration from these countries was feared and considered less desirable. On the other hand, there was no regulation of immigration from Denmark, Norway, England, France, and Spain. The protection of the Swedish labor market and the preservation of the purity of the Swedish race lay behind these restrictions.[67]

The global contraction of trade, of the movement of capital, and of migration during the 1930s also left their mark upon the inter-Nordic exchange of people. Traditional patterns, however, were preserved. Immigration from border areas to the major cities dominated, for example, from the rural areas of western Sweden to Oslo and from the southern Swedish countryside to Copenhagen, as well as emigration from Finland's Swedish-speaking areas. Immigrants to Sweden from the other Nordic countries found employment primarily in agriculture and lumbering. Immigrants from the non-Nordic countries during this period were primarily specialized laborers in industries that were in need of foreign expertise. The majority within that category, however, reemigrated after less than one year in the country.[68]

After 1933 Nazi Germany's expansion and its increasing repression of Jews and other ethnic groups led to a large number of refugees. Sweden, which had little experience of immigration by ethnic minorities, sought above all to safeguard its own national interests. During the 1930s its immigration policy was characterized by inertia and unwillingness to make any commitments. Entry into Sweden was more tightly controlled, and in 1938 a general visa requirement was introduced. From 1938 through 1941 less than 10,000 refugees came to Sweden. Only when the German fascist policy of annihilation of the Jewish race became known did the Swedish authorities turn to an active and generous refugee policy. One hundred and fifty Norwegian Jews who survived the brutal German deportation as well as the Danish Jews were given asylum.[69] In-migration from occupied Denmark and Norway increased and was now encouraged. The overwhelming majority of these migrants returned at the end of the war, although many—after having received paramilitary training—returned even earlier in order to contribute to the liberation. Within the context of labor migration, these movements were insignificant.

In May 1945 there were 194,000 foreigners in Sweden, of whom more than half were refugees. The majority had fled from neighboring countries. There were no less than 43,000 Norwegians, 18,300 Danes, and about 65,000 children evacuated from Finland as well as between 20,000 and 40,000 adult Finns who had come over the border along the Torne River. The refugees also included 30,000 from the Baltic area, above all Estonians and displaced persons, mainly East Europeans from camps in Austria, Italy, and, to a lesser extent, from Germany, Turkey, Greece, and Yugoslavia.[70]

After 1945 migration patterns changed and Sweden, Denmark, and Norway were gradually transformed into immigration countries. The movements between the Nordic nations have been large and have been dominated by Finnish immigration to Sweden. The economic and cultural effects of this migration have become one of the most widely debated questions in Nordic cooperation. Furthermore, considerable numbers of labor migrants from Southern Europe arrived on their own initiative or through active recruitment.

CONCLUSION

Certain major trends stand out in the movement of population within Scandinavia during the course of the centuries. An example of continuity is the pattern of age-old contacts across the Gulf of Bothnia and the Baltic Sea, which has led to the existence of a Swedish-speaking population in Finland since the Middle Ages. The intensity of these east-west contacts has varied. From the sixteenth century onward, however, westward movements have dominated, and since the Second World War, emigration from Finland to Sweden has been especially large.

The population in border areas has generally migrated either temporarily or permanently in order to seek work. It was natural for the residents of the southern

Swedish provinces of Skåne, Halland, and Blekinge, which were transferred from Denmark to Sweden in 1658, to leave for places of employment on the other side of the Öresund strait, just as the Danes made their way to southern Swedish areas. The same has been true of the areas along the Swedish-Norwegian border. Major cities, located close to borders, had labor markets extending beyond the respective country's limits. Thus the in-migration of Swedish labor to Copenhagen and Oslo has been considerable, as has that of Finns to Stockholm (which was the Finnish capital until 1809). The establishment in 1954 of a free Nordic labor market may be regarded as an adaptation to historical conditions of population mobility in the Nordic countries, where market forces have been subjected to very little restraint and the influence of administrative regulations has been negligible.

Mobility between the Nordic countries has been facilitated by linguistic similarities (with the exception of Finnish) and religious homogeneity, which has also meant that the effects of the movements have been limited on the social and cultural planes. Where the moves have been definitive, assimilation has been rapid.

In the exchange of people with countries outside Scandinavia, there have been differences over the years in both the extent and directions of migration. The geographical locations of Denmark and Norway have meant that they have traditionally had their greatest exchange of migrants with the areas surrounding the North Sea, while the corresponding movements for Sweden and Finland have, for the most part, affected the countries around the Baltic.

In Swedish history the "Age of Greatness" stands out as a period of more lively contacts with other countries apart from Nordic nations. During the years 1610-1720 foreigners were recruited with the intention of strengthening the nation's economy, armed forces, and public administration. The period following the Second World War has a similarly clear profile in that regard, as Sweden, Denmark, and, to a certain extent, even Norway, have attained the character of immigrant nations.

Between these periods of immigration lies a century characterized by departures for the New World. Transatlantic migration must be seen within the context of other migration tendencies, that is, urbanization and colonization within the countries. There are three waves of migration that partially go in opposing directions; they can be explained by the mechanization of agriculture, the growth of industry, and the shifts in the international market economy. This transformation of society coincided with the rapid natural increase in the population, which had far-reaching social consequences. The proportion of the population not possessing land increased, and the rural population was proletarianized. That the official reaction to emigration was so long in coming can be attributed to the fact that transoceanic emigration relieved the pressure on the food supply and functioned to a certain extent as a safety valve in a situation where social disruption could have been the result. The transatlantic migration of 2.5 million during the course of a century must, from the European point of view, be seen as an element in the transformation from an agrarian to a modern, urban society; the departure of the rural population for the cities formed the greatest migration movement in the Nordic countries.

NOTES

1. Ingrid Semmingsen, *Veien mot Vest. Utvandringen fra Norge til Amerika* [The way west. Emigration from Norway to America], vol. 1: *1825–1865* (Oslo, 1941), vol. 2: *1865–1915* (Oslo, 1950). The terms *Scandinavia* and *the Nordic countries* are used interchangeably and include Denmark, Finland, Iceland, Norway, and Sweden.

2. Theodore D. Blegen, *Norwegian Migration to America, 1825–1860* (Northfield, Minn., 1931) and *Norwegian Migration to America: The American Transition* (Northfield, Minn., 1940); George M. Stephenson, *The Religious Aspects of Swedish Immigration. A Study of Immigrant Churches* (Minneapolis, 1932).

3. A. William Hoglund, *Finnish Immigrants in America* (Madison, Wis., 1960); John I. Kolehmainen, *The Finns in America. A Bibliographical Guide to Their History* (Hancock, Mich., 1947).

4. Helge Nelson, *The Swedes and the Swedish Settlements in North America*, 2 vols. (Lund, 1943).

5. Dorothy Swaine Thomas, *Social and Economic Aspects of Swedish Population Movements, 1750–1933* (New York, 1941).

6. *La emigración europea a la América Latina. Fuentes y estado de investigación: Informes presentados a la IV. Reunión de Historiadores Latinamericanistas Europeos* (Berlin, 1979).

7. When the project reached its conclusion in 1976, it had produced some twenty doctoral and licentiate dissertations. For a bibliography of the project, see Harald Runblom and Hans Norman, eds., *From Sweden to America. A History of the Migration. A Collective Work of the Uppsala Migration Research Project* (Minneapolis, Uppsala, 1976).

8. Hans Norman and Harald Runblom, *Nordisk Emigrationsatlas*, 2 vols. [Nordic emigration atlas] (Gävle, 1980); Bo Kronborg, Thomas Nilsson, and Andres A. Svalestuen, *Nordic Population Mobility. Comparative Studies of Selective Parishes in the Nordic Countries 1850–1900*, special issue of *American Studies in Scandinavia* 9 (1977), nos. 1–2.

9. Olavi Koivukangas, ed., *Scandinavian Emigration to Australia and New Zealand Project. Proceedings of a Symposium, February 17-19, 1982, Turku, Finland* (Turku, 1983).

10. Michael G. Karni, Matti E. Kaups, and Douglas Ollila, eds., *The Finnish Experience in the Western Great Lakes Region. New Perspectives* (Turku, 1975).

11. A good example is the volume *American Labor and Immigration History* (Urbana, Ill., 1983), edited by Dirk Hoerder.

12. Birgitta Odén, "Ekonomiska emigrationsmodeller och historisk forskning" [Economic emigration models and historical research], *Scandia* 37 (1971), 1–70 and "Emigrationen från Norden til Nordamerika under 1800–talet. Aktuella forskningsuppgifter" [Emigration from Scandinavia to North America during the 19th century. Current tasks of research], *Historisk Tidskrift* 83 (1963), 261–77.

13. Sune Åkerman, "Theories and Methods of Migration Research," Runblom and Norman, eds., *From Sweden to America*, pp. 19–75.

14. *Norges Historie. Bind 15: Historisk atlas* [History of Norway. Vol. 15: Historical atlas] (Oslo, 1979).

15. Knut Mykland, "Gjennom nødsår og krig 1648-1720" [Through famine years and warfare, 1648–1720] *Norges Historie*, vol. 7 (Oslo, 1977), pp. 1–447.

16. Lars-Olof Larsson, *Kolonisation och befolkningsutveckling i det svenska agrarsamhället 1500-1640* [Colonization and population development in the Swedish agrarian society, 1500–1640] (Lund, 1972), pp. 153–54.

17. Rolf Fladby, "Gjenreisning 1536–1648" [Reconstruction, 1536–1648], *Norges Historie*, vol. 6 (Oslo, 1977), pp. 118ff.; Mykland, "Gjennom nødsar og krig," pp. 166ff.

18. Sten Carlsson, "Tyska invandrare i Sverige" [German immigrants in Sweden], *Fataburen. Nordiska Muséets och Skansens årsbok 1981* (Stockholm, 1981), pp. 9–31.

19. Jonas Berg and Bo Lagercrantz, *Scots in Sweden* (Stockholm, 1962); Bernt Douhan, "Vallonerna i Sverige" [The Walloons in Sweden], in *Fataburen*, pp. 66–90.

20. Sven Lundkvist, "Rörlighet och social struktur i 1610–talets Sverige" [Mobility and social structure in Sweden in the 1610s], *Historisk tidskrift* (1974), 192–258.

21. Larsson, *Kolonisation*, p. 155; Ståle Dyrvik, "Den lange fredstiden 1720–1784" [The long period of peace, 1720–1784], *Norges Historie*, vol. 8, pp. 220ff.

22. Max Engman, *S:t Petersburg och Finland. Migration och influens 1703–1917* [St. Petersburg and Finland. migration and influences, 1703–1917] (Helsinki, 1983).

23. Richard Broberg, "Invandringar från Finland till Sverige före 1700–talet i verklighet och tradition" [Migrations from Finland to Sweden before 1700: reality and traditions] in *Migrationen mellan Sverige och Finland* (Stockholm, 1970), pp. 91–112; K. Østberg, *Finnskogene i Norge* [The Finn woods in Norway] (Grue, Norway, 1978).

24. Semmingsen, *Veien mot Vest*, vol. 2., p. 145.

25. Sten Carlsson, "Norrmän i Sverige 1814–1905" [Norwegians in Sweden], *Historielärarnas förenings årsskrift 1963–1964* (Uppsala, 1964), pp. 47–63.

26. Lars-Olof Larsson, "Utvandring från södra Småland fram till 1870" [Emigration from Southern Småland until 1870] in Ulf Beijbom, ed., *Utvandring från Kronoberg. En temabok. Kronobergsboken 1978* (Växjö, 1978), pp. 171ff, 199–200.

27. Richard Willerslev, *Den glemte indvandring. Den svenske indvandring til Danmark 1850–1914* [The forgotten immigration. The Swedish immigration to Denmark, 1850–1914] (Copenhagen, 1982).

28. Unless otherwise noted, this part is based primarily upon Helge Nelson, "Säsongvandringar och svenskt näringsliv under 1800– och 1900–talen" [Seasonal migration and Swedish economic life during the 19th and 20th centuries] in *Ekonomisk–geografiska studier tillägnade Olof Jonasson på hans sextiofemårsdag 22 januari 1959* (Göteborg, 1959), pp. 134–54; and Göran Rosander, *Herrarbete. Dalfolkets säsongvisa arbetsvandringar i jämförande belysning.* [The seasonal labor migrations of the Dalecarlia Population in comparative perspective] (Uppsala, 1967), pp. 54–61, 91–116.

29. Anders Norberg, *Sågarnas ö. Alnö och industrialiseringen 1860–1910* [The sawmill island. Alnö and the industrialization, 1860–1910] (Uppsala, 1980). Note that seasonal migrants are sometimes difficult to trace since the parish registers did not list them consistently. Many appeared in the records only after the permanent move was completed.

30. Eric De Geer and Holger Wester, "Utrikes resor, arbetsvandringar och flyttningar i Finland och Vasa län 1861–1890" [Travels abroad, seasonal migrations and migrations

in Finland and Vasa county 1861–1890], *Österbotten 1975* (Vasa, 1976), pp. 5–116; Engman, *St Petersburg och Finland*.

31. Helgi Skúli Kjartansson, "The Onset of Emigration from Iceland," *American Studies in Scandinavia* 9, nos. 1–2 (1977), 87–94.

32. Note that Ireland's highest rate of emigration occurred during the years 1846–1854.

33. Norman and Runblom, *Nordisk Emigrationsatlas*.

34. Semmingsen, *Veien mot Vest*.

35. Lars Ljungmark, *Swedish Exodus* (Carbondale, Ill., 1979), pp. 15–27.

36. Hans Norman, *Från Bergslagen till Nordamerika. Studier i migrationsmönster, social rörlighet och demografisk struktur med utgångspunkt från Örebro län 1851–1915* [From Bergslagen to North America. Studies in the migration pattern, social mobility, and demographic structure on the basis of Örebro county, 1851–1915] (Uppsala, 1974), pp. 78ff.

37. Reino Kero, *Migration from Finland to North America in the Years between the United States Civil War and the First World War* (Turku, 1974), p. 50.

38. Hans Norman, "Causes of Emigration. An Attempt at Multivariate Analysis," in Runblom and Norman, eds., *From Sweden to America*, pp. 149–64; Eric De Geer, *Migration och influensfält. Studier av emigration och intern migration i Finland och Sverige 1816–1972* [Migration and fields of influence: studies of internal migration, labor migration and emigration in Sweden and Finland, 1816–1972] (Uppsala, 1977); Kero, *Migration from Finland*, pp. 52ff.; Andres A. Svalestuen, "Professor Ingrid Semmingsen—emigrasjonshistorikern," in Sivert Langholm and Francis Sejersted, eds., *Vandringer. Festskrift til Ingrid Semmingsen på 70-årsdagen 29. mars 1980* (Oslo, 1980), p. 30; Engman, *S:t Petersburg och Finland*, p. 30. A similar pattern was established in Hungary, where an early tradition to migrate plus urban influence decided the intensity of emigration from various regions. See Julianna Puskás, *From Hungary to the United States, 1880–1914*. (Budapest, 1982), pp. 56ff.

39. Sune Åkerman, "From Stockholm to San Francisco," *Annales Academiæ Regiæ Scientiarum Upsaliensis* 19 (1975), 5–46.

40. Lars-Göran Tedebrand, *Västernorrland och Nordamerika 1875–1913. Utvandring och återinvandring* [Emigration from Västernorrland County to North America and re-migration, 1875–1913] (Uppsala, 1972), pp. 143ff.; Norman, *Från Bergslagen till Nordamerika*, pp. 47ff.

41. Holger Wester, *Innovationer i befolkningsrörligheten. En studie av spridningsförlopp i befolkningsrörligheten utgående från Petalax socken i Österbotten* [Innovations and population mobility. A study of diffusion patterns in the emigration from the parish of Petalax in Österbotten, Finland] (Uppsala, 1977), pp. 76ff.; Semmingsen, *Veien mot Vest*, vol. 2, pp. 220–21; Kristian Hvidt, *Flugten til Amerika eller Drivkræfter i masseudvandringen fra Danmark 1868–1914* [The flight to America or push factors in mass emigration from Denmark] (Odense, 1971), pp. 145–47.

42. Norberg, *Sågarnas ö*, p. 46.

43. Semmingsen, *Veien mot Vest*, vol. 2, pp. 497–99; Fred Nilsson, *Emigrationen från Stockholm till Nordamerika 1880–1893. En studie i urban invandring* [Emigration from Stockholm to North America, 1880–1893. A study in urban emigration] (Uppsala, 1970), p. 241; Hvidt, *Flugten til Amerika*, p. 495.

44. Norman, *Från Bergslagen till Nordamerika*, pp. 68–73.

45. See especially Berit Brattne, *Bröderna Larsson. En studie i svensk emigranta-gentverksamhet under 1880–talet* [The Larsson brothers: A study of the activity of Swedish emigrant agencies during the 1880s] (Uppsala, 1973), pp. 143ff.; also Björn Rondahl, *Emigration, folkomflyttning och säsongarbete i ett sågverksdistrikt i södra Hälsingland 1865–1910. Söderala kommun med särskild hänsyn till Ljusne industrisamhälle* [Emigration, internal migration, and migrant labor movements in a sawmill district in Southern Hälsingland with special regard to the industrial town of Ljusne] (Uppsala, 1972), pp. 190ff.; Norman, *Från Bergslagen till Nordamerika*, pp. 92ff.; Berit Brattne and Sune Åkerman, "The Importance of the Transport Sector for Mass Emigration," in Norman and Runblom, eds., *From Sweden to America*, pp. 176ff.

46. Sten Carlsson, "Flyttningsintensiteten i det svenska agrarsamhället" [Migration intensity in the Swedish agrarian society], *Turun Historiallinen Arkisto* 28 (1973), 114–48; Kero, *Migration from Finland to North America*, pp. 51–52; Hvidt, *Flugten til Amerika*, pp. 186–91.

47. This section is based on Lars-Göran Tedebrand, "Strikes and Political Radicalism in Sweden and Emigration to the United States," pp. 221–34 in Hoerder, ed., *American Labor and Immigration History*; quote on p. 226.

48. Ibid., pp. 226–32, quote on p. 232.

49. Sune Åkerman and Hans Norman, "Political Mobilization of the Workers: The Case of the Worcester Swedes," ibid., pp. 235–58.

50. Ibid., pp. 243 (quote), 249–50.

51. Ann-Sofie Kälvemark, *Reaktionen mot utvandringen. Emigrationsfrågan i svensk debatt och politik 1901–1904* [The Swedish reaction against emigration. The issue of emigration in Swedish debate and politics, 1901–1904] (Uppsala, 1972); Hvidt, *Flugten til Amerika*, pp. 270–80; Svalestuen, "Professor Ingrid Semmingsen," p. 11.

52. Arne Hassing, "Norway's Organized Response to Emigration," *Norwegian-American Studies* 25 (1972), 54–79.

53. This portion is partly based on Norman and Runblom, *Nordisk Emigrationsatlas*.

54. Ulf Beijbom, *Swedes in Chicago. A Demographic and Social Study of the 1846–1880 Immigration* (Växjö, 1971), pp. 110–18.

55. Harald Runblom, "The Swedes in Canada. A Study of Low Ethnic Consciousness," *The Swedish-American Historical Quarterly* (1982), 4–20.

56. Runblom and Norman, eds., *From Sweden to America*, pp. 301–10.

57. Olavi Koivukangas, *Scandinavian Immigration and Settlement in Australia before World War II*. (Turku, 1974); Ulf Beijbom, *Australienfararna* [The Australia migrants] (Stockholm, 1983).

58. Kero, *Migration from Finland to North America*, pp. 60–61.

59. Norman, "Causes of Emigration," p. 272.

60. Beijbom, *Swedes in Chicago*, pp. 298ff.

61. Jon Wefald, *Norwegians in American Politics, 1890–1917* (Northfield, Minn., 1971).

62. Peter A. Munch, "Norwegians," in Stephan Thernstrom et al., eds., *Harvard Encyclopedia of American Ethnic Groups* (Cambridge, Mass., 1980), pp. 750–61.

63. Ulf Beijbom, "Swedes," in Thernstrom, *Harvard Encyclopedia*, pp. 971–81.

64. Dirk Hoerder, comp., *The Immigrant Labor Press in North America, 1846–1976. An Annotated Bibliography* (Westport, Conn., forthcoming), sections on Swedes by Michael Brook, on Norwegians by Robert L. Mikkelsen, on Danes by Jens-Bjerre Dan-

ielsen, and on Finns by Auvo Kostiainen.

65. Reino Kero, "The Canadian Finns in Soviet Karelia in the 1930s," in Michael G. Karni, ed., *Finnish Diaspora I: Canada, South America, Africa, Australia, Sweden* (Toronto, 1981), pp. 203–214.

66. Tomas Hammar, *Sverige åt svenskarna. Invandringspolitik, utlänningskontroll och asylrätt 1900–1932* [Sweden for the Swedes. Immigration policy, immigrant control and right of sanctuary 1900–1932] (Stockholm, 1964), pp. 233–59. Scandinavia had been very little affected by the movements of people resulting from World War I and the Russian Revolution. But these belong to the category of involuntary rather than labor migration. Political refugees came in spite of the fact that Swedish immigration law did not permit their classification as such. The Russians, whose number may not have exceeded 1,000 persons, belonged to the intelligentsia. The majority moved on after a short time.

67. Ibid., pp. 210–27; Hans Lindberg, *Svensk Flyktingpolitik under internationellt tryck* [Swedish refugee policy under international pressure] (Stockholm, 1973), pp. 48–74.

68. Sven Nordlund, "Invandringen till Sverige *1920–1945*, I–II" [The immigration to Sweden, 1920–1945, I–II] (licentiate thesis, Dept. of Economic History, University of Gothenburg, 1970).

69. Lindberg, *Svensk flyktingpolitik*, pp. 278–85; Hugo Valentin, *Judarna i Sverige* [The Jews in Sweden] (Stockholm, 1964), pp. 193–97.

70. *Sverige och flyktingarna* [Sweden and the refugees] published by Arbetsmarknads-departementet [Ministry of labor] (Stockholm, 1978).

A SURVEY OF PATTERNS AND STRUCTURES OF MIGRATION IN AUSTRIA, 1850–1900

3

Heinz Fassmann

APPROACH

Surveys demand generalizations, and in choosing what information to include and what to omit one cannot avoid a certain feeling of uncertainty. This applies more to the first part of this essay, which tries to give a survey of migration around 1890, than to the second, which consists of a primary statistical analysis of the social and demographical structure of this migration. Although there are a large number of different angles from which research into migration can be approached, here the emphasis is on a few basic aspects. Where did migrants come from? Where did they go to? What changes occurred in patterns of migration during the nineteenth century? What were the social and demographical structures of the migration? What was the position of migrants in relation to economic and social developments in the areas they moved to?

The area covered by the analysis presented in this essay is the Austrian half of the Austro-Hungarian monarchy. The reasons for this choice were of a purely pragmatic nature, the most important one being the lack of access to Hungarian statistics. The period of analysis is the second half of the nineteenth century. One disadvantage here is that the aggregated data on the complex patterns of migration date from a different period than the main analysis of individual migrants.

TERMINOLOGY AND SOURCES

One problem that must be dealt with initially is the definition of what a migrant is. It is not always clear whether a person should be counted as a migrant, especially when one is working with historical statistical data. The sources used for this essay permit the following two definitions. A person was counted as a migrant when

1. his/her place of birth was not the same as the place where he/she was at the time of the census or

2. the community of which he/she had official membership (Heimatberechtigung) was not the same as the one in which he/she was resident at the time of the census.

These two definitions have the following shortcomings: In the case of 1, if a child was born in a maternity home this was registered as its place of birth. No further information is available to indicate when migration occurred or what course it took—it might have consisted of several stages. In the case of 2, official membership in a community could be acquired by birth or marriage or it could be granted after a certain period of residence. Hence it was more common for female migrants than males to acquire official membership in a community by marriage. This status entitled its holders to certain social and political rights. When a child was born it became an official member of the same community as its father unless the mother was unmarried, in which case the child became a member of the same community as she was. Take, for example, the children of a migrant from Prague, who were born in Vienna. Since the father was an official member of the community in Prague, so were the children, and hence they were incorrectly counted as migrants. In spite of its disadvantages, the use of official membership in the community to determine who was a migrant seems to be the more practicable approach. It makes visible those migrants who had only been in the target area for a short period of time, as a longer period of residence was required before a person was entitled to official membership in the new community (in Vienna, for example, the minimum period was ten years). Migrants defined in this way are more homogeneous in the date of their migration than if place of birth is used as the basis for a definition. Whichever definition is used, however, the empirical findings are structurally similar, so that the results presented here can be regarded as methodologically safe.[1]

The sources for this essay are the census of 1890 and conscription lists of 1857 and 1880 for Vienna. Until 1857 censuses only included the native population. Although foreigners were entered in so-called lists of aliens (Fremdenbögen), they were often not included in total figures. From 1869 onward censuses were based on the resident population, and an additional note was made of those who did not have official membership in their community of residence ("nichtheimatberechtigt"). As the census of 1869 and the following one in 1880 were not processed centrally, however, it was not possible to carry out a detailed analysis of migration for these years. It was not until the census of 1890, when all the forms were sent to the Central Statistical Commission in Vienna, that a uniform analysis of details of origin could be carried out. It should be noted that in 1890 for the first time this analysis was carried out "using electric calculating machines, a technique which revolutionized the whole process of counting and increased its efficiency to an unimaginable extent."[2] The second source, the conscription lists, allow a primarily statistical approach. As part of a research project on the social history of the family at the Institute for Economic and Social History in Vienna, a clustered sample was selected from the high-quality original data on the conscription of 1857 and analyzed using a computer.[3] The following details about the residents (including those on the aliens' list) were collected: age, marital status, sex, occupation, position in household, and origin. This essay examines those 38,229 people from the sample for Vienna conscription of 1857 whose origin is given (about 8 percent of the total population of Vienna) and a further smaller sample of 4,171 people from a district of Vienna in 1880. This is an especially suitable source for a varied and complex picture of the structure of the migration that will be studied in the second part of this essay.

Some Hypotheses on Migration in the Second Half of the Nineteenth Century

Parallel to the model of demographic transition, the concept of the development of migration involves a climax in regional mobility toward the end of the nineteenth century, the most important aspect of which was migration from the country into the cities.[4] It is not possible to enter into a serious discussion of this approach within the limits of this essay as this would have to include an empirical examination of the concept. Hence, only selected aspects of this migration will be considered.

Toward the end of the nineteenth century mobility became a mass phenomenon. In 1869, 80 percent of the people resident in a community had official membership in that community, but by 1880 this figure had fallen to 70 percent, by 1890 to 65 percent. Peripheral regions, which lagged behind central areas in terms of modernization and development, continued to have considerably higher proportions of people who had official membership in the community in which they resided. Hence in 1890, 84 percent of the people in Galicia and Bukowina had official membership in the communities in which they resided at the time of the census, whereas for Lower Austria the figure was only 42 percent, for Upper Austria 49 percent, and for Bohemia 52 percent. A comparison of the balance of migration in the years 1869, 1880, and 1890 reveals an increase in migration both into and out of all of the regions covered. Lower Austria, including Vienna, as well as Salzburg, Trieste, Vorarlberg, and Styria, had the highest gains from migration, while Bohemia, Moravia, Silesia, Carinthia, and Carniola had the highest losses.

Toward the end of the nineteenth century, regional mobility was affecting the whole area studied. A map of the patterns of migration shows a very complex picture. (See Figure 3.1). The following patterns are noticeable:

- The area within the pull of Vienna and Lower Austria includes the whole of the Austrian half of the Empire, with the exception of such distant areas as Dalmatia. The dominant flow of migration came from Bohemia (especially its southern parts), Moravia, Silesia, Galicia, and—to a lesser extent—from Upper Austria, Styria, and the other Alpine areas.
- Bohemia was divided into a southern area of emigration and the industrial north west, where the balance of migration was positive. The area around Prague acted as the regional center of migration for Bohemia.
- The areas of out-migration toward Moravia were to be found in southeastern and northeastern Bohemia, Silesia, Hungary, and Western Galicia. There was a considerable amount of migration to Silesia from Northern Moravia and Western Galicia. Galicia

Figure 3.1
A Survey of Migration in Austria

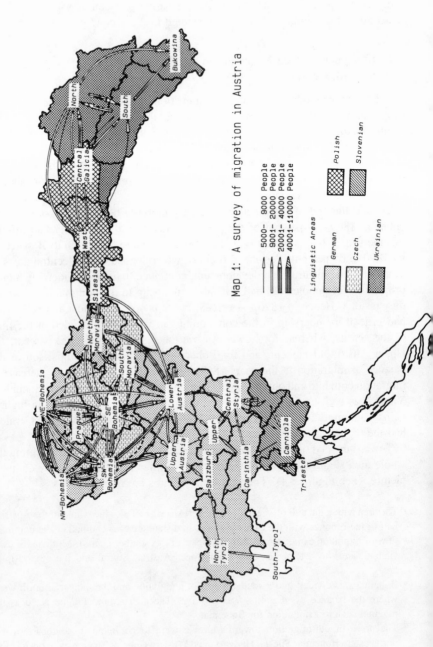

Map 1: A survey of migration in Austria

5000–   9000 People
9001– 20000 People
20001– 40000 People
40001–110000 People

Linguistic Areas

German   Polish

Czech   Slovenian

Ukrainian

itself had only interregional migration, although movement from the southeastern areas gave the Bukowina a positive balance of migration.

- In the South of the Austrian monarchy, Trieste was a center for migration affecting the provinces of Carniola, Gorizia, and Istria. North of the Karawanken, however, the target of migrants from Carinthia and Lower Styria was the industrialized area of the Northern Styria and Central Styria with the administrative center of Graz.
- A predominantly northward flow of migration can also be observed in the Tyrol, but a large proportion of this was emigration abroad.[5]

This movement consisted first and foremost of migration by workers. The direction of migration was therefore toward the economic centers of the area of study (e.g. Lower Austria, Styria, Northwestern Bohemia). The surplus population came mainly from agricultural areas that had reached the limits of their economic capacity as a result of developments that had taken place in farming during the nineteenth century. The geographical nature of these areas varied greatly. In the Alps, for example, mountain farming areas were particularly affected, and their marginal economic situation led to their increasing impoverishment. At the same time, however, the farming areas of the fertile southern districts of Moravia, which were constantly being divided up into smaller sections, also came under increasing pressure. Economic conditions (which varied from region to region) coupled with changes in the structure of agriculture, a long-term upward trend in population, and increasing mobility all led to a rise in migration away from rural areas. As migration increased during the course of the nineteenth century, linguistic and cultural barriers declined in importance, although basic ethnic and cultural structures continued to be effective (Moravia-Silesia, Western-Central-Northern-Southern Galicia, Southern Moravia-Lower Austria, etc.). The division of the region into linguistic areas in Figure 3.1 shows, however, that the direction of migration was not as a rule influenced by linguistic considerations.

The drawback of urbanization is that it leads to the abandonment of country areas, especially outlying districts situated in the high mountains. Hence it can be generally said that the maximum altitude of settlement decreased toward the end of the nineteenth century. In addition to this, new groups of urban society entered the market for property situated close to the industrializing areas. This led to an increase in the process of desettlement, which is a feature of the transformation in agrarian society that took place in the nineteenth century and continues to the present day (the "agrarian revolution"). The various aspects of this question have been discussed in detail by E. Lichtenberger in connection with the problem of mountain farming.[6] She distinguishes between three patterns according to the area involved:

1. In Lower Austria and Styria the intrusion of groups not connected with farming (industrialists, bankers, the educated middle classes) led to an increase in the sales of farms. With the decline in the market for agricultural goods that accompanied the so-called early Gründerzeit (till 1870), many farmers were

tempted to accept the enticing offers made for their property by members of the urban upper classes. This resulted in the development of tourist centers just outside Vienna (e.g., Semmering). The ownership of summer houses or hunting rights covering a wide area were typical of the almost feudal life-style of the new property-owning classes.

2. In the Tyrol and Salzburg areas, where farms were passed on undivided to one heir, the perseverance of the agrarian population was considerably greater. Ulmer gives a figure of only 9 percent for the number of farms that were forced to cease operation between 1857 and 1940.[7] Other studies (e.g., on East Tyrol) also show the structures of agrarian society to have been remarkably stable.[8] They were only marginally affected by developments which occurred in the "Gründerzeit."

3. The situation is, however, very different in West Tyrol and the Vorarlberg, where farms were divided up among a number of heirs. There the number of farms declined by 29 percent in the period between 1857 and 1940. Most of these had less than two hectares of land available. This led to a process of concentration of ownership or at least of management.

It must be assumed that similar processes were at work in other former crown territories, although with regional variations and at different periods.

Some Aspects of a Typology of Migration: Migration from Rural to Urban Areas

During the second half of the nineteenth century migration from rural to urban areas was the most important form of regional mobility. In 1843 about 81 percent of the population still lived in places with fewer than 2,000 inhabitants, but in 1890 this figure had fallen to 68 percent. The trend toward an increase in the urban population is more apparent in places with over 20,000 inhabitants, which showed a four-fold increase in their share of the population. Table 3.1 shows the growth of the six largest cities in the Austrian monarchy.

Table 3.1
Average Yearly Increase in Population of the Six Largest Cities in the Austrian Monarchy in Percentages

Period	Vienna		Graz	Trieste	Prague		Brünn	Lemberg
1831–40	1.6	(6.4)	2.2	3.7	1.7	(2.2)	0.7	1.4
1841–50	2.4	(4.4)	2.1	4.9	2.8	(7.6)	0.3	0.8
1851–60	2.2	(6.0)	2.0	−1.6	1.5	(4.4)	3.5	0.4
1861–70	1.7	(4.1)	2.4	−1.5	2.4	(16.4)	2.1	2.0
1871–80	2.6	(6.0)	1.3	1.6	2.5	(6.3)	0.6	1.7
1881–90	2.0	(3.5)	1.6	0.7			1.5	1.5

Source: Heinrich Rauchberg, "Der Zug nach der Stadt," *Statistische Monatsschrift* (1893),135–171.

Note: Figures in parentheses for Vienna and Prague include the growth of their suburbs. The percentage rates are calculated on the basis of the population in the first year of each period. Figures refer to the first year of the respective interval period.

The rapid growth can only be explained by migration to cities. Although it varied in intensity and began at different times, it led to a sudden increase in the population of all of the cities mentioned. Unlike in the cities of the agricultural east, the increase in those of the north, west and south was above average.

Especially in the case of medium-sized and small cities (e.g., Steyr, Linz, Wiener Neustadt, Innsbruck, Laibach Ljubljana, Reichenberg, Fridek), the degree to which migrants were drawn in depended on the opportunities available in the industrial and craft labor markets. Such cities were, however, often only intermediate stages in what was frequently a long series of migrations from place to place.

As a result of their intermediate position these areas, such as the district of Krems, seem almost predestined to be stages leading on to further migration. The reason for this is that they absorb elements from areas with a related but less intensive economic life, and at the same time they release their own workers to other areas with more specialized industry. The latter areas can make use of these workers, but not the less skilled workers. . . . Hence the district of Krems, which seems to be very little affected by migration, is in fact likely to be an area in which there is a considerable amount of immigration by less well-qualified workers from the districts of Lower Austria, Bohemia and Moravia further north. This immigration, however, only serves the purpose of filling the gaps left by the migration of more highly trained workers to the Vienna area with its more highly developed economy and culture.[9]

The size of the area within the pull of a city also depends on its position as a regional center and hence it is the result of a number of complex factors. As examples, Figures 3.2 and 3.3 show the patterns of migration to Vienna and Prague. The area of origin of migrants to Prague is in fact only the city's extended surroundings, but in the case of Vienna it includes the whole of the monarchy. The figures also show immigrants from abroad. Approximately 10 percent of the people counted in Vienna were born abroad, but in Prague this was only the case with circa 2 percent. Brünn (Brno) played a role similar to that of Prague in Bohemia as a regional center in Moravia, but its attractiveness to the south was affected by the proximity of Vienna. Graz as a regional center south of the Semmering drew mostly migrants from Central Styria, Upper and Lower Styria, Carinthia, Carniola, and Lower Austria. To the south the attractiveness of Graz was affected by Trieste. For Cracow, the center for Western Galicia, and Lemberg (Lvov), the center for Central and Eastern Galicia, the same influences apply as for Prague and Brünn. The areas of attraction for these cities only extended as far as the national boundary.

The emigration statistics revealed by the census of 1890 should also be considered here. About 12 percent of the people with official community membership in Vienna were elsewhere at the time of census. Most of them were registered in Lower Austria, the rest in the cities of Graz, Brünn (Brno), Prague, and Trieste. The census does not, however, show the probably considerable number of migrants who had left again before it was taken. It seems justified to assume that on account of personal connections, there were close links between emigration and immigration areas.

Figure 3.2
Migration to Vienna

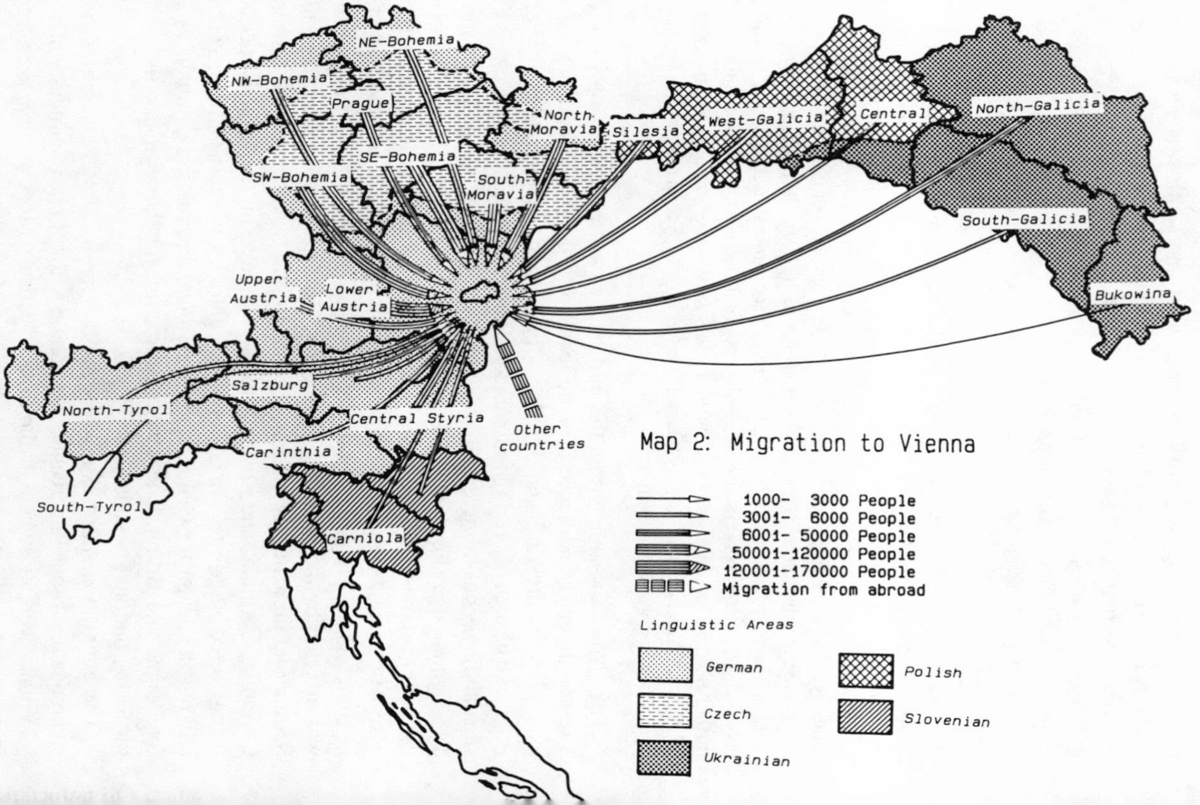

Map 2: Migration to Vienna

1000– 3000 People
3001– 6000 People
6001– 50000 People
50001–120000 People
120001–170000 People
Migration from abroad

Linguistic Areas

German   Polish

Czech   Slovenian

Ukrainian

Bukowina
North-Galicia
South-Galicia
Central Galicia
West-Galicia
Silesia
North-Moravia
South-Moravia
NE-Bohemia
Prague
SE-Bohemia
NW-Bohemia
SW-Bohemia
Upper Austria
Lower Austria
Salzburg
Central Styria
Carinthia
Carniola
North-Tyrol
South-Tyrol
Other countries

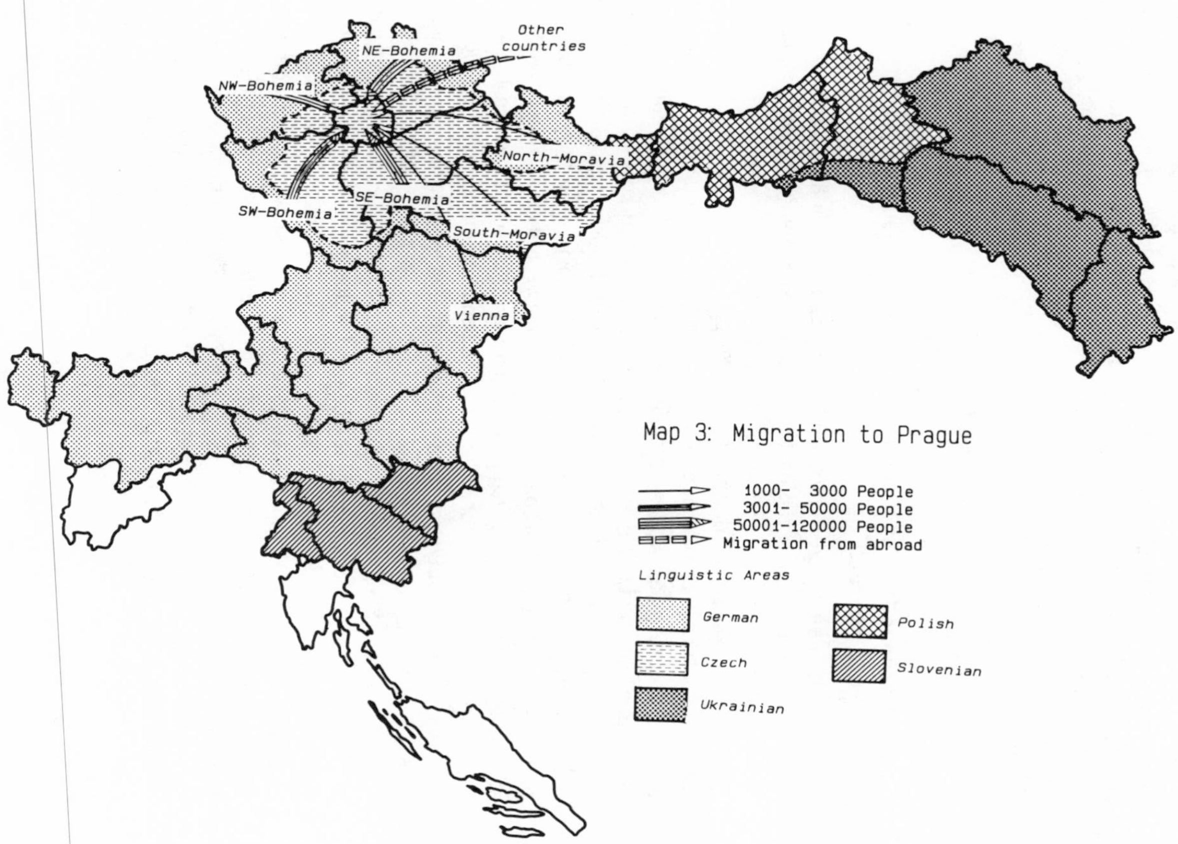

Map 3: Migration to Prague

1000- 3000 People
3001- 50000 People
50001-120000 People
Migration from abroad

Linguistic Areas

German
Czech
Ukrainian
Polish
Slovenian

Other
countries

North-Moravia

NE-Bohemia

NW-Bohemia

SW-Bohemia

SE-Bohemia

South-Moravia

Vienna

Suburban communities had a higher rate of growth than the inner city areas, because new industries were situated there and living costs were reasonable. The figures given in brackets for Vienna and Prague in Table 3.1 have been computed by including the growth of their suburbs. Hence within the limits of the city of Prague there was little change in the rate of growth, but in the whole Prague area there was a clear increase in population. In Vienna, too, the rates of increase for the whole area are constantly higher than for the city within its official boundaries.

MIGRATION TO VIENNA

The Economic Role of Vienna and Its Image among Prospective Migrants

Migration in the nineteenth century, based as it was on the search for a better life, must be seen against the background of the economic role of Vienna. The following are a few brief aspects of this situation:

1. Typical features of the manufacturing period that lasted until about 1840 were the decentralized structure of production (putting-out system) in the textile and silk industries as well as centralized functions of organization of labor, production and trade. Apart from the demand for workers in the traditional occupations, qualified labor was needed for new fields of production.

2. The Industrial Revolution as a phase of transition to the organization of production on an industrial basis took place between the 1820s and 1860s. The silk industry moved out of Vienna, and small industries organized on a traditional basis expanded, keeping their domestic, dependent conditions of employment. The expanding economy opened up the labor market to large numbers of migrants from small towns and rural areas.

3. From the 1870s onward the leading sectors of the economy (mechanical and electrical engineering and the chemical industry), which consisted for the most part of large firms, began to exert a decisive influence. The change to free, capitalist conditions of employment together with the booming economy of the last decade of the nineteenth century led to a further wave of migration. Apart from this expansion of the labor market due to the development of the economy, the dominating central role played by the old capital of a great and powerful absolutist empire over the whole period also must be seen as a driving force behind the migration.[10]

As the centuries-old capital of the Habsburg monarchy with its centralized political structure, Vienna had an unusually large proportion of nobles and officials amongst its population. Especially the expansion of the central government authorities during the reign of Joseph II led to a rapid increase in the size of the bureaucracy and the transformation of the nobility from a group of courtiers to a caste of public officials and military officers whose ranks were constantly being swelled by bourgeois who had moved up in society. This increase in the size of the aristocracy and the public service led on the one hand to the migration of many thousands of servants, but on the other hand it meant a concentration of the consumption of income from property and taxes within a limited area.[11]

The trade and craft structure of Vienna was closely linked with the needs of the court, the aristocracy, and public service. The structure of the Viennese labor market was very diverse and offered the chance to earn a living to a wide range of people. In spite of this, these aspects of the labor market are not sufficient to explain the popularity of Vienna as a target for migration. We can only understand the decision made by thousands of people to migrate if we have some knowledge of the ideas current at that period. To argue that the labor market was the only reason would not correspond to reality.

Biographies and travel reports give some impression of what were frequently stereotyped ideas about the capital. They involve promising visions of a rich and lively city full of architectural masterpieces and a confusing multitude of people and languages.[12] Here is an example from Bohemia: 'In Bohemia Vienna was looked upon as a kind of Eldorado and people sent their children there to make their fortune. Of course, one or two came back on a visit from Vienna acting like cavaliers. They had made their fortune in Vienna''.[13] There are obvious parallels such as the "rich uncle" in the United States or the "guest-workers" of today who return home with the symbol of their new-found wealth—the automobile.

Changes in the Sources of Migration during the Course of the Nineteenth Century

A typical feature of the development of migration to Vienna was the change that took place in the area of origin. Until the beginning of the nineteenth century migrants came from southern and central Germany: the dominant flow of migrants was from west to east. During the nineteenth century they came from the Sudeten area (the southern parts of Bohemia and Moravia) and thus a flow from north to south occurred. A similar increasing tendency can be seen among Jewish migrants from the east (Galicia, Hungary). This change was connected with railroad construction, (which first made the north accessible), the widening political gap between Austria and Germany, and finally the various phases of the economic development of Vienna. Figure 3.4 shows the development of migration from a selection of towns to Vienna.[14] The index is based on the figures for 1810. Hence the development shown is relative and not absolute, as the selection of towns is by no means random or representative.

A phase in which migration steadily rose from 1810 to 1860 is followed by a first high between 1860 and 1870. Slowing down after 1870, migration again increased rapidly from the 1890s onward. The migration from German towns stagnated during the nineteenth century, falling in some cases below the figures for 1810.

The dynamic increases in migration from the towns of Bohemia and Moravia underline the importance of the north as an inflow area for Vienna. The migration from Austrian towns (Graz, Innsbruck, Linz, Salzburg, and Klagenfurt) also reveals a considerable upward trend toward the end of the nineteenth century. In the decades following 1860 and 1880, however, the number of migrants from these towns declined in contrast to those from the German, Bohemian, and Moravian towns.

The Areas of Origin and Social Profile of the Migrants

The relationships between the emigration areas and the towns that were centers of migration were determined by the nature of the social groups that tended to be released in the area of origin and the social qualities for which there was most demand in the center. Hence these two poles also played a major role in determining the profile of the migrants and their position in the receiving society.

Area of Origin	**Center of Migration**
defined by its economic and political structure	defined by the structure of its labor market and its attractivity
releases migrants	attracts migrants

with the following
typical features
demographic
structure
social status
position in
household

The purpose of this schematic representation is to show the dependent relationships between centers of migration and areas of origin and also to emphasize the selective effect of demand for certain types of migrants. In the following the emigration areas will be divided into three groups according to their distance and the type of migrant provided by each group will be analyzed. For Vienna the three groups are as follows:

short distance migrants (from areas surrounding Vienna)
middle distance migrants (from Bohemia, Moravia, the Alps)
long distance migrants (from abroad, Galicia, Bukowina, etc.)

There are a number of differences between these three groups which can be measured in quantitative terms. Apart from these differences it can also be assumed that the biographies of the migrants varied according to the distance of their areas of origin. Any attempt to use the sources to reveal the individual motivation structure of the migrants meets with considerable obstacles. Although accounts of migration given by long distance migrants, especially German crafts-men, do exist, the great majority of those who came from the north said nothing about their decision to migrate, the reasons behind it, and their reception in Vienna. Reference to the relevant literature and interviews with old people show why this is the case. For those who came from the surrounding areas or the middle distance, the decision to migrate was a perfectly normal phenomenon. The very fact that so many people came from these areas meant that there was very little that was unusual about it. Hence this form of migration with its individual, cognitive decision structure contrasted sharply with long-distance and overseas migration both in this respect as well as in its demographic structure. The latter forms of migration generally required a longer period of preparation in which property had to be sold to raise money to pay for the journey. A large number of family members often took part, and the whole neighborhood became involved in the preparations. A further aspect of long-distance migration was the role played by socio-cultural differences and the distance that separated the migrants from their home areas. Short- and middle-distance migration was, however, a completely different matter. It was based on a long tradition of

Figure 3.4
Migration from Towns to Vienna, 1810–1910

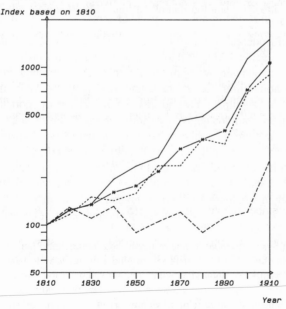

Index based on 1810

·——·	*Overall development*
------	*Towns in Germany*
———	*Towns in Bohemia and Moravia*
··········	*Towns in Austria*

seasonal agricultural labor (e.g., as a reaper or gleaner at harvest-time), journeymen's travels, or transfer for military or governmental purposes, and it was
frequently undertaken by individuals. Often it was more a matter of chance than
careful planning. Here is one example of such a case:

Rudolf Tamele was born in 1854. After he had completed his apprenticeship as a baker
in 1868 he traveled on foot with another journeyman from Policka (Southern Bohemia)
to Brünn (Brno) in Moravia. As they had used up all their money they had to work there
before they could go any further. Tamele's brother, who had stayed at home, looked
after the bakery in the mean time. Six months later they left Brünn for Vienna. The call
of the metropolis was hard to resist. They had been taught the German language at
elementary school, so they were able to find their way around. When Rudolf met the
woman who was to become his wife and she refused to return to the "provinces" with
him, it was only natural that they should stay in Vienna.
The biography of Mr. Merinsky also reveals aspects of this specific form of migration.
The youngest of twelve children, he set off to travel from Bohemia to Moravia and then
on to Vienna after completing his apprenticeship as a plumber. His eldest sister already
lived in Vienna and so he could stay with her at the beginning. The woman who was to
become his wife also came from Bohemia. She had been attracted by the letters of a
friend of hers in which she described the better living conditions in Vienna, the rich
people, and good positions.[15]

Even though these examples are not representative and do not constitute statistical
evidence, they do reveal important aspects of short- and middle-distance migration. The following three sections deal with the differences between short-,
middle-, and long-distance migration.

Demographic Structure. In general migration leads to an overproportional
increase in urban population between the ages of fifteen and thirty-five. This
shows that the main function of migration is to fulfill the urban economy's labor
requirements. The extent to which this phenomenon is apparent among the three
categories of migrants varies. Age distribution among the short-distance migrants
is similar to that of the long-distance group, and both differ from middle-distance
migrants. Among the latter there is a particularly large concentration of those
between fifteen and thirty-five years of age (62.3 percent of the migrants from
this area), whereas the short- and long-distance groups both include an overproportional number of older migrants. (See Figures 3.5 and 3.6.) A similar
structure is revealed if the marital status of the 3 is examined. Large numbers
of middle-distance migrants were not married in contrast with the short- and
long-distance migrants among whom the proportion who were married was comparable with that of the local population. Among the long-distance group, however, there were a remarkable number of people living separately from their
wives or husbands (38 percent of this category). (See Table 3.2)

The distribution of migrants according to sex varies. As has been observed
elsewhere, in Vienna the mobility of women declined the greater the distance

involved. A large surplus of men is, however, only characteristic of the middle decades of the nineteenth century. (See Table 3.3.) During this period the socio-economic structure of Vienna was determined by the expansion of small industries whose traditional craft methods of working required male labor. Both at the beginning and at the end of the nineteenth century women were in the majority. The same results show that in 1880 there was a less marked process of selection among the migrants with regard to the distance of their migration. Although the middle-distance migrants were also concentrated within the fifteen to thirty-five age group, the proportion of women among the short-distance migrants was greater than in the other groups, and there was more family migration among the short- and long-distance migrants than in the middle-distance group, the quantitative differences had become smaller. At this late stage in the development of migration, the number of women involved had risen considerably.

Social Position of the Migrants. An examination of occupational distribution among the migrants confirms some features of the picture we already have, but

Figure 3.5
Age Distribution in Vienna, 1857

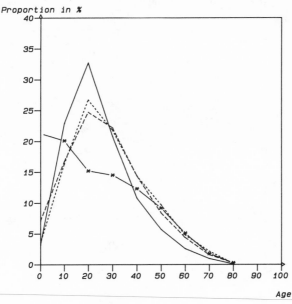

—— Vienna
`------` Surrounding Area
`———` Middle Distance
`··········` Long Distance

it also reveals a new form of differentiation. Whereas the demographic structure of the short-distance migrants was in some respects similar to that of the long-distance group, the two categories differed widely in their social position. (See Table 3.4.) Among the short-distance group the number of unqualified laborers was overproportional (the majority of those listed under the heading of hired labor were day-laborers, manual laborers, and factory workers); there were an equally overproportional number of domestic servants, especially women (farm-workers, maids), but also a smaller number of men (farmworkers, living-in employees). The middle-distance group consisted of people employed in small-scale industry, especially in craft production. In the 1850s and 1860s it was by no means rare for master craftsmen, especially in the wood- and metal-processing and clothing industries, to employ between one and two dozen journeymen and apprentices and to provide them with bed and board. It was not uncommon for at least two-thirds of these workers to be from Bohemia and Moravia. Both the short- and middle-distance migrants displaced the lowest class of the towns to which they migrated . Long-distance migrants differed from the other two groups

Figure 3.6
Age Distribution in Vienna, 1880

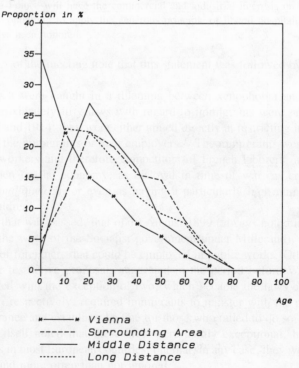

Table 3.2
Origin and Marital Status

	Vienna		Short Dist.		Middle Dist.		Long Dist.	
	1857	1880	1857	1880	1857	1880	1857	1880
Unmarried	66.1	73.2	65.7	45.2	73.8	49.7	64.1	53.2
Married	26.1	21.3	26.8	44.0	21.3	41.8	64.1	37.9
Widowed	6.9	4.6	6.7	8.9	4.7	7.4	6.6	7.9
Others	.7	1.0	.7	1.8	.8	1.0	2.7	1.5
TOTAL	38.9	46.2	16.0	12.7	31.0	29.5	14.0	11.5

Table 3.3
Origin and Sex

	Vienna		Short Dist.		Middle Dist.		Long Dist.	
	1857	1880	1857	1880	1857	1880	1857	1880
Male	51.1	46.4	48.2	43.2	58.6	51.0	61.7	44.3
Female	58.5	53.6	51.8	56.8	41.4	49.0	38.3	55.7
TOTAL	38.9	46.2	16.0	12.7	31.0	29.5	14.0	11.5

Table 3.4
Origin and Occupation

	Vienna		Short Dist.		Middle Dist.		Long Dist.	
	1857	1880	1857	1880	1857	1880	1857	1880
Unknown and Marginal Occupations	6.9	—	4.6	—	3.1	—	7.1	—
Property and Business Ownership	8.8	1.6	2.2	2.6	1.7	0.9	6.9	2.9
Civil Servants and Self-employed	11.9	7.5	4.0	6.6	3.7	5.5	7.4	8.9
Small-scale Industry	41.3	39.3	28.9	40.0	48.2	53.3	38.3	43.7
Hired Labor	21.9	44.5	27.1	32.2	18.8	25.5	22.8	31.4
Domestic Service	8.8	7.2	32.3	18.6	23.8	14.8	17.0	13.1
Agriculture	4.0	—	.9	—	.7	—	.5	—
TOTAL	26.5	34.2	19.1	14.5	38.5	39.4	16.0	11.9
Proportion Employed	44.0	41.0	72.2	63.2	82.6	74.0	73.1	57.5

in that an overproportionally large number of them had occupations requiring a high level of qualification or were business or property owners or aristocrats. The long-distance migrants also included a large number of people with small-scale industrial occupations. There is evidence that the tradition for journeymen craftsmen to travel long distances had not yet died out, although it had already begun to decline. In the sample of 1880 the majority of middle-distance migrants continued to be employed in small industry. The proportion of the local population in the category of hired labor had increased. For all three groups of migrants domestic service had to a large extent ceased to provide a minimum level of existence, but this applied especially to the short-distance migrants. This led to a shift toward employment in small industry and as hired labor. There continued to be an overproportional number of businessmen, members of the profession and so forth, among the long-distance migrants. As might be expected, the rate of employment among migrants was considerably higher than that of the whole population, although the figures reveal a downward tendency toward the end of the century. It may be of interest to note that the proportion of migrants then employed is similar to that of "guestworkers" now in Vienna. There is another remarkable similarity: the number of employed "guestworkers" was also higher during the early stage of this migration than during the peak and later stages. There has also been a marked decline in the dominating role played by men emigrating on their own. Increasingly, whole families emigrated together.

The Position of Migrants in the Household. The social position of migrants, influenced by their demographic structure, also determined their position in the households of the center to which they migrated. Most short-distance migrants were living-in employees, but there were frequently also heads of households. This means that there was a fairly wide range of employment conditions and possibilities of finding living accommodation available to members of the lower classes who had come from the surrounding area. It can also be assumed that whole families were involved in short-distance migration. (See Table 3.5) The distribution of positions in the household is especially polarized among the long-distance migrants. On the one hand there is evidence of migration by individual people on their own, some of whom, however, may have left their families at home for a period, so that most of them were registered in Vienna as sharing accommodation as sub-tenants. The large number of heads of households, but also of sons and daughters, reveals that, especially in the case of the property-tied classes, large family groups also migrated to Vienna.

On the other hand, migration from the middle-distance areas seems especially to have involved migrants with the status of living-in employees, in particular journeymen or apprentices in small-scale industry. Family migration was least probable among this group of migrants. The difference in orientation between female short-distance migrants, who tended to find work of an unspecified nature in domestic service, and male middle-distance migrants employed in craft production is also revealed in the age distribution. In domestic service living-in tended to be a condition of employment regardless of one's age; in small industry living-in was likely to be a requirement that mainly applied only to young people. By 1880 there had already been a marked decline in the number of positions involving dependent conditions of employment. In 1857, 27 percent of the entire population were registered as living-in employees, but in the small sample of 1880 this figure had fallen to 14 percent. The short- and middle-distance migrants profited most from this change and increasingly had their own households. This factor also corresponded with the change in their occupational structure. A decline in the number of people living in and an increase in the number of migrants with their own household is least observable among the long-distance group.

Segregation and Integration

One feature of urban development in the nineteenth century was the rapid increase in population, which led to expansion into the surrounding area and considerable demand for living accommodations. This was heightened by the long-term trend toward smaller households and the increasing tendency to separate living accommodations from working places. The establishment of public transport facilities and the building of houses and tenement blocks that provided accommodations varying considerably in size, comfort, and price led to the increasing segregation of the population. Groups of people began to be concentrated in certain areas, and in extreme cases this resulted in the formation of ghettos.

If the degree of segregation is calculated for each district of the city according to the area of origin of the population, a strong concentration of migrants from Galicia and Bukowina is revealed (index of segregation = 31).[16] As is well known,

Table 3.5
Origin and Position in Household

	Vienna		Short Dist.		Middle Dist.		Long Dist.	
	1857	*1880*	*1857*	*1880*	*1857*	*1880*	*1857*	*1880*
Head of Household	16.9	11.4	18.5	21.9	14.7	22.8	20.0	20.5
Housewife	14.9	14.6	13.4	30.8	8.9	24.3	11.3	22.6
Children	44.2	55.4	6.4	10.2	5.7	6.1	9.7	8.3
Relatives	1.7	3.7	1.1	4.1	.9	3.5	1.8	3.0
Children Not Belonging to Family	3.5	—	.8	—	.6	—	.8	—
Servants	6.5	4.4	39.6	16.6	46.4	22.3	26.3	17.2
Other Members	12.4	10.5	20.1	16.4	22.8	21.0	30.1	28.4
TOTAL	38.9	45.9	16.0	12.9	31.0	29.7	14.0	11.5

Jewish migration played an important role here. Migrants from Hungary also reveal an above-average level of segregation (index of segregation = 18), and they also had a similar local structure to that of the Jewish immigrants from Galicia. Migrants from other countries abroad (index of segregation = 16) were concentrated in central districts and finally there were the migrants from Bohemia (index of segregation = 14), in the southern suburban districts of the city. Calculations of the degree of segregation of Czech-speaking migrants in 1910 revealed an index of over 20.[17] In interpreting the increase in segregation (1890:14-1910:20), the fact that segregation was at its climax before the First World War and also that German-speaking migrants from Bohemia had less difficulties than those who spoke Czech when it came to finding places to live must be considered. Figure 3.7 shows in simplified form the local distribution of migrants in Vienna around 1890. The migrants from the surrounding area and the north (Bohemia and Moravia), who displaced the lowest class of workers, found living accommodations in the cheaper areas on the edge of the city. Concentrations occurred in districts that provided large numbers of working places (Favoriten). The Jewish migrants from Galicia and Hungary lived chiefly in the second district of Vienna (Leopoldstadt), the location of two railheads. Around the turn of the century and especially after the First World War, this concentration reached a fairly high level (circa 35 percent of the district's population were Jews). Long-distance migrants from other places abroad lived mostly in the middle- and upper-class districts of the city center. Taking the whole of Vienna into consideration, however, the degree of segregation was low, especially when it is compared with local patterns of distribution in other cities (studies of European migrant groups in North American cities reveal indices of segregation ranging from c.35 to 45). One explanation for this is to be found in the specific nature of the economic development of Vienna in the nineteenth century. The important role played by employment in small industry and work in which employees lived in prevented the formation of local concentrations of certain sections of the population. There were a few cases in which such concentration did occur toward the end of the nineteenth century, but even during the period of high industrialization it was never a widespread phenomenon. This argument is seen in a new light, however, when it is examined on the basis of aggregates from a small area. Thus there is evidence that regional origin exerted an influence on the composition of households not only in individual cases but also to such an extent as to be significant in statistical analyses.

Because of the lack of other data comparable in quality, the following examples are taken from the conscription list of 1857, but the basic trends should also be valid for subsequent decades. One example of a house in which there was a concentration of people similar in origin was no. 1 Josefsgasse in the eighth district of Vienna:

A maker of plaster figures from Tuscany lives there with his wife and five children, who have all come from Italy, and also a maid from just outside Vienna. In the same house two other workers are registered, both of whom also come from Tuscany. The owner of the house who also lives at no. 1 Josefsgasse was born in Vienna, but his wife is Italian.

The way in which people found accommodations helped to bring about such concentration. The most important channel of information in the search for accommodations consisted of offers passed on informally via personal contact.

An analysis at the household level also reveals regional preferences in the composition. Calculation of the endogamy rates shows that there was a strong tendency for married couples to come from the same region (Cramers V:0.81. Cramer's V is a statistical measure indicating the correlation between two features in a cross-table, its range can be 0-1, e.g. V:0.81 demonstrates a rather high degree of correlation). Those migrants who did not get married until they came to Vienna were to a large extent restricted in their choice of mates to other migrants. An almost perfect state of endogamy existed between local married couples from Vienna. There were some exceptions to this strong pattern of endogamy among long-and short-distance migrants, about 8 percent of whom had Viennese wives, and also among the middle-distance migrants, of whom 8

Figure 3.7
Schematic Representation of the Local Distribution of Migrants in Vienna, 1890

percent were married to women from the area surrounding Vienna. All together 95 percent of the married heads of household who came from Vienna had Viennese wives, 84 percent of short-distance migrants were married to women who belonged to the same group, 82 percent of the middle-distance migrants, and 78 percent of the long-distance migrants. The local population clearly isolated itself from the migrants, but this endogamy was often an expression of the continuing hope of the migrants to return home one day. This was sufficient reason to marry someone who was acquainted with one's own background. The longer the distance of migration, the more the level of endogamy declined. This was perhaps an expression of the fact that the migrants accepted their new home, but perhaps because it was more difficult to find someone from the same region to marry. It should also be noted that the endogamy rates show a variation in the level of social selection. There are especially high rates of endogamy at the upper and lower ends of the social scale, that is, among property owners and businessmen as well as among hired laborers. The figures are low for the petit bourgeois middle classes. Especially in small-scale industry there had never been a tradition of endogamy; journeymen's travels and marriages to widows led to more mixing.

Although the largest group of migrants, workers involved in craft production and those in domestic service who lived in with their employers, were integrated into a household, there was a fixed social distance between them and the head of the household, and they occupied a subordinate position. This ambivalence between integration into a household and social segregation is also expressed in the statistics. In general there is only a low level of correlation between the origin of the head of the household and that of the employees living in, but it is enough to be significant (Cramers V: 0.14; n = 8,820). An above-average number of migrants from the surrounding area and living-in employees from Vienna were to be found in households together with local people. This also applies to the great majority of living-in employees from the middle- and long-distance regions, but a large proportion of these also lived in households headed by people who came from the same region as they did. This can be interpreted as a form of "identification" by the migrants, who were ethnically foreigners to the local population, but also as a sign that complete households migrated together.

An examination of other members of households who shared accommodations reveals a similar picture. (This group consists of people who were neither relatives nor employees of the head of the household.) The level of correlation is also significant (Cramers V:0.15; n = 6,478). Among both the local population and the long-distance migrants there is a marked tendency for the head of the household and those sharing the accommodations to be from the same region.

A comparison with the sample of 1880 shows how patterns developed. There was a marked tendency away from strict endogamy (Cramers V:0.32; n = 580); it remained relatively high among the local population and middle-distance migrants. Yet there had been a sharp increase in the preference of heads of house-holds for living-in employees from the same region of origin (Cramers V:0.21; n = 476) and similarly for others sharing their accommodations, too (Cramers V:0.28; n = 342). The middle-distance group reveals an above-average prefer-ence. The question of nationality was becoming an increasing problem in Vienna toward the end of the nineteenth century.[18]

SUMMARY

As a result of the increase in regional mobility during the nineteenth century, clearly defined patterns of migration developed involving movement from the peripheral areas to the center. This freedom of movement was fostered by the liberal-capitalist social order of the period. In the process of this development, various sub-systems of migration appeared. Of these, migration from one region to another was more important than that within the same region (e.g., Trieste-Gorizia-Istria, Galicia-Bukowina, Tyrol-Vorarlberg), and Vienna, the Imperial capital, became the center of migration. Distinguishing between the migrants according to the distance of their migration three categories have become ap-parent: short-distance, middle-distance, and long-distance. Generally it can be concluded for Austria that short-distance migrants corresponded more closely to the lower classes of urban social structure, whilst long-distance migrants were more likely to correspond to the upper classes. Within these social categories, however, the two groups of migrants reveal a relatively wide range of demo-graphic characteristics and positions in the households of the cities to which they moved. In contrast, the possibilities available to the middle-distance migrants seem to have been more constrained. In their case, there was the closest rela-tionship between the demand for labor of a city and the specific range of workers offered by a region. Migration in this group was also more restricted to people with certain social and demographic characteristics and its members were more rigidly assigned to dependent positions in the households of their employers than those of the other two groups.

Even though the two census samples involve different areas, a comparison with the sample of 1880 permits us to conclude that as the number of working places that did not involve living-in increased, the process of demographic se-lection among the migrants and the determination of their situation declined, especially in the case of the short- and middle-distance migrants.

The 1857 profile of the population shows an initial stage in the development of migration, whereas the survey of 1880 tends more to represent a peak. In-dividual migration by people going to work as living-in employees has been replaced by migration that increasingly involves families. They may set up their own households in Vienna, fewer of them are employed, and they are subject to less demographic and social segregation.

NOTES

1. Cf. Heinrich Rauchberg, "Die Gebürtigkeitsverhältnisse der Bevölkerung Österreichs nach den Ergebnissen der Volkszählung vom 31. December 1890," *Statistische Monatsschrift* (1892), 514–74.

2. Heinrich Rauchberg, "Die Heimatsverhältnisse der Bevölkerung Österreichs nach den Ergebnissen der Volkszählung vom 31. December 1890," *Statistische Monatsschrift* (1892), 345–405.

3. The term "clustered sample" means a random sample in which – a priori – certain spatial limits are given for the survey so that the source of data is not a matter of pure chance.

4. Wilbur Zelinsky, "The Hypothesis of the Mobility Transition," *Geographical Review* 61, 219–49.

5. The 359 districts and autonomous towns of the Austrian half of the Empire were grouped as follows:

Vienna and Lower Austria separately;

Styria
Upper Styria: Bruck/Mur, Gröbming, Judenburg, Leoben, Liezen, Murau
Central Styria: Graz (town and district), Deutsch-Landsberg, Feldbach, Hartberg, Leibnitz, Radkersburg, Weiz
Lower Styria: Cilli (town and district), Marburg (town and district), Pettau (town and district), Rann, Windisch-Graz

Tyrol
North Tyrol: Innsbruck (town and district), Bozen (town and district), Brixen, Bruneck, Imst, Kitzbühel, Kufstein, Landeck, Lienz, Meran, Reutte, Schwaz
South Tyrol: Trient (town and district), Rovereto (town and district), Ampezzo, Borgo, Cavalese, Cles, Primiero, Riva, Tione

Bohemia
Center: Prague, Böhmisch-Brod, Karolinenthal, Königl. Weinberge, Smichow
North West: Asch, Aussig, Brüx, Eger, Falkenau, Graslitz, Joachimsthal, Kaaden, Karlsbad, Komotau, Kralowitz, Laun, Luditz, Plan, Podersam, Rakonitz, Raudnitz, Saaz, Schlan, Tepl, Teplitz
North East: Reichenberg (town and district), Böhmisch-Leipa, Braunau, Dauba, Friedland, Gabel, Gablonz, Hohenelbe, Jicin, Jung-Bunzlau, Königgrätz, Königinhof, Leitmeritz, Melnik, Münchengrätz, Neubydzow, Neustadt/Mettau, Podebrad, Rumburg, Schluckenau, Semil, Starkenbach,Tetschen, Trautenau, Turnau
South East: Beneschau, Caslau, Chotebor, Chrudim, Deutsch-Brod, Hohenmauth, Kolin, Kuttenberg, Landskron, Ledetsch, Leitomischl, Mühlhausen, Neuhaus, Pardubitz, Pilgram, Policka, Reichenau, Selcan, Senftenberg, Tabor, Wittingau
South West: Bischofteinitz, Blatna, Budweis, Horowitz, Kaplitz, Klattau, Krumau, Mies, Moldautein, Pilsen, Pisek, Prachatitz, Prestitz, Pribram, Schüttenhofen, Strakonitz, Tachau, Taus

Moravia
South: Brünn (town and district), Iglau (town and district), Ung.Hradisch (town and district), Znaim (town and district), Auspitz, Boskowitz, Datschitz, Gaya, Göding, Groß-Meseritsch, Mähr.Kromau, Neustadtl, Nikolsberg, Trebitsch, Wischau
North: Kremsier (town and district), Olmütz (town and district), Hohenstadt, Holleschau, Littau, Mähr.-Trübau, Mistek, Neutitschein, Prerau, Prossnitz, Römerstadt, Mähr.-Schönberg, Sternberg, Ung.Brod, Wall.-Meseritsch, Mähr.-Weißkirchen

Galicia
Western Galicia: Krakau (town and district), Biala, Bochnia, Brzesko, Chrzanow, Dabrowa, Gorlice,

Grybow, Jaslo, Limanowa, Mielec, Myslenice, Neumarkt, Neu-Sandec, Pilzno, Ropezyee, Saybusch, Tarnow, Wadowicw, Wieliczka

Central Galicia: Brzozow, Dobromil, Jaroslau, Kolbuszow, Krosno, Lancut, Liske, Mosciska, Nisko, Przemysl, Rzeszow, Sanok, Tarnobrzeg

North East: Lemberg (town and district), Bobrka, Borszczow, Brody, Brzezany, Buczacz, Cieszanow, Czortkow, Grodek, Hussiatyn, Jaworow, Kamionka-strumilowa, Podhajce, Przemyslany, Rawa Ruska, Rohatyn, Rudki, Skalat, Sokal, Tarnopol, Trembowla, Zaleszezyki, Zbaraz, Zloczow, Zolkiew

South East: Bohorodczany, Dolina, Drohobycz, Horodenka, Kalusz, Kolomea, Kossow, Nadworna, Sambor, Sniatyn, Stanislau, Stare-Miasto, Stryj, Tlumacz, Turka, Zydaczow

6. Elisabeth Lichtenberger, "Die Sukzession von der Agrar-zur Freizeitgesellschaft in den Hochgebirgen Europas," *Innsbrucker Geographische Studien* (1979), 401–36, and "Das Bergbauernproblem in den österreichischen Alpen," *Erdkunde* (1965), 39–57; Michael Mitterauer, "Auswirkungen der Agrarrevolution auf die bäuerliche Familienstruktur in Österreich," in *Historische Familienforschung*, ed. M. Mitterauer (Frankfurt/M., 1982), pp. 241–70.

7. F. Ulmer, *Die Bergbauernfrage*, Schleunschriften, 1958.

8. Josef Kytir, "Bevölkerungsgeographische Untersuchungen in einem peripheren Raum: Osttirol" (Ph.D. diss., Vienna, 1984).

9. Heinrich Rauchberg, "Dichtigkeit, Zunahme, natürliche und Wanderbewegung der Bevölkerung Österreichs in der Periode 1881–1890," *Statistische Monatsschrift* (1892), 217–32.

10. Josef Ehmer, "Familie und Klasse. Zur Entstehung der Arbeiterfamilie in Wien," *Historische Familienforschung*, ed. Michael Mitterauer (Frankfurt/Main, 1982), pp. 300–326.

11. Peter Feldbauer, *Stadtwachstum und Wohnungsnot. Determinanten unzureichender Wohnungsversorgung in Vienna 1848–1914* (Vienna, 1977), p. 30.

12. Cf. Erich Zöllner, "Wien um die Mitte des 19. Jahrhunderts aus der Sicht seiner fremden Gäste," *Wiener Geschichtsblätter* (1979), pp. 120–36.

13. Monika Glettler, *Die Wiener Tschechen um 1900* (Vienna, 1972), p. 40.

14. The figures are from Rudolf Till, "Zur Herkunft der Wiener Bevölkerung," *Vierteljahrsschrift für Sozial- und Wirtschaftsgeschichte* 34 (1941), 15–37. This is an analysis of death certificates from Vienna. It only includes the death certificates of migrants from selected towns (11 of these towns were in what is now Austria, 9 in Bohemia/Moravia, 1 in Hungary and 13 in the German Reich) and of these only figures for every decade from 1810 to 1910 are included. On the basis of the known mortality rate, the number of people from each of thirty-four towns was calculated. Note that this assumes an equally spread mortality rate.

15. Michael John, *Hausherrenmacht und Mieterelend 1890–1923* (Vienna, 1982), pp. 164–81.

16. The index of segregation measures the extent of the deviation in distribution of a group of the population in a particular area from its distribution in the total area. The index has a range of 0 to 100, whereby 0 means no segregation and 100 complete segregation. Broadly speaking, the index of segregation can also be interpreted as the percentage of the minority that would have to move to achieve a proportional distribution.

17. Helga Leitner, *Gastarbeiter in der städtischen Gesellschaft* (Frankfurt/Main, 1983), pp. 104–6.

18. See the chapter by Monika Glettler in this volume.

ITALIAN MIGRATION TO EUROPEAN COUNTRIES FROM POLITICAL UNIFICATION TO WORLD WAR I

4

Gianfausto Rosoli

EUROPEAN VERSUS OVERSEAS DESTINATIONS OF ITALIAN MASS EMIGRATION (1876-1915)

Contrary to common opinion, sometimes even that of some scholars, Italian emigration abroad—during its one-century duration—had Europe as its main destination. In fact, if we add up all the expatriations throughout the entire century, according to Italian statistical sources—which give us emigration data only from 1876 on—we find that expatriations towards Europe exceed those towards the rest of the world: in fact more than 13 million Italian emigrants towards Europe versus 11 million and a half towards America. (See Figure 4.1 and Table 4.1.)

If we also add various other East European and Mediterranean destinations, then we see that European destinations have clearly always been favored by Italian emigration, especially in the last fifty years.[1] (See Figure 4.2.)

Nonetheless, Italian observers themselves refer to Italian emigration as "the American fever." But in reality Italian emigration to the Americas predominated only toward the turn of this century. Instead, during the initial period of Italian emigration—after the unification of Italy in 1861—and again after the closure

Table 4.1
Major Destinations of Italian Emigration to European and Extra-European Countries in One Century, 1876–1976

Major European Countries		Extra-European Countries	
France	4,117,394	USA	5,691,404
Switzerland	3,989,813	Argentina	2,969,402
Germany	2,452,587	Brazil	1,456,914
Benelux	535,031	Canada	650,358
G. Britain	263,598	Australia	428,289
Austria	1,188,135	Venezuela	285,014
TOTAL	12,546,558	TOTAL	11,481,381

Figure 4.1
Destinations of Italian Out-Migration

1876-1900

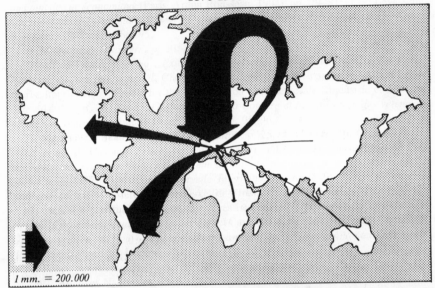

1901-1915

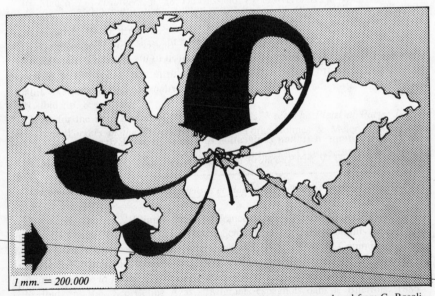

Source: Figure 4.1 and all other figures and tables in this chapter are reproduced from G. Rosoli, ed., *Un secolo di emigrazione italiana: 1876–1976* (Rome:CSER, 1978) unless otherwise noted.

Figure 4.2
A Comparison of European and Overseas Migration by Italians, 1876–1976

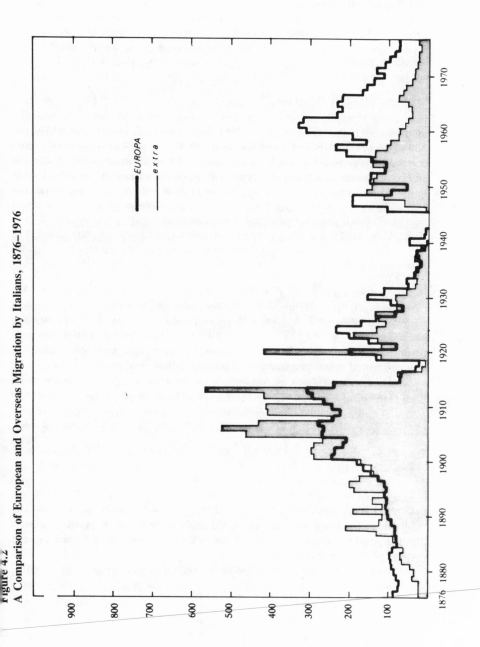

of the American borders in the 1920s, there was a growth of Italian emigration to European countries.

The stress on American emigration derives from the prejudice, current and scientific, that saw departure for America as the only major indicator of economic plight, as the real dramatic and definitive choice of the people of poor regions. In fact, however, the regions that were beginning to become the most advanced (Piedmont, Liguria, and Lombardy) in the first period (1870–1890) provided the greatest number of emigrants. What is interesting to note about these migrations is the very marked regional preference for particular countries of destination. Northern Italy has always shown a growing preference for European destinations, while the south preferred transoceanic emigration. During the period of mass emigration, the south sent almost all its emigrants overseas. Geographical position, economic structures, and cost of transportation had a determining role in these regional choices. A trip from Sicily to northern Germany on an average cost more than a trip to New York. One also had to consider the cost of living abroad, in relation to salaries and duration of expatriation. There also existed elements of "professionalism" in relation to the various markets for foreign labor, with the possibility of combining work in Italy with work abroad to supplement one's income. Moreover, "chain migration" with the system of letters calling for particular people, prepaid trips, the support system of relatives and *paesani* (country people), and the luring policies of some foreign countries led to a certain amount of stability in the range of destinations selected. As early as the beginning of the 1880s, Italian emigration was able to establish its international labor market in Europe and in America. Among European countries, France showed a great capacity for attracting Italian workers. During the 1890 economic crisis, the labor markets of Switzerland and Germany benefited from the French policy against Italian immigration. In these two countries there has been an "anti-cyclical" absorption of Italians in productive sectors, such as housing construction, public works, and railroad construction. After the 1890 crisis the flows of Italian manpower generally tended to concentrate on a few big labor markets in Europe and overseas.

By and large, emigration to other countries in Europe has traditionally been underestimated, even in official evaluations. The terminology of the last century contrasted this emigration with emigration "as such," namely, transoceanic emigration. Emigration to Europe was simply regarded as temporary, almost like the seasonal work across the border that was rooted in the traditions of various northern Italian regions.

As a result of the temporary nature of Italian emigration to European countries and in the absence of a policy of integration in the receiving countries, the Italian communities abroad gradually developed certain characteristics that sharply differentiate transoceanic and European emigration. The decisive and most evident factor is that emigration to Europe rarely led to the formation of real colonies that were vital, compact, and geographically definable with specific residential, professional, and linguistic characteristics, as was the case with transoceanic emigration. The colonies of Italian emigrants in Europe, when they did exist, enjoyed little demographic, cultural, and political independence in their development vis-à-vis the country of origin and the receiving country just as they today hardly seem to be touched by the process of ethnic identity that characterizes the emigrant communities in America.

This brief essay focuses on Italian emigration to Europe during the period of mass emigration and begins with a description of the quantitative aspects. The stress on the three countries of France, Switzerland, and Germany is due to the importance these countries have had and still have in the development of Italian emigration. In fact, Italian emigration after World War II has become more and more "Europeanized," consolidating destinations already achieved and strengthening already existing communities.

A QUANTITATIVE OUTLINE OF THE ITALIAN MIGRATION FLOWS, 1876–1915

The forty-year period from 1876 to the outbreak of World War I registered the expatriation of 14 million Italians, with an average yearly outflow of 350,691, an amount greater to that of any other European country over such a long period of time. The increase was constant: from 1,314,689 Italian emigrants in the decade 1876–1885 to 2,391,049 in the following decade, from 4,322,425 in the decade at the turn of the century to 5,999,497 in the 1906–1915 period. (See Table 4.2.)[2]

Of the Italian emigration for the whole period, European countries received 44 percent while 54.5 percent went overseas. The Italian regions which have greatly contributed to the migratory movement are Veneto (13 percent) with almost 2 million emigrants, Piedmont (11 percent) with more than a million and a half, Campania (10.5 percent) with almost a million and a half and Friuli (Venezia Giulia) with a similar proportion (10 percent). (See Figure 4.3 and Table 4.3.) Considering the two periods 1876–1900 and 1901–1915 separately, we can clearly perceive the social and geographical dynamics of the Italian movement abroad. During the first period there were 5,257,911 emigrants with an average of 210,316 per year. Of the flow, 48.5 percent was directed toward other countries in Europe, manifesting a certain balance between Europe and overseas. An average of 108,554 emigrants a year went to overseas countries, 101,763 to Europe.(See Table 4.4.)

The major European countries that imported Italian labor were France (817,633, i.e., a third of the total Italian emigration to Europe), Austria-Hungary (600,407), Germany (353,897) and Switzerland (326,647). (See Table 4.4.) During this first period the outflow was predominantly from northern regions, particularly from Veneto (about one million emigrants) and Friuli (Venezia Giulia). The

Venetian area as a whole supplied more than one third (34 percent) of the total expatriates of the period (See Table 4.5.)

Emigration rates of the Italian regions reached a figure of ten per thousand inhabitants on average during 1876–1900. In Veneto they reached a peak of forty per thousand during the 1888–1891 period, when there was a huge exodus of peasants (*contadini*). In the province of Udine alone, which used to comprise the major part of today's region of Friuli-Venezia Giulia, emigration rates were approximately twenty-five per thousand, and in 1899 they reached a peak of sixty-three per thousand, that is, fifty emigrants a year per thousand inhabitants during the decade 1890–1900.

Migration almost exclusively involved male workers. Female participation rose from 17 percent in the first five years (1876–1880) to 25 percent at the end of the period (1896–1900). Agricultural laborers made up 37 percent of the total during the first five-year period, constituted nearly half the total outflow (49 percent) at the height of the Venetian migration (1886–1890), and fell to 40 percent in the following five-year period.

The second period, 1901–1915, registered the maximum Italian mass migration marked by evident pathological features: emigration was damaging to demo-

Table 4.2
Italian Expatriation according to Destination, 1876–1915

Destination	Number	Percent of Total	Yearly Average
Great Britain	69,483	0.5	1,737
Benelux	37,489	0.2	937
Germany	1,225,847	8.7	30,646
France	1,715,566	12.2	42,889
Switzerland	1,340,292	9.6	33,507
Austria-Hungary	1,128,490	8.0	28,212
Europe	*6,137,386*	*43.6*	*153,434*
Canada	148,565	1.1	3,714
USA	4,156,944	29.6	103,923
Brazil	1,225,171	8.7	30,629
Argentina	1,795,916	12.8	44,898
America	*7,622,790*	*54.4*	*190,570*
Africa	237,966	1.7	5,949
Asia	10,245	—	256
Oceania	19,273	—	482
Total Expatriates	14,027,660	100.0	350,691

Source: ISTAT.

Note: In tables 4.2, 4.4, and 4.6, subtotals and totals are larger than the sum of the countries listed because of residual geographical categories not shown in the table.

Figure 4.3
The Republic of Italy

Source: Istituto Centrale di Statistica

graphic (reproductive) and socio-economic structures. (See Table 4.6.) Indeed, more than one-third of the total outflow over the century 1876–1976 occurred during this fifteen-year period: 8,769,749 emigrants with a yearly average of more than half a million (584,649). The Americas exerted the maximum attraction for Italians, with five million emigrants (57 percent of the total). The United States constituted the major labor importing nation: it received about three and a half million Italians (400,000 in 1913 alone), namely, two-fifths of all the Italian expatriates of this period.

The Italian emigration to Europe (41 percent of the total for the period) had Switzerland as its main destination (one million Italian immigrants, corresponding to 28 percent of the total number of emigrants to Europe); France and Germany followed with about 900,000 immigrants each, Austria-Hungary received 528,083. Other European countries, like Belgium, Holland, Luxembourg and Great Britain, received lesser Italian flows. (See Table 4.6.)

The prevalence of overseas flows was due to the growing importance of southern and insular emigration. Sicily, with 1,126,000 emigrants, reached 13 percent of the total, Campania 11 percent with one million, Veneto 10 percent

Table 4.3
Expatriation from Italian Regions, 1876–1915

Regions	Number	Percent of Total	Yearly Average
Piedmont	1,540,164	11.0	38,504
Lombardy	1,342,759	9.6	33,569
Veneto	1,822,793	13.0	45,570
Trentino-Alto Adige	—	—	—
Friuli-Venezia Giulia	1,407,793	10.0	35,195
Liguria	223,156	1.6	5,579
Emilia Romagna	690,175	4.9	17,254
Tuscany	763,156	5.4	19,079
Umbria	164,540	1.2	4,114
Marche	390,157	2.8	9,754
Lazio	205,055	1.5	5,126
Abruzzi	595,556	4.2	14,889
Molise	308,035	2.2	7,701
Campania	1,475,979	10.5	36,899
Puglia	382,897	2.7	9,572
Basilicata	385,693	2.7	9,642
Calabria	879,031	6.3	21,976
Sicily	1,352,962	9.6	33,824
Sardinia	97,759	0.7	2,444
Total Expatriates	14,027,660	100.0	350,691

Source: ISTAT.

with 900,000 emigrants, followed close by Piedmont and Lombardy. (See Table 4.7 and Figure 4.4). In 1913 the emigration rate for Sicily was 40 emigrants per 1,000 inhabitants, for Calabria 45. In 1905 the corresponding figure for Basilicata was 37. The number of female emigrants tended to be low, at about 20 percent of the total emigration.

Data on returnees are available from 1905 onward but only from overseas countries. From 1905 to 1915 about two million Italians returned home, 1,200,000 of them from the United States. Returns affected southern regions, which were the greatest contributors to the emigration to America. Data on return migration from European countries are not available till 1921.

During the 1900–1915 period, agricultural laborers decreased in the outflow, falling from 35 percent at the beginning of the century to 26 percent in the period 1911–1915. The phenomenon of progressive proletarization of Italian emigration is evident. The order of emigration was first the traditional *contadini*, then farm hands and unskilled laborers – who constitute an enduring component of Italian emigration – and finally a quota of industrial workers. The intense fluctuation of Italian migration flows during this fifteen-year period was determined by economic cycles and international difficulties. Italian emigration to the rest of Europe was one of the principle vehicles of subordinate integration of the Italian economy into that of the most industrialized countries.

Table 4.4
Italian Expatriation according to Destination, 1876–1900

Destination	Number	Percent of Total	Yearly Average
Great Britain	16,027	0.3	641
Benelux	7,338	—	294
Germany	353,897	6.7	14,156
France	817,633	15.6	32,705
Switzerland	326,647	6.2	13,066
Austria-Hungary	600,407	11.4	24,016
Europe	*2,544,064*	*48.4*	*101,763*
Canada	12,326	0.2	493
USA	772,792	14.7	30,912
Brazil	814,388	15.5	32,576
Argentina	801,362	15.2	32,054
America	*2,614,691*	*49.7*	*104,588*
Africa	91,046	1.7	3,642
Asia	2,623	—	105
Oceania	5,487	—	219
Total Expatriates	5,257,911	100.0	210,316

Source: ISTAT.

ITALIAN EMIGRANTS IN FRANCE

By the end of the nineteenth century, Italians had become the largest foreign group in France according to official publications.[3] In 1851 there were 63,307 Italians living in France, about one-sixth of all foreigners; in 1886 they numbered 264,568, about one-fourth of all foreigners. By 1911 there were 414,234 Italians in France: more than one-fourth of the entire foreign population, enough to form a city with the combined population of Genoa and Venice at that time. With its population at zero growth and a humming industrial complex, pre-war France was attracting large numbers of immigrants from various countries.

In the field of industrial production, Italians represented 40 percent of the foreign workers engaged in agriculture and forestry, according to the 1906 census. Even in manufacturing, Italians made up 40 percent, while in transportation they actually represented two-thirds of the foreign workers, and in commerce one-third. More specifically, in 1906 Italians made up 7 percent (about 24,000) of all the quarry workers and miners and 8 percent of the chemical workers.

The importance of the Italian contribution is underestimated even in the censuses themselves. Italians represented three-fourths of foreign workers. Every

Table 4.5
Expatriation from Italian Regions, 1876–1900

Region	Number	Percent of Total	Yearly Average
Piedmont	709,076	13.5	28,363
Lombardy	519,100	9.9	20,764
Veneto	940,711	17.9	37,628
Trentino-Alto Adige	—		—
Friuli-Venezia Giulia	847,072	16.1	33,883
Liguria	117,941	2.2	4,718
Emilia Romagna	220,745	4.2	8,830
Tuscany	290,111	5.5	11,604
Umbria	8,866	—	355
Marche	70,050	1.3	2,802
Lazio	15,830	0.3	633
Abruzzi	109,038	2.1	4,362
Molise	136,355	2.6	5,454
Campania	520,791	9.9	20,832
Puglia	50,282	1.0	2,011
Basilicata	191,433	3.6	7,657
Calabria	275,926	5.2	11,037
Sicily	226,449	4.3	9,058
Sardinia	8,135	—	325
Total Expatriates	5,257,911	100.0	210,316

Source: ISTAT.

Figure 4.4
Out-Migration Rates from Italian Regions, 1876–1915

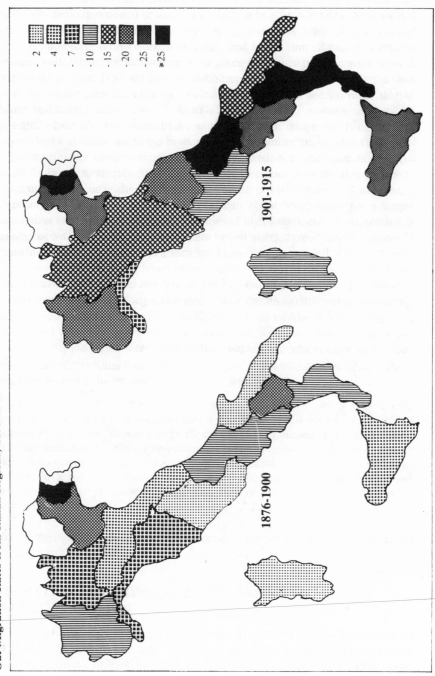

year about 15,000, especially from the neighboring provinces of Liguria and Piedmont, were employed beyond the Maritime Alps in seasonal work: the olive harvest, cultivation and picking of flowers and vegetables (for which many women were used), while men were used especially for tilling and grape-harvesting or gardening, particularly in the Department of Var.[4] In Provence Italians had taken the place of the mountain people who had been coming down for the harvest. In tilling and land reclamation, they had become indispensable. In 1912 a French economist, C. F. Caillard, called their work a real "agricultural tour de force" that had transformed the Camargue region into a vineyard. Within a few years some of them had become small property owners.[5] Most of them, however, were temporary wage earners.

As for their main city settlements, in Paris there were about 34,000 Italians in 1911, spread out in about a half-dozen neighborhoods. They represented the largest and most colorful foreign colony. Artists, itinerant musicians, models, and cooks were numerous.[6] But, for the most part, they were construction and glassworkers, who were preferred to the French because even minors were available. Still, Italians generally did not make it a practice to reside in Paris for good.

Marseilles had taken in about 125,000 Italians before the First World War. The beginnings of Italian emigration to Marseilles go back many decades. The

Table 4.6
Italian Expatriation according to Destination, 1901–1915

Destination	Number	Percent of Total	Yearly Average
Great Britain	53,456	0.6	3,564
Benelux	30,151	0.3	2,010
Germany	871,950	9.9	58,130
France	897,933	10.2	59,862
Switzerland	1,013,645	11.6	67,576
Austria-Hungary	528,083	6.0	35,206
Europe	*3,593,322*	*41.0*	*239,555*
Canada	136,239	1.6	9,083
USA	3,384,152	38.6	225,610
Brazil	410,783	4.7	27,385
Argentina	994,554	11.3	66,304
America	*5,008,099*	*57.1*	*333,973*
Africa	146,920	1.7	9,795
Asia	7,622	—	508
Oceania	13,786	—	919
Total Expatriates	8,769,749	100.0	584,650

Source: ISTAT.

majority were Tuscans and Piedmontese, though the Southern Italians were also numerous, especially in the suburbs, where they were in control of small businesses. Of the 2,400 fishermen in Marseilles, the majority were Italian; and in summer many Neapolitans joined them. Italians held most of the hardest and least remunerative jobs in the city: they were stevedores and workers in salt production, on highways, in soapworks, and potteries.[7]

At the beginning of the century, the Italian colony in Lyons was made up mostly of women and minors; in the Loire region, in fact, the number of workers who were minors exceeded women workers. The silk industry, which had grown considerably, began employing increasing numbers of Italians, while the glassworks – which were of Italian origin – employed three or four thousand Italian minors. The French did not allow their minors to do this kind of enervating work.[8] Minors who had been contracted back in Italy first walked to France; later they were transported from Naples to Marseilles by boat. Against this inhumane exploitation the Bonomelli Association fought long and hard, first by using explosive investigative reporting and then by denouncing the speculators and defending the minors in France.[9]

Table 4.7
Expatriation from Italian Regions, 1901–1915

Region	Number	Percent of Total	Yearly Average
Piedmont	831,088	9.5	55,406
Lombardy	823,659	9.4	54,911
Veneto	882,082	10.1	58,805
Trentino-Alto Adige	—	—	—
Friuli-Venezia Giulia	560,721	6.4	37,381
Liguria	105,215	1.2	7,014
Emilia Romagna	469,430	5.4	31,295
Tuscany	473,045	5.4	31,536
Umbria	155,674	1.8	10,378
Marche	320,107	3.7	21,340
Lazio	189,225	2.2	12,615
Abruzzi	486,518	5.5	32,435
Molise	171,680	2.0	11,445
Campania	955,188	10.9	63,679
Puglia	332,615	3.8	22,174
Basilicata	194,260	2.2	12,951
Calabria	603,105	6.9	40,207
Sicily	1,126,513	12.8	75,100
Sardinia	89,624	1.0	5,975
Total Expatriates	8,769,749	100.0	584,650

Source: ISTAT.

Toward the end of the last century, rich mineral deposits were discovered in the Briey Basin (the Meurthe-et-Moselle and Meuse Departments). The area experienced a sudden population increase due to the influx of foreigners. Cities rose up as if by magic; quiet areas became bustling centers and at times worrisome hotbeds of "subversion": Joeuf, Homécourt, Auboué, Hussigny, Pienne, Longwy, Jasny, and Moutiers gained immediate prominence. The natives supplied only one-fifth of the workers in heavy industry, while two-thirds of all the workers were Italians. In the Department of Meurthe-et-Moselle alone the Italians numbered 6,000 in 1901, around 30,000 in 1910, and 46,755 in 1913, out of a foreign population of 74,043 consisting of about 18 nationalities.[10]

As a rule, Italians were contracted directly in Italy by the interested businesses or through employment agencies. French businesses paid for the trip. Italians came from Lombardy, the Veneto region, Piedmont, Tuscany, Abruzzi, and Sardinia. Permanent residence was not common. They would often reside in a place for a few months and then move on elsewhere in groups. Though most of the Italian workers were miners, others labored in steel mills, others (four or five thousand) worked for the Compagnie de l'Est railroads. Italians contributed considerably to the development of French industry, more than for which they were given credit. They did the most menial and heaviest work. In a survey of living conditions among Italian miners, a French writer, M. Bonneff, calls them "tragic" because of the disturbing social, sanitary, and moral conditions of the men and women workers.[11]

Employers were interested in having cheap and plentiful labor and, because of its availability, were able to undermine worker resistance. It was generally accepted that Italian workers were much more amenable, more docile, and worked for lower wages than French workers.

French workers never looked favorably on this labor competition. With their trade unions, they aimed at a labor aristocracy of sorts and tried to put into practice a form of labor protectionism.[12] Occasionally, French workers managed to pursue a common cause with the foreigners, especially the Italians, who represented the most formidable competition. Gide and Lambert called the Italians "the Chinese of Europe."[13] On some occasions, the tensions smoldering between French and Italian workers blew up spectacularly. In 1882 trouble broke out against the Italians in Marseilles. In 1893 French miners savagely attacked the Italians at the salt-works of Aigues Mortes, killing 50 of them and seriously wounding another 150.[14]

As for social and living conditions, the food and lodging of the Italians in France were the bare minimum, which often happens when workers are forced to save at all costs. In Paris as well as in Marseilles they crowded into humid, airless rooms. Children from seven or eight years of age upwards often shined shoes to earn money.

Lodgings for the Italians in the Briey area were especially bad. There they had to resign themselves to abandoned farms and barracks. Many families took in workers, who were lodged from four to six per room. The mines owned their own hostels or houses, but they were not much used. The usual thing was the "cantine," a sort of boarding-house with the ground floor for eating, drinking, and amusement and the upper floor for sleeping. There were two men per bed, with the beds being used around-the-clock.

During the period of France's greatest economic growth, serious social and health problems plagued Italian workers in that country, judging by the incidence of labor-related sicknesses and of tuberculosis. Educational and cultural conditions also left much to be desired, judging by the belated interventions, often by the employers themselves, on behalf of schooling for the children of immigrants. Despite this marginal existence in France, for more than thirty years, some people fought to have immigrants taxed and their entry restricted – an important sign of public opinion and general attitudes of French society toward foreigners.[15]

ITALIAN EMIGRANTS IN GERMANY

As far back as 1860 several hundred Italians worked in the mines of Westphalia. In southern Germany there was a large number of brass workers, chair weavers, traveling vendors from Northern Italy, sellers of marble or alabaster statuettes from Lucca, and, from Caserta, keepers of trained bears. But what began to attract many workers from the Veneto region was the construction of the Brenner railroad (1867) and the St. Gotthard railroad. As early as 1872 there were several thousand Italians in Württemberg. Before the end of that decade, many arrived in Bavaria, Baden, and Alsace-Lorraine.

The censuses do not show accurately the size of the Italian emigration, since statistics were taken in December, when many Italians had already returned home after the season's work. In 1880 statistics revealed a total of 7,841 Italians, in 1890 of 13,080, in 1900 of 69,738, in 1905 of 98,165, and in 1910 of 104,204. Before World War I, Italians were believed to number around 175,000 during summer.[16] According to the industrial census of 1907, there were 121,000 Italians, making them the third largest immigrant group. They were almost all unskilled and concentrated in manufacturing, mining, and construction. Twenty-three hundred Italians worked in mines and steel mills, about 3 percent of all the workers in this field. Over 30,000 worked in excavation and masonry, 5.7 percent of all workers. In construction the Italians numbered 57,400 (almost half of all the foreign workers), 6.3 percent of the working force.[17]

Emigration to Germany was different from Italian emigration to France during the same period, especially because Italian workers did not settle down in the large cities, did not form large concentrations – such as on the outskirts of Paris and Marseilles – and kept away from farm work, involving themselves almost exclusively in the industrial or business sector.

In Germany, like in France, Italian women and children settled mainly in the south, in the areas closest to the border. Many were itinerant vendors. Italians worked in the brick factories of Bavaria, Württemberg, and the Rhine Palatinate.

Even before the snows melted, agents of German companies, especially the "contractors" (middlemen who contracted for the production of a set amount of bricks, tiles, etc.), would go to Udine and other parts of the Veneto region to recruit workers. In upper and lower Saxony there were about one thousand furnaces, two-thirds of which were manned by Italians. While Germans worked in factories and used machines, the Italians were ready to work all day long with their hands in the wet clay.[18]

Historical documentation shows the situation of Italian kilnmen in Bavaria to have been particularly dramatic. They worked longer hours than local people: an average of eleven to twelve hours a day without interruption. Even women and children were used to clean furnaces, to load and unload them, to move heavy trolleys, and to do night work. Minors were indiscriminately employed because many emigrants were in financial straits and needed immediate gain. Moreover, back in their own country it was traditional for minors to be hired, albeit for lighter work.

The German areas that took in Italians in greatest numbers were those in the west, where the largest iron and coal deposits in Europe had been discovered: the Ruhr, Lorraine and the Saar basin. The Italians worked mostly in the iron and steel industries, as well as in the textile factories. By and large, Italian workers were tools in the industrial growth of Germany, which needed abundant manpower to build up its infrastructure in public works, mines, and other industries.[19]

In the beginning the Italians came from the Veneto region and from Lombardy. But later large numbers from Central and Southern Italy sought work in the industrial areas of Germany. The emigrants traveled in special trains, which took several days to reach their destination (40 hours from the border village of Ala to Dortmund at the beginning of the century). During the winter months representatives of German companies or, more often, agents, recruited Italian workers in their native land. When spring came, the Italians flocked to Germany in great numbers. Every year 50,000 to 70,000 would come from the Veneto area, Lombardy, and other regions of Italy to do the unskilled work for which they had been hired.[20]

In Westphalia and the Rhine only Austrians exceeded Italians, but Italians had to do the heavier work. In Baden and Alsace, numbers of Italian women and children began working in the cotton, silk, and jute industry. Gradually the immigration of women to work in this industry turned from temporary to permanent in the Baden and Württemberg factories.

In northern and western Germany, Italian immigration never became very large, even though it had begun back in the 1880s. The expense of the trip, which exceeded that of a trip to the United States, discouraged emigration that far north. In Silesia Italian workers worked in the coal mines. Between 1880 and 1890 they also worked on the construction of the Kiel Canal, where they formed a colony.

The situation regarding integration of the Italians, especially because of language problems, was different from that in France. The persistence of anti-Italian prejudice (more deeply rooted than elsewhere), little signs of social advancement, and the small number of mixed marriages all go to prove that there was little integration into local society and that Italian residency had a temporary character. The regimentation of foreign labor (employment, control, etc.) in Germany encouraged this trend. Before World War I, almost all the Länder (except for those in the south) had introduced systems of rigid control of foreign labor, all to the advantage of employers, who dictated the conditions for professional mobility. Every foreign worker had to have a document that qualified him for the required job (Legitimations-Karten) and cost two Marks. In the case of a change of jobs, he got a new document with his name and that of his new employer. Anyone found looking for a new job without an indication on his work document confirming his dismissal from his previous job was expelled from the country. In the beginning, this system had been introduced for farm workers but was later extended to all job categories.

The health of Italians in Germany is marked by a high rate of illness and of job-related sicknesses due to the sanitary and hygienic conditions of their environment. To achieve up to thirty-five working days a month, miners would work "double" days, that is to say, sixteen hours a day. There were understandable serious health consequences. But, because of the high cost of living, savings were not commensurate to the work done. Italians scrimped especially on their housing, which, as a rule, was squalid and overcrowded: little more than barracks with six to eight men per room and two men taking shifts in a bed. Under these conditions it was, as a rule, hard to achieve a certain degree of well-being.

The German trade unions generally considered Italian workers as an element of weakness or failure in their effort. There was a certain attitude of contempt not only for Italian workers but also for their trade-union and political leaders. Even at Socialist meetings, Italian workers were looked down upon. They were constantly being accused of accepting salaries below the agreed-on salaries or accepting piece-work for certain jobs. There was little understanding of their precarious institutional status, for their fear of expulsion in the case of strikes, and for the language barrier. Still, in no other European country did the local trade unions put on such a massive struggle to organize the Italian workers into trade unions. As far back as the end of the last century, the central federation of trade unions had been publishing an Italian trade-union newspaper, *L'operaio italiano*. Worker secretariats and trade-union representatives also worked in Italy, particularly for organizational purposes during the winter months. In this work of sensitization, a great deal of help was given by Milan's "Società Umanitaria" (a Socialist foundation that was active in the field of emigration) and by the "Consorzio," a cooperative established by some trade unions and the "Umanitaria" for the protection of Italian migrants.[21]

ITALIAN EMIGRATION IN SWITZERLAND

In the winter of 1860, census figures showed that 9,000 Italians were already living in Switzerland, but in the following decades their number increased considerably. In the canton of Ticino especially, there were many people of Italian nationality or origin. Starting in 1872, with the building of the St. Gotthard Tunnel, Italians began to flock to Switzerland in ever increasing numbers. In 1880 there were 41,500. This figure increased slowly in the following years. But toward the end of the century there was a great upsurge in the influx of Italians. By the end of the century there were 95,000 Italians in Switzerland, and from work on the railroads and tunnels they branched out into all the industrial fields. Census figures show that in 1910 there were half a million foreigners in Switzerland; more than 15 percent of the entire population came from abroad. But in certain cantons it would reach 30 or 40 percent. This little mountain country had the same percentage of immigrants as the United States. In 1910 the Germans and Italians together accounted for four-fifths of the foreign population, with an equal number of each nationality: more than 200,000 of each. Italians alone made up 6 percent of the entire Swiss population, not counting the seasonal workers who came every summer. In no other European country was the Italian factor proportionally more important.[22] Italians were also important in agriculture. In 1905 there were 10,000 in this sector. Four thousand worked on farms, but many others came in summer for seasonal farm work.

The development of modern Switzerland is due to this work force, which performed the heaviest and most dangerous jobs, jobs that were indispensable for the modernization of the country, which required the creation of an infrastructure (roads, railroads, tunnels). In a mountainous country like Switzerland, these improvements were of prime importance. Swiss nationals accounted for only three-fourths of those engaged in construction and manufacturing. The Italians made up about 14 percent of the total. In construction, out of a total of 85,000 foreigners, they numbered 65,000. In 1914, in the construction field, one-third of the total labor force were Italians. In manufacturing, they numbered 20,000. But the 44,000 Italians working on railroad construction represented the vast majority of all the workers of this category in the entire country. Most of the Italians came from Northern Italy, but many were also from Southern Italy and Tuscany.

It is hard to list the undertakings and projects to which Italians contributed in those years. Among the more important ones are those of Mont Cenis (1857–1871), St. Gotthard, and the Alpine railroads of Rigi, Pilatus, Albula, including the Brig-Furka-Disentis railroad begun in 1914. Work on the Simplon Tunnel began in 1898 with the recruitment of Sicilians, Calabrians, and Romagnoli, who were later joined by Piedmontese and Venetians. Later the Loetschberg railroad was built. At the peak of construction, from 6,000 to 7,000 Italians were working on it. Many of these, after finishing one tunnel, went on to work in the building of another one. The endurance of Italians was remarkable; they worked even during winter, taking advantage of the fact that the tunnels were not as cold as outdoors.[23]

Another field in which Italians were massively represented was the brick industry. Italians worked also in the silk, cotton, chocolate, footwear, and tobacco industries and were second only to the more numerous and more skilled German group.

Despite the usual attitude of contempt for Italians, their work was appreciated, especially by employers, who used the Italians as a counterforce to offset workers' demands. They were often called scabs. On occasion, proletarian hatred would explode, like at Zürich (July 1896), when Swiss workers assaulted Italian workers.

Italian residence in Switzerland was generally temporary. There was no desire whatsoever to assimilate or integrate the Italians. Public opinion and Swiss law did not encourage naturalization, although it did happen on a reduced scale. Some welfare organizations in the cantons of Basle and St. Gallen even refused to help Italians. The Italians were contemptuously called *crispi*, and *macaroni* and considered necessary rather than desired guests.[24] Italians did not generally join worker and trade-union organizations in large numbers. However, in Switzerland the important and powerful "Federazione Muraria Italiana", a union of Italian masons, had many members. There was also an organization of granite workers, and a considerable number of active mutual benefit societies.[25]

Italians living in Switzerland lived more poorly than any of the other ethnic groups. In particular, the harshness of their work had a deleterious effect on their health, and the housing situation was dismal. To save a few pennies, they had to accept serious hardships. As far as their savings are concerned, we can say that, despite the fact that they remitted 25 million francs, according to the Commissariat General of Emigration in Rome, and despite the fact that they brought home much strong currency every year, their savings were never very high, especially because of the high cost of living and transportation.

At times Italians preferred to create little ghettos in the big cities to overcome isolation. Italian organizations were fairly numerous and of different kinds. Schooling for the children of the emigrants, however, was inadequate. For women and girls, especially in smaller centers, *Heime* (more than thirty throughout Switzerland) were set up. In Switzerland, the welfare program of the Bonomelli Association had its greatest success with the setting up of nurseries, welfare secretariats, worker organizations (sometimes in opposition to the Socialist ones), recreational centers, and a whole gamut of social programs, including the hospices at Chiasso, Domodossola, and Lucerne.[26]

CONCLUDING REMARKS

The analysis of the causes of Italian emigration is much more complex than the mere description of flows of people. Without entering into a question intertwined with the political, economic, and social history of Italy, we must stress the territorial and chronological differentiation of the phenomenon and the difficulty in distinguishing economic from noneconomic factors and pull from push factors. The Italian economy has been characterized by an incomplete and time-fractioned industrial takeoff spanning the period from 1873 to the "economic miracle" of the early 1960s and its diffusion in marginal regions and sectors during the 1950s. Here was almost a century of economic development accompanied by emigration. The paradox of the direct relationship between economic growth and the number of emigrants – when the economy was growing faster more people were leaving the country – can be explained by the consolidated experience of other European countries witnessing emigration taking place at the same time as industrial growth. The fact was due to the impact of the factory system and of agricultural reorganization, together with qualitative and subjective contradictions between labor supply and demand, typical of a phase of drastic shifts in workers' social and professional status.

The Italian experience was marked by the 1880 agricultural crisis, which accelerated the massive emigration from Italy. This agricultural crisis was preceded and followed by an economic policy that strengthened the pressure to emigrate. First of all there was the free trade policy that especially damaged industry in Southern Italy, then the agricultural and industrial protectionism of the late 1880s, which prevented the backward sections of the Italian economy from reorganizing and from increasing the average level of efficiency.

The artificial and partial character of the various moments of industrial modernization, concentrated in few small districts and few different kinds of industries, facilitated emigration abroad. Among the various factors affecting emigration were demographic pressure, the crisis of small farmers and mountain agriculture, the crisis of artisans and rural manufacture, money erosion in the countryside forcing farm laborers to move in order to pay their obligations, and the international labor market. In fact, during the Atlantic economy system Italian labor was also widely used, after the beginning of the 1873 depression, to keep wages low and to replace national workers. A large number of Italian emigrants were oriented to temporary work abroad. This unstable labor supply came in very handy when labor demand reached exceptionally high peaks. The Italians followed public works projects and harvests all over Europe and other continents. A further feature of Italian emigrants was their willingness to work as common laborers and the preindustrial quality of their skills, which allowed them to fill certain voids in the labor markets of fast growing industrial countries.

NOTES

1. For more general information, see G. Rosoli, ed., *Un secolo di emigrazione italiana: 1876–1976* (Rome, 1978); F. Assante, ed., *Il movimento migratorio italiano dall'Unità nazionale ai giorni nostri* (Geneva and Naples, 1978); Z. Ciuffoletti, and M. degl'Innocenti, *L'emigrazione nella storia d'Italia, 1868–1975* (Florence, 1978); E. Sori, *L'emigrazione italiana dall'Unità alla seconda guerra mondiale* (Bologna, 1979); E. Franzina, *La grande emigrazione. L'esodo dei rurali dal Veneto durante il secolo XIX*

(Venice, 1976); A. Lazzarini, *Campagne venete ed emigrazione di massa (1866–1900)* (Vicenza, 1981).

2. L. Favero, and G. Tassello, "Cent'anni di emigrazione italiana (1876–1976)," in Rosoli, ed., *Un secolo di emigrazione italiana* (Rome, 1978) pp. 9–63; R. Paris, "L'Italia fuori d'Italia," *Storia d'Italia*, vol. 4 (Turin, 1975), pp. 509–620.

3. R. F. Foerster, *The Italian Emigration of Our Times* (Cambridge, Mass., 1919), pp. 129–31; S. Wlocevski, *L'installation des italiens en France* (Paris, 1934); P. Milza, *Français et italiens à la fin du XIXe siècle* (Turin, 1981).

4. E. Blanchard, *La main-d'oeuvre étrangère dans l'agriculture française* (Paris, 1913).

5. C. F. Caillard, *Les migrations temporaires dans les campagnes françaises* (Paris, 1912).

6. R. Paolucci de' Calboli, *Larmes et sourires de l'émigration italienne* (Paris, 1909).

7. P. Milza, "L'intégration des italiens dans le mouvement ouvrier français à la fin du XIXe siècle et au début du XXe siècle: le cas de la région marseillaise," *Affari Sociali Internazionali*, 3–4 (1977), 171–207.

8. C. Bonnet, "Les italiens dans l'agglomération lyonnaise à l'aube de la 'Belle Epoque,' " ibid., 3–4 (1977), 87–103.

9. U. Cafiero, "Inchiesta nei circondari di Sora e di Isernia," *Bollettino dell'Opera di assistenza*, I, 1 (1901), 1–17; E. Schiaparelli, "Il traffico dei minorenni italiani per le vetrerie francesi," ibid., 3–4, (1901), 11–25; 5–6, (1902), 10–22.

10. S. Bonnet, C. Santini, and H. Barthélemy, "Les italiens dans l'arrondissement de Briey avant 1914," *Annales de l'Est* (Nancy, 1962); S. Bonnet, E. Kogan, and M. Maigret, *L'homme du fer (1889–1930)* (Nancy, 1975).

11. M. Bonneff, *La vie tragique des travailleurs: enquêtes sur la condition économique et morale des ouvriers et ouvrières d'industrie* (Paris, 1914).

12. R. Paris, "Le mouvement ouvrier français et l'immigration italienne (1893–1914)," in B. Bezza, ed., *Gli italiani fuori d'Italia* (Milan, 1983), pp. 633–78; Z. Ciuffoletti, "Il movimento sindacale italiano e l'emigrazione dalle origini al fascismo," ibid., pp. 203–19.

13. C. Gide, and M. Lambert, "Les troubles d'Aigues Mortes," *Revue d'Economie Politique* (Sept.–Oct. 1893), 839–41.

14. T. Vertone, "Antécédents et causes des événements d'Aigues Mortes," *Affari Sociali Internazionali* 3–4 (1977), 107–38.

15. E. Serra, "L'emigrazione italiana in Francia durante il primo governo Crispi (1887–1891)," "e il secondo governo Crispi," ibid., 41–61, 139–70.

16. G. Pertile, "Gli italiani in Germania," *Bollettino dell'Emigrazione* nos. 11 and 15 (1914); S. Jacini, "Die italienische Auswanderung nach Deutschland," *Weltwirtschaftliches Archiv* 5 (1915), 121–43; H. Schäfer, "L'immigrazione italiana nell'Impero tedesco (1890–1914)," in Bezza, ed., *Gli italiani fuori d'Italia*, pp. 737–62.

17. A. Knoke, *Ausländische Wanderarbeiter in Deutschland* (Leipzig, 1911); W. Böhmert, "Die Ausländischen Arbeiter in Deutschland," *Arbeiterfreund* 5(1913), 16–46; A. Sartorius von Walterhausen, *Die italienischen Wanderarbeiter* (Leipzig, 1903); I. Britschgi-Schimmer, *Die wirtschaftliche und soziale Lage der italienischen Arbeiter in Deutschland. Ein Beitrag zur ausländischen Arbeitsfrage* (Karlsruhe, 1916).

18. P. Sandicchi, "I fornaciai italiani in Baviera," *Bollettino dell'Emigrazione* 12 (1912), 3–34; P. Mondini, "L'immigrazione italiana nella Baviera meridionale," ibid. (1904), 10–13.

19. G. Pertile, "Le condizioni degli operai italiani nei distretti consolari di Colonia, Düsseldorf, Saarbrücken e Lussemburgo," *Bollettino dell'Emigrazione* 19 (1908), 3–51.

20. G. Cosattini, "L'emigrazione temporanea del Friuli," *Bollettino dell'Emigrazione* 3 (1904), 3–107; V. Merx, "Ausländische Arbeitskräfte im Deutschen Reich und in der Bundesrepublik," *Wirtschaftspolitische Chronik*, Universität Köln, no. 1 (1967), 65–91.

21. *L'Umanitaria e la sua Opera* (Milan, 1922); M. Punzo, "La Società Umanitaria e l'emigrazione. Dagli inizi del secolo alla prima guerra mondiale," in Bezza, ed., *Gli italiani fuori d'Italia*, pp. 119–44.

22. *Résultats statistiques du recensement fédéral de la population du 1er déc. 1910* (Berne, 1915); see also Foerster, *The Italian Emigration*, pp. 171–88.

23. E. Sella, *L'emigrazione italiana nella Svizzera* (Turin, 1899); G. De Michelis, "Gli operai italiani al Sempione," *Giornale degli Economisti* (Feb. 1899), 138–54.

24. A. Picot, *Un problème national. La population étrangère établie en Suisse* (Geneva, 1914); H. Amman, *Die Italiener in der Schweiz. Ein Beitrag zur Fremdenfrage* (Basel, 1917); C. Raymond-Duchosal, *Les étrangers en Suisse. Etude géographique, démographique et sociologique* (Paris, 1929); D. Demarco, *"L'emigrazione italiana in Svizzera dal 1860 al 1914,"* in *Le relazioni del pensiero italiano risorgimentale con i centri del movimento liberale di Ginevra e Coppet* (Rome, 1979), pp. 77–101. See also the numerous articles in the official publications of the Italian Foreign Ministry: *Bollettino dell'Emigrazione* and *Emigrazione e Colonie* (Rome, 1905).

25. G. De Michelis, *L'emigrazione italiana nella Svizzera* (Rome, 1903); idem "Le associazioni italiane nella Svizzera, politiche, artistiche, di istruzione, di convegno e di sport," *Bollettino dell'Emigrazione* 22 (1908), 3–23; idem, "La mutualità fra gli italiani nella Svizzera," ibid., 10 (1908), 3–49.

26. Among the numerous publications, see G. Rosoli, "L'emigrazione italiana in Europa e l'Opera Bonomelli (1900–1914)," in Bezza, ed., *Gli italiani fuori d'Italia*, pp. 163–201.

GERMAN EMIGRATION TO THE UNITED STATES AND CONTINENTAL IMMIGRATION TO GERMANY IN THE LATE NINETEENTH AND EARLY TWENTIETH CENTURIES

5

Klaus J. Bade

Up to the end of the nineteenth century Germany was a country of emigrants. Until recently the nineteenth- and early twentieth-century transatlantic migration of more than five million Germans, mostly to North America, has been largely forgotten in contemporary Germany, except by a few historians. That is all the more true for the mass movement of foreign migrant workers into the German labor market in the decades preceding World War I. Of immediate interest in West Germany today is the so-called "guest-worker question" (*Gastarbeiterfrage*) which is now becoming an immigration issue in contrast to the earlier "foreign-worker question" in pre-World War I Germany. In recent years West Germany witnessed the transition from a country hiring "guest workers" to one possessing a genuine immigrant minority. This ongoing experience has contributed to a new interest in the historical development of transnational migration in both of its manifestations, as emigration and as immigration. In the late nineteenth and early twentieth centuries Germany experienced alternating waves of the two forms of transnational mass migration, both of which were dwarfed by the internal migration streams.[1]

Migration within imperial Germany and across its borders was intimately related to the transformation of the Reich from an agrarian state with a dynamic industrial sector into an industrial state with a strong agricultural base. This transformation was accompanied by the shift from a land of emigration—still producing more than one million emigrants during the 1880s—to one with a reserve army of foreign laborers, whose numbers were fast approaching the million mark in the decade preceding World War I. However, these laborers did not become immigrants in the sense of acquiring citizen rights, but remained "foreign migrant workers," for Germany did not turn into a land of immigration, but rather became what contemporaries euphemistically termed a "labor-importing country."[2]

The transition from an agrarian to an industrial state and from a land of emigration to a "labor-importing country" was in part the result of interrela-

This chapter was first published in *Central European History*, Emory University (December 1980), 348–77. It is reprinted with the permission of the author and of the publisher.

tionships in the complex of labor market, population trends, and migration. In turn, the framework of the migration process itself was characterized by the intrinsic coherence and mutual interactions of overseas emigration, internal migration out of agriculture, and continental immigration. The shift from agriculture to industry in imperial Germany at the turn of the century is clearly reflected in Figures 5.1 and 5.2,[3] which show the changing sectoral shares of total labor force and national income. By the end of the 1880s the secondary had overtaken the primary sector in its contribution to the national income, and by 1905 it employed a larger share of the labor force as well. The trend lines of the two sectors cross, suggesting an inverse relationship. In terms of demographic trends late nineteenth- and early twentieth-century Germany experienced the crucial period of demographic transition, shown in Figure 5.3.[4] The combined effects of falling death rates and persisting high birth rates swelled the population of Germany from 45 million in 1880 to 56 million at the turn of the century, an increase of nearly 25 percent. Up until that point birth rates had fallen only minimally. The first two decades of the twentieth century saw a decisive break, the transition to the demographic patterns of modern industrial societies.[5]

Figure 5.1
Sectoral Shares (%) of National Income, 1871–1913

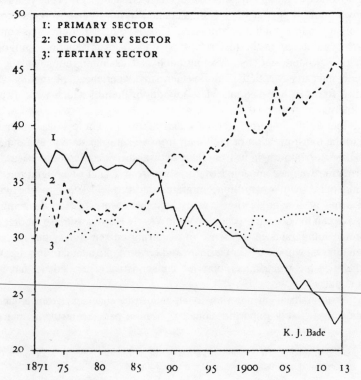

The extraordinary dynamism of mass migrations resulted from inconsistencies in the processes of modernization. The international and internal mass migrations during the decades of rapid industrialization before World War I were above all labor migrations and as such primarily "proletarian mass migrations."[6] In imperial Germany mass migration took three different forms: (1) overseas emigration, mainly directed to the United States, but also, less extensively, to Latin America; (2) internal migration within Germany, especially the long-term migration from rural to urban areas reaching its climax in the vast urban growth around the turn of the century, and the long-distance migration from east to west transforming millions of landless poor and small peasants into an industrial proletariat; and (3) continental immigration into Germany especially from eastern but also from southern Europe.[7] Historically, the waves of overseas emigration, internal migration, and continental immigration developed differently and began at varying times. All of them, however, reached a climax before World War I and faded away or came to a temporary halt in the late 1920s. Together they formed a more or less interdependent system. The intensity, coherence, and interdependence of these mass movements were most noticeable in the predom-

Figure 5.2
Sectoral Shares (%) of Labor Force, 1871–1913

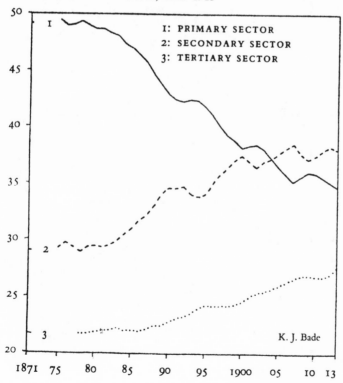

inantly agricultural areas of northeast Germany, shown in Figure 5.4.[8] In the decades preceding World War I the northeast served as the main recruiting ground for overseas emigration as well as internal migration and, in addition, was the focus of continental immigration across the eastern borders of Prussia. This is why our analysis concentrates primarily on this region.

The correspondence of these three waves is shown in the accompanying figures. Figure 5.5,[9] dealing with overseas emigration during a period of a hundred

Figure 5.3
Natural Population Increase in Germany, 1872–1970

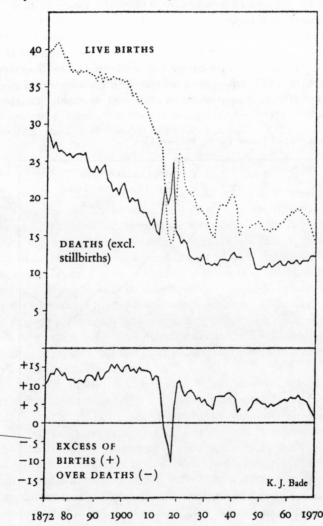

Figure 5.4
Areas of Origin of German Overseas Emigration

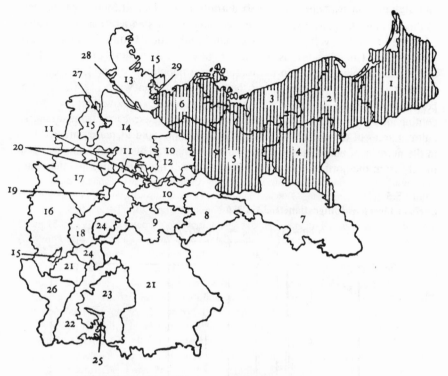

NORTHEAST GERMANY
1. East Prussia
2. West Prussia
3. Pomerania
4. Posen
5. Brandenburg
6. Mecklenburg

SOUTHEAST GERMANY
7. Silesia
8. Kingdom of Saxony

MIDDLE GERMANY
9. Thuringia
10. Province of Saxony
11. Brunswick
12. Anhalt

NORTHWEST GERMANY
13. Schleswig-Holstein
14. Hanover
15. Oldenburg

WEST GERMANY
16. Rhineland
17. Westphalia
18. Hesse-Nassau
19. Waldeck
20. Lippe

SOUTHWEST GERMANY
21. Bavaria
22. Baden
23. Württemberg
24. Hesse
25. Hohenzollern-Sigmaringen
26. Alsace-Lorraine

HANSE TOWNS
27. Bremen
28. Hamburg
29. Lübeck

years, shows that the third emigration wave occurred between 1880 and 1893. In absolute numbers it was the greatest exodus from nineteenth-century Germany, and also the longest, directed almost entirely to the United States. At the end of this exodus Germany ceased to be a country of mass emigration. This is also confirmed by the development of German immigration within the total immigration to the United States, as shown in Figure 5.6. Accordingly the percentage of German immigrants within the foreign-born population of the United States declined from 30.1 percent during the third emigration wave (1890) to 18.5 percent in 1910 and to 11.3 percent in 1930.[10] Figure 5.7[11] shows that the largest contingent of Germans during the third emigration wave came from the agricultural areas of the northeast. Figure 5.8[12] shows a rapid increase, since 1880, in the number of people going west within Germany. This stream, too, was fed mostly from the northeastern part of the country. Finally Figure 5.9[13] puts into

Figure 5.5
German Overseas Emigration, 1830–1932

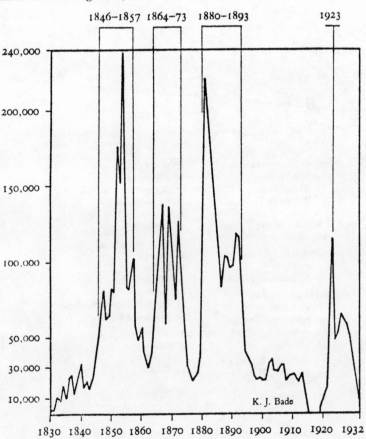

focus the massive continental immigration which also showed up first of all in the northeast.

To explain why people in the northeast left their homes, heading overseas or going west, it is helpful to analyze (1) the structural ''push'' - factors responsible for creating a willingness to migrate and (2) the reasons why some headed overseas while others went west within Germany.

Up to the 1860s the agrarian regions of the northeast had contributed only minimally to overseas emigration and internal outmigration. The long-term structural push-factors operating in the northeast since the late 1860s were, in particular, continuing population growth, combined with the rigidity of the traditional form of land distribution. The distribution of land in the northeast was, as shown in Figure 5.10,[14] almost the exact opposite of what it was in southwest Germany, the region which had been the main source of overseas emigration during the first and second emigration waves in the nineteenth century. In both regions the agrarian middle class was very small. In the southwest, the most important push-factor for emigration had been the constant splitting of farms due to customs of equal division among heirs. In the northeast, where the large estates were pre-

Figure 5.6
Total Immigration and German Immigration to the United States, 1820–1919
(in thousands; from American immigration statistics)

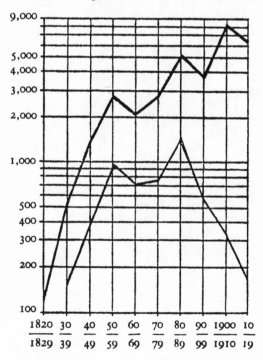

dominant and the right of inheritance among small farmers was completely different, the farmland was usually not divided, but taken over entirely by the oldest son. For the younger brothers who were not able to marry into another farm there were two possibilities. First, if the father's farm was large enough to pay out hereditary portions while remaining above the level of subsistence production, the younger brothers had the chance of buying a new, though smaller,

Figure 5.7
German Overseas Emigration by Area of Origin, 1871–1910

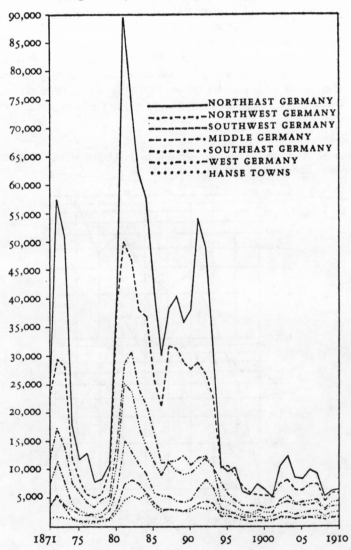

farm. This opportunity, however, was limited by the high costs of buying or renting farmland. Otherwise there was only one way of maintaining the social status and economic way of life: the exodus to the "New World." Frequently, entire families emigrated in order to preserve the family unit. Second, the farm might be too small to pay out hereditary portions. This was, as Figure 5.10 clearly shows, very often the case, given the fact that an independent existence as a farm in the northeast usually required about twenty acres of tillable land because of the climate and poor quality of the soil. In such a case, the younger brothers, who regarded industrial labor as social degradation, were left only with social descent into the class of farmhands or rural proletariat. Of course, this was often regarded as a mere temporary state of dependency in order to save enough money to buy a small farm at home or in the United States.

Figure 5.8
East-West Migration within Germany: Migration to Rhineland-Westphalia, 1880–1910

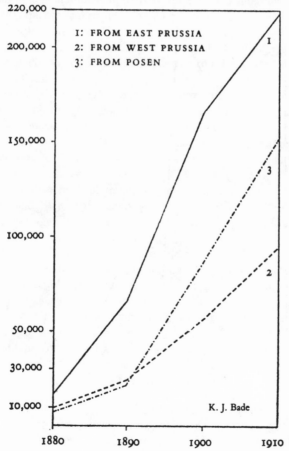

I: FROM EAST PRUSSIA
2: FROM WEST PRUSSIA
3: FROM POSEN

K. J. Bade

The driving force of population growth and land distribution in the northeast was reinforced by the crisis of agriculture since the late 1870s and the deterioration of the traditional economic and social way of life due to modernization of the agrarian structure. The living conditions of the farmworkers and small peasants, who earned additional income by working on the large estates in eastern Prussia, worsened. The decline of wheat prices due to competition on the world market induced a growing number of estate owners to convert from extensive cultivation of wheat to intensive forms of agricultural production. The advance of the threshing machine in the wheat-producing areas left the harvest hands without work in winter. The trend towards root crops, in particular sugar beets,

Figure 5.9
Registered Foreign Labor in Germany, 1910–1932 (in thousands)

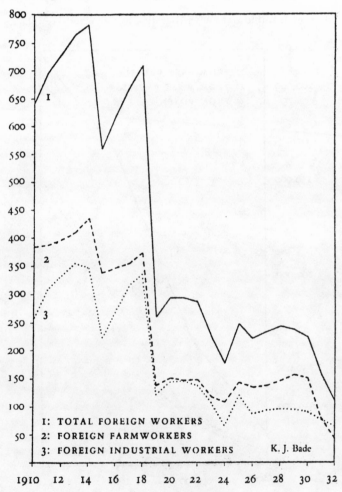

I: TOTAL FOREIGN WORKERS
2: FOREIGN FARMWORKERS
3: FOREIGN INDUSTRIAL WORKERS   K. J. Bade

did indeed increase the demand for seasonal workers during the summer, but at the same time it lowered the demand in winter. The combined result was a constant increase in seasonal employment on the agrarian labor market of the northeast. In the short summer season there was a lack of manpower despite higher wages and hard piece-work. In contrast, there was little work, with low wages, during the long winter. Thus, for anyone who could obtain a "prepaid ticket" from American relatives or afford at least the passage, the idea of emigration despite a lack of initial capital was not very farfetched. Many emigrated hoping they could earn enough money in industrial and urban employment in the United States to buy the farm they had unsuccessfully tried to obtain at home. For the same reasons, small peasants had difficulties maintaining their farms because of the lack of opportunities for earning additional income by working on the large estates. During the summer they could not leave their own small farms, and out of season they found no jobs. Many of them therefore sold their farms expecting they could acquire new ones in the United States with the money earned from the sale. This would enable them to attain something they could no longer maintain in their own country: an independent existence as a farmer. Thus, during the 1870s and 1880s the alternatives were either social demise or emigration to the United States.

In the early 1890s German emigration dropped abruptly, as shown in Figure

Figure 5.10
Distribution of Farmland in Northeast (1), in Southwest (2), and in All of Germany (3)

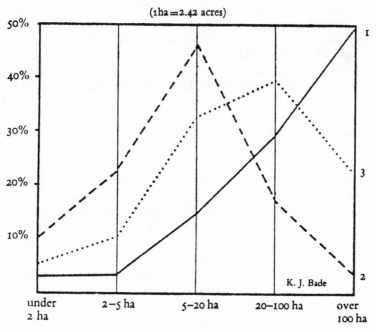

(1ha = 2.42 acres)

K. J. Bade

under 2 ha   2–5 ha   5–20 ha   20–100 ha   over 100 ha

5.5. For the following two decades it remained a trickle and was practically nonexistent after the outbreak of the war. Although emigration in the 1920s once again assumed significant proportions, this must be interpreted mainly as a consequence of the war. By 1930, the number of Germans returning to Germany even exceeded the number leaving the country, first as a result of the depression in the United States and then of full employment in Germany; and in the mid-thirties German emigration once again became numerically insignificant. The Jewish flight from Nazi Germany in the 1930s forms a unique—and tragic—chapter in German emigration history.

The debate on the question why emigration ceased so abruptly in the mid-1890s has emphasized several arguments. The most comprehensive explanation, although not entirely adequate, is offered by W. Köllmann and P. Marschalck. They argue that "since the frontier was practically closed by 1890" the surplus population of the agricultural eastern provinces of Prussia no longer had a chance of realizing the dream of peasant life without capital in the United States. Left with the choice between American and German urban industrial employment they opted more often for the more familiar environment. Hence the currents of migration, pointing overseas before, by the mid-1890s became part of the internal German migration streams, while Germany as a whole experienced the period of rapid transition to industrial mass society.[15]

The connection between the decline in overseas emigration and the increase in internal migration is obvious. This is especially true for the long-distance internal migration from the predominantly agricultural areas of northeast Germany to the industrial centers of the west, particularly the Ruhr district, as shown in Figure 5.8.

The German-style "frontier thesis," however, has to be modified. In order to successfully establish a farm, even on free homestead land, a considerable amount of capital for supplies and machinery was required. Moreover, during the third emigration wave the pattern of settlement for the German-born population in the United States was already far more extensively urbanized than the settlement pattern in Germany, despite the fact that a majority of German immigrants came from the country. According to the United States census, in 1900 more than 51 percent of all German-Americans lived in cities with a population of 25,000 or more, as compared to only 35 percent of all Germans in cities of more than 20,000.[16] This seems to indicate that even during the third emigration wave the majority of the German emigrants from agricultural areas left their rural way of life, never to find it again. Instead they engaged in industrial and urban occupations in the United States. By 1920 this development had created a situation—as shown in Figure 5.11[17]—in which only slightly more than 20 percent of the German-born population in the United States lived on farms.

This tendency was already apparent in the 1880s. During the third emigration wave the number of German immigrants in the United States employed in all occupational branches, including agriculture, increased in absolute numbers. A look at Figure 5.12[18] shows, however, that the rate of growth in agrarian occupations continually fell further behind the enormous increase in employment in the secondary and tertiary sectors. Also this transition in the occupational makeup of the German-born population in the United States during the third emigration wave took place earlier and more intensively than in Germany. There is some historical evidence that the decision to move to an urban area was frequently made in order to earn enough money to buy a farm. There is just as much evidence, however, that the intention remained unfulfilled and emigration ended with urban employment. Without doubt, many of the emigrants, particularly those from the predominantly agrarian areas of northeast Germany, migrated to the United States expecting to export their traditional form of agricultural

Figure 5.11
European Immigrants in the United States by Country of Birth and Percentage Living on Farms, 1920

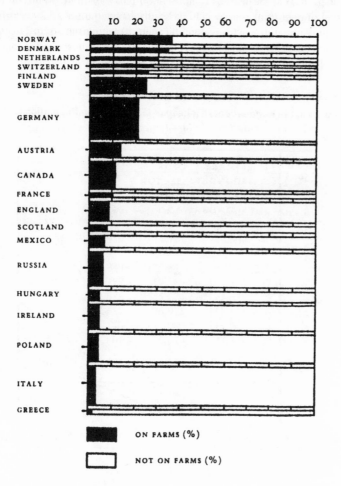

ON FARMS (%)

NOT ON FARMS (%)

existence and rural social status, that is, to reconstruct their old way of life in the "New World." By the time of the third emigration wave, however, this was a dream which, as the American statistics show, no longer corresponded to the reality in the promised land.

Obviously already in the 1880s most German newcomers in America by choice or necessity took employment outside of agriculture. Thus it appears that the precipitous drop at the end of the third emigration wave had more to do with the bust of the 1890s, especially the Panic of 1893 in America, and the simultaneous beginning of the prewar boom period in Germany, than with the alleged closure of the frontier.[19] The German mining industry had already begun to compete with the United States in attracting migrants during the 1880s. The prewar boom period starting in the mid-1890s not only enabled German industry to absorb most or all of the available skilled and unskilled labor, but demand even outgrew supply. The rapid rise of German industry allowed the rural migrants, especially from the northeast, to escape from their agrarian misery while still remaining in their native land. The declining margin of existence in the agriculture of the northeast had done its share in taking the stigma from joining the industrial proletariat. The rural proletariat of the northeast had in fact nothing to lose by moving from east to west.

Figure 5.12
Sectoral Increase in Occupational Makeup of German-Born Population in the United States, 1870–1890 (in thousands; 1870 = 0)

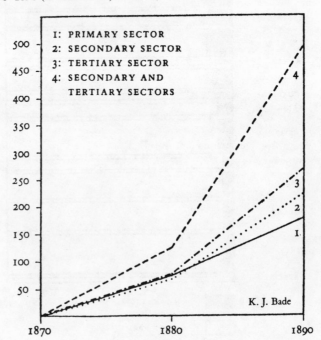

With the growing attraction of the industrial labor market in the west, the pattern of migration from the northeast began to change during the 1880s. The more industry took the lead, the more internal migration from the east to the west turned into the domestic equivalent of overseas emigration. Besides the option of permanent internal migration, it was now also possible to earn enough money through temporary industrial employment to buy a small farm, or stabilize and expand the old one at home. This was particularly evident in the temporary migration of the Masurians to the Ruhr district.[20] Migrants from northeast Germany first went to the industrial center of Berlin, then, in the 1870s, to the industrial areas of central Germany such as Leipzig and Dresden and to a lesser extent already to the Rhineland and Westphalia. During the 1880s and even more so after 1890, internal east-west migration in Germany was characterized by the long-distance exodus from areas of economic stagnation in the agricultural northeast to the industrial centers of the west, especially to the Ruhr district. Disregarding the numerous regional differences within the northeast, we can say in general that not just towards the end of the third wave of emigration but already during the 1880s the currents of migration from the northeastern areas, formerly flowing overseas, became part of the internal migration streams from rural to urban areas and especially to the far west of Germany.

Decisive for the regional differences during this transition were the varying strengths in the traditions of emigration in the particular provinces and the resulting degree of transatlantic communication. For example, in areas such as Mecklenburg, with a long tradition of emigration and therefore intensive transatlantic communication, overseas emigration and internal migration were both considered equal alternatives during the third wave of emigration.[21] Many people had relatives, everyone had acquaintances in the United States, who could be asked to purchase a "prepaid ticket." Nevertheless, even in Mecklenburg the volume of internal migration during the 1880s was greater than that of overseas emigration. In East Prussia, the province with the lowest wages for farmworkers and the lowest standard of living for the small peasants, there was hardly any tradition of overseas emigration. Overseas emigration, therefore, offered little hope of escape from rural misery. Thus, during the third emigration wave East Prussia registered the lowest intensity of overseas emigration within the northeast, but an extremely high intensity of internal east-west migration. In East Prussia, the "prepaid ticket" did not come from the United States, but as early as the 1880s from the industrial areas of the German far west.[22]

It should be noted that this internal east-west migration corresponded to transatlantic emigration not only in the sense that both movements took the same directions. We also find migrants exposed to similar problems of alienation and integration, partly balanced by the help of family and friends. The migrants from the eastern provinces faced a foreign environment when they arrived in the industrial melting pot of the Ruhr, even more so if they were Poles from the eastern provinces of Prussia, unable to speak German and isolated in the subculture of the so-called "Ruhr Poles" (*Ruhrpolen*).[23] There is a certain parallel between their situation and the formation of German-speaking "colonies" in the United States. But one would assume that a Polish-speaking farmworker from eastern Prussia found it even more difficult to adjust to the mining industry of western Germany than a German-speaking farmworker to one of the German agricultural settlements of the American Midwest. That is why one could call the internal long-distance migration of farmworkers speaking Polish or Masurian a kind of internal emigration.[24]

Except for the Masurians, however, the decision to go west was for most—in particular the farmworkers from the northeast—a road without return. Apparently, this was also true for those who had initially migrated in order to earn the money for buying a farm back home or in the United States. These migrants from the east found their "America" in western Germany. They experienced the same fate as their counterparts who went to the United States without any financial resources expecting to earn the money for a farm there and then became bogged down in urban and industrial employment. For the majority of rural migrants from the northeast the dream of an independent life as a farmer was lost in the rising tide of the industrial mass society on both sides of the Atlantic.

Overseas emigration from Germany and internal migration within Germany were closely linked to the development of continental immigration into Germany, especially from eastern European countries. This linkage too was most noticeable in the German northeast. Despite all the differences in the intensity of overseas emigration and internal outmigration, all areas of the northeast had one thing in common: between the 1880s and World War I the northeast suffered the highest loss of population through migration, both overseas and internal. In areas where overseas emigration was less severe, internal outmigration was all the more devastating. Moreover, the internal "flight from agriculture" (*Landflucht*) took other forms besides interregional migration. Where urban employment was available nearby, as in Brandenburg, or where there was industrial employment, as for instance in the Upper Silesian mining district, part of the rural surplus population stayed in the area, but left agricultural jobs for urban and industrial employment. In Germany this pattern came to be known as "flight from agriculture without changing location" (*berufliche Landflucht*).[25]

Together, overseas emigration, the various forms of internal outmigration, and the "flight from agriculture" soon resulted in a transition from a relatively overpopulated northeast to an area plagued by a lack of agricultural manpower, a situation which was balanced from the 1890s on by the growing continental immigration of foreign migrant workers from across the eastern borders of Prussia. The Upper Silesian mining industry aside, this immigration headed first for the agricultural labor market of the northeast. In particular, laborers from central Poland, at that time under Russian domination, and workers from Galicia, then part of the Austro-Hungarian Empire, took jobs in agricultural areas formerly held by German farmworkers. The rural proletarians from the overcrowded agricultural areas of central Poland and Galicia found the same living conditions that had driven away the Germans still highly attractive. What pushed one group pulled the other. Agrarian employers, plagued by labor shortage, welcomed the newcomers, who recommended themselves by being "undemanding," "willing," and "cheap" (*bescheiden, willig und billig*).[26]

As early as 1906 the agricultural capacity of eastern Prussia had become directly dependent on foreign labor from across the eastern borders. The Prussian administration had to concede that the absence of foreign migrant workers in the northeast "would almost mean the death knell for agriculture."[27] That was also true for the Upper Silesian mining district, where, reportedly, the mining industry could "not continue to operate without foreign labor."[28] Beginning in the agricultural northeast the continental immigration from eastern Europe found its goal continuously further west and southwest, finally arriving at the industrial centers of the west. During the prewar boom period, industry in the western parts of Germany also offered jobs not only to German workers leaving the land but also to more and more foreigners. Because of political considerations, the employment of foreign laborers from eastern Europe, especially from central Poland and Galicia, in the western provinces of Prussia was allowed only in exceptional cases. The rationale was to prevent a "polonization of the west," which it was feared would follow the "polonization of the east" if foreign Poles were allowed to mingle with their Prussian brethren in the Polish "colonies" of the Ruhr. As a result, laborers of other nationalities were recruited with all the more zeal. This was particularly true in the brickworks and the construction industries, where Italians made up the main contingent.[29]

Figure 5.9 depicts the increasing influx of foreign migrant labor especially in the northeast. From 1910 to 1920 the annual average of foreign labor in Germany amounted to more than 700,000. Poles from Russia and Austria formed the biggest group (43.7 percent), while Ruthenians from Galicia were the second largest (11.8 percent). On the national level this must, however, be understood as a conservative figure, as foreign workers outside Prussia were not fully listed. Figure 5.13 gives the net migration balance in Germany.[30] It relates the natural population growth to the net gain or loss from transnational migration movements, which includes, of course, all the movements on the continent and across the Atlantic. This opened up the prospect, shocking at the time, that Germany might cease to produce large numbers of emigrants and instead be faced with growing numbers of immigrants. However, this tendency never materialized. The Prussian administration, being more upset by this prospect than any other authority in Germany, evolved a sophisticated system whereby insiders could get out, but outsiders from across the eastern borders could only temporarily get in.

Germany was liberal on emigration but, of course, not on immigration. This position had emerged in the course of the nineteenth century. The German debate on emigration[31] had gathered some momentum in the 1830s and became heated in the following decade, culminating in the passage of the Emigration Bill (*Reichsauswanderungsgesetz*) of 1849, which even envisaged an emigration office. However, no emigration act on the Reich level came into legal existence

before 1897. Even then, except for tight controls against young men escaping
their military duties, German policy on emigration remained liberal, and the
brakes that were applied were less important, as mass emigration by that time
was a closed chapter. Apart from obstacles to immigration created by overseas
countries during the immediate postwar era, German overseas emigration remained an essentially free and self-regulating movement determined by the forces
of socioeconomic push and pull.

Figure 5.13
German Net Migration Balance, 1871–1910

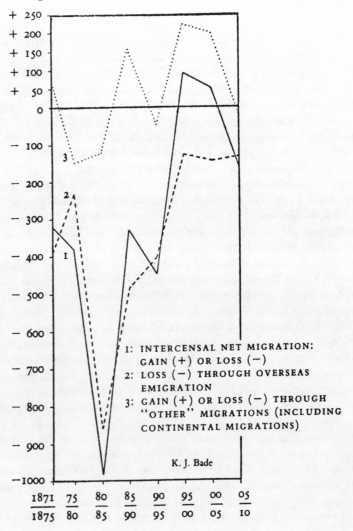

I: INTERCENSAL NET MIGRATION:
   GAIN (+) OR LOSS (−)
2: LOSS (−) THROUGH OVERSEAS
   EMIGRATION
3: GAIN (+) OR LOSS (−) THROUGH
   "OTHER" MIGRATIONS (INCLUDING
   CONTINENTAL MIGRATIONS)

K. J. Bade

The contrary, however, was true when it came to continental immigration to Germany.[32] This movement, too, was mainly determined by socioeconomic factors. But it was not left to the migrants from eastern Europe to decide whether they wanted to stay or come in temporarily. Immigration policies and alien legislation tended to curb permanent immigration and to favor the existence of a "reserve army" of foreign workers, responsive to the changing needs of industry and the seasonal demands of agriculture. The result was a highly mobile force of foreign labor which, when necessary, could be controlled by limited work as well as by residence permits. Foreign workers had to carry identity cards specially devised for that purpose. This practice was called *Legitimationszwang* (mandatory identification) and was directed, most of all, against Polish workers from across the eastern borders, who accounted for half of the foreign migrant labor force. Moreover, they were not allowed to come in with their families but only as single laborers. Their work permits were issued at the German border and expired every December. They tied the foreign worker to his employer, as both their names were entered into the foreign workers's passport. Special permits, mostly requested by industrial employers, were required for residence throughout the winter. Thus agricultural employers did not have to pay for their workers during unproductive winter months, whereas industrial employers were free to apply for an extension for their low-wage foreign workers whenever they needed them. Figure 5.14[33] shows the result of these state-imposed restrictions. They prevented Germany from becoming an immigration country by turning what would have been a permanent immigration into an annual ebb and flow of foreign labor crossing the eastern borders of Prussia. Thus the shift from permanent to temporary migration was not only a result of the general rise of temporary transnational labor migration in Europe. It was above all the result of deliberate government intervention into migration movements and the labor market in Germany and especially in Prussia ever since the 1890s.

In this way a dual labor market emerged. Foreign workers entered it on the internationalized lower-skill levels of employment like heavy manual labor and piece-work, in both industry and agriculture, where Germans preferred not to make their living. Here the reserve army of aliens, nearly one million people, operated as a buffer against structural changes and market fluctuations. Thus Germany did not have to conform to the tradition of classical immigration countries of eventually granting full citizen status to immigrants in return for their labors. By 1893 Germany ceased to be an emigration country; but rather than becoming an immigration country, it turned into a "labor-importing country." If, in spite of all this, a considerable number of immigrants from eastern Europe managed to stay, this was mainly a matter of illegal immigration which the Prussian Ministry of State tried to prevent with all the means at its disposal.

The system which had emerged by the turn of the century was bound to create serious conflicts among various economic, political, and social agencies on the national as well as on the international level. On the national level agrarian and industrial employers fought for a free-for-all admission of foreign workers, according to their specific needs and interests, while the trade unions vacillated between internationalism and their protective instincts. On the one hand trade unions failed to organize the unstable army of foreign workers and lost the battle for equal pay and equal rights; on the other hand they lamented the existence of foreign "strike breakers," "dirty competitors," and "wagecutters." The same conflict existed on the international level, where collisions occurred between the trade unions of both sides, the respective employers in industry and agriculture, and the governments of Germany, Austria-Hungary, and, above all, Russia. On the national level, however, public discussion of the "foreign-worker question" in imperial Germany manifested sharp conflicts of interest to an extent and intensity otherwise experienced only in the controversies over immigration policy in countries of immigration. World War I brought an abrupt end to this development.

When the war broke out, the eastern European workers who were in Germany at the time were forced to stay. That was especially true for the foreign migrant workers in agriculture. Without these foreign farmworkers (still 374,000 in October 1918), whose numbers were soon to be augmented by prisoners of war (900,000 in October 1918), the crisis of the German war economy would have culminated much earlier than it did in 1916. In the time of the Weimar Republic the number of foreign workers in Germany declined steadily. There were many reasons for this trend. The eastern borders of Germany had been moved west by the peace treaty of Versailles. Many Polish workers either returned to the

Figure 5.14
Annual Fluctuation of Registered Foreign Labor in Germany, 1910-1920

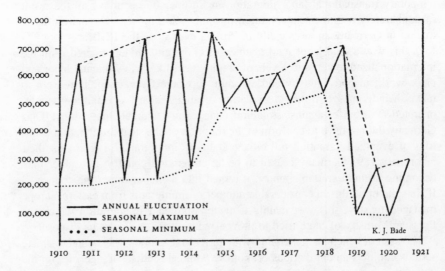

new Poland or went further west to France. Even more important, however, was that, in view of mass unemployment in the Weimar Republic, the Prussian system of *Legitimationszwang* for laborers from across the eastern borders was expanded to a yearly work-permit system (*Genehmigungspflicht*) for all foreign laborers in Germany. Visas for foreign laborers were now given out only if the employment offices had confirmed that there was no equivalent native labor available for the job. Thus the reserve army of foreign workers was also legally restricted to a buffer function on the German labor market. Thus too, the curve on foreign employment, shown in Figure 5.9, serves as a sort of crisis barometer for Weimar Germany, indicating the changing supply-and-demand relationships in the labor market.[34]

The contradictions between the policy of liberalism towards German emigration and protectionism with regard to continental immigration became even more crass. The protectionistic new quota system of the United States was sharply criticized in Weimar Germany. At the same time, however, the "labor-importing country" of Germany ran a restrictive system of entrance visas that went considerably further in its protectionistic intentions than the new American immigration policy. "Today the economy of international migration is on the road from liberalism to state-planned national economies," observed K. C. Thalheim in 1930. "Since the World War, the majority of states ruthlessly follow their own interests when it comes to regulating the right of their citizens to emigrate or of foreigners to immigrate," commented I. Ferenczi on the one-sided regulations of the labor market, "and their demands on other nations here stand in even greater contradiction to their own policies than in the case of tariffs."[35]

The Great Depression brought a precipitous decline in the number of foreign workers in Germany. The few who remained in 1932 may have carried a foreign passport, but a third of those employed in agriculture and nearly all those in industry were of German descent and had lived in the Reich for years. Thus most of them had been freed from the restrictive Weimar work-permit system and were on an equal footing with German laborers. For a while, the time had passed when foreign migrant labor had helped to balance the German labor market and had served to secure growth in good times, and social peace in bad ones.

The "foreign-worker question" of imperial and Weimar Germany experienced a modified revival half a century later, though under different conditions, in the "guest-worker question" in the Federal Republic.[36] Again it was a reserve army of foreign workers, this time exclusively industrial workers coming mainly from southern and southeastern Europe, which assumed a buffer function on the internationalized lower level of the dual labor market of West Germany in times of boom and bust. They were brought into the country during the boom period of the 1960s and in the 1970s their numbers had to be reduced with the beginning of a recession caused by structural changes and market fluctuations; but their replacement function on the lower level of the dual labor market continued. Characteristic for this situation was the considerable number of unemployed, unskilled German workers despite the large number of job opportunities on this lower level. These jobs had to be filled by foreign workers because the majority of unqualified German workers would rather receive unemployment compensation than enter into these employment areas. This system of a dual labor market rested on the shoulders of millions of foreign laborers, who worked in Germany without being able to become Germans.

In imperial Germany and the Weimar Republic the number of highly skilled and specialized foreign workers remained rather small. The mass of foreign laborers worked on the lower level of the dual labor market. In the Federal Republic and especially during the 1970s, the boundaries between these two levels have become more flexible for foreigners. Many of them moved upward through skills acquired in Germany, while others started out right away on the upper level as skilled workers. Many of them have been employed for more than one decade in Germany and have settled down with their families. This is one of the important differences between the "foreign-worker question" in imperial Germany and the "guest-worker question" in the Federal Republic. It also points up the shift from a "guest-worker question" to a genuine "immigration question." This is especially true for the hundreds of thousands of children of these families, who can't speak the native language of their parents any better than they can speak German. The so-called "guest-worker children" are in fact Germans with a foreign passport and constitute a new subculture in Germany. What will become of them when they have to compete with the last German baby boom on the overcrowded labor market of the next few years, only time will tell. To cope with this future it would be wise to recognize the historical consequences of "labor importing" and to enact them into law, and to risk the decisive step from a mere "foreigner policy" (*Ausländerpolitik*) to a genuine immigration policy.

NOTES

Notes 1, 13, 31, 36 have been updated for this volume.

1. References have purposely been kept short. For a more extensive discussion of the wide array of literature see K. J. Bade, "Massenwanderung und Arbeitsmarkt im deutschen Nordosten von 1880 bis zum Ersten Weltkrieg: Überseeische Auswanderung, interne Abwanderung und kontinentale Zuwanderung," *Archiv für Sozialgeschichte* 20 (1980), 265–323; idem, "Politik und Ökonomie der Ausländerbeschäftigung im preussischen Osten 1885–1914: Die Internationalisierung des Arbeitsmarkts im Rahmen der preussischen Abwehrpolitik," *Geschichte und Gesellschaft*, Sonderheft 6, 1980, pp. 273–99; idem, "Arbeitsmarkt, Bevölkerung und Wanderung in der Weimarer Republik," in M. Stürmer, ed., *Die Weimarer Republik—belagerte Civitas* (Königstein, 1980), pp. 160–87; idem, "Transnationale Migration und Arbeitsmarkt im Kaiserreich: Vom Agrarstaat mit starker Industrie zum Industriestaat mit starker agrarischer Basis," in T. Pierenkemper and R. H. Tilly, eds., *Historische Arbeitsmarktforschung* (Göttingen, 1982), pp. 182—221; idem, "Arbeitsmarkt, Ausländerbeschäftigung und Interessenkonflikt: Der Kampf um die Kontrolle über Ausländskrutierung und Inlandsvermittlung ausländischer Arbeitskräfte in Preußen vor dem Ersten Weltkrieg, in *Fremdarbeiterpolitik des Imperialismus*,

H. 10, (Rostock, 1981), pp. 27–47; idem," 'Kulturkampf' auf dem Arbeitsmarkt: Bismarcks 'Polenpolitik' 1885–1890," in O. Pflanze, ed., *Innenpolitische Probleme des Bismarckreichs* (München, 1983), pp. 121–42; idem," 'Preußengänger' und Abwehrpolitik': Ausländerbeschäftigung, Ausländerpolitik und Ausländerkontrolle auf dem Arbeitsmarkt in Preußen vor dem Ersten Weltkrieg," *Archiv für Sozialgeschichte* 24 (1984), pp. 91–162; idem, ed., "Arbeiterstatistik zur Ausländerkontrolle: Die 'Nachweisungen' der preussischen Landräte über den 'Zugang, Abgang und Bestand der ausländischen Arbeiter im preußischen Staate' 1906–1914," *Archiv für Sozialgeschichte* 24 (1984), pp. 163–283; idem, "Land oder Arbeit: Massenwanderung und Arbeitsmarkt im deutschen Kaiserreich" (Habilitationsschrift, University of Erlangen, 1979). For their helpful criticism I would like to thank Prof. K. Neils Conzen, Dr. R. H. Dumke, Prof. W. D. Kamphoefner, Prof. F. C. Luebke, Prof. A. McQuillan, Prof. O. Pflanze, and Prof. M. Walker, who commented on my paper in San Francisco 1978.

2. I. Ferenczi, *Kontinentale Wanderungen und die Annäherung der Völker* (Jena, 1930), p. 21.

3. Source of data for calculating sectoral shares of total labor force and national income: W. G. Hoffmann, F. Grumbach, and H. Hesse, *Das Wachstum der deutschen Wirtschaft seit der Mitte des 19. Jahrhunderts* (Berlin, 1965), pp. 205, 454f.

4. Source of data: Statistisches Bundesamt, ed., *Bevölkerung und Wirtschaft 1872–1972* (Wiesbaden, 1972), pp. 101ff.; compare the diagrams in G. Mackenroth, *Bevölkerungslehre* (Berlin, 1952), p. 56, and W. Köllmann, "Bevölkerungsgeschichte," in W. Zorn and H. Aubin, eds., *Handbuch der deutschen Wirtschafts- und Sozialgeschichte*, vol. 2 (Stuttgart, 1976), p. 24.

5. Statistisches Bundesamt, ed., *Bevölkerung und Wirtschaft 1872–1972*, pp. 101f.

6. I. Ferenczi, "Proletarian Mass Migrations, 19th and 20th Centuries," in F. W. Willcox, ed., *International Migrations*, vol. 1 (New York, 1929), pp. 81ff.

7. On German overseas emigration, see W. Mönckmeier, *Die deutsche überseeische Auswanderung* (Jena, 1912); F. Burgdörfer, "Die Wanderungen über die deutschen Reichsgrenzen im letzten Jahrhundert," *Allgemeines Statistisches Archiv* 20 (1930), 161–96, 383–419, 536–51; M. Walker, *Germany and the Emigration, 1816–1885* (Cambridge, Mass., 1964); P. Marschalck, *Deutsche Überseeauswanderung im 19. Jahrhundert* (Stuttgart, 1973); W. Köllmann and P. Marschalck, "German Emigration to the United States," *Perspectives in American History* 7 (1974), 499–554; G. Moltmann, ed., *Deutsche Amerikaauswanderung im 19. Jahrhundert: Sozialgeschichtliche Beiträge* (Stuttgart, 1976), see also note 31. On international migration within Germany, see W. Köllmann, *Bevölkerung in der industriellen Revolution: Studien zur Bevölkerungsgeschichte Deutschlands* (Göttingen, 1974); D. Langewiesche, "Wanderungsbewegungen in der Hochindustrialisierungsperiode: Regionale, interstädtische und innerstädtische Mobilität in Deutschland 1880–1914," *Vierteljahrschrift für Sozial- und Wirtschaftsgeschichte*, 64 (1977), 1–40. On continental immigration into Germany see notes 32 and 34.

8. Figure 5.4 is modeled on J. Knodel, *The Decline of Fertility in Germany, 1871–1939* (Princeton, N.J., 1974), p. 12. The division of Germany into economic regions on the basis of emigration patterns is based on Mönckmeier, *Die deutsche überseeische Auswanderung* and Burgdörfer, "Die Wanderungen über die deutschen Reichsgrenzen" (above, note 7).

9. Source of data: Burgdörfer, "Die Wanderungen über die deutschen Reichsgrenzen," pp. 189, 192; *Statistisches Jahrbuch für das deutsche Reich* 52 (1933), 49. The second dip in the second emigration wave at the end of the 1860s results from a shortened

fiscal year (for a corrected emigration curve see Moltmann, ed., *Deutsche Amerikaauswanderung*, p. 201).

10. N. Carpenter, *Immigrants and Their Children 1920*, Census Monographs, 7 (Washington, 1927), p. 47; *12th Census 1900, Population*, 1 (Washington, 1901), clxxi; *Statistical Atlas* (Washington, 1903), p. 57; *13th Census 1910, Population*, 1 (Washington, 1913), 718; *15th Census 1930, Abstract* (Washington, 1933), p. 129.

11. The data, from *Statistik des Deutschen Reiches*, and the diagram come from Mönckmeier, pp. 127–33.

12. Cumulative data from Chr. Klessmann, *Polnische Bergarbeiter im Ruhrgebiet, 1870–1945* (Göttingen, 1978), p. 260.

13. The data, from *Statistik des Deutschen Reiches*, come from Burgdörfer, "Die Wanderungen über die deutschen Reichsgrenzen," p. 542; *Statistisches Jahrbuch* 50 (1931), 305; 51 (1932), 295; 52 (1933), 294. The data were gathered by the German *Feldarbeiterzentrale/Arbeiterzentrale*. For the secret data on foreign workers in Prussia gathered by the Prussian Ministry of the Interior, 1906–1914, see my editing "Arbeiterstatistik zur Arbeiterkontrolle," cited in note 1.

14. Calculated, from the data of *Statistik des Deutschen Reiches*, by Mönckmeier, *Die deutsche überseeische Auswanderung*, p. 94.

15. Köllmann, "Bevölkerungsgeschichte", pp. 20, 31 (compare idem, *Bevölkerung in der industriellen Revolution*, pp. 39f., 115); Marschalck, *Deutsche Überseeauswanderung*, pp. 10, 12, 44, 82, 97.

16. *Statistisches Jahrbuch* 53 (1934), 11; *13th Census 1910, Population*, 1 (Washington, 1913), 844, 902; compare *14th Census 1920, Abstract* (Washington, 1923), p. 318; *15th Census 1930, Abstract* (Washington, 1933), p. 131; and *Population*, 2 (Washington, 1933), 232. Compare Knodel, *The Decline of Fertility*, p. 193, who erroneously asserts that as early as 1900 over 70 percent of all German-Americans lived in cities of more than 25,000.

17. L. E. Truesdell, *Farm Population of the United States*, Census Monographs, 6 (Washington, 1926), p. 105.

18. *9th Census 1870, Compendium* (Washington, 1872), pp. 578–602; *11th Census 1890, Population*, 2 (Washington, 1897), cxlvi. It should be noted here that the strong gains of the secondary and tertiary sectors at the expense of the primary sector in the occupational makeup were even more dramatic than they appear in the diagram, since the American statistics aggregate the more agrarian German immigration of earlier decades with new arrivals. (For the method of calculation see my forthcoming book, cited in note 1.)

19. For the United States, see S. Resneck, "Unemployment, Unrest, and Relief in the United States during the Depression of 1893–1897," *Journal of Political Economy* 61 (Aug. 1953), 324–45; Ch. Hofman, "The Depression of the Nineties," *Journal of Economic History* 17 (June 1956), 137–64; R. Fels, *American Business Cycles, 1865–1897* (Westport, Conn, 1959), pp. 179–219. For Germany see J. J. Lee, "Labour in German Industrialization," in *Cambridge Economic History of Europe*, vol. 7 (Cambridge, 1978), pp. 442–91.

20. H. Linde, "Die soziale Problematik der masurischen Agrargesellschaft und die masurische Einwanderung in das Emscherrevier," in H.-U. Wehler, ed., *Moderne deutsche Sozialgeschichte* (Cologne, 1968), pp. 456–70.

21. On the history of emigration from Mecklenburg, see E. Czalla, "Die Auswanderung aus Mecklenburg nach Nordamerika in der zweiten Hälfte des 19. Jahrhunderts" (Ph.D. diss., University of Rostock, 1974).

22. E. Franke, *Das Ruhrgebiet und Ostpreussen* (Essen, 1936); W. Brepohl, *Der Aufbau des Ruhrvolkes im Zuge der Ost-West-Wanderung* (Recklinghausen, 1948).

23. See note 12.

24. For a regional case study, see K. Neils Conzen, *Immigration Milwaukee, 1836–1860: Accommodation and Community in a Frontier City* (Cambridge, Mass., 1976); see also her study on the Germans in America, in Stephan Thernstrom, ed., *Harvard Encyclopedia of American Ethnic Groups* (Cambridge, Mass., 1980), p. 405–25. For a comparative regional study with a more rural focus, see W. D. Kamphoefner, "Transplanted Westphalians: Persistence and Transformation of Socioeconomic and Cultural Patterns in the Northwest German Migration to Missouri" (Ph.D. diss., University of Missouri, 1978).

25. P. Quante, *Die Flucht aus der Landwirtschaft* (Berlin, 1933); L. Schofer, *The Formation of a Modern Labor Force: Upper Silesia, 1865–1914* (Berkeley and Los Angeles, 1975); R. A. Dickler, "Organization and Productivity Change in Eastern Prussia," in W. N. Parker and E. Jones, eds., *Economic Essays in European Agrarian History* (Princeton, 1975), pp. 269–92.

26. M. Weber, *Die Verhältnisse der Landarbeiter im ostelbischen Deutschland*, Schriften des Vereins für Socialpolitik, 55 (Leipzig, 1892), passim; idem, "Die ländliche Arbeitsverfassung," in *Schriften des Vereins für Socialpolitik*, 58 (Leipzig, 1893), 62–86.

27. W. A. Henatsch, *Das Problem der ausländischen Wanderarbeiter unter besonderer Berücksichtigung der Zuckerproduktion in der Provinz Pommern* (Greifswald, 1920), p. 17.

28. Zentrales Staatsarchiv, Historische Abteilung II, Merseburg, Rep. 120, VIII, 1. Nr. 106, vol. 10, pp. 109f.

29. A. Knoke, *Ausländische Wanderarbeiter in Deutschland* (Leipzig, 1911); A. Sartorius von Waltershausen, "Die italienischen Wanderarbeiter," in *Festschrift für A.S. Schultze* (Leipzig, 1903), pp. 51–94.

30. Net migration balance, according to *Statistik des Deutschen Reiches*, from Burgdörfer, "Die Wanderungen über die deutschen Reichsgrenzen," p. 539.

31. On the discussion of the emigration issue in Germany, see H. Fenske, "Die deutsche Auswanderung in der Mitte des 19. Jahrhunderts: Öffentliche Meinung und amtliche Politik," *Geschichte in Wissenschaft und Unterricht* (1973), 221–36; K. J. Bade, *Friedrich Fabri und der Imperialismus in der Bismarckzeit: Revolution—Depression—Expansion* (Freiburg i.Br., 1975); idem, "Die deutsche Kolonialexpansion in Afrika: Ausgangssituation und Ergebnis," in W. Fürnrohr, ed., *Afrika im Geschichtsunterricht europäischer Länder: Von der Kolonialgeschichte zur Geschichte der Dritten Welt* (München, 1982), pp. 7–47; idem, ed., *Imperialismus und Kolonialmission: Kaiserliches Deutschland und koloniales Imperium* (Wiesbaden, 1982, second edition, Stuttgart, 1984), 1–28, 103–41; idem, "Das Kaiserreich als Kolonialmacht: ideologische Projektionen und historische Erfahrung," in J. Becker, A. Hillgruber, eds., *Die deutsche Frage im 19. und 20. Jahrhundert* (München, 1983), pp. 91–108.

32. On political issues of foreign labor in Germany before World War I, see J. Nichtweiss, *Die ausländischen Saisonarbeiter in der Landwirtschaft der östlichen und mittleren Gebiete des Deutschen Reiches* (Berlin, 1959).

33. Source of data: "Denkschrift über die Ein- und Auswanderung nach bzw. aus Deutschland in den Jahren 1910 bis 1920," *Stenographische Berichte über die Verhandlungen des deutschen Reichstags*, 372 (1920), 4382ff.

34. On the political issues of foreign labor in Germany during World War I and in the

Weimar Republic, see L. Elsner, "Die ausländischen Arbeiter in der Landwirtschaft der östlichen und mittleren Gebiete des Deutschen Reiches während des 1. Weltkrieges," (Ph.D. diss., University of Rostock, 1961); F. Zunkel, "Die ausländischen Arbeiter in der deutschen Kriegswirtschaftspolitik des 1. Weltkrieges," in G.A. Ritter, ed., *Entstehung und Wandel der modernen Gesellschaft: Festschrift für H. Rosenberg zum 65. Geburtstag* (Berlin, 1970), pp. 280–311; J. Tessarz, "Die Rolle der ausländischen landwirtschaftlichen Arbeiter in der Agrar- und Ostexpansionspolitik des deutschen Imperialismus in der Periode der Weimarer Republik, 1919–1932" (Ph.D. diss., University of Halle, 1962).

35. K. C. Thalheim, "Gegenwärtige und zukünftige Strukturwandlungen in der Wanderungswirtschaft der Welt," *Archiv für Wanderungswesen* 3 (1930), 47; I. Ferenczi, "Weltwanderungen und Wirtschaftsnot," *Soziale Praxis* 36 (1927), 890.

36. For a sample of current discussion of this issue, see E. Gehmacher et al., eds., *Ausländerpolitik im Konflikt: Arbeitskräfte oder Einwanderer? Konzepte der Aufnahme- und Entsendeländer* (Bonn, 1978); R. C. Rist, *Guestworkers in Germany: The Prospects for Pluralism* (New York, 1978); J. Blaschke and K. Greussing, eds., *Dritte Welt in Europa: Probleme der Arbeitsimmigration* (Frankfurt, 1980); K. J. Bade, *Gastarbeiter zwischen Arbeitswanderung und Einwanderung* (Akademie für Politische Bildung, Tutzing, Reihe: Zur aktuellen Diskussion, 1983/H. 1) (Tutzing, 1983); idem, *Vom Auswanderungsland zum Einwanderungsland? Deutschland 1880–1980* (Berlin, 1983); idem, ed., *Auswanderer–Wanderarbeiter–Gastarbeiter: Bevölkerung, Arbeitsmarkt und Wanderung in Deutschland seit der Mitte des 19. Jahrhunderts*, 2 vols. (Ostfildern, 1984).

"FILLING THE VOID": IMMIGRATION TO FRANCE BEFORE WORLD WAR I   **6**

Nancy L. Green

It is perhaps not surprising that it was a French economist who wrote "Il n'est force ni richesse que d'hommes." Although Jean Bodin wrote this phrase in the sixteenth century, the preoccupation of the French government with demographic politics remains to this day, as any *livret de famille* (marriage certificate in the form of a booklet) attests. The twelve expectant and optimistic pages waiting to be filled in with children's names are but one sign of this concern.

The relationship between population growth, labor needs, and migration policies has become increasingly explicit in the twentieth century.[1] However, already at the end of the nineteenth century, attention began to turn to the possible control and regulation of migration, its desirability, its inconvenience. The discourse on migration reveals not only changing attitudes toward migration itself, but a turning point in the development of liberal capitalism. Classical laissez-faire theories were giving way to increasing appeals for state intervention and other forms of organization by the end of the nineteenth century. The "spontaneous" period of labor migration prior to World War I, corresponding to that "spontaneous" equilibrating mechanism of supply and demand, would after that period be subject to increasing controls.[2] But already before World War I there were attempts to regulate that supply and demand in order to aid economic development.[3] The French case is especially pertinent, as concern over lagging population growth led to explicit appeals in favor of immigration on the part of some business leaders and government officials. The period before 1914 is a crucial one in which the seeds of later politics of migration are sown and the role of immigrants in French economic growth is (however begrudgingly at times) acknowledged.

THE INTERNATIONAL CONFERENCE ON IMMIGRATION, 1889

It was in Paris during the World Fair of 1889 that an International Conference on Governmental Intervention with regard to Emigration and Immigration took place. Conference delegates came from France, Belgium, and Spain for the "Old World," Argentina, Brazil, Chile, Guatemala, Paraguay, El Salvador, Venezuela and Hawaii for the "New World." In many ways the debates reflected the divergent views between the former, countries of emigration, and the latter,

Table 6.1
Total Numbers of French Abroad and Immigrants in France, 1851–1911

	French Elsewhere[a] (estimates)	Immigrants in France[b] (absolute numbers)
1851		379,285
1861	318,000	
1866		655,036
1876		801,754
1881	426,000 (1881-86)	1,001,090
1886		1,126,531
1891		1,130,211
1896		1,027,421
1901	495,000	1,037,778
1906		1,046,905
1911	600,000	1,159,835

[a]Service National des Statistiques, Mouvements Migratoires entre la France et l'étranger (Paris: Imprimerie Nationale, 1943), pp. 34, 36 and 70.

[b]Georges Mauco, Les étrangers en France (Paris: Armand Colin, 1932), p. 38; cf. Service National des Statistiques, p. 70.

Table 6.2
Annual Average of Emigrants and Immigrants, 1851–1911

	Annual Average Number of	
	Emigrants	Immigrants
1851-61	25,100 (1851-60)	30,000
1861-66		60,000
1866-72	17,700 (1861-70)	50,000
1872-76		30,000
1876-81	35,300 (1871-80)	60,000
1881-86		60,000
1886-91	47,200 (1881-90)	40,000
1891-96		45,000
1896-1901	28,600 (1891-1900)	45,000
1901-06		70,000
1906-11	44,500 (1901-10)	100,000

Source: Service National des Statistiques, Mouvements Migratoires
        entre la France et l'etranger (Paris: Imprimerie Nationale,
        (1943), pp. 34, 36, and 70.

Table 6.3
Destinations of French Emigrants
(annual averages)

	Overseas		French Colonies		Europe		Total	
	No.	(%)	No.	(%)	No.	(%)	No.	(%)
1851-60	11,100	(44.2)	7,000	(27.9)	7,000	(27.9)	25,100	(100.0)
1861-70	7,200	(40.7)	3,500	(19.8)	7,000	(39.5)	17,700	(100,0)
1871-80	13,900	(39.4)	6,400	(18.1)	15,000	(42.5)	35,300	(100.0)
1881-90	21,300	(45.1)	7,900	(16.8)	18,000	(38.1)	47,200	(100.0)
1891-1900	10,000	(35.0)	8,600	(30.0)	10,000	(35.0)	28,600	(100.0)
1901-10	16,000	(36.0)	4,500	(10.1)	24,000	(53.9)	44,500	(100.0)

SOURCE: Service Nationale des Statistiques, Mouvements Migratoires
entre la France et l'étranger (Paris: Imprimerie Nationale, 1943), p. 36.

NOTE: It may be noted that emigration to the French colonies did
not increase considerably until the interwar period, when it accounted for
35.6 percent from 1921-1930 and 43.5 percent from 1931-35 of total French
emigration. Service National des Statistiques, p. 39.

countries of immigration. Yet the attitudes of the French delegates reflected both
positions, for while France had a positive immigrant balance, it was also sending
emigrants to the "New World" and to French colonies. (See Tables 6.1, 6.2
and 6.3.) .

What is striking about the convention reports is the juxtaposition of concern
as to whether and how migration should be controlled with a free market ideology
precluding any control whatsoever. Should the governments encourage or discourage migration? All of the advantages of "wise" emigration (to get rid of
excess population, to get rid of paupers or even criminals, to open up new
markets, etc.) and "useful" immigration (to develop colonies, people new countries, aid industrial and agricultural prosperity with working "arms") were discussed. Various methods of regulating or controlling emigration/immigration
were evoked, particularly in the areas of transportation and recruitment. But in
the end, and perhaps for the last time, the delegates hesitated and ultimately
reemphasized faith in the free market as the best regulator of both state and
individual interests in three important resolutions:

1. Emigration and immigration, considered in and of themselves and *free of any abnormal conditions*, offer advantages both for the state and for the individual.
2. The state should not intervene *directly* in the emigration movement *except* in order
to *inform* and *protect* the emigrant. . . .
3. [The Conference proposes] the creation of public utility companies which would
serve, free of charge, as links between the country of emigration, from which they would
choose the emigrants, and the country of immigration, to which they would send the
emigrants, upon the request of duly accredited agents, acting, as the companies themselves, in the sole aim of protection and humanity.[4]

Thus, after three days of debates concerning possible regulatory measures, the laissez-faire market was once again defended.

Yet at the same time the conference conclusions indicate possible areas for future control: first, in the case of "abnormal conditions," many of which had already been discussed throughout the Conference (such "frictional obstacles" as recruiting agents, shipping companies, etc., that interfered with the free market mechanism); second, in order to inform and protect migrants (from the anarchy and vagaries of the market mechanism).[5] Finally and perhaps most significantly, the "choosing" function appears: the possibility on the part of migration regulators to choose the candidates best adapted to conditions in the country of destination.

THE DEMAND FOR IMMIGRANT LABOR IN FRANCE

The case of France is instructive. Although regulation and control would not appear so starkly until the bilateral treaties between the wars, even before World War I the discourse on migration was changing. At the basis of that change was the recognition that immigration was doubly useful to France to right the demographic (im)balance and to help the French economy keep up with competitors.

Alone of the Western European countries that were by and large exporting labor to the New World throughout the nineteenth century, France was a country

Figure 6.1
Comparative European Populations, 1810–1910

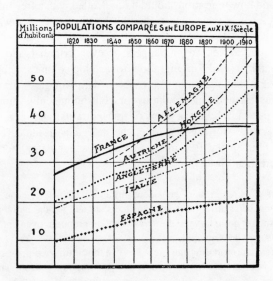

Source: George Mauco, *Les étrangers en France* (Paris: Armand Colin, 1932), p. 26. Used with permission of the publisher. Photograph courtesy of Bibliothèque Nationale de Paris.

of *im*migration in Europe, particularly after mid-century. Demographic woes largely account for this. Whereas from 1850 to 1900 the populations of the United Kingdom and Ireland, Germany, and Italy increased by amounts varying from 35 to 60 percent, the French population only grew a paltry 11.5 percent in that period (see Figure 6.1 and Table 6.4).[6] At the same time population density in France increased from 66 to 73 people per square kilometer while in Germany the population density grew from 66 to 103 people per square kilometer and in Great Britain from 92 to 163.[7]

The demographic problem was blamed on several factors, including inheritance laws, taxes, military service (which delayed marriages), and even child labor laws. Whereas children had once been seen as productive, they could now only be seen as a luxury since labor laws prevented them from working before the age of fourteen or fifteen.[8] In sum, the declining birth rate was blamed on the "développement de l'esprit du calcul."[9]

After the Franco-Prussian War, with the loss of men not only on the battlefield but through the annexation of Alsace and Lorraine by Germany, decreased manpower became of utmost concern. Demographic difficulties were blamed for not only political but also economic weakness. France, once a world leader, saw

Table 6.4
French Population Growth and Immigration

	Population Increase (%)[a]			Immigrants[b]	
	in France	as compared to		as percentage of Total Population	
		U.K.+Ire.	Germany		
1800–				1.05	1851
1850	29.6	69.0	45.1	1.7	1866
				2.1	1876
				2.6	1881
1850–				2.9	1886
1900	11.5	51.3	59.2	2.8[c]	1891
				2.6	1896
				2.6	1901
1900–				2.5	1906
1949	1.2	25.2	68.0	2.86	1911

[a]Hilde Wander, The Importance of Emigration for the Solution of Population Problems in Western Europe (The Hague: Martinus Nijhoff, 1951), p. 51. Compare George Mauco's figures of French population growth by 20-year periods, which are less dramatic but nonetheless telling of constant declining growth: 1801-21: 4.9%; 1821-41: 5.6%; 1841-61: 3.4%; 1861-81: 2.7%; 1881-1901: 1.8%. Les étrangers en France (Paris: Armand Colin, 1932), p. 18.

[b]Mauco, Les etrangers en France, p. 38.

[c]See Figure 6.1 for statistical effects of the 1889 nationality law.

growing industrial competition from Germany, England, and the United States threaten its goods in world markets and even in some sectors of the domestic market. Industrial reports lamented the factors that had caused this, including the low birth rate, which did not provide enough producers or consumers. At the same time it was noted that French labor costs were often considerably higher than those of other industrializing countries.[10]

Immigration would be seen by some as an inevitable result of this state of affairs. One contemporary so lamented, giving the following osmotic interpretation of migration:

If we do not face [other countries] with a population density approximately equal to theirs, it is inevitable [*fatalement*] that we will always be invaded, for the difference in populations of neighboring countries is like communicating vessels where the liquids will necessarily flow to the same level.[11]

But others increasingly saw immigration more optimistically as a way of solving France's labor problems. One of the French delegates to the 1889 conference stated:

If it is proven that the French nation will soon cease to grow by itself, then let us open our frontiers even wider than before, let us attract foreigners, instead of repelling them! ... This time France will have the commercial and industrial interests on her side and the merit of continuing to apply the generous principle of liberal hospitality for which she has always been honored.[12]

(The minutes of the meeting note that this statement was followed by prolonged applause.)

The French were caught in a dilemma between xenophobia and economic needs. Approximately fifty laws with regard to immigrants were proposed between 1883 and 1914; they were either aimed directly at restricting immigration or at taxing the immigrants or their employers.[13] The immigrants were variously labeled as workers and therefore competitors of French laborers, as poor and thus a burden on the economy, as disloyal in time of war, as criminals (or evildoers—*malfaiteurs*), or even as having a particularly high number of illegitimate children!

One law that was passed, that of 10 August 1899 (always noted ironically to have been the work of the Socialist government under Millerand), limited the percentage of foreigners that could be employed in public works. Otherwise, all of the other restrictive proposals suggested in the period before World War I were defeated with the exception of two, which became the laws of 1888 and 1893. They, respectively, required immigrants to register with the police upon arrival in France and established a fine for those who failed to do so. The police department itself noted that these laws were hardly exceptional, having their counterparts in most European countries, but that, in any case, they were difficult to enforce and more often than not ignored.[14]

The mixed blessing of migration and the continuing dilemma between fear and need of foreigners were summed up in such ambivalent phrases as the "phénomène de pénétration et d'invasion pacifique" or "cette invasion [ou infiltration] . . . [qui] nous est salutaire et nécessaire."[15] If immigrants were often looked upon as invaders and infiltrators, they were also recognized for their utility. Ultimately immigration to France in the period before World War I was tacitly encouraged, industrial interests winning out over fears that were xenophobic at worst, protectionist at least. The immigrant population in France almost tripled from 1851 to 1886, from approximately 380,000 to 1,130,000, or roughly 1.1 to 2.9 percent of the population (see Table 6.4).[16]

The relation of immigration to demographic concerns became evident with the law of 26 June 1889, which widened the definition of French nationality by declaring that birth on French soil conferred French nationality. Thus immigrants' children who were born in France would henceforth be considered French (and therefore liable to military service). The law also made naturalization easier, decreasing the waiting period from five to three years and allowing naturalization after only one year for those foreigners who had "rendered important services to France," brought in "distinguished talent," introduced an industry or useful invention or had served in the French armed forces (a path to French citizenship that would be used by World War I survivors).[17]

The demographic problem had been described as "le mal constaté par la statistique," and the statistical implications of the 1889 law are clear.[18] From the 1876 to 1881 censuses, the immigrant population grew by almost 200,000 people, a 24 percent increase; from 1881 to 1886, the immigrant population grew by approximately 125,000 people, a 13 percent increase. But from the census of 1886 to that of 1891, the number of foreigners grew by only 3,680 persons, a 0.3 percent increase, and in succeeding censuses the absolute number of foreigners actually declined. This represented a decrease from the high of 2.9 percent of the French population in 1886 down to 2.5 percent in 1906 (before the immigrant figures climb again). But the statistical decrease in foreigners only "masked the contingent of new arrivals," according to a comment in the *Résultats statistiques du recensement de la population*,[19] and the law of 1889 got a round of applause at the international conference that year after one French delegate praised foreigners for "fill[ing] a void" in France.[20] Certainly, as another delegate had acknowledged, temporary inconveniences due to immigration were inevitable, but they were outweighed by the permanent advantages that the immigrants provided to the French economy (another round of applause).[21]

IMMIGRANT ORIGINS AND EMPLOYMENT

Who were the immigrants in France before 1914? Table 6.5 provides the breakdown by nationality, which shows the importance above all of France's neighbors. The largest contingents of immigrants to France throughout the second half of the nineteenth century came from those countries bordering on the multifrontiered hexagon: Belgium, Italy, Germany, Spain, Switzerland, and England.[22] And, with the exception of Germany, the immigrants came from France's present and future allies, including the Russian Empire.

Similarly, as seen in Table 6.6, the immigrants for the most part settled in the border provinces, with the notable exception of the Seine (Paris) department, which, in absolute numbers, came in second with 153,600 immigrants in 1907 (after 191,700 in the Nord and followed by 123,500 in the Bouches-du-Rhône).[23] Paris, the pole of the *métropole* and renowned for its manufactured goods, had always attracted a large number of immigrants, foreign and provincial.[24] But, basically, just as the foreign immigrants came from bordering countries, they settled for the most part in the border provinces, a geographic distribution cor-- responding not only to home ties but to manpower needs in the French economy (see Figure 6.2). Thus the Spanish and Italian immigrants helped agricultural

Table 6.5
Immigrants in France by Country of Origin

	Belgians		Italians		Germans		Austro-Hungarians		Spaniards		Swiss	
	No.	(%)	No.	(%)	No.	(%)	No.	(%)	No.	(%)	No.	(%)
1851	128,103	(33.8)	63,307	(16.7)	57,061	(15.0)			29,736	(7.8)	25,485	(6.7)
1866	275,888	(42.1)	99,624	(15.2)	106,606	(16.3)			32,650	(5.0)	42,270	(6.4)
1876	374,498	(46.7)	165,313	(20.6)	59,028	(7.4)	7,498	(0.9)	62,437	(7.8)	50,303	(6.3)
1881	432,265	(43.2)	240,733	(24.0)	81,986	(8.2)	12,090	(1.2)	73,781	(7.4)	66,281	(6.6)
1886	482,261	(42.8)	264,568	(23.5)	100,114	(8.9)	11,817	(1.0)	79,550	(7.0)	78,584	(7.0)
1891	465,860	(41.2)	286,082	(25.3)	83,333	(7.4)	12,909	(1.1)	77,736	(6.9)	83,117	(7.3)
1896	395,498	(38.5)	291,886	(28.4)	90,746	(8.8)	10,952	(1.1)	76,819	(7.5)	74,735	(7.3)
1901	323,390	(31.2)	330,465	(31.8)	89,772	(8.7)	11,730	(1.1)	80,485	(7.8)	72,042	(6.9)
1906	310,433	(29.7)	377,638	(36.1)	87,836	(8.4)	13,021	(1.2)	80,914	(7.7)	68,892	(6.6)
1911	287,126	(24.8)	419,234	(36.2)	102,271	(8.8)	17,851	(1.5)	105,760	(9.1)	73,422	(6.3)

	English		Dutch and Luxembourgeois		Russian subjects		Others *		TOTAL	
	No.	(%)	No.	(%)	No.	(%)	No.	(%)	No.	(%)
1851	20,357	(5.4)			9,338	(2.5)	45,902	(12.1)	379,289	(100.0)
1866	29,856	(4.6)	16,158	(2.5)	12,164	(1.8)	39,820	(6.1)	655,036	(100.0)
1876	30,077	(3.7)	18,099	(2.3)	7,992	(1.0)	26,509	(3.3)	801,754	(100.0)
1881	37,006	(3.7)	21,232	(2.1)	10,489	(1.1)	25,227	(2.5)	1,001,090	(100.0)
1886	36,134	(3.2)	37,149	(3.3)	11,980	(1.1)	24,374	(2.2)	1,126,531	(100.0)
1891	39,687	(3.5)	40,326	(3.6)	14,357	(1.3)	26,894	(2.4)	1,130,301	(100.0)
1896	36,249	(3.5)	-		15,251	(1.5)	35,285	(3.4)	1,027,421	(100.0)
1901	36,948	(3.6)	27,814	(2.7)	16,061	(1.5)	49,071	(4.7)	1,037,778	(100.0)
1906	35,990	(3.4)	-		25,605	(2.4)	46,576	(4.5)	1,046,905	(100.0)
1911	40,378	(3.5)	25,611	(2.2)	35,016	(3.0)	53,166	(4.6)	1,159,835	(100.0)

SOURCE: Derived from Georges Mauco, Les étrangers en France (Paris: Armand Colin, 1932), p. 38.

*Portuguese, Scandinavians, Greeks, Rumanians, Serbs, Bulgarians, Turcs, Africans, Asians, none representing over 3200 people/year + Mauco's category of "Others."

production in the south while Belgians, Germans, and Italians aided industrial development in the north and east.

The increase of immigrants into the agricultural south corresponded with the development of wine-growing following the double effect of the "railroad revolution" and the phylloxera crisis of the last third of the nineteenth century.[25] The advent of the railroad opened up markets and encouraged the shift toward a monoculture based on vineyards, wine being more profitable than wheat. Spanish immigrants in particular took part in this expansion, largely as seasonal migrants, along with French rural migrants from surrounding mountain regions. The phylloxera epidemic (caused by lice which attacked the vines at the root), which began in 1865 and reappeared over the next twenty years, in turn accelerated this movement. With the emigration of many French winegrowers (some to Algeria) and the increasing concentration of winegrowing into a more capitalist and less family-oriented structure, the result was an increase in permanent foreign in-migration, relaying and replacing the slowed-down mountain and seasonal migrations. More immigrants were brought in during the First World War, which hit the rural communities particularly hard (many more peasants were drafted and killed than industrial workers, who were often exempt), and the number of Spaniards and Italians had in some places doubled or tripled by 1921.[26]

Nonetheless, as can be seen in Table 6.7, foreign migration to France before the war was particularly directed to the industrial sector. Rather than filling its

Table 6.6
Immigrant Destinations in France as Percentage of Departmental Population

Department	1886[a]	1906[b]
Alpes-Maritime	19.1	28.5
Nord	18.9	11.0
Bouches-du-Rhône	12.8	15.0
Ardennes	11.3	6.6
Belfort	10.5	10.0
Var	8.7	
Meurthe-et-Moselle	7.6	7.7
Seine	7.2	5.2
Corse	6.0	
Pyrénées-Orientales	5.1	5.2

[a]Prince De Cassano, Procès verbaux sommaires du Congrès international de l'intervention des pouvoirs publics dans l'émigration et l'immigration, tenu à Paris du 12 au 14 août 1889 (Exposition Universelle Internationale de 1889) (Paris: Imprimerie Nationale for the Ministère du Commerce, de l'Industrie et des Colonies, 1890), p. 10.

[b]Maurice Didion, Les Salariés étrangers en France (Paris: V. Giard & E. Brière, 1911), p. 10.

factories with a rural exodus similar to other industrializing countries, France was already importing foreign labor, while French agricultural workers remained stubbornly and proudly on the farm. Once again, the slow demographic growth already noted was one reason for the limited pressures toward rural emigration; the particular effects of World War I would reinforce that trend in the post-war period.

The breakdown of occupations (Table 6.7) exercised by the different foreigners in France before World War I clearly indicates the important immigrant input to industry. Industrial activity accounted for over 40 percent of the jobs held by foreigners, with a high of over 51 percent of the Belgians and 62 percent of Russian subjects (Jews for the most part) in France working in this sector. At the same time 27 percent of the Spanish immigrants aided French agriculture; 25 percent of Italians were involved in transportation and heavy labor; over 20 percent of the Germans, Swiss as has been seen; and the English were merchants of one sort or another; while 26 percent of Germans and 21 percent of the English served as domestic servants or "nannies."

It is interesting to note that mining had not yet become a major "choice" for

Figure 6.2
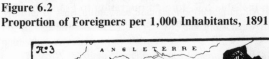
Proportion of Foreigners per 1,000 Inhabitants, 1891

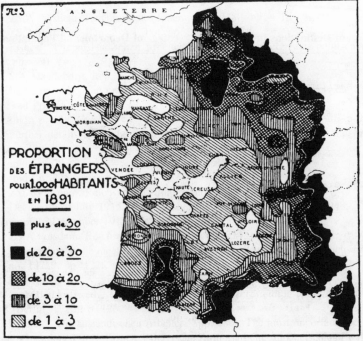

Source: Mauco, *Les étrangers en France*, (Paris: Armand Colin, 1932), p. 41. Used with permission of the publisher. Photograph courtesy of the Bibliothèque Nationale de Paris.

immigrant workers, as it would in the interwar period. As seen in Table 6.8, only 3 to 4 percent of Belgians, Italians, and Spaniards worked in the mines before 1914. However if it could be said that mining was not yet the choice of the immigrants, immigrants were clearly already becoming the choice of the mine owners. Table 6.9 shows that immigrants already represented some 13 percent of the work force in mining and metallurgy, prefiguring the important numbers of Italians and Poles who would work in those fields in the interwar period.

We can also see in Table 6.9 how immigrants were being increasingly employed in new and expanding fields such as chemicals, lighting, and clothing. More generally, it is important to note that the immigrants were by and large greatly overrepresented in the industrial work force as compared to their percentage of the total population (2.8 percent in 1891).

Prior to World War I the use of immigrant labor was thus in its incipient stage. Immigrants were increasingly recognized as potentially valuable aids in the face of relative demographic and industrial lag. This meant that implicit if not explicit acceptance of control to insure that aid was already being envisaged. As the spontaneous, osmotic flow into France of her relatively more populated neighbors became insufficient, the idea began to take shape that such important matters as labor-force recruitment could not be left to the marketplace. Starting in 1906 Polish agricultural workers and then Italian as well as Polish mine workers were recruited through French employers' unions. By 1913 there were already 14,000 Italians in the Lorraine iron ore fields.[27]

The war would accelerate the trend toward the organization and control of migration. Manpower shortages during the war led to three types of organized migrations. Over 220,000 colonial workers were brought in to aid the war industries; about 160,000 Spanish, Portuguese, and Italian farm workers were hired to replace the vast numbers of conscripted peasants; and approximately 80,000 European industrial workers were recruited.[28] The Service de la Main

Table 6.7
French and Immigrant Work-Force Participation in 1891 and 1911

	1891		1911	
	French	Immigrant	French	Immigrant
AGRICULTURE	47 %	19 %	42 %	12 %
INDUSTRY	26	50	30	43
COMMERCE	14	20	16	29
OTHER	13	11	12	16
	100	100	100	100

SOURCE: Georges Mauco, Les étrangers en France, (Paris: Armand Colin, 1932), p. 48.

d'Oeuvre Etrangère was created during the war under the Armament Ministry, and, as of January 1, 1918, it was made part of the Labor Ministry.

After the war, with 1.3 million dead, 1.1 million wounded, and the northern industrial areas of the country largely destroyed or damaged, the twin problems of demography and development became even more critical than before. The legalization of the eight-hour workday (in 1919) was also criticized as further

Table 6.8
Immigrant Occupations, 1911

Occupations	Belgians		Italians		Germans		Spaniards	
	No.	(%)	No.	(%)	No.	(%)	No.	(%)
Agriculture	19,421	(11.5)	32,008	(12.5)	3,382	(5.4)	16,401	(26.9)
Mining	6,373	(3.7)	10,242	(4.0)	837	(1.3)	1,982	(3.3)
Industry	86,931	(51.3)	100,232	(39.0)	19,884	(31.3)	21,055	(34.5)
Transportation	22,231	(13.1)	63,749	(24.8)	4,706	(7.4)	6,913	(11.3)
Commerce	18,261	(10.8)	27,180	(10.6)	13,212	(20.8)	9,346	(15.3)
Domestic Service	11,713	(6.9)	19,106	(7.4)	16,526	(26.0)	3,744	(6.1)
Education	492	(0.3)	464	(0.2)	1,720	(2.7)	184	(0.3)
Liberal Professions & Administration	4,026	(2.4)	3,830	(1.5)	3,251	(5.1)	1,388	(2.3)
TOTAL	169,448	(100.0)	256,811	(100.0)	63,518	(100.0)	61,013	(100.0)

Occupations	Swiss		English		Russians		Total[*]	
	No.	(%)	No.	(%)	No.	(%)	No.	(%)
Agriculture	6,880	(14.7)	217	(1.4)	758	(4.6)	82,200	(12.1)
Mining	154	(0.3)	15	(0.1)	85	(0.5)	20,620	(3.1)
Industry	17,501	(37.3)	2,570	(16.3)	10,333	(62.0)	276,219	(40.7)
Transportation	3,128	(6.7)	1,537	(9.7)	404	(2.4)	105,829	(15.6)
Commerce	10,198	(21.7)	3,179	(20.2)	514	(3.1)	94,794	(14.0)
Domestic Service	5,482	(11.7)	3,346	(21.2)	2,512	(15.1)	65,918	(9.7)
Education	374	(0.8)	2,045	(13.0)	304	(1.8)	6,467	(1.0)
Liberal Professions & Administration	3,185	(6.8)	2,856	(18.1)	1,744	(10.5)	26,042	(3.8)
TOTAL	46,902	(100.0)	15,765	(100.0)	16,654	(100.0)	678,089	(100.0)

SOURCE: Derived from Georges Mauco, Les étrangers en France (Paris: Armand Colin, 1932), p. 562.

[*]Includes "Others".

decreasing available labor power. Frontier immigrants, spontaneous or not, were no longer enough. The government signed several bilateral treaties with Poland, Italy, and Czechoslovakia in 1919 and 1920 in order to assure the needed labor force.[29]

Thus, in the 1920s, while the most important of the New World immigrant-receiving countries, the United States, was closing its doors, France was opening

Table 6.9
Immigrants as Percentage of Work-Force by Branch of Activity and Sex, 1891

Occupation		Men	Women
AGRICULTURE		3.3	1.2
INDUSTRY		8.7	4.7
Textile	5.5		4.3
Metallurgy	12.9		3.6
Mining	13.4		6.6
Machine tools	8.3		3.3
Leather	4.5		2.3
Ceramic	9.6		5.4
Wood	5.0		4.8
Chemical Products	22.0		9.6
Construction	9.2		3.5
Lighting	11.7		6.1
Furniture	8.2		3.6
Food	10.1		3.8
Clothing	10.6		5.1
Luxury Items	7.1		6.0
Printing, Paper Goods	5.0		4.4
State manufacture	0.4		0.4
TRANSPORTATION		5.2	2.0
COMMERCE		6.6	4.2

SOURCE: Yves Le Febvre, <u>L'ouvrier étranger et la pro-tection du travail national</u> (Paris: C. Jacques et Cie., 1901), p. 19; the same figures are found in Jean Mesnaud de Saint-Paul, <u>De l'Immigration étrangère en France considérée au point du vue économique</u> (Paris: Arthur Rouseau, 1902), pp. 12-13. Cf. Service National des Statistiques, <u>Mouvements migratoires entre France et l'étranger</u> (Paris: Imprimerie Nationale, 1943), p. 73.

its. France continued in its immigration/emigration (to the colonies) tradition already evident at the time of the 1889 conference. But alone of all European countries, France's immigrant balance remained positive.

A COMPARISON OF PRE- AND POST-WAR MIGRATION

The immigration to France before 1914 of hundred of thousands of its European neighbors prefigures the interwar period. However, at the same time there are important differences between the pre-1914 and post-1914 periods, both with regard to the sectors in which the immigrants were employed and the immigrant populations concerned.

In the first place, the industry category must be broken down into heavy and light industry. The numerous Belgians and Russians counted in the industrial sector before the war were often skilled craftsmen in the manufacturing sector. Industrial development in France before World War I took place in a country where one-third of the total establishments had only one to ten employees.[30] In the interwar period the industrial immigrants were rather to be found largely in the extractive industries, in the mines in the north and east of France.

There was a corresponding shift in labor needs. The earlier immigrants were valued for their skills. In the interwar period employers were looking instead for simply docile, hard workers. The change from skilled to unskilled labor also corresponded to a shift in immigrant populations. The Italians, who had been among the less skilled of France's immigrating neighbors, continued to come. By 1926 they clearly outdistanced the Belgians as the most important immigrant group in France.[31] But France also now looked farther afield to Central Europe. As emigration to the United States was halted, France provided a viable alternate destination for those populations, encouraged, as has been seen, by labor treaties.

This interwar migration of unskilled laborers was perhaps France's new immigration as compared to the old, pre–1914 one. Certainly the immigrant question of the 1919–1931 period (when the depression hit) was tied up with the predominant image of Poles and Italians.[32] And by comparison to this large-scale and organized immigration of entire colonies of foreigners, the pre-1914 immigrants already seemed assimilated.

In fact, adaptation to France before 1914 for the Belgians, Swiss, and Luxembourgers could not have been too difficult. Just as there were no formidable administrative barriers, there were no linguistic barriers to migration for these three groups. The best proof of their acculturation to French society is perhaps the fact that these groups never became the butt of anti-immigrant campaigns, either before 1914 or after (although jokes about their accents are legion).

The commonality of Romance languages undoubtedly also eased the way for Italians and Spaniards.[33] However, several other factors have been cited as helping acculturation. The labor movement, for one, offered an ideology of internationalism and workers' unity along with a practical terrain for social and political encounters between French and foreign workers. Italian workers even became the avant-garde of strike activity in some places, while social conflicts also served to integrate Spanish immigrants into the village communities in which they had settled.[34] More generally, participation in the labor movement implied a desire for betterment of conditions in the new country and thus a perspective toward settlement, which was reflected in other factors attesting to the immigrants' stabilization in France. They sent for their families, purchased property, and even were naturalized.[35] Spanish immigrants in the Languedoc region purchased vineyards little by little in the 1920s. The possession of a "bit of land of one's own" was an important step toward becoming rooted in the area. And even when the immigrants did not become naturalized themselves, they made sure their children were French, because "We came here to live." Finally, of course, acculturation would happen via the second generation and the effect of French schools on immigrant children: "Spanish parents, French kids."[36]

As for the Germans, it could be said that the question of long-term German acculturation to French society never really existed. German immigration to France varied as a function of political events. The German colony in Paris was quite important before 1871. However, with the Franco-Prussian War, the majority of these workers were expelled. And as Germany began its own process of industrialization, German emigration declined. In any case, the life of a German in France in the period between the Franco-Prussian War and World War I could not have been easy.

In fact, each immigrant group had to face a certain amount of xenophobia that contrasts strikingly with the calculation of the importance of immigrant labor. Between the Franco-Prussian War and World War I the climate of nationalism was particularly strong.[37] At the factory and workshop level, labor competition was sometimes expressed in anti-immigrant slogans and even violence. The massacre of Italian immigrants at Aigues-Mortes in August 1893 is the most tragic case in point.[38]

The question of immigrant acculturation is thus tied up with cultural, political, and economic factors. At the same time, indigenous evaluation of that acculturation varied over time. Whereas in the United States a debate over the relative merits of an "old" (Western and Northern European) immigration versus the "new" (Southern and Eastern European) immigration took place at the end of the nineteenth century, in France the comparable images of "new" and "old" immigrant waves occurred later on and in two stages.

First, by the 1930s, when the depression led to xenophobic reactions and discriminatory legislation, the pre-1914 immigrants seemed to have melted into French society with little trace. Antipathies were now aimed at the Italians, Poles, and Polish Jews. Yet these latter new immigrants in France between the wars would in turn become old, integrated, and less subject to attack once the decolonization period brought yet more new immigrants to the Hexagon after World War II. The constant renewal of immigrant waves may have favored the acculturation of the previous population, although it remains to be seen how far acculturation will be permitted for the twentieth-century colonial immigrants.

Indeed, France is renowned for her "cultural homogeneity," which was reflected in assimilatory politics with regard to immigrants up until the 1950s.[39] This attitude was consistent with the factors favoring immigration in the first place and particularly the perceived need to "fill the void." Whether France was enthusiastic about immigration or resigned to it as a response to the low birth rate, the country quickly realized that the immigrants had come to stay and would become more than just statistics increasing the overall population. To the extent that the immigrant population before World War I was a Western European one, this did not present too great a problem, and in retrospect those Belgians, Spaniards, Italians, and even the later-arriving Poles have become well-integrated into the French population.

The question remains, Why are there virtually no Spanish or Polish restaurants in Paris, culinary hegemony in France being perhaps but one symbol of cultural hegemony? (Italian restaurants have always been abundant, but for reasons that have less to do with the Italian community than with the possibilities of the restaurant business.) The point is that the old immigrants to France have become acculturated without maintaining the ethnic communities that one finds in the United States. Perhaps this is because their Western European cultures were too similar to French society. More likely, however, it is because acculturation in France and acculturation in the United States have been very different experiences.

The "modèle américain" of cultural pluralism, which allowed ethnic groups to survive "beyond the melting pot," has been juxtaposed to the French model of cultural homogeneity.[40] Pressures toward cultural unification in France, one of the oldest *nation*-states, have existed since the Capetians and have been exercised over French regional groups as well as over foreigners. Cultural unity after Napoleon was reinforced by political centralization in the nineteenth century. Consequently, the Belgian, Italian, Spanish, and Polish communities in France have largely adopted French society and the universal values of the civilization which it represents, as their own. Little margin for cultural individualism was available in French society. Even the Frenchification of Eastern European Jews occurred to a more encompassing extent than the Americanization of those who went to the United States.

Ultimately the pre-World War I immigrants did indeed do what they were hoped to do: fill the void. That void was in fact culturally specific, but to the extent that the immigrants joined French society, they had served their purpose.

NOTES

1. See, in particular, the recent works of Michael J. Piore, *Birds of Passage* (New York: Cambridge University Press, 1979); Georges Tapinos, *L'Economie des migrations internationales* (Paris: Presses de la Fondation Nationale des Sciences Politiques, 1974); Christian Mercier, *Les Déracinés du Capital: Immigration et Accumulation* (Lyon: Presses Universitaires de Lyon, 1974); as well as William H. McNeill and Ruth S. Adams, eds., *Human Migration: Patterns and Policies* (Bloomington, Indiana University Press, 1978),

and particularly Aristide Zolberg's article there, "International Migration Policies in a Changing World System," pp. 241–86.

2. See Gary S. Cross, "Toward Social Peace and Prosperity: The Politics of Immigration in France During the Era of World War I," *French Historical Studies* 11 (Fall 1980): 610–32; and his *Immigrant Workers in Industrial France: The Making of a New Labor Class* (Philadelphia: Temple University Press, 1983); cf. Joseph Lugand, *L'Immigration des ouvriers étrangers en France et les enseignements de la guerre* (Paris: Librairies-Imprimeries Réunies, 1919), p. 55, who argues that the lessons of the war "convergent toutes vers une condamnation du libéralisme économique et vers une formule interventionniste," and Louis Chevalier, *Problèmes français de l'immigration* (Paris: Les Cours de Droit, 1947), p. 58, who argues that there were some controls after the war but no real policy. See also Jean-Charles Bonnet, *Les Pouvoirs publics et l'immigration dans l'entre-deux guerres* (Lyon: Centre d'Histoire économique et social de la région lyonnaise 7, Université de Lyon II, 1976), who also emphasizes the lack of a coherent policy.

3. In this regard I differ with Richard Kuisel's emphasis in the first chapter of his otherwise excellent *Capitalism and the State in Modern France* (Cambridge: Cambridge University Press, 1981), in which he maintains that the liberal order before World War I remained intact (in order to better contrast it with state intervention in the 1930–1950 period). Kuisel seems to define state intervention largely as "macro-economic management" (p. 29), which, of course, he does not find before 1914. I would argue that the move toward state intervention as well as employer concertation was already taking place before World War I particularly with respect to labor relations and labor needs, and that the motives underlying this move were the same that Kuisel emphasizes for the later period: self-examination; worry over national decline in the face of demographic problems; the Franco-Prussian War; growing industrial competition from the United States, Great Britain, and Germany; and so on. The industrial reports of the World's Fairs in Paris in 1889 and 1900 are important testimony in this regard. See note 10.

4. *Congrès international de l'intervention des pouvoirs publics dans l'émigration et l'immigration, tenu à Paris, les 12, 13 et 14 août 1889* (Paris: Bibliothèque des Annales Economiques Société d'Etudes Scientifiques, 1890) (hereafter cited as *Congrès*), p. 142, emphasis added.

5. See Julius Isaac, *Economics of Migration* (New York: Oxford University Press, 1947), pp. 41–48, on "frictional obstacles" to free labor migration.

6. Hilde Wander, *The Importance of Emigration for the Solution of Population Problems in Western Europe* (The Hague: Martinus Nijhoff, 1951), p. 51. Although the classic interpretation of French economic development has relied heavily on slow demographic growth to explain France's relative backwardness compared to its industrializing competitors in the late nineteenth century, newer interpretations have challenged this idea on two grounds: first that in absolute terms, French economic development proceeded apace and second that, given the low birth rate, per capita production was not so bad after all. For a discussion of the relation between demographic and economic growth in France in this period, see Fernand Braudel and Ernest Labrousse, eds., *Histoire économique et sociale de la France*, tome 4, vol. 1: *Années 1880–1914* (Paris: Presses Universitaires de France, 1979), pp. 21–30. Regardless of whether demographic sluggishness was *the* cause for slow relative industrial growth, what is important is that many contemporaries thought it was and furthermore linked the issue to that of immigration.

7. Chevalier, *Problèmes français*, p. 52; see also Georges Mauco, *Les étrangers en France* (Paris: Armand Colin, 1932), p. 18.

8. Jean Mesnaud de Saint-Paul, *De l'Immigration étrangère en France considérée au point de vue économique* (Paris: Arthur Rousseau, 1902), pp. 79–81; cf. E. Levasseur, *Questions ouvrières et industrielles en France sous la Troisième République* (Paris: Arthur Rousseau, 1907), pp. 280–95.

9. Mauco, *Les étrangers*, p. 20.

10. Alfred Picard, gen. ed., *Exposition universelle internationale de 1889 à Paris: Rapports du Jury international*, Classe 36: *Habillement des deux sexes*, by Albert Leduc (Paris: Imprimerie Nationale for the Ministère du Commerce, de l'Industrie et des Colonies, 1891), pp. 25, 32–33; Gaston Worth, *La Couture et la confection des vêtements de femmes* (Paris: Imprimerie Chaix, 1895), pp. 95–96.

11. Mesnaud de Saint-Paul, *De l'Immigration*, p. 25; cf. *Congrès*, p. 60.

12. Prince de Cassano, *Procès-verbaux sommaires du Congrès international de l'intervention des pouvoirs publics dans l'émigration et l'immigration, tenu à Paris du 12 au 14 août 1889 (Exposition Universelle Internationale de 1889)* (Paris: Imprimerie Nationale for the Ministère du Commerce, de l'Industrie et des Colonies, 1890), p. 11.

13. Mauco, *Les étrangers*, pp. 58–59; Yves Le Febvre, *L'ouvrier étranger et la protection du travail national* (Paris: C. Jacques et Cie., 1901), pp. 28–29; Gaston Chandèze, *De l'Intervention des Pouvoirs publics dans l'Emigration et l'Immigration au XIXe siècle* (Paris: Imprimerie Paul Dupont, 1898), pp. 118–22.

14. Police report entitled, "Les réfugiés révolutionnaires russes à Paris," pp. 12–15, F⁷12894, Archives Nationales, Paris.

15. Mesnaud de Saint-Paul, *De l'Immigration*, pp. 13, 136, 59.

16. Mauco, *Les étrangers*, p. 38; De Cassano, *Procès-verbaux*, p. 9.

17. Ministère de la Justice, *Code de la Nationalité française* (Melun: Imprimerie Administrative, 1946), 1:62–66.

18. De Cassano, *Procès-verbaux*, p. 25.

19. *Résultats statistiques du recensement de la population—1911* (Paris: Imprimerie Nationale, 1913), vol. 1, part 1, p. 41.

20. De Cassano, *Procès-verbaux*, p. 25.

21. Ibid., p. 8.

22. As for the immigration of "Russian subjects," see *The Pletzl of Paris; Jewish Immigrant Workers in the Belle Epoque* (New York: Holmes & Meier, 1985; Paris: Fayard, 1985).

23. Maurice Didion, *Les Salariés étrangers en France* (Paris: V. Giard & E. Brière, 1911), p. 9.

24. Louis Chevalier, *Classes laborieuses et classes dangereuses* (Paris: Librairie Général Française, 1978).

25. Georges Dupeux, "L'immigration en France de la fin du XVIIIe siècle à nos jours" (report of a Centre National de la Recherche Scientifique conference on this subject held in Montpellier in October 1972, hereafter cited as CNRS, 1972), in Commission internationale de l'Histoire des mouvements sociaux et des structures sociales, *Les Migrations internationales de la fin du XVIIIe siècle à nos jours* (Paris: CNRS, 1980), pp. 165–66.

26. Ibid., p. 166. See Céline Azas, "Migrants espagnols dans le Biterrois, 1886–1934" (thèse de IIIe cycle, Université de Paris-V, 1981); and J. Fornairon, "Les Etrangers d'origine méditerranéenne en Languedoc Roussillon: 1850 à nos jours" (Paper presented at CNRS, 1972), pp. 6–8.

27. Dupeux, "L'immigration," p. 167. See Rolande Trempé, "La Main d'oeuvre étrangère dans les mines françaises de 1914 à 1958" (Paper presented at CNRS, 1972).

28. Cross, "Toward Social Peace," pp. 615–16.

29. Cross, *Immigrant Workers in Industrial France*, chapter 3.

30. Braudel and Labrousse, *Histoire économique*, p. 259.

31. In 1926 the Italians comprised 32 percent of all immigrants in France, while the Belgians only accounted for 14 percent. Next came the Spaniards (13 percent) and the Poles (12 percent). Cross, "Toward Social Peace," p. 632.

32. See Alain Girard and Jean Stoetzel, *Français et immigrés: L'attitude française, l'adaptation des Italiens et des Polonais*, INED-Travaux et Documents, Cahiers 19 et 20 (Paris: Presses Universitaires de France, 1953, 1954); Ralph Schor, "L'opinion française et les étrangers en France, 1919–39" (Doctoral thesis, Université de Provence, Aix-Marseille I, 1980), the recent book by Gérard Noiriel, *Longwy: Immigrés et prolétaires, 1880–1980* (Paris: Presses Univérsitaires de France, 1984) on Italian immigrant workers in Longwy and Janine Ponty's work in progress on Polish immigrants to the north of France between the two world wars.

33. Christiane Mora, "Les milieux agricoles et l'immigration rurale dans le Sud-Ouest de la France entre les deux guerres mondiales" (Paper presented at CNRS, 1972), p. 7, particularly noting the similarity of Italian to the Gascon dialect.

34. Azas, "Migrants espagnols," pp. 290–303, 354, 403; Pierre Milza, *Français et Italiens à la fin du XIXe siècle* (Rome: Ecole Française de Rome, 1981), ch. 10.

35. See Emile Témime's interesting analysis of these factors in "La colonie espagnole à Marseille de 1890 à 1936 (implantation réelle ou migration provisoire)" (Paper presented at CNRS, 1972). Interestingly, what Témime does not find in the urban environment Azas does find in the rural case.

36. Azas, "Migrants espagnols," pp. 404, 362, 369; cf. Milza, *Français et Italiens*, p. 833; and Dominique Schnapper's analysis of contemporary Italian immigrants who "after ten years [in France] have lost all of their specific characteristics." "Quelques réflexions sur l'assimilation comparée des travailleurs émigrés italiens et des Juifs en France," *Bulletin, Société Française de Sociologie* 3 (July 1976), 11–18.

37. See Raoul Girardet, *Le nationalisme français, 1871–1914* (Paris: Armand Colin, 1966).

38. Preceded by anti-Italian violence in 1882, the "chasse à l'italienne" or rampage through the Italian neighborhood of Aigues-Mortes in 1893 was sparked by a quarrel between French and Italian workers in the salt mines. Mounting tensions due to the degeneration of Franco-Italian relations over Tunisia also furnished the background to this violent manifestation of labor competition which resulted in the death of between eight (according to official reports) and fifty Italians and the wounding of over one hundred. See R. Paris, "L'Italia fuori d'Italia," *Storia d'Italia*, vol. 4, tome 1 (Turin: Einaudi, 1975), pp. 525–52, published in French in *Pluriel*, no. 36 (1983) pp. 92–145; T. Vertone, "Antécédents et causes des événements d'Aigues-Mortes," *Affari Sociali internazionali* no. 3–4 (1977), 107–38; and Jean-Michel Gaillard, "Les manifestations de xénophobie anti-italienne dans le Gard à la fin du XIXe siècle," (Paper presented at CNRS, 1972).

39. As discussed by René Gallissot in Dupeux, 'L'immigration,' pp. 172–73.

40. For example, Dominique Schnapper, "Centralisme et fédéralisme culturels: les émigrés italiens en France et aux Etats-Unis," *Annales E.S.C.* (October 1974), 1141–59.

7

LABOR MIGRATION OF SKILLED WORKERS, ARTISANS, AND TECHNICIANS AND TECHNOLOGY TRANSFER BETWEEN SWEDEN AND GERMANY BEFORE WORLD WAR I

Claudius H. Riegler

Research into transnational labor migration within Europe by skilled workers and technicians and the resulting transfer of knowledge is only just beginning. This may be explained by the difficulty of integrating the highly achievement-oriented migration of qualified industrial workers and engineers to undergo training into the heterogeneous patterns of European migration in the late nineteenth century. Labor migration by skilled industrial workers and technicians is, to some degree, comparable to the traditional travels of craftsmen, but it nonetheless had its own characteristics. Parallel to the process of industrialization, internal migration in most European countries involved working people seeking a better standard of living. It led to an increase of production at the local and regional levels.[1] According to Thistlethwaite, this "close relationship between migration and occupation" was already apparent before America's attraction as an overseas migration goal began to take effect.[2] Because of the division of the European continent into numerous nation-states, these movements involved (labor) migration across national boundaries even before the beginning of the nineteenth century.[3] It is, however, advisable to avoid speaking of the internationalization of labor markets until the advent of cross-border migration by free wage workers at the beginning of the period of high industrialization.[4] Beneath this threshold, the limits of which are difficult to determine, the transnational migration in search of new labor markets can be discussed. This opening of labor markets means the comprehensive and partly permanent redistribution of people in their function as workers. It is one aspect of the disintegration of the pre-capitalist method of production. This deep-reaching process of mobilization must not be regarded as the inevitable triumph of the most rational form of human economic activity.[5] It is a deeply antagonistic process, which has had functional economic, political, and social effects that continue up to the present day.[6]

Especially during the period in which freedom of movement was virtually unlimited (1860–1914), migration between northern and central Europe was frequent, it was goal-directed and geographically highly complex. People were

I wish to acknowledge my deep appreciation for the comments and suggestions that Dirk Hoerder and Christiane Harzig proposed for the final version of this essay. Of course, the final product is, for better or for worse, my sole responsibility.

all on the move for new jobs—whether they had been recruited or were taking a chance at finding them. This "confusion" was a marked feature of the dynamics of disintegration of the traditional rural society; it resembled the English model of industrialization.[7]

Temporary and permanent migration by skilled workers and technicians formed one element of this process. In Sweden it began at an earlier date than overseas emigration to the United States, which can be characterized by the following phases: the introductory phase (c. 1850–1869), the growth phase (c. 1870–1883), the saturation phase (c. 1884–1892), and the regression phase (c. 1893–1930).[8] It reached its climax during the saturation and regression phases of emigration overseas. In the years from 1850 to 1930, a total of about 1.5 million people emigrated, about 300,000 of them went to European countries. A total of about 40,000 Swedish labor migrants were residing in Germany in this period.

The first part of this essay gives a brief account of the migration of craftsmen, skilled workers, and technicians to German-speaking areas before the German Reich was established in 1871. Parts 2 through 4 deal with the recruitment of labor in Sweden by German firms between 1868 and 1911, the migration of individual journeymen and skilled workers between 1870 and 1914, and migration by mostly skilled industrial workers and technicians seeking further training. This analysis is based mainly on unpublished Swedish sources containing material on specific aspects of continental migration by individuals. In addition, extensive use was made of the standard Swedish and German social history literature.

MIGRATION OF CRAFTSMEN, SKILLED WORKERS, AND TECHNICIANS TO GERMANY BEFORE 1871

The migration of trained workers from Sweden to Germany from the beginning of the modern age to the establishment of the German Reich involved comparatively small numbers.

As a result of decades of war and confusion during the first half of the seventeenth century, Swedish towns and cities had been invaded by German-speaking journeymen and master craftsmen. The size of this group of foreign skilled workers gradually declined by the end of that century. Around 1650, 42 percent of all journeymen craftsmen in Stockholm were German migrants, but this figure had decreased to about 33 percent by 1689. In the wake of this labor migration, "fashionable innovations and technical improvements" reached Sweden from the continent.[9] The eighteenth century brought a rise in the number of Swedish journeymen coming to central Europe. Increases were registered in all occupations. For those occupations that relied on close contact for information about technical innovations in Germany, migration was supported by the state. Hence around the middle of the eighteenth century Swedish journeymen gunsmiths were sent to Germany, France, Holland, and England with the support of the Manufakturkontoret (Chamber of Trade) and the Krigskollegium (Ministry of War) "to increase their skills and to learn new methods." Since the Swedish (and also the Danish) craft system was based on the guild system of German towns and cities, the German-speaking countries of central Europe as well as Denmark were especially suitable destinations for journeymen. In some cases a stay in one of these countries was compulsory and brought a great deal of prestige.

Special routes and destinations were characteristic for each occupation, and up to the second half of the nineteenth century they were generally followed.[10] The main routes were via Danish islands or Jutland to Lübeck and Hamburg, where they split, with the members of some occupations heading eastward to the towns of Mecklenburg, Pomerania, and the Baltic states and from there often via St. Petersburg and Finland back to Sweden. Others traveled via Hanover and Westphalia to the Rhineland and then southward as far as Nuremberg and Augsburg. Returning after an absence frequently as long as ten years, they received the respect due to widely traveled men skilled in their trades.

In many of the Swedish guilds (as in Germany) it was still compulsory for journeymen to travel well into the nineteenth century. In spite of the vehement protests of parliament (*Riksdag*), the Swedish government was unable to abolish this custom. It was part of the requirements for qualification in various occupations, was "highly important for finding work," and furthered transfer of technology, for example, in the Swedish brewing industry.

At the end of their apprenticeship, the vast majority of Swedish brewers went to Germany to work and study for several years. Two returnees introduced the new method of bottom fermentation to their home country in the late 1840s.[11] Not until 1877, however, did the first Swede qualify as a master brewer upon return form Germany, where he had received most of his training at the Faculty of Brewing at the College of Technology at Weihenstephan near Munich. This man was Carl Gustaf Piehl, a member of a family that had immigrated from Pomerania during the first half of the nineteenth century. Previously he had worked in breweries in Hamburg and Karlsruhe and found temporary employment in Oslo and London. Other brewers spent periods in Weihenstephan during the 1880s, and when they returned they immediately obtained influential positions in the large number of Stockholm breweries.

The procedure for the approval of craftsmen's travels in Sweden was similar to that of the German guilds. When a journeyman was ready to set off, he had to take leave of the master who had employed him. Then he applied to the master of his guild for a traveling card and—from the 1680s on—he needed a certificate of good conduct, which he then handed in to the municipal authorities in order to obtain a passport.

Even after the abolition of the Swedish guild system in 1846, journeymen continued to travel, but in 1844 the government issued a decree against "vagrancy." It prevented the granting of a passport to journeymen who had had a job for less than three months if work was still available locally. With the introduction of general freedom of trade in 1864, the number of journeymen going on traditional travels began to decline. In spite of the gradual development of an international exchange of ideas via specialized trade publications, people continued to migrate from Sweden to Germany (and vice versa) to look for work or to undergo training. While temporary migration of workers in search of jobs requiring few skills, if any, increased, the international transfer of craft and technical skills, of new forms of work organization, and of innovations in production processes as a result of personal contact continued to be of considerable importance.

RECRUITMENT OF LABOR FOR WORK IN GERMANY

In addition to individual migration based on social patterns, such as guild rules, large-scale campaigns had been launched since the middle of the nineteenth century to recruit workers for industry and construction whenever demand developed in Germany. The occupational composition of the migration changed from servants and agricultural laborers between the end of the 1860s and the middle of the 1880s to industrial workers in the 1890s.

Swedish Workers Employed in the Construction of Railroads, Fortifications, and Ships in Sleswig-Holstein

In the late summer of 1868, 1,200 to 1,500 Swedes, mostly from the southern provinces, arrived in Sleswig-Holstein.[12] No details of their journey south are available, but it may be assumed that in contrast to the mainstream of contemporary migration of agricultural laborers (Gesinde) and servants, most of them came via Denmark (Copenhagen, Korsør). Reportedly, traveling agents, who demanded fees, had provided them with documents assuring "work on railroad construction now in progress and the like." Upon arrival, this proved to be a gross deception. They were not given employment. Many had returned to Sweden by fall 1868, and at the beginning of April 1872 there were only 300 Swedish workers still employed in railroad construction in Sleswig-Holstein. Similarly, Swedish construction workers were recruited in 1868 for the erection of the fortress of Friedrichsort at the entrance of the harbor of Kiel. In November 1871 there were still at least 250 Swedish emigrant workers involved in building fortifications in Kiel. Finally, industrial workers were recruited to replace striking German workers. Unlike the Swedish agricultural laborers and servants scattered over wide areas of the north German plain, this concentrated group of industrial workers formed a closed ethnically unified community that was to have considerable influence on the industrial labor force of Kiel.

The whole labor force of the Norddeutsche Werft near Kiel, demanding increases of 25 Silbergroschen (Sgr.) to one Taler, had struck in September 1871. The strike failed but the majority of the workers later found employment at the Kaiserliche Werft in Kiel. The management of the Norddeutsche Werft, on the other hand, sent an agent to Sweden to recruit workers. This operation was probably carefully planned and deliberately aimed at exploiting the uncertain situation of the workers in Karlskrona, the most important Swedish naval port in the province of Blekinge. Here the shipbuilding industry was in a state of stagnation. Within a short time about 250 Swedish workers—by no means all of them qualified shipbuilding workers—had been recruited. They were given contracts for one year, free passage, and daily wages equivalent to those paid to the German workers before the strike. Hence these Swedish workers were brought to Kiel as strikebreakers by the Norddeutsche Werft in one of the first industrial disputes to occur in the area. Desperate for workers, the shipyard management even recruited Swedes who were "less suitable"—tailors, brick-layers, cabinet makers, painters. The managing director explained that they were given jobs as riveters, work that could be done by anyone who was strong enough. As a result, acculturation was difficult. A few of them, "those who were suffering most from homesickness," were sent back to Sweden at the expense of the shipyard, but the majority remained. A Swedish colony was established consisting of a group of barracks (still used in the 1880s) to house these workers and their wives or German girl friends. At the end of November 1871, a battle with German workers occurred in the streets outside the Swedish quarters because the Swedes refused to join the strike. Several Swedes were injured by stones thrown at them, and it only ended when Prussian soldiers were called in. The unexperienced foreigners were quick to learn, however, and there was a joint strike by German and Swedish shipbuilding workers in April 1872. By that time there were only about 200 Swedes left working for the Norddeutsche Werft. Employers wanted to prevent them from leaving at all cost. They often refused to return to the labor migrants their identification documents. Frequently the Swedish consul had to intervene on their behalf with protests to the local chief of police.

In spite of their relatively high status as much sought after skilled industrial workers in an era of expansion of the imperial economy, the Swedish immigrants were constantly faced with disasters against which they had little or no protection. In November 1872 when gales and high tides devastated the whole of the Baltic coast, the Swedes were to discover the double disadvantage of being members of a foreign labor force. Their quarters were situated in the areas of the harbor that were most susceptible to flooding, however, as foreigners they were not eligible for social welfare. Each of the following winters was to bring a new catastrophe for the inhabitants of the Swedish colony, and in 1872 and 1873 it was only as a result of relief funds collected in Sweden and of the assistance of the Swedish consul that they were able to make some kind of recovery.

In the winter of 1877–1878 the situation of the Swedish construction and shipyard workers in Kiel was particularly grave. The extensions to the naval harbor were almost completed, and a large number of workers, particularly the Swedish labor migrants, were given notice by the Norddeutsche Werft. Their situation was disastrous and left them and their families destitute. The general decline in the German economy made it impossible for many immigrants to stay on. Since they did not receive any kind of assistance, such as return fare or poor funds from the German authorities or their employers, the Swedish public was aroused. For a while the consulate acted as an employment agency, but it had to devote most of its attention to arranging the transport of workers and their families back to Sweden. Frequently wives and children, deserted by their bread-winners, had to apply to the consulate. Prevented from begging by the threat of severe punishment by the German police, the Swedes were forced to take refuge in their consulate. In the spring of 1878 the labor market situation in Kiel turned even worse, and the winter of 1878–1879 completely ruined the majority of the Swedish immigrants in Sleswig-Holstein outside of those in the agricultural sector.

Neither the hopes with which the Swedish workers embarked on this emigration nor the expectation of the Swedish authorities that the population pressure would be reduced were fulfilled. An intensive publicity campaign in *Post-och Inrikes Tidningar* and later in most of the newspapers in central and southern Sweden warned people against emigrating to Germany. For this reason "a large number of young working people" abandoned their plans of emigrating to Germany in search of work at least temporarily.[13] Thus the first period of continuous Swedish industrial migration and intended long-term settlement came to a premature end. The Swedes discovered that they were wanted only to fulfill the typical functions of migrant workers in industrializing economies, that is, to do work that was dangerous, badly paid, and required mobility. After 1880 jobs were available to them especially on the canal projects increasingly being undertaken in North Germany, in railroad construction, and other earthworks. They obtained jobs because they had no families and were prepared to accept constant changes of work place and long periods of unstable living conditions, characteristics that put them at a competitive advantage to German workers, who were less inclined to work far from settlements, from their families and friends. Their numbers increased during the 1880s and 1890s.

Swedish Metalworkers in Stettin and Bremen

From the beginning of August 1886 onward about 400 Swedish workers left Stockholm, Malmö, and other towns for Stettin to work at the Maschinenbauan-stalt and Schiffbauwerft Vulcan (a shipyard), especially in the mechanical engineering department in Bredow. From 1884 to 1885 the size of the Vulcan labor force had doubled to about 5,000. Since wages had stagnated since 1885—fitters, ship's carpenters, and blacksmiths earned between 12 and 21 Reichsmarks per week—this firm as well as other metalworking companies in Stettin continued to hire more workers in 1886. Qualified Swedish metalworkers came over the Baltic to Stettin, partly as a result of active recruitment by the firm and partly "merely as a result of advertisements in Swedish newspapers and without any prior arrangement with the agents of 'Vulcan.' "[14]

According to the Swedish consul-general in Stettin, however, the majority of these 400 workers returned at their own expense by October 1886. Most of the remainder were dismissed in January, April, and June 1887. A few skilled workers attempted to find work in Hamburg and Berlin, but all except one were unsuccessful. Forty migrant workers were given assistance by the consul-general in Stettin. In June 1887 he concluded his report by saying, "that of the 400 Swedish ironworkers engaged by 'Vulcan' last fall there are no more than a dozen still living there now."[15] Most of the dismissed workers returned to Sweden, especially to its industrial center Stockholm, which had been the last stage of their internal migration in search of work before leaving for Germany.

The third major German shipyard to employ Swedish workers was the Weser-Werft in Bremen. In July 1911 the Swedish vice-consul in Bremen reported, "that a certain Koenemann, a language teacher in Helsingborg . . . , has been recruiting metalworkers and also people with other occupations for a major shipbuilder here by making enticing promises of high wages, etc."[16] An unknown number of Swedish workers, among them "even married men" and "a printer," came to Bremen as a result, but after a short time they demanded of the consulate "that they should be taken home immediately." A few days later the Swedish Foreign Ministry informed the district government of Malmöhus, the authority responsible, of the recruiting campaign and of the dissatisfaction expressed by the recruited workers who had gone to Bremen. In the middle of July the Swedish vice-consul then sent a report on an agreement with the management of the Weser-Werft. He stated that "most of the people then carried on working, but others stopped work and have left." With regard to the way in which the workers had been recruited he wrote:

As there is no written evidence available, it was unfortunately no longer possible to determine whether the foreman sent by the management of the shipyard to Copenhagen to recruit workers or his friend Koenemann, the language teacher in Helsingborg already mentioned, promised the people higher wages, etc., or whether there was a misunderstanding on the part of the Swedish workers. In any case, some kind of precise agreement in either written or printed form would have been of some use to the Swedes in the negotiations.[17]

No information is available on the subsequent fate of the workers who stayed on at the shipyard.

MIGRATION BY INDIVIDUAL JOURNEYMEN AND SKILLED WORKERS, 1870–1914

Parallel to the recruitment of large groups of workers in Sweden, migration of individuals took place. After 1870 more and more Swedish skilled workers went to Germany to look for work or undergo further training. Glovers, cork cutters, and those in the tobacco industry could rely on both material assistance for the journey from their craft unions in Sweden as well as on a friendly reception and financial assistance from the German unions. Blomkvist called this information and support system an "Internationale en miniature."[18] Looking for work in Denmark and Germany was accepted as a means of achieving higher wages in Sweden in the long term and of ensuring workers on strike of further employment in their occupation. Hence sixty-five glovers from Scania received financial support from their union in 1876 to enable them to seek work in Denmark and Germany after their strike in Lund had been called off without achieving any improvements. A worsening of the situation on the craft-oriented labor market as a result of the economic situation could, according to Blomkvist, be countered by means of a comprehensive international system of providing jobs that was based on the trade unions. The periodicals of the Swedish glovers regularly printed detailed information on job opportunities in Germany. As a result of the good international relations, many local union organizations in Sweden had a copy of the German glovers' publication. According to a resolution passed by the general assembly of the German glovers' union in 1877, Scandinavian workers had the right to claim assistance for their traveling expenses.

Evidently considerable numbers of Swedish (and Danish) skilled workers poured into Northern Germany during the 1870s. In 1878 earlier migrants to that area suggested to their newly arrived compatriots to move to the labor markets of Central and Southern Germany in order to avoid forcing down wages in the north. The German unions welcomed the Swedish skilled workers since they preferred qualified foreigners to unqualified Germans. They particularly wanted to maintain their level of qualifications and so preserve their occupational ethos. In contrast to this positive attitude to foreign workers, there were some incidents similar to the events of 1871 in the shipbuilding industry of Kiel, but they remained isolated cases.

Swedish tobacco workers were attracted to Denmark (Copenhagen) by advertisements and recruiting trips in 1874 and 1875. In Malmö there was a tobacco industry of some importance that involved all of the traditional processes and products and that continued to expand until 1875. In that year the first strikes for more pay occurred. Their aim was to achieve the same piecework rates as were normally paid in Copenhagen, and they went on until the beginning of 1876. These strikes by the "first socialist-inspired trade union movement in Sweden," which had been founded on the initiative of Danish workers, were unsuccessful in spite of the considerable amount of solidarity shown by the Danish and German unions. Up to one hundred workers left the factories of Malmö and were recruited for work in Copenhagen. Others went to Germany, where they obtained employment mainly in the tobacco industry of Hamburg and the surrounding area.

Skilled Swedish cigar and tobacco workers trained in the factories of Stockholm, Göteborg, and Malmö, had already emigrated to Hamburg before 1868.[19]

In the 1870s this flow increased. As a result of the vulnerability of the industry to financial crises, however, there were frequent dismissals, which always affected the Swedish immigrants in particular. In addition, the job opportunities for foreigners were limited owing to the custom of employing large numbers of "women, people on probation and convicts."[20] The strike of 3,000 tobacco workers from 28 factories in Hamburg, Altona, and Wandsbek, which lasted from November 1890 to March 1891, also precluded employment opportunities.

Between 1882 and 1894, thirty-eight cigar workers who had come from Hamburg were given assistance by the Swedish consulate in Lübeck either in obtaining work or in returning to Sweden. Many had been dismissed because of a decline in production and of labor conflicts. Lack of qualifications may have been a further reason for dismissals. A destitute, skilled immigrant worker from Malmö stated in 1903 that "but as a result of my lack of skill in the German method of working (using your hand and not a mold) I could not get a permanent job."[21] The tobacco industry in Hamburg also employed female migrants. A Swedish woman came to Hamburg in 1893 and found work in a cigar factory but was dismissed in 1894 when she became pregnant. In many other North German towns Swedish tobacco workers found employment. One reason for this emigration was the change over in the Swedish tobacco industry to the employment of women and unskilled laborers.[22] The Danish capital of Copenhagen, where almost all of the migrants had first worked, acted as a kind of springboard for this transnational emigration. Frequent unemployment in Germany forced most of them to return to Sweden.

Though cork cutters had no well-developed network of international contacts such as those of the glovers and the tobacco workers, it was not unusual for unemployed men in this craft to seek work in Germany. In 1872, five Swedish cork cutters were working in Lübeck, others were living in Hanover and in the towns of Mecklenburg. But they had to rely for help on the consulate in Lübeck when they were unemployed and destitute. One of them "had been expelled by the police in Breslau as he was a socialist and arrived with a passport containing a ban."[23]

These examples do not cover the full range of workers of many occupations who reacted to the lack of opportunities in Sweden by emigrating to Germany. An examination of the official lists of Swedish migrants to Germany reveals the diversity of these occupations. For example, there were a considerable number of male immigrants employed in industrial work in the towns of Mecklenburg, especially as factory and building workers, cork cutters, basket makers, brewers, and in other craft occupations. The list of all the Swedes resident in Mecklenburg-Schwerin compiled in 1892 on the basis of the census of 1890 shows that about four-fifths of them worked in agriculture, and that less than 20 percent of all immigrants had settled in the towns of Mecklenburg, where their main concentration was in the coastal towns of Rostock and Wismar.[24] The high proportion of craftsmen involved (shoemakers, tanners, brewers, cork cutters, and glass-makers) reveals that the immigration to towns originally consisted of temporary migration by in-transit journeymen. This pattern is confirmed by some examples taken from records of people requiring assistance: in 1886 a twenty-six-year-old Swedish distillery worker from Ramdala (Blekinge) who had spent two years in Germany; in 1897 a lithographic printer who had been in Schwerin; in 1877 a forty-two-year-old quarry worker from Blekinge who had turned down a job because of low pay. In 1903 a twenty-three-year-old grinder who had worked in Karlshamm and then as a mechanic on a steamship had to be helped to return to Sweden after a short period of casual work in Rostock.

In 1873 there were over forty women from Sweden working at a paper mill in Oldesloe. In the same year a number of male and female emigrants from Sweden were sent to work at a spinning mill in Linden near Hanover. Individual Swedish workers were to be found, for example, at a factory in Freiburg/Baden in 1869, at a sugar refinery in Itzehoe in 1875, at a match factory in the Hanover area around 1884, and at a cement works in 1887. Others worked as lithographers (in Schwerin); painters (in Neustrelitz and Hanover); rope makers, tilers, bakers (in Kiel); butchers, cabinetmakers and brewery workers (in Lübeck); dyers, tanners, bricklayers, and gardeners (in Neumünster). As late as 1897 stonemasons from the Swedish province of Blekinge came to seek work in Lüneburg. Glass-blowers came to look for employment in Northern Germany around 1885 and at the turn of the century because of the lack of work in the large number of Swedish glassworks. Finally, there were over two hundred Swedes working at the rubber factory in Harburg in 1879.

After 1877 large numbers of steel- and metalworkers came to Germany. They found work in the foundries of the Ruhr district (Dortmund and Mülheim) and Northern Germany (Magdeburg, Hanover, Bremen, Harburg, Hamburg, and Lübeck). Most of the metalworkers came via Copenhagen, where they obtained their first temporary jobs and then went southward overland via Flensburg. Among them were grinders and filers who had previously worked for specialized firms in Stockholm.

The decade from around 1899 to 1909 was a time of increasing labor conflicts in Sweden.[25] Especially during this period transnational migration became increasingly common among skilled workers affected by lockouts. Of around 9,000 Swedes who were permanently resident in Germany during the first decade of the twentieth century or who were constantly shuttling back and forth between Sweden and Germany in search of work, 1,100 were still engaged in agricultural work, 2,700 in industry and mining (in this case especially metalworkers), 1,100 in the transport industry, and 1,000 in other occupations.[26] These migrants were also extremely mobile between various regions and towns of Germany. On the initiative of the Danes, a fund was therefore set up in 1899 to provide assistance for migrant workers from the whole of Scandinavia (Den Skandinaviske Central-Understöttelses-Kasse i Udlandet), which had local branches in eleven Swiss and twenty-one German towns, published its own periodical for its members, and in 1912 had about 1,000 members, most of them Danish. The variety and the significance of this temporary migration may be outlined by taking Swedish skilled workers in Hamburg and Berlin as examples.

In 1871 the Swedes (including Norwegians), with their almost 1,400 members, made up the largest group of foreigners in Hamburg. (See Table 7.1.) Until 1885 the Swedish population grew in proportion to the increase in the whole of the resident foreign population. In contrast to the decline in the number of Swedish citizens in other North German states, their share of the population continued to increase slightly until 1910. These figures indicate that although migration from Sweden to the industrial metropolis of Northern Germany was increased by the two great waves of rural emigration from Sweden to Germany (1868–1873 and 1879–1885), the driving forces behind it were relatively independent of these waves. In particular, the constant migration from the surrounding areas (Sleswig-Holstein, Mecklenburg, and Hanover) to Hamburg and other towns may explain this increase. After World War I, in spite of the high rate of unemployment in Sweden during the 1920s, migration decreased. For the period 1910–1925 the official statistical report stated that "the greatest decline has affected the citizens of the three Nordic countries, Denmark, Sweden and Norway, whose share fell from 23.6 percent in 1910 to 15 percent in 1925."[27]

Nonagricultural workers began to migrate from Sweden in the 1870s. According to a police report of 1879, about 170 Swedish workers registered in Hamburg every year. The decline in the number of male immigrant servants was

Table 7.1
The Swedish Population of Hamburg Compared to Total Foreign Population, 1871–1910

Total Foreign Population		Number of Swedes		
Year	*Total*	*Total*	*Male*	*Female*
1871	7,348	1,364[a]	930	434
1875	9,236	– [b]	–	–
1880	10,844	1,538	–	–
1885	13,228	2,403	1,387	1,016
1890	16,748	2,020	1,131	889
1895	14,576	1,460	793	667
1900	16,299	1,480	845	635
1905	22,855	1,618	925	693
1910	28,149	1,647	940	707

Note: [a] Includes Norwegians.
[b] The census of 1875 did not record the nationality and place of birth of foreigners.

Source: Statistik des Hamburgischen Staates, vol. 4 ff. (Hamburg 1872ff.)

to be explained by the fact that men "were anxious to join the class of free wage laborers which enabled them to find jobs on projects involving earthworks."[28]

In 1879 the employment prospects of immigrants in Hamburg were extremely bleak, as a report of the consul-general in Hamburg demonstrates. The building of the central prison in Fuhlsbüttel and dredging of the Elbe River had almost been completed. The earthworks at the Dammtor area in Hamburg and the beginning of the construction of the railroad from Hamburg to Cuxhaven were hardly likely to provide enough jobs for Swedish immigrants, as there was a broad stream of workers coming from other German states and Poland at the same time. The situation in the factories was just as hopeless. Only in Harburg, which then belonged to Hanover and where an increasing amount of capital from Hamburg was invested in the 1870s, did about 200 Swedes manage to find work in the rubber factories.

Long before 1868 Swedish seamen had sought work in Hamburg on British, German, and Norwegian merchant ships. Access to employment on board the ships was via the German recruiting agents, so-called *Schlafbaase*. These used the same kind of organization and business methods as the contemporary agencies for agricultural laborers and domestic servants. When "an unusually large number of Swedish and Norwegian seamen" arrived in the fall of 1884, for the first time the consul-general circulated a warning to prevent further inflow of seamen.[29] But the temporary migration to Hamburg of men from nonmaritime trades in search of a berth continued after the turn of the century. The records contain open recommendations from the years 1901 and 1904 urging unemployed metalworkers and unskilled laborers from Stockholm to go to Hamburg and seek work on board ships.

Around 1880, when foreign workers in the areas surrounding Hamburg were often forcibly sent home, city authorities also increasingly deported Swedish immigrants to their home country merely on the grounds that they were destitute. The case of a servant woman who came to Hamburg in 1880 from a nearby area in search of work and who had to pay bond, as well as the inability of three Norwegian foremen at the (Norwegian-owned) shoeing-nail factory of Sande near Bergedorf to pay a bond of 100 Reichsmarks, illustrates the methods adopted by the Hamburg police at that time to limit the inflow of workers from abroad by administrative means.

Although the Swedish consul-general in a detailed comparison of the German and Swedish economies bitterly criticized the fact that "we export our people because we do not know how to occupy them" and although competition for jobs increased considerably, labor migration from Sweden to Hamburg continued even after 1900.[30] Especially in periods of high unemployment but also when idled by labor disputes in Sweden, industrial workers sought work on the urban labor markets of Germany, especially in Berlin and Hamburg. The brief reports submitted by the consul-general in Hamburg to the Swedish Foreign Ministry show that a large number of the Swedish migrants failed in their attempts to gain access to the Hamburg labor market. In 1908, during a period of increased emigration and unemployment as a result of the growing labor conflicts that came to a climax in Sweden with mass lockouts and a general strike, the consulate-general became the center of the daily stream of destitute Swedes who had vainly spent long periods of time looking for work ashore or on board ship.

In Berlin Swedish migrants tried to find work especially in the service and metalworking industries. While no detailed information is available until the turn of the century, the subsequent period is covered by a number of surveys and reports.

In January 1887 Swedish metalworkers who had lost their jobs in Stettin went to Berlin. Since the middle of the 1880s small numbers of destitute Swedish workers in Berlin had required the help of Swedish consulates to return home. Before the turn of the century mainly craftsmen and members of service occupations were involved, but soon skilled industrial workers also began to be affected by the insecurity of the Berlin labor market. Migration to other German towns also provided no relief, and as early as 1901 the Swedish consul-general started to issue serious warnings against coming to Berlin. Unlike in Hamburg, there was no possibility of finding alternative employment in shipping, agriculture, canal construction, or on coastal dikes.

In 1906 the Swedes in Berlin were, according to the Swedish envoy, "for the most part" engineers. In view of the increasing migration of workers to Berlin, the consulate again warned in December 1907:

Since large numbers of Swedish workers have been here in recent months in search of work and they have had to return home without finding any, and as crowds of workers returning from America are now expected, it is to be feared that the situation will continue to deteriorate.[31]

At the beginning of 1908 the Swedish embassy reported the announcement of an employment program by the Prussian Ministry of Public Works. It was aimed especially at the construction industry, which had around 30,000 unemployed, and "as far as possible the use of foreign workers [was to be] avoided."[32] The consul in Lübeck demanded that information on the lockout planned by the building industry in Berlin on 1 April 1908 "must be given to Swedish workers and the public labor exchanges in Sweden."[33] In spite of these warnings, in the fall of 1908 every day "a large number of unemployed and destitute Swedish subjects who have traveled here" came to the consulate in Berlin.[34] This flow of migrants had not eased by spring 1909 on account of the continuing unemployment caused by the worsening of the labor conflict in Sweden. In the summer of that year warnings against migrating to Berlin were again sent to Sweden, where the mass lockout and general strike had laid off around 300,000 workers.

A summary of emigration from Sweden to the various regions of Germany yields an extremely heterogeneous picture. While agricultural laborers and servants went to Schleswig-Holstein, Mecklenburg, and the northern areas of the Prussian province of Hanover up to the end of the 1890s, Swedish immigration to the North German towns and cities consisted partly of highly qualified skilled workers and technicians. Between these two extremes Swedes found employment in practically every kind of occupation. Individual migrants wandered as far afield as Saxony and Silesia, and others even went to Southern Baden. Active recruitment took place in Sweden for rural workers as well as for shipbuilding and metalworkers. However, the majority sought work on their own, a venture that involved a considerable amount of personal risk. Owing to the nature of sources used here, most of the examples are of migrants who were unsuccessful; however, it is clearly evident that Swedish workers were even more susceptible than Germans to the effects of economic crises on the labor market.

MIGRATION FOR TRAINING PURPOSES

From 1861 onward the Swedish government encouraged labor migration by various groups and offered financial support. In that year the Kommerskollegium for the first time offered travel grants enabling craftsmen to spend periods abroad for the purpose of training. In 1887 grants were also made available to technicians. This temporary migration for training purposes paralleled the movements of urban and rural lower class workers to Denmark, Norway, and Germany in search of employment. The purpose of the grants and subsequent migration was to give workers more comprehensive training in their occupations and to introduce them to methods and new developments not yet practised in Sweden. The applicants for the travel grants were highly motivated craftsmen and skilled workers who wanted to visit the continental countries, Britain, and the United States. Most of them had permanent jobs in Sweden. They had detailed knowledge of where training could be undertaken, what it involved, and what employment conditions to expect.

Laborers and Craftsmen

The extent and importance of Swedish migration for training purposes and its importance for the development of craft work and industry in Sweden has already been described in detail.[35] Further information will help to show migration trends and will illustrate the sudden change that took place in the pattern of Swedish migration to Germany in the late 1880s. Between 1861 and 1907 around 12,000 persons applied for travel grants for training abroad, mainly in European countries. Only a fraction of these were successful. Table 7.2 shows the increase in the number of applications and the attraction exerted by industrial exhibitions and world fairs. The applications frequently included a list of periods spent abroad previously or planned for the future. They provide a good picture of the mobility of craft and industrial workers during this period. Sometimes new applications were even made while workers were still abroad.

Random samples show that from about 1876 on Germany was the main country favored by the applicants. In 1886, for example, it was chosen by 76 of the 165 applicants. In that year the majority, 101 people, came from Stockholm and towns in Central Sweden. Only 17 were from the south, an area which played a dominant role in labor emigration to the continent. When in 1896 it became possible for laborers and technicians already abroad to make collective applications via the Swedish consulates, the largest number came from the consulate in Berlin. The popularity of Germany as a goal continued to increase after the turn of the century.

Technicians and Engineers

A large portion of the 40,000 Swedish migrants to the German labor market between 1850 and 1930 were technicians and engineers.[36] Gårdlund has provided important information on the extent and the effects of their labor migration and on the considerable influence that technical impulses from abroad had on the process and extent of industrialization in Sweden. He emphasized the role played by industrial exhibitions, at which technicians and inventors got to know foreign production processes. In the years when industrialization was making its breakthrough in Sweden (1850–1870), "forward-looking workers and engineers" went to England often for several years at a time to obtain further training. In the subsequent decades more and more Swedish mechanics visited the United States, where the World's Fair of 1876 in Philadelphia proved to be of great interest.[37] On their return the technicians, most of whom had gone to America on state grants, were very enthusiastic in their verdicts on new methods across the Atlantic.[38] Gårdlund notes "an ever-increasing interest in American technology and organization." The foremen and workers who had been to the United States played an important role in the "Americanization of the Swedish mechanical engineering industry."[39] Of 23,000 workers in this industry who were interviewed around the turn of the century, 1,423 had spent some time working abroad, 1,043 for more than a year. Six hundred and ninety had been to neighboring countries in Scandinavia, 176 to Germany, 47 to England, and 437 to the United States.

For the period up to 1870 Gårdlund concentrates on the technological and organizational influence exerted by British industry. After that he places more stress on American industry and allots a decisive role to the visits of Swedish technicians to both countries. Without going into further details, he wrote: "By the turn of the century Germany had also become the leading supplier of machines to a number of other Swedish industries, but this did not mean that it had become our master."[40]

While the impact of the increasing export of machinery is well known the influence of large firms and training facilities in Germany on skilled Swedish workers and technicians will be analyzed here.[41] During their stay in Germany, they encountered both new techniques of production and methods of organization that were adopted by Swedish industry upon their return. Gårdlund does not connect organizational innovations with migration, but rather makes them appear to be the ideas of individual managers and theorists. In his comprehensive survey, however, he stresses the importance of periods spent working abroad:

It is difficult to assess the importance of studying and working abroad for engineers in relation to other factors in their training, but it can be said that it was very great. During the period in which Swedish industry was being established and the revolutionary changes which followed, repeatedly decisive impulses were provided by technicians who had been abroad.[42]

Recent research has particularly emphasized the outstanding role played by the recruitment of foreign labor in the development of industrial firms in Europe.[43] Pollard states that access to the most up-to-date technology of rival foreign countries was often vital if firms were to be able to compete.[44] In accordance with Pollard's theory, Sweden was able to imitate the process of industrialization in other countries of Western and Central Europe and to make use of new developments. There were, however, some difficulties that had to be overcome. Berner, for example, has shown that until after the First World War it was common for Swedish industrialists to show a complete lack of interest in theoretically trained chemists. This situation led to sharp criticism, especially from one of the initiators of what was later to become the Academy of Engineering Sciences (Ingejörsvetenskapsakademi, IVA). He pointed out that "engineering in Sweden continued to suffer from the fact that it was not permeated by that spirit of research which has, for example, played such a great role in the industrial expansion of Germany and most recently in its conduct of the war."[45]

Table 7.2
Number of Applications Made to the Kommerskollegium for Assistance with Traveling Expenses, 1861–1907

Year	Laborers and Craftsmen	Technicians	Special Occasions
1861	13	–	
62	90	–	
63	18	–	
64	30	–	
65	48	–	
66	15	–	
67	60	–	
68	60	–	
69	70	–	
70	77	–	

Table 7.2—Continued

Year	Laborers and Craftsmen	Technicians	Special Occasions
1871	54	–	
72	200	–	1872: Of these 124 were for visits to industrial
73	441	–	exhibitions in London, Moscow and
74	57	–	Copenhagen.
75	69	–	1873: Of these 358 were for visits to the
76	87	–	world fair in Vienna.
77	86	–	
78	181	–	
79	196	–	
80	186	–	
81	182	–	
82	163	–	
83	121	–	
84	102	–	
85	152	–	
86	165	–	
87	169	15	1888: Of these 207 were for visits to the
88	435	42	industrial exhibition in Copenhagen.
89	746	11	
90	148	17	1889: Of these 400 were for visits to the
91	206	25	world fair in Paris.
92	184	23	
93	434	6	1893: Of these 192 were for visits to the
94	59	43	world fair in Chicago.
95	350	51	
96	213	63	
97	269	48	
98	351	–	
99	784	186	1899: Of these 620 were for visits to the
1900	323	79	world fair in Paris (1900).
1901	247	64	
02	359	98	
03	357	192	1904: Of these 99 were for visits to the world
04	408	140	fair in St. Louis.
05	357	162	
06	454	277	1906: Of these 58 were for visits to the
07	455	200	industrial exhibition in Milan.

Source: Riksarkivet Stockholm, Kommerskollegium. Huvudarkivet E XVIIf, vols. 1–89.

At the end of 1918 there were several thousand Swedish immigrants in the industrial towns of Germany, especially the large cities. They included a considerable number of technicians. In Berlin, for example, they had their own organization, the Svenska tekniska klubben (Swedish Technicians' Club), which they used to resist attempts to force them out of the German labor market. At the end of the First World War, the Swedes united to protest against the efforts of such groups as the Bund technischer Berufsstände (Federation of Technical Occupations) to secure the dismissal of all foreign architects, engineers, chemists, technicians, and foremen. The Swedes demanded "that such measures must be taken as will protect us from an assault on the positions and situations we occupy here in Germany."[46] The confidence expressed here and the degree of acculturation were the results of decades of continual migration to the industrial centers of the Reich.

Mobility of Technicians According to Branch of Industry

From the end of the 1860s onward an increasing number of qualified skilled workers and technicians emigrated to Germany, and some envisaged spending long periods there.[47] In 1887 most of the applicants who wanted to go to Germany were technicians from the traditional industries (iron, steel, printing, and building), but they also included chemists. It is remarkable how well-informed they were about everything they could learn in Germany, including reproduction techniques in the printing industry and the production of water glass, saltpeter, and hydrochloric acid in the chemical industry. Civil engineers were interested in the traditional industries of building and mechanical engineering (including agricultural machinery) and later in the electrical industry, paper manufacture, and boilermaking. Three examples will show how attractive prosperous German industries were at this time for Swedes seeking further training.

The range of employment available in Sweden to qualified chemists was still restricted in the 1890s, as firms were often traditionally against employing "theorists." On the other hand, even people with practical experience, such as those working at the various large sulphite plants, required knowledge of the technology and processes employed in the major pulp factories of Central Europe. In their applications they frequently stressed the economic advantages of technical innovations they could contribute as a result of visits abroad. They could aid Swedish firms faced with increasing foreign competition to produce goods as cheaply and of as high a quality as foreign ones. The processing of wood pulp according to the sulphite method, the use of electricity in methods of bleaching paper, techniques of chemical analysis and material testing, tanning chemistry, and beet-sugar production received particular attention. After gaining experiences at American and Canadian factories, one engineer remarked that, there, too much emphasis was placed on quantity to the detriment of quality. Since in Germany the opposite was the case, he wanted to put his American experience to the test by spending some time there.[48]

One branch of industry that was traditionally strong and especially so during the consolidation phase of industrialization in Sweden was mechanical engineering. As an export industry it had to be highly competitive. Large numbers of Swedish technicians spent years working for leading European mechanical engineering firms abroad, especially in Germany, in the hope of being able to make use of their skills acquired when they returned to Sweden. Most of those in Germany worked for the railroads and in locomotive construction or in the field of equipment for energy production and distribution. A number of other applicants had very concrete ideas of what they wanted to learn. One engineer who applied from the United States who enclosed excellent references from General Electric and other firms and who had worked in Reval (Tallinn), was interested in "studying the construction and management of power stations for electric railroads and streetcar systems in Germany and Switzerland."[49] In the field of equipment for energy construction and distribution, there was a great demand for training in specialized factories in Germany and Austria. On a more general level, the teaching methods of the German technical universities attracted special attention as well.[50]

The progress made in the German electrical industry in the two decades before the First World War was also reflected in the attraction that it exerted among foreign technicians and engineers. Swedish engineers went to Berlin because of the excellent production and development facilities of Siemens & Halske. One engineer, for example, had been trained by Siemens & Halske in fitting and testing machines in 1902–1903 after taking courses at the Technical University in Berlin. From 1899 to 1901 he had worked for the Swedish branch of this German firm and a number of Swedish firms. In 1903–1904 he went to work for Western Electric, Milwaukee Electric, and National Electric in the United States. Swedish engineers also worked for the Allgemeine Elektrizitätsgesellschaft (AEG) in Berlin and Schuckert AG in Nuremberg. Scholarships for foreign study were often provided by Swedish firms and the Technical University of Stockholm.

As far as can be judged from the incomplete material available, there was also a considerable amount of migration by Swedes to work and train in the German iron and steel industry, in mining, underground and surface engineering, the food and drink industry, the wood and textile industries, and the German shipbuilding industry. One shipbuilding engineer from Malmö spent some time in Kiel followed by a period with the AG Weser in Bremen. He declared his intention of discovering the trade secrets of two of the largest German shipyards and of the best workshops in England before "turning his back on countries abroad."[51] This and other cases show that the aims of such forms of migration were more or less on the borderline between technology transfer and industrial espionage. This also explains why many of the highly qualified workers from Sweden tried to work their way from the bottom. They wanted to be in positions to receive the most useful kinds of information.

Mobility of Technicians and the Organization of Work

As early as 1894 a few technicians and engineers were complaining of the backwardness of their industries in their letters of application to the Kommerskollegium. Such complaints included both technical production processes and the rational employment of human labor as seen from the point of view of trained technicians. In that year a shipbuilding engineer from Malmö wanted to study "working methods in shipbuilding" in addition to recent naval design.[52] At the same time the manager of the largest Swedish cement works at Degerhamn on the island of Öland eloquently described the risks of competition from foreign cement works "which by using more modern methods can manufacture a product more cheaply."[53] As this involved standards of quality and in order to maintain the Swedish share of the market it was essential "to get to know their more rational methods of production and introduce them" in Sweden.

In 1905 the subject of rationalization was mentioned in greater detail in a number of applications: An engineer from Stockholm with letters of recommendation from the leading mechanical engineering firms of his country—Atlas in Stockholm and Vulcan in Norrköping—wanted "to study modern methods of working in mechanical engineering workshops" in England and Germany.[54] A chemist wanted "to make a study of innovations which can simplify and lower the costs of production."[55] An engineer wanted to study the French, British, and German industries to observe "what may be of use to our own motor industry" and to publish details "not only in our specialist journals but also in those newspapers that have a wider circulation among the workers in our mechanical engineering workshops."[56] By this time specialists from Sweden and the industrial centers of Europe had been traveling to the United States to study methods of rationalization in their everyday application to see if they were practicable.[57]

At this point a number of questions arise. The most important of these seems to be that of the qualification standards and efficiency of the Swedish (industrial) working classes and of technicians and engineers. In a case study of the qualifications of Swedish steelworkers during the last decades of the nineteenth century, Wohlert came to the conclusion "that the professional skill of the workers did in fact play a large role in the successful introduction of the new technique" (i.e., the Bessemer process).[58] Larsson, Johansson, and Runeby, on the other hand, emphasize in their studies that Swedish employers and their ideological leaders considered their own workers to be inefficient and constantly inclined to interrupt production. They argue that the power elite encouraged visits of Swedish technicians and engineers to the United States and the simultaneous introduction of modern American methods of rationalization and management in order to solve these problems.[59] It is not possible to examine in detail Runeby's carefully documented study of the introduction of Taylorism, Johansson's evidence of the Swedish employers' increasing consciousness of efficiency from around 1908, and Larsson's arguments on corporate tendencies and social integration, but we can mention some of their most important conclusions.[60] Evidently Swedish industrial workers had a wide knowledge of their occupations, including the industrial organization of labor. This gave rise to an attack from one of the supporters of the "new rational efficiency," who declared that the old-fashioned system of organizing labor, which left many of the technical operations to the individual worker, was "bankrupt."[61] How had skilled industrial workers obtained this knowledge and how had they managed to preserve it for so long? Not only technicians but also a large number of production workers had acquired knowledge and practical experience during periods of training in the leading industrial countries of the Continent and Britain. Migration to work abroad was one of the most important means available to industrial workers to improve their qualifications, acquire experience, and hence increase the value of their labor on the home labor market. In the long run, however, the workers could not prevent the devaluation of such qualifications.[62] In the 1920s at the latest the organization of labor according to "scientific principles" finally became the responsibility of a new breed of engineers.[63]

Mobility of Technicians and Protection of Workers

The aims of some governmental efforts to gain information abroad were diametrically opposed to the general tendency toward "more rational" working methods and the introduction of "scientific" methods of production that led to the disqualification of labor. In addition to the measures taken by the workers in self-defense, inspectors from the Swedish state industrial safety authority (yrkesinspektionen) tried to ensure the protection of the workers by means of a comprehensive system of regulations. This authority had been founded in 1889 and in 1900 employed nine inspectors. Evidently its members were very interested in examples and ideas from abroad, for in 1894 one of the inspectors (yrkesinspektor) who came from Jönköping applied for state assistance for a visit to Germany "to study safety regulations in some of the factories of Central Germany." Rationalization and safety measures, two opposing tendencies of the "progress" of industrial capitalism, were introduced simultaneously in a number of countries, or in some cases with a short period of delay between the two.[64] Not only journals but also the direct experience of workers abroad helped to ensure that this was the case.

One of Runeby's arguments, which Fridenson has placed in an international context, deals with the specific role of the Swedish engineers' organizations in the spread of "American methods."[65] He states that, as in Germany and the United States, the engineers' organizations were in the forefront of the rationalization movement. Swedish engineers greeted the new form of labor organization with even more enthusiasm than employers, whose organization did not take over the leadership of the rationalization movement until years later. Logically this meant that corporativism and technocracy were to be the ways in which the state and industry would have to enter into a new relationship with each other. In contrast with the German "pure" engineer as defined by Kocka, however, a large number of Swedish engineers and technicians showed evidence of active interest in economic and organizational questions in spite of their experience of and contact with German firms.[66] Following Gårdlund's line of argument, it is possible to speak of a model based on the typical American engineer in this context and hence to confirm the persistence of American influence, but with some reservations.

In spite of a number of gaps, the material available shows that the average engineer was extremely interested in organizational problems.[67] Many of them, especially those who were newly trained or who worked for export firms, argued that these problems should be solved according to the principles of "scientific labor organization," and that "progress" and rationalization at the expense of the workers should be accepted. Opposed to them were a few others, often employed by the state, who were above all interested in the possibilities of increasing the amount of protection available to workers. Both groups relied on—among other factors—the international exchange of workers and the transfer of knowledge and experience that this encouraged.

CONCLUSION

In the course of industrialization nonagricultural workers became more conscious of the discrepancy between the limited opportunities that they had of providing for themselves locally and their knowledge about prospects of achieving lasting improvements in their social situation elsewhere. With the spread of the railroad network throughout the whole of Sweden and the development of the first export-oriented mass production industry (the sawmills of Norrland), opportunities for employment outside the primary sector had gradually increased from the 1860s onward for those who were prepared to leave home for a period of time or even permanently. A change in behavior took place in that feelings of social deprivation were transformed into action, even though this frequently led to failure.[68] Hence it became more common for people to accept and try out offers of employment from abroad.

At the beginning of the 1890s there was a broad thrust toward industrialization. Parallel to this the workers began to organize themselves, and these two movements led to a change in the social behavior of the lower classes. What had previously been workers' experience on an individual basis aimed at achieving a share in the expanding economy by means of increases in income, gradually gave way to the development of collective forms of expressing their interests within the national framework. One result of this was that pure (seasonal) labor migration did not lead to further qualifications or social mobility, and soon even permanent emigration lost its attraction. They were replaced by demands of a political nature, which were pressed on employers by an increasingly more organized labor force.[69] Only for training and as an alternative in the case of labor disputes did continental migration and to a larger and larger extent migration overseas still serve a purpose.

NOTES

1. See R. Braun, *Sozialer und kultureller Wandel in einem ländlichen Industriegebiet (Züricher Oberland) unter Einwirkung des Maschinen- und Fabrikwesens im 19. und 20. Jahrhundert* (Erlenbach, Zürich, 1965), pp. 38ff., pp. 258ff.; A. Redford, *Labour Migration in England 1800-1850* (Manchester, 1964).

2. F. Thistlethwaite, "Migration from Europe Overseas in the Nineteenth and Twentieth Centuries," *XIe Congrès International des Sciences Historiques, Stockholm 1960,* Rapport V (Uppsala, 1960), pp. 32–60.

3. D. S. Landes, *The Unbound Prometheus. Technological Change and Industrial Development in Western Europe from 1750 to the Present* (Cambridge, 1972), pp. 147ff.

4. K. J. Bade, "Politik und Ökonomie der Auslanderbeschäftigung im preußischen Osten 1885–1914. Die Internationalisierung des Arbeitsmarkts im Rahmen der preußischen Abwehrpolitik," *Geschichte und Gesellschaft,* special issue no. 6 (1980), 273–99.

5. See, for example, J. Hughes, *Industrialization and Economic History: Theses and Conjectures* (New York, 1970), p. 147.

6. H. Elsenhans, "Geschichte und Struktur des internationalen Systems," in H. Haftendorn, ed., *Theorie der internationalen Politik. Gegenstand und Methode der internationalen Beziehungen* (Hamburg, 1975), pp. 150–70.

7. See S. Pollard, "Industrialization and the European Economy," *Economic History Review* 26 (1973), 636–48 and some reflections on this problem in R. Fremdling, T. Pierenkemper, and R. Tilly, "Regionale Differenzierung in Deutschland als Schwerpunkt wirtschaftshistorischer Forschung," in R. Fremdling, R. Tilly, eds., *Industrialisierung und Raum. Studien zur regionalen Differenzierung im Deutschland des 19. Jahrhunderts* (Stuttgart, 1979), pp. 9–26.

8. See S. Åkerman, *From Stockholm to San Francisco. The Development of the Historical Study of External Migrations* (Uppsala, 1975), p. 20; C. H. Riegler, "Emigrationsphasen, Akkumulation und Widerstandsstrategien. Zu einigen Beziehungen der Arbeitsemigration von und nach Schweden, 1850–1930," in H. Elsenhans, ed., *Migration und Wirtschaftsentwicklung* (Frankfurt/New York, 1978), pp. 31–69.

9. See E. Andrén, "Arbetarvandringar. I staden," in A. Lindblom, ed., *Arbetaren in helg och söcken II. Vardag och fest* (Stockholm, 1944), pp. 29–58.

10. See K.J. Bade, "Altes Handwerk, Wanderzwang und Gute Policey: Gesellenwanderung zwischen Zunftökonomie und Gewerbereform," *Vierteljahrschrift für Sozial- und Wirtschaftsgeschichte* 69 (1982), pp.1–37, see especially p. 17.

11. See S. E. Bring, *Anders och Pehr Bjurholms bryggerier* (Stockholm, 1949), pp. 177ff.

12. This part is a revised and shortened version of a chapter in C. H. Riegler, "Die 'deutsche Krankheit': Emigration und Arbeitswanderungen aus Schweden nach Deutschland, 1868–1914" (Ph. D. diss., University of Erlangen-Nürnberg 1982), forthcoming as a book under the title *Emigration und Arbeitswanderung aus Schweden nach Norddeutschland, 1868-1914* (Neumünster 1985).

13. This and the other case histories are from the Riksarkivet (Swedish National Archives, hereafter RA); The Kommerskollegium Huvudarkivet (Authority of Commerce, main archive, hereafter KK Ha) collections contain reports by Swedish embassies abroad (series E VI a) and individual applications for travel grants to foreign countries (series E XVII f), the Utrikesdepartementet (Ministry of Foreign Affairs, hereafter UD) collections also contain reports by Swedish embassies abroad.- RA, UD vol. 3 019 b, 54 C 1, I, 13 June 1879.

14. RA, KK Ha E VIa, vol. 448, 9 October 1886.

15. Ibid., 10 June 1887.

16. RA, Utrikesdepartementet (hereafter, UD), vol. 3019 b, 54 C 1, I, 8 July 1911.

17. Ibid.

18. See B. Blomkvist, *International i miniatyr. Studier i skånsk arbetarrörelse före 1880 och dess internationella kontakter* (Lund, 1979), especially pp. 118 ff.

19. H. Elmquist, *Arbetsstatistiska studier rörande den svenska tobaksindustrien* (Stockholm, 1899).

20. Zentrales Staatsarchiv Merseburg (hereafter ZSTA), Rep. 120 BB VII 1, Nr. 1 b, vol. 13 p. 73.

21. RA, KK, Ha E VI a, vol. 324, 1903 (Appendices).

22. L. Olsson, "Barnarbete i de svenska tobaksfabrikerna," *Scandia* 44 (1978), 257–88.

23. RA, KK Ha E VI a, vol. 314, 29 March 1882 (appendix).

24. See note 12.

25. B. Schiller, *Storstrejken 1909* (Stockholm, 1967).

26. E. Kumm, *På vandringsväg och arbetsfält. En kulturhistorisk studie* (Stockholm, 1944), pp. 101f.

27. *Statistik des Hamburgischen Staates* No. 32 (Hamburg, 1926), p. 34.

28. RA, UD vol. 3 019 b, 54 C 1, I, 14 June 1879 (appendix).

29. RA, KK Ha E VI a, vol. 114, 23 October 1884.

30. RA, KK Ha E VI a, vol. 119, 23 June 1896.

31. RA, UD, vol. 3019 a, 54 C 4, 5 December 1907.

32. Ibid., 10 February 1908.

33. Ibid., 6 March 1908.

34. Ibid., 20 October 1908.

35. T. Gårdlund, *Industrialismens samhälle* (Stockholm, 1955).

36. See note 47.

37. I. Jansson, "Svensk rapportering av amerikansk teknologi pa världsutställningen i Philadelphia 1876," *Stockholm Papers in History and Philosophy of Technology* TRITA-HOT 2006 (Stockholm, 1980).

38. M. Hagerman, "Berättelser från utlandet. Svenska tekniker och arbetare pa studieresor i Europa och Amerika under 1800-talets senare hälft," *Stockholm Papers in History and Philosophy of Technology* TRITA-HOT 2008 (Stockholm, 1980).

39. T. Gårdlund, *Industrialismens samhälle*, p. 245.

40. Ibid., p. 234.

41. J. Kuuse, "Foreign Trade and the Breakthrough of the Engineering Industry in Sweden, 1890–1920," *Scandinavian Economic History Review* 25 (1977), 1–36.

42. T. Gårdlund, *Industrialismens samhälle*, p. 259.

43. N. Horn and J. Kocka, eds., *Recht und Entwicklung der Großunternehmen im 19. und frühen 20. Jahrhundert* (Göttingen, 1979) p. 423.

44. Pollard, "Industrialization."

45. B. Berner, *Teknikens värld. Teknisk förändring och ingenjörsarbete i svensk industri* (Lund, 1981), p. 106.

46. RA, UD, vol. 4591, 97 G 16, 3 April 1919.

47. See details in C. H. Riegler, "Transnationale Migration und Technologietransfer: das Beispiel der schwedisch-deutschen Arbeitswanderung von Technikern und Ingenieuren vor dem Ersten Weltkrieg," in K. J. Bade, ed., *Auswanderer—Wanderarbeiter— Gastarbeiter: Bevölkerung, Arbeitsmarkt und Wanderung in Deutschland seit der Mitte des 19. Jahrhunderts. Beiträge des internationalen wissenschaftlichen Symposiums an der Akademie für politische Bildung Tutzing, 18.–21.10.1982* (Ostfildern, 1984), pp. 506–26.

48. RA, KK Ha E XVII f, vol. 76 (1905), no. 1194.

49. Ibid., no. 1192.

50. Ibid., no. 519.

51. Ibid., vol. 36 (1894), no. 705.

52. Ibid., 13 April 1894.

53. Ibid., no. 447.

54. Ibid., vol. 76 (1905), no. 658.

55. Ibid., no. 1018.

56. Ibid., no. 1089.

57. J. Kocka, "Industrielles Management : Konzeptionen und Modelle in Deutschland vor 1914," *Vierteljahrschrift für Sozial- und Wirtschaftsgeschichte* 56 (1969), 332–72.

58. K. Wohlert, "Svenskt yrkeskunnande och teknologi under 1800–talet. En fallstudie av förutsättningar för kunskapstransfer," *Historisk Tidskrift* (1979), 398–421.

59. H. de Geer, *Rationaliseringsrörelsen i Sverige. Effektivitetsidéer och socialt ansvar under mellankrigstiden* (Stockholm, 1978); K. Jonsson, "Taylorismen och svensk arbetarrörelse 1913–1928," *Arkiv för studier i arbetarrörelsens historia* 19/20 (1981), 3–30; C. Berggren, "Slog taylorismen aldrig igenom i Sverige?" ibid. pp. 31–50; idem, "Ingenjörer, marxister och teknisk utveckling," *Häften för kritiska studier* 4 (1981), 56–61.

60. N. Runeby, "Americanism, Taylorism and Social Integration. Action Programmes for Swedish Industry at the Beginning of the Twentieth Century," *Scandinavian Journal of History* 3 (1978), 21–46; A. Johansson, *Den effektiva arbetstiden. Verkstäderna och arbetsintensitetens problem 1900–1920* (Uppsala, 1977); J. Larsson, "En ny rationell effektivitet. Några perspektiv på svensk industri historia 1895–1920," *Historieforskning på nya vägar. Studier tillägnade S. Carlsson* (Lund, 1977), pp. 121–41.

61. Cited in Runeby "Americanism."

62. For the general line of argument, see H. Braverman, *Labor and Monopoly Capital* (New York, 1974).

63. See Kocka, "Industrielles Management," and R. Locke, "Industrialisierung und Erziehungssystem in Frankreich und Deutschland vor dem 1. Weltkrieg," *Historische Zeitschrift* 225 (1977), 265–96; B. Sundin, *Ingenjörsvetenskapens tidevarv. Ingenjörsvetenskapsakademin, Pappersmassekontoret, Metallografiska Institutet och den teknologiska forskningen i början av 1900–talet* (Umeå, 1981).

64. See, for example, the historical parts in S. Kelman, *Regulating America, Regulating Sweden: A Comparative Study of Occupational Safety and Health Policy* (Cambridge, Mass., 1981), pp. 113 ff.

65. Runeby, "Americanism"; P. Fridenson, "Unternehmenspolitik, Rationalisierung

und Arbeiterschaft. Französische Erfahrungen im internationalen Vergleich, 1900 bis 1929," in Horn, and Kocka, eds., *Recht und Entwicklung*, pp. 428–50.

66. Kocka, "Industrielles Management."

67. R. Torstendahl, "Vom Berufsstolz zum Angestelltenbewußtsein in Schweden, 1900–1940," in J. Kocka, ed., *Angestellte im europäischen Vergleich. Die Herausbildung angestellter Mittelschichten seit dem späten 19. Jahrhundert* (Göttingen, 1981), pp. 142–68.

68. W. G. Runciman, *Relative Deprivation and Social Justice* (London, 1966).

69. See, for example, W. M. Lafferty, *Economic Development and the Response of Labor in Scandinavia. A Multi-level Analysis* (Oslo, 1971), pp. 205 ff.

FOREIGN WORKERS AND FORCED LABOR IN GERMANY DURING THE FIRST WORLD WAR

8

Lothar Elsner

INTRODUCTION

It is impossible to understand fully the changes that took place in Germany during the First World War with regard to migrant labor policies and the employment of foreigners without a firm grasp of the essential nature of this war. Both the class system and the continuity of imperialist immigrant labor policies since the 1890s must be taken into consideration as well as the links between pre-war and wartime policies. The following description is based on a view of the First World War as an imperialist war caused by the ruling classes of all of the powers involved, but for whose preparation and outbreak German imperialism in particular was responsible.[1]

In accordance with their aggressive policies the ruling classes of these countries were eager to recruit foreign labor in larger numbers than in the pre-war period and to utilize it in the war economy. As far as the Central Powers are concerned, this was especially true of Germany and Austria-Hungary and within the Entente of Britain and France. During the war France imported additional labor, especially from its colonies.[2]

German imperialism made particularly extensive and brutal use of forced labor between 1914 and 1918. This cannot simply be regarded as the result of war. The imperialist struggle for extra profit has been going on ever since monopoly capitalism emerged, and it involves the exploitation of the cheapest labor available. The nature of German imperialism and its aggressiveness resulted in a policy aimed at achieving an ambitious program of expansion for a country that occupied an unfavorable geographical situation and had relatively limited economic and military means at its disposal. This discrepancy between aspirations and the means of fulfilling them produced the Blitzkrieg strategy and under war conditions caused Germany to resort to a policy of forced labor. On the one hand the exploitation of forced labor and foreign peoples was an integral objective of the war, but it was also the necessary prerequisite for achieving expansionist aims.[3]

This essay is a revised and translated version originally appearing in German in Klaus J. Bade, ed., *Auswanderung–Wanderarbeiter–Gastarbeiter: Bevölkerung, Arbeitsmarkt und Wanderung in Deutschland seit Mitte des 19. Jahrhunderts* (Ostfildern, 1984). Translation by Andrew Winter.

Reliable data are available on foreign labor and immigrant labor policies in Germany before 1914—at least as far as foreigners employed in agriculture and the situation in the labor market are concerned.[4] These data confirm the general observations made by Lenin in 1917 that the exploitation of badly paid workers from backward countries is typical of imperialism. He also said that these workers form the prey on which the rich imperialist countries feed like parasites, never failing to exploit the situation of the imported foreign workers, who have no rights whatever.[5]

In connection with policies affecting foreigners, J. Nichtweiß states that long before the war the German government "had decided on a way of employing foreigners which took into consideration the economic aspirations of the land-owners and the political interests in all reactionary groupings."[6] Before 1914 German imperialists could rely on economic pressure when recruiting and importing hundreds of thousands of foreign workers; unemployment, underemployment, and overpopulation forced these workers to leave their home countries. By 1914 about 1.2 million such workers were employed in Germany. These imported workers were subjected to special legislation that discriminated against them and ensured their exploitation. These laws varied according to the nationality of the immigrant workers, the Poles suffering most of all. Following the example of Prussia, most of the other German states introduced mandatory identification, which compelled foreigners to work for specific firms, placed them at the mercy of the firms' owners, and made it possible to keep them under systematic control. In addition to this, the length of time for which Poles could stay was limited, the intention being to prevent them from settling premanently, to keep wages down, and to split the working class by making it more difficult for the migrant workers to develop economic and cultural needs similar to those of German workers. These measures were the most important elements of the system that was used to exploit and oppress foreign workers; within this system the Deutsche Arbeiterzentrale (DAZ), a semi-official institution that worked in close contact with the police, played a particularly important role in supervising foreigners and keeping them under control.

In the pre-war period German authorities did everything possible to ensure an unlimited supply of immigrant labor by exerting pressure on the governments of countries of origin, especially Russia and Austria-Hungary. At the same time they tried to prevent these countries from intervening to protect their citizens working in Germany from unrestricted exploitation.[7]

During the First World War the reactionary and imperialist immigration labor policies developed under the Wilhelmian empire intensified and found their logical conclusion in the open brutality of forced labor.[8] One of the most important preconditions both for this and the achievement of those war objectives that sought to ensure the unrestricted recruitment, import, and exploitation of foreign labor in the post-war period was the accelerated development of state monopoly capitalism, which took place during this period.

This essay begins with a description of the transition from migratory to forced labor in 1914. The next three parts deal with forced labor from Belgium, from the occupied territories in the east, and with the recruitment of workers in the neutral countries. We then deal with the differences over recruitment between Germany and the Austro-Hungarian Empire and analyze the attempts to guarantee a continuous inflow of foreign labor after the war. Finally, we discuss the exploitation of Russian and Polish workers in the period 1915 to 1918 and the resistance of foreign workers to deportment and forced labor.

THE TRANSITION TO FORCED LABOR IN 1914

Although not fully prepared for war from the economic point of view, the ruling class in Germany had considered the labor question before the war in connection with the measures it had adopted to ensure that the country was in a state of military readiness and had decided what use was to be made of foreign workers in case of war. As far as industry was concerned, there was no apparent labor problem, except for the fact that if there was unemployment, as was expected, this was to be regulated by such measures as sending foreign workers home or making them available for agricultural work. However, in accordance with the increasingly pressing demands made by the big landowners during the last few years before the war, the relevant departments of the Reich, the Prussian ministries, and the representatives of the large-scale agricultural interests all agreed that foreign workers employed on farms should be forced to stay in Germany if war broke out. This is clearly shown by such discussions as those that took place on 13 March 1914 at the meeting of the Permanent Commission on Questions of Economic Mobilization in the Reich's Department of the Interior (Ständige Kommission für Fragen der wirtschaftlichen Mobilmachung),[9] on 26 May 1914 at the meeting of the Committee for Economic Affairs (Wirtschaftlicher Ausschuss),[10] and in the materials used to prepare these meetings.[11] As a result of this, on 27 July 1914, five days before Germany declared war on Russia, Secretary of State Delbrück asked the Prussian Minister of War to recommend to the military commanders not to resort to a general deportation of Russian workers.[12] The same recommendations were passed on to the governments of the other German states.[13]

When war broke out, there were approximately 1.2 million foreign workers in Germany, about half of them in the industrial sector and the other half in agriculture.[14] Tables 8.1 and 8.2 give information on the number of foreign workers in Prussia in 1913 and 1914, their countries of origin, and the sector in which they were employed. At the same time these data show how the situation had changed in 1914 compared with the previous year.

Before and during the war foreign workers were usually employed as unskilled labor doing hard manual work that was dangerous to their health. In the pre-war period those in the industrial sector were employed especially in mining;

structural and civil engineering; railroad, canal, and road construction; brick-making; and peat cutting.[15]

Imme.liately after the war broke out workers from the so-called enemy alien territoiies were confined to their places of work and subjected to forced labor;

Table 8.1
The Number of Foreign Workers in Prussia at the End of 1913 and the End of 1914 according to the Country of Origin, Nationality, and Sector of Employment

Country of Origin and Nationality	Agriculture		Industry		Mining		Total	
	1913	1914	1913	1914	1913	1914	1913	1914
I Russia comprising:	6,139	184,122	7,435	13,550	1,153	4,336	14,727	202,008
1. Germans	4,671	8,156	4,951	5,955	695	592	10,317	14,703
2. Poles	791	173,251	523	5,631	67	3,382	1,381	182,264
3. Lithuanians	208	1,288	451	506	120	138	779	1,932
4. Others	469	1,427	1,510	1,458	271	224	2,250	3,109
II Austria-Hungary comprising:	16,211	53,582	105,104	86,493	54,531	38,345	175,846	178,420
1. Germans	6,265	6,844	60,017	54,545	16,694	13,563	82,976	74,952
2. Poles	459	21,158	1,176	1,723	197	1,225	1,832	24,106
3. Czechs	720	946	14,008	11,687	6,042	4,915	20,770	17,548
4. Ruthenians	7,811	22,962	9,528	4,529	23,488	4,957	30,827	32,448
5. Others	956	1,672	20,375	14,009	18,110	13,685	39,441	29,366
III Italy	215	214	50,496	25,591	8,878	6,465	59,589	32,270
IV Belgium comprising:	634	563	4,122	3,352	518	339	5,274	4,254
1. Flemish	356	330	2,039	1,689	246	94	2,641	2,113
2. Others	278	233	2,083	1,663	272	245	2,633	2,141
V Netherlands	22,414	21,675	50,987	47,785	5,514	5,285	78,915	74,745
VI Denmark	5,554	5,396	5,506	4,805	20	20	11,080	10,221
VII Others	3,955	4,016	10,644	8,829	480	435	15,079	13,280
Total number of foreigners	55,122	269,568	234,294	190,405	71,094	55,225	360,510	515,198

Source: Lists of arrivals, departures and total numbers of foreign workers in the state of Prussia during 1914, Zentrales Staatsarchiv (ZStA) Merseburg, Rep.87 B, Arbeitersachen, no. 21 B.

Note: A number of small mistakes which occur in the original records have been corrected in this table.

this involved especially the Russian-Polish workers and some of the Poles and Ruthenians from Galicia (Austria), who were not liable for military service. Workers liable for military service in the allied army of Austria-Hungary were allowed to return to their homes. Industrial workers from neutral countries who had lost their jobs were in some cases deported to their home countries, as occurred in the first few weeks of the war with Italian workers and their families, 72,000 people in all.[16]

On 31 July 1914 martial law, transferring executive power to the general staff of the army, was declared.[17] In cooperation with the civilian government, the military authorities at once established a rigid system of controls over foreigners and took brutal measures against anyone who attempted to resist increased exploitation. Thousands of foreign workers, especially Russian Poles, were arrested and confined to prison camps either because they were unemployed or had been deported to Central Germany on account of the fighting in the east, or because they had resisted exploitation and oppression. The measures taken against Russian-Polish workers were particularly harsh. They were forbidden to leave their local police districts or to return to their home country and thus found themselves even more at the mercy of business employers and big farmers than before the war. The threat or use of physical violence forced them to work. Their legal

Table 8.2
Arrivals, Departures, and Numbers of Foreign Workers Remaining in Prussia in 1913 and 1914 according to Country of Origin

	1913			1914		
Country of Origin	Arrivals	Departures	Numbers remaining at the end of the year	Arrivals	Departures	Numbers remaining at the end of the year
1. Russia	231,686	216,959	14,727	242,667	46,947	202,008
2. Austria-Hungary	400,895	225,049	175,846	391,469	212,835	178,420
3. Italy	118,761	59,172	59,589	109,346	77,057	32,270
4. Belgium	7,960	2,686	5,274	7,671	3,417	4,254
5. Netherlands	116,602	37,687	76,915	111,115	36,370	74,745
6. Denmark	16,220	5,140	11,080	15,204	4,986	10,221
7. Others	23,880	8,801	15,079	23,308	9,940	13,280
Total	916,004	555,494	360,510	900,780	391,552	515,198

Source: Lists of arrivals, departures and total numbers of foreign workers in the state of Prussia during 1914, ZStA Merseburg, Rep. 87 B, Arbeitersachen, no. 21 B

Note: A number of small mistakes which occur in the orginal records have been corrected in this table.

status was that of civilian prisoners. Contrary to Zunkel's statement that the terms of their employment remained a matter of civil law, it is important to note the practice of the military authorities and the relevant ministries, who not only forbade the workers to change jobs but directly influenced the level of their wages and from the fall of 1914 also the terms of their contracts of employment.[18]

In September and October the government departments involved came to a decision on whether the Russian-Polish and Galician workers should remain in Germany. At the beginning of the discussion opinions varied. Originally Beth-mann Hollweg, Chancellor of the Reich, intended that the Polish workers should be used to carry out land improvement projects after the harvest and cultivation work in fall had been completed.[19] Similarly a meeting in the Department of the Interior of the Reich on 28 August 1914 advised that the limit on the period for which a foreigner could work in Germany should be removed by abolishing the "Karenzzeit," the annual forced departure from Germany during the winter months.[20] In contrast to this, however, the "general principles" issued by the Prussian Ministry of the Interior[21] and a meeting of the ministries responsible held on 5 September 1914[22] spoke out in favor of sending home all Polish workers who were neither liable for military service nor needed in industry or agriculture. The only exception was to be the coal-mining industry of Upper Silesia. There was to be no limit on the period of stay of Polish workers from Austria, but if they lost their jobs they too were to be deported.

With the Battle of the Marne, it was becoming clear that the Blitzkrieg strategy of the German general staff had failed and all the signs indicated a war that was going to last for some time with consequent effects on the war economy. This, together with pressure from the big farmers and increasingly also from big industrialists, led to a change in the attitude of the government authorities. Although a decree issued by the Prussian ministers responsible on 28 September 1914,[23] orders issued by the general staff of the Prussian army corps on about 5 October 1914,[24] and similar measures in the other German states[25] still spoke of restrictions on the period of employment of Russian-Polish workers who were not liable for military service, landowners were allowed to retain those workers with whom they signed contracts for the winter. As the big landowners and their organizations were clearly in favor of forced labor and did not want the avail-ability of foreign workers to be dependent on whether contracts of employment could be arranged, they expressed their "gravest misgivings" about the measures decreed at the end of September and the beginning of October.[26] As a result the Prussian Ministers of Agriculture and of the Interior issued a further decree on 12 October 1914 in which they stressed that it was their aim, "as far as possible to retain all of the presently employed Russian seasonal workers over the winter" and to make arrangements which would mean that their relations with "their" exploiters were as "favorable and peaceful as possible."[27] A decree issued by the Prussian Minister of the Interior on 7 November 1914 stated that, contrary to the decree of 28 September 1914, no further attempt would be made to force

Russian-Polish workers to leave.[28] A similar decree affecting Polish workers from Austria-Hungary had already been issued on 12 October 1914. This meant that Russian-Polish workers and Galicians who were not liable for military service were, apart from a small number of exceptions, to be subjected to a system of forced labor for the rest of the war period. Thus a group of especially discriminated workers were placed by governmental authority at the disposal of monopolists and big landowners, who made handsome extra profits by their exploitation.

Tables 8.1 through 8.3 at the same time show that a considerable number of workers employed in the industrial and agricultural sectors came from other occupied countries (e.g., Belgium) and from neutral countries.

From the fall of 1914 onward, the industrial sector began to increase its demands for foreign labor; one suggestion was that Russian-Polish workers who were no longer needed on the land in the winter should be sent to work for industrial firms. Such demands were bound to lead to disputes with the big land proprietors. Although some landowners tried to burden the government with the cost of keeping the harvest workers over the winter and demanded among other things that these workers should be confined to prison camps, most of the farmers who employed foreigners were prepared to retain them over the winter and force them to accept new contracts acknowledging the decline in working and living conditions that had in the meantime occurred.[29] In most cases they rejected the idea of temporarily employing the Russian-Polish workers in the industrial sector. The Prussian government, on the other hand, tried to negotiate a compromise between big industrialists and landowners over the question of foreign workers. Eventually they arrived at a solution. In response to an application made by the Association for the German Brown Coal Industry (Deutscher Braunkohlen-Industrie-Verein) on 16 October 1914 for the ban on the use of Russian-Polish workers in the industrial sector to be removed, on 7 December 1914 the Prussian Minister of the Interior gave the brown coal industries of Saxony and Brandenburg permission to employ foreign Poles, initially for the winter months.[30] They were not, however, to take on workers otherwise employed in agriculture but civilian prisoners liable for military service from the camps controlled by the military administration.[31] A decree of 30 January 1915 allowed such workers to be employed in all sectors of large-scale industry in Prussia.[32] Under certain conditions it was also permissible to employ on a temporary basis Poles who had previously worked in agriculture. Other organizations of large-scale industry including the coal-mining industry of the Ruhr, the Chamber of Commerce in Düsseldorf, and the representatives of other interests, especially those of the Rhenish-Westphalian industries, then made vociferous demands insisting that they too should be given access to the reserves of Russian-Polish workers.[33] In response to the demands a decree of 11 May 1915 also permitted the use of newly imported Russian-Polish workers in large industrial plants in the central and western provinces of Prussia.[34] This was, however, not to apply to workers

Table 8.3 Identity Cards Issued to Foreign Workers in Germany by the Deutsche Arbeiterzentrale in the Years 1913/1914–1917/1918 according to Sector of Employment

	Agriculture					Industry				
	1913/14	1914/15	1915/16	1916/17	1917/18	1913/14	1914/15	1915/16	1916/17	1917/18
1. Russia comprising:	286,413	275,972	311,658	326,683	24,838	35,565	75,938	133,913	147,676	154,073
Poles	269,000	246,572	276,500	278,469	29,108	22,538	55,737	103,643	116,635	117,841
Germans	11,184	24,329	27,522	31,931	36,200	7,650	16,840	26,998	27,498	29,882
Others	6,229	5,071	7,636	16,283	21,106	5,377	3,361	3,272	3,543	6,360
2. Austria comprising:	130,577	49,442	26,371	19,130	14,117	167,756	72,982	56,204	47,897	51,106
Poles	58,244	20,011	8,841	6,497	4,406	17,266	4,512	2,123	1,621	1,120
Ruthenians	68,236	26,090	14,228	9,485	6,274	46,017	4,821	2,459	1,675	1,276
Germans	3,033	2,707	2,545	2,449	2,779	57,772	41,822	34,483	30,437	35,343
Czechs	951	567	696	618	551	27,194	13,361	10,442	8,511	8,037
Others	133	67	61	81	87	19,507	8,466	6,697	5,653	5,330
3. Hungary comprising:	5,291	349	210	174	145	21,235	7,816	5,786	4,474	3,582
Germans	1,023	96	60	40	42	5,827	2,777	2,159	1,728	1,396
Others	4,268	253	150	134	103	15,408	5,039	3,627	2,746	2,186
4. Switzerland	1,534	1,660	1,905	2,013	2,197	2,608	4,003	5,285	4,404	6,402
5. Italy	45	21	41	49	128	64,992	12,935	11,399	10,591	13,556
6. Netherlands/Belgium	9,633	7,916	6,208	5,533	5,547	46,245	42,349	50,009	88,602	104,630
7. Denmark/Sweden/Norway	3,199	2,315	2,318	1,598	1,203	4,714	3,842	3,988	3,615	2,912
8. France/Luxemburg	18	57	61	236	385	789	1,000	1,979	3,324	4,343
9. Other countries	26	20	45	67	166	2,218	1,879	1,924	2,555	2,829
Total	436,736	337,752	348,817	355,483	372,274	346,122	222,762	270,487	313,138	343,496

Source: Statistisches Jahrbuch …

who had already been employed in Germany before 1 May 1915. A further decree of 14 December 1915 stated that "agriculture must be protected from the danger of losing large numbers of Russians who up to now have primarily been employed in this sector"; on the other hand, "the question which is becoming more and more acute of recruiting sufficient numbers of workers for the industrial sector (especially for the war industry) made it necessary to further relax the regulations governing the employment of foreign workers in industry."[35] Hence permission was granted for the employment of all foreign Polish and Ruthenian workers throughout Prussia. This included those who had been working in Germany before 1 May 1915 but not those who had been employed in agriculture. This not only applied to large-scale industry but also to medium-sized firms, including those employing craftworkers. The only exception was that Poles and Ruthenians could not be employed as journeymen or apprentices in small workshops owned by one master craftsman working on his own, as it did not seem likely that the segregated accommodation required for foreigners could be provided in such cases. This regulation was, however, also repealed in the decree of 10 November 1916.[36]

Decrees issued by the Prussian Minister of the Interior on 20 July 1915 and 16 December 1915 also gradually made it possible for Jewish workers from Russia to be employed in industry during the war, although a decree of 23 December 1905 had reinforced the ban on their entry into Germany.[37] These Jews were for the most part skilled workers who were not, however, allowed to bring members of their families with them, unless they too were under contract. A decree of 10 November 1916 also permitted their employment by small firms and master craftsmen.[38] Further investigation is required to determine why after two meetings in the Department of the Interior of the Reich on 9 March and 15 April 1918[39] the Prussian Minister of the Interior decreed on 23 April 1918 that there should be no further recruitment of Jewish workers in the general government area of Warsaw (Generalgouvernement Warschau).[40]

FORCED LABOR BY BELGIANS IN GERMANY 1915-1918

German imperialism made every effort to use the countries that it had occupied to the best possible advantage of the war economy. As far as foreign labor was concerned, the statement made by the Prussian Ministry of War in October 1916 was valid for the whole period of occupation: "Whatever doubts there may be about principles of international law, they must give way to the absolute necessity that every worker under German control should be employed in the most productive capacity possible and to the best advantage of the war economy."[41]

The recruiting of forced labor and deportation to Germany, both of which were in violation of international law, especially affected Belgian and Polish workers but also those of the Ukraine and the Baltic states. Tables 8.3 through

8.5 give information on the numbers and countries of origin of the foreign workers recruited or employed. Belgian workers were employed in the arms industry mainly in Rhineland-Westphalia, a few thousand of them temporarily in agriculture.

Bourgeois historians hardly deal with forced labor and the policies behind it during the First World War.[42] Although they condemn the recruiting of forced labor in the occupied territories, they try to claim that it was restricted to the period from October 1916 to February 1917.[43]

Zunkel refuses to accept the term "forced deportation" in connection with Belgium for the period before 26 October 1916 and, in spite of all his reservations, considers the use of the expression "volunteers" to be "rather more accurate a description of the Belgian workers recruited."[44] This argument also goes hand in hand with the failure to deal with the resistance to forced labor on the part of deported Belgians, evidence of which is available from the very beginning. In addition to this, as Zunkel also clearly shows, while Rhenish-Westphalian heavy industry is described as the initiator of forced labor, it is not named as its main beneficiary, and differences of opinion between the various departments of the government and the military authorities about specific forms and methods of forced recruitment are described as opposing positions based on matters of principle. The explanation of this lies in the general failure to recognize the class character of the state and in the desire to demonstrate the ability of the state to develop and pursue "liberal labor policies."

The question of forced labor by Belgians has been discussed elsewhere.[45] Analyses of economic policies in the occupied territories are also available.[46] A few brief remarks about the deportation of Belgian workers and their subjection to forced labor will suffice.

From spring 1915 on Belgians were deported to Germany and subjected to forced labor at first only for a few firms. After June 1915, however, assistance was available from the Bureau of German Industry (Deutsches Industriebüro) established by the Northwestern Group of the German Association of Iron and Steel Producers (Verein Deutscher Eisen-und Stahlindustrieller) in Brussels, which was supported by the occupying authorities of the general government area of Brussels (Generalgouvernement Brüssel). From July 1915 to October 1916 over 30,000 workers were deported. At first it was intended that appearances should be kept up that the work was voluntary and only indirect force was to be used. When this is referred to as forced recruitment and forced labor, it is not only because the economic pressure of the pre-war years had increased enormously since the Germans had occupied the country, for example, as a result of deliberate attempts to ruin certain sectors of industry, the plundering of raw materials, and the unemployment that this caused. It is also because the often forgotten "Decree against Shirkers" ("Verordnung gegen die Arbeitsscheu") of 15 May 1916 was not the first measure to be taken by the Governor General in matters of employment. This decree provided a legal basis for the mass deportations that large-scale industrialists, landowners, and the army had increasingly been demanding since spring 1916. Further evidence of this is provided by discussions that took

Table 8.4

Numbers of Foreign Workers Supplied to the Agricultural Sector in Germany in 1914–1918

Country of origin/Nationality	1914	1915	1916	1917	1918	Total
I Russia comprising:						
1. Germans	60,113	40,807	41,550	43,893	48,014	234,377
2. Poles	1,620	16,264	5,748	3,008	5,588	32,228
II Austria-Hungary comprising:	58,493	24,543	35,802	40,885	42,426	202,149
1. Poles	63,626	10,905	1,547	538	270	76,886
2. Hungarians	22,365	5,627	605	357	219	29,173
3. Czechs	4,092	4	6	2	5	4,109
4. Ruthenians	180	46	101	49	5	381
III Others	36,989	5,228	835	130	41	43,223
	3,068	1,816	3,430	11,361	5,533	25,208
Totals	126,807	53,528	46,527	55,792	53,817	336,471

Source: Statistisches Jahrbuch für das Deutsche Reich, (Berlin), 1915, p. 475; 1916, p. 107; 1917, p. 149; 1918, p. 125; 1919, p. 313.

Table 8.5
Numbers of Foreign Workers Supplied to the Industrial Sector in Germany in 1914–1918

	1914	1915	1916	1917	1918	Total
Country of origin/Nationality						
I Russia comprising:	1,212	20,121	30,153	31,502	26,039	109,027
1. Germans	97	3,610	917	760	2,733	8,117
2. Poles	1,115	16,511	29,236	30,742	23,306	100,910
II Austria-Hungary comprising:	2,908	50	237	41	57	3,293
1. Poles	373	15	152	15	16	571
2. Hungarians	163	—	26	2	4	195
3. Czechs	20	2	53	14	6	95
4. Ruthenians	2,352	33	6	10	31	2,432
III Others	2,048	553	4,815	5,753	16,486	29,655
Totals	6,168	20,724	35,205	37,296	42,582	141,975

Source: Statistisches Jahrbuch für das Deutsche Reich, (Berlin), 1915, p. 475ff; 1916, p. 107ff; 1917, p. 148; 1918, p. 124; 1919, p. 312.

place in the Department of the Interior of the Reich and the Prussian Ministry of War in March and May 1916.[47] The first "Decree against Shirkers" of 15 August 1915 threatened Belgians who refused to carry out or continue work offered to them with imprisonment or fines.[48] Threats and actual physical force were used to make Belgians work; for many of them it was of secondary importance whether they had to work for the occupying power in Belgium or in Germany.

Further evidence that the Belgians who were brought to Germany in 1915–1916 were not volunteers is provided by their resistance, a subject that requires more detailed research. Bittmann noted that enquiries about Belgians in the coal-mining, iron, and mechanical engineering industries produced mainly complaints "about lack of training, lack of the will to work, and lack of interest."[49]

After discussion about forms and methods of forced labor the government authorities responsible and the representatives of the occupation administration agreed in September 1916 to take measures leading to mass deportation. The main subject of a meeting that also took place in September 1916 was the question of "whether legal grounds could be found for forced labor which were not too obvious a breach of the Hague Convention."[50]

From October 1916 to February 1917 especially brutal methods were used to deport 60,000 Belgians to Germany; in the same period the threat of possible deportation was used to persuade a further 17,000 Belgians to "volunteer" to go and work in Germany.[51] After the mass deportation had been completed, 70,000 more Belgians went to Germany in 1917, to be followed by a further 28,000 in the first six months of 1918; hence a total of at least 206,000 Belgians were subjected to forced labor in Germany during the war. This figure does not include those who were forced to work for the occupation forces in logistics and close to the front; during the last two years of the war in the so-called Civilian Labor-Battalions (Zivil-Arbeits-Bataillone) alone, there were 62,155 Belgians.

The discontinuation of mass deportation in February 1917 after it had been practiced for several weeks and the return to the use of indirect force to recruit Belgian workers are generally attributed by bourgeois historians to resistance in Belgium, protests at the international level, and the alleged opposition to deportation of the governor general and the civilian administration of the general government area (General gouvernement). This view overlooks another factor —the resistance of the Belgians who had already been deported to Germany where they were put in camps and attempts were made to force them to sign contracts of employment as if they were volunteers.

In order to achieve this, use was made of "firm discipline and forced labor for camp duties at the distribution center."[52] Writing about the situation in the camps, a representative of the Department of the Interior of the Reich observed in February 1917 that the food was "below standard, the people are terribly thin, the state of their health is bad and the number of deaths high."[53]

In spite of increased pressure, only a small number of those who had been deported in 1916–1917 were prepared to work. Not even attempts made during the final years of the war to provide certain incentives to work by offering short-term contracts and leaves of absence or bounties and family allowances succeeded in breaking the resistance of the Belgians to forced labor. As a result of this, a considerable number of industrialists and big landowners refused to employ Belgian workers. They preferred to do without these workers, who did not seem sufficiently cheap and willing, and concentrated their efforts on obtaining labor from other occupied territories.

RECRUITMENT OF FORCED LABOR IN THE OCCUPIED TERRITORIES OF THE EAST

The German occupiers made every effort to recruit as much labor as possible from the territories that they occupied in the east, in particular from the general government area of Warsaw, the Ukraine, and the Baltic states. Contrary to what Zunkel and also Conze[54] have stated, it should be pointed out that in Poland too the use of economic force, which had deliberately been increased since the occupation, was accompanied more and more by the use of other forms of force, whether direct or indirect.[55] Every means was used in pursuit of the single aim of gaining control of the maximum possible number of workers who were completely at the mercy of the ruling class. A closely knit system of recruitment developed in which the DAZ, whose agencies were attached to the German local occupation authorities and which worked in close contact with the police, played an important role.[56] The decree of 4 October 1916 aimed at the "shirkers" was not only meant to provide a seemingly legal basis for deportation but was also used to put pressure on Polish workers to make them sign contracts "voluntarily."[57]

With the increase in the power of the military dictatorship marked by the creation of the III. Oberste Heeresleitung (Supreme Command) and with the Hindenburg Program of 1916, the monopolists, big landowners, and the state set about deporting vast numbers of workers using especially brutal methods. At the beginning of the war there were at least 300,000 to 350,000 Russian-Polish workers in Germany.[58] According to the figures given by the director of the DAZ, approximately 100,000 to 120,000 workers were recruited from the general government area of Warsaw between January 1915 and February 1916.[59] This means that according to the official data contained in Tables 8.4 and 8.5 the DAZ supplied about 140,000 Russian-Poles for work on German farms and 150,000 for work in the German industrial sector. The number of workers involved in forced labor increased every year, and at the end of the war there were from 500,000 to 600,000 Russian-Poles working in Germany.

At no time, however, were the occupiers satisfied with the results of their campaigns to recruit workers. Nevertheless, in choosing the forms of force required to recruit labor they had to take into consideration the growing resistance of Polish workers, who were influenced by the Russian Revolution of 1917. At the conference of the relevant departments of civilian and military authorities on 30 March 1917, which recommended that more use should be made of indirect forms of force, the following statement was made: "The effects of the Russian Revolution in the occupied territories are becoming noticeable in a state of growing agitation among the population. It would therefore be most inopportune to resort to the use of force at the present moment."[60] In spite of this, various forms of force were used to recruit labor up to the very end of the war.

After the signing of the peace treaty with the Ukrainian central council (Zentralrada) on 9 February 1918, the German occupation forces recruited 10,000 to 12,000 workers in the Ukraine.[61] This they considered unsatisfactory.

An intensive campaign to recruit labor was also carried out in the Baltic and Russian territories that had been occupied in 1917–1918. As Table 8.1 shows, there were only around 2,000 Lithuanians in Prussia when war broke out, and the numbers of Latvians and Estonians were far smaller. According to the DAZ, a total of 34,108 workers were deported to Germany during the war from the territories under the control of the High Command East (Oberkommando-Ost, often abbreviated to Ober-Ost), including 24,239 from Lithuania and 3,650 from the other Baltic states.[62] In May 1918 Ludendorff confirmed that the choice of the methods used to recruit these workers always depended on the aim of the occupiers: "The forces in the field always take whatever measures are possible in order to put the workers there to use, either in the service of the army or of our country."[63] These measures included close cooperation between the DAZ, the Supreme Command, and the High Command East, which led to an agreement in spring 1918 that the territories in which recruitment was allowed should be divided into three areas by the DAZ; 1. Livonia, Estonia, Riga, Dwinsk (now Daugavpils) and district; 2. the military government area of Minsk and the refugee camp of Baranowitschi; 3. the military government area of Volhynia.

Increased economic force and other forms were used simultaneously. A circular issued by the rear area headquarters (Etappen-Inspektion) of the Eighth Army on 18 February 1917 and addressed to the German local government heads (Kreishauptmänner) declared unequivocally: "It is absolutely necessary that all available labor should be put to the fullest possible use. If necessary, force is to be used to carry out these measures. No one is to remain without employment."[64] The occupying power tried to deny the use of force other than that of an economic nature, and the records of the military authorities frequently refer to political reasons that prevented the use of force. However, in discussions of the labor question held at the High Command East on 17 December 1917 it was taken for granted that workers could not be recruited without the use of force.[65] The need to maintain appearances that work was voluntary was explained as follows: "Criticism at home: Reichstag statement, constant complaints, the reaction from abroad, both from enemy and neutral states. In fact: the forced labor system has been a fiasco. . . . " Further details were added to justify this last statement: "Workers subjected to forced labor do the absolute minimum. . . . Many escape. . . . We have no administrative facilities required to carry out the compulsory registration of all workers. . . . '' One person who attended the meeting correctly summarized the discussion and the guidelines given by the High Command East as follows: "All that matters is the form of forced recruitment that is employed." Baron v.d. Gayl, High Command East, stated in conclusion: "Everything possible is to be done to encourage people to volunteer, but with the proviso that anyone who does not come of his own free will will be forced to come."

There is a considerable amount of evidence of forced recruitment available. Thus, after Riga was occupied, 700 workers were rounded up within a few days and subjected to forced labor.[66] Even the Lithuanian National Council (Landesrat), which cooperated closely with the occupying authorities, was moved to protest against forced labor.[67] A memorandum dated 20 November 1917, which was handed in to the Chancellor of the Reich giving many examples of forced labor, described the ending of this practice as "the most important matter for Lithuania."[68]

The use of workers from the Baltic states also shows that monopoly capitalists and big landowners profited most of all from deportation and forced labor. Records in the archives confirm, for example, that workers recruited in Livonia and Estonia in 1918 were supplied to such firms as AEG in Berlin, Gewerkschaft Deutscher Kaiser in Hamborn, Farben-Fabrik Wolfen, Deutz in Cologne, Krupp in Essen, Kaiserliche Werft in Stettin, Kaiserliche Schiffswerft in Danzig, Schwartzkopf in Wildau, and so on.[69] A considerable number of these and other firms played an important role in preparing German imperialism for war so as to be able to exploit foreign countries and their workers.[70]

The German occupation authorities did not hesitate to set up DAZ offices directly behind the German-Russian front in the hope of recruiting people crossing over. This hope was based on speculation about the economic situation in Soviet Russia; the discussion at a meeting in the departments responsible on 19 March 1918 put this hope into words: "When these people see that they cannot live on Bolshevik ideas they will have to start looking for work."[71] After an officer had been sent to Moscow to make enquiries, however, the German consulate-general recommended that the idea of recruiting labor in Soviet Russia should be abandoned. This was not only because wages in Moscow and other industrial areas were too high, but also because "there was a danger of Bolshevik ideas being spread."[72] As the sections of heavy industry and the land-owning classes that were interested in employing foreigners did not simply want workers but the cheapest and most willing workers, the German government decided to abandon this plan altogether, which in any case had no chance of success.

THE RECRUITMENT OF LABOR IN NEUTRAL COUNTRIES, 1915–1918

At the same time as workers were being deported from the occupied countries, the German government attempted to support efforts that were being made to attract workers, especially skilled workers, from the countries that remained neutral during the war. Special attention was paid to those countries from which workers had migrated to Germany in the pre-war period. Tables 8.1 through 8.3 confirm that in the fall of 1914 there were still several thousand workers from Switzerland and the Scandinavian countries in Germany as well as 65,000 from Italy, which was neutral at the beginning. Most of these were employed in the industrial sector. Using Sweden as an example, Riegler shows how attempts were made to obtain more workers from these countries with the help of the DAZ.[73] According to DAZ records, agents of this institution brought 810 workers from Denmark to Germany in 1916–1917; in Germany the DAZ issued identity cards to 3,505 workers from Denmark, Norway, and Sweden between 1 January 1918 and 25 May 1918.[74] Most of these workers were employed in the industrial sector. Evidence of the support given to the war policies by right-wing German trade union leaders is provided by the fact that the General Committee (General-kommission) of the unions tried to recruit skilled workers in Denmark and Switzerland with the help of the unions there.[75] In a telegram dated 24 May 1918, Ludendorff recommended to the Department of the Interior of the Reich that, because of the danger of the spread of Bolshevik ideas, workers from Denmark and Sweden should be kept under observation "by the authorities but also by the organs of the trade unions which could use this opportunity to show their loyalty to the state."[76] On the whole it can be said that the results of the recruitment campaigns in neutral countries and the performance of the workers from these countries did not fulfill the expectations of the German ruling circles.

DIFFERENCES BETWEEN GERMANY AND AUSTRIA-HUNGARY OVER MIGRANT WORKERS[77]

The pre-war conflicts between the governments in Vienna and Berlin in connection with the employment of workers from the Danubian monarchy in Germany reached a climax during the war; they confirmed the imperialist nature of the alliance between the two monarchies.[78]

After Russia, Austria-Hungary was the second largest supplier of labor to German industry and agriculture—Table 8.2 shows that in 1913 alone over 400,000 workers came from the Danubian monarchy to work in Prussia. At the outbreak of war all citizens liable for military service were summoned home; other workers, for the most part Poles and Ruthenians from Galicia, were left in the hands of the German imperialists for the time being. After a new recruitment campaign had initially also been carried out in the normal way, the government authorities of Prussia and of the Reich agreed to the repatriation of those workers who had become unemployed. At the end of 1914 there were more than 200,000 workers from the Danubian monarchy in Prussia (cf. note 14); in the following years this number declined.

The ruling circles in Germany expressed a desire to continue recruiting workers in Austria-Hungary during the war. Beginning with its note of 9 February 1915, the government in Vienna made this conditional on the Germans fulfilling its pre-war demands—that all of the problems associated with seasonal migration should be settled first.[79] The most important of these were that citizens of Austria-Hungary living in Germany should be granted the same rights as Germans and that the mandatory identification should be abandoned. During the war the German government continued to reject such demands categorically, and it was not prepared to allow the government in Vienna to exert any kind of influence that might have led to the improvement of the disgraceful working and living conditions under which its citizens employed in Germany were forced to exist. At the same time, the German government tried to put pressure on its ally to allow the recruitment of Galician workers. To this end the Germans tried to make use of negotiations that took place on 19 April 1915 with the Austrians over the distribution of customs duties from the Russian-Polish territories, which the troops of the two countries had occupied. These negotiations ended in an agreement that permitted the recruitment of labor in the occupied territories, but the Germans were not granted access to the labor reserves of Galicia as they had hoped.[80] As a result of constant pressure from the German government, negotiations resumed on 14 May 1915 over the recruitment of Galician workers who had been put to flight by Russian troops and were now in Austrian refugee camps.[81] In the course of the negotiations, the Germans again rejected the demands made in the Austrian note of 9 February 1915, but finally had to agree to a general settlement of all of the problems connected with migrant workers before the end of 1915 if they were to be allowed to recruit Galician workers from the refugee camps for a limited period.[82]

After the DAZ had recruited several thousand Galician workers in the following weeks, it soon became clear that the ruling circles in Germany were not prepared to make any concessions.[83] Differences over the agreement that had been made in April 1915 on customs duties and especially over the recruitment of labor in the general government area (Generalgouvernement) of Warsaw and the military government area (Militärgouvernement) of Lublin served to strengthen the resolve of the Vienna government to reject German recruitment of labor in Galicia.[84] At the same time, it complained that the Austrians were being prevented from recruiting labor in the general government area of Warsaw.[85]

The conflicts that followed confirmed that the German government preferred to abandon its attempts to recruit labor in Galicia and the military government area of Lublin rather than allow Austria to recruit in the general government area of Warsaw and grant its ally the right to be consulted on the working conditions of seasonal labor. At a meeting on 1 February 1916 the departments involved decided that each side should be allowed to recruit in that section of Russian-Polish territory that it had occupied; beyond that it was considered that there was no point in further negotiations.[86] In spite of this, further demands were made that Austria should allow the recruitment of Galician workers. Austria-Hungary reacted to such activities on the part of the German government with a note dated 18 February 1916 in which it stated that if there was to be any recruitment at all then only on condition that there were measures enacted in advance to ensure the social and political protection of Austrian seasonal workers employed in the German Reich and [secondly] on condition that the state of affairs relating to the recruitment of workers from the territories occupied by the Germans, which did not fulfill the provisions of the agreements should be radically improved. . . . [87]

In spite of constant complaints about the shortage of workers, however, the ruling circles in Germany were not prepared to make any social or legal concessions. Instead they tried to recruit labor in other countries and to prevent all foreigners already in Germany from leaving the country. After 1915 they attempted to stop workers from Austria-Hungary from returning home. Although it was not possible to seal the border, everything was done to achieve this aim without revealing the use of force to the outside world.[88] This plan was put into operation, although the Prussian Minister of War admitted on 2 January 1917 that there was ''no legal reason whatever to refuse Austrian migrant workers resident in Germany the general right to return home.''[89] The Germans also strictly rejected the request of the Austrians that those people who had originally come from the Russian territories occupied by Austria during the war should be allowed to return. According to Austrian figures, 95,000 workers had migrated from what was later to become the military government area of Lublin to Germany, where they had been retained against their will since the beginning of the war.[90] As a result of the ''friction'' between the two monarchies, the German government considered that it was making a major concession in allowing Polish workers from the military government area of Lublin leaves of absence if substitutes were provided in advance.[91] The government in Vienna rightly considered this suggestion to mean a rejection of its basic demands. Right up to the end of the war, the German imperialists stubbornly rejected all the suggestions and demands made by Vienna for a solution of the problem of seasonal workers. Finally there were also differences beginning in May 1918 between Austria-Hungary and Germany over the recruitment of workers in the occupied Italian territories. Although there were between 10,000 and 12,000 Italian workers in Germany from 1915 to 1918, only about 2,000 workers could be recruited by the DAZ after May 1918. Of these 834 had been taken to Germany by 19 September 1918.[92]

ATTEMPTS TO ACHIEVE GUARANTEED RECRUITMENT, IMPORTATION, AND EXPLOITATION OF FOREIGN WORKERS IN THE POST-WAR PERIOD

At the same time as efforts were being made to recruit and exploit as many foreign workers as possible, the German imperialists attempted to ensure that there would be no obstacles in the way of recruiting, importing, and exploiting foreign workers without restriction during the post-war period too.[93] Countries that were directly or indirectly dependent on Germany were to be compelled to accept the demands that were part of the program of war objectives in the form of a dictated peace or a treaty. The Prussian Minister of War agreed with the monopolists and big landowners who based their demands for the annexation of foreign territories, for example, Belgium and parts of Russian Poland, on their interest in exploiting the labor available there.[94] In the middle of 1918 he declared that

in the case of a future economic mobilization the immigration of foreign workers [would] seriously have to be considered to replace Germans who have been called up for military service. The War Department has therefore long considered it to be one of its paramount duties to encourage in every way possible from some areas under its control the immigration of foreign workers to Germany now and in the period after the war.[95]

The most important demands made by the ruling circles during the war with a view to ensuring supplies of foreign labor in the post-war period were incorporated in the various detailed plans for a peace treaty with Russia that were prepared after 1915 and in the drafts of treaties that were to be signed with various countries.

The most important of these demands were summarized in the petition handed in to the Chancellor of the Reich on 25 November 1917 by the War Committee of German Agriculture (Kriegsausschuss der deutschen Landwirtschaft) in connection with the employment of Polish workers.[96] This petition culminated in the following demand:

All of the questions connected with the importation of Polish workers must be settled so completely in the treaty that there is no opportunity for future discussion and so that a constant flow of Polish workers is available and remains so irrespective of changes in the economic and political situation of the new state and of the effects of Polish national and religious aspirations and passions.

The German government endeavoured to include these demands in such treaties as were being prepared for Poland and Austria, but the war ended before they could be signed.[97]

It was also the aim of the German government to ensure that its ideas on migrant workers were included in the peace and commercial treaties that the Ukraine, Finland, Soviet Russia, and Rumania were forced to accept in 1918. The peace treaty with the Ukraine was concluded on 9 February 1918 with the Central Council,[98] a government without a country, which hoped that the German occupiers would reinstate it in Kiev.[99] Neither this nor the additional German-Ukranian treaty signed on the same day contained any reference to the migration of workers. The big landowners, the DAZ, the Ministry of War, and the Supreme Command of the Army all agreed that a separate military and economic treaty, which was to be signed with the Ukraine, should ensure that the latter could not prevent seasonal migration to Germany and would have to admit German recruiting organizations. The German ambassador in Kiev was instructed by the Foreign Ministry to see that these demands were included in the treaty.[100] The model for this was the equivalent section of the trade and shipping agreement between Germany and Finland that was signed on 7 March 1918 at the same time as the peace treaty between the two countries.[101]

It should be mentioned that the peace treaty and the trade agreement were concluded at a time when the German imperialists were preparing to intervene in Finland at the request of reactionary elements there. This intervention was to be the deciding factor in favor of the bourgeoisie in the struggle between revolution and counter-revolution in Finland.[102] In return for help in the struggle against the revolutionary movement, the Finnish bourgeoisie was prepared, among other things, to allow the recruitment of labor for German industry and agriculture. In January 1918 the Prussian Ministry of War/War Department had written: "At the moment the most important way in which Finland can serve German interests is by supplying workers, and the readiness we have shown to recognize Finland should go some considerable way towards making it easier for the Finnish government to grant this concession."[103] Article 16 of the trade agreement signed on 7 March 1918 contained the same demands as those which had been made of Russia and Poland and stated the following:

Each party to this agreement shall permit the temporary migration of its citizens to the territory of the other for the purpose of working in the agricultural and industrial sectors and in no way shall this be prevented, especially not by means of passport restrictions. The representatives of organizations established within the territory of one party to act as agents for the recruitment of such workers, and who are officially certified as such to the government of the second party, shall be admitted to the territory without further formalities and permitted to carry out their task of recruiting without hindrance.[104]

As Finland was not interested in the immigration of foreign workers, it was clear that the German imperialists had forced the Finnish government to accept its demands on the question of migrant workers in spite of the formulations of reciprocity of the agreement, which followed diplomatic usage. The draft version of a military and economic agreement with the Ukraine dated summer 1918 also contained a similar stipulation.[105] Going beyond what was stated in the German-Finnish agreement, the Ukraine was to be obliged not only to permit the Germans to recruit workers there but also to give them active support in doing so.

The Treaty of Brest-Litovsk, which Soviet Russia was forced to accept on 3 March 1918[106] also contained the same demands on the question of migrant workers as the treaty with Finland. The desire of extreme elements of German imperialism, put forward by the Ministry of War/War Department and supported by Ludendorff, was that Soviet Russia should also be obliged to give active support to recruiting campaigns and to offer no resistance to the removal of recruited workers.[107] This, however, was to be taken into consideration at a later date in a further agreement.

In the dictated peace treaty signed in Bucharest on 7 May 1918, Rumania was obliged to agree to the recruitment of "agricultural workers and manual workers" and not to hinder their migration to Germany.[108] In the same way Courland, Lithuania, Belgium, and Italy were to be compelled to enable part of their labor forces to be exploited.[109] As a result of the defeat of German imperialism in the war, the ruling circles in Germany were unable to fulfill their objective of guaranteeing the unrestricted recruitment, importation, and exploitation of foreign workers in the post-war period.

THE TREATMENT OF RUSSIAN-POLISH WORKERS, 1915–1918

The legal status of foreign workers during the war was subordinated to the aim of using them for as long as possible in the interest of profits to be made in the war economy.[110] This was the case whether they had been detained in Germany at the beginning of the war, deported from the occupied territories, or recruited in Austria-Hungary or neutral countries. The diversity of the legal regulations cannot conceal the fact that force other than that of an economic nature was also used against workers from neutral countries or the allied Danubien monarchy whenever they offered resistance to the system of oppression and exploitation. The Polish workers from the general government area of Warsaw and the military government area of Lublin suffered the most brutal treatment of all.

The Russian-Polish workers were subjected to forced labor and were tied to a fixed place of work by rules forbidding them to change jobs, to leave their local police district, or to return home. The decrees on mandatory identification issued every year from 1915 onward by the Prussian Minister of the Interior not only ensured that strict control was maintained by the DAZ and the police but also strengthened the hold that firms had on workers and exerted pressure on them to sign contracts.[111] Orders issued by the Second-in-Command of the Army Staff threatened all of those who did not submit unconditionally to this discipline with the use of force. Dohse rightly speaks of the "vicious circle of state and private repression": "Force exerted by the state permitted employers to increase the pressure on their workers, which in turn required the state to continue to exert force."[112]

As the domestic political crisis worsened and the military dictatorship increased its power, two different but not essentially opposing viewpoints began to become apparent in the discussions about the treatment of Russian-Polish workers that took place among the ruling class after the fall of 1916. Conservative and imperialist elements supported the idea of maintaining or increasing the use of force. In this context these elements included the big landowners from east of the Elbe, representatives of heavy industry (e.g., from Upper Silesia), most of the Deputy Commanding Generals of the Army Corps, as well as influential representatives of the ministerial bureaucracy. This view found its expression in the petition handed in by the War Committee of German Agriculture on 25 November 1917. Other more flexible representatives of the ruling class pursued the same aim of exploiting labor reserves as effectively as possible, but they wanted to cover up the policy of forced labor by means of concessions, promises of reform, and various forms of appeasement. This grouping included representatives of the civilian administration of the general government area of Warsaw, the Department of the Interior of the Reich, and the Prussian Ministry of War. The Undersecretary of State in the Department of the Interior of the Reich, for example, spoke out in support of alleviating the conditions of forced labor, because otherwise "instead of willingness to work [there would be] an atmosphere of bitterness open to incitement . . . which would have an extremely negative effect on the success of our war economy and destroy our chances of recruiting more workers after the war."[113]

After the proclamation of an allegedly independent Polish state on 5 November 1916,[114] nothing was done initially to improve the situation of the Poles in Germany.[115] A meeting of the departments involved on 18 November 1916,[116] a decree issued by the Prussian Minister of War on 7 December 1916,[117] the regulations for its execution of 5 February 1917,[118] and similar orders from the Army Corps provided for a slight relaxation of the conditions of forced labor. The aim of these measures was "to make the fullest possible use of Polish workers for the German war economy."[119] In connection with the effects of the Russian Revolution of 1917 on the Polish workers' struggle for national and social liberation and as a result of growing resistance to deportation and forced labor, the representatives of the relevant departments in Prussia and the Reich agreed to modify the conditions of forced labor.[120]

This decision was reflected in the decree of the Ministry of War on the treatment of Polish workers dated 15 October 1917[121] and in the regulations for its execution of 21 November 1917.[122] Vigorous protests from the conservative and imperialist elements[123] did not succeed in getting these measures rescinded but nevertheless ensured that the concessions granted to the workers were not put into practice.[124] The aim of the ruling class in modifying the policy of forced labor is well expressed in an order issued by the High Command of the Marches (Oberkommando in den Marken) on 14 December 1917 according to which the new regulations had

only been issued to increase the willingness of the Polish workers to work. It is and always has been the paramount duty of all authorities and employers to ensure that the maximum amount of work is done by the Polish workers and that peace and order are maintained among them. All other aspects of the matter must be subordinated to this.[125]

The available material from the archives refutes Zunkel's claim that the modification of the forced labor policy led to a "certain amount of pacification of the Polish workers and their political representatives."[126]

There was no question of there being a "liberal labor policy," and the Polish workers, in fact, rarely experienced any of the promised alleviations. For this reason the Prussian Minister of Agriculture was obliged to observe in January 1918 that the new regulations had "unfortunately not served to pacify them, but rather the opposite. . . . "[127] And in July the Prussian Ministry of War stated that the promised measures were not yet sufficiently well known to the local authorities everywhere or appreciated by them. . . . People are still being punished even with imprisonment to try and compel them to renew contracts of employment which have expired and they are maltreated or refused food if they do not work hard enough. The wrong treatment and insufficient wages for strenuous work serve to embitter a Pole in the long run and make him restive and unwilling to work. . . . [128]

Especially under the influence of the Russian Revolution of 1917, there was an increase in the resistance of the Polish workers to deportation and forced labor.

THE RESISTANCE OF FOREIGN WORKERS TO DEPORTATION AND FORCED LABOR

It is beyond the scope of this study to deal in any detail with the ''explosive contradiction'' involved in the system of forced labor created by the ruling class during the First World War; this must form the subject of a separate study. The observation made by Eichholtz in connection with the Second World War also applies to the First World War: ''It was impossible to put an end to the antagonism between the masses in the plundered occupied countries and the workers subjected to forced labor on the one hand and the imperialist German conquerors on the other.''[129] This is demonstrated by the foreign workers' struggle against occupation, deportation, and forced labor, a struggle that existed in various forms from the beginning of the war but that grew especially during the final years.[130] The ruling circles had to take this struggle into consideration, for example, when modifying their forced labor policy.

Whatever their social origins (which require closer examination) the foreign workers became part of the working class and basically had the same class interests as the German proletariat. They made up a section of the working class that was especially discriminated against, and as a result of their concrete situation, for example, their different nationalities, legal status, and historical traditions, they also had specific interests.[131] The objective class interests of the proletariat made it necessary to weaken and destroy the state monopoly system of government and to use the war to bring about the collapse of the bourgeoisie; this had to include the struggle against occupation, deportation, and discrimination.

The attitude of the German working-class movement to their foreign-class brothers played an important role in the development of the foreign workers' class consciousness and organization. Initial studies of this attitude reveal that there were two basic tendencies. First, there were right-wing SPD and trade-union leaders who had openly supported the bourgeoisie and the imperialist war since its beginning. They betrayed proletarian internationalism as, for example, expressed in the resolution on immigration and emigration adopted by the Stuttgart Congress of the Second International in 1907.[132] They did not firmly reject occupation and forced labor, and they did not seek to involve the foreign workers in the revolutionary struggle.[133] This also impaired the resistance of the German working-class movement to the war and imperialism. Second was the German left wing, headed by the Spartakus group, class-conscious members of the SPD and the USPD, and workers who were not members of parties. They attempted to involve the foreigners in the developing struggle of the people to end the war and to do all in their power to oppose forced labor and discrimination against foreigners. As a result of growing war-weariness and the effects of the Russian Revolution of 1917, there were an increasing number of joint campaigns in the final years of the war.

Material in the archives shows that foreign workers were actively involved in the large-scale strikes of the German proletariat that took place in 1917 and 1918; for example, the strikes of April 1917 in the arms industry and those of January and February 1918 that affected most industries. In July 1917 the deputy commander-in-chief of the VII. Armeekorps in Münster remarked: "It is interesting to note that in the recent disturbances of which there are reports from Düsseldorf but also other places a leading role was played by foreign workers, especially Poles and Belgians."[134]

On the other hand, German workers also supported foreigners who resorted to strikes or similar measures. An example of this is the close cooperation of members of the Association of German Farmworkers (Deutscher Landarbeiterverband) with those Polish workers who organized a strike affecting several estates in the district of Franzburg in the spring of 1918. A further expression and also a result of this cooperation was the fact that around 2,000 Polish agricultural workers in Mecklenburg joined the association at that time.[135]

CONCLUSION

The German imperialist policy of forced labor during the First World War is one link in the chain of imperialist policies involving migrant workers in Germany.[136] The basis of this continuity is the aggressive nature of German imperialism and the enduring domination of the same class elements in the twentieth century—elements which were and still are the main beneficiaries of the import and exploitation of foreign workers. During the Weimar Republic monopoly capitalists and big landowners imported up to 300,000 foreign workers into Germany during a year.[137] After the fascist dictatorship of German imperialism had been set up in 1933 the number of foreign workers, which had declined during the world economic crisis, gradually began to rise again, especially after 1937–1938, and just before the Second World War there were around 500,000 foreigners employed in Germany.[138] During the war the German imperialists developed a system of mass forced labor involving millions of deported foreign workers.[139] Finally, the monopoly capitalists of the Federal Republic began to import foreign workers in the middle of the 1950s until a record number of 2.6 million—excluding the workers' families—was reached in 1973. The forms and methods of recruiting foreign workers as well as their countries of origin have changed to conform with changes in international power relationships and in class relationships within the various industrialized capitalist countries importing foreign labor. Periods in which the German ruling class made use of the economic pressure that compelled workers from underdeveloped countries to leave their homes because of unemployment and social deprivation in order to seek work abroad alternated with times such as during the two world wars, when German imperialists, in their attempts to rule the world, made use of force other than that of a purely economic nature to recruit and exploit foreign workers.

These changes in the forms and methods used to recruit and exploit reserves of foreign labor cannot, however, conceal the fact that the reactionary traditions of the foreign labor policies of German imperialism continue throughout the twentieth century, though in modified form. Created in the Wilhelmian Empire, they extend through the subsequent decades, reached an appalling climax in the policy of mass forced labor during the Second World War, and are carried on in the discrimination against foreign workers in the Federal Republic.[140] For anyone who is aware of developments since the turn of the century, an examination of the present policies toward foreigners in other imperialist countries such as France, Great Britain, or Switzerland confirms that this continuity in foreign labor policies corresponds to the nature of imperialism.

NOTES

1. For the First World War, cf. Institut für Geschichte an der Akademie der Wissenschaften zu Berlin, Arbeitsgruppe Erster Weltkrieg, Leitung F. Klein, ed., *Deutschland im Ersten Weltkrieg*, 3 vols. (Berlin, 1970 ff.); D. Baudis and H. Nussbaum, *Wirtschaft und Staat in Deutschland vom Ende des 19. Jahrhunderts bis 1918/19* (Berlin, 1978); H. Mottek et al., *Wirtschaftsgeschichte Deutschlands. Ein Grundriss*, vol. 3, 2d. ed., (Berlin, 1975); A. Schröter, *Krieg-Staat-Monopol, 1914–1918. Die Zusammenhänge von imperialistischer Kriegswirtschaft, Militarisierung der Volkswirtschaft und staatsmonopolistischem Kapitalismus in Deutschland während des ersten Weltkrieges*, (Berlin, 1965). The following works give surveys of Marxist and bourgeois literature on the First World War: W. Gutsche et al., "Forschungen zur deutschen Geschichte vom Ausgang des 19. Jahrhunderts bis 1917," in *Historische Forschungen in der DDR 1970–1980, Analysen und Berichte*, special issue, 1980 of the *Zeitschrift für Geschichtswissenschaft (ZfG)*, (Berlin, 1980), pp. 204ff.; F. Klein, "Erster Weltkrieg," in G. Lozek et al., eds., *Unbewältigte Vergangenheit, Kritik der bürgerlichen Geschichtsschreibung in der BRD*, 3d. ed. (Berlin, 1977), pp. 304ff.

2. For France, cf. Gary S. Cross, "Towards Social Peace and Prosperity: The Politics of Immigration in France during the Era of World War I," *French Historical Studies* 11 (1979–1980); N. M. Frolkin, *Trudowaja immigrazija wo Franzii w nowejscheje wremja* [Immigration of Workers to France in Recent Times], (Kiev, 1975), p. 32; Y. Moulier and G. Tapinos, "Frankreich," in E. Gehmacher, D. Kubat and U. Mehrländer, eds., *Ausländerpolitik im Konflikt, Arbeitskräfte oder Einwanderer? Konzepte der Aufnahme– und Entsendeländer* (Bonn, 1978), p. 139.

3. Cf. the basic principles of a definition of forced labor in D. Eichholtz, *Geschichte der deutschen Kriegswirtschaft 1939–1945*, vol. 1 ((Berlin, 1971), pp. 88ff.

4. J. Nichtweiss, *Die ausländischen Saisonarbeiter in der Landwirtschaft der östlichen und mittleren Gebiete des Deutschen Reiches* (Berlin, 1959); K. J. Bade, "Massenabwanderung und Arbeitsmarkt im deutschen Nordosten von 1880 bis zum Ersten Weltkrieg," *Archiv für Sozialgeschichte*, 20 (Bonn, 1980). Cf. also K. Dohse, *Ausländische Arbeiter und bürgerlicher Staat. Genese und Funktion von staatlicher Ausländerpolitik und Ausländerrecht. Vom Kaiserreich bis zur Bundesrepublik Deutschland* (Königstein/Ts., 1981), pp. 29ff.

5. W. I. Lenin, "Zur Revision des Parteiprogramms," in *Werke*, vol. 26 (Berlin, 1974), p. 155.

6. Nichtweiss, *Die ausländischen Saisonarbeiter*, p. 54.

7. Ibid., pp. 197ff.

8. Cf. for the whole period of the First World War: L. Elsner, "Die ausländischen Arbeiter in der Landwirtschaft der östlichen und mittleren Gebiete des Deutschen Reiches während des 1. Weltkriegs" (Ph.D. diss., Rostock, 1961); L. Elsner, "Die polnischen Arbeiter in der deutschen Landwirtschaft während des ersten Weltkriegs," manuscript (Rostock, 1975); F. Zunkel, "Die ausländischen Arbeiter in der deutschen Kriegswirtschaftspolitik des I. Weltkrieges," in G. A. Ritter, ed., *Entstehung und Wandel der modernen Gesellschaft*, essays in honor of H. Rosenberg presented to him on his sixty-fifth birthday (Berlin, 1970), pp. 280ff. Cf. also relevant sections of *DDR-Literatur über Arbeiterwanderungen und Fremdarbeiterpolitik im Imperialismus, Forschungsstand und Bibliographie* (Rostock, 1979), no. 5, in the series "Fremdarbeiterpolitik des Imperialismus."

9. Minutes of the meeting: Zentrales Staatsarchiv (hereafter, ZStA) Potsdam, Reichswirtschaftsamt, no. 7611, pp. 83ff.

10. Minutes of the meeting: ZStA Potsdam, Reichswirtschaftsamt, no. 7613, pp. 13ff. Cf. also R. Zilch, "Zur wirtschaftlichen Vorbereitung des deutschen Imperialismus auf den ersten Weltkrieg. Das Protokoll der Sitzung des 'Wirtschaftlichen Ausschusses' bei der 'Ständigen Kommission für Mobilmachungsangelegenheiten' vom Mai 1914," in *Zeitschrift für Geschichtswissenschaft* 2 (1976), 202ff.

11. Memorandum on questions of economic mobilization dated January 1914, see ZStA Potsdam, Auswärtiges Amt, no. 3623, pp. 75ff.; notes on questions of economic mobilization dated May 1914, see ZStA Potsdam, Auswärtiges Amt, no. 3624, pp. 8ff.

12. ZStA Potsdam, Reichsamt des Innern, no. 12361, pp. 2f.

13. Ibid., pp. 2, 4: Prussian Minister of War to Second-in-Command of the Army Corps, 31 July 1914; Department of the Interior of the Reich to the governments of the states of the Reich, 1 August 1914.

14. Precise statistical data on the employment of foreigners in the pre-war and wartime periods are not available. Apart from population and occupational censuses, the main sources are the yearly lists of arrivals and departures and total numbers of foreign workers that were kept in Prussia from 1906 to 1914. (These lists, which have not been published up to now, were based on information supplied by the heads of the local authorities. They are to be found in ZStA Merseburg, Rep. 87 B, Arbeitersachen, no. 21 B). A further source is the annual list of the number of identity cards issued to workers by the DAZ (cf. Table 8.3). As the annual issue of identity cards did not include all workers and since some states of the Reich did not adopt the identity card system, the figures given cannot be considered to be exact. According to the director of the DAZ, in 1917, for example, the number of workers without identity cards was about 20 percent of the

number who had one. (ZStA Merseburg, Rep. 87 B, Arbeiter-und Angestelltensachen, no. 23, vol. 5, director of the DAZ to the Prussian Minister of Agriculture, dated 16 October 1917). This problem must be taken into consideration when analyzing the figures in the tables given. The figures in this chapter are based on the sources given here and statistics contained in a considerable number of other archive sources.

15. Dohse, *Ausländische Arbeiter*, pp. 43ff. The author of this paper is at present working on a study of the employment of foreigners in the industrial sector. Exact figures will be provided there.

16. Zunkel, "Die ausländischen Arbeiter," p. 285.

17. Dohse, *Ausländische Arbeiter*, p. 79, is mistaken when he speaks of "dictatorial powers given to the staff of each Army Corps" only after the War Department had been established.

18. Zunkel, "Die ausländischen Arbeiter," p. 288.

19. Ibid., p. 286.

20. Notes, see ZStA Potsdam, Reichsamt des Innern, no. 12361, pp. 88ff.

21. Ibid., p. 110ff.

22. Notes, see ZStA Potsdam, Reichsamt des Innern, no. 12380, pp. 18ff.

23. Ibid., pp. 38f.

24. For a model for these orders, see ibid., p. 39.

25. Ibid., pp. 72ff.

26. Telegram and letter sent by v. Wangenheim on 2 October 1914 to the Prussian Minister of Agriculture, see Staatsarchiv (hereafter StA) Greifswald, Rep. 60, no. 1455. For further protests, see Elsner, "Die ausländischen Arbeiter," pp. 55ff.; Elsner, "Die polnischen Arbeiter," pp. 19ff.

27. ZStA Potsdam, Reichsamt des Innern, no. 12380, pp. 47ff.

28. ZStA Potsdam, Rep. 2 A I, Pol. no. 2844, pp. 50f.

29. Elsner, "Die ausländischen Arbeiter," pp. 63ff.; Elsner, "Die polnischen Arbeiter," pp. 25ff.

30. StA Magdeburg, Rep. C20 I b, no. 1948, VI, pp. 47ff.

31. Ibid., pp. 43f. The only area in which this ban did not apply was the eastern provinces of Prussia.

32. Ibid., p. 188.

33. Further details are to be found in ZStA Potsdam, Reichsamt des Innern, no. 13713, pp. 40ff.

34. Ibid., p. 78.

35. Ibid., p. 225.

36. ZStA Potsdam, Reichsamt des Innern, no. 13714, pp. 367f.

37. Decree of 20 July 1915, see StA Magdeburg, Rep. C20 I b, no. 1948, VII, p. 15; decree of 16 December 1915, see ibid., pp. 78f.

38. ZStA Potsdam, Reichsamt des Innern, no. 13714, p. 367.

39. Notes taken at the meeting on 15 April 1918, see ZStA Potsdam, Reichsamt des Innern, no. 13719, pp. 122f.

40. Ibid., p. 198.

41. E. Ludendorff, ed., *Urkunden der Obersten Heeresleitung über ihre Tätigkeit 1916/18* (Berlin, 1922), p. 126.

42. Zunkel, "Die ausländischen Arbeiter," pp. 280f. The most important bourgeois literature is mentioned in L. Elsner, "Belgische Zwangsarbeiter in Deutschland während

des ersten Weltkrieges," in *ZfG* 11 (1976), pp. 1256ff. A very recent work deals with the attempt of right-wing SPD leaders to present deportation in a favorable light: A. Blänsdorf, *Die 2. Internationale und der Krieg. Die Diskussion über die internationale Zusammenarbeit der sozialistischen Parteien 1914–1917* (Stuttgart, 1979), pp. 338ff.

43. Cf., for example, G. Ritter, *Staatskunst und Kriegshandwerk Das Problem des "Militarismus" in Deutschland*, vol. 3 (Munich, 1964), pp. 433ff.; P. Graf Kielmannsegg, *Deutschland und der Erste Weltkrieg* (Frankfurt/Main, 1968), pp. 274f.

44. Zunkel, "Die ausländischen Arbeiter," pp. 259.

45. Elsner, "Belgische Zwangsarbeiter," cf. also W. Gutsche, "Zu einigen Fragen der staatsmonopolistischen Verflechtung in den ersten Kriegsjahren am Beispiel der Ausplünderung der belgischen Industrie und der Zwangsdeportation von Belgiern," in *Politik im Krieg 1914–1918, Studien zur Politik der deutschen herrschenden Klassen im ersten Weltkrieg* (Berlin, 1964), pp. 66ff.

46. *Deutschland im ersten Weltkrieg*, vol. 2, pp. 141ff.; Baudis and Nussbaum, *Wirtschaft und Staat*, pp. 277ff.

47. There are two different sets of notes on the meeting that took place at the Ministry of War on 2 March 1916: see ZStA Potsdam, Reichsamt des Innern, no. 2797, pp. 5ff. and pp. 13ff.

48. Gutsche, "Zu einigen Fragen der staatsmonopolistischen Verflechtung," p. 83.

49. K. Bittmann, *Werken und Wirken, Erinnerungen aus Industrie und Staatsdienst*, vol. 3 (Karlsruhe, 1924), p. 133.

50. Ritter, *Staatskunst und Kriegshandwerk*, p. 442.

51. For figures, see ZStA Potsdam, Reichsamt des Innern, no. 2797, pp. 119f.; memorandum on the movement of Belgian workers from the general government area of Belgium to Germany, prepared by the Department of Trade and Industry of the general government area of Belgium (23 January 1917) in ZStA Potsdam, Reichsamt des Innern, no. 19388, pp. 290ff.; memorandum on the utilization of Belgian workers in the German economy after the war prepared by the Department of Trade and Industry in the general government area of Belgium, edited by Dr. phil.et jur. W. Asmis (foreword dated 10 January 1918) in ZStA Potsdam, Reichsamt des Innern, no. 13718, p. 163.

52. ZStA Potsdam, Reichsamt des Innern, no. 19388, pp. 85f., guidelines on the allocation of work-shy Belgians to work in Germany, issued by the War Department in October 1916.

53. Ibid., p. 343.

54. Zunkel, "Die ausländischen Arbeiter," pp. 301ff.; W. Conze, *Polnische Nation und deutsche Politik im ersten Weltkrieg* (Cologne/Graz, 1958), p. 135.

55. On the economic exploitation of Poland, cf. W. Basler, *Deutschlands Annexionspolitik in Polen und im Baltikum 1914–1918* (Berlin, 1962), pp. 108ff.; *Deutschland im Ersten Weltkrieg*, vol. 2, pp. 160f., 493ff.; Baudis and Nussbaum, *Wirtschaft und Staat*, pp. 277ff., and Conze, *Polnische Nation*, pp. 125ff. do not give a true description of the extent to which Poland was exploited.

56. ZStA Potsdam, Reichsamt des Innern, no. 1280, pp. 407ff., decree issued by the head of the administration of the general government area of Warsaw to the heads of local government on 12 March 1916.

57. For details, see Elsner, "Die polnischen Arbeiter," pp. 77f.

58. Cf. Tables 8.1 to 8.3; for further information see Zunkel, "Die ausländischen Arbeiter," pp. 289, 310; Elsner, "Die polnischen Arbeiter," p. 81 and notes 109, and

110. Veltmann, who worked in the War Department at the time, confirms our figures: ZStA Potsdam, Reichsamt des Innern, no. 13722, pp. 170f., Kammergerichtsrat Veltmann to the Secretary of State of the Department of the Interior of the Reich, dated 5 June 1919.

59. Shorthand report on the meeting convened by the DAZ on 21 February 1916, p. 14, contained in ZStA Potsdam, Reichsamt des Innern, no. 13715, p. 177.

60. Notes taken at this meeting, which was attended by representatives of the Departments of the Reich, involved the general government area of Warsaw and the military government area of Lublin, the administration of High Command East, the Foreign Ministry of Austria-Hungary, the Chief of the Reserve Army, and the Chief of the Austrian General Staff and of the DAZ. See ZStA Potsdam, Reichs-Justizamt, no. 7764, pp. 48f.

61. ZStA Potsdam, Auswärtiges Amt, no. 30006, p. 168; Reichsamt des Innern, no. 13721, p. 5.

62. ZStA Merseburg, Rep. 87 B, Arbeiter- und Angestelltensachen no. 21 A, special vol. 4, Government Commission on Labor Affairs in the Ministry of Agriculture to the Commission on Compensation of the Reich, dated 5 June 1919.

63. ZStA Potsdam, Reichsamt des Innern, no. 13720, p. 2, Ludendorff to the Department of Economic Affairs of the Reich, the Chancellor of the Reich and the Ministry of War, dated 17 May 1918.

64. Central Archives of the Latvian SSR, Riga, Fonds no. 6414, Apr. 1, Arch. 9, p. 30.

65. Notes, see ibid., Fonds no. 6428, Apr. 1, Arch. 37, pp. 42ff.

66. Ibid., Fonds no. 6418, Apr. 1, Arch. 203, p. 76.

67. For the Lithuanian National Council, cf. F. Fischer, *Griff nach der Weltmacht*, 3d. ed., (Düsseldorf, 1964), pp. 617ff.

68. Letter and memorandum, see ZStA Potsdam, Reichskanzlei, Film 13093/13094, no. 2404, pp. 167ff., 193ff.

69. Central Archives of the Latvian SSR, Riga, Fonds no. 6418, Apr. 1, Arch. 202, pp. 6ff., 22ff., 29ff., 42ff.

70. In addition to the literature already mentioned, cf. W. Schumann and L. Nestler, eds., *Weltherrschaft im Visier. Dokumente zu den Europa- und Weltherrschaftsplänen des deutschen Imperialismus von der Jahrhundertwende bis Mai 1945* (Berlin, 1975).

71. Notes, see ZStA Merseburg, Rep. 87 B, Arbeiter- und Angestelltensachen no. 18 A, p. 6.

72. ZStA Potsdam, Auswärtiges Amt, no. 30006, p. 170, German Consulate-general to the Chancellor of the Reich, dated 8 October 1918.

73. C. H. Riegler, "Arbeitskräfterekrutierung für die deutsche Kriegswirtschaft in neutralen Ländern unter besonderer Berücksichtigung Schwedens, 1915–1919," in *Arbeiterwanderungen, Ausländerbeschäftigung und Ausländerpolitik in den kapitalistischen Ländern Europas im 20. Jahrhundert* (I) (Rostock, 1981), no. 10 in the series "Fremdarbeiterpolitik des Imperialismus," pp. 63ff.

74. ZStA Potsdam, Reichsamt des Innern, no. 13719, p. 251.

75. P. Umbreit, *Die deutschen Gewerkschaften im Weltkrieg* (Berlin, 1917), pp. 125ff.; ZStA Potsdam, Reichsamt des Innern, no. 12368, pp. 70ff., 102f.; no. 13718, pp. 250ff.; no. 13719, pp. 33f., 253f.; no. 13720, p. 492.

76. ZStA Potsdam, Reichsamt des Innern, no. 13719, p. 252.

77. Only a brief description is given here. For a more detailed account, see Elsner, "Die ausländischen Arbeiter," pp. 79ff.; Elsner, "Die polnischen Arbeiter," pp. 52ff.;

Elsner, "Zu den Auseinandersetzungen zwischen Deutschland und Österreich-Ungarn über die Saisonarbeiterfrage während des ersten Weltkrieges," in *Wissenschaftliche Zeitschrift der Universität Rostock, Gesellschafts-und Sprachwissenschaftliche Reihe* 1 (1969), 101ff.

78. Nichtweiss, *Die ausländischen Saisonarbeiter*, pp. 187ff.

79. ZStA Potsdam, Reichsamt des Innern, no. 13713, pp. 50f.

80. Agreement and appendix, see ZStA Potsdam, Auswärtiges Amt, no. 30005, pp. 116ff.

81. Notes, see ibid., pp. 121f.

82. Ibid., p. 122.

83. The DAZ mentioned 5,000 Galician workers being recruited; ZStA Merseburg, Rep. 87 B, Arbeiter-und Angestelltensachen, no. 18 A, I, vol. 1, p. 105, the director of the DAZ to the Prussian Minister of Agriculture, dated 9 August 1915.

84. ZStA Potsdam, Reichsamt des Innern, no. 13713, pp. 239f., note dated 23 October 1915.

85. Ibid., p. 140; no. 19898, pp. 25ff.

86. Notes, see ZStA Potsdam, Reichsamt des Innern, no. 19798, pp. 101ff.

87. ZStA Potsdam, Reichsamt des Innern, no. 13713, pp. 337f.; cf. also no. 13714, pp. 210ff., note dated 6 March 1916.

88. For examples, see Elsner, "Zu den Auseinandersetzungen," pp. 106f.

89. ZStA Potsdam, Reichsamt des Innern, no. 13715, p. 107.

90. According to the list given by the High Command of the Austrian Army dated 4 November 1916, 95,084 workers from the military government area of Lublin had been detained in Germany since the outbreak of war, and 5,983 had been newly recruited between the beginning of the war and 15 May 1916: see ZStA Potsdam, Reichsamt des Innern, no. 13715, p. 113.

91. Ibid., pp. 139ff., notes on the meeting of 26 February 1917. Cf. also ibid., p. 220, note sent by the Foreign Ministry on 31 March 1917; for Austria's rejection, see the Austrian note of 1 June 1917, ibid., pp. 277f.

92. On the recruitment of Italians, cf. ZStA Potsdam, Reichsamt des Innern, no. 3718, pp. 307ff.; no. 13719, pp. 7ff.; no. 13720, pp. 343, 423ff.

93. Cf. L. Elsner, "Sicherung der Ausbeutung ausländischer Arbeitskräfte. Ein Kriegsziel des deutschen Imperialismus im ersten Weltkrieg," in *ZfG* 5 (1976), 530ff.

94. For evidence of this see ibid., pp. 532f.

95. ZStA Potsdam, Auswärtiges Amt, no. 29873, p. 128.

96. ZStA Potsdam, Reichskanzlei, no. 1146, pp. 58ff.

97. Elsner, "Sicherung," pp. 535ff.

98. *Der Friedensvertrag mit der Ukraine vom 9.2.1918, der Zusatzvertrag und der deutsch-ukrainische Handelsvertrag nebst der amtlichen Denkschrift. Die wirtschaftliche Bedeutung der Ukraine* (Berlin, 1918).

99. For the peace treaty and the exploitation of the Ukraine, cf. F. Klein, ed., *Deutschland im ersten Weltkrieg*, vol. 3, pp. 187f.; G. Rosenfeld, *Sowjetrußland und Deutschland 1917–1922* (Berlin, 1960), pp. 55f.

100. For details see Elsner, "Sicherung," pp. 542f.

101. The texts of the peace treaty and the trade and shipping agreement are in *Verhandlungen des Deutschen Reichstages, Anlagen zu den stenographischen Berichten* XIII. Legislaturperiode, II. Session, Vol. 323, paper no. 1396 (Berlin, 1914/18).

102. M. Menger, *Die Finnlandpolitik des deutschen Imperialismus 1917–1918* (Berlin,

1974); F. Klein, ed., *Deutschland im ersten Weltkrieg*, vol. 3, pp. 214ff.

103. ZStA Potsdam, Auswärtiges Amt, no. 30006, p. 84, Ministry of War/War Department to Foreign Ministry, dated 22 January 1918.

104. *Verhandlungen des Reichstages*, vol. 323, paper no. 1396, 21/22.

105. For draft, see ZStA Potsdam, Büro Staatsminister Dr. Helfferich, no. 19294, pp. 5ff.

106. For the text of the treaty and appendices, see *Verhandlungen des Reichstages*, vol. 323, paper no. 1395.

107. ZStA Potsdam, Reichsamt des Innern, no. 13720, pp. 485ff.

108. Text of the treaty, of the special agreement, the additional treaties, and the official memorandum in *Verhandlungen des Reichstages*, vol. 324, paper 1616. On the conclusion of the treaty, see M. Hegemann, ''Der deutsch-rumänische Friedensvertrag im Mai 1918 —ein Vorstoss der imperialistischen Reaktion gegen die junge Sowjetmacht,'' in *ZfG* 5 (1957).

109. For evidence, see Elsner, ''Sicherung,'' pp. 544f.

110. Cf. Elsner, ''Die ausländischen Arbeiter,'' pp. 103ff., 197ff.; Elsner, ''Die polnischen Arbeiter,'' pp. 73ff., 120ff.; L. Elsner, ''Liberale Arbeiterpolitik oder Modifizierung der Zwangsarbeitspolitik? Zur Diskussion und zu den Erlassen über die Behandlung polnischer Landarbeiter in Deutschland 1916/1917,'' in *Jahrbuch für Geschichte der sozialistischen Länder Europas*, vol. 22/2 (Berlin, 1978), pp. 85ff.

111. Decree of 13 January 1915, see ZStA Potsdam, Reichsamt des Innern, no. 13713, p. 8; decree of 1916, see ibid., p. 202.

112. Dohse, *Ausländische Arbeiter*, p. 81.

113. ZStA Potsdam, Reichskanzlei, no. 1146, pp. 77f.

114. On the proclamation of 5 November 1916, cf. Basler, *Deutschlands Annexionspolitik*, pp. 154ff.; F. Klein, ed., *Deutschland im ersten Weltkrieg*, vol. 2, pp. 494ff.; L. Grosfeld, ''Die Proklamation des Königreichs Polen am 5.11.1916,'' in *Neue polnische Geschichtswissenschaft, Aufsätze und Studien*, supplement 3 of the *ZfG* (Berlin, 1956), pp. 135ff.; H. Lemke, *Allianz und Rivalität, Die Mittelmächte und Polen im ersten Weltkrieg (bis zur Februarrevolution)* (Berlin, 1977). Conze, *Polnische Nation*, supports the Anti-Polish proclamation and attempts to portray the policies behind it as forward-looking.

115. Elsner, ''Liberale Arbeiterpolitik,'' pp. 87f.

116. ZStA Potsdam, Reichsamt des Innern, no. 12381, p. 145.

117. ZStA Potsdam, Reichsamt des Innern, no. 12381, pp. 119ff.

118. Ibid., pp. 165ff.

119. Ibid., p. 122.

120. Notes, see ibid., pp. 281ff.

121. Ibid., p. 277.

122. Ibid., p. 278.

123. Cf. Elsner, ''Die polnischen Arbeiter,'' pp. 135ff.

124. Elsner, ''Die polnischen Arbeiter,'' pp. 145ff; Elsner, ''Liberale Arbeiterpolitik,'' pp. 100ff.

125. ZStA Potsdam, Rep. 2 A 1, Pol. no. 2845, p. 123.

126. Zunkel, ''Die ausländischen Arbeiter,'' p. 309.

127. L. Stern, ed., *Die Auswirkungen der Großen Sozialistischen Oktoberrevolution auf Deutschland*, Archivalische Forschungen zur Geschichte der deutschen Arbeiterbewegung, vol. 4/II (Berlin, 1959), 956.

128. StA Schwerin, Rep. 41, no. 17254, p. 72.

129. Eichholtz, *Geschichte der deutschen Kriegswirtschaft*, p. 90.

130. The resistance has been described in detail by the author elsewhere. Cf. Elsner, "Der Aufschwung des Kampfes der in Deutschland befindlichen polnischen Arbeiter gegen die Großgrundbesitzer nach der Großen Sozialistischen Oktoberrevolution," *Wissenschaftliche Zeitschrift der Universität Rostock, Gesellschafts-und Sprachwissenschaftliche Reihe* 2 (1977), 215ff.; L. Elsner, "Zur Haltung der rechten SPD- und Gewerkschaftsführer in der Einwanderungsfrage während des 1. Weltkrieges," ibid., 9 (1976), pp. 687ff.; Elsner, "Belgische Zwangsarbeiter," pp. 1963ff.; Elsner, "Zur Lage und zum Kampf der polnischen Arbeiter in der deutschen Landwirtschaft während des ersten Weltkrieges," in *Politik im Krieg 1914–1918*, pp. 167ff. Elsner, "Die polnischen Arbeiter," pp. 73ff., 120ff.

131. In contrast to such historians as H. Mommsen, who seek to set theories of stratification against Marx's class concept on the grounds that the latter allegedly cannot express social and legal heterogeneity as outlined in H. Mommsen's introduction to H. Mommsen and W. Schulze, eds., *Elend der Handarbeit, Probleme historischer Unterschichtenforschung* (Stuttgart, 1981), pp. 10ff., we believe that the concept of class can certainly be used to show the differences within the inner structure of the working class and the wide variety of divisions, groups, and strata that it includes. Cf. the definition of class in W. I. Lenin, "Die Grosse Initiative" in *Werke*, vol. 29 (Berlin, 1973), p. 410; for the situation nowadays cf. also *"Multis," Proletariat, Klassenkampf* (Berlin, 1981), pp. 181ff.; L. Elsner, "Integration sozialer Unterschichten statt Klassen und Klassenkampf," *Wissenschaftliche Zeitschrift der Universität Rostock, Gesellschafts- und Sprachwissenschaftliche Reihe*, 1 (1983), 67ff.

132. Resolution recently printed in *Über die Stellung der Arbeiterbewegung zu Migrationen und zur Ausländerbeschäftigung in Westeuropa* (Rostock, 1978), no. 4, in the series "Fremdarbeiterpolitik des Imperialismus," pp. 50ff.

133. Dohse, *Ausländische Arbeiter*, p. 7, is putting it too simply when he reduces internationalism to the acceptance of freedom of movement within the capitalist world and the demand for the abolition of emergency legislation, and when he also fails to mention in this context the organization of foreigners and development of their consciousness by involving them in the revolutionary struggle.

134. ZStA Potsdam, Reichsamt des Innern, no. 12381, p. 246.

135. Cf. Elsner, "Zur Lage und zum Kampf der polnischen Arbeiter," p. 186.

136. Bourgeois historians reject the concept of the continuity of an imperialist foreign labor policy in Germany. Cf. most recently K. J. Bade, *Gastarbeiter zwischen Arbeitswanderung und Einwanderung* (Tutzing, 1983), pp. 19, 28f.

137. Cf. Dohse, *Ausländische Arbeiter*, pp. 85ff.; W. Hennies, "Bemerkungen zur Beschäftigung ausländischer Arbeiter im Deutschen Reich während der Weimarer Republik," in *Arbeiterwanderungen, Ausländerbeschäftigung und Ausländerpolitik in den kapitalistischen Ländern Europas im 20. Jahrhundert* (II) (Rostock, 1981), no. 11, in the series "Fremdarbeiterpolitik des Imperialismus," pp. 21ff.; J. Tessarz, "Die Rolle der ausländischen landwirtschaftlichen Arbeiter in der Agrar- und Ostexpansionspolitik des deutschen Imperialismus in der Periode der Weimarer Republik (1919–1932)" (Ph.D. diss., Halle, 1963).

138. Cf. J. Lehmann, "Ausländische Arbeitskräfte in Deutschland 1933 bis 1939. Zum Umfang, zur Entwicklung und Struktur ihrer Beschäftigung," in *Zur Haltung der herrschenden Klasse und der Arbeiterbewegung zur Beschäftigung ausländischer Arbeiter*

(Rostock, 1980), no. 8, in the series "Fremdarbeiterpolitik des Imperialismus," pp. 5ff.

139. Eichholtz, *Geschichte der deutschen Kriegswirtschaft*, pp. 88ff.

140. For the literature published in the German Democratic Republic on foreign labor and policies toward foreigners in Western Europe, cf. *DDR-Literatur über Arbeiterwanderungen und Fremdarbeiterpolitik im Imperialismus, Forschungsstand und Bibliographie* (Rostock, 1979), no. 5, in the series "Fremdarbeiterpolitik des Imperialismus." For the publications on the subject that have appeared in the Soviet Union, cf. T. Tschernowa and L. Elsner, "Neuere sowjetische Arbeiten zur Ausländerbeschäftigung in Westeuropa," in *IPW-Berichte*, Berlin 9 (1979), pp. 58ff.

Part II

ACCULTURATION IN EUROPE AND NORTH AMERICA

Few migrants could live in a new culture without being influenced by it. Seasonal migrants coming and working in crews and living separately might perhaps escape such influences temporarily. But even those who returned home after a few months usually did so in reaction to the new culture. By culture we mean the whole of everyday life and work; the social, economic, and political aspects of a society; its continually changing customs and traditions. Acculturation then means the acceptance of parts of a new culture by individuals and groups who have received their primary socialization in a different culture and now share the traditions and modes of behavior of their new surroundings. Acculturation is a two-way process.

In the first essay. W. H. Sewell, Jr., deals with internal migration in France, taking Marseille as an example. Native and migrant workers do not mix easily and aside from the work place, recreational facilities were segregated. Although some grievances were common, both groups nevertheless were able to cooperate in strike situations by taking on different roles. Sewell's French migrants do show certain similarities with the migrants in the Industrial Workers of the World. They were ready for action without going through union hierarchies. Mary Nolan, in her recently published study of working-class radicalism in Düsseldorf, Germany, on the other hand, demonstrates the organizing capacity of skilled migrant workers. With the image, projected by Sewell, of the migrants as more prone to direct action than the resident workers, the danger of a return to the old middle-class war cry of "dangerous classes" necessitating the institution or expansion of a police force looms large. But after all, why should oppressed classes or groups not be dangerous? And as to their oft-criticized unsteady work habits, that is exactly what the economy demanded of them as recent labor-market theorists have demonstrated. It is also a way of life that could be relished, as social historians have shown. The question was, who determined when to work— the worker or the employer.

Two essays are concerned with Polish migrants. Polish agricultural laborers in Germany, France, and Denmark were the first to migrate, industrial workers followed. The miserable conditions under which seasonal agricultural workers lived had been recorded by interviews among German migrants in 1865. Poles in the 1890s and later fared worse. Christoph Kleßmann shows that on the other hand, migrating industrial workers, especially miners, who did not have to return to their country in winter, did have a chance, all discrimination notwithstanding, to organize and to live a life between the cultures, accepting parts of both and fighting to be accepted in their own different ways. Many still live in the Ruhr district; others continued to the mines of France and Belgium. In Milwaukee Poles and Germans were in the same position—they had also carried their ethnic antagonisms with them. Robert Mikkelsen shows that under certain conditions these ethnic tensions could be surmounted in an attempt to obtain political power. In the Ruhr the separate organization of the Polish migrants had made them a factor to be reckoned with, as it did in Milwaukee, but they could achieve lasting influence only by combining with Germans, since all ethnically based labor organizations had to join forces against employers.

Czechs in Vienna achieved a multitude of organizational goals though they faced the same discrimination as Poles did in Germany. In their attempts to form an ethnic group based on their nationality, they failed. Neither the socio-economic realities of their position in Vienna nor their feeling of national identity permitted separatism. The German Austrians were quick to realize their opportunity. By making nationalist separatism a key issue, they passed assimilation regulations that made life for the migrants, particularly social organization and economic advancement, more difficult. Just as the Dillingham Commission and other U.S. organizations used pretended "racial" differences as a pretext for discrimination so did the Lueger administration in Vienna.

All chapters in this part deal with class, though it sometimes is only implicit, given the multi-class character of ethnic groups. None deals with "fragmentation" as an interpretive concept. This never became a paradigm in European scholarly discourse. The tensions between belonging to one class and aspiring to another or having norms of consumption strongly suggested by another (or its well-meaning social workers) is taken up by Lizabeth Cohen. As in the case of unsteady work habits, conspicuous consumption is not simply a question of embourgeoisement, it is a question of who decides for what purposes the consumption is being done. Who appropriates to himself the power to set the norms? Again we find a two-way acculturation process, this time between classes.

NATIVES AND MIGRANTS: THE WORKING CLASS OF REVOLUTIONARY MARSEILLE, 1848–1851

9

William H. Sewell, Jr.

Until the Revolution of 1848, the working class of Marseille was one of the most quiescent and conservative in France. Marseille's workers had been staunchly royalist during the Restoration, and were touched only slightly by the widespread agitation of the early 1830s. While republican and socialist political sentiments may have made some progress among the workers in the 1830s and 1840s, there were no signs of significant organized working-class political activity until the outbreak of the February Revolution. The establishment of the Second Republic, however, evoked an immediate and massive response in Marseille, where once apathetic workers were soon marching in the streets, forming revolutionary political clubs, and shouting republican and socialist slogans. In spite of fluctuations in the fortunes of the movement, working-class political activity was sustained at a high level for the duration of the Second Republic. The activities peaked in June 1848, when there was a working-class insurrection simultaneous with the June Days in Paris. During the period of repression that followed, the movement declined, and then built steadily until it was dismantled by Louis Napoléon's coup d'état in 1851.[1] Yet even the repression of the early Second Empire could not reverse the effect of the revolutionary years of the Second Republic. The working class of Marseille could not be restored to its state of prerevolutionary docility; and when republican and socialist activity returned to France in the late 1860s, the Marseillais workers were in the vanguard of the movement.[2]

In this study we will subject the democratic and socialist movement of the Second Republic's crucial years to a social analysis,[3] identifying the groups of workers who participated actively in the movement, determining their place in the social structure of the working class, and contrasting the groups of workers who were radicalized and politicized with those who remained aloof. We believe that this analysis will lead to a better understanding of the social and political changes which took place in Marseille—and perhaps elsewhere in France— during the Second Republic.

This chapter is an abbreviated version of "The Working Class of Marseille Under the Second Republic: Social Structure and Political Behavior," first published in *Workers in the Industrial Revolution: Recent Studies of Labor in the United States and Europe*, ed. Peter N. Stearns and Daniel J. Walkowitz (New Brunswick, N.J.: Transaction Books, 1974), pp. 75–116. It is reprinted with the permission of the author and the publisher.

SOCIAL STRUCTURE OF THE WORKING CLASS

Between the restoration of the Bourbons and the flight of Louis-Philippe, Marseille grew at an unprecedented rate. From 1821, the first date for which we have undisputed population figures, to 1851, the city grew from 109,483 to 195,138, an increase of 77 percent. This rate of increase was higher than that of either Paris or Lyon during those years, and one of the highest rates anywhere in France.[4] Migration, rather than natural increase, was the main source of population growth; during the 30 years from 1821 to 1851, only 2,718 more people were born in Marseille than died, yet the total population grew by 88,263.[5] Many of the immigrants were drawn from the small towns and villages of southeastern France, but a substantial proportion came from more distant parts of the country and from abroad—the latter mainly from Italy.[6] Immigrants made up the majority of the adult population of the city by mid-century: according to figures taken from the 1,130 *actes de mariage* (marriage certificates) that were registered in 1846, 59 percent of Marseille's adult men and 55 percent of its adult women were immigrants.

The force that drew so many immigrants into Marseille was its expanding economy, and the most important factor in the city's economic advance was its maritime commerce, which more than tripled in volume from the early Restoration to the late July Monarchy.[7] But while Marseille remained above all a great port city, its industry was also increasingly important, especially in the 1830s and 1840s, when Marseille experienced a genuine industrial revolution. The most progressive industries were mechanical construction and oil pressing, both creations of the 1830s, and sugar refining, an old industry which experienced extraordinary concentration and mechanization in the 1830s and 1840s.[8] Between 1830 and 1848, the number of factory workers in Marseille grew from 1,550 to 4,185, and by 1848 the factory industries accounted for over half of the city's industrial production. The remainder of Marseille's industrial production was accounted for by a large number of artisan industries. The artisan sector produced for local demand, either servicing the maritime sector (crate and barrel making, rope and sail making, ship repairing) or servicing the population at large (building, manufacture of garments and household objects, food processing, the luxury trades). This sector expanded during the Restoration and July Monarchy, but only to the extent required by local demand.

The working class of Marseille was as diversified as the city's economy. In 1848, the National Assembly's *Enquête sur le travail agricole et industriel* enumerated 131 different industrial specialties being practiced in Marseille, and even then there were some omissions.[9] The differences among these various working-class occupations were often extensive. Wages ranged from 1.75 to 8 francs a day; skills ranged from simple lifting and carrying to the fine adjustment of steam engines, or the manufacture of watches. Some occupations had powerful and elaborate trade organizations, while others had none at all; the length of the working day ranged from 6 to 12 hours, and the average number of days worked per year ranged from 150 to 365. The organization of production was equally diverse, ranging from tiny shops where self-employed artisans made jewelry, cooking pots or shoes, to huge factories with heavy machinery powered by steam engines, employing hundreds of workers and having a complex hierarchy of command. It is impossible to talk about the social structure of such a vast and diverse collection of trades without classifying workers into general, relatively homogeneous occupation groups. A number of possible criteria might be used: the sector of the economy in which they worked, their level of remuneration, the nature of their work situation, their level of skill, their prestige in the community. We have decided to use two criteria: level of skill and patterns of recruitment.

SKILLED AND UNSKILLED TRADES

There were many gradations of skill in the working-class world of mid-nineteenth century Marseille. A ditch-digger or cart-loader needed almost no skill, whereas a clockmaker or a carver needed a high level of skill that could be acquired only by a long period of training. But most trades fell in between these extremes, and it is often difficult to know where to draw the line between skilled and unskilled occupations. There is no difficulty with workers such as ditch-diggers or cart-loaders, whose jobs required nothing but muscular strength, nor in the case of *journaliers* (day-laborers) and *manoeuvres* (manual laborers), whose very occupational titles imply a lack of skill. Factory workers present a more ambiguous case, since they had to learn certain techniques and develop some degree of precision. Nevertheless, except for very highly skilled and well-paid workers in the machine construction industry, factory workers fit more comfortably into the unskilled than the skilled category. The vast majority of the city's skilled workers were employed in small-scale handicraft trades and in building. The exceptions were the workers in the mechanical construction industry, and one very special case, the dockworkers. The dockworkers did not need much skill; but they were the best organized, the most stable, the highest paid, the most exclusive and all in all the most privileged workers in Marseille.[10] Because they not only shared but epitomized nearly all the distinctive characteristics of the city's skilled workers, they must be ranked among the ''skilled'' trades. Defined in this manner, skilled workers accounted for about two-thirds of the working class of Marseille in the middle of the nineteenth century.[11] Unskilled workers tended to move about from job to job and from industry to industry according to the whims of the labor market, while skilled men tended to change jobs more rarely and to move into new trades only under highly unusual circumstances.

To properly measure the rate of turnover in different working-class occupations, we would have to follow the same men through all the stages of their careers, noting all their changes in jobs—something we cannot do with the data at hand. But the *listes nominatives* of the census—which list all the inhabitants of the city by street, address, and household—and the *actes de mariage* give us some indirect evidence that turnover must have been high in the unskilled trades. When unskilled workers were asked by the census taker or the keeper of the *état civil* to state their occupations, they replied in over half the cases that they were *journaliers*, rather than identifying their specific jobs. According to the *enquête sur le travail* of 1848, there were some 500 oil industry workers, some 600 soap makers, some 1,000 sugar refiners and some 750 ditch-diggers employed in Marseille.[12] Yet in 1851, when the population was probably somewhat larger than in 1848, the census found only a handful of men who identified themselves as oil industry workers, only 390 soap makers, only 500 sugar refiners and only 80 ditch-diggers. The figures from the *actes de mariage* are comparable. The remaining men who worked in these trades must have identified themselves simply as *journaliers*. This vagueness on the part of unskilled workers contrasts sharply with the exact occupational titles given by skilled men. The difference presumably indicates that most unskilled men felt no commitment to their particular occupations, and that they were not sure what kind of work they would be engaged in even in the relatively near future.

Unskilled occupations also seem to have suffered from another kind of turnover in personnel: the continuing movement of men into and out of the city. Once again, our sources do not allow an exact measurement of this turnover, but there are indirect indications that it must have been relatively rapid. Three fourths of the city's unskilled workers had been born outside of Marseille, as opposed to half of the skilled workers.[13] Thus it seems likely that their roots in the city seldom went very deep. Contemporary observers noted that it was common for men to come from Italy or the French countryside to work in the factories of Marseille, and then to return to their homes after a year or two.[14] Also, the *enquête sur le travail* of 1848 estimated that 31 percent of the city's unskilled workers, as against only 18 percent of the skilled workers, had no permanent domicile in Marseille.[15]

Parallel to this difference in stability of personnel was an equally marked difference in the workers' ability to form and sustain labor organizations. Virtually all the unskilled trades were unorganized, while most skilled trades had some form of collective organization. It is difficult to determine exactly what form this organization took, since coalitions were illegal and trade union organizations were therefore necessarily clandestine. Some of these organizations took the form of *compagnonnages*, the traditional associations of itinerant journeymen. We have been able to identify *compagnonnages* in 16 of Marseille's skilled trades, and there may have been others.[16] Trade union organizations sometimes took another form, registering with the authorities as a mutual aid society and carrying on trade union activities under the cover of the authorized society. On the eve of the February Revolution there were registered mutual aid societies in 37 of Marseille's working-class occupations, and 34 of these were in skilled trades.[17] There were also other types of labor organizations in mid-nineteenth century Marseille; the proof is that the members of one trade, the tailors, were able to mount two strikes in the 1830s and 1840s, even though they had neither a *compagnonnage* nor a mutual aid society.[18] Despite the gaps in our documentation, we have positive evidence of trade union organizations in 43 skilled trades, including all but four of those that employed over 100 workers, and a number of smaller trades as well.

If organization was ubiquitous in the skilled trades, it was virtually nonexistent in the unskilled trades. We have uncovered no evidence that any unskilled trade had either a *compagnonnage* or a *société de secours mutuels*, and have discovered only one strike by unskilled workers in the 1830s and 1840s, an unsuccessful and ill-organized affair involving *terrassiers* employed on the railway line.[19] By contrast, we have uncovered 16 strikes among the skilled trades during the same years, at least seven of which were successful.[20] (Another five are known to have failed, and the outcome of the other four is unknown.) The lack of labor organization in unskilled trades was largely the result of their instability in personnel. It was extraordinarily difficult to maintain a continuous and effective organization when a high proportion of the workers in a trade changed jobs or moved out of the city in the course of a year. To make matters worse, unlike the skilled workers, the unskilled workers were not committed to any particular trade.

The unskilled trades' inadequate salary level was partly the cause and partly the effect of their instability in personnel and lack of labor organization. According to the *enquête sur le travail* of 1848, wages ranged from 1.75 francs to 3 francs a day for unskilled labor, and from 2.50 to 4.50 for skilled labor. The average wage for the unskilled trades was 2.20 francs a day, while the average for skilled trades was 3.40 francs a day (See Appendix 1 for more detailed figures). Taking seasonal unemployment into account, these daily wages meant annual earnings of about 610 francs for the average unskilled laborer, and about 960 francs for the skilled laborer.[21] According to contemporary estimates,[22] the unskilled man's earnings were barely sufficient to support himself, while the skilled men's earnings were more than sufficient for a couple without children. In other words, an unskilled laborer could not adequately provide for a family even with his wife working full time, while a skilled man with a working wife could raise a family with a certain margin of comfort.

Thus, Marseille's unskilled workers were badly paid, uncertain about the future, chronically unemployed, and had few family attachments in Marseille; they changed jobs frequently, moved about from city to city, and had no defense against the whims of their employers or of the labor market. In addition, most of them lived in the oldest, most crowded, and least sanitary district of the city;[23] fewer than half of them (as opposed to almost four-fifths of the skilled workers) could sign their names on their *actes de mariage*; and they were much more likely to engage in criminal behavior than any other group in the population.[24] The lot of Marseille's unskilled laborers was inferior to that of the city's skilled laborers in almost every respect.

MEASURES OF EXCLUSIVENESS

There were also some important differences among the trades within the skilled category. Perhaps the most important difference was that, while nearly all the skilled trades maintained some degree of labor organization, only a minority were strong enough to significantly control the recruitment of new members into their trades. Workers in trades which had achieved such control felt themselves distinct from and superior to other skilled workers. They constituted an "aristocracy of labor" which not only enjoyed a higher level and a greater security of earnings than ordinary skilled laborers, but which also possessed a distinct culture and way of life. This aristocracy of exclusive trades can also be distinguished from ordinary skilled laborers by a systematic exploitation of the *actes de mariage*.

The *actes de mariage* contain two types of information which are useful in determining the exclusiveness of different occupational groups[25]—the groom's birthplace and the occupation of his father. From these two types of information we can construct three distinct measures, each of which identifies a different variety of exclusiveness: the percentage of men in an occupation who were born in Marseille—this measures an occupational group's ability to keep out immigrants; the percentage of men in an occupation whose fathers had the same occupation—this is a measure of the extent to which trades were passed on from father to son; and the percentage of men in an occupation whose fathers were peasants or *journaliers*—this measures the extent of penetration into a trade by men of low social origins. These measures of exclusiveness are difficult to compare if they are left as raw percentages. For example, a score of 50 percent on the second measure is well above average, but a score of 50 percent on the first measure is a little below average. To make the three measures comparable, we have used the simple statistical technique of converting the percentages into scores which express their standard deviations from the mean. Thus, an occupational group whose percentage of native Marseillais is exactly average will have a standardized score of zero on measure one; a group whose percentage is above average will have a positive score; and a group whose percentage is below average will have a negative score, with the size of the positive or negative score depending on how far the group's percentage deviates from the average.[26] This technique allows us to make exact comparisons of the three measures.[27]

Table 9.1 demonstrates that the three different measures of exclusiveness are all statistically related; that is, occupations which have high standardized scores on one measure tend to score high on the others as well. This correspondence is far from perfect, however, which leads to a problem in categorizing occupations, since the categories would differ somewhat depending on which measures were used. We have attempted to avoid this problem by adding the three scores together to form a composite index of exclusiveness. Using this index, we can separate the skilled occupations into a minority of exclusive trades, defined as those with a positive score, and a majority of open skilled trades, defined as those with a negative score. The trades in these two categories, together with their percentage scores, their standardized scores, and their composite scores, are listed in Table 9.1

The differences between the open and exclusive trades were sharpest on measure one, where 79 percent of the men in the exclusive trades, and only 37 percent of those in the open trades, were native Marseillais. Indeed, the differences were so sharp that there was no overlap between the exclusive and the open category; masons, with 69 percent natives, were the lowest of the exclusive trades on this measure, while the stonecutters, who ranked at the top of the open category, had only 50 percent natives. The contrast was only a little less striking on measure two, where 45 percent of the men in the exclusive trades, as opposed to 24 percent in the open trades, had the same occupations as their fathers, and where the overlap between categories was only slight. On measure three, the difference between exclusive and open trades was rather small, with 16 percent of the men in the former group, and 24 percent of those in the latter, having been recruited from sons of peasants or *journaliers*; overlap between these categories was considerable.

Although our measures of exclusiveness were developed to make a division within the general category of skilled workers, they may also be used to determine the characteristics of unskilled occupations. All the occupations in the unskilled category had extremely low composite indices of exclusiveness; indeed, there is only a small amount of overlap between the lowest of the open skilled trades and the highest of the unskilled trades (See Table 9.1). On the composite measure the unskilled trades stood well below the open skilled trades. However, most of the overall difference between unskilled trades and open skilled trades is explained by measure three, the percentage of men whose fathers were peasants or *journaliers*. Otherwise, the open skilled trades did not differ greatly from the unskilled trades in their patterns of recruitment. In terms of their ability to exclude migrants and to pass their occupations along to their sons, the working-class men fell into only two groups: the exclusive skilled trades on the one hand, and all the rest of the trades, skilled and unskilled alike, on the other.

Surprisingly, workers in the exclusive skilled trades also stood far above men in bourgeois occupations in their ability to keep out migrants and to pass on their occupations to their sons. Only 38 percent of the bourgeoisie were natives of Marseille—as opposed to 37 percent of the workers in the open skilled trades, 25 percent in the unskilled trades, and 79 percent in the exclusive skilled trades. On measure two, the percentage of bourgeois who had the same occupation as their fathers was only 18 percent, less than either the open skilled trades or the unskilled trades. Even on measure three, the bourgeoisie had a slightly higher percentage of men from low social backgrounds than did the exclusive skilled trades; 17 percent of the former, as opposed to 16 percent of the latter, were sons of peasants or *journaliers*. This comparison between the exclusive trades

Table 9.1
Measures of Exclusiveness

Occupations	No. in Sample	Percent Born in Marseille	(1) Standard Deviations	Percent With Same Occupation as Father	(2) Standard Deviations	Percent Sons of Peasants or Journaliers	(3) Standard Deviations*	Composite Index of Exclusiveness
Exclusive Trades								
Dockworkers	40	90	1.73	73	2.55	2	1.82	6.10
Maritime Industries	17	88	1.69	53	1.34	6	1.40	4.43
Shipbuilders	17	82	1.36	41	.61	6	1.40	3.37
Coopers	26	73	.95	31	.00	0	2.00	2.95
Tanners	21	80	1.27	38	.43	29	-.64	1.06
Packagers	10	80	1.27	30	-.06	30	-.73	.48
Masons	58	69	.77	38	.43	33	-1.00	.20
Total Exclusive	189	79		45		16		
Open Trades								
Joiners and Cabinet-makers	41	39	-.59	24	-.44	17	.45	-.58
Miscellaneous Building Workers	20	35	-.72	25	-.38	20	.18	-.90
Shoemakers	64	33	-.86	42	.67	30	-.73	-.92
Miscellaneous Skilled Workers	114	46	-.27	19	-.73	21	.09	-.91
Metallurgists	35	37	-.68	20	-.67	23	-.09	-1.44
Bakers	25	24	-1.27	32	.06	36	-1.27	-2.48
Housepainters	12	33	-.86	8	-1.40	25	-.27	-2.53
Stonecutters	22	50	-.09	5	-1.58	36	-1.27	-2.94
Tailors	16	6	-2.09	19	-.73	25	-.27	-3.09
Total Open Trades	354	37		24		24		
Total Skilled Trades	543	52		31		22		

Table 9.1—Continued

Occupations	No. in Sample	(1) Percent Born in Marseille	Standard Deviations	(2) Percent With Same Occupation as Father	Standard Deviations	(3) Percent Sons of Peasants or Journaliers	Standard Deviations*	Composite Index of Exclusiveness
Unskilled Trades								
Carters	10	20	-1.45	50	1.19	40	-1.64	-1.90
Miscellaneous Unskilled	20	27	-1.14	27	-.25	40	-1.64	-3.03
Soapmakers	13	62	.45	23	-.50	69	-4.27	-4.32
Day Laborers	62	24	-1.27	42	.69	65	-3.91	-4.49
Sugar Refiners	17	24	-1.27	0	-1.94	47	-2.45	-5.66
Total Unskilled Trades	122	26		30		57		
Miscellaneous								
Miscellaneous Service	16	12	-1.82	19	-.75	25	-.27	-2.84
Waiters and Cooks	15	20	-1.45	7	-1.50	40	-1.64	-4.59
Sailors	30	27	-1.14	40	.56	17	.45	.13
Fishermen	13	85	1.50	85	3.47	0	2.00	6.97

*The figures in this column are the negative of the actual standard deviation scores.

and the bourgeoisie points up the unique position of the exclusive trades in the social structure of mid-nineteenth-century Marseille. In every other segment of the city's occupational structure, the labor market was kept in a constant state of flux by the expansion of the economy and the population. In the face of this overall fluidity, it was extremely difficult for any occupation, at any social level, to remain exclusive. At the mid-point of the nineteenth century, the exclusive skilled trades were the only occupational groups in the city which were able to seal themselves off from the liberating currents that flowed in the labor market as a whole and to effectively restrict the entry of outsiders.

EXCLUSIVE TRADES AND OPEN TRADES: CULTURAL DIFFERENCES

There were many similarities between skilled workers in open and exclusive trades. For example, there was no significant difference in their levels of literacy—79 percent of the workers in open trades could sign their names on the *actes de mariage*, and 78 percent of those in exclusive trades could do so. Furthermore, virtually all skilled trades in both categories had some form of labor organization. The labor organizations in the exclusive trades were usually more powerful and prominent, as one might expect from their ability to restrict entry into their trades. Here one thinks above all of the dock workers, who in 1814 managed to reconstitute their ancient corporation in all but name, and who retained absolute control over all work done on the quays until their organization was broken in an unsuccessful strike against Paulin Talabot's *Compagnie des docks* in 1864.[28] But there were some open trades which had more active and aggressive labor organizations than some of the exclusive trades: for example, the bakers organized four strikes against their masters between 1823 and 1848.[29] In the realm of trade union action, the difference between exclusive and open trades was one of degree rather than of kind.

There was also a great deal of overlap between exclusive and open trades in levels of earnings; the best paid workers in Marseille were certain highly skilled specialists in the machine construction industry, who made as much as 8 or 10 francs a day. But in the open trades, wages were high only when the required skills were genuinely scarce, as was the case for printers, machine builders or clockmakers, while in the exclusive trades the scarcity of labor resulted, not from an intrinsic difficulty of learning the required skills, but from an artificial restriction of the labor market. Thus, the exclusive trades formed a "labor aristocracy" not only in the sense that they were economically privileged, but also in the much stricter sense that they formed a closed class, a class whose members obtained and maintained their privileges not by being the most successful competitors in an open market, but by employing a systematic policy of exclusiveness. The result was that in 1848, wages in the exclusive trades ranged from 3 francs a day for fishing net makers to 4.50 for dock workers, with an average daily wage of 3.80 francs and an average annual salary of 1,055 francs, for the entire category of exclusive trades. By contrast, wages in the open skilled trades ranged from 2.55 francs for plumbers to 4 francs for typographers and smelters, with an average wage of 3.20 francs per day and average annual earnings of 880 francs for the entire category.[30] In short, the average worker in an exclusive trade made some 20 percent more than the average worker in an open trade.

The sharpest difference between workers in open and exclusive trades was not in their material life, however, but in their cultural and social life. Workers in the exclusive trades lived in a cultural and social sphere of their own, regarding workers in the other trades as their inferiors; thus they had the pride as well as the economic privileges of "aristocrats." This aristocratic pride was noted in a remarkable book by François Mazuy, a self-educated former shoemaker and a native of Marseille, who was a faithful observer of the traditional working-class culture of his city. Mazuy noted that between "the Marseillais who belonged to the free and lucrative trades"[31] and the "poor itinerant workers of the other trades" there existed "a line of demarcation that degenerated into pride on one side and rancor on the other."[32] According to Mazuy, the native Marseillais worker, whom he implicitly identifies with the privileged trades of the labor aristocracy,[33] considered migrants to the city his inferiors, and the women of Marseille "would have considered it a misalliance to marry a *françiot*"—that is, a native French-speaker.[34]

Hence the native Marseillais working in the exclusive trades avoided contact with strangers in his recreation, as well as in his labor. Both his favorite forms of recreation, the *cercle* and the *cabanon*, were closed to outsiders. The *cercle* was a social club which maintained a meeting place where members gathered in the evenings. The Marseillais, according to Mazuy, preferred the *cercle* to the café or other establishments open to the public because, in the confines of the *cercle*, "one could always feel at home in the evenings, without fear of having strangers at his side."[35] The *cabanon* was a small fishing cabin on the sea, usually owned in common by several workers. Every Sunday during the warm season the workers and their families would go to the cabanon, where the men would fish while the women cooked and supervised the children's play. According to Mazuy, the *cabanon* was strictly a family institution, in which no drunkenness or debauchery was allowed; it was therefore far superior to the country taverns, which he felt demoralized the working classes of other French cities.[36] But, whether or not the *cabanon* was a moralizing force, it certainly contributed to the segregation of the native Marseillais in the exclusive trades from the immigrant worker in the open trades. The latter could join in the *cabanon* only by invitation, and such invitations were very rare. Consequently he spent his Sundays drinking and carousing in the country taverns, which were also to be found in the countryside surrounding Marseille, and which were patronized mainly by other men like himself.

Mazuy remarked that this coldness and exclusiveness on the part of the native population "was very displeasing to workers from the North," because it made it difficult for them to "form intimate friendships in Marseille."[37] However, the difficulty of getting to know native Marseillais was not limited to workers from the North. Agricol Perdiguier, who spent some time in Marseille as a journeyman joiner, was from nearby Avignon, yet he too was conscious of being regarded as an outsider by the natives of the city: "It is in their families that they eat their bouillabaisse and take their recreation. As for the stranger, he is seldom admitted to their celebrations or to their joys."[38] All strangers, then, were subjected to this segregation of leisure-time activities. Furthermore, as Perdiguier remarks, the segregation was exaggerated by the difference of language: strangers, even those from as nearby as Avignon, were baffled by the peculiarities of Marseille's dialect. At the same time, the segregation the Marseillais practiced both in their work and in their leisure made it possible for their dialect to be maintained "in all its purity."[39] The importance of the difference in language should not be overstated; Perdiguier lived in Marseille in 1824, and all observers agree that as the nineteenth century progressed, the use of standard French became more and more universal and the patois of Marseille began to lose its eccentricities.[40] Nevertheless, the language barrier contributed to the mutual isolation of natives in the exclusive trades and immigrants in the open trades. It reinforced the existing patterns of segregated recreation and occupational exclusiveness, and thereby helped to mold the exclusive trades into a self-conscious, traditional and haughty aristocracy of labor.

In addition to these three main categories of working-class occupations—the unskilled trades, the exclusive skilled trades and the open skilled trades—there were two other groups of workers: sailors and fishermen, and service workers. Both stood somewhat apart from the rest of the working class; service workers because they were engaged in serving other men rather than in the manufacture or transportation of goods, and because they often spent their working day in contact with higher strata of the population rather than with men of their own trade and class; sailors and fishermen because they spent their working days at sea and were segregated from other workers by their patterns of residence even when ashore.[41] Service workers bore some resemblance to unskilled workers in their patterns of recruitment, and were generally poorly organized. Sailors and fishermen were closer to the exclusive trades in their recruitment patterns: fishermen, in fact, had the highest index of exclusiveness in the working class of Marseille (See Table 9.1). It is not clear, however, how much of this exclusiveness was due to a conscious attempt to restrict entry into their trades, and how much was due to the fact that a seafaring life was not very appealing to most young men. In any case, there is another good reason for keeping sailors and fishermen distinct from the exclusive skilled trades—only 50 percent of the sailors and a mere 8 percent of the fishermen were literate, as opposed to 78 percent of the workers in the exclusive trades (See Appendix at end of chapter.) Their cultural level was thus far below that of skilled workers, and was actually nearer to that of peasants or unskilled laborers.

THE SOCIAL COMPOSITION OF THE DEMOCRATIC AND SOCIALIST MOVEMENT

How did these different types of workers respond to the great movement of political liberation that was set off in Marseille by the coming of the Second Republic? The archives of Marseille contain several lists of men who participated in some way in the revolutionary movement of these years; by analyzing these lists, we can determine which social categories were prominent in the movement, and which remained apathetic or conservative. The most important documents in this regard are the police and judicial records created by the repression of the insurrection in June 1848, and the repression of the republican movement following Louis Napoléon's coup d'état in December 1851.[42] Relatively complete dossiers were drawn up for each man arrested in these affairs, and although nothing approaches the detail reported by Gossez and Rougerie for the Parisian insurrectionaries of the June Days and for the Communards, the dossiers contain the name, occupation, age, place of birth and residence for all men arrested, and give the marital status of a few of the insurrectionaries of June 1848. Such information is available for 270 men arrested in June 1848, and for another 297 who were arrested after the coup d'état in 1851. Comparable but less complete information for the rest of the 1850s may be drawn from lists of dangerous individuals which were maintained by the police in case of an insurrectionary movement or other threat to the regime. Such a list was first drawn up in 1853, and subsequently revised in 1855, and again in 1858. These lists give the name, occupation, and address of some 346 men, and occasionally include age, place of birth, or prior police record as well.[43] In addition to these three sources, the departmental archives list the members of three republican political clubs which were active at various times under the Second Republic. One of these lists gives the names, ages, occupations, and addresses of 172 members of the *Club de la Montagne*, one of the most active and revolutionary clubs of the spring of 1848. There are also lists of members of two smaller and more moderate political clubs, the *Cercle de Noailles* and the *Cercle de la Paix*, each giving the names, occupations, and addresses of 97 members.[44] Finally, the police and judicial archives have records of proceedings against a number of men accused of diverse political offenses, which may also be used to identify participants in the democratic and socialist movement. We have found such records for 39 men arrested between 1848 and 1851, and for another 80 arrested between 1852 and 1859.[45] By putting together the information taken from all these sources, we can identify 1,398 men who participated in some way in the democratic and socialist movement during the Second Republic and the early years of the Second Empire.

Owing to the diversity of these documents, the list of militants which they give us is also extremely varied. Some of the men listed were important leaders of the movement; others were only sporadic and casual participants. Some were theoretical and romantic revolutionaries, while others were hard-bitten street fighters who kept guns hidden in their closets, in anticipation of an insurrectionary outburst. Some were arrested for firing on the troops or the police in a genuine insurrection, while others were arrested for shouting *"cris séditieux"* in a moment of drunken enthusiasm. This diverse collection of men makes up a valuable—albeit a highly unscientific—sample of nearly all types of republicans and revolutionaries. The problem, of course, is that certain types may be overrepresented in the sample—for example, the leaders of the movement, or those most prone to acts of violence. But this problem can be overcome to some degree by searching out patterns in the socio-occupational makeup of lists taken from all the sources. When this is done, we find that certain social types were prominent in nearly all kinds of revolutionary or republican activity, while others participated only rarely.

The occupations of the 1,398 militants identified through these lists are summarized in Table 9.2. In that table, we have given both the total number of militants in each occupational category and the percentage which each category contributes to the total. We have then compared these percentages with the percentage of the adult male population employed in each category. The ratio of the first percentage to the second is a convenient measure of each occupational category's involvement in the democratic and socialist movement. A ratio of 1.0 means that men in a given category accounted for the same proportion of militants as they did of the population at large. A ratio of more than 1.0 indicates a relatively high degree of involvement in the movement, and a ratio of less than 1.0 indicates a relatively low degree of such involvement. As Table 9.2 indicates, one occupational category stood out from all the others: workers in the open skilled trades were nearly twice as likely to be militants as men in any other category. Furthermore, their prominence in the movement seems to have extended to all kinds of activity, since the open skilled trades were strongly represented in all of the different lists of militants which we have used to compile our overall statistics.

The contrast between open and exclusive skilled trades is especially striking and consistent. In every one of the lists of militants, from the insurrectionaries of June 1848 to the quiet habitués of the *Cercle de la Paix*, workers in open trades outnumbered workers in exclusive trades by a wider margin than one would expect, judging from their proportions in the population. Our figures indicate that workers in open skilled trades were nearly three times as likely as workers in exclusive trades to participate in some form of radical politics. This striking difference in political behavior cannot be accounted for by the greater prosperity of the exclusive trades. The difference in earnings was relatively small,

Table 9.2
Occupations of Militants

	Exclusive Skilled	Open Skilled	Unskilled	Service	Sailors and Fisherman	Bourgeois	Miscellaneous
Number of Militants n = 1,398	105	653	140	143	19	395	43
Percent of Militants	8	47	10	4	1	28	3
Percent of Population	13	28	17	3	6	30	4
Ratio of Percent Militants to Percent Population	0.6	1.7	0.6	0.8	0.2	0.9	0.8

From the census of 1851.

while the difference in political behavior was great. Furthermore, there is little correspondence between high earnings and abstention from revolutionary politics within either the exclusive or the open category. Thus, the bakers and the metallurgists were among the most revolutionary occupations in the city, even though their earnings were higher than those of most workers in the exclusive category. Similarly, the dock workers, who were the best-paid workers in the city, were more frequent participants than the masons, who were the worst-paid workers in the exclusive category.[46] Nevertheless, the privileged position of the exclusive trades probably contributed to their political conservatism. After all, they owed their privileges to their control over recruitment into their trades, not to the possession of any unusual skills, and in a time when the economy and the population of Marseille was expanding rapidly, their precarious control over recruitment was under constant threat. Because they had managed to succeed in controlling access to their trades where others had failed, and because they knew their own successes were so fragile, the workers in the exclusive trades naturally feared any proposals for sweeping social and economic changes, including those of the socialists, which might imperil their hard-won gains. This gave them even more reason to distrust a socialist movement dominated by the less fortunate workers, who were jealous of their privileges.

More important, however, was the fact that the exclusive trades were a traditional, culturally distinct and socially self-sufficient community. Recruitment was from within the group, and they avoided contact with outsiders in both their work and their leisure; hence group members remained insulated against the changes in political and social attitudes which took place in other segments of the populations. In this voluntarily isolated community, the old corporative and conservative cultural traditions of Marseille retained all their vitality. In the less restricted environment of the open trades, where men were recruited from all types of social backgrounds, and where many had spent their formative years in rural or quasi-rural villages, the old urban traditions were weaker, social prescriptions were less definite and less binding, and novel ideas received a friendlier hearing. Thus the democratic and socialist movement won more converts among the open than among the exclusive trades; and, at the same time, the spread of the new political ideas and styles from the open to the exclusive trades was inhibited by the lack of social ties between the two categories.

The overall difference between workers in the open skilled trades and the unskilled trades was just as sharp as the difference between the open and exclusive trades: workers in the open trades were almost three times as likely to be actively involved in the movement. However, the level of participation on the part of unskilled workers varied a great deal more than that of workers in the exclusive trades. For example, unskilled workers made up less than 2 percent of the members of the *Cercle de Noailles* and the *Cercle de la Paix*, but accounted for 18 percent of the men arrested for diverse political offenses in the early years of the Second Empire. As a general rule, unskilled workers were much more prominent in sporadic and violent political activities than in activities which required sustained attention, hard work and organizational skills. We can see this by breaking down our list of militants into two categories: the first including all men who engaged in insurrectionary violence, political riots or other acts of public defiance; the second including members of political clubs and secret societies, and men who were arrested for their prominence in the democratic and socialist movement in December 1851 or placed on the subsequent police lists of dangerous individuals. As Table 9.3 indicates, unskilled workers were nearly twice as likely to engage in acts of public defiance as in organizational activities. The one exception to this general pattern was the extremely radical *Club de la Montagne*, where unskilled workers made up 22 percent of the members, more than their percentage in the population at large.

Unskilled workers thus followed a very different pattern of political activity than workers in the exclusive trades. They were fairly prominent in the most violent and radical kinds of political action, but only rarely participated in more moderate or highly organized branches of the movement. Nevertheless, the large contingent of unskilled workers in the *Club de la Montagne* indicates that many may have been formally affiliated with democratic and socialist organizations, at least in the euphoric spring of 1848. Indeed, some may have kept such formal affiliations right up to the coup d'état in 1851, or even beyond it. But they did not play a prominent enough role in the movement's organization to be arrested after the coup d'état, or to figure on the lists of "dangerous individuals." The instructions of the minister asking the prefect to draw up the first of these lists in 1853 is revealing in this respect. The instructions ask for "a list of the men in your department who belong to political parties hostile to the Government of the Emperor, who should be considered men of action, capable of personally directing an insurrectionary movement, of carrying along the masses by their influence and their personal courage."[47] Thus it is not the mass of the movement but its leaders and militants who are envisaged in the instructions, and the men

Table 9.3
Participants in Acts of Public Defiance vs. Participants in Organizational Activities, by Occupation

	Exclusive Skilled	Open Skilled	Unskilled	Service	Sailors and Fishermen	Bourgeois	Miscellaneous
Public Defiance n = 404							
No. of Militants	30	221	59	26	9	39	20
Percent of Militants	7	55	15	6	2	10	5
Ratio of Percent Militants to Percent Population	.5	2.0	.9	2.0	.3	.3	1.2
Organization n = 994							
No. of Militants	75	432	81	17	10	356	23
Percent of Militants	8	43	8	2	1	36	2
Ratio of Percent Militants to Percent Population	.6	1.5	.5	.7	.2	1.2	.5

rounded up by the police after the coup d'état of 1851 were no doubt of the same stamp.

Given what we know about the unskilled laborers of Marseille, it should not surprise us that few attained positions of leadership in the democratic and socialist movement. Many were illiterate, and even those who could sign their names on *actes de mariage* were probably too ill-informed and inarticulate to play prominent roles in the debates of political clubs or secret societies. Finally, in contrast to skilled workers of all kinds, they had no prior experience in labor organizations, which could serve as a training school for political cadres and as an organizational model for political movements. But when it came to crowds of semi-inebriated workers singing revolutionary songs in the streets late at night, or angry crowds hurling insults at the police or at the Emperor, or armed bands waiting for a call to insurrection, or to pitched battles with the national guard and the troops of the line, a good share of the assembly was bound to be made up of unskilled workers. Despite their low cultural level and their lack of organizational skills, a substantial portion of the city's unskilled workers had been reached by democratic and socialist propaganda, had learned the new political slogans, and were ready to fight for the cause when an opportunity presented itself.

But while unskilled workers had an aggressive political style when they participated in politics at all, they remained far behind the members of the open skilled trades in the amount of their violent, as well as organizational, political action. As George Rudé has demonstrated in his studies of political crowds, most political violence is the outcome of extensive and well-organized political activity. So it was in mid-nineteenth century Marseille; the revolutionary political crowds were dominated by the same social types as the democratic and socialist movement in its day-to-day existence. The "*classes dangereuses,*" in the person of the unskilled workers, had some role in Marseille's political violence, but the self-respecting, moderately prosperous, well-organized skilled worker of the open trades made up the shock troops of the revolution, as well as the bulk of its political cadres.

The role of the bourgeoisie in the democratic and socialist movement was precisely the opposite of the unskilled workers' role. Although most of Marseille's bourgeois were Orleanists, Legitimists or Conservative Republicans, bourgeois also filled nearly all the top-level leadership positions in the democratic and socialist movement and provided a good portion of the political cadres as well. They were second only to the open skilled trades in their level of participation in the organizational activities of the movement. But for all their prominence in the meeting-room, the bourgeois were rarely on the streets; their rate of participation in political violence and other forms of public defiance was even lower than that of the exclusive trades. The importance of the bourgeois in the movement's affairs was far out of proportion to their numbers. With their education, superior oratorical and debating skills, greater financial resources, command of the techniques of organization, and superior political experience, the relatively small bourgeois element provided the bulk of the ideological and organizational leadership of a movement composed primarily of unsophisticated political novices from the working class.

Of the remaining occupational categories, service workers were moderately active in the movement, while sailors and fishermen had the lowest rate of participation of any group in the population. Sailors and fishermen combined the traditionalism and social isolation of the exclusive trades with the low literacy rates and absence of organizational skills characteristic of the unskilled trades; in addition, they were frequently at sea, physically removed from the arena of politics and political organizations. Their political apathy therefore comes as no surprise. The higher level of activism in the service trades, which was most notable in acts of political violence and public defiance, was due entirely to one sub-group in the service category—the waiters and cooks who accounted for less than a third of all service workers, but for nearly half the militants. One suspects that their political activism resulted from the political importance of their work-places. It was in the wineshops, cabarets, and cafés of Marseille that most political organizations met, both on a formal and an informal basis, and it was there that most political discussions took place. It is only natural that the employees of such establishments—and their proprietors, many of whom were also militants—should share the politics of their customers.

One final observation can be made about the social composition of the democratic and socialist movement: men who had migrated to Marseille from elsewhere in France were much more likely to be involved in the movement than men who were born in Marseille. Even immigrants from Italy, who had little stake in French society or politics and who frequently lacked a command of the French language, were somewhat more likely to be politically involved than were natives of Marseille. Such, at least, is the conclusion resulting from an analysis of the June 1848 and December 1851 lists, the only ones which give a place of birth for most of the men concerned. Immigrants were especially numerous in the insurrection of 1848 and among the men arrested for insurrectionary preparations or for acts of public defiance in 1851, but this predominance was less pronounced among men arrested as leaders and political cadres in 1851 (See Table 9.4). The immigrants' penchant for revolutionary politics was not simply a byproduct of their numerical prominence in the most politically active occupations of Marseille. Within each of the major occupational groupings, immigrants were more likely to participate in the democratic and socialist movement than their native-born compatriots. Thus, both a man's occupation and his status as a native or an immigrant affected the likelihood of his involvement in the democratic and socialist movement. The fact that a man worked in an open skilled trade was likely to draw him into revolutionary politics, especially if he was an immigrant; conversely, most workers in exclusive trades avoided revolutionary politics, but they were more certain to avoid it if they were also natives of Marseille.

The immigrants' enthusiasm for the new politics was part of their general lack of traditionalism and willingness to accept new values and standards of behavior.

As immigrants, they were far removed from their original small-town or village communities and had not yet been integrated into urban society. Furthermore, many of the values and social assumptions which they had taken for granted in their native villages were not applicable in the new urban environment. As a consequence, the immigrants were more open to new values and life styles than the natives of Marseille, who had experienced no sharp discontinuities in their lives and whose inherited social assumptions continued to be adequate. This difference between traditional and socially restricted natives and adventurous and socially liberated immigrants held true in several different areas of behavior. As the Abbé Charpin has demonstrated in his massive study of religious practices in Marseille, the "de-Christianization" of the working class, which began around 1848, advanced particularly rapidly among migrants to the city.[48] Paradoxically, the same freedom from traditional social assumptions that made immigrants more likely to join in the democratic and socialist movement also made them more ambitious for social advancement and more willing to abandon their own class of origin to enter the bourgeoisie. Thus in 1846, 13 percent of all immigrants of working-class origins, as opposed to only 6 percent of all natives of working-class origins, had bourgeois occupations when they signed their *actes de mariage*. But the greater openness and freedom of immigrants also made them far more

Table 9.4
Militants by Place of Birth

		Marseille	Other France	Foreign Country	
Insurrection, June, 1848					
	No.	44	185	30	n = 259
	Percent	17	71	12	
Acts of Public Defiance December, 1851					
	No.	18	53	10	n = 81
	Percent	22	66	12	
Organizational Activities December, 1851					
	No.	55	126	13	n = 194
	Percent	28	65	7	
Total, December, 1851					
	No.	73	179	23	n = 275
	Percent	27	65	8	
Total, 1848 and 1851					
	No.	117	364	53	n = 534
	Percent	22	68	10	
Percent of Population, 1846		41	43	16	

open to the temptations of crime than native Marseillais. Natives made up only 17 percent of the men convicted of theft by the *Tribunal correctionnel* (criminal court) of Marseille from 1845 to 1847, at a time when they accounted for 41 percent of the city's population. During the same period immigrants, who made up 59 percent of the population, accounted for 83 percent of all thefts.[49] It appears, in short, that migration undermined traditional behavior in all areas of life—in politics, in religion, in the labor market and in personal morality.

CONCLUSIONS

Just as economic transformations begin and progress most rapidly in certain leading sectors, and only later spread to the rest of the economy, so there are often leading sectors in the processes of social and political transformation. To understand these processes of historical change, we must seek out and identify those sectors of the economy or the social structure where the transformations in behavior and mentalities begin, and where the new patterns of thought and action first expand. Our statistics on participation in the democratic and socialist movement enable us to identify the leading sector in one such social and political change: the revolutionary transformation of working-class politics which took place in Marseille during the Second Republic. Workers in the open skilled trades, and above all workers in the open trades who had immigrated to Marseille from elsewhere in France, first embraced the ideology and the political style of the democratic and socialist movement, and provided the bulk of the organizers, missionaries and enthusiasts who were essential to its continued growth and development.

There are a number of reasons why immigrants working in the skilled trades were especially responsive to the call of democratic and socialist ideology, and were especially fitted to play a dominant role in that movement. To begin with, they had serious enough material dissatisfactions to make them unhappy with the existing social, economic and political arrangements. They also had attained a sufficiently high cultural level to grasp the relevance of politics to their daily lives, and through their labor organizations they had had invaluable experience in running complex associations. Because of the diversity of their social and cultural backgrounds, and because of the uprooting experience of immigration, they were not prisoners of tradition, but were willing to experiment with new ideas and new styles of life. Finally, the immigrants working in the skilled trades were sufficiently numerous for any change in their political attitudes and behavior to have a profound impact on the rest of society. Other groups in the population shared some of these characteristics, of course, but only the open skilled trades united all of them. Workers in the exclusive trades also had a high cultural level, and were experienced in the arts of political organization, but they were too jealous of their privileged position among the workers of Marseille to feel a general sense of disaffection, and their social isolation and strong attachment to an older cultural tradition kept them apart from new forms of political thought and action. Workers in the unskilled trades were oppressed and disaffected, and they were not averse to democratic and socialist ideas, but they were prevented from playing a leading role in the movement by their low cultural level and their lack of organizational skills and experience. As for workers in the service trades and sailors and fishermen, there were too few of them to have had a significant impact on society as a whole. The bourgeoisie had a superior cultural level and a superior command of organizational skills, but few of them were disaffected enough to join in a movement that posed a potential threat to their privileges and property. The small fraction of the bourgeoisie that did join the democratic and socialist movement monopolized most of its top leadership positions, but until the open trades provided them with a mass following in the spring of 1848, the bourgeois republicans were no more than an isolated sect.

Were these patterns of political behavior peculiar to Marseille under the Second Republic, or were they repeated in other cities of France and in other periods of time? This is an important question, but the answer remains obscure at the present time. Indeed, until more research has been done, we will not even know whether the working classes of other cities had the same kinds of social-structural groupings as the working class of Marseille, let alone whether the differences in social structure always had the same consequences for political behavior. To be sure, unskilled workers existed everywhere, and the similarity in the nature of their work—with its insecurity, low wages and ease of changing personnel—probably caused unskilled workers in other cities to share the characteristics of their brethren in Marseille—a low cultural level, a lack of labor organizations and a general lack of stability and predictability in their lives. Furthermore, some information is available on the social composition of revolutionary movements in Paris and Lyon and there, as in Marseille, unskilled workers seem to have been distinctly less prominent than skilled workers. J. Rougerie's figures on the Communards show that *journaliers* made up a smaller percentage of arrested insurrectionaries than they did of the population at large,[50] and figures in the "Statistique de l'insurrection de décembre 1851" in the *Archives nationales* indicate that unskilled workers made up only 11 percent of the men arrested after the coup d'état in the department of the Rhône, and only 5 percent of those arrested in the department of the Seine—surely less than their percentage within the total population.[51] By contrast, skilled workers made up the majority of those arrested in all three of these cases.

It is much more difficult to generalize, at this point, about the difference which we found in Marseille between the open and the exclusive trades. Until research on patterns of recruitment has been carried out elsewhere, we can only guess which trades were exclusive and which were open in other cities; indeed it is possible that there was no distinct category of exclusive trades in some cities. Nor do we know whether exclusive trades in other cities had a special cultural pattern which distinguished them from the rest of the working class. It is even possible that in cities with longer traditions of political insurgency—for example, Paris or Lyon—the members of those occupations which recruited from within the trade and within the city may have been more radical than the workers in occupations with more heterogeneous patterns of recruitment. There is no reason why a revolutionary political stance cannot be passed on from father to son just as a stance of political indifference was passed on in Marseille. But our research demonstrates one thing conclusively: an imaginative use of quantitative data can genuinely illuminate our understanding of nineteenth-century workers.

NOTES

1. No adequate history of the Second Republic in Marseille has yet been written. The best accounts are in *Les Bouches-du-Rhône: Encyclopédie départementale*, ed. P. Masson, vol. 5, *La Vie politique et administrative* (Paris and Marseille, 1829), pp. 157–81; and vol. 10, *Le Mouvement social* (Paris and Marseille, 1823), pp. 28–36.

2. On the political movement of the late Second Empire and the Commune, see Antoine Olivesi, *La Commune de 1871 à Marseille et ses origines* (Paris, 1850); "Marseille" in Louis Girard, ed., *Les élections législatives de mai 1869*, vol. 21 of the *Bibliothèque de la Révolution de 1848* (Paris, 1860), pp. 77–127; and "L'Evolution de l'opinion politique à Marseille sous le Second Empire, 1852–1870," in *Marseille sous le Second Empire* (Paris, 1961), pp. 143–64.

3. The main sources used for the analysis of the social structure of the working class are the *actes de mariage* as well as the *listes nominatives*. The *actes de mariage* for Marseille in the nineteenth century are in series 201 E of the Archives départementales des Bouches-du-Rhône. For this study we have analyzed the information given for all men who married in 1846. The year 1846 was chosen as the last normal year before the social and economic crisis of 1847–1851. The *listes nominatives* of the 1851 Marseille census are in the Archives de la Ville de Marseille, 2 F 161. Several of the registers were misfiled with the *listes nominatives* of the census of 1836, 2 F 131–36. In our analysis of the census, we took a systematic sample of 10 percent of the households that appeared on the registers.

4. Charles Pouthas, *La Population française pendant la première moitié du XIXe siècle* (Paris, 1956), pp. 98–107.

5. Figures for the number of births and deaths in Marseille from 1806 through the 1870s are given in Joseph Mathieu, *Marseille: statistique et histoire* (Marseille, 1879), pp. 34–35.

6. The departments of the Var, Vaucluse, and Basse-Alpes, together with a part of the department of Bouches-du-Rhône, lying outside the commune of Marseille, accounted for 38 percent of all male immigrants in 1846. Another 34 percent came from elsewhere in France, and the remaining 28 percent came from foreign countries. These figures are taken from the *actes de mariage* of 1846.

7. Figures for the carrying capacity of the ships entering the port of Marseille show an increase of 267 percent from the period 1825–1829, the first for which figures are available, to 1843–1847. Jules Julliany, *Essai sur le commerce de Marseille*, 2d ed. (Marseille, 1842), vol. 1, p. 162; Bousquet et Sapet, *Etude sur la navigation, le commerce*

et l'industrie de Marseille, pendant la période quinquennale de 1850 à 1854 (Marseille, 1857), pp. 23–29. Figures for customs duties collected by the *Douane de Marseille*, a rough index of the value of goods entering the port, and on the whole a less reliable indicator of traffic, increased by 450 percent from 1815–1819 to 1843–1847. Julliany, vol. 1, p. 145; *Travaux de la société de statistique de Marseille*, vol. 1 (1837), p. 70 and vol. 19 (1855), p. 92.

8. For the development of industry, see Julliany, *Essai sur le commerce*, vol. 3.

9. Archives Nationales (hereafter abbreviated as AN): C947. For Marseille, at least, this is by far the most accurate and the most extensive of the governmental *enquêtes* of the midnineteenth century. For each industry, the *enquête* gives the number of establishments, the number of workers (men, women, and children), their wages, an estimate of how many workers in each industry are permanent and how many are temporary residents, the hours worked per day and the days worked per year, and the quantity and value of each industry's product. Unfortunately, Marseille is the only major city in France where the *enquête* was carried to completion.

10. For information on the *portefaix*, see the excellent study by Victor Nguyen, "Les Portefaix marseillais. Crise et déclin, survivances," *Provence historique*, vol. 12 (1926), pp. 363–97.

11. More precisely, there were 8,100 unskilled workers and 18,950 skilled workers in Marseille when the census was taken in 1851.

12. AN: C947.

13. These figures come from our analysis of the *actes de mariage* of 1846.

14. See the *enquête sur le travail* of 1848, AN: C947; Armand Audiganne, *Les Populations ouvrières et les industries de la France*, 2d ed. (Paris, 1860), vol. 2, pp. 248–49; and François Mazuy, *Essai historique sur les moeurs et coutumes des Marseillais au XIXe siècle* (Marseille, 1833), p. 179.

15. AN: C947.

16. The identification of *compagnonnages* is based on two different types of evidence. First, a number of trades are spoken of as having *compagnonnages* in police or judicial archives or in the press. *Compagnonnages* of hatters, locksmiths, bakers, shoemakers, joiners and cabinetmakers, wheelwrights, harnessmakers and saddlers, foundry workers, cutlers, coppersmiths, plumbers, house painters, and stonecutters were identified in this manner. We have also identified in the *listes nominatives* of the census all the rooming houses in Marseille of which all or nearly all the residents were in a single trade, on the assumption that they were *mères* (houses of call) of *compagnonnages*. There were three such rooming houses of joiners and cabinetmakers; one of locksmiths, joiners, and cabinetmakers combined; one of foundry workers, coppersmiths, plumbers, and cutlers combined, and one each of carpenters, painters, glaziers, blacksmiths, and wheelwrights.

17. Some of these societies are listed in *Les Bouches-du-Rhône: Encyclopédie départementale*, vol. 10, pp. 806–09. The rest may be found in the Archives départementales des Bouches-du-Rhône (Hereafter abbreviated as ADBdR): M 6/1045–50 and M 6/1636–1635.

18. J.-P. Aguet, *Les Grèves sous la Monarchie de Juillet* (1830–1847) (Geneva, 1954); and ADBdR: M 6/26.

19. ADBdR: 403 U52, Jugements du Tribunal correctionnel, 1845.

20. There were three strikes by coopers, two each by tanners, shoemakers, tailors, and printers and one each by turners, bakers, joiners, stonecutters, and crate makers. The

strikes of the tanners and coopers were all unsuccessful; the shoemakers, joiners, and printers each succeeded once. Information about most of these strikes can be found in Aguet, *Les Grèves sous la Monarchie de Juillet*; Octave Festy, *Le Mouvement ouvrier au début de la Monarchie de Juillet* (1830–1834) (Paris, 1908), pp. 283–85; and Office du Travail, *Les Associations professionnelles ouvrières*. 4 vols. (1899–1904).

21. These figures are from the *enquête sur le travail* of 1848, AN: C947.

22. We have estimates from two sources representing very different social and political points of view: one from the *enquête sur le travail*, which was carried out by Marseille's *juges de la paix* (justices of the peace); and the other from a socialist tract entitled "*Les Misères du peuple*," by Antoine Agenon, the editor of Marseille's leading democratic and socialist journal in the spring of 1848. The tract was published in the journal, *Le progrès social*, beginning on March 30, 1848. Happily, the two estimates are consistent with each other. The *juges de la paix* estimated that a single man could get by on 600 to 900 francs a year, and that a couple with two small children could manage on 900 to 1,200. Agenon put minimum expenses for a couple with no children at 700 francs and for a couple with small children at 1,050 francs.

23. Fifty-eight percent of the unskilled workers lived in the *vieille ville* (old city), as opposed to only 30 percent of the skilled workers, according to our analysis of the *listes nominatives* of the census of 1851.

24. Although they accounted for only 17 percent of the adult male population of Marseille, unskilled workers made up 40 percent of all the men convicted of theft by the *Tribunal correctionnel* of Marseille from 1845 through 1847. Skilled workers, who made up 40 percent of the population, accounted for only 31 percent of the men convicted of theft.

25. In carrying out the calculations done here, we have grouped certain of the smaller occupations into somewhat larger categories. The categories entitled maritime industries, shipbuilders, metallurgists, miscellaneous building workers, miscellaneous skilled, miscellaneous unskilled, and waiters and cooks are all, in fact, composite categories. The occupational titles included in these categories are indicated in the Appendix. Trades represented in the *actes de mariage* sample by fewer than ten men are included in either the category of miscellaneous skilled or miscellaneous unskilled, whichever is appropriate, on the grounds that such small samples would not give us any reliable indication of the actual characteristics of the occupations.

26. On measure three, plus and minus signs of the standard deviation scores have been reversed, since in this case a low percentage, not a high one, indicates greater exclusiveness.

27. For example, we can say that an occupation in which 37 percent of the members were born in Marseille is almost exactly as exclusive on measure one as another occupation is on measure two if 20 percent of its members had fathers in the same occupation. We can make this statement because the figure of 37 percent on measure one yields a score of − .68 standard deviations, and the figure of 20 percent on measure two yields a score of − .67 standard deviations.

28. Nguyen, "Les Portefaix marseillais."

29. *Les Associations professionnelles ouvrières*, vol. 1, pp. 488–90, and G. and H. Bourgin, *Le Régime de l'industrie en France de 1814 à 1830*, vol. 3 (Paris, 1941), pp. 161–71.

30. These figures are from the *enquête sur le travail* of 1848, AN: C947.

31. Mazuy, *Essai historique*, p. 180.

32. Ibid., p. 181.

33. This identification of natives with the exclusive trades is in fact quite accurate. As we have seen, 79 percent of the workers in the exclusive trades were born in Marseille, as opposed to only 37 percent in the open skilled trades and 26 percent in the unskilled trades. To approach this question from another angle, nearly half (47 percent) of all the native Marseillais in the working class were employed in the exclusive trades. Furthermore, it is likely that some of the men in the open trades who were born in Marseille were in fact sons of immigrants and therefore probably had little in common with men from old Marseillais families. In short, it is likely that a sizeable majority of Marseillais workers *de vieille souche* (from old families) were in the exclusive trades. It is also likely that Marseillais in the open trades lost many of their distinctive cultural and linguistic traits as a result of their continual interaction with immigrants.

34. Mazuy, *Essai historique*, p. 181.

35. Ibid., p. 197.

36. Ibid., pp. 188–93.

37. Ibid., p. XV.

38. Agricol Perdiguier, *Mémoires d'un compagnon* (Paris, 1964), pp. 90–91.

39. Ibid., p. 91.

40. Victor Gelu, *Chansons provençales*, 2d ed. (Marseille, 1856), pp. 5–6; Emile Ripert, *La Renaissance provençale, 1800–1860* (Paris, 1917), p. 305; and Mazuy, *Essai historique*, p. 75.

41. Most of the city's sailors and fishermen lived on a narrow strip of land along the northern edge of the port, as can be seen from an examination of the *listes nominatives* of the 1851 census.

42. Those arrested in 1848 are listed in ADBdR: M 6/367. Those arrested in 1851 are in M 6/356.

43. ADBdR: M 6/366 and 14 U 89.

44. ADBdR: M 6/949 includes the members of the *Club de la Montagne* and the *Cercle de la Paix*. The members of the *Cercle de Noailles* are listed in M 6/29.

45. Archives de la Ville de Marseille: I 1/489; and ADBdR: 14 U 89, 403 U 63–65.

46. Figures on each trade's participation in the democratic and socialist movement are given in Appendix 1.

47. ADBdR: M 6/366. *Circulaire du Ministère de la Police Générale*, 13 June 1853.

48. F. L. Charpin, *Pratique religieuse et formation d'une grande ville: le geste du baptême et sa signification en sociologie religieuse* (Marseille, 1806–1958; Paris, 1964), Chapter 5.

49. ADBdR: 403 U 52–57, *Jugements du Tribunal correctionnel de Marseille*.

50. "Composition d'une population insurgée: La Commune," *Le Mouvement social*, 48 (July–September 1964), 41.

51. AN: BB 30/423.

Appendix: Selected Characteristics of Marseille's Working-Class Occupations

	Number in Census 1851	Percent of Total Population 1851	Number in Sample, Actes de Mariage 1846	Percent of Total Sample Actes de Mariage 1846	Index of Exclusiveness	Daily Wage in France*	Yearly Earnings in France*	Percent Literate†	Labor Organization‡	Percent of Militants	Ratio of Percent Militants to Percent Population
Exclusive Skilled Trades											
Dockworkers	1,390	2.9	40	3.5	6.10	4'50	1,350	85	(1)	3.0	1.0
Maritime Industries♦	510	1.1	17	1.5	4.43	3.25	895	59	(1)	0.4	0.4
Shipbuilders¡¡	440	0.9	17	1.5	3.37	4.00	1,120	76	(1)	0.4	0.4
Coopers	980	2.0	26	2.3	2.95	3.60	1,160	85	(1,3)	0.6	0.3
Tanners	580	1.2	21	1.9	1.06	3.25	975	67	(1,3)	1.2	1.0
Packagers	190	0.4	10	0.9	.48	4.50	1,350	80	(1)	0.1	0.5
Masons	1,770	3.2	58	5.1	.20	3.25	812	69	(1)	1.7	0.6
Total, exclusive Skilled Trades	5,860	12.4	189	16.7		3.80	1,055	78		7.4	0.6
Open Skilled Trades											
Joiners & cabinet-makers	1,450	3.1	41	3.6	-.58	3.00	900	90	(1,2,3)	4.9	1.6
Shoemakers	2,430	5.1	64	5.7	-.92	3.00	600	64	(1,2,3)	7.4	1.4
Bakers	930	2.0	25	2.2	-2.48	3.25	1,182	84	(1,2,3)	6.0	3.0
Tailors	1,000	2.1	16	1.4	-3.09	4.00	600	88	(3)	3.5	1.7
Housepainters	350	0.7	12	1.1	-2.53	3.00	810	83	(2)	2.2	3.1
Metallurgists#	1,080	2.3	35	3.1	-1.44	3.75	1,125	86	(1,2)	5.7	2.5
Stonecutters	500	1.1	22	1.9	-2.94	3.75	938	77	(2,3)	3.0	2.7
Miscellaneous Building Workers**	1,060	2.2	20	1.8	-.90	3.25	895	75	(1,2)	4.0	1.8
Miscellaneous Skilled Workers	4,510	9.5	114	10.0	-.91	3.25	970	80	(1,2,3)	10.2	1.1
Total, open Skilled Trades	13,310	28.3	354	31.3		3.20	880	79		46.7	1.7

	Number in Census 1851	Percent of Total Population 1851	Number in Sample, Actes de Mariage 1846	Percent of Total Sample Actes de Mariage 1846	Index of Exclusiveness	Daily Wage in France*	Yearly Earnings in France*	Percent Literate†	Labor Organization‡	Percent of Militants	Ratio of Percent Militants to Percent Population
Unskilled Trades											
Soapmakers	390	0.8	13	1.2	-4.32	3.00	900	62	—	0.1	0.1
Sugar Refiners	500	1.1	17	1.5	-5.66	2.50	750	65	—	0.7	0.6
Carters	1,010	2.1	10	0.9	-1.90		—	20	—	1.3	0.6
Day Laborers††	4,500	9.5	62	5.5	-4.49	2.10	580	45	—	5.2	0.5
Miscellaneous Unskilled Workers	1,720	3.7	20	1.8	-3.03			64		2.7	0.7
Total, Unskilled Workers	8,120	17.2	122	10.8		2.20	610	48	(3)	10.0	0.6
Waiters and Cooks	510	1.1	16	1.8	-2.84	—	—	73	(1)	1.6	1.5
Miscellaneous Service‡‡	230	2.6	15	1.7	-4.59	—	—	69	(1)	1.6	0.6
Sailors	1,890	4.0	30	3.4	.13	—	—	50	(1)	1.3	0.3
Fishermen	590	1.2	13	1.5	6.59	—	—	8	◆◆	0.1	0.1

*From the *enquête sur le travail* of 1848, AN: C 947.

†From the *actes de mariage* of 1846.

‡The number (1) means the trade in question had a registered *société de secours mutuals*, (2) means it had a *compagonnage*, and (3) means there was a strike in the trade between 1830 and 1850.

◆Includes sailmakers, ropemakers, and fishnet makers.

ⅱIncludes carpenters, caulkers and tarrers.

#Includes mechanical workers, forgers, founders, puddlers and coppersmiths.

**Includes locksmiths, sawyers, marble cutters, carpenters, carvers, plasters and paperchangers.

††Includes *journaliers* and *manoeuvres*.

‡‡Includes guards, domestics, valets, coachmen, stable boys, shoeshine boys and barbers.

◆◆The fishermen were organized, but not in any of the forms considered here. The ancient corporation of the fishermen, with its elected *prud'hommes* who settled all disputes between fishermen, remained intact well beyond the middle of the nineteenth century. *Les Bouches-du-Rhône: Encyclopédie départementale*, Toma VII (Paris and Marseille, 1928), 704-431.

POLISH MINERS IN THE RUHR DISTRICT: THEIR SOCIAL SITUATION AND TRADE UNION ACTIVITY

10

Christoph Kleßmann

For many years German historians devoted all their attention to leading politicians, administrators, scholars, and industrialists. "Simple, ordinary people" escaped their notice; but then rank and file workers do not leave written records, neither diaries nor autobiographies. This is even truer of a working-class minority who speaks a foreign language. Such was the case of the Polish mineworkers of the Ruhr district. If the Prussian police and a section of the contemporary German press had not shown a particular interest in this group and had not reported on them in comparatively great detail, it would be almost impossible to describe anything but their physical living conditions and forms of organization. In addition to these reports, which are by no means always reliable and are politically very biased, there are, however, a few notes and memoirs written by Polish industrial workers who migrated to the Ruhr district temporarily or who settled there. The four brief biographical sketches presented here are intended to provide a picture of the social situation and political life of Polish immigrants in the Ruhr district. In spite of the differences in detail, it is possible to recognize certain typical characteristics in the course of these biographies.[1]

BIOGRAPHICAL SKETCHES

Jakub Wojciechowski came from the small village of Nowiec in the district of Schrimm in Posnania, where he grew up in extreme poverty. In his autobiography, which has attracted a great deal of attention in Poland, he describes the different places he lived in during the restless wanderings of his life, including two periods in the Ruhr district.[2] His father worked in a brickworks near Berlin. However, only a small proportion of the money he earned there reached his family at home in Nowiec; most of it was spent on drink. When Jakub was fifteen he too left the village to earn money to support the family and at first found work in the same brickworks as his father. After various other jobs he migrated to the Ruhr in 1904, where he was employed as a coalman (Schlepper)

Revised and enlarged version of my article in H. Mommsen, U. Borsdorf, eds., *Glückauf Kameraden!* (Köln, 1979).

at the "Pluto" mine in Wanne. Because this work was too hard he moved to a coking plant in the same year and then finally to the gasworks in Wanne. When a German insulted him by saying "Shut your mouth, you lousy Pole!" there was a fight and he lost his job, and he left the "merry Polish village" (Wanne) again in 1905 and went to work in the copper mines at Mansfeld (Saxony). He did not stay there very long either. He then worked for a builder in a number of brown coal mines and on the streetcars in Magdeburg. After being wounded in France at the beginning of the war and put on the reserve list, he returned to the Ruhr in 1915 and worked as a coal cutter (Hauer) and blaster (Schießmeister) at the "Hibernia" mine in Gelsenkirchen until 1918. After working in several other places he left Germany in 1924, having opted for Polish nationality. This step corresponded with his marked sense of national consciousness, which— together with his close relationship with the Roman Catholic church—provided him with a constant point of orientation throughout his life, in spite of all his outward restlessness.

In contrast with this extreme example of constant movement from one work place and domicile to another—one of the main characteristics of this period, not only of workers who spoke a foreign language—the biography of Antoni Lasinski, a Polish mineworker of the second generation, is quite different.[3] His father, who also came from Posnania, migrated to the Ruhr in 1893. He only changed his domicile and workplace twice. From 1911 until 1956 Antoni lived and worked at the "Friedrich Thyssen II/V" mine in Hamborn/Marxloh. At home they only spoke Polish and there were only Polish newspapers, which, as Lasinski remembers, "I had to read aloud to my father every Sunday even when I was only ten as he had never been to school. That was why he drew three crosses when he had to sign anything." In "Posnan on the Rhine," as Hamborn/ Marxloh was often called by the Germans because of the size of its Polish population, Antoni Lasinski joined several Polish associations, and he was also a member of the parish council of his church. In 1922 he did not opt for Poland but in spite of this remains—right up to the present day—conscious of his Polish origins. His brother, by contrast, had his name changed from Lasinski to Las- inger. As his activities were restricted to church and cultural associations, and also due to fortunate circumstances, he escaped persecution during the Nazi period and renewed his interest in the club activities after 1945.

These few biographical details are enough to show that Antoni Lasinski is a good example of the social integration of a second-generation Pole, in spite of the fact that he kept up his national traditions and identity.

In some respects the life of the family of Jan Kocik, a mineworker who has returned to Poland, is similar.[4] They came from the district of Gostyn (Posnania) and his parents migrated to the Ruhr in 1898, where his father worked as a smith at the "Ewald" mine in Herten (district of Recklinghausen) until 1923.

The owners of the "Ewald" mine built housing for their workers in the working-class district. Whole streets of workers' houses belonged to the mining company. From 1906 until 1923 we lived in one of these houses, at 7d Spichernstrasse. It was a house for four families. Each tenant had a four-room apartment with a little outhouse for animals, a cellar, and a small garden. The apartments did not have bathrooms or toilets, there was only an outhouse closet. There was no sewerage at that time and each apartment had a cess pit that had to be emptied regularly. Petroleum was used for lighting. It was not till the twenties that gaslights were put in.

Talking of his parents Jan Kocik, who was born in 1900, said:

My father also spoke German, but my mother could only speak a little German. At home we only spoke Polish. We children learnt the German language at school. My father always read the Polish newspaper *Wiarus Polski*, which had been published in Bochum since 1902. [In fact *Wiarus* had been published since 1890] My father read a lot about history. At home we had a Polish book about the history of Poland and Polish songbooks. Even before I started school my father gave me lessons in Polish using a little book called *Elementarz Polski*. When I started school I could already read and write Polish and I also knew the alphabet in Gothic script.

After leaving school and completing his apprenticeship, Jan Kocik started work at the mine during the First World War. He was given a job as a horse boy underground.

After about a year I gave up this job. I went to Essen and wanted to be trained as a fitter at the Krupp works. Instead of this I was given a construction job erecting factory shops. It was hard work out in the open. The winter of 1917 was very hard and after a few months I stopped working there. I went back to Herten and looked for another job. I got one working as a fitter at the chemical works attached to the "Pluto Wilhelm" mine in Wanne. After the war had ended the boss fired me, however, he counted my time as an apprentice so that I could take the fitter's exam of the Chamber of Trade in Recklinghausen. I went back to the "Ewald" mine again and worked as a pit fitter underground.

After the war the seven-hour day was introduced in the mining industry. This meant that I had more spare time. I was interested in technical things, and I thought about becoming an engineer. I took two correspondence courses in mechanical engineering and technical drawing. I came to the conclusion that I was not getting anywhere as I had had no secondary education. I turned to teachers from the high school (Realgymnasium) in Herten for help and they gave me private lessons to prepare me for the high school diploma (Abitur). At the same time as I was working as a pit fitter I studied hard for two and a half years, and on 9 April 1924 I took my final exam before the examination board of the secondary school (Oberrealschule) in Recklinghausen. The certificate enabled me to enter the senior high school.

Kocik had to abandon his plans of continuing school when he lost his job. His parents emigrated to France, where Polish mine workers were promised a better future. He remained in Herten at first and, because of his situation, applied to the "Alliance of Poles in Germany," which had been founded in 1922 to help finance further training. The Alliance gave him assistance but at the same time urged him to move to Berlin. In 1924 Jan Kocik left the Ruhr and went to work for the Alliance of Poles in Berlin.

The fourth biography presents a completely different picture. Whereas most of the Poles came from Posnania, Hans Marchwitza is a representative of the smallest but at the same time very important contingent of immigrants that came from Upper Silesia, an area famous for its coal mines.[5] Because of the mixed Polish and German settlement patterns in Upper Silesia—a situation similar to that of the Masurians in East Prussia—they could hardly be distinguished regardless of the objective and subjective criteria employed and in spite of the fact that they spoke Polish.[6]

There is no doubt that Marchwitza's autobiography "My Youth" reveals a great deal about the atmosphere in which he grew up, and the polished style and the political consciousness of the later writer are clearly evident in his description. His ancestors over several generations had been miners. He grew up together with a large number of brothers and sisters in miserable conditions. At home Polish was spoken and family life was marked by deep Catholic piety and petty bourgeois ideas about "good morals" and "what people think." When he was fourteen he went to work at the mine, which for a youth meant eight hours underground. His hopes of being released from his toil by military service were crushed when he was only put in the reserve list because of ill health. In 1910 he was recruited by a mine agent for work in the Ruhr district. "We went to the Ruhr. It was a new dreamland we were all longing for, a kind of 'Cape of Good Hope' for the many who were in distress." His drastic descriptions of working and living conditions show clearly how soon such illusions were destroyed. Marchwitza's first years in the Ruhr are marked by constant moves from one work place and residence to the next and by problems in finding the right political orientation. He was careful to avoid the terminology of class struggle and in the end joined both the Old Union (Alter Verband), which was the miners' trade union associated with the Social Democrats, and the Christian Miners Union (Christlicher Gewerkverein) so as to avoid offending his personal friends. The First World War was to be a deciding factor in his life; at first he looked upon it as a kind of "liberation," but then he experienced the trench warfare before Verdun and tried to escape it by deserting to the French army. After the collapse of Germany he found a political home in the USPD (Unabhängige Sozialde-mokratische Partei Deutschlands—the Independent Social Democratic Party of Germany) and the KPD (Kommunistische Partei Deutschlands—the Communist Party), which was completely atypical of Poles in the Ruhr district.

POLISH MIGRATION

The Poles in the Ruhr district formed one section of the broad flow of ethnically mixed migrants from the eastern territories of the German Reich. It is impossible to say exactly how many of them there were. The Miners' Friendly Society (Allgemeiner Knappschaftsverein—AKV) in Bochum counted all of the migrants who came from the eastern provinces of Prussia as "Poles" and in doing so—

unintentionally, at least—conformed to the widespread popular usage according to which no distinction was made between Poles, Masurians, and Germans from the East. With its negative connotations this stereotype corresponded to the insulting use of the word "Pollacken," a term that has survived tenaciously and which was still in frequent use after the Second World War to describe German refugees working as newcomers to mining in the Ruhr district.[7] From the point of view of the creation of prejudices or the social effects of the uprooting of these people, it may be legitimate to use a general term for all of the migrants from the eastern territories, but if one wishes to examine specific forms of behavior and problems of organization, then precise distinctions have to be made between Poles, Masurians, and Germans.

The great period of internal migration from East to West had its first beginnings in the 1870s, but really began to function in huge bursts in the 1890s. All together around two million people had come to the West by 1914.[8] The origins of this process were, on the one hand, the overpopulation of the agricultural areas of the East, for which there was no industrial area within easy reach to act as an overflow, and, on the other hand, the rapid development of West German heavy industry. The rural lower classes who had no regular work were forced and were in many cases also prepared to seek a better way of life in areas where there were plenty of jobs. Coal mining at a greater depth than before required high capital investments, which in turn made concentration necessary, and the surplus produced resulted in the creation of large mines employing a huge labor force. When the supply of labor from the surrounding areas was exhausted, the mining companies turned their attention to the eastern provinces, where labor was available. Apart from the natural attraction exerted by the higher wages offered on the Rhine and in Westphalia, systematic recruitment campaigns were used to encourage migration to the Ruhr, and they in turn had a snowball effect. There were a number of distinct phases in this process. From early on the East Prussians were in the majority. It is not possible, however, to distinguish clearly between Masurians and Germans until 1902. Presumably the first mine workers in the Ruhr district who spoke a foreign language came from Upper Silesia. Especially Bottrop was a center of this early immigration.[9] Local records in Bottrop report that after the war of 1870–1871 a Pole named Karl Sliwka, who worked as a foreman (Steiger) in the "Prosper I" mine, was twice sent to Rybnik on recruiting campaigns and that he brought several hundred Polish workers back to Bottrop on each occasion. Although most of them returned to the East after a strike, Bottrop became the core of the first permanent Polish settlement in the Ruhr district.[10] One of these recruitment campaigns is described by a contemporary observer:

In January recruiting agents come to East and West Prussia, to Posnania and to Upper Silesia . . . to hire labor for the western provinces. Cigars, beer, and schnaps are distributed among the workers by the agent, each recruit receives a mark as earnest money and after the contracts have been signed the agent organizes a dance for everybody.[11]

Immigration from Posnania really began in the 1890s and rose steadily from then on. It was in this group that the majority of "genuine" Poles came to the Ruhr. As far as their social situation was concerned, there was little difference among the immigrants from the East, but as regards their national consciousness and their attitude to organization in trade unions, it is important to distinguish between the Masurians, the Poles, and the Germans. The Polish trade union, which was founded in 1902, was only open to ethnic Poles. The Masurians were a group from southern East Prussia who had undergone a separate political and confessional development and who spoke a dialect of old Polish. Hence linguistically they were closer to the Poles. As a result of their Protestant faith and their support of the Prussian monarchy, however, there were clear differences between them and the Poles, and it was this factor that in the end was decisive. As a result, all attempts by the Polish nationalists to persuade the Masurians to give their support to Poland ended in complete failure.[12] The total number of Poles and Masurians including those who had been born in the Ruhr district must have been about 450,000 to 500,000 before the First World War broke out. Of these, 300,000 to 350,000 were Poles, and the rest Masurians.[13]

The data available on age structure and distribution of the sexes provide a considerable amount of information about the character of the migration to the Ruhr. Initially it was meant to be a temporary labor migration, but it increasingly led to more permanent settlement. The statistics show that the first immigrants were for the most part unmarried men or men who left their families behind. The rapid increase in the proportion of women, however, demonstrates that the men soon sent for their families or their fiancées or that they married mainly women who had also come from the East.[14] The proportion of women among the Poles is, however, considerably lower than that among the East Prussians. The high figures for East Prussia reflect the different stages of migration already mentioned.[15] The East Prussians formed the largest group of migrants during the early period and were the first to settle; it was not until later that large groups of Poles from Posnania did the same. An analysis of the age structure of the immigrants confirms that they were "in the best years of their lives" when they arrived—in 1890 over 40 percent were between twenty and thirty years of age.[16]

The regional and local concentration of Poles in the Ruhr district was influenced by the extension of the mining area northward and the situation of mines in areas that were formerly country districts. Table 10.1 gives an impression of the distribution of the Polish population throughout the various areas of the Ruhr district and their concentration in rural areas. The concentration of Poles in the rural areas of the northern Ruhr district permits certain inferences about the occupational structure of the migration. Coal mining required above all physical strength and less skill and training. To that extent the industry was especially suitable for unskilled immigrants coming from the country. It may, however, be assumed that Polish workers had just as much opportunity as German miners to make their way up through the job hierarchy from being a coal man (Schlepper) to coal cutter (Vollhauer).[17] The chances of moving to other industries were limited, though, as there was hardly any need for other workers within the boundaries of the Ruhr district. It is therefore not surprising that the number of immigrants from the East who were socially immobile in that they remained in the job they had initially chosen was especially high. For over two generations there were far more of them than there were miners of western origin.[18] In this situation the Polish miners found themselves at the point of intersection of two tendencies that were opposed to each other. For the former farm worker from east of the Elbe, a job in the mining industry was doubtless a step up the ladder of social mobility. At the same time, however, the occupation of a miner lost part of the high status it originally had among the native inhabitants. "Work in the mines became the first job of immigrants from the East, a step down for the local people."[19]

The proportion of Polish workers in mining and in the iron and steel industries always remained fairly high in the Westphalian section of the Ruhr—according to the census of 1905, it was over 80 percent—whereas in the provincial government district of Düsseldorf in the Rhineland, which had a wider range of jobs available, large numbers of Poles were also employed in other industries. For the year 1926 a Polish newspaper estimated that of all the Polish workers remaining in the Ruhr about 75 percent were miners and about 25 percent were factory workers.[20]

It is difficult to arrive at an accurate picture of the living conditions of the Poles in the Rhineland and the Ruhr district. In the northern areas of the district at least, where most of the large mines were situated, the "colony" was the most frequent form of housing to be found. Although this company-owned housing, which many German workers did not at all like, meant undesirably close links with the mine to which it belonged, it turned out to be popular, especially with immigrants who had a lot of children. The rent was around 40 percent lower than that of comparable private apartments.[21] Generally there was a garden and it was possible to keep small animals, and above all the Poles usually made contact immediately with people of their own nationality there.

This very point, however, was also the source of a great deal of criticism. The liberal *Frankfurter Zeitung* accused the mine owners of being politically inconsistent in 1902 as they supported the government proposals for the settlement law (Ansiedlungsgesetz) for the eastern provinces aimed at restricting Polish influence, but at the same time they were creating "Polish enclaves on German territory" as a result of their company-housing policies.[22] The German unions were also critical, saying that it was the deliberate policy of the employers to form these enclaves with the intention of keeping "every breath of modern ideas" away from the Polish workers and hence of keeping them in their role as useful tools at the service of company interests. "The vendor of the *Bergarbeiter-Zeitung* is threatened with being prosecuted for trespassing," reported the Old Union in 1899, "if he should disturb the idyllic calm of the mine houses

Table 10.1

Distribution of Polish Groups in the Areas of the Ruhr Containing the Largest Number of Poles (excluding Masurians and Bilinguals)

Proportion of the Total Population	1890		1900		1905		1910	
	absolute	*%*	*absolute*	*%*	*absolute*	*%*	*absolute*	*%*
Provincial Government District of Münster								
Recklinghausen (City)	716	5.1	6389	18.8	9250	20.8	12404	23.1
Recklinghausen (Rural Area)	3988	5.8	15495	12.3	23777	13.3	40847	15.7
Buer (City)	553	5.0	4115	14.4	4895	12.2	7259	11.8
Provincial Government District of Arnsberg								
Hamm (City)	11	0.04	66	0.2	145	0.4	198	0.5
Hamm (Rural Area)	183	0.3	737	1.0	1005	1.2	1982	2.0
Dortmund (City)	626	0.7	3803	2.7	5701	3.2	9722	4.5
Dortmund (Rural Area)	1699	2.2	10787	7.3	18423	10.2	26024	12.2
Hörde (City)	177	1.1	703	2.8	1052	3.7	1466	4.5
Hörde (Rural Area)	338	0.5	1355	1.5	1571	1.6	2268	2.1
Bochum (City)	1120	2.4	1841	2.8	4673	3.9	6269	4.6
Bochum (Rural Area)	2038	2.7	11095	8.4	13054	11.3	10834	9.0
Witten (City)	195	0.7	1098	3.3	1253	3.5	1693	4.5
Herne (City)	2121	15.2	3452	12.4	4521	13.6	12364	21.6
Gelsenkirchen (City)	1930	6.9	1880	5.1	13889	9.4	15065	8.9
Gelsenkirchen (Rural Area)	7064	7.1	24542	13.1	16923	14.1	25383	17.7
Hattingen	492	0.8	1784	2.2	2418	2.7	3238	3.3

Provincial Government
District of Düsseldorf

Duisburg (City)	74	0.1	484	0.5	4224	2.2	7199	3.1
Oberhausen (City)	668	2.6	2743	6.5	4898	9.4	8641	9.6
Mülheim (City)	12	0.04	176	0.5	1276	1.4	2089	1.9
Hamborn (City)	27	0.6	3055	9.4	10493	15.6	17432	17.1
Dinslaken	242	0.3	1188	1.6	1304	2.1	2288	2.9
Essen (City)	211	0.3	1657	1.4	2601	1.1	3805	1.3
Essen (Rural Area)	1887	1.2	9049	3.2	12035	4.9	17699	6.4

Source: M. Broesike, "Einiges über Polen und Deutsche nach der Volkszählung von 1912," *Zeitschrift des statistischen Landesamtes* 48 (Dortmund 1979).

with his cries for our paper."[23] In fact the housing situation of the Poles, especially in the basically rural areas of the northern section of the district, did have an ambivalent effect. It made it more difficult to establish contacts with the German population and encouraged national isolation. On the other hand it reduced the amount of fluctuation among the labor force and hence helped the immigrants to get used to their new surroundings and made it easy for Polish organizations to recruit members. This placed an increased burden of responsibility on the Polish trade union for the fate of the Polish miners, who for the most part kept to themselves.

SOCIAL INTEGRATION AND NATIONAL ISOLATION

The low level of upward mobility among the immigrants from the East—among the Masurians it even was considerably lower than among the Poles—in comparison with that of the local people can be explained not only by the conditions already mentioned but also by the low degree of integration and the long time it took to achieve fuller integration into the new social environment. This leads us to a complex problem that did not simply involve a conflict between two concepts—on the one hand, integration, which in the long run could mean Germanization or assimilation, on the other, conscious national isolation, including a system of organization that was to a large extent autonomous. The German administrative authorities and the general public considered Polish immigration within this frame of reference. But making what was to a large extent a social question a matter of politics only led to an increase in the tensions that already existed. As was the case in the eastern provinces, the official policy toward Poles in the Ruhr district was governed by the political objective of Germanizing them. At first, however, the result of this was the opposite of what was intended. The first Polish associations had been formed in the 1870s, but these were apolitical societies catering to social needs or religious interests. It was therefore typical for them to be organized by the local German priest. Initially hardly any notice was taken of the Polish groups as a national minority, since there were so few of them and they were so scattered. The district administrator (Landrat) in Bochum was correct in stating in 1884 that "as a result of the elementary schools, marriages and constant contact with the German population the Poles in this area will in any case be Germanized in the long run".[24]

The mass immigration of the 1890s changed this situation. In 1890 Franciszek Liss, a Polish priest working in Bochum, founded the first Polish newspaper *Wiarus Polski* (The Polish Champion). A few years later a first attempt was made to form a central organization—the Polish Alliance (Polenbund)—to link the existing societies, but this soon failed. To what extent these activities developed beyond a natural requirement for contact and communication in an alien environment to become a kind of second "Polish question" in the west of Germany depended, however, to a very large extent on the reaction of the German authorities and the general public. There was by no means one general reaction.

But what was of considerable importance was the fact that the authorities and above all the Pan-German press, especially the *Rheinisch-Westfälische Zeitung* which was published in Dortmund, spoke out in favor of a strict policy of Germanization. A typical example of this view is the detailed memorandum written in 1896 by the provincial governor of Westphalia and former district administrator of Obornik (Posnania) Heinrich Konrad von Studt, who was later to become Minister of Education. Summing up, he wrote:

The societies should therefore be looked upon as one organization all under a single leadership which—as long as the number of Polish workers continues to rise at the present rate—within the near future will constitute a considerable political force. In the interest of the state I therefore consider it necessary that suitable measures should be taken to reduce the number of Poles working in the West drastically, as has been done in the East of the monarchy.[25]

These "suitable measures" involved the following: Polish priests should not be allowed to settle among their people; there should be strict control of the Polish press and Polish societies, including the banning of processions accompanied by Polish flags and emblems; the school authorities should pay special attention to Polish pupils; and there should be no translations into Polish of safety regulations and notices in the mines. Two years later Studt observed that they were doing the Poles a favor by Germanizing them, "for instead of an inferior element which is always inclined to resort to excess, whose female section has a very doubtful reputation, it will become one which can fully profit from the economic and moral superiority of Germany".[26]

In view of the constantly increasing struggle over nationality in the eastern provinces, it was hardly surprising that the political treatment recommended for the Ruhr district in the long run only led to similar reactions and that the bitterness of the conflict in the "Eastern Marches" (Ostmarken) was also felt in the West, although the social and ethnic situation in the Ruhr district was totally different. It was only as a result of this anti-Polish policy of the German authorities that a process involving the formation of a minority took place among the Poles of the Ruhr. What were formerly farm workers with hardly any political consciousness and little interest in national questions became Poles who were conscious of their nationality and who no longer saw the complex system of organizations as simply a welcome opportunity to maintain social contacts but as a means of preserving national identity. Although narrow-minded nationalistic observers from both sides failed to recognize it, a complex mixture of social integration and national isolation took place, such as has also been established in the case of other minorities like the Irish in New York or the Czechs in Vienna.[27] The growth of Polish nationalism did not by any means lead to a clear division between the nationalities, in spite of all the urgent pleas to emphasize the separate identity of the Poles, which came especially from their press, but it meant that people also partly succeeded in adapting themselves to a new environment that was often hostile toward them and was certainly felt to be so. The process of becoming politically and socially conscious was accompanied by a strengthening of the ties between this group, which came from less developed areas, and the industrial surroundings that they found in the west of Germany. For this reason it was very difficult for the Ruhr Poles to come to a decision after 1918 when a Polish state once again came into existence and they had the opportunity to return and opt for Polish nationality. It was like tearing oneself apart to have to make this choice.

Clear evidence in support of the argument that there was a complex mixture of integration and separation is provided by an examination of the Polish trade union, the most important social and political institution of the Ruhr Poles and at the same time the most successful organization.

THE DEVELOPMENT OF THE POLISH MINERS' UNION

On 9 November 1902 the Zjednoczenie Zawodowe Polskie (ZZP—Polish Trade Union) was founded in Bochum.[28] (See Table 10.2 for membership figures.) The initiative for this can be traced back to the proprietor and editor of the *Wiarus Polski*, and the support and protection provided by this paper was very important for the launching of the new organization. In spite of this, the ZZP was by no means the creation of "priests and businessmen" as its opponents liked to claim in their polemic attacks.[29] The last chairman of the ZZP in Bochum, Franciszek Kolpacki, later saw the reason for the development of an independent Polish union to have been the shabby way in which the Poles were treated by the German unions. There is no doubt that the lack of recognition within the German organizations did play a role, but this reproach is only justified to a certain extent. At least the so-called Old Union, the miners' union associated with the Social Democrats, also tried to take the interests of its Polish members into consideration at a relatively early date. Hence the Polish *Górnik (Miner)*, whose editor was a member of the executive committee of the Union, was first published in 1897. In 1902 this newspaper was replaced by a four-page supplement in Polish to the union publication *Berg- und Hüttenarbeiter-Zeitung*. These efforts, however, did not meet with a great deal of success. The German rival organization of the Old Union, the Christian Miners' Union, which in 1903 also issued a newspaper in Polish, did not do much better. One important reason for this was that the Poles were very annoyed about a mine inspection decree (Bergpolizeiverordnung) issued in 1899, which made knowledge of a certain amount of German a condition of employment in the mining industry. The authorities had rejected the idea of translating the most important safety regulations into Polish for political reasons.[30] Although the German unions had always demanded such translations but without success, they now expressly applauded the decree as a step toward preventing accidents, even though they were not convinced that it would be effective. But this decree, which was made into an issue by *Wiarus Polski*, is not sufficient explanation for the development of the ZZP. It is probable that the underlying reason was the inability of the two German unions to provide suitable concepts for the organizational integration of the Polish miners.

Although the ZZP was first and foremost a union for miners, it was by no means restricted to them, and in practice it was open to all Poles. In its statutes the ZZP closely followed the example of the Christian Miners' Union. "It is the task of the union," stated paragraph two, "to secure the moral and material improvement of its members, sufficient and steady wages and an adequately respected position in society." In order to achieve this aim, it should "resort to all means permissible under the Christian faith and not forbidden by the law." Although this vague formulation did not directly mention the right to strike, it did not exclude it either but limited it to cases in which it was to be used as a last resort. Paragraph four expressly stated the union's opposition to Social Democracy: "Disputes of a religious or political nature and all forms of agitation

Table 10.2
Membership Figures for the ZZP

Year	Total Membership	Miners' Total	Branch Ruhr District	Metal workers' Branch Bochum
1902				
1903	4,616			
1904	11,500			
1905	25,000			
1906	40,962			(35,863)
1907	47,926			(39,256)
1908	48,000			(40,842)
1909	57,000	22,243	17,772	
1910	66,970	38,387	26,309	
1911	70,583	46,995	30,164	
1912	77,322	50,903	30,354	
1913	75,171	50,047	28,936	
1914	50,512	29,512	16,137	
1915	34,590	17,295	9,130	
1916	33,884	16,942	9,027	
1917	43,984	21,992	12,746	
1918	73,720	36,860	20,834	
1919	480,100	51,722	46,261	
1920	570,537	67,000	45,000	11,140
1922	—	—	45,018	11,200
1923	—	ca.60,000	33,200	—
1924	—	13,400		—
1925	—	4,792		3,017
	—	3,180		2,880

Source: Christoph Klessmann, *Polnische Bergarbeiter im Ruhrgebiet 1870-1945* (Gottingen, 1978), p. 283.

in favor of Social Democracy are under no circumstances permissible."[31] From the mixed membership at the beginning, which cannot be assigned to particular occupations for the first few years, various occupational branches developed after 1909, which were all linked by the central organization. This lack of separation in the initial period played an important role in the development of the organization in that it enabled the ZZP to spread surprisingly quickly beyond the Ruhr district to the East. From the fall of 1904, that is, two years after it had been founded, the ZZP began to agitate in the eastern provinces, and by 1906 it had over 2,000 members in the provincial government districts of Danzig, Marienwerder, Posnan, Bromberg, Oppeln, and Allenstein. This figure was not overwhelmingly high, but it did denote considerable organizational success. As a result of the financial and organizational strength of the Bochum union, it was logical that the existing Polish unions in Prussia should join together to form a central organization. After strong internal political resistance had been overcome, a merger with the existing Polish unions in Posnania and Upper Silesia in 1908 was achieved. This was made easier by the creation of three branches with a great deal of autonomy within the central organization, which kept the name "ZZP" of the Bochum union. The three branches were the miners in Bochum; the craftworkers in Posnan; and the iron, steel, and factory workers in Königshütte.

The central executive committee had its headquarters at first in Bochum and then in Kattowitz from 1911 onwards. The leader of the miners in Bochum, the largest and also still by far the most important branch, was Franciszek Mańkowski. There were always tensions within the central organization which resulted especially from the different histories of the individual branches and the social interests which they represented. These tensions, however, never seriously threatened the unity of the ZZP; it presented itself to the outside world as a strong union, which made it easier to inspire confidence and organize Polish workers in large numbers. Although the paragraph of the German Empire's Association Law (Reichsvereinsgesetz) of 1908 that regulated the use of foreign languages and forbade public meetings with speeches in Polish (except in areas where 60 percent of the population were Polish) placed a considerable obstacle in the way of the ZZP, its membership continued to grow steadily. However, at the outbreak of the First World War the union found itself on the verge of ruin, in spite of its previously successful attempts to strengthen the organization, as is shown especially by the rapid decline in membership and income after 1914. In addition to this, the Polish union was subjected to tight control by the police. Although the administrative authorities did show a certain tendency to cooperate politically with the Poles to a limited extent, especially since the Polish group in the Reichstag had voted unanimously in favor of the war credits, this by no means put an end to the very varied and frequently arbitrary behavior of the police. Moreover, any kind of undesirable union activity could be sabotaged under the martial law regulations by a ban issued by the representative of the Deputy-General Command of the army in Münster or by threatening to send the workers involved to the front.

This worsening of the political situation within Germany forced the miners' unions and hence also the ZZP to cooperate more closely if they were to succeed in gaining acceptance at least for their basic demands. A further factor was the "Patriotic Auxiliary Service Law" (Vaterländisches Hilfsdienstgesetz) of 5 December 1916, which introduced the general duty to work, but which also recognized the unions as organizations with an important role to play in the war effort. This gave them more power in their relations with employers and allowed their officials to be exempted from military service. The rapid rise in the membership numbers of all unions can hence be attributed partially to this law. In 1919 the ZZP already had more members than it had had before the war, and in 1921 the Christian Polish unions from the former Prussian, Austrian, and Russian partition areas all joined together under the ZZP banner. This central organization, which had its headquarters in Posnan, thus formed the union with by far the highest membership in Poland. Its chairman was Franciszek Mańkowski, one of the initiators of the ZZP in the Ruhr district. The Bochum branch also belonged to this central organization, a situation that initially did not present any major organizational or political difficulties in view of the large measure of autonomy that the various branches had in relation to the central organization. Together with the Upper Silesian miners' branch, however, it was given an exceptionally autonomous status in that it was independent of the central miners' branch in Posnan.

THE PROGRAM OF THE ZZP

Many points on the program of the ZZP were similar to those of the Christian Miners' Union, especially the strictly anti-socialist position in the statutes. The ZZP had its own attitude toward the question of nationalization, a matter that was of particular importance to the mining industry and that was the subject of a great deal of discussion. In contrast to the great majority of the delegates to the international mine workers' congresses at which the ZZP was also represented along with the Old Union and the Hirsch-Duncker Union (associated with the liberal Progressive Party) from 1907, those of the Polish organization consistently adopted a negative stance. It was not without good reason that the Poles feared that a takeover of the mining industry by the Prussian government would lead to further disadvantages for them as a national minority.

It was not until the conference of the chairmen of the union branches on 27 October 1917 in Posnan that a general program of basic principles was introduced. This consisted of five points, which maintained the basic guidelines that had governed the union since it came into existence, although practice had by no means always conformed to these principles. This program was very much a compromise, which took into account the internal tensions within the whole organization. According to the preamble, "The ZZP as the representative of the working classes desires close links with Polish society together with all the obligations and rights which this involves. For this reason the ZZP rejects the concept of class struggle based on the idea of internationalism as harmful to the development of a healthy society."[32] The program made express reference to the Christian faith and as in 1902 rejected "all forms of agitation in favor of Social Democracy." It even gave express approval to private property and private enterprise, merely protesting against the misuse of economic freedom and demanding the participation of workers in profits within the framework of a partnership with employers.

If one examines the relationship between the ZZP and the two large German mining unions—because of its small membership the Hirsch-Duncker Union can be ignored—what is striking is the low respect for, and rudeness toward, one another. Before the ZZP was founded, both the Christian Miners' Union and the Old Union were accused of being "Hakatists," especially as a result of their positive attitude toward the mine inspection decree of 1899.[33] After the formation of the ZZP, the journalistic feuds continued unabated. At the same time the other unions tried to undermine the ZZP by increasing the publicity for their own organizations.

But what is more important—and now let us return to the question of why the ZZP was so successful—is that neither of the two German unions ever managed to develop a viable positive concept for the integration of Polish miners, and, given their own assumptions, it would hardly have been possible for them to do so. In the case of the Christian Miners' Union, the obstacle was their close link with the Catholic Center Party, with which the Poles quarreled increasingly bitterly after the turn of the century over the question of the right of Polish priests to minister to their people. Although the Old Union, with its links with the SPD, in theory had room for national minorities as part of its internationalist orientation, in practice the strong religious and nationalist links of the Poles were an insurmountable obstacle for them. It is true that the Social Democrats contrasted sharply with all the other parties on account of their demand for the "maximum amount of tolerance" to be shown toward the Polish workers in the Ruhr district, but this demand was not a sufficient basis for a practicable program of action.[34] Julius Bruhns was completely correct when he wrote of the "Polish question and the Social Democrats" in *Die Neue Zeit*:

People wanted to keep the party free of tendencies that were petty-bourgeois, nationalistic and not socialist, a motive which in fact should be welcomed. But the trouble was that they often acted without discretion. They forgot or at least did not sufficiently consider the fact that the national element had unavoidably to play an extremely important role among the Poles as a repressed nationality and that the worse the national repression of the Poles was, the greater its effect would be.[35]

THE "COOPERATIVE DISTRIBUTION OF LABOR"

If the ZZP hence outwardly appeared to have helped to cause further divisions within the mine-workers' movement, it did at the same time fulfill an important function, which could hardly have been taken over by the German unions, and in this way it did more in the long run to strengthen organized labor than to weaken it. For although the continuous flow of new immigrants from the eastern provinces, which went on up to 1914, consisted neither of strikebreakers nor of workers ready to accept lower wages, there was a danger that these newcomers, who had not yet got used to the new industrial surroundings, would allow themselves to be intimidated more easily. In view of difficulties with the language and because of a mentality formed in a totally different social situation, it was more likely that a Polish organization would be successful in approaching them, organizing them, and, when necessary, in mobilizing them. The increasing importance of the ZZP was not only reflected in the growth of its membership, but also in the successes it gained in elections to various offices in the mining industry, for example, the Miners' Friendly Society (Knappschaftsälteste), as safety inspectors (Sicherheitsmänner), and to workers' councils (Betriebsräte).[36] The success of the Polish candidates in these elections proves that the ZZP had worked its way up to becoming a respected third force among the miners' unions by the beginning of the twentieth century.

The argument that the mine-workers' movement was in fact strengthened by the "cooperative distribution of labor" among the unions in spite of the gap that continued to separate the ZZP from the German unions is perhaps most clearly supported by the Polish union's behavior in the two great strikes of 1905 and 1912.[37]

The strike of 1905 had a large number of causes: mine closures, arguments about whether pay should be stopped while workers were being treated for worms, truckloads of coal that were not counted because they contained too much stone, the rate for piecework, bad treatment of workers by the pit inspectors. It broke out spontaneously at the Stinnes mine in Bruchstrasse, Langendreer (Bochum), initially because of a unilateral change in working regulations by the employers. Although the unions did their best to restrict the strike to this mine, it rapidly spread throughout the whole Ruhr. At its climax on 19 January, 217,539 men were on strike; that is 78 percent of the total labor force and as many as 87.4 percent of the underground workers, among which the Polish immigrants were concentrated. Although police reports give a contradictory picture from area to area, there is no doubt that the Poles generally participated actively in the strike. According to the district administrator of Gelsenkirchen, an area with an especially high percentage of Polish residents, the Poles followed the Social Democrats, who were "the first to welcome the outbreak of the strike."[38] The ZZP was represented by Jan Brzeskot and Jósef Regulski in the central Committee of Seven that was set up to organize the strike. On behalf of the Polish members in the Reichstag, Jan Brejski delivered a declaration of solidarity with the striking Polish workers with the provision that they continue to use legal means to fight for their rights and those of the working classes in general.[39]

When the strike had to be called off by the unions after it had lasted several weeks, the leadership of the ZZP even tried to give the impression in a resolution passed by shop stewards (Vertrauensmänner) that the strike had only been called off as a result of the initiative of the other unions. The resolution expressed regret and stated: ''But in view of the fact that a lack of unity at the present time would destroy the organization which is the worker's only means of defence, we must go back to work now that the decision has been made, even if we do so against our will.''[40]

After the strike the membership of all the unions rose sharply, since many workers realized that success was only possible if there was a high degree of organization. In the case of the ZZP, its membership more than doubled. Another reason for this successful mobilization was probably the fact that the strike had not been a complete failure—one small success was the establishment of workers' committees (Arbeiterausschüsse) under the revision of the Prussian General Mining Law.

Even more information about the ZZP's attitude toward strikes is provided by its behavior in the short but very bitter struggle of 1912. Contrary to the spontaneous action of 1905, it was started deliberately by the leaderships of the Old Union, the ZZP, and the Hirsch-Duncker Union, which had joined together in a loose ''alliance of three.'' What was remarkable about this strike was that it was partly of a political nature and that the Christian Miners' Union did not take part. It was these characteristics that made the active participation of the ZZP into an event of special importance. The Polish union now clearly occupied a position to the left of the Christian Miners' Union, and this shows that it had succeeded in emancipating itself from the Catholic influence that had dominated it at the beginning. Obviously disappointed about the ''renegades,'' whom his union had once looked upon as potential supporters, Heinrich Imbusch, the editor of *Der Bergknappe*, the newspaper of the Christian Miners' Union, was moved to write somewhat exaggeratedly:

In their hearts most of them have long been close to the Social Democrats, although they themselves still consider themselves to be Christians. It is only their exaggerated sense of nationalism that keeps them from taking the last step. . . . The Polish union and also the Polish party are standing on the brink. The strike has shown this once again. Either they turn round now, or they will be swept away by the red wave sweeping through the Ruhr district.[41]

The ZZP was also heavily criticized by the Polish press in the East and even by some of its own members. Apart from violent attacks by the bourgeois press in Posnan, Sosinski, the chairman of the central organization of the union, tried to wipe out the impression that they had any contact with ''the Reds.'' While the strike was still on, he took great care to emphasize the independent role of the ZZP in the conflict. After the failure of the strike, he launched a regular campaign against the Old Union using more or less the same arguments as the Christian Miners' Union. In the face of this, the Bochum branch stressed the pressure on them to represent the interests of the Polish miners energetically, especially in view of the competition from the Old Union. In spite of initial reservations, they were even supported in this by the Polish press in the Ruhr district against the attacks from Posnan and Upper Silesia.

THE POLISH MINERS' UNION AFTER THE FIRST WORLD WAR

In contrast with the strikes of 1905 and 1912, it is difficult to assess the precise role played by the Polish miners and the ZZP in the mass movements of 1918–1919. What is clear is that there were closer contacts between the ZZP in the Ruhr district and the German unions and their policies than during the pre-war years, even though the central ZZP kept to its Polish nationalist position. The leadership of the ZZP, like that of the German miners' unions, came out publicly against the strikes and the workers' council movement (*Rätebewegung*), as these endangered its position. As a result of their recognition as equal partners with the employers for the purposes of wage negotiations, the Polish miners had suddenly gained something that they had been fighting for in vain for years. This situation, which was manifested most clearly in the *Arbeitsgemeinschaft* (an association of employers and trade unions), was put in jeopardy by the workers' councils and the syndicalist union movement. An alliance of the existing unions seemed to be a question of self-preservation. As a result of this, the four recognized unions that had joined together for the purpose of negotiations in 1918 not only spoke out against the great strike in February 1919 but they also demanded protection from the government for those who wanted to work against the "heavily armed Spartacist bands."[42] The four also launched an extremely sharp attack on the "Committee of Nine" (consisting of three deputies each from the SPD, USPD, and KPD), which had been given the task of preparing the nationalization of the coal industry, as they considered the committee's independent way of acting to be an open affront.

The ZZP also continued its close cooperation with the German unions together with an extremely anti-communist attitude during the Kapp Putsch of 1920 and the occupation of the Ruhr district by the French in 1923. In spite of the significant short-term flow of new members in the period up to 1921, the main internal problem of the Polish union in the Ruhr district after 1918 was, however, the dwindling basis of its authority. Just at the moment when the national question lost its significance owing to the restoration of the Polish state and the union's membership was rapidly decreasing as the workers returned to Poland or emigrated to France, it set about making itself more or less redundant by cooperating closely with the German unions.

"Our workers have come to expect a wide variety of material and spiritual rewards here," observed Kotpacki, the ZZP chairman in Bochum, "which they will under no circumstances give up in Poland. . . . There are unlikely to be any but a few who are still prepared to work 'pod pana' [for a landed proprietor], that is, as farm workers."[43] This was precisely the dilemma of the Ruhr Poles at the beginning of the Weimar Republic. In a way they were the victims of a conflict of loyalties. It is impossible to say for sure how this conflict between their national desires and their social links would have ended. After 1918 a large proportion of the Ruhr Poles returned spontaneously to Poland. It is, however, almost impossible to estimate exactly how many were involved, as no record was kept of their numbers, and, in addition, some of them—again it is impossible to say how many—returned to the Ruhr once more because they were disappointed with the wretched working and living conditions they found in the new Polish state.

When the process of opting for German or Polish nationality that was provided for in the Treaty of Versailles came into operation in 1921–1922, the internal situation of Poland, which had only just managed to consolidate its external boundaries to a certain extent, was enough to stifle many people's preparedness to take on its nationality. Even the comparably small number who opted in favor of Poland did not go there for the most part, but emigrated to the coal-mining areas of northern France, which had been recruiting labor even before the rationalization crisis led to mass dismissals in the Ruhr coalfields beginning in 1924. The pressure to emigrate was sharply increased by direct reactions in the Ruhr district to the quarrels over German Polish nationality in the border areas and districts that were subject to a plebiscite. This was especially the case with the plebiscite in Upper Silesia in the spring of 1921, which led to waves of national emotion on both sides and also poisoned the climate between Germans and Poles in the Ruhr district.

This tense situation worsened during the national emergency caused by the occupation of the Ruhr in 1923, when the Germans suspected the Polish minority collectively of being potential collaborators because of the close diplomatic relations between France and Poland. It is true that there were occasional cases of cooperation with the French occupiers, but what was of more importance was that the ZZP joined with the German unions to attack sharply the invasion of the "French and Belgian imperialists."[44]

From the middle of the 1920s on the size of the Polish minority in the Ruhr district shrank to 150,000, that is between a half and a third of what it had been before the war. The various societies fought a hard battle that was by no means without success to preserve the Polish language and to keep up national, cultural, and religious traditions, but the Polish union soon lost all importance. It was formally dissolved in the Ruhr district in July 1934 because of the lack of members.

POLES IN THE RUHR DISTRICT—"GUEST WORKERS" IN THE FEDERAL REPUBLIC

Placing the historical subject of "Polish workers in the Ruhr district" in the greater context of labor migration of workers speaking a foreign language reveals a number of aspects similar to those of the current "guest-worker problem." The movement from the country into the cities, the abrupt change from backward agricultural districts to highly developed industrial areas, the problems of getting used to a new and harder pace of working, experiencing discrimination, disadvantages in various working and living situations that encourage the natural tendency to fall back on one's own ethnic group, the difficulty of achieving adequate union representation because of a language barrier—all of these are points that clearly show structural similarities between the situation of the "guest workers" today and that of the Poles in the Ruhr district before the First World War. There are, however, two major differences. Firstly, the Poles were citizens of the German Reich. This meant that legal and organizational means of improving their situation were available to them that are not necessarily available to foreigners. Secondly, the social problem of the immigrants was given its own special national hallmark as a result of the unsolved "Polish question" in the East, one of the most serious sources of crisis in the Reich. It is important to emphasize this in order to make clear once again where the accent of this interpretation lies.

For Polish historians the Poles of the Ruhr district are one section of the worldwide Polish emigration. From the Polish viewpoint dominating aspects are the struggle against loss of nationality and repression and also a kind of pioneer role played by the Polish workers on the Ruhr in the history of the Polish working class and the unions. The strong emphasis on the national element of the history of the Ruhr Poles does not, however, do full justice to the complexity of the subject. On the other hand the approach employed by Richard Murphy, who tends to argue from the opposite perspective, is not convincing either. His study, which takes Bottrop as an example, is entirely based on the social historical perspective. In his work the attempts made by the Poles through their organizations to resist tendencies toward Germanization are seen primarily as efforts "to create a German version of a pluralist society," and hence the history of the Ruhr Poles is for him "a success story of American dimensions."[45]

As important as it is that the history of the Polish working-class minority in the Ruhr district should not only be described in terms of conflicts between two nationalities, the specific nature of the national conflict between Germans and Poles nevertheless remains of paramount significance for an adequate interpretation. Both the Polish national view and Murphy's, with its stronger comparative and social historical elements, must be taken into consideration. Such a dualist interpretation does not only correspond to the perspective required of the historian of today looking back through time but it also seems to be reflected in the experiences of the people involved, as they were outlined at the beginning of this essay.

NOTES

1. For a comprehensive description of the history of the Poles in the Ruhr district see, Christoph Klessmann, *Polnische Bergarbeiter im Ruhrgebiet 1870–1945. Soziale Integration und nationale Subkultur einer Minderheit in der deutschen Industriegesellschaft* (Göttingen, 1978). This includes detailed bibliographical references.

2. J. Wojciechowski, *Życiorys własny robotnika* [Autobiography of a worker], 2d ed. (Posnan, 1971; first published in 1930).

3. A. Lasinski in a letter to the author in 1975.

4. An autobiographical account sent to the author by Jan Kocik on 8 February 1983 from Złotów in Poland.

5. H. Marchwitza, *Meine Jugend* (East Berlin, 1964).

6. See below, p. 258.

7. See R. Schmitz, "Das Gedinge. Seine Bedeutung und seine Wirkung auf die zwischenmenschlichen Beziehungen im Ruhrkohlenbergbau" (Ph.D. diss., Erlangen, 1952).

8. K. E. Born, "Der wirtschaftliche und soziale Strukturwandel in Deutschland am Ende des 19. Jahrhunderts," in E.-W. Böckenförde, ed., *Moderne Deutsche Verfassungsgeschichte 1815 bis 1918* (Cologne, 1972), p. 456.

9. R. Murphy, *Gastarbeiter im Deutschen Reich. Polen in Bottrop 1891–1933* (Düsseldorf, 1982).

10. "Geschichte einer polnischen Kolonie in der Fremde," published on the occasion of the jubilee of the St.-Barbara-Verein in Bottrop (1911), in "Kirche und Religion im Revier, Beiträge und Quellen zur Geschichte religiöser und kirchlicher Verhältnisse im Werden und Wandel des Ruhrgebiets," issue 4, mimeographed (Essen, 1968), 3f.

11. C. A. Zakrzewski, "Zur ländlichen Arbeiterfrage im Osten Deutschlands," *Schmollers Jahrbuch* 14 (1890), 166.

12. For the question of the Masurians and the problems of Polish historians in assigning them to the correct nationality, see H.-U. Wehler, "Zur neueren Geschichte der Masuren," *Zeitschrift für Ostforschung* 11 (1962), 147–72.

13. For details of the statistical basis of this estimate, see Klessmann, *Polnische Bergarbeiter*, p. 22.

14. W. Köllmann, "Die Bevölkerung Rheinland-Westfalens in der Hochindustrialisierungsperiode," in idem, *Bevölkerung in der industriellen Revolution* (Göttingen, 1974), pp. 240f.

15. W. Köllmann, "Binnenwanderung und Bevölkerungsstrukturen der Ruhrgebietsgroßstädte im Jahre 1907," ibid., pp. 173f.

16. K. Murzynowska, *Polskie wychodźstwo zarobkowe w zagłębiu Ruhry w latach 1880–1914* [Polish labor emigration to the Ruhr district] (Warsaw, 1972), p. 28, German translation: *Die polnischen Erwerbsauswanderer während der Jahre 1880 bis 1914* (Dortmund, 1979).

17. J. V Bredt, *Die Polenfrage im Ruhrkohlengebiet, eine wirtschaftliche Studie* (Leipzig, 1909), p. 98.

18. G. Tölle, "Wandlung und Krise der Belegschaft im Ruhrbergbau in ihren Auswirkungen auf die Produktivität" (Diss., Erlangen, 1952).

19. H. Croon, "Die Einwirkung der Industrialisierung auf die gesellschaftliche Schichtung der Bevölkerung im rheinisch-westfälischen Industriegebiet," *Rheinische Vierteljahresblätter* 20 (1955), 309.

20. See Klessmann, *Polnische Bergarbeiter*, pp. 69f.

21. E. Oberschuir, *Die Heranziehung und Sesshaftmachung von Bergarbeitern im Ruhrkohlenbecken* (Düsseldorf, 1910), p. 63.

22. Quoted in L. Pieper, *Die Lage der Bergarbeiter im Ruhrrevier* (Stuttgart, 1903), pp. 243f.

23. *Deutsche Berg- und Hüttenarbeiter-Zeitung*, 8 July 1899.

24. Quoted in M. Heinemann, "Die Assimilation fremdsprachiger Schulkinder durch die Volksschule in Preussen seit 1880," *Bildung und Erziehung* 28 (1975), 59f.

25. Memorandum dated 31 October 1896, copy in the Staatsarchiv Düsseldorf, Reg.Düss.Präs. 867, pp. 228ff.

26. Quoted in Klessmann, *Polnische Bergarbeiter*, p. 63.

27. See N. Glazer and D. P. Moynihan, *Beyond the Melting Pot, the Negroes, Puerto Ricans, Jews, Italians, and Irish of New York City* (Cambridge, Mass., 1963); M. Glettler, *Die Wiener Tschechen um 1900. Strukturanalyse einer nationalen Minderheit in der Großstadt* (Munich, 1972).

28. For the following see Klessmann, *Polnische Bergarbeiter*, p. 110f.

29. As in the *Correspondenzblatt der Generalkommission der Gewerkschaften Deutschlands* 20 (1910), 348.

30. Pieper, *Die Lager der Bergarbeiter*, pp. 159f., mentions a particularly grotesque example. In April 1903 a meeting was held at the Ministry of Trade and Industry that was attended by doctors and representatives of the mining companies and the Miners' Friendly Society. (The unions were not represented.) In discussions of measures for the prevention of worms, the authorities expressly refused to publish the proposed hygiene regulations in Polish—for "political reasons."

31. Quoted in F. Mańkowski in *Cwierć wieku pracy dla narodu i robotnika, Zjednoczenie Zawodowe Polskie 1902–1927* [A quarter of a century of service to the nation and the workers, the Polish trade union 1902–1927] (Posnan, 1927), pp. 55f.

32. The Polish text is to be found in M. Chelmikowski, *Związki zawodowe robotników polskich w królestwie pruskim 1889–1918* [The Polish trade unions in the kingdom of Prussia] (Posnan, 1925), pp. 273ff.

33. The expression "Hakatism" comes from the German pronunciation of the first letters of the names of the initiators of the Association for the Eastern Marches (Ostmarkenverein) that was founded in 1894—*H*ansemann, *K*ennemann and *T*iedemann.

34. As stated in a resolution passed at the district conference of the SPD in Western Westphalia in 1901, *Vorwärts* 30 October 1901, supplement.

35. J. Bruhns, "Polenfrage und Sozialdemokratie", *Neue Zeit* 26 (1907–1908), 763.

36. Klessmann, *Polnische Bergarbeiter*, pp. 284f.

37. For the strikes, see M. J. Koch, *Die Bergarbeiterbewegung im Ruhrgebiet zur Zeit Wilhelms II. 1889–1914* (Düsseldorf, 1954); A. Gladen, "Die Streiks der Bergarbeiter im Ruhrgebiet in den Jahren 1889, 1905 und 1912," in J. Reulecke, ed., *Arbeiterbewegung an Rhein und Ruhr* (Wuppertal, 1974), pp. 111–48. For the participation of the Poles, see Murzynowska, *Polskie wychodźstwo*, pp. 147ff., 241ff. Klessmann, *Polnische Bergarbeiter*, pp. 121ff.

38. Report dated 28 February 1905, Staatsarchiv Münster, Reg.Münster VII 35b.

39. Shorthand reports of the proceedings of the German Reichstag, 1905, vol. 5, pp. 3970f.

40. Quoted in Murzynowska, *Polskie wychodźstwo*, p. 161.

41. H. Imbusch, *Bergarbeiterstreik im Ruhrgebiet im Frühjahr 1912* (Cologne, 1912), p. 44.

42. Quoted in H. Spethmann, *Zwölf Jahre Ruhrbergbau*, vol. 1 (Berlin, 1928), p. 241.

43. Quoted in J. Kaczmarek, "Die polnischen Arbeiter im rheinischwestfälischen Industriegebiet, eine Studie zum Problem der sozialen Anpassung" (Ph.D. diss., Cologne, 1922), p. 63.

44. Appeal made by the four miners' unions on 7 February 1923, quoted in Spethmann, *Zwölf Jahre Ruhrbergbau*, vol. 4, p. 16.

45. Murphy, *Gastarbeiter*, pp. 183, 17.

IMMIGRANTS IN POLITICS: POLES, GERMANS, AND THE SOCIAL DEMOCRATIC PARTY OF MILWAUKEE

11

Robert Lewis Mikkelsen

When analyzing the relationship between ethnicity, socialism, and political structures in the United States during the first decades of the twentieth century, Milwaukee proves to be a rather special case. Though the growth of municipal socialism was not wholly unique in this era, the strength and durability of the Social Democratic Party of Milwaukee (SDM) stands in contrast to the development of other working-class-oriented third-party movements in the United States. However, neither the expansion of the city nor its industrial development would seem exceptional in its American context. It paralleled the development of other urban centers in the Midwest and encountered the same problems caused by rapid and extensive growth.

THE GERMAN AND THE POLISH IMMIGRANTS

The most readily identifiable factor unique to the city was its ethnic composition. Compared with other Midwestern cities, Milwaukee's population was remarkably homogeneous. Excluding native Americans and a small and declining contingent of Irish, there were only two ethnic communities of any size in the city prior to World War I: the German-Americans and the Polish-Americans. The German-Americans were the first to arrive and by far the larger of the two groups. Germans began immigrating to Wisconsin in the 1840s and took part in the founding of Milwaukee, which gradually became known as the "Deutsche-Athen" of the United States. They quickly established their own schools, newspapers, social organizations, and churches. Many of their leaders referred to themselves as "forty-eighters," men who had taken part in the German Liberal Revolution. Though political refugees were only a minority, they were exceptionally active and well educated. This made them almost natural leaders of a community that in sheer numbers dominated the development of the city. Between 1850 and 1890, Americans of German birth never made up less than one-fifth of Milwaukee's total population. As late as 1910, German immigrants made up 15 percent of the city's total population of 373,847 or some 55,000. Moreover, an additional 30 percent of Milwaukee was of German parentage (mixed or both), making the German-American community roughly half the size of the city or some 167,000 strong.

The German-Americans were, in short, an ethnic community that played a major role in the founding of the city and made up half of its population. This created rather unusual conditions when compared with ethnic communities within the other, more heterogeneous, Midwestern urban centers. By 1890 Milwaukee's German-Americans spanned all classes and embraced third generation managers and owners and newly arrived skilled and semi-skilled workers alike. German-Americans were evident in both major parties and, in addition, had begun a tradition of third-party politics. Thus, being a German-American in Milwaukee neither determined one's socio-economic position nor one's political loyalties.[1]

The situation of the Polish-Americans was quite different. They first began arriving in numbers in the 1880s. By 1890 there were ten to fifteen thousand in the city. Unlike German immigrants, they were a distinct and identifiable minority from the outset and were subject to stereotyping and discrimination. In turn, their Polish cultural heritage led them to view the dominant German-American ethos of the city with suspicion. Furthermore, they were almost exclusively working class in composition and overwhelmingly unskilled. Scanty immigration data suggest many were probably of peasant background. Nor were they as numerous as the German-Americans. In 1910, after three decades of uninterrupted growth, the Polish-American community comprised only 16 percent of Milwaukee's total population or some 58,000 members—as compared with 167,000 German-Americans. They quickly formed a tight-knit community on Milwaukee's south side, where large industrial complexes like the Bay View steel rolling mills offered ready employment. As in Poland, the Roman Catholic Church played a central role in community life through its affiliated social organizations. Politically, the Polish-Americans gravitated to the Democratic Party and adopted what amounted to a bloc voting pattern. The Democrats afforded them, as Adolf Korman put it, "in the distinction of office . . . a compensation for lack of recognition in economic and social spheres of the city's life." Thus, being Polish-American determined one's socio-economic status and political loyalties in Milwaukee to a much greater degree than being German-American.[2]

Given the size and breadth of the German-American community in Milwaukee, an analysis of the impact of ethnicity on the SDM may seem an exercise in the obvious. The rise and decline of socialism in Milwaukee might easily be interpreted as a function of its German political culture, successful so long as that culture received fresh impetus from newly arrived immigrants, but doomed to decline as assimilation into American political culture progressed.[3] Seductive as this explanation may seem, its very simplicity serves more to mask than to illuminate the impact of ethnicity on the SDM. Rather than being viewed as an importation into a set political context, the SDM should more properly be approached as an intrinsically American phenomenon shaped to fit specifically American problems. Accordingly, this essay will explore the roots of the party in its American context and in its German-American heritage, particularly with regard to its relationship with the Social Democratic Party of Germany. This will explicate the manner in which ethnicity supported the growth of socialism in the city. The chapter also will examine the relationship between the German-American and the Polish-American working-class communities, and point out the way in which ethnicity hindered the development of a unified labor movement. The central thesis presented will be that ethnicity did not so much determine the growth of socialism in Milwaukee through the specific heritage of German-American political culture as through the ethnic homogeneity that the sheer size of the German-American community induced in Milwaukee when it is compared with other American cities. This provided the basis for the development of a working-class political tradition that drew upon a German-American heritage. Ethnic homogeneity, it will be argued, was the primary cause of the SDM's rise and decline.

VOTING ALLIANCES IN MILWAUKEE

Leon Fink has pointed out that the twentieth-century American substitute for the mass party of the urban working class so prevalent in Europe was often some form of political organization based on ethnic brokerism.[4] The clearest and most famous form of such organization is, of course, the political boss and his machine. The boss stepped into the political power vacuum created by the inability of traditional, decentralized American municipal government to cope with the explosive growth of the nation's urban centers in the late nineteenth century. He forged an extra-legal organization based on graft and patronage and dependent upon a diverse alliance of interest groups. Central to this alliance were the numerous ethnic working-class communities dotting the American urban landscape. Within the ethnic heterogeneity of the nation's urban centers, each of these communities found itself a minority. Together, however, they formed a majority or near majority of urban voters. Through his position of central authority, the boss drew these communities into alliance, providing them with much needed services as well as patronage and the opportunity to achieve political recognition. In return he gathered in their votes. The relationship was reciprocal and self-perpetuating and created a strong link between political machines and working-class communities.[5]

Excluded from political power and outmaneuvered in gaining the support of the working class in American urban centers, the middle classes became the logical focus of resistance to what they viewed with justification as the illegal and inefficient system of "bossism." Thus, by the turn of the century the two main antagonists of the Progressive Era of politics were fully developed. The political boss and his working-class allies were aligned against middle-class urban reformers. Whether they were "structural reformers" bent on transforming municipal government into a tight, efficient, businesslike operation or "social reformers" aiming at undermining the alliance of boss and working-class communities through a program designed to meet working-class needs in a more efficient manner, both fought a long and largely successful battle to replace the entrenched boss system with "clean government."[6]

In considering the roots of the SDM during this era, it is essential to bear in mind that the very basis of the boss form of political organization was absent in Milwaukee. The division of Milwaukee's working class into only two major groups precluded multiple ethnic bloc voting patterns of the kind found within political machines elsewhere in the United States. This removed one of the basic underpinnings of a strong political machine in the city and, in fact, none ever developed. Equally, however, it deprived the German-American and Polish-American working-class communities of a readily acceptable extra-legal central authority with which they might have traded votes for services. In Milwaukee, as elsewhere, the working class suffered from many deficiencies in municipal services including bad water, poor housing, haphazard zoning and inadequate or expensive transportation. In seeking to address these needs, the two communities making up Milwaukee's working class reacted differently. The longer established German-American workers, constituting one part of a multi-class ethnic community, gradually came to define themselves as a distinct working-class community within the larger German-American community and created a class rather than an ethnic political cleavage within the city. The Polish-Americans adopted a bloc voting pattern for the Democratic party in the city. Thereafter, the Polish-American community became a battleground between the associational politics practiced by the Democrats and the third-party labor politics of the German-American working-class community. In the former they voted as an ethnic group, in the latter on the basis of class interest. The ambivalence of Polish-American voters facing this choice will be viewed more closely in the course of this chapter. Initially, however, it might be argued that it reflected the lack of a strong central authority of the kind the boss offered elsewhere. Had the Democrats been in a position to offer more goods, perhaps the Polish-Americans would have remained more firmly in the fold.[7]

The organized expression of the class cleavage that developed within the German-American community was a series of working-class voters' alliances that replaced one another with varying degrees of success between 1877 and 1897. These included the Workingman's Party (1877), the Milwaukee Trades Assembly Ticket (1881), the People's Party (1886), the Union Labor Party (1887–1888), the Citizen's Ticket (1890), and the Cooperative Labor Ticket (1893–1896). In the same manner that the absence of a political machine in the city had forced the German-American portion of Milwaukee's working class back onto its own resources, this absence also led them to champion issues of municipal betterment or urban reform that elsewhere became increasingly the province of the middle classes. From the outset these alliances addressed the immediate needs of their working-class constituency in the city. The Milwaukee Trades Assembly Ticket called for "just, impartial, and efficient administration of law and of every public trust," for "the reorganization of court procedures, strict economy in public improvements, reform in methods of assessing and collecting property taxes [and] elimination of 'ring' rule." The People's Party and Union Labor Party advocated public ownership and management of municipal services and a host of specific suggestions for improvements in the city. The Citizen's Ticket combined "a long-standing radical reform program with an appeal to efficient, businesslike administration of government." The Cooperative Labor Ticket continued this tradition and added elements of a socialist analysis to the program.[8]

As the names of these alliances suggest, they revolved around the union movement of the city that developed during these years of rapid industrialization. From the middle 1880s the central focus of activity was the Knights of Labor under the leadership of Robert Schilling. From the early 1890s, however, the Knights' place was taken by the Federated Trades Council of Milwaukee (hereafter the FTC), which became the local branch of the national American Federation of Labor. The strength of the alliances reflected the fortunes of these labor organizations. Labor's strength, in turn, reflected its ability to deal with the problem facing union organizations throughout the United States: how to unify under one economic or political leadership an ethnically heterogeneous working class divided not only by language and culture, but by date of arrival, numbers, neighborhood, and level of skill. The latter posed particularly difficult questions, since the division of skilled and unskilled often paralleled the division into ethnic communities.

In Milwaukee, as elsewhere in the United States, the Knights of Labor attempted to deal with this issue by including both skilled and unskilled workers in their organizations. Skilled German-Americans dominated the early years of the establishment of the Knights. In 1886, however, unskilled Polish-Americans were mobilized in large numbers to support the drive for the eight-hour day.[9] This was the first appearance of Polish-Americans in the city's labor movement, and the results of the Knights' efforts were so explosive as to affect the course of the labor movement for sixty years and to present the SDM with a predetermined set of conditions within which it was forced to work.

Like the greater portion of Milwaukee's established powers, the union movement had ignored the Polish-Americans. When in 1886 the Knights tapped this group during their drive for the eight-hour day, they found that it was seething with frustration over its social and economic position. Despite calls for moderation in pressing union demands, the Polish-Americans took matters into their own hands. They formed a crowd that swept through the southern section of the city and attempted to shut down larger industrial firms and draw their employees out on strike. Their failure to heed union leadership in part reflected their distaste and suspicion of the Knights' practice of accepting different gains for groups of employees according to skill or sex. In their view, "skilled laborers had started the labor movement but were leaving the onerous tasks to fall upon the common laborers after manufacturers had granted concessions to the skilled." When Polish-Americans stormed the Bay View works on May 5, they were met by units of the National Guard, who fired on the demonstrators, killing nine.[10]

The Bay View incident galvanized the labor movement and the Polish-American community as nothing had ever done before. The initial consequences were

the destruction of the eight-hour campaign and the repression of the labor movement in the city. But both the unions and the Polish-Americans vowed to take
revenge at the polls for the rough treatment given them by city and state authorities. The People's Ticket of 1886 and its successor, the Union Labor Party,
were the direct offspring of this desire. The united forces of the skilled German-
Americans and the unskilled Polish-Americans were at first successful in their
election efforts. In 1886 the People's Party carried almost its entire Milwaukee
County slate and sent Henry Smith (originally Schmidt) to Congress. The alliance
of the two proved short-lived, however. Beyond a common desire for vengeance,
the People's Party offered little that was substantial to either group. Its successor,
the Union Labor Party, went on to suffer defeat by narrow margins in 1887 and
1888. Thereafter the movement floundered. Its fortunes paralleled the decline
of its founder, the Knights of Labor.[11] The decline of the Knights of Labor and
the failure of the Union Labor Party to continue the electoral successes of the
People's Party determined the main legacy of the events of 1886 for Milwaukee's
labor movement: the isolation of the Polish-American community from the German-American working-class community. Disillusioned by repeated election de-
feats, the Polish-Americans gradually drifted back to the Democratic fold. With
the disappearance of the Knights, they lost the only form of union organization
that could encompass both skilled and unskilled workers. In its place arose the
Federated Trades Council, which was dedicated to organizing on the basis of
skill and trade. By the early 1890s the division between skilled, German-American trade unionists and unskilled, Polish-American laborers was institutional-
ized. Henceforth the labor movement in Milwaukee concentrated its efforts within
the German-American working-class community.

The rise of the People's Party had illustrated that it was possible to forge a
third-party movement capable of capturing electoral power in the city. But its
rapid decline had spotlighted the weaknesses of working-class voters' alliances.
This was primarily due to their lack of a clear program and an independent
political organization capable of translating electoral gains into concrete improvements. Successive alliances after the Union Labor Party were forced by
these deficiencies to seek electoral alliances with political organizations outside
the labor fold, further clouding their programs and weakening their influence.
Yet their very existence illustrated the abiding need for such an organization to
represent working-class needs.[12]

POLITICS, CULTURE, AND ETHNICITY: THE SDM

The organization, programs, and ideology of the SDM were formed to meet
these conditions and needs. To this end it turned to the tradition of socialist
thought embedded in its German-American heritage. In a sense this was odd.
Under the auspices of the Socialist Labor Party (SLP) socialism had been the
wild card of the working-class voters' alliances up to the 1890s. In 1888 the
SLP, under the leadership of Paul Grottkau, had cost the Union Labor Party the

election by fielding its own slate and gaining 964 votes to the ULP's 15,033. This tipped the election to the opposition Citizen's Ticket, which won by a margin of only 945.[13] Socialism's continued legitimacy may be explained in part by the fact that socialist thought had been evident in Milwaukee long before the advent of the SLP and was not solely identified with the movement. As early as 1877 Lassallean Social Democrats in the city had out-polled their Greenback-Labor rivals.[14] Social organizations within the German-American community had acted as conduits for such thought from even earlier times. Prior to the Civil War the Milwaukee *Turnverein* had been affiliated with the *Sozialistischer Turnerbund* of North America. After the war it divided into a conservative and radical faction in Milwaukee, reflecting the developing class cleavage in the community. In addition, the ethnic German-American press had a tradition of radical papers ranging from Joseph Bruker's short-lived *Der Sozialist* (1876) to Paul Grottkau's *Arbeiter Zeitung* (1885), which was succeeded by *Vorwärts*, published by Victor L. Berger.[15]

Victor Berger was the architect and leading light of the SDM. In the early 1890s he had established a philosophical discussion group called the "Sozialistischer Verein," which had established close ties with the FTC and become the basis of the team leadership around which the party took form.[16] Once established, the SDM quickly set about forming an independent and durable political organization. As a model it chose the most prestigious party in the international labor movement of the time, the Social Democratic Party of Germany (Sozialdemokratische Partei Deutschlands, hereafter the SPD). The extra-parliamentary structure of the SPD provided the blueprint for a centralized and democratic organization that could exist quite apart from the electoral system. This centralization met a pressing need for the German-American working class of the city—it provided a possible source of authority to order the chaos of urban growth. Elsewhere this need was met by the boss and his extra-legal machine. In Milwaukee, however, the German-American working class tended more toward creating an extra-parliamentary organization designed to derive its power through the electoral system and fueled not by graft and patronage, but by ideology and common interest.

The extra-parliamentary structure of the SDM functioned as the framework of Milwaukee's working-class community, as its model of government, and as its training ground for future public service. Like the SPD, the SDM made party membership a privilege and a duty. Membership applications were scrutinized by a reviewing board to ensure commitment and reliability. Dues were then paid monthly, which provided the party with a secure economic basis. The backbone of the party organization was its local branches, organized to correspond to the political division of the city into wards. Branches elected representatives to the County Central Committee, which functioned as the party's unicameral legislature. Members were in turn selected from this body to serve on the County Executive Board, which was the party's administration. All positions within this hierarchy were filled by democratic elections, and all political decisions were taken by majority vote. Once a political program was adopted, however, all were bound to respect it. Recalcitrants could be sanctioned or, ultimately, excluded from the party by its Vigilance Committee, though this rarely happened.[17]

In order to clothe this skeleton and consolidate its hold on the working-class community apart from the larger German-American ethnic community, the SDM again emulated the SPD in setting up a maze of social organizations designed to give the individual members the opportunity of fully expressing themselves without straying too far outside community boundaries. These organizations filled other functions as well. They provided a ready source of income that normally exceeded party dues, they acted as social centers for political education and as channels through which new party members might be recruited. Some organizations were created by detaching the socialist or working-class portion of earlier social organizations, others by creating parallel socialist organizations anew. This process had begun before the SDM was established. When, for example, Victor Berger was elected "Erster Sprecher" (President) of the South Side Turnverein, it was promptly dubbed by more conservative elements the "Red Turn Society." Later examples are the *Sozialistischer Verein* itself, clearly deriving from the larger Turnverein; the Socialist Männerchor (male-voice choir), created to parallel the existing Männerchor Germania; and the Socialist Liedertafel (choral society), derived from the Milwaukee Liederkranz. In addition, the SDM sponsored, through its party units, innumerable picnics, mask carnivals, bazaars, minstrel shows, card tournaments, dramas, vaudeville shows, fancy-dress balls, dances, get-togethers, and entertainments.[18]

The SDM also borrowed a leaf from the SPD's book in forging its relationship with organized labor under the leadership of the FTC. By 1902 the SDM and the FTC found themselves on the horns of a dilemma. Previous to that date the SDM had gradually gained ascendency in that body with the substantial assistance of its chief officer, Frank J. Weber, and early member of the Sozialistischer Verein. By 1899 the SDM had won the formal endorsement of the FTC's executive board. By 1901 Victor Berger's *Herald* had become the FTC's official newspaper. However, in supporting a third-party labor ticket, the FTC was moving against the tide of organized labor on the national level. Samuel Gompers and the American Federation of Labor were moving away from third-party endorsements toward a strategy of pressure-group trade unionism, of "rewarding friends and punishing enemies" irrespective of party affiliations. The SDM could not hope to retain its grip on the German-American working-class community without the FTC's active support. Yet, if it persisted in soliciting formal support, it ran the risk of destroying the FTC's relationship with its national organization and undermining the city's labor movement. When the socialists were soundly defeated in an attempt to gain the AFL's endorsement for the Socialist Party of America at the national level in 1902, it was clear that some accommodation would have to be made in Milwaukee.[19]

The solution the SDM hit upon was the tactic of "Dual Status." Dual Status had been developed by the SPD in order to protect Germany's fledgling union movement from the political repression under which the party suffered. According to this "all leaders and officials of the Trade Unions, theoretically independent, had to be chosen by party members."[20] In Milwaukee, in contrast, Dual Status was adopted in order to bridge the gap between the SDM and a preexisting union movement, itself a potential source of anti-socialist activity by virtue of its national affiliation. In this way it was hoped that internal division in the city's union movement might be avoided. Berger enunciated the new policy in 1902 in an article entitled "The AF of L and Socialism":

Each branch of the labor movement has its own sphere of usefulness and he who tries to force one upon the other is trying to hurt them both. In the PERSONAL UNION OF BOTH; i.e., in having the same persons take an active interest in both the trade unions and the political labor movement we find the strongest connecting link between the Socialist Party and trades union organizations, wherever the true relationship between Trade Unionism and Socialism is rightly understood."[21]

The tactic of Dual Status reinforced what Marvin Wachman has aptly described as an "interlocking directorate" between the leadership of the SDM and the FTC. The FTC routinely appointed committees to visit local unions to urge support of the SDM in virtually every election. It contributed funds to the party's campaigns and to its many projects and was particularly heavily engaged in the Social Democratic Publishing Company, which published the SDM's English daily newspaper, *The Milwaukee Leader*. The party reciprocated by supporting union activities. Its members were formally required to take part in the work of their appropriate unions. Moreover, only members of the party who were trade unionists were eligible for nomination to public office. Of eighteen SDM candidates for the Wisconsin state legislature between 1904 and 1910, six were officials in their unions and another ten were members. The benefits to both organizations were great. As Fredrick Olson has put it, "By means of the Milwaukee Socialist party, labor was elevated to a position of prestige and power in government long before such recognition became general in the United States."[22] The rapid growth of the SDM at the polls attests to its profit from the relationship. Yet it is also clear that in binding itself to the established trade union movement of the city, the SDM was acquiescing to the division of the city's working class into skilled and unskilled sections.

Though the SDM had modeled its structure, organizations, and relationship to the trade unions on the labor movement in Germany, it should not be mistaken for a pint-sized SPD transplanted to the American urban landscape. It fashioned these elements to meet its immediate circumstances, rejecting other aspects of the German movement that did not correspond to American conditions. This can be most clearly seen in the SDM's ideology. Whereas the SPD repeatedly rejected the doctrines of revisionism as championed by Eduard Bernstein prior to World War I, the SDM embraced and in some important ways anticipated these ideas. The SPD had developed a tradition of nonparticipation in society after having been systematically excluded from political power for decades in Germany through tactics ranging from outright suppression to inclusion in a democratically elected, but essentially powerless Reichstag. Logically it had come to view election campaigns and parliamentary representation as podiums from which it could spread its tenets of revolutionary Marxism, rather than as channels to political power to be used to change the social and political system. In this manner the SPD could engage in electoral activities while at the same time remaining theoretically aloof and uncorrupted by its host society.[23] In contrast, the SDM represented the culmination of a long tradition of working-class voters' alliances dedicated precisely to gaining political power through the electoral system with the aim of improving working-class conditions. These had been led by practical men—trade unionists, professionals, labor journalists, and organizers—who were concerned with the immediate needs of their constituency. The close relationship between the SDM and the FTC exemplifies this. As Duverger has pointed out, wherever the trade unions have formed a close relationship with socialist parties, they have had a tendency to draw the party away from doctrinaire Marxism and give precedence to immediate reforms. This is certainly the case in Milwaukee, where the SDM found the SPD's traditions of nonparticipation and revolutionary Marxism alien to its situation.[24]

As early as 1893 Victor Berger had written in *Vorwärts* that, "Nothing more ought to be demanded than is attainable at a given time and under given circumstances." By the turn of the century he had elaborated on this stance; "Considered in itself capitalism has by no means reached that stage of development where it becomes impossible. On the contrary, in the trust system, capitalism has just stepped into a new phase, the duration of which is unlimited according to our present light." Therefore it was, "nonsense to talk of a sudden bloody revolution until the power of the ballot [has] at least been tried." "Socialism," Berger was fond of saying, "is coming all the time. It may be another century or two before it's fully established."[25]

This brand of evolutionary revisionism held clear advantages for the SDM. Primarily it justified socialism's heavy engagement in the electoral system of the city. It further allowed the party to take up the threads of urban reform from earlier working-class voters' alliances by addressing the immediate needs of its working-class constituency. The logical place to begin evolutionary socialism was on the local level. "To evolve socialism," wrote Berger, "the city, state and national governments should acquire and manage those services necessary for their life and development."[26] To the calls of earlier movements for municipal ownership of utilities, the extension of state services to the poor and working class, public bathhouses, free textbooks, and public works for the unemployed, the SDM added demands for free legal and medical services for the needy, city condemnation of slum properties, the opening of schools after hours as social centers, and the expansion of public parks. Finally, when coupled with urban reform, revisionism gave the party a posture of pragmatic flexibility when appealing to Milwaukee's voters outside the German-American working-class community. This was necessary, for in itself this community was not strong enough numerically to gain a majority in the city.[27]

ETHNIC POLITICS IN MILWAUKEE

Elsewhere in urban America the middle classes were rallying to the standard of urban reform to wage war on the boss and his machine. In Milwaukee there had been no basis for such a strong political machine. In the resulting power vacuum, however, a local variant had arisen. Though weakened by the lack of an ethnically heterogeneous working-class alliance, this man was recognizable in his role as a power broker. He was Mayor David G. Rose, a Democrat who held office five times. Originally elected on a "Popocratic" ticket in 1898 with the intention of instituting reforms, "All-the-time-Rosy" quickly turned to a more personalized form of politics. Despite a series of cases of exposure of municipal corruption under his administration, Rose managed to defeat his Republican opponents repeatedly at the polls. The city's middle class grew increasingly disenchanted with his rule but lacked a center around which their opposition could be made effective. The SDM shrewdly took advantage of this dissatisfaction, presenting itself to the electorate as the party of "honest government" and gradually forming a thoroughgoing program of urban reform. In doing so, it was again following up the traditions of earlier working-class voters' alliances, which had long called for honest and open government and supported such reform measures as direct elections and home-rule bills.[28] At the same time, it attacked its rivals for the reform impulse in the Republican Party, the structural reformers. "We want to warn our readers," wrote Berger in the *Milwaukee Leader*,

not to be caught by the current drivel about "business methods" and "business principles." A government is not a personal contrivance like a business. It should not be administered from the point of view of economy as businessmen understand the term. It should bring about the greatest good to all regardless of expense, as long as there is a way to make ends meet.

The programs of the SDM bore a closer resemblance to those of social reformers like Samuel Jones of Toledo or Tom Johnson of Cleveland but proved more enduring, given the solid backing of the German-American working-class community and the durable organization and ideology of the SDM.[29]

As Table 11.1 illustrates, by 1908 the SDM had reached the threshold of power in the city. In the space of a decade it had increased its portion of the vote from 5.2 percent to 31.1 percent, becoming the city's second largest party. Its rapid growth reflects its successful adaptation of the German-American working-class community's ethnic and political heritage to American conditions, to the subsequent consolidation of that community under its leadership in both the trade union and political spheres, and to its development of an ideology and

political program that could both meet its constituency's pressing needs and
appeal beyond the boundaries of this community to Milwaukee's middle-class
voters. In 1904 the party had proclaimed the slogan "What Milwaukee Needs
is a Socialistic Housecleaning" and followed this up with promises to set up an
administration of experts beyond corruption. By 1908 the normally Democratic
Milwaukee Journal endorsed the Socialist ticket on the anti-corruption issue.
The SDM had successfully captured the reform impulse that elsewhere had
devolved to the middle classes.[30]

Yet the party was defeated in 1908 by incumbent Mayor Rose. According to
the party's own analysis, this defeat was caused, paradoxically, by the failure
of the SDM to capture the vote of one portion of the very working class it
purported to represent, the Polish-Americans. The SDM now found itself paying
the price for concentrating its efforts within the German-American working-class
community and forging such a tight alliance with the FTC and automatically
excluding the majority of the unskilled Polish-Americans.[31] In the intervening
years after 1886, the Polish-Americans had remained securely in the Democratic
Party, which worked in tandem with the Roman Catholic Church in opposing
the growth of the SDM in the community. The church played a role in the Polish-
American community analogous to that played by the SDM in the German-
American class community; it provided a network of ethnic social organizations
that acted as structural fences within which its flock might be held and as
springboards for the development of Polish-American political leaders who served
both as models for their community and as mediators between it and the city as
a whole. This reflected the double role of the church, as a sanctuary for the
language, culture, and traditions of ethnic groups and as a mechanism for integrating these groups into what it viewed as the American mainstream.[32]

In Milwaukee these functions meshed to produce an elite of Polish-American
Catholic Democratic political leaders whom the church heavily supported in

Table 11.1
The Votes and Percentage of Total for the Democratic, Republican, and SDM Parties

	DEMOCRATIC		REPUBLICAN		SDM	
	Votes	%	*Votes*	%	*Votes*	%
1898	26,219	55.4	18,207	38.5	2,444	5.2
1900	25,166	49.5	22,772	44.7	2,584	5.1
1902	28,971	49.5	20,906	35.7	8,457	14.4
1904	23,515	39.4	17,598	29.5	15,056	25.3
1906	21,332	34.9	22,850	37.4	16,784	27.5
1908	23,106	36.6	18,411	29.2	20,887	33.1
1910	20,513	34.5	11,262	19	27,608	46.5

Source: Frederick I. Olson, "The Milwaukee Socialists 1897–1941" (Ph.D. diss., Harvard University, 1952), pp. 161, 183–85.

opposing the incursions of the SDM, which it viewed as atheist and lawless. In 1904 Archbishop Sebastian Messmer forbade Catholics to join or vote for the SDM. In 1904 and 1908 priests in Polish-American parishes invited Mayor Rose to speak against socialism in their churches the Sunday before elections, arranging staggered meetings so all might be reached. The trade-union movement was viewed with equal skepticism, given its German-American and socialist character. Yet the FTC had not been particularly active in the community. It had almost ignored the Polish-Americans since its establishment. Only in 1905 had it felt strong enough to launch an organization drive in the community, with disappointing results. Only one affiliate was established. Though this in part reflects the occupational structure of the unskilled Polish-Americans, it also undoubtedly reflects the opposition of the community's leadership to the union movement. As Adolf Korman has noted, the church was "a serious obstacle to the growth of socialism and trade unionism in the city."[33]

Without Polish-American votes the SDM could not achieve electoral power. Accordingly it made an all-out effort to break the grip of the alliance of the Democratic Party and the Roman Catholic Church in that year. Lacking trade-union allies in the Polish-American community, it concentrated its efforts through its extra-parliamentary organization. Branches had been established in the Polish-American wards of the city. These were now used to flood the community with innumerable pamphlets, flyers, and leaflets. The object of these efforts was to educate the Polish-Americans in the tenets of evolutionary socialism through a combination of the written and spoken word. To combat English- and Polish-language periodicals supporting the Democrats, the party published a special campaign paper entitled *Voice of the People* printed in two editions, one in English/German and the other in English/Polish. In 1909 it established the Polish-language newspaper *Naprzod* to further spread its programs. Both papers were distributed to virtually every household in the city according to its ethnic background through a system of 500 to 1,000 volunteers called the "Bundle Brigade." During the campaign of 1910, the party imported Polish-American socialist speakers to appear at branch meetings—including a sympathetic Roman Catholic priest.[34] The SDM's efforts did not go unrewarded. In 1910 it captured the Polish-American Fourteenth Ward, allowing the party to achieve a majority in the city and sweep the election. In addition to the mayor's office, the SDM had its entire city ticket elected, as well as fourteen of twenty-seven contested seats in the city's Common Council, giving the party a majority of twenty-one in that body of thirty-five.[35]

Had the SDM then finally breached the barrier of ethnicity within Milwaukee's working class? The answer is, not thoroughly, not finally, and not solely through its own efforts. At the same time as the SDM was making its greatest efforts to break the grip of the Democratic-Roman Catholic leadership, this leadership was shaken by an internal division in the Polish-American community based not on class, but on ethnic identity. The focus of this conflict was the Roman Catholic Church. For years Polish-Americans had chafed under a Roman Catholic hierarchy manned by entrenched German-American clergy. They had repeatedly requested that a Polish-American be appointed bishop for them. The church hierarchy viewed this with disfavor. Archbishop Messmer rejected the notion in 1905 on the grounds that, "Wherever a bishop would have any difficulty in a Polish parish, *their bishop* would be appealed to. The Polish are not yet American enough and keep aloof too much from the rest of us." Polish-Americans resented this policy and the doctrine of assimilation that lay behind it. For them, nationalism and Catholicism were so interwined that the one was naturally seen as nourishing the other. The proper role of the church, from their perspective, was to protect their heritage. The last thing they wanted in America was to lose their identity as a separate group. This inherent conflict between the assimilative and particularistic function of the church in Milwaukee reached a head shortly before 1910, when a portion of the Polish-American community openly rejected the church's policies and broke away to form a Polish National Church.[36]

Though no study has been made of the effects of this division, it is reasonable to argue, as Adolf Korman does, that it disrupted the social and political leadership of the community, much as a division in the extra-parliamentary organizations of the SDM would have weakened the leadership of the German-American working-class community. In the ensuing confusion of ethnic, religious, and class loyalties, the SDM stood as a salient alternative for disgruntled Polish-Americans. The votes gathered by the SDM among the Polish-Americans did not, of course, solely reflect a protest vote. The party had made progress in recruiting Polish-Americans during its years of growth. These voted for the SDM on the basis of class interest. Given the lack of trade-union allies in the community, this was in itself a remarkable accomplishment for the SDM.[37] Nonetheless, as in 1886, this alliance of German-American and Polish-American workers reflected fortuitous circumstances more than commitment to common ideals and was destined to be short-lived.

When faced by the combined forces of the Republicans and Democrats in a "Non-Partisan" fusion ticket in 1912, the SDM again lost the Fourteenth Ward. Though it won the ward once more in 1916 under the leadership of its popular candidate for mayor, this was to prove the SDM's last successful venture into the Polish-American community. The advent of World War I lent new intensity to ethnic loyalties in the city. The Polish-Americans, rallying to Woodrow Wilson's support of an independent Poland, supported the war. The German-American working class opposed it, as did many middle-class German-Americans, who rallied to the SDM's anti-war position. Though the party regained a portion of the Polish-American vote after the war, it never again reached the strength it had shown in 1910. As after 1886, the Polish-Americans returned to the Democratic fold during the inter-war years. The rise of the Congress of Industrial Organizations (CIO) with its close ties with the Democrats in the 1930s, served to solidify this position in the union as well as the political sphere. But by that time the SDM was in any case in decline.[38]

This decline was not evident during the second decade of the twentieth century nor in the years directly following the war. On the contrary, the SDM had clearly arrived on the political scene to stay for the foreseeable future. It survived reverses at the hand of the Non-Partisans in 1912, retained between 35 percent and 45 percent of the vote, and rebounded to capture the mayor's office in 1916, an office it was destined to hold under Daniel Webster Hoan until 1940. During World War I it withstood intense harassment by state and federal authorities for its anti-war stand. Furthermore, it avoided the divisions that ripped apart the Socialist Party of America in the wake of the Russian Revolution, maintained its moderate brand of evolutionary socialism, retained its alliance with the FTC, and emerged in the city elections of 1920 with a near majority of fourteen out of thirty-one seats on the newly apportioned Milwaukee County Council. In part the wartime strength of the party reflected purely ethnic support given to it by German-Americans. As Victor Berger remarked during these years, "There are three things one need not be ashamed of in Milwaukee; To be fat, to be German and to be Socialist." This situation was of a transitory nature, however. The fundamental sources of the party's durability lay in the continued relevance of its urban programs and, more importantly, in the health of its extra-parliamentary organization. This had emerged from the war years intact. Though party membership had dipped during the decade, the number of branch organizations had actually increased from sixty-eight to seventy-five between 1910 and 1919. According to its reports, most of its members were men between the ages of twenty-one and thirty-five—a point that augured well for the future. The party had also managed to save its principal political organ in the city, *The Milwaukee Leader*, despite the federal government's continued refusal to give it second-class mailing privileges.[39]

Yet within the space of a decade the power of the SDM was drastically reduced in the city. This was partly masked by increasing majorities given to Mayor Hoan (51.3 percent in 1920 and 58.1 percent in 1928), through whose offices major portions of the SDM's urban program were implemented. Within the County Council, however, the SDM representation decreased from thirteen to fourteen out of thirty-one in 1920 to six out of twenty-five in 1928. The party found itself permanently placed in the position of being an administrative majority and a legislative minority. Increasingly Mayor Hoan, forced to work with hostile majorities, became the lonely standard-bearer of the party. This situation continued until the dissolution of the party and its absorption into the Democratic Party in 1941.[40]

Ironically, the causes of the decline of the SDM may be traced to the very source of its strength; the homogeneous German-American working-class community from which it sprang. Three factors were at work in this decline, all related to the shifting forces of ethnicity in the city. First there was the inability of the SDM to unite the entire working class of the city; unskilled as well as skilled, Polish-American as well as German-American. Second, there was the inability of the party to break out of its national isolation caused by the destruction of the Socialist Party of America. Finally, there was the fossilization of the party induced by an isolation encouraged by its particular background. Of these three factors, ethnicity is most clearly at work determining the first. It is interesting, though ultimately fruitless, to speculate what the fate of the party might have been had it been able to develop an industrial policy capable of including both skilled and unskilled among its union allies. In fact it did not and probably could not do so. The failure of the SDM to unite the entire working class doomed it to remain a perpetual minority in the city. Without a united labor movement behind it, the SDM did not have the requisites for continued growth as a social democratic mass party. The SDM's inheritance of trade-union policies had intertwined with ethnicity to form a seemingly impenetrable barrier between the German-Americans and the Polish-Americans. Yet, the alternative remained to try to widen the base and scope of the SDM in the post-war era. If this could have been accomplished, perhaps the continued division of the city's working class could have been ameliorated or even mended.

Anticipating the division and disintegration of the Socialist Party of America before the national Chicago Convention of 1919, Victor Berger had written, "What the outcome of our convention in Chicago will be, I do not care—because Wisconsin is in a good position to go it alone for a while, and form a new *center* for *crystallization*." The SDM was not, however, a viable model for socialist organization throughout the United States. Its ideology and organization had derived from an unusually homogeneous working-class community and been shaped by that commmunity's particular ethnic heritage. The mass-based, extra-parliamentary SDM was not an exportable item. If the party was to form a center for crystallization in the post-war era; it had to form alliances or coalitions with other progressive political organizations in place of the crippled Socialist Party. This the SDM attempted to do so as soon as the national party removed constitutional blocks to such coalitions in 1921. It soon encountered political opposition to this policy within the party, however. The rank and file of the SDM viewed alliances and coalitions with extreme skepticism. They feared their movement would be exploited or absorbed by larger, non-socialist forces beyond the boundaries of Milwaukee. They therefore insisted that high standards of security for the party's independence be set in all negotiations, standards so high that they repeatedly frustrated efforts by the leadership to form coalitions in the early 1920s. In this tug-of-war with the membership, the leadership of the party was seemingly damned if they did and damned if they did not. They could induce the party to enter into coalitions to achieve national scope at the risk of the party's ideological and organizational cohesion on the local level. Or they could agree to avoid entering wider coalitions and maintain party organization and ideology intact at the price of national isolation.[41]

In practice the leadership heeded the rank and file and the German-American working-class community they represented. The SDM elected to go it alone. When it was finally forced to enter a coalition with the Conference for Progressive

Political Action (CPPA) in 1924 by order of what was left of its national organization, the Socialist Party, the deepest fears of its membership were realized. Both locally and nationally the socialists were exploited and (after a poor showing by the CPPA's presidential candidate, Wisconsin Senator Robert M. La Follette) then abandoned by a partner over whom they exercised no control whatsoever. Confirmed in their suspicions, Milwaukee's socialists were driven deeper into an isolation from which they never emerged. Gradually their party wound down. Without a national movement to lend vitality to its ideology of the gradual transformation of capitalism, the SDM was left with little beyond its local programs and local power to inspire new members to work within its extra-parliamentary structure. Indeed, it became increasingly difficult to know what to work for. It was not necessary to "recruit" in order to maintain the popularity of the SDM's municipal program. Mayor Hoan kept it in the public eye and thereby kept both the SDM and himself in power. The educational, social, and propagandizing functions of the party apparatus fell away. Membership decreased, with a brief upswing in the 1930s, while the Communist Party of the city grew. Trade union allies defected to the Democratic Party, which was able to offer increasingly important national connections. The CIO and the Polish-Americans remained beyond the party's grasp. The SDM and the German-American working-class community it represented had remained true to themselves. Unfortunately, this had served to set both adrift. Ethnicity had played its last wild card on the SDM.[42]

NOTES

1. Thomas William Gavett, "The Development of the Labor Movement in Milwaukee" (Ph.D. diss., University of Wisconsin, 1957), pp. 51–52; Frederick I. Olson, "The Milwaukee Socialists, 1897–1941" (Ph.D. diss., Harvard University, 1952), p. 4; *U.S. Eighth Census*, 1860, Vol. I (Washington, D.C., 1864), p. XXXII; *U.S. Ninth Census*, 1870, vol. I (Washington, D.C., 1872), pp. 377, 386; *U.S. Tenth Census*, 1880, vol. I. (Washington, D.C., 1883), pp. 538–41; *U.S. Eleventh Census*, 1890, vol. I, Part I (Washington, D.C., 1895), pp. XCII, 670–77; *U.S. Twelfth Census*, 1900, Population, Part One (Washington, D.C., 1901), pp. CX, 800–803; *U.S. Thirteenth Census*, 1910, vol. I (Washington, D.C., 1913), pp. 178, 732, 989.

2. Leon Reynold Fink, "Workingmen's Democracy: The Knights of Labor in Local Politics, 1886–1896" (Ph.D. diss., University of Rochester, 1977), pp. 313–14, 365; Adolf Gern Korman, "A Social History Of Industrial Growth; A Study with Particular Reference to Milwaukee, 1880–1920" (Ph.D. diss., University of Wisconsin, 1959), p. 27, published under the title *Industrialization, Immigrants and Americanizers: The View From Milwaukee, 1866–1921* (Madison, 1967). Quotations will be taken from the original dissertation in this chapter. See also Kathleen Neils Conzen, *Immigrant Milwaukee, 1836–1860: Accommodation and Community in a Frontier City* (Cambridge, Mass., 1976).

3. Lest I be thought to be only setting up a man of straw let me quote political scientist Leon D. Epstein regarding the decline of socialist movements in New York and Mil-

waukee, "Both the East European Jews of New York and the Germans of Milwaukee were bound to become less heavily influenced politically by their backgrounds." Leon D. Epstein, *Political Parties in Western Democracies* (New York, 1967), pp. 141–42.

4. Fink, "Workingmen's Democracy," p. 377.

5. Kenneth T. Jackson and Stanley K. Schultz, "Introduction: Part Six: Bosses, Machines, and Urban Reform," *Cities in American History*, ed. Jackson and Schultz (New York, 1972), pp. 357–62; Robert K. Merton, "Latent Functions of The Machine," *American Urban History*, ed. A. B. Callow (New York, 1973), pp. 221–25.

6. Alexander B. Callow, "The City in Politics," *American Urban History*, ed. A. B. Callow (New York, 1973), pp. 217–18.

7. Korman, "A Social History," p. 23.

8. Gavett, "Development of the Labor Movement," pp. 61–64, 85–90, 137–41, 147–48, 191, 194–97; Fink, "Workingmen's Democracy," p. 363.

9. Fink, "Workingmen's Democracy," pp. 320–21.

10. Gavett, "Development of the Labor Movement,", pp. 122–34, 131; Fink, "Workingmen's Democracy," pp. 317, 320–21.

11. Fink, "Workingmen's Democracy," pp. 341–60. Fink gives a fascinating and detailed account of these events. His coverage of internal splits within the Polish-American community is of particular interest. The division between reform leaders, union leaders, and the Roman Catholic leadership lends insight to the later division of the community in 1910.

12. Ibid., pp. 363–64.

13. Ibid., pp. 355–57.

14. Ibid., pp. 314, 356, 365.

15. Ibid., pp. 356, 365; Olson, "Milwaukee Socialists," pp. 6–10; Gavett, "Development of the Labor Movement," pp. 54–56; Henry Frederick Bedford, "A Case Study in Hysteria, Victor L. Berger, 1917–1921" (M.A. thesis, University of Wisconsin, 1953), pp. 8–9.

16. Olson, "Milwaukee Socialists," p. 10; Gavett, "Development of the Labor Movement," pp. 189–90, 207.

17. Olson, "Milwaukee Socialists," pp. 57–62, 65.

18. Ibid., p. 10; Peter Nettl, "The German Social Democratic Party, 1890–1914, as a Political Model," *Past and Present* (1965), pp. 76–77. Examples of parallel organizations may be found by comparing "German Activities" and "Socialist Activities" notices in any pre-World War I *Milwaukee Leader*.

19. Fink, "Workingmen's Democracy," p. 366; Olson, "Milwaukee Socialists," p. 47; Edward J. Muzik, "Victor L. Berger, A Biography" (Ph.D. diss., Northwestern University, 1960), p. 115.

20. Maurice Duverger, *Political Parties: Their Organization and Activity in the Modern State* (London, 1962), p. 51.

21. Gavett, "Development of the Labor Movement," p. 204.

22. Ibid., pp. 144, 204, 206; Olson, "Milwaukee Socialists," p. 16; Muzik, "Victor L. Berger," p. 115; Fink, "Workingmen's Democracy," p. 366.

23. Nettl, "The German Social Democratic Party," pp. 65–67; Duverger, *Political Parties*, pp. 366–77; Einhart Lorenz, *Arbeiterbevelgelsens historie, 1789-1930; en inføring* (Oslo, 1972), p. 62; Gavett, "Development of the Labor Movement," p. 190; Muzik, "Victor L. Berger,", p. 11.

24. Duverger, *Political Parties*, p. 71.

25. David A. Shannon, *The Socialist Party of America, A History* (New York, 1955), p. 267; Muzik, "Victor L. Berger," pp. 7–8; Fink, "Workingmen's Democracy," p. 365.

26. Muzik, "Victor L. Berger," p. 8.

27. Sally M. Miller, "Victor Berger and The Promise of Constructive Socialism, 1919-1920" (Ph.D. diss., University of Toronto, 1966), p. 30; Fink, "Workingmen's Democracy," pp. 370–72.

28. Olson, "Milwaukee Socialists," p. 41; Muzik, "Victor L. Berger," p. 146; Fink, "Workingmen's Democracy," pp. 367–68, 372.

29. Marvin Wachman, "History of the Social-Democratic Party of Milwaukee, 1897–1910," *Illinois Studies in The Social Sciences*, vol. 28 (1945), pp. 51, 61.

30. Ibid., pp. 53, 64; Fink, "Workingmen's Democracy," p. 368.

31. Wachman, "History of The Social-Democratic Party," p. 65.

32. Korman, "A Social History," p. 5.

33. Wachman, "History of The Social-Democratic Party," pp. 52, 53, 65; Gavett, "Development of the Labor Movement," pp. 222–23; Korman, "A Social History," pp. 10, 16.

34. Olson, "Milwaukee Socialists," pp. 57, 73–74, 81, 176–77.

35. Ibid., pp. 73–74, 183–85; Fink, "Workingmen's Democracy," p. 369.

36. Korman, "A Social History," pp. 12, 13, 15, 24.

37. Ibid., p. 24; Gavett, "Development of the Labor Movement," pp. 117, 137; Fink, "Workingmen's Democracy," p. 369.

38. Olson, "Milwaukee Socialists," pp. 239, 243, 244, 318, 331, 332; Donald Pienkos, "Politics, Religion, and Change in Polish Milwaukee, 1900–1930," *Wisconsin Magazine of History*, 61 (Spring 1978), pp. 179–209.

39. Olson, "Milwaukee Socialists," pp. 239, 243, 244, 318, 331, 332, 354, 356, 365, 366, 378, 379, 381, 396, 397, 420-426; Gavett, "Development of the Labor Movement", pp. 263, 303; Muzik, "Victor L. Berger," pp. 282, 286; H.C. Peterson and Gilbert Fite, *Opponents of War, 1917–1918* (Seattle, 1968), pp. 77–80; *Hearings Before The Special Committee Appointed Under the Authority of House Resolution No. 6 Concerning The Right of Victor L. Berger to Be Sworn in as A Member of The Sixty-Sixth Congress*, Vol. II (Washington, D.C., 1919), pp. 345, 351; The Social-Democratic Party Papers, Milwaukee County Historical Society, August 11, 1917, Letter to Morris Hillquit from Victor Berger; *The Milwaukee Leader*, December 31, 1918, Part II, p. 7, "1000 Members Gained By Party in County in 1918." This apparently represented a gain of some 16 new branches directly after the war, after a low ebb in December 1918 of 59 branches. The SDM would seem to have been in a period of expansion; James Jerome Weinstein, *The Decline of Socialism in America, 1912-1925* (New York, 1967), pp. 50, 131, 143.

40. Olson, "Milwaukee Socialists," pp. 406, 415–17; Gavett, "Development of the Labor Movement," pp. 140–51, 171–75.

41. Muzik, "Victor L. Berger," pp. 322, 356, 361–62; Olson, "Milwaukee Socialists," pp. 401–406.

42. Weinstein, *The Decline of Socialism*, pp. 276–78, 319; Olson, "Milwaukee Socialists," pp. 82, 409, 410–11, 414, 416; Shannon, *The Socialist Party of America*, pp. 176–78, 180–81; Muzik, "Victor L. Berger," p. 319.

THE ACCULTURATION OF THE CZECHS IN VIENNA

12

Monika Glettler

Historiography abounds with examples of what are but popular myths. Thus German-language historical writing emphasized that the Czechs in Vienna organized active and politically effective clubs that represented their interests against the German-speaking majority in the city. In fact, the Czechs did organize over 450 clubs, societies, trade unions, and other organizations but their activities had other motives and were of limited impact only. A structural analysis will be useful in debunking this misconception.

After briefly analyzing the social and migration structure of the Czech population of Vienna, the role played by ethnic organizations in the development of national consciousness will be discussed. In the second part of this essay the reasons for and the basis of Czech assimilation in Vienna and then the elements of Czech nationalism involved will be examined. Finally, an attempt will be made to show the extent to which the opposition between national ideology and social reality made the assimilation of the middle classes more or less unavoidable.

MIGRATION AND SETTLEMENT IN VIENNA

In the sixties of the last century clear changes began to appear in the geographical distribution of nationalities in Austria. Above all, there were distinct signs of an increased migration from the Czech lands of Bohemia and Moravia to Vienna and Lower Austria.[1] The attraction was economic: higher earnings, particularly in manual occupations. In 1890 at least half of the inhabitants of Bohemia were no longer in their birthplaces. The situation was similar in Moravia; that is, horizontal mobility had already fundamentally changed the social structure of the Bohemian lands before the turn of the century.[2] The attraction of the capital city was so strong that migration from the natural hinterlands took place even when the population lived under good conditions.[3] The number of people who had lived in Vienna ten years or longer—those with Heimatrecht—decreased, while the number of recent immigrants—those with Heimatrecht in the Bohemian lands—increased.[4] Between 1860 and 1880 Vienna grew by 35.5 percent, but between 1880 and 1900 it grew by 130.8 percent. The legal residents had decreased from 70 percent of the total population in 1830 to 35.2 percent in 1880[5]—a phenomenon that must be explained as a result of the mobility of the peasants after emancipation in 1848.[6]

Beginning with 31 December 1880, the migration can be traced every ten years in the official statistics.[7] These statistics recorded a person's language of communication, that is, either German or Bohemian-Moravian-Slovakian, which was to be reported by the heads of households. It is obvious that this registration system alone carried many factors of uncertainty with it. The census of 1880 listed 68,158 Czechs in Vienna and Lower Austria (the areas around Vienna). Ten years later, in 1890, there were already 44 percent more than in 1880, and in 1900, 46 percent more than 1890. At the turn of the century, the Czechs in Lower Austria had reached their largest number—officially 102,974 out of a total Viennese population of 1,650,000.[8] The concentration of Czech job-hunters in Vienna was considerably overestimated[9] by public opinion at that time because official statistics showed a higher birthrate among the Czechs than among the German-speaking population of Austria.[10] Nevertheless, there was by no means a flooding of the labor market because of the migration. The important thing was the conviction that a change in the proportion of Czechs and Austrian-Germans could considerably change the face of the city.

The question is how relations had developed between the two peoples before the migration started. The integration of the Czechs into daily life and relations between them and the natives are factors just as important and basic as the numbers of immigrants and reasons for the influx. Indeed, the exact number of the Viennese Czechs could not be determined, not only because the Slovaks were subsumed in the Czech category in the registration of languages, but because the registration had at times been arbitrarily changed or influenced for purposes of agitation on the part of the Austrian-Germans. The basic problems were twofold. One of them was assimilation. In regard to national origin, approximately one-fourth of the inhabitants of Vienna were of Czech or Slovak nationality; but in regard to national consciousness as determined by census questions on the language of communication, the figure was hardly one-tenth. The second unknown factor was fluctuation.[11] Neither of these factors was taken into consideration in the local Viennese census. However, they both contributed decisively to tensions between the government, the city adminstration, the German-speaking population, the Viennese Czechs, and Czechs in Bohemia.

The number of Czech brickyard workers or construction workers, servants in mostly noble, large landowning households, apprentices, students, civil servants, artists, and military men fluctuated, since such employment was temporary or seasonal. There is no way to separate these temporary groups from the Czechs permanently resident in Vienna. Despite the fact that the censuses always took place in late December, at a time when the seasonal workers had already left Vienna, the fluctuating element decisively strengthened the backbone of both the Czech and German national movements. Since the constant coming and going—be it to the new German or the old Czech homeland—was balanced, the population base of the Viennese Czechs changed very little. However, within a twelve-month period there could be a 100 percent turnover in the membership of individual Czech clubs.

The situation of the Czechs of Vienna may be compared with a hotel that is indeed always occupied, but always by different people. A few of them had just arrived, a few had already been living there for a longer time, and only a common club administration or management united them. Until 1900 the growth continued. But in the following decade, there was a generally unexpected retrogression, both in absolute and relative terms, which was only partially due to assimilation.[12] There was not only the influence of the increasing industrialization of the Czech-speaking areas in Bohemia, which stemmed the migration to Vienna and resulted at the same time in a decrease in the birthrate in the Czech-speaking territories; there was also a decline in trade in Vienna, which halted the growing influx of industrial workers. Moreover, at the time of the 1900 census, large numbers were employed in building the city's elevated railroad. It can be said of these workers, as of many others, that as soon as they had reached the pecuniary goal that they had set for themselves in Vienna, most of them returned home. Vienna not only emptied the Bohemian regions of many people, it also returned many with the means for further economic development. Such returnees came home with changed attitudes: they were more experienced and had been exposed to industrial time and discipline. Thus they altered the social and intellectual climate of the Bohemian Crown Lands immediately and directly.

A comparison of the sex ratios of the Czech and German-speaking sections of the population reveals a surplus of Czech males. In 1900 for every 100 Viennese German men there were 112 women; in the case of the Viennese Czechs for every 100 there were only 82 women.[13] In the marriageable age group from twenty-one to fifty, there was a 25 percent surplus of Czech men. Only in the forty-and-over age group were there more women. This cannot be explained exclusively by the temporary presence of Czech apprentices, craftsmen, and factory workers; it is rather one of the clearest indications of Czech men marrying into German families. From among the Czechs who were scattered throughout the twenty Viennese districts, it was only in the 10th district— Favoriten—that there were Czechs living side by side. In 1910 one-fifth of the people in this district were Czechs; however, this figure represented a maximum concentration.[14] There is no indication that Czechs strove to live and work alongside their countrymen. The social differentiation between the Czech and German-speaking sections of the population was evidently not great enough to create a nationally closed Czech settlement.

A comparison of the employment and class structures of Czechs and Germans in Vienna in 1910 shows that Czechs were overproportionally represented in the industry and trades sector and in the working class. The distribution by branch of employment was (German figures in parentheses): 73.5 percent (45.9 percent) in industry and trades, 13.8 percent (29.8 percent) in commerce and transport, 12.2 percent (23.3 percent) in civil service and the professions, 0.5 percent (1.0 percent) in agriculture and forestry. The working-class section of the Czech population amounted to 79.1 percent (69.4 percent workers, apprentices, and day-laborers, plus 9.7 percent in domestic service and similar occupations like porters, etc.). The respective section of the German population comprised only 56.7 percent of the whole. Of the Czechs 3.6 percent were employees or civil servants, as compared to 12.0 percent of the Germans. The self-employed and employers comprised 17 percent of the Czech but 30 percent of the German population, the rest being family members employed in family businesses (0.3 percent and 1 percent, respectively).[15] Thus two-fifths of the Czech migrants belonged to the working class, but many of them worked in the small shops so traditionally rooted in the imperial capital. In general, they preferred the clothing trades (27.6 percent of the employed Czechs worked as tailors or as cobblers) and in some areas the brickyards attracted Czech workers. There was hardly a trade in which Czechs could not be found.

ETHNIC ORGANIZATION

The above analysis of basic social statistics of the Viennese Czechs according to age and sex, as well as economic and area distribution, gives only superficial insight into social conditions. The analysis does not indicate the attitude of the individual toward his or her national homeland or the motivations behind decisions and actions. The institutional network, however, which was organized by the Czechs and acted upon them reflected their behavioral attitudes and norms.[16] The Czechs on the Danube expressed their national identity through religious societies, trade unions, chess clubs, and political parties.[17] Their common denominator consisted of a clearly defined circle of members of a similar inner structure, and of a clearly defined purpose, which was apparent to members and non-members alike. Each of these organizations emphasized a special aspect of Czech identity.

The question of whether the Czechs in Vienna and Lower Austria represented a native population (i.e., with Heimatrecht) and whether the Czech language was according to the Imperial Laws of 1877, 1880, and 1882 "a language which is spoken in daily intercourse by a significant number of people," started the discussion on national identity. To support their claim to this, the Czechs quoted official census material that showed that the Czech-speaking proportion of the national population remained constant. In addition to this, the Czechs tried to demonstrate that they were a native group because of their common national consciousness, as expressed in their language and their sense of identity vis-à-vis non-Czechs.[18]

This consciousness was expressed in a multitude of clubs, the full number of which were registered neither by the government officials nor by the Viennese

Czechs themselves. The role that the clubs played in forming national consciousness is described by Josef Karásek, the first historian of the Czech minority in Vienna, in 1895:[19] "What do the clubs mean for the Czechs of Lower Austria? The great importance of these institutions can be appreciated best by saying that the clubs are for us what the community and state are for other people and nations. All that we have been able to do, to accomplish up to now in a national sense, had its origins in the clubs."[20] Through these remarks we can understand the value of these organizations, with their simultaneous disintegrating and integrating effects on the Czechs of Vienna. A stable society that is also a community will have an integrating effect by creating a coherent way of life, whereas scattered work conditions have a disintegrating effect on the society by dividing people according to employment. The Czech organizations in Vienna reflected the problem of instability in this society, and they showed evidence of social disintegration.[21]

The integrating forces in the society of the Viennese Czechs were only partially able to provide an arena for individual fulfillment. Therefore special groups arose in order to fulfill these limited purposes. It seems to be a general principle that increasing integration undermines the effectiveness of such communities of interests, in that their functions are coopted in other ways by the society as a whole. It becomes clear that the newly developing social structure of the Czech community found its expression in the growing variety and form of such clubs. The Czech organizations reflected the customs and traditions of the homeland. They were an intermediary stage, providing a substitute for the familiar things that were lacking in the new home, where no mutual acquaintanceship existed among the inhabitants.[22] Here we see the other side of the phenomenon of disintegration: the positive function of organizational structure. Karásek's statement confirms that the clubs were one of the most important integrative elements for the Viennese Czechs and for their political life; yet nobody recognized the concrete political importance of the clubs.

Data were abundant, however; the crisis was developing in the failure to find social alternatives to the excess of club life in the Czech community.[23] For the Czechs of Vienna the organizational complex signified undeniable proof of their loyalty to their Czech nationality. Here the consciousness of belonging together was manifested, and here the care and cultivation of the mother tongue took place; in other words, they were evidence of the existence of the Czech ethnic group in Lower Austria.[24] Such enduring organizations were empirical proof, and the failure of the Austrian-Germans to acknowledge this fact meant that all Czech political demands had to remain unfulfilled.[25] Even though the clubs as a whole had little to do with a common political desire, they were nevertheless homogeneous enough to smooth over splits in their own national-political program. It was common discontent that made them homogeneous, and this phenomenon was neither new nor limited to Austria: it was built into the structure of all European industrial societies. In Vienna it became apparent when provoked by especially critical challenges. In the first three decades after their beginnings in the middle 1860s, the Czech clubs were by no means a "fortress" against the German-speaking inhabitants. The most influential factors in the life of the Czech club members were contemporary circumstances that brought about vast changes in their whole style of living. At no time in history did social interaction have such an impact as it did in the age of industrialization. The work process and even the workers' motivations were imposed from outside and had a further impact on others. Therefore the Czechs and Germans in Vienna interacted with each other more intensively than did the rural people in the Czech regions, a fact which nationalist propaganda from both sides sought to deny and which also served to undermine the mutual solidarity among the working class of the factories. According to the class structure of the industrially employed population, the Viennese Czechs were a part of the population of a large city, and the conditions of work dictated the nature of the community structure. This also modified the national problem.

These remarks seek to illustrate how Czech clubs developed mainly out of the rhythm of everyday life and were therefore indicative of a social life in a national context. As an indicator of everyday social life, no club was really superfluous. Some of them went further in their influence on national life, and in some cases this influence was decisive. All reestablished connections with the homeland; all the clubs arose, stabilized themselves, or disintegrated in proportion to their momentary importance to the individual and to the extent of the significance of a common social program. Therefore, in analyzing the significance of the organizations within the total complex of the Czech national community in Vienna, one should not reduce this problem to a question of ideologies or look at these organizations from a merely political standpoint.

SCHOOLS, ETHNIC IDENTITY, AND THE LANGUAGE QUESTION

We shall examine the language question in education with an example of a club which was the national and political center of the Viennese Czechs, the Komenský Schulverein (school association). The support of this organization was an unwritten law for all Czech clubs. All their efforts, political, social, and economic, were more or less centered around it. The Komenský Schulverein was created on Easter Day 1872 by the Czecho-Slav labor club, which had been founded in 1868. In 1883 it opened its first private school in the tenth district, where the majority of the Czechs lived. In 1885 it began a long series of vain attempts to get official approval to establish a regular public school, that is, to obtain government support. Its requests were based on Article 59 of the Reichs-volksschulgesetz, by which a public school could be opened provided that over a five-year period at least forty children of a certain nationality were registered as living within a half-mile radius. The teaching language in the school was to be determined exclusively by the responsible school board. In those provinces with several nationalities, the public schools were to be established in such a way that every nationality would be guaranteed an education in its mother tongue. Three decisions of the Reichsgericht (Imperial Court) in 1877, 1880, and 1882 had explicitly guaranteed the establishment of public schools for Czech students in three villages in Lower Austria.[26] The Komenský association made its applications on the basis of these precedents.

On the whole, the spokesmen of the Viennese Czechs proved to be substantially freer from ideological prejudice and more realistic than they appeared in German nationalist propaganda. Never, neither in the 1870s, the 1880s, nor shortly before the outbreak of World War I, did the Czechs demand an education only in Czech, nor did they perceive knowledge of the German language as national betrayal. On the contrary, they only wanted their children to start learning in their mother tongue because most of them came from purely Czech-speaking areas and spoke no German at all. Beginning with the second year of school they should then systematically acquire fluency in the language of the region, in the Viennese case, German. This was nothing more than a gradual acclimatization to Viennese circumstances. The perspective of the Prague politicians is shown in the opinion of the office manager of the Czech Central School Organization (Ústřední matice školská, ÚMŠ). In June 1910 he wrote in his report the following about the Komenský association in Vienna: "My visit confirms my opinion that our efforts have had only very little success. The children go to the Czech schools only because their parents think they would learn German there earlier and better. In my opinion, we must first resolve whether or not we should work for the maintenance of the Czech nationality in Vienna at all."[27] He also sharply criticized the teaching methods, the teaching staff, and the school administration. The hidden root of these problems lay in the poor financial situation of the staff in the Komenský schools. Their years of employment at a Komenský private school did not count toward retirement benefits. The salary of the Oberlehrer (the highest level of teacher) was significantly lower than that received by assistant teachers in Viennese public schools. As a result of the rapidly increasing deficit of the club, thirty-one (out of forty-six) teachers were fired in 1914, and the salary of the remaining fifteen was reduced by half. Nevertheless, German nationalists maintain even today that "since 1909 Komenský built up its educational system with renewed energy and increased revenues."[28]

The situation was quite similar in the leading political organization of the Viennese Czechs: the Czech National Council of Lower Austria (Národní Rada Dolnorakouská). Its predecessors had been the political clubs, Klub Rakouských národností (1881) and První Politická Jednota ve Vídni (1885), both founded on a supra-party basis.[29] There were two reasons why the Czechs of Vienna founded the National Council. First, it was to be a counterpart to the Deutsche Volksräte, which came into existence around the same time; and second, it was a reaction of the Czech minority in Vienna to the most important statement of German nationalistic politics in the pre-war period, the so-called Whitsun-Program (Pfingst-Programm) of May 1899.[30] The Pfingst-Programm was drawn up by the German opposition in the Reichsrat and comprised five diverse political parties. The program concerned the settlement of the language question and demanded for the German Hereditary Lands (including Lower Austria), a legal statement that the German language should be the only language in all schools, whether these schools received government support or not.

Thus, it is certainly not accidental that the secretary of the Komenský association, Josef Urban, proposed the formation of a large organization that would be empowered to represent the interests of all the Viennese Czechs. Such a political organization, however, did not fit the needs of the Viennese Czechs. In Vienna office workers and shopkeepers were not politically organized, and the bourgeois clubs insisted on their political neutrality. Urban doubted whether the authorities would recognize the new organization, and, therefore, it was illegal at first. The leading associations, such as Slovanská Beseda and Slovansky Zpěvácký Spolek, which presented entertainment, the Czech language, music and customs, and the gymnastic society, Sokol, and Komenský, did not even send official representatives in order not to provoke official dissolution of the organization. Although the Czech National Council in Vienna had solicited funds for years from Czech banks in Vienna, it received no financial support from these sources. The council claimed, however, to be the only national self-help organization that looked after ''the widest variety of interests of the whole Czech nation on the Danube, being far above all narrow-minded party standpoints.''[31]

Its program included district committees, actions on the school issue, on the census and franchise issues, and negotiations with the Slovaks. The program, however, stood in sharp contrast with the practical results of its efforts. In March 1914 President Drozda informed the central office in Prague that at the latest elections in the tenth district, in which 18,489 Czechs lived, only 160 votes were cast for Czech candidates. In comparison, in 1911 Czech candidates in the same district received 1,300 votes. Such facts bring into question the conclusion reached in both Czech and German sources, that the Czech National Council in Vienna was the most important center of Czech influence, that it was the leader of the whole Czech national movement in Vienna, or even that it was created by Prague and not by the Viennese Czechs themselves.[32] Nevertheless, the Christian Socialist slogans about Czech expansionism have enjoyed a long-standing popularity and have found their way into many publications, though even the Viennese police were not convinced by such slogans.

ACCULTURATION OR FORCED LOYALTY

Writing on the lack of effectiveness of Czech organization in representing the interests of the community, Hanuš Sýkora, the editor of the nationalist party organ Česká Vídeň, stated the following in a lead article dated June 1913:

We have to admit it: there is no organization which links the Czech crowds here in Vienna. As a result of this unsatisfactory state of affairs we have suffered such losses over the last years that it can almost be said that we are the witnesses of a great Czech funeral in the middle of a huge Czech cemetery.[33]

According to Sýkora, who has been quoted here as a representative of the Czech nationalists in Vienna, the leading intellectual circles had to bear the full responsibility for this state of affairs.[34] The members of the Czech intelligentsia living in Vienna were neither prepared to use their numbers nor to change their attitudes in such a way as to help combine the one hundred thousand officially registered Bohemians, Moravians, and Slovaks into one united Czech national bloc. This had very little to do with their own pride of place or lack of trust in their fellow countrymen, for in most cases Czech intellectuals only spent a limited period in Vienna before returning home to take up leading positions there.[35] If, however, they wanted to stay in Vienna or had to do so, they soon found themselves victims of discrimination. They were discredited as nationalist exponents of Czech minority ideas. At the very least they were thrown into a dilemma among professional aspirations (assimilation), cultural heritage, and leadership of an ethnic minority.

But there are further reasons why most of the Czech immigrants could not escape the process of adaptation and acculturation. Two social systems confronted each other—on the one hand the aspiring industrial society of Vienna, on the other the constant stream of Czechs pouring in from the country in search of work—and one was bound to dominate the other. First of all, the industrial city, with its metropolitan milieu, demanded rapid and passive adaptation of the Czechs, a kind of *Arrangez-vous* or accommodation.[36] Secondly, pressure was put on them to assimilate, in the sense that they were made to accept external norms and expectations and apply them in their own households. In effect, this meant that if Czech newcomers succeeded early on in adapting their expectations and attitudes to conform with those of the German-speaking Christian-Social majority, they might come to believe that they had chosen of their own volition to accept the norms decreed by the city government under the mayoralty of Karl Lueger and to recognize the "German character of the city of Vienna," as the law demanded.

The penalty for refusing to do so was social, economic,[37] and psychological degradation.[38] The new city by-laws (Gemeindestatut) introduced by Lueger on 28 March 1900 were a combination of patriarchal sentiment and nationalistic arrogance. Until then the law of 19 December 1890 had applied, according to which it was only necessary for a person to make a kind of declaration of loyalty to the city in order to be granted citizen's rights.[39] Each applicant had to swear an oath to the mayor "that he would conscientiously fulfill all the duties of a citizen in accordance with the city by-laws and do his best to further the interests of the city."[40] Since the new by-laws had come into force, however, every Czech who applied for citizen's rights had to swear an additional oath that he would *"do his utmost to preserve the German character of the city of Vienna."*[41]

This brings us to the issue that forms the root of all the political disagreements and quarrels concerning the Czechs in Vienna and their acculturation, an issue that was also to have a substantial effect on the whole of their national and political ideas: were the Czechs who wanted to, or for career reasons had to, become citizens of Vienna prepared or even obliged to take an oath of loyalty couched in such terms or was it essential for them in order to succeed? Viennese people "of Bohemian descent" were, for example, expected to swear that they did not belong to any kind of Czech association and that they did not intend to form any such organization, although this would have been perfectly legal according to the Austrian national constitution. A Czech migrant knew that if he refused to swear the oath he would not be granted citizenship and would suffer social and occupational disadvantages and be subject to other forms of reprisals.[42] If he took the oath to avoid these sanctions, he could be punished for perjury or even for "causing a Czech provocation" if he merely engaged in legal activities in which only Czechs were involved, such as the foundation of a Czech loan-fund. In most cases there was not even a right of appeal against such a punishment. The problem was even worse for Czechs who had no other choice but to live in Vienna. Refusal to swear the oath would have meant that Czech civil servants who had been employed in Vienna for years and other Czechs, such as the large number of businessmen and factory owners, would have had to abandon everything they had built up over the years and lose the whole basis of their existence.

The question we have to ask is whether the rigorous policies of the mayor and the city council were not in fact successful. For the political reality of life for the Czechs in Vienna was far less influenced by nationalistic and social aggressiveness than by factors compelling social adaptation and assimilation.[43] Nevertheless, if Mayor Lueger is to be given the credit for achieving a de facto reduction in the size of the so-called Czech problem by means of his successful social policies—that is, increased assimilation as a result of economic prosperity—then a clear distinction must be made between his effectiveness as a flexible politician and his rigorous ideological intentions. But it was this oath compelling acknowledgment of the German character of the city that had been one of the starting points of the growing volume of Czech protests since the turn of the century. However, it was only occasionally, somewhat more frequently since 1910, that the voices of protest united to form any kind of national movement.[44] The resignation of the nationalistic Czech political leadership in Vienna does not only have its origins in the trend toward assimilation resulting from socio-economic conditions. (This trend ensured from the very beginning that the national propagandists within the Czech camp would remain a tiny minority.) The lack of an upper class was also a problem. If Czech nationalist politics in Vienna had no aims, this was explained at least partly by the absence of a publicly accepted personality who embodied and expressed such ideas and by the lack of common objectives among all of the nationalist organizations, which paralyzed them. Left alone, the spokesmen of Czech national demands isolated themselves for fear of having to face reality, thus increasing the gap between themselves and the majority of the migrants, including the Czech deputies in the Reichsrat, who represented the Crown Lands.[45] A feeling of senselessness and aimlessness grew up among the politically active Czech nationalists in Vienna, adding fuel to internal conflicts.[46] Bourgeois nationalists even accused the Viennese Czech Social Democrats of playing down the reality of adaptation and of disguising their policy as a question of historical necessity.

In view of the countless number of clubs and societies, the idea of a Czech power vacuum in Vienna was, of course, hard to accept, but there simply was no social or political upper class or even any kind of ethnic consensus among Czechs in Vienna. There was, however, an "establishment"—if this term is used in the sense that Ralf Dahrendorf has given it—that is, that "buffer zone of modern social structures" in which customs, claimed to be the result of conscious decisions, are stubbornly defended. (A good example here would be the long tradition of holding Czech language services in Viennese churches.)[47]

Even worse than the comparatively low socio-economic status of the Czechs in Vienna were the constant slights reminding them that they were not welcome in the Habsburg capital. There were the minor inhumanities of everyday life, such as tenants being given notice to vacate an apartment because they listed "Bohemian" rather than "German" as their nationality in the census forms.[48] There were also the more important inhumanities inflicted on them by institutions, such as the compulsive registration of Czech children in German schools after their own school had been closed down. To this the authorities added the demand that the parents should be punished for registering their children in a Czech school.[49] The consequences of this situation were on the one hand protests, on the other resignation or assimilation, which was more expedient. The records and club reports do not mention many examples of Czech nationalists engaging in "subversive activities", but when this did occur it was almost always as *a result of miserable living conditions*. On the one occasion when the Viennese Czechs did join together in 1903 to demand improvements in their situation in the form of a complaint to the Reichsgericht, the Austrian authorities and party organs were quick to accuse them of nationalist agitation.[50] But does it involve nationalistic extremism when a group of 100,000 adults, all speaking the same language and with 13,500 children of school age, express the desire to found their own privately financed bilingual school and are prepared to fight for this aim against considerable resistance?

During the two or three decades before 1914 it was almost always in cases of genuine need and difficulties that the national issue came to the fore, and to this extent the national issue was in fact a social issue for the Czech migrants. As a result of this Vienna provides us with an example of an important phenomenon that has all too frequently been ignored. There was obviously an overwhelming difference between the historical importance and the political consequences of national consciousness and the minor role which it played in the private lives and activities of the Viennese Czechs.[51] How strong are the links forged by language, national customs, and ethnocentrically oriented programs if substantial sections of a people can simply cast them off? The range of possibilities available to the Czechs in Vienna as a so-called marginal group extended from assimilation into the new environment to their continuing existence as a separate community isolated from this environment.[52]

THE RHETORIC OF NATIONALISM

Those characteristics that were to turn the idea of Czech nationalism in Vienna into an ideology of integration of the minority—according to the proponents of the nationalistic wing—reflect precisely the attributes analyzed by Eugen Lemberg in his work on the sociology and politics of nationalism.[53] In the case of the Viennese Czechs, it seems useful to deal with the first two of the characteristic conditions named by Lemberg together, as they are closely connected with each other. The first of these involves *a clear delimitation of the group from its surroundings*, that is, a dominating characteristic that assigns either membership in the minority group or exclusion from it. The second involves *the assignment of a role that is not and cannot be assumed by any other group*. This requires continuous existence and survival of the Viennese Czechs as a group and makes it both honorable and advantageous to belong to it.[54] The special feature of the Viennese Czechs' consciousness of their role or mission was that it did not take the usual form of a "crusade" but was in fact more or less exactly the opposite in that it involved a kind of isolationism in the sense of a mission addressed to the members of their own group. This was combined with a readiness to welcome Czech newcomers from Bohemia into their ranks. But the more the real basis of their isolationism crumbled away—that is, the smaller the number of Czechs migrating to the city on the Danube became—the more the inward oriented mission became a battle cry.

In accordance with their political status as a national minority, the more actively nationalist sections of the Czech population of Vienna took on the passive role of heroic martyrs. Feeling themselves to be pioneers working for a promised land in which subsequent generations would no longer be underprivileged, they considered justice and the future to be on their side.[55] In order to draw attention to their own suffering, they were constantly finding new examples taken from their experiences in a wide variety of situations. Their position in relation to Austrian-German society was generally characterized by pointing out the assigned "inferiority" of the Czech element in Vienna, but mostly they were more concrete. They regarded themselves as "a nation of domestic servants," "a mob of newcomers," "slaves not allowed to raise their heads unless they wanted a taste of the whip," mistreated wretches "condemned to mental and physical servitude" whose "only rewards were kicks," "stepchildren subject to systematic persecution,"[56] "an element completely without rights similar in status to vagrant gypsies and helot slaves"[57] sentenced to a "long period of Babylonian imprisonment"[58] and also as "weeds in Teutonic fields,"[59] "defenseless victims in an unequal fight,"[60] and "bloodily hunted helpless deer."[61]

At the same time the nationalists felt themselves to be the representatives of the whole of the Czech people, and it hurt them the more that they were not only the victims of the Austrian Germans' scorn[62] but that their Bohemian land of origin also played "a perfect comedy" with the Czech minority in Lower Austria and did not hesitate to send them into the lions' den.[63] For the development of their self-perception, it was of considerable importance that they realized that in Vienna they were no longer part of the Bohemian nation. At the beginning of the 1890s Josef Svatopluk Machar, a Czech poet in Vienna, first used the expression "opuštěná větev" (forlorn branch), a motif that does not only pervade the writings of the Viennese Czechs prior to 1914 but is still to be found in 1946 in Antonín Machát's *Naši ve Vídni* (Our Compatriots in Vienna).[64] Jan Auerhan, the Czech expert on minorities who was at that time the correspondent of the foreign section of the Czech National Council (Národní Rada Česká, NRČ) in Prague, explained that the forlorn "branch" was in fact an "offshoot," for the Viennese Czechs were destined to put down their own roots *detached* from the main stem.[65]

On the other hand, the nationalist Czechs in Vienna did add some elements to their ideology, which made positive identification both possible and effective. Lemberg calls these elements consciousness of superiority in relation to the surrounding world and the feeling of being threatened by the outside world.[66] Nationalists declared the Czech people to be the most "nationally conscious" of all the Slav peoples and the Czech language to be the most beautiful:[67] "Forget about foreign languages and speak your own! It is more beautiful than a thousand others."[68] In addition to this, particular emphasis was placed on specific accomplishments of the Czechs in Lower Austria. Under the influence of the Sokol, a paramilitary gymnastic mass organization, and its ideology, which was based on Darwin's principles of the survival of the fittest, they considered their community in Vienna to be "an outpost of the Czech nation" on the Danube[69] or "the foremost bulwark against which the first waves would break when the vast floods of the Teutonic ocean were unleashed."[70] If this bulwark were breached the result would be the destruction of the whole nation. But the qualities of the nation were also expressed in the form of quantities. Vienna became the "largest Czech city where the fate of the whole of the Czech people is decided."[71] In 1893 there were forecasts that the number of Viennese Czechs would have doubled within the next ten years[72] and it was claimed that there were 470,000 migrants in the city in addition to the 130,000 Czechs who had long been resident there.[73] Allegedly more than one-twelfth of the inhabitants of the Crown Lands and one-fifth of the population of Vienna were Viennese Czechs,[74] and no less than 73 percent of the workers in the Imperial capital were supposed to hold Czech nationality.[75]

The more assimilation occurred, the more superlatives were produced that were supposed to prove the opposite. This constant assertion of the group's own potential superiority, which was based on what it had achieved and was intended to act as a stimulus for what it still hoped to achieve, also played an important role among the Viennese Czechs themselves. In answer to the Czech Social Democrats' proud claim of "We are the nation!"[76] the bourgeois parties proclaimed: "We are proud to declare ourselves the champions of the Czech ideal in Lower Austria."[77] Memories of the sufferings and achievements of past generations of Czechs in Lower Austria were revived in an attempt to increase their own self-esteem. For this reason support was given to the idea of printing pamphlets in Czech and German that described the extent to which Lower Austria had been affected by Czech or Slavonic influences.[78] As the nationalistic movement got into a crisis, especially from 1910 onward, such publications became more and more common, whereas previously there had only been occasional references to Slavonic place names in Lower Austria or the original Slavonic population of the Austro-Hungarian monarchy.[79] Such literature was considered to be the best form of protection for the Czech minority.[80] The very word "protection," however, shows that here too the idea of a common danger from without again played a role—a further element in the composition of their national ideology. The "bloodthirsty hydra of German nationalist intolerance," the "insatiable Teutonic Moloch," the "most ruthless terrorism" and "rape" are just some examples of the vocabulary that was used to bring about a kind of truce among the feuding Czechs in Vienna, as the existence of a common enemy to a certain extent justified their own existence as a group.[81]

The more dangerous the "furor Teutonicus" appeared, the more necessary it became to unite against it, and the more meritorious it seemed to oppose it, to fight and defeat it.[82] The Czechs were urged to suppress their internal conflicts and divisions and warned not to expect "tolerance and justice" from their Teutonic neighbors. The bourgeois Viennese Czechs declared that "patriotism and nationalism" did not mean privately boasting that one was a member of a nation but of openly fighting for it against the enemy.[83] But here a clear line must be drawn between the enemy without and the enemy within. While the continuing existence of the enemy without, that is, the Austrian Germans, was a precondition for national identity, the enemy within could split their ranks. By failing to attempt to bring about the ideological integration of the great majority of the Czech population, that is, the Czech Social Democrats, the nationalism of the bourgeois Czech leaders in Vienna proved foreseeably to be an unsatisfactory concept. The *Vídeňský Denník* thus explained the split that resulted in mutual accusations of anti-Czech behavior:

Our attitude to the enemy without is obvious and self-evident. This is not the case with the enemy within. . . . The old symptoms of which the Slavs complain in their conflicts with the Germans have appeared in the body of the Czech people in relation to the Social Democrats. Especially for us Czechs, internationalism means exactly the same as German culture for the Slavs. The main enemy inside our Czech body, the enemy within, is the idea of internationalism, which is just as much a danger to our survival as a nation as the efforts to Germanize us. There is one difference, that the efforts to destroy our national individuality come from the Germans, from our declared enemies, whereas we ourselves are responsible for the second danger. So it stems from our midst and grows among us, often even with our indirect support.[84]

Hence there were two opposing interpretations of the nature of the Czech question in Vienna and the solutions to it. In bourgeois circles the nationally inspired struggle against assimilation was of foremost importance, whereas the Social Democrats devoted their attention to social injustices such as discrimination and their lack of equality with the Austrian Germans. The bourgeois nationalist preoccupation with the unity and purity of the basic national conception proved how much the existence of the Viennese Czechs as a national group was dependent on a mere ideology.[85] National unity and homogeneity[86] required a form of *group morality* of which the most important maxim was love of one's nation.[87] The identification of love of one's nation with love of one's neighbor guaranteed the binding force of the former, making service to one's people and one's nation into a sacred commandment.[88] As a result, words such as "morals," "honor," "immorality," and similar expressions frequently formed part of the Czechs' slogans addressed to the masses.[89]

This system of morality leads us to the last aspect of the ideology of integration: *the demand that the individual should submit his interests to those of the group.*[90] Bourgeois morality with its self-conceit gave no quarter to divergents. Antonín Hubka, a national-social deputy and sharp critic of the political leadership of the Viennese Czechs, called the Czech "renegades" the "refuse of a demoralized Vienna."[91] The members of the bourgeois Czech leadership themselves also looked upon their Social Democrat fellow countrymen as renegades with whom they basically had nothing in common, although they did make one or two attempts to come to terms with them. Generally their motto was "Whoever is not with us is against us!"[92]

This analysis of the elements of nationalism among the Viennese Czechs, which slowed down the process of acculturation, shows that the nationalist ideological system was only intact externally; internally it lacked the ability to act as an integrating force. The nationalists' attempts to mobilize their own people always revealed a tendency to pass off as historical reality matters that were intended to be developed by propaganda and agitation. The nationalists placed less emphasis on the common pursuit of certain objectives than on the feelings of solidarity that allegedly existed within the group.[93] But the nationalist ideology never gained acceptance as an absolute moral code for the whole of the minority. This was neither the result of ideological tensions within nationalists' ranks nor was it due to the lack of sustained policy of settlement or economic interest by the Prague leadership. The frustrated and hence aggressive nationalism to be found in Vienna did not succeed in making the breakthrough to become an integral form of nationalism. Nationalist ideology could not protect the Czech minority from assimilation because if its members wanted to succeed at work as workers and middle-class professionals, they had to disavow this very ideology. Beneath a surface which seemed to indicate that Czechs in Vienna had found some kind of national identity, the basic problems remained unsolved. According to Karl Marx, being determines consciousness. The nationalist ideology of the Viennese Czechs was a vain attempt to reverse this relationship.

THE PRESSURE FOR INTEGRATION

Finally, it is important to mention once again those factors that can be considered to be the reasons why Czechs in Vienna failed to develop an adequate form of national consciousness. One point that contributed to their assimilation was the way in which they settled in the city. They were scattered over all the districts of Vienna and it was only in Favoriten (the tenth district) that almost every house contained Czechs who knew each other from work or because they were neighbors. The process of assimilation was also accelerated by living in a comparatively open social structure. In contrast, in the Baltic provinces, the upper and lower classes were also clearly separated according to nationality. In Lithuania, for instance, the three main social classes (nobility, middle class, peasantry) were each made up of three different ethnic groups before 1918: Poles, Jews, and Lithuanians.[94] The Austrian socialist Otto Bauer, who propagated the idea of national assimilation as a modern means of class formation, came to the conclusion that the "middle strata," that is, apprentices, craftsmen, self-employed masters, small entrepreneurs, housemaids, and workers, were most easily assimilated. The social structure of the Viennese Czechs fulfilled all of these conditions. To use Bauer's terminology, the immigrants were recruited from the upper section of the agricultural/domestic service economy and the lower section of the industrial capitalist economy.[95]

Czech historian Miroslav Hroch came to the conclusion that participation in patriotic activities was not the result of "membership in a certain class, a certain social group or a certain profession" and that it did not depend on a person's position in society either.[96] Hroch observed that the urban milieu was more open to nationalist agitation than the rural and that it was easier to gain the support of young people for the idea of a national awakening than it was to win over the middle and older generations.[97] If this were true, the nationalist movement ought to have had more resonance among the Viennese Czechs, as they were a socially mobile and highly communicative group that consisted mostly of young people. But here, too, there is no causal relationship between communication, social mobility, and national consciousness. Hroch names Wales, the Oberlausitz district, and Slovakia as examples of areas in which the most industrialized, that is, communicative and mobile, sections were assimilated particularly fast.[98] For Vienna it is difficult to try to fit the forces and counterforces of Czech nationalism into a model of explanation. Vertical mobility depended on integration with the Austrian-German population. This was not always the case, however, and Germanization was not necessarily the conscious political and ideological objective of the state organs. But Czechs in Vienna who wanted to improve their social or financial standing were more or less compelled to seek access to the German-speaking ruling structure. Assimilation also accelerated a number of socio-psychological aspects of the process of industrialization.[99] According to American research, a pluralistic industrial society encourages its members to develop realistic expectations that do not lead to either Utopian hopes or despair. Workers become an integral part of this society, adapt themselves to their situation in it, and their potential to protest declines.[100]

To what extent did industry, with its great power to unite people, help to moderate the strength of national feeling? An important feature of the period of mechanization was the division of labor.[101] Even if factory work leads to the isolation of the individual, each worker is at the same time dependent on many others. The term "division of labor" conceals the fact that this process involves passing on work from one person to another, or one person working with or for another. In this chain the impetus to work always comes from other workers and is then passed on to the next. The workers must also adapt to the machines they are using. This means that the 70 percent of the Viennese Czechs who were workers not only had to adapt to machines but also to their (Austrian-German) colleagues if they wanted to get their own work done.[102] The a priori result of this was that they were not influenced by nationalist ideals but simply by the "work ethos." They had come to Vienna to earn good wages, not to earn praise for helping to build up the nation.

The transition to a new way of life in an industrial world placed a further burden on the Czechs seeking work in Vienna: the loss of their home, which they left voluntarily and in many cases permanently. From the psychological point of view Czech migration from the Bohemian lands meant their removal from the centuries-old framework of their culture. Their experiences, their sense of security, and their knowledge of their surroundings no longer influenced their lives and lost value. It is therefore essential to take into account that this process of losing their home played a central role in the history of the Viennese Czechs. Until migration all of them had lived within the limits of a geographical area whose features they had known since their youth: Their ideas, their whole imaginations were closely linked with this area. Hence "home" in this case did not only mean the geographical area of the Bohemian Crown Lands but also a system of norms and values.[103] The move from the country districts of Bohemia and Moravia to the capital of the monarchy did not only involve alterations in their way of life but dramatic social and psychological changes.

If the term "home" is interpreted as a social system, as a closely meshed network of relationships with members of the family, neighbors, and authorities, there still remains the question of why the dissolution of this network of relationships led to a tide of assimilation and not—as in England—to a tide of nationalism.[104] It is not sufficient simply to observe that the migration of the Czechs to Vienna caused dislocation and general disorientation.[105] All of the migrants' social relationships were severed, and it took some time to readapt to a new social system with its new values. At this point it is, however, important to emphasize the double character of the Czech ethnic group in Vienna. There were the long-term migrants and the short-term ones. The temporary residence of apprentices, students, civil servants, soldiers, or artists did not make them into members of the Viennese Czech community, even if they were counted as such in the official statistics. Left to themselves, deprived of friends and relations, they all began their new life as strangers, outcasts isolated from many forms of communication and contact.[106] By force of circumstances Czech newcomers to Vienna retreated into the paling world of their past home, they spoke or wrote of things remembered, their memories often clouded by their emotions. This only increased their isolation, and the local people, with their mockery, mercilessly exposed the situation of the Czechs.[107] The reaction of the migrants to this was resentment [108] but also a secret wish to be like the local people.[109]

The more their old home faded into the past, the more the Czechs resorted to the small circle of their compatriots in the various clubs and groups as the only support that they could rely on in their new world. But ethnic and national traditions had little authority and did not provide the newcomers with any kind of orientation.

One symptom of the advanced stage that assimilation had reached was the lack of effectiveness of Czech organizations whose functions duplicated non-ethnic organizations. The organization representing the interests of the 54,000 Czech tradesmen in Vienna, for example, had only 50 members, whereas social clubs, and drama and choral associations were much more popular, since they catered to the tradition of Czech theatrical and musical performances, a welcome change to everyday life and assimilation in Vienna.[110] Economic integration and cultural distinctiveness were the two opposite poles of Czech life in Vienna.

The generation gap also played an important role. The second generation of Viennese Czechs remained only partly adjusted to their new surroundings. School children characterized their situation as follows: "Nejsem Němec, nechci býti Čechem, jsem Vídeňák a vy jste Češi" (I'm not a German, I don't want to be a Czech, I'm Viennese and you're Czechs).[111]

But the decisions made by the second generation can also be more radical, as Irwin Child has shown with his use of the term "rebel-reaction" in his work on the Italians in the United States. Child argues that the second-generation Italians in the United States overemphasize the fact that they are Americans and do their best to avoid being recognized as Italians.[112] In the case of Vienna, however, it would be going too far to adopt Child's concept. There was not such a clamor for the way of life and language of the old-established "echte Wiener" (genuine Viennese) to justify the term "rebellion" against everything that was Czech. What nationalist ideologists condemned as rural exodus or the actions of renegades was in fact more of a reconstruction of a Czech-Austrian community based on the opportunities for employment in the Imperial capital. Whenever Czech migrants made a successful career for themselves and decided to stay in Vienna, they either deliberately or unconsciously came close to the local population.[113]

The one question that remains to be asked is how the transition from the old to the new surroundings actually occurred. While occasional visits to Moravia or reading Czech periodicals available from the ethnic organizations made it clear to the Czech population of Vienna that they no longer completely belonged to their old home, their day-to-day experiences on the Danube made them realize that they were not yet quite at home in their new social surroundings either.[114] They found themselves somewhere between the two.[115]

Nationalist historians have frequently argued that the loss of national culture was the result of some kind of weakness of character among the Czechs.[116] This is true neither for the intellectuals nor for Czech housemaids, wet-nurses, workers, apprentices, or tradesmen. On the contrary, it was the one and only way open to them if they wanted to settle and survive in Vienna. Thus, far removed from the domain of ideologists, subconscious change took place in their values— in those values that we are sometimes inclined to judge according to theoretical criteria without taking the lower classes and the social pressures on them into consideration.

In addition to the two extremes—on the one hand the nationalists, on the other the ''renegades''—a large proportion of the Viennese Czechs must be assigned to the so-called floating ethnic group that had no definite preference for either the new or the old culture. This combined the claims of both nations, had close contacts with both of them, and came into conflict with both of them, too. To a certain extent they lacked a point of crystallization but also the will to form an independent group. Ethnologists have indicated that there are a number of stages in the process of ethnic alienation, one of which in the case of the Viennese Czechs was bilingualism. Thus many of them claimed to use German for the purposes of everyday communication but in spite of this they felt themselves to be Czechs. They adjusted their language according to the topic of conversation and who their interlocutor was. They also were unable or unwilling to understand national differences as they were inclined to be extremely tolerant. Such a group, poised between two nations, is bound to arouse the disdain of and be subject to persecution by the two extreme groups, the nationalists and the ''renegades,'' simply as a result of the instability of its system of norms and values. This intermediate group endangered the existence of the Viennese Czechs as a group. Its lack of group consciousness precluded the opportunity to integrate others; in politics it endangered the effectiveness of ethnic demands and certainly of nationalist political principles.[117]

In conclusion, a very general observation comes to mind. Sometimes it can and must be the task of the dispassionate historian to defend an ethnic group or minority in great social difficulties against the extreme postulates of its own political ideology. Such an ideology is only all too easily and purposely misunderstood by the numerically dominant majority. The Viennese Czechs, even at the peak of their political effectiveness, represented chiefly their own legitimate social interests and in no way followed any of their overblown nationalistic slogans.

NOTES

1. Monika Glettler, *Die Wiener Tschechen um 1900. Strukturanalyse einer nationa-Len Minderheit in der Großstadt* (Munich/Vienna, 1972) pp. 32–44. Parts of this chapter appeared in *East-Central Europe* 9, pts 1-2 (1982), 124–36.

2. Heinrich Rauchberg, *Der nationale Besitzstand in Böhmen*, 3 vols. (Leipzig, 1905), and Erika Fischer, "Soziologie Mährens in der zweiten Hälfte des 19. Jahrhunderts als Hintergrund der Werke Marie von Ebner-Eschenbachs" (Diss., University of Leipzig, 1939).

3. Gustav Otruba and L.S. Rutschka, "Die Herkunft der Wiener Bevölkerung in den letzten 150 Jahren," *Jahrbuch des Vereins für Geschichte der Stadt Wien* 13 (1957), 227–74, here, 230.

4. "Heimatrecht," the right to live in a certain place, included (1) the right to remain there permanently, and (2) the right to aid (early "social security") in distress. It was in the language of the time "the personal relationship to the community from which stems the right to unimpaired sojourn in the whole area of the community and the right to support in case of poverty." Ernst Mischler and Josef Ulbrich, *Österreichisches Staatswörterbuch*, 2 vols. (Vienna, 1906), pp. 809–43, here, p. 810.

5. Reinhard Petermann, *Wien im Zeitalter Franz Josephs I* (Vienna, 1908), p. 142; Rudolf Till, "Zur Herkunft der Wiener Bevölkerung," *Vierteljahresschrift zur Sozial- und Wirtschaftsgeschichte* 34 (1941), 15-37, here, 21.

6. František Kutnár, *Počátky hromadného vystěhovalectví z Cech v období Bachová absolutismu* (Prague, 1964); Christoph Stölzl, *Die Ära Bach in Böhmen. Sozialge-schichtliche Studien zum Neoabsolutismus 1849–1859* (Munich/Vienna, 1971); for Vienna see p. 270–75.

7. G.A. Schimmer, "Die einheimische Bevölkerung Österreichs nach der Umgangssprache," *Statistische Monatsschrift* 8 (Vienna, 1882), p. 105.

8. Of interest is the officially confirmed percentage of Czechs in several villages in Lower Austria in 1900: Bischofswart, 99.5 percent Czechs; Unterthemenau, 93.3 percent; Oberthemenau, 92.8 percent; that is, remaining settlements of Slovaks and Croats under the reign of Maria Theresa and Joseph II. Anton Schubert, *Ziffern zur Frage des niederösterreichischen Tschecheneinschlags* (Vienna, 1909), pp. 51-62. Until 1920 Vienna belonged administratively to Lower Austria.

9. Otto Wittelshöfer, "Politische und wirtschaftliche Gesichtspunkte in der österreichischen Nationalitätenfrage," *Preussische Jahrbücher* 76 (1894), 445–601, here, 491.

10. Rauchberg, *Der nationale Besitzstand*, I, pp. 193f; III, charts V, VII, VIII.

11. Glettler, *Die Wiener Tschechen*, pp. 31–62.

12. Compared to Prague from 1880 to 1890, that is, twenty years earlier–1880: 20.59 percent Germans, 79.27 percent Czechs; 1890: 16.44 percent Germans, 83.55 percent Czechs. Wittelshöfer, "Politische und wirtschaftliche Gesichtspunkte," 473.

13. Wilhelm Winkler, *Die Tschechen in Wien* (Vienna, 1919), p. 20.

14. Glettler, *Die Wiener Tschechen*, pp. 51–60.

15. Ibid., pp. 60–72.

16. Renate Mayntz, *Soziologie der Organisation* (Reinbek near Hamburg, 1967); Franz Klein, *Das Organisationswesen der Gegenwart* (Berlin, 1913).

17. Friedrich Fürstenberg, *Die Sozialstruktur der Bundesrepublik Deutschland. Ein soziologischer Überblick* (Cologne/Opladen, 1967), p. 39.

18. Glettler, *Die Wiener Tschechen*, pp. 31, 89, 102.

19. Josef Karásek was a Slavist and publicist (1868–1916). In 1894 he was working for the *Wiener Zeitung*; in 1895, at the library of the Ministry of the Interior; in 1896, *Pražské noviny*. He was a friend of V. Jagić, translated M. Ebner-Eschenbach and Otto Ludwig, and edited the works of Petr Chelčický. In addition he wrote a Slavic history of literature and was a teacher with the great aristocratic families of Harrach, Windischgrätz, Hohenlohe-Schillingsfürst, Thun-Hohenstein, and Metternich.

20. Josef Karásek, *Sborník Čechů dolnorakouských 1895* (Prague, 1895), p. 149. (Anthology of Czechs in Lower Austria).

21. Wilhelm Brepohl, *Industrievolk im Wandel von der agraren zu der industriellen Daseinsform, dargestellt am Ruhrgebiet* (Tübingen, 1957), p. 153.

22. With emphasis on the "self-help" character.

23. Wittelshöfer, "Politische und wirtschaftliche Gesichtspunkte," p. 478; Karl Hugelmann, *Das Recht der Nationalitäten in Österreich und das Staats-Grundgesetz über die allgemeinen Rechte der Staatsbürger: Zwei Vorträge* (Graz, 1880).

24. The *Reichsgerichtserkenntnis* of 19 October 1904 (Hye, No. 473) deprived the Vienna Czechs of the status of a *Volksstamm*. See Karl Gottfried Hugelmann, ed., *Das Nationalitätenrecht des alten Österreich* (Vienna/Leipzig, 1934), p. 448.

25. Glettler, *Die Wiener Tschechen*, pp. 476–85.

26. Ibid., pp. 90–111.

27. Ibid., pp. 70–140.

28. Hugelmann, *Das Nationalitätenrecht*, p. 454.

29. Glettler, *Die Wiener Tschechen*, pp. 121–32.

30. German nationalistic protective societies (*Schutzvereine*).

31. Hůrecký (Josef Drozda), "O významu u úkolech Nár. rady," *Vídenský Nár. Kalendář* 1 (1906), 43f.

32. Hugelmann, *Das Nationalitätenrecht*, pp. 430, 438, 447.

33. *Česká Vídeň*, no. 25, 21 June 1913.

34. *Nár. Politika*, 23 February 1906.

35. Ibid., 13 April 1906.

36. Alexander Mitscherlich, "Aggression und Anpassung," in Herbert Marcuse, Anatol Rapoport and Klaus Horn, eds. *Aggression und Anpassung in der Industriegesellschaft* (Frankfurt/M., 1969), pp. 80–127, here, p. 109.

37. Glettler, *Die Wiener Tschechen*, pp. 232–40.

38. Richard Kralik, *Karl Lueger und der christliche Sozialismus* (Vienna, 1923), p. 231.

39. *Niederösterreichische Landesgesetze*, vol. 2, *Gemeindestatut für Wien* (Vienna, 1897).

40. Law of 19 December 1890, *Niederösterreichische Landesgesetze*, vol. 2, p. 16 § 10.

41. *Gemeindestatut für die k.k. Reichshaupt- und Residenzstadt Wien* (Vienna, 1900), §10; Hugelmann, Das Nationalitätenrecht, pp. 444, 487.

42. Glettler, *Die Wiener Tschechen*, pp. 232–40.

43. For both terms, see Mitscherlich, "Aggression und Anpassung," pp. 80–127.

44. Glettler, *Die Wiener Tschechen*, pp. 265, 352, 375.

45. This is also true for the Czech socialists. Karl Renner, "Über Innsbruck hinaus," *Der Kampf* 5 (1912), 145–54, here, 147.

46. *Vídeňský Denník*, 15 June 1907; *Ceská Vídeň*, 21 June 1913; *Vídeňský Denník*, 19 May 1905; *Vídeňský Kalendář* 2 (1893), 95.

47. See "Denkschrift des DONRČ an Ministerpräsident Gautsch," 28 November 1905, in Glettler, *Die Wiener Tschechen*, Appendix, p. 544.

48. Ibid., p. 369.

49. Ibid., p. 362.

50. Ibid., pp. 277–83 and Appendix, pp. 526–37.

51. *Kalendář Čechů Vídeňských* 4 (1895), 64; Walter Sulzbach, "Zur Definition und Psychologie von 'Nation' und Nationalbewußtsein," *Politische Vierteljahresschrift* 3 (1962), 139–58, here, 156.

52. Terminology: see Eugen Lemberg, *Nationalismus II. Soziologie und politische Pädagogik* (Reinbek near Hamburg, 1964), pp. 113–19; and *Nationalismus I*, ibid., p. 258; Friedrich Fürstenberg, "Randgruppen in der modernen Gesellschaft," *Soziale Welt* 16 (1965), 236–45.

53. Lemberg, *Nationalismus II*, pp. 65–69.

54. Ibid., II, pp. 66, 69; Peter Robert Hofstätter, *Sozialpsychologie* (Berlin, 1956), p. 164.; Boyd C. Shafer, *Nationalism, Myth and Reality* (London, 1955), p. 45.

55. *Vídeňský Denník*, no. 77, 23 May 1907.

56. Various editions of the *Vídeňský Denník* appearing in 1907.

57. *Národní Kalendář* 1 (1906), p. 88.

58. *Vídeňský Denník*, no. 67, 9 May 1907 (leader).

59. Josef Václav Drozda, *Paměti z mého života* (Vienna, 1919), p. 22.

60. *Vídeňský Denník*, no., 8, 26 February 1907.

61. *Politik*, 18 November 1900.

62. Ibid., no. 5, 22 February 1907, no. 25, 17 May 1907.

63. *Vídeňský Denník*, no. 10, 28 February 1907.

64. Josef Svatopluk Machar, "Opuštěná větev," in Karásek, *Sborník Čechů Dolnorakouských*, p. 3; Antonín Machát, *Naši ve Vídni* (Our compatriots in Vienna) (Prague, 1946), p. 10.

65. Jan Auerhan, *Československá větev v Jugoslavii* (Prague, 1930), p. 352.

66. Lemberg, *Nationalismus II*, pp. 73, 82.

67. *Vídeňský Denník*, no. 79, 25 May 1907.

68. *Kalendář Čechů Vídeňských* 8 (1899), 78.

69. *Národní Kalendář* 3 (1908), 80.

70. *Vídeňský Denník*, no. 8, 26 February 1907, no. 7, 24 February 1907.

71. *Kalendář Čechů Vídeňských* 3 (1893), 120.

72. *Vídeňský Kalendář* 2 (1893), 120.

73. *Kalendář Čechů Vídeňských* 9 (1902), 62.

74. Drozda, *Paměti*, p. 22, František Pazourek, "Čechové ve Vídni," *Časopis Turistů* 20 (1908), 106.

75. *Vídeňský Denník*, 23 August 1907.
76. Ibid., no. 84, 1 June 1907.
77. Ibid., no. 78, 24 May 1907.
78. Glettler, *Die Wiener Tschechen*, p. 426, note 61 (literature!).
79. *Vídeňský Kalendář* 1 (1892), 41 and 57-59; Nö. Präs. J 12, 51 (1898).
80. Drozda, *Paměti*, p. 19.
81. Various editions of the *Vídeňský Denník* that appeared in 1907.
82. Ibid., no. 72, 16 May 1907.
83. *Kalendář Čechů Vídeňských* 9 (1900), 65; 11 (1902), 39. *Vídeňský Denník*, no. 24, 16 March 1907.
84. Ibid., no. 78, 24 May 1907.
85. Lemberg, *Nationalismus II*, p. 91.
86. *Vídeňský Denník*, no. 2, 19 February 1907, no. 12, 2 March 1907.
87. Lemberg, *Nationalismus II*, p. 86.
88. *České dělnické listy*, 14 January 1898, *Vídeňský Kalendář* 1 (1892), 59.
89. *Vídeňský Denník*, no. 22, 14 March 1907; no. 24, 16 March 1907; no. 40, 13 April 1907.
90. Lemberg, *Nationalismus II*, p. 95.
91. Antonín Hubka, *Čechové v Dolních Rakousích* (Prague, 1901), p. 26.
92. NRČ. Agenda of the DONRČ 1910-1912.
93. Walter Sulzbach, "Zur Definition und Psychologie von 'Nation' und National-bewußtsein," *Politische Vierteljahresschrift* 3 (1962), 139-58, here, 153.
94. Hans Rothfels, "Grundsätzliches zum Problem der Nationalität," *Historische Zeitschrift* 174 (1952), 339-58, here, 348.
95. Otto Bauer, "Die Bedingungen der nationalen Assimilation," *Der Kampf* 5 (1912), 246-63, here, 256.
96. Miroslav Hroch, *Die Vorkämpfer der nationalen Bewegung bei den kleinen Völkern Europas. Eine vergleichende Analyse zur gesellschaftlichen Schichtung der patriotischen Gruppen* (Prague 1968), here pp. 141, 166.
97. Ibid., pp. 166, 147.
98. Hroch, *Die Vorkämpfer*, p. 169.
99. Rauchberg, *Der nationale Besitzstand I*, p. 303; III, charts 27 and 28; *Kalendář Slovanů Vídeňských* 21 (1912), 64: assimilation quota: 5/6!
100. Clark Kerr, John T. Dunlop, and Frederick H. Harbinson, *Der Mensch in der industriellen Gesellschaft. Die Probleme von Arbeit und Management unter den Bedingungen wirtschaftlichen Wachstums* (Frankfurt/M., 1966), p. 334.
101. Brepohl, *Industrievolk*, p. 116.
102. Glettler, *Die Wiener Tschechen*, chart on p. 61.
103. Brepohl, *Der Aufbau des Ruhrvolkes im Zuge der Ost-West Wanderung. Beiträge zur deutschen Sozialgeschichte des 19.und 20. Jahrhunderts* (Recklinghausen, 1948), p. 26.
104. Ibid., p. 31.
105. Brepohl, *Industrievolk*, p. 140.
106. *Vídeňský Denník* no. 79, 25 May 1907.
107. Ibid., no. 5, 22 February 1907; no. 25, 17 May 1907.
108. Glettler, *Die Wiener Tschechen*, p. 226 (Visit of a Czech midwife in a Viennese circus).

109. This was true for both, for the assimilated Czechs as well as for the nationalistic circles. *Vídeňský Denník*, no. 56, 25 April 1907; no. 62, 3 May 1907.

110. *Vídeňský Merkur*, no. 8, 15 May 1905.

111. Josef Sulik, *Proč máme vychovávati své děti v českých školách?* (Vienna, 1914), p. 13.

112. Irvin Child, *Italian or American? The Second Generation in Conflict* (Princeton, 1943).

113. Brepohl, *Der Aufbau des Ruhrvolkes*, pp. 193–98; Paul F. Secord and Carl W. Backman, *Social Psychology* (New York, 1964), pp. 190, 415, 569.

114. In 1893–1894 in the Akademický Spolek (Academic Club) alone one could read 166 periodicals (143 were Czech). *Výroční správa Akademického spolku ve Vídni 26* (1893–1894), 17–23.

115. Marie-Luise Lehmkühler, "Umformungsprozesse in Kultur und Gesellschaft. Das Schicksal der Auswanderer in der Sozialdynamik," Walther Gustav Hoffmann, ed., *Beiträge zur Soziologie der industriellen Gesellschaft* (Dortmund, 1952), pp. 101–8, here, p. 106; Brepohl, *Industrievolk*, p. 147.

116. *Vídeňský Denník*, no. 43, 10 April 1907.

117. Lemberg, *Nationalismus II*, p. 78.

13

EMBELLISHING A LIFE OF LABOR: AN INTERPRETATION OF THE MATERIAL CULTURE OF AMERICAN WORKING-CLASS HOMES, 1885–1915

Lizabeth A. Cohen

The material life of American urban workers from 1885 to 1915, as revealed in patterns of home furnishings and organizations of domestic space, provides a new way of understanding the historical development of working-class culture. While in recent years historians have pursued the often elusive lives of working people, they have almost totally ignored domestic settings and the material culture within them as sources. Instead, historical investigation has focused on the work place and local community. Only a few sociologists have examined home environments for evidence of the values and social identities of workers.[1]

Historians have examined working-class homes primarily in the context of the Progressive Era housing reform movement. The keen interest that these early twentieth-century social reformers displayed in workers' home environment, however, should alert us to the significance of the home, the most private and independent world of the worker, in expressing the working-class family's social identity and interaction with middle-class culture.

Studies of the material culture of the working-class home have much to contribute to our understanding of workers' experience beyond the outlines sketched by social historians who have quantified occupations and family events such as births, marriages, and deaths. Although workers were often constrained in their household activities and consumption by low incomes and scarcity in housing options, they still made revealing choices in the process of ordering their personal environments. This chapter, therefore, addresses issues relevant to current debates in immigration history as well. It clearly supports the revisionist premise that immigrants were active agents in their own acculturation and offers new insights into the nature of that process. Historians have stressed the assistance of ethnic organizations and newspapers as immigrants assimilated into American life within their own communities; in contrast they have usually viewed the home

This chapter is a considerably revised and expanded version of a paper first published in the *Journal of American Culture* 3 (Winter 1980), 752–75. It is used with the permission of the author and The Popular Press, Bowling Green State University.

I would like to thank Kenneth Ames for his initial encouragement of this project and Lawrence Levine for his invaluable criticism.

as a bastion of traditional culture. Evidence presented here suggests that, on the contrary, the home was a central arena for the acculturation process.

The common impression that the immigrant home retarded assimilation may stem from the prevailing assessment of the role of the immigrant woman. Historians have generally shared the Progressive Era reformers' view that women made the slowest adjustment to the American environment. Examining the often ignored sphere of domestic material life and consumption may, however, grant the immigrant woman a more active role in assisting her family's transition, serving as validation for Robert J. Lifton's thesis that the traditional woman is often a crucial agent for social change, particularly during periods of historical pressure.[2]

This essay explores developments in the consumption preferences of urban working-class families from 1885 to 1915 and interprets how these choices reflected and affected workers' social identity. An investigation of working-class homes places them in the context of the material standards of the larger society in which the workers lived. Only a comparison between working-class and middle-class homes can elucidate the degree to which working-class material culture was distinctive or part of a larger cultural system.

During the period 1885–1915 new people joined the ranks of the American working class as industry expanded.[3] Foreign-born and native American workers commonly shared the experience of having recently left rural, small-town settings for the urban industrial work place. This chapter examines the homes both immigrant and native American workers made within the city environment, although the "new immigrants" from Southern and Eastern Europe figure most prominently in this story, as they did in the manual trades of the era.

First, the development of interior styles among the middle class during this period will be traced, probing particularly how esthetic trends reflected middle-class social attitudes. While the middle class was by no means a clear-cut group with uniform tastes, still its trend setters and reflectors, such as popular magazines and home decoration advice books, articulated a consistent set of standards. Second, efforts by reformers and institutions to influence the tastes of workers toward these middle-class norms will be examined. Finally, an analysis of working-class homes in the light of workers' experiences and values and in relation to middle-class society will be undertaken.

Herbert Gutman urged at the close of his seminal essay on the integration of pre-industrial peoples into nineteenth- and early twentieth-century America that "much remains to be learned about the transition of native and foreign-born American men and women to industrial society, and how that transition affected such persons and the society in which they entered."[4] The study of the material life of American working people as expressed in consumption patterns and the arrangement of domestic interiors may offer some new insights toward that goal. Workers who left no private written records may speak to us through the artifacts of their homes.

THE CHANGING LOOK OF THE MIDDLE-CLASS HOME

American homes from the 1840s through the 1880s mirrored the nation's transformation from an agricultural to an industrial society. Just as industrialization affected people and places in the country in different ways and at various rates, so too homes reflected an individual's or family's degree of integration into the industrial economy. Location, occupation, and financial status all affected the quantity and quality of consumption. The middle classes, with a status and income often attributable to an expanded economy and the mechanized means of production, were the most enthusiastic purchasers of mass-produced objects for their homes.[5] Meanwhile, technologically advanced products were less abundant in the houses of those who lived more self-sufficient economic lives.

The home served as an accurate indicator of one's relationship to the industrial economy not by accident but as a result of the Victorians' contradictory attitude toward economic and technological change. Enthusiasm for, as well as anxiety toward, industrialization provoked both an appetite for new products and a need to incorporate them carefully into private life. At the same time that new kinds of objects transformed the home, the Victorians loudly proclaimed the sanctity of the family refuge in a menacing, changing world. As John Ruskin wrote:

This is the true nature of home—it is the place of peace; the shelter, not only from injury, but from all terror, doubt and division. In so far as it is not this, it is not home; so far as the anxieties of the outer life penetrate into it, and the inconsistently-minded, unloved, or hostile society of the outer world is allowed by either husband or wife to cross the threshold, it ceases to be a home.[6]

The home embodied a contradiction as both the arena for and refuge from technological penetration. Insofar as people could tolerate this contradictory domestic environment, the home provided a setting for gradual adaptation to a technological and commercial world.

The parlor best represented this accommodation to industrial life. As the room reserved for greeting and entertaining those beyond the family circle, the parlor permitted controlled interaction with the outside world. Similarly, a typical parlor overflowed with store-bought mass-produced objects, carefully arranged by family members: wall-to-wall carpeting enclosed by papered and bordered walls and ceilings; upholstered furniture topped with antimacassars; shawl-draped center tables displaying carefully arranged souvenir albums and alabaster sculptures; shelves and small stands overloaded with bric-a-brac and purchased mementos. Technology made much of this decor possible: carpeting, wallpaper, and textiles were ever cheaper and more elaborate, and the invention of the spiral spring encouraged the mass distribution of upholstered furniture. Artificial covering of surfaces and structural frames thus replaced the painted walls and floors and the hardwood furniture of an earlier era.[7]

After about 1885, popular magazines, home decoration manuals and architectural journals revealed a gradual but dramatic rejection of the cluttered spaces of the Victorian home in favor of two stylistic trends unified around a common concern for traditional American symbols. The Colonial Revival and the Arts and Crafts Movement both sought an American esthetic to replace European-inspired and technologically sophisticated styles. In the early twentieth century, an up-to-date middle-class family almost anywhere in America most likely lived in a Colonial Revival house, perhaps along newly extended trolley lines, or in a craftsman-style bungalow, often in a recently developed housing tract.[8]

The Colonial Revival had its debut at the Philadelphia Centennial Exposition in 1876 amid the salute to American technological progress; the style reached full maturity in the 1920s with the opening of the American Wing of the Metropolitan Museum of Art in New York and the restoration of Williamsburg.[9] Middle-class Americans encountered the Colonial Revival style more intimately, however, not at these public sites, but within their own homes and neighborhoods. Just as house construction had dominated colonial American building, the domestic setting most engaged the attention of the revival style. While for some people Colonial Revival meant "accurately" re-creating early American interiors replete with spinning wheels and antique furniture, for most middle-class Americans, adoption entailed purchasing new, usually mass-produced items in the colonial style, such as a house or parlor set.

The Arts and Crafts Movement, also referred to at the time as the "craftsman" or "mission" style, evolved concurrently with the Colonial Revival. Exteriors and interiors boasted natural materials such as wood, shingle, and greenery, exposed structural elements and surfaces, and open, flexible spaces. Elbert Hubbard's Roycraft Industries, Henry L. Wilson's Bungalow House Plan business, and similar firms popularized on a mass level the unique work of such artists as furniture-maker Gustav Stickley and architects Greene and Greene.

This craftsman style, justified in contradictory terms, met varied pressures of the day. On the one hand, the style depended on technological innovations in heating, lighting, and windowglass and was merchandised as a solution to the household problems of dust, germs, and inefficiency.[10] On the other hand, the Arts and Crafts Movement invoked and sought to replicate such traditional American symbols as the farmhouse and its furnishings. In the Hingham, Massachusetts Arts and Crafts Society, as elsewhere in the country,

bits of old needlework and embroidery were brought down from dusty attics for admiration and imitation. Chairs and tables, of exquisite design and honest purpose, took the place of flimsy and overdecorated furniture.[11]

Middle-class people's attraction to the Colonial Revival and Arts and Crafts Movement corresponded to prevailing social attitudes, particularly toward workers and immigrants. Nativism, anti-industrialism, and a propensity toward environmental solutions for social problems were values incorporated into the new esthetic. Patriotic organizations such as the Daughters of the American Revolution and the National Society of Colonial Dames, both formed in the early 1890s, frequently encouraged the preservation of colonial artifacts and buildings.[12] Architects and client congregations found in the Colonial Revival an appropriate architecture for Protestant churches to replace the Catholic-associated Gothic style.[13] Founders of the Society for the Preservation of New England Antiquities blamed immigrant residents for the destruction of historical areas like Boston's North End.[14] Outspoken xenophobes like Henry Ford, Abbott Lawrence Lowell, and Henry Cabot Lodge were important patrons of the preservation and Colonial Revival movements.[15]

The Arts and Crafts style satisfied the anti-industrial instincts of many middle-class Americans. Montgomery Schuyler, organizer of an arts and crafts production studio outside Philadelphia, argued that this new style was not only wholesome, but it revived the accomplishment of the colonial craftsman, "an educated and thinking being" who loved his work without demanding a wage or labor union membership.[16] Instruction manuals for making mission furniture at home encouraged the de-mechanization of furniture-making. Earlier, middle-class Victorians had handled ambivalence toward industrialism by monitoring, while increasing, their interaction with industrial products within the home. Now, the next generation was employing technological advances to restrain and deny the extent to which industrialism affected private life.

Supporters of the craftsman and Colonial Revival styles had confidence in the moral effect of this new physical environment. Stickley's *Craftsman Magazine* declared in a 1903 issue:

Luxurious surroundings . . . suggest and induce idleness. Complex forms and costly materials have an influence upon life which tells a sad story in history. On the other hand, chasteness and restraint in form, simple, but artistic materials are equally expressive of the character of the people who use them.[17]

The new domestic ideal represented a search for a truly American environment, in Stickley's words, "American homes exclusively for American needs."[18]

SPREADING THE MIDDLE-CLASS MESSAGE

Progressive Era reformers seized upon this new American domestic esthetic, contributing to its popularity and using it to assist in their campaigns to "uplift," "modernize," and "Americanize." Though social reform efforts in this period were broad in scope, a surprising range of reformers made use of the new styles as they sought to transform people's home environments in order to promote social improvement and cultural homogeneity. Often behind their pleas for cleaner, simpler, more sanitary homes for working people lay a desire to encourage more middle-class American environments. In a twist that would have shocked any colonial farmer, the "early American look" became linked with a dust-, germ- and disease-free scientific ideal. Reformers and associated organizations made efforts to influence workers in their homes, their neighborhoods, and their work places through promulgating domestic models; elsewhere, workers encountered these new middle-class style standards more indirectly.

Both public institutions and privately funded organizations conveyed the new esthetic to working-class girls within model classrooms created for housekeeping instruction. By the 1890s, particularly in urban areas, domestic science classes in public schools promoted ideal domestic environments. Similarly, settlement houses in workers' neighborhoods fostered middle-class home standards through "Housekeeping Centers."

In a guide to planning Housekeeping Centers, *Housekeeping Notes: How To Furnish and Keep House in a Tenement Flat: A Series of Lessons Prepared for Use in the Association of Practical Housekeeping Centers of New York*, reformer Mabel Kittredge perfectly stated the new esthetic. The section "Suitable Furnishing for a Model Housekeeping Flat or Home for Five People" recommended wood-stained and uncluttered furniture surfaces, iron beds with mattresses, and un-upholstered chairs. Walls must be painted, not papered; floors should be oak stained; window seats must be built in for storage; shelves should replace bulky sideboards ("the latter being too large for an ordinary tenement room; cheap sideboards are also very ugly"); screens provide privacy in bedrooms; a few good pictures should grace the walls, but only in the living room.[19] One settlement worker who gave domestic science instruction observed, "The purpose in our work is to help those in our classes to learn what is the true American home ideal, and then do what we can to make it possible for them to realize it for themselves."[20] (Figure 13.1)

After 1914, governments on the local, state, and national level became increasingly involved in domestic housekeeping instruction, often linking it to the teaching of English.[21] This new offensive resulted in the swarming of "Home Teachers," "Visiting Housekeepers," and "Home Demonstration Agents" into communities bearing the message of the Housekeeping Center to those workers who had failed to patronize similar programs of their own accord. This stage in the domestic reform effort corresponded with more structured Americanization programs, the home economics movement, and the professionalization of social work.

Settlement workers further promoted middle-class styles through the didactic power of the house itself. Furnishing the settlement house interior became a self-conscious process for its residents. In a letter to her sister, a young Jane Addams exclaimed,

Madame Mason gave us an elegant old oak side-board . . . and we indulged in a set of heavy leather covered chairs and a 16" cut oak table. Our antique oak book case and my writing desk completes it.[22]

Figure 13.1
Illustrations to "Homemaking in a Model Flat" by Mabel Kittredge, *Charities and the Commons*, 4 November 1905, 176.

Edith Barrows, a settlement worker in Boston's South End House, recorded in her diary, "The pretty green sitting-room with its crackling fire and gay rugs and simple early American furniture is a good setting for all that transpires. I find that it has a spiritual and, I think, almost a physical reaction in the neighborhood."[23] Settlement workers hoped that community patrons would incorporate the styles observed at the house into the furnishing of their own homes (Figure 13.2).

Industries were also involved in the business of setting standards for workers' homes through company housing, welfare programs, and the creation of domestic-like spaces in the factory.

Companies sought to communicate middle-class values through housing provided for workers. Frequently, individual entrances, even in multiple or attached dwellings, sought to reinforce nuclear family privacy.[24] Interiors promoted the specialization of rooms in an effort to discourage the taking in of boarders and to enforce a middle-class pattern of living revolving around parlor, kitchen, dining room, and bedrooms.

Some companies offered employees welfare programs that also affirmed middle-class domestic standards. Amoskeag Mills' employee benefits, for example, included a Textile Club (established to compete with ethnic organizations), a Textile School, a Cooking School, and a Home Nursing Service.[25]

Within the factory, workers were frequently treated to domestic-like environments deliberately planned along middle-class esthetic lines. Employee lounges and lunchrooms were an innovation in the early twentieth century and frequently provided models for light, airy rooms with hardwood floors and simple furniture (Figure 13.3). Thus, McCormick Harvesting Machine Company hired a social worker to survey factories nationwide and recommend proper recreation, education, luncheon, and lounge facilities, which they proceeded to install.[26]

In the minds of the reformers, simple, mission-style furniture and colonial objects, associated with the agrarian world of the pre-industrial craftsman, seemed the obvious—and most appropriate—material arrangement for all Americans, particularly for industrial workers newly arrived from rural areas. And they tried with a vengeance to impose it.

Despite the missionary zeal of middle-class reformers, however, they did not succeed very well in communicating new standards for domestic interiors to workers. In part, they were responsible for their own failure through ineffective organizational techniques and flawed programs.[27]

Many reform programs, particularly those aimed at immigrant workers, suffered from the narrow perspective of the reformers. Model housing projects dependent on private investment put profits and demonstrable success above workers' housing needs.[28] Domestic science classes often were offered in high schools, which many working-class girls never attended, because they were busy instead contributing to their families' incomes. Settlement houses cut themselves off from many members of their potential communities by having few foreign language-speaking staff members. Native Americans and immigrant children

Figure 13.2
Interior of Hull House, Chicago, 1895. From *Hull House Maps and Papers* (New York: Crowell, 1895).

Figure 13.3
Recreation Room in the McCreary Store, Pittsburgh, Pennsylvania, c. 1907. By Lewis Hine. From *Women and the Trades*, by Elizabeth Beardsley Butler (New York, Russell Sage Foundation, 1909), p. 322.

were hence more likely to attend programs than foreign-born adults.[29] Reformers clearly did not convey as coherent a program as they intended.

But blaming the failure of the reforms to affect working-class people solely on reformer ineptitude deprives workers and their families of a role in opposing these middle-class values. While some workers obviously had little exposure to reform programs, evidence suggests that many workers in contact with them resisted in different ways. Some immigrant women, like those from Southern Italy, viewed the acceptance of any charity as a disgrace.[30] Immigrant husbands often opposed their wives attending activities outside the home, particularly in the evenings.[31] Other women avoided reformers' clubs and domestic science classes because they perceived condescension on the part of instructors, who often had low opinions of their students' abilities.[32] Some people suspected domestic science courses of attempting to make servants out of their daughters in order to solve middle-class America's "Servant Problem."[33]

Although many neighborhood people patronized settlement houses and other reformer establishments, they did so on their own terms, partaking of the programs and recreational facilities without taking the social message to heart.[34] Other working-class people were more outspoken in their rejection, at least among peers. Elizabeth Hasonovitz recounted a heated discussion about the YWCA's country place among the young women working with her in a garment industry factory.

Never again to them "charity pleasures!" . . . There is rules for everything—sleep, eat, wake up—all rules. We get to think we are nothing but rules. . . . Them charity institutions t'ink they do you a lot o' favors, but they don't, 'specially when you work for the rest of the expense, and it's still charity favor.

Why should you live at the Y.W.'s? I would never stay there, even if they kept me for nothing. . . . They keep charity homes for poor working-girls. Why don't they see that the working-girl gets paid properly for the work she is doing, and need not live in a charity home? Our rich employers give charity by underpaying us, for our money they get fame and praise—eh, if they only paid us what we deserved, we could get comfortable homes without their help; with our money they are kind and charitable.[35]

Some people made their objections known directly to the reformers. Miss Jane E. Robbin, M.D., reported that during her first year at the College Settlement another resident encountered a patient on a home visit who said "that she had had her breakfast, that she did not want anything, and that she did not like strange people poking around in her bureau drawer anyway."[36] Others used more tact but rejected the attentions of reformers nonetheless. A Boston settlement worker recalled her neighbors' response to a circulating collection of photographs of famous paintings:

South End House had a loan collection of photographs of paintings which were given to the House to use in acquainting our friends with great works of art. These were sent from tenement to tenement to stay for a period of time and then removed while others took their place. The "Holy Pictures," as all of the Madonnas were called, were always mildly welcomed, but the lack of color made them unattractive, and the "unholy" pictures were usually tucked away to await the visitor's return. Some of our earliest calls became very informal . . . when the visitor joined the whole family in a hunt, often ending by finding us all on our knees when the missing photographs were drawn from beneath the bed or bureau.[37]

More than working-class rejection of middle-class tastes, however, separated the worlds of the worker and the reformer. Workers' homes themselves hold the key to the nature and sources of their material preferences, apparently at odds with those held by the middle class. This conflict of value systems was powerfully perceived by a young participant in settlement-house programs when she was faced with furnishing her own home at marriage.

We had many opportunities to talk quite naturally of some of the problems of home-making and house-furnishing [wrote settlement worker Esther Barrows]. . . . The lack of plush and stuffed furniture [in our house] was a surprise to many, whose first thought would have been just that. One of our club girls who was about to be married sat down to discuss the matter in relation to her own new home. She seemed convinced by all the arguments brought forward to prove its undesirability from the point of view of hygiene and cleanliness. Months afterward she invited us to her home, much later than would have seemed natural, and as she greeted us rather fearfully she said, "Here it is, but you must remember you have had your plush days." Her small livingroom was overfilled by the inevitable "parlor set," while plush curtains hung at the windows and on either side of the door. The lesson learned by us from this incident was never to be forgotten.[38]

A commitment to a classless America, achievable through educational and environmental solutions to social problems, blinded settlement workers like Esther Barrows to the strength of workers' own cultures. Reformers had little conception of how deeply rooted these material values were in working-class life.[39]

THE WORKING CLASS BECOMES "AT HOME" IN URBAN AMERICA

Workers in this period had few options in selecting their housing. Whether home was an urban slum or a model tenement block, a milltown shack settlement or a company town, families frequently lived in substandard housing far below the quality that middle-class residents enjoyed and had few alternatives. Furthermore, workers found themselves forced into low-rent districts separated from middle-class residential neighborhoods. Proximity to other working-class people of similar job and income status typified workers' experience more than the ethnic isolation we commonly associate with working-class life. Often, ethnic enclaves were no more than islands of a few blocks within a working-class community.[40] Limitations of housing choices, however, may have encouraged workers to value interior spaces even more.

Within these working-class neighborhoods and homes, workers expressed a distinctive set of material values. An examination of attitudes toward home ownership; space allocation within the house or flat; the covering of the structural shell—floors, walls, and windows; furniture selection; and decorative details illuminate the meanings workers attached to the artifacts of their homes.

The view that workers should own their homes provided a rare convergence of opinion between reformers and working people, though each group advocated home ownership for different reasons. Some reformers felt that a home-owning working class would be more dependable and less radical, and thus America would be "preserved" as a classless society. Others hoped that meeting mortgage payments in America might discourage immigrants from sending money home and hence stem the tide of further immigration.[41] In short, reformers saw home ownership as a strategy for directing worker ambition along acceptable middle-class lines.

Workers, on the other hand, sought to purchase homes for reasons more consistent with their previous cultural experience than with American middle-class values.[42] In Russia, even poor Jews often had owned the rooms in which they lived.[43] Jews in many cases left Eastern Europe in response to Tsarist regulations prohibiting their ownership of property and interfering in their livelihoods as artisans, merchants, and businessmen.[44] For these immigrants, the flight to America was a way of resisting "peasantizing" forces. Recent work on Italian immigrants has shown that they, too, came to America hoping to preserve their traditional society and to resist efforts at making them laborers.[45] They viewed a sojourn in the States as a way of subsidizing the purchase of a home upon return to Italy.[46] Many Italians both in Europe and America sacrificed in order to leave their children a legacy of land, which supports David Riesman's theory that pre-industrial families trained and encouraged their children to "succeed them" rather than to "succeed" by rising in the social system.[47] In America, owning a home allowed Italians to uphold traditional community ties by renting apartments to their relatives or paesani, and in less urban areas, to grow the fresh vegetables necessary to maintain a traditional diet.[48] Furthermore, Slavic immigrants, property-less peasants in the old country, eagerly sought homes in America to satisfy long-standing ambitions.[49] Native American workers, moreover, descended from a tradition that equated private property ownership with full citizenship and promised all deserving, hard-working persons a piece of land. Thus, working-class people of many backgrounds sent mother and children to work, took in boarders, made the home a workshop, and sacrificed proper diet in order to save and buy a house, compromises too severe to substantiate some historians' claims that workers were merely pursuing upward social mobility toward middle-class goals.[50]

Once workers occupied purchased homes or rented flats, their attitudes toward the utilization of interior space diverged markedly from those of the middle class. Reformers advocated a careful allocation of domestic space to create sharp divisions between public and family interactions and to separate family members from one another within the house. Reformers often blamed working-class people for contributing to unnecessary overcrowding and violations of privacy by huddling in the kitchen, for example, while other rooms were left vacant.[51]

While the middle classes were better equipped with, and could more easily afford, housewide heating and lighting than the working classes, a difference of attitudes toward home living was more at issue. Many people from rural backgrounds were used to sharing a bedroom—and sometimes even a bed—with other family members.[52] And for those working people whose homes were also their work places, the middle-class ethos of the home as an environment detached from the economic world was particularly inappropriate. Jewish, Irish, Italian, and Slavic women frequently took in boarders and laundry, did homework, and assisted in family stores often adjoining their living quarters. For former farmers and self-employed artisans and merchants, this integration of home and work seemed normal.[53] Among Southern Italian women, doing tenement homework in groups sustained "cortile" (shared housekeeping) relationships endangered in the American environment of more isolated homes.[54]

The reformer ideal of the kitchen as an efficient laboratory servicing other parts of the house found little acceptance among workers. Even when workers had a parlor, they often preferred to socialize in their kitchens. Mary Antin fondly recalled frequent visits in her married sister's kitchen in East Boston where after dinner dishes were washed,

Frieda took out her sewing, and I took a book; and the lamp was between us, shining on the table, on the large brown roses on the wall, on the green and brown diamonds of the oil cloth on the floor . . . on the shining stove in the corner. It was such a pleasant kitchen—such a cosy, friendly room—that when Frieda and I were left alone I was perfectly happy just to sit there. Frieda had a beautiful parlor, with plush chairs and a velvet carpet and gilt picture frames; but we preferred the homely, homelike kitchen.[55]

When investigators surveyed working-class people for their housing preferences in 1920, most still rejected small kitchens or kitchenettes in favor of ones large enough for dining.[56] A second generation Italian married daughter, returning to her mother's tenement flat kitchen at about this date, appreciated its superiority over her own more modern one.

It was a room to live in and to work in and to eat in. Octavia missed it. Her immaculate Bronx apartment had a table of porcelain with chromium chairs. The sink glistened white as a wall. Here was the debris of life.[57]

Workers kept their old-world hearths burning bright in their new American homes.[58]

Reformers applauded all attempts by workers to create parlors in their homes. They viewed such spaces as evidence of civilization, self-respect, and acceptance of American middle-class standards.[59] A home with a parlor was more likely, they felt, to instill the middle-class image of the family as an emotional, sentimental unit. Margaret Byington's investigation of Homestead workers' homes reflected this bias:

It has been said that the first evidence of the growth of the social instinct in any family is the desire to have a parlor. In Homestead this ambition has in many cases been attained. Not every family, it is true, can afford one, yet among my English-speaking acquaintances even the six families each of whom lived in three rooms attempted to have at least the semblance of a room devoted to sociability.[60]

Worker interest in creating parlor space at home varied, though often it correlated with occupational status. People who did little income-producing work at home, such as Jews and native Americans, most often established sitting rooms. Among Italians and Slavs, where men frequently had low status jobs and women brought work into the home, the combination living room/kitchen, so similar to their European homes, survived the longest. When George Kracha left the Homestead steel mills and established his own butcher business, his home soon reflected his change in status in a way that his neighbors all recognized:

They still lived in Cherry Alley and much as they had always lived, though Elena no longer kept boarders. . . . Kracha had bought new furniture and the room adjoining the kitchen, where the girls had slept, was now a parlor. Its chief glories were a tassled couch, a matching chair with an ingenious footrest that slid out like a drawer from inside the chair itself, and an immense oil lamp suspended from the ceiling by gilt chains. The lampshade was made of pieces of colored glass leaded together like a church window; it seemed to fill the room and was one of the most impressive objects Cherry Lane had ever seen. On the walls were colored lithographs in elaborate gilt frames of the Holy Family and of the Virgin with a dagger through her exposed heart. Drying ribbons of Easter palm were stuck behind them. On the floor was flowered oilcloth.[61]

Kracha's adoption of a parlor, however, did not entail acceptance of middle-class modes of furnishing. Rather, his parlor presented an elaborate collage of traditional and technological symbols.

Nevertheless, reformers were not mistaken in recognizing a relationship between the presence of a parlor and some acculturation to middle-class ways. The expression of sentiment toward family and community through consumption involved in "parlorization" could indicate a favorable nod to middle-class values. For many workers, though, their usage of kitchen and parlor still respected long-established patterns of sociability. As Mary Antin's comment indicated, people with parlors did not necessarily abandon a preference for the kitchen. Likewise, workers' parlors frequently doubled as sleeping rooms at night.[62] Often when workers accommodated middle-class concepts of space in their homes, they imbued them with different social expectations. For example, Byington noted that even when a native American worker in Homestead had a dining room, "it did not live up to its name."

In five-room houses we find an anomaly known as the "dining room." Though a full set of dining room furniture, sideboard, table and dining chairs, are usually in evidence, they are rarely used at meals. The family sewing is frequently done there, the machine standing in the corner by the window; and sometimes, too, the ironing, to escape the heat of the kitchen; but rarely is the room used for breakfast, dinner or supper. The kitchen is the important room of the house.[63]

Whereas the middle-class home provided a setting for a wide range of complex interactions related to work, family, and community, and therefore required distinctions between private and public space, workers conceived of home as a private realm distinct from the public world. Because workers only invited close friends and family inside, the kitchen provided an appropriate setting for most exchange. Relationships with more distant acquaintances took place in the neighborhood—on the street or within shops, saloons, or churches. The transference of these traditional patterns of socializing from an intimate pre-industrial community to the city had the impact of increasing the isolation of the working-class home. It is not surprising, therefore, that historians have noted that among many immigrant groups, the American home became a haven as it had never been in the old world.[64]

When addressing working-class people, reformers justified the new esthetic primarily in terms of cleanliness; specifically they promoted a simple house shell free of "dust-collecting" carpets, drapes, and wallpaper. The 1906 Tuberculosis Exhibition that toured the nation made this point dramatically with a life-sized model contrasting a disease-breeding room with a "proper" interior. Texts in Yiddish, Italian, and English explained why bare floors, uncurtained windows, and painted walls were preferable to carpets, drapes, and wallpaper.[65] For most working-class people, however, these decorative treatments were signs of taste and status that they hated to forsake. In almost all European rural societies, as in comparable places in America, only upper-class people had carpets and curtains.[66] Workers embraced the accessibility of these products in urban America with delight.[67] In her autobiography, Mary Antin significantly remarked, "we had *achieved* a carpet since Chelsea days"[68] Given alien and institutional-looking housing facades, curtained windows were often a family's only way to make a personal statement to the world passing by.[69] Wallpaper—the worst demon of all to reformers—was for workers a privilege possible with prosperity and a relief from otherwise dull home walls. The behavior of one family occupying company housing that prohibited wallpaper near U.S. Steel's Gary, Indiana, plant spoke for many others:

"If you'll give us the colors we want, Sophie will do the painting herself." This broken up into foreign-sounding English, ended the parley with the company decorator. . . . And in the "box" occupied by her family she had her way. Outside it remained like all the rest in the row, but indoors, with stencil designs, such as she had learned to make at school, she painted the walls with borders at the top and panels running down to the floor.[70]

This young girl replicated in paint the borders and backgrounds of wallpaper design; though learned in school, this long-standing form of rural folk art satisfied the esthetic tastes and status needs of her family (Figure 13.4).

Workers' selection of furniture perhaps best demonstrates their struggle to satisfy both traditional and new expectations with products available on the mass market. The middle-class preference for colonial-inspired natural wood furniture, built-ins, and antiseptic iron bedsteads satisfied neither of these needs.

As indicated earlier by Mabel Kittredge's despair in her *Housekeeping Notes* at "cheap" and "ugly" sideboards, workers valued case pieces like bureaus, chiffoniers, and buffets. This preference evolved out of a long tradition of dowry chests and precious wardrobes, often the only substantial furniture in rural homes. Workers, however, did not necessarily consider their acquisition of such furnishings in urban America a conscious perpetuation of traditional material values. An uncomprehending settlement worker noted that

There were the Dipskis, who displayed a buffet among other new possessions, and on the top of it rested a large cut-glass punch bowl. Mrs Dipski said proudly, "And so I become American," as she waved her hand toward the huge piece of furniture, which took an inordinately large place in her small room.[71]

While reformers counseled against unhealthy wood bed frames as vermin-infested and expensive, feather bedding for causing overheating of the body, and fancy linens as unsanitary, working-class people sought to bring all three items into their homes.[72] Byington found a "high puffy bed with one feather tick to sleep on and another to cover" typical of native American homes in Homestead.[73] An observer in Lawrence, Massachusetts, in 1912 described the interior of an Italian mill-worker's home as boasting "pleasant vistas of spotless beds rising high to enormous heights and crowned with crochet-edged pillows."[74] (Figure 13.5.)

Immigrants carried feather bedding with them on the long trek to America more frequently than any other single item.[75] Antin recalled her Russian neighbor's warnings before the family departed for the United States.

In America they sleep on hard mattresses, even in winter. Haveh Mirel, Yachne the dressmaker's daughter, who emigrated to New York two years ago, wrote her mother that she got up from childbed with sore sides, because she had no featherbed.[76]

Jews, Italians, Slavs, and most other groups shared a native experience which prized feather bedding and viewed "the bed"—unveiled at marriage—as an emotional symbol of future family happiness.[77] The bed was the dominant feature of most peasant homes, often overpowering all other furniture, which usually was very minimal. Elizabeth Hasonovitz nostalgically remembered her mother in Russia, "bending over a boxful of goose feather, separating the down, preparing pillows for her daughters' future homes."[78] Italian marriage rituals pre-

Figure 13.4
"Where Some of the Surplus Goes," 1907. By Lewis Hine. From *Homestead: Households of a Mill Town* by Margaret Byington (New York: Russell Sage Foundation, 1910).

Figure 13.5
"Finishing Pants," c. 1900. By Jacob Riis. The Museum of the City of New York. Used with permission.

scribed that the bride's trousseau would provide hand-sewn, heavily embroidered linens along with the marital bed. Pride often produced beds so high that a stool was needed to climb into them.[79]

At least for Italians, the bed played a part in the rituals of death as well. While in Italian villages an elaborate funeral bed commonly was carried into the public square, in America, Italian families laid out their dead ceremoniously at home.[80]

The embellished bed, then, was an important family symbol of birth, marriage, and death, not an object to abandon easily.

We have seen throughout this chapter that workers' homes were crowded with plush, upholstered furniture, a taste that may have emerged out of valuing fluffy, elaborately decorated beds. As the parlor appeared on the home scene, workers brought traditional bed-associated standards to their newly acquired and prized possessions. Well aware of this working-class market for Victorian-style furniture, Grand Rapids furniture factories produced their cheapest lines in styles no longer fashionable among middle-class consumers.[81]

Since domestic reformers were promoting a simpler esthetic at the turn of the century, they denounced workers' taste for ornamentation. Photographs of working-class homes nevertheless reveal the persistence of abundant images on the walls (if only cheap prints, torn-out magazine illustrations and free merchant calendars), objects on tabletops, and layering in fabric and fancy paper of surface areas such as mantles, furniture, and cabinet shelves. One three-room Slavic home in Jersey City was typical of the attention to detail common among the working class:

The walls are hung with gorgeous prints of many-hued saints, their gilt frames often hanging edge to edge so that they form a continuous frieze around the walls. This mantle is covered with lace paper and decorated with bright-colored plates and cups, and gorgeous bouquets of homemade paper flowers are massed wherever bureaus or shelves give space for vases. Gayly figured cotton curtains at the windows and in doorways complete a bright and pleasing picture and numerous canaries in cages—I have found as many as four in a single kitchen—lend vivacity to the scene.[82]

If framed pictures in the kitchen upset reformer Mabel Kittredge, what would she have said about live canaries?

Pre-industrial experience encouraged workers to make creative use of the abundant printed images available in American cities. Farm people who had coveted scarce pictures to cover their walls were overwhelmed by the sheer number of visual images available at low or even no cost.[83] In its campaign to rectify tenement conditions contributing to disease, the Committee for the Prevention of Tuberculosis of the New York Charity Organization exploited this appetite for pictures by printing advice about consumption prevention on the margin of posters depicting sentimental scenes. A committee agent would call on Italian families, explain the dangers lurking in their household habits, and offer them a picture of a Venetian landscape.[84]

Pictures and objects with religious significance dominated homes of workers of all ethnic groups. A housing investigator recorded the emotion and pride toward this art expressed by black residents of Washington, D.C.'s alley houses.

Mrs. Keefe, pointing to a forbidding chromo of a bleeding Christ with His Crown of thorns, declares that this is her "favo-right" picture and she "jes likes to set an' look at it—coz it's so natchral!"[85]

Others cherished their cheap, store-bought prints of Christ before Pilate and da Vinci's Last Supper.[86] Even Stanley Behrman, a Jewish boy from Worcester, Massachusetts, vividly remembered the engravings of "Jewish saints from the Middle Ages" hanging in his childhood home, the only "family portraits" he could claim.[87]

In Catholic homes, people often assembled home shrines upon their mantle shelves and bureau tops, at times combining traditional religious symbols with newly purchased secular objects. A New York social worker described the Morelli family's iconographic display.

Over the mantelpiece hung a large, shiny photograph of the last baby lying in its casket . . . and pictures of the royal family, the Pope, the Saints, and the Holy Virgin; under this last a candle burned, an offering for Tony's return (missing son).[88]

Carla Bianco recalled visiting the Brooklyn home of an elderly Italian woman from Ciocciaria who had placed a cheap little Statue of Liberty sculpture, which she called "Santa Liberata," next to that of the Madonna of Montevergine on her bureau; framing both were a perennial lamp and artificial flowers.[89]

The fabric valance which appears in almost every photograph of a working-class interior demonstrates how a traditional symbol took on new applications in the American environment of industrial textile manufacture (Figure 13.6). In cultures such as the Italian, for example, where people treasured the elaborate bed, they adorned it with as much decorative detailing as possible. In fact, it was often the only object warranting such art and expense in the home. A visitor to Sicily in 1905 shared with his travelogue readers a peek into a typical home where

you are greeted by a bed, good enough for a person with a thousand a year, of full double width, with ends of handsomely carved walnut wood or massive brass. The counterpane which sweeps down to the floor is either hand-knitted, of enormous weight, or made of strips of linen joined together with valuable lace, over which is thrown the yellow quilt so handy for decoration. The show pillows are even finer, being smaller.[90]

Under this spread, women fastened a piece of embroidered linen in a deep frill to cover any part of the bed's frame that might show. Even when families could afford attractive, wood frame bedsteads, they still used this "turnialettu," or valance, its original purpose forgotten.[91] In America, where fabric was cheap, the valance of gathered fabric found even more applications, adorning every

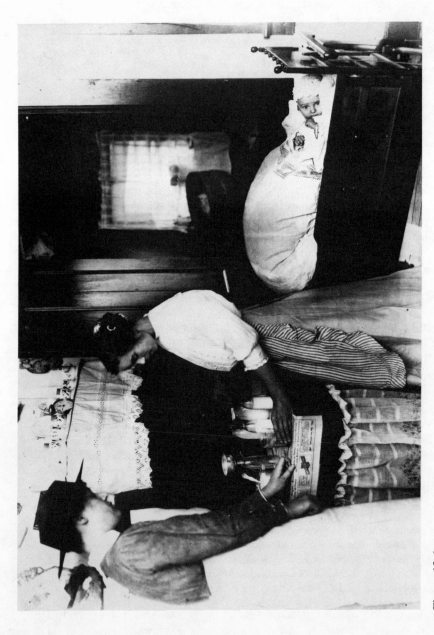

Figure 13.6
Infant Welfare Society Nurse with Immigrant Mother and Baby, c. 1910-1920, Chicago Historical Society. Used with permission.

possible surface and exposed area; in the 1930s Phyllis Williams even discovered valances over washing machines in second-generation Italian-American homes.[92] Fabric was draped and decoratively placed in a multitude of other ways as well. Thus a French-Canadian woman who ran a boarding house for shoe factory workers in Lynn inappropriately adorned the inexpensive craftsman-style Morris Chairs in her cluttered parlor with antimacassars, an affront to any Arts and Crafts devotee (Figure 13.7).

The reformer strategy of trying to change working-class values through the women of the family, if not successful, at least was astute, though for reasons reformers might not have understood. Usually reformers argued that they should aim programs at the immigrant woman because she was the least acculturated member of the foreign-born family, since she was removed from school or a job. While in many ways this was true, the working-class woman, as both keeper of traditional values and the family's chief agent of consumption, orchestrated cultural transitions within the home. By bringing cultural artifacts into the new urban environment, by handling the family's purchases of new items, and by transmitting traditional values to her daughters through the example of her own compromises, the immigrant woman was a powerful mediator between an old and new world.

Women, particularly among immigrant families, transported familiar objects to the new homesite. The image of the newly disembarked immigrant woman loaded down with bundles of clothes, pots, and featherbeds often recurs in literature and photographs.[93] Wooden chests bearing a woman's dowry frequently accompanied her on the train or boat, soon finding a place as furniture in her new home.[94] In *Call It Sleep*, David's mother introduced an American-raised son to her Austrian homeland by purchasing a ten-cent landscape picture from a pushcar vendor.[95]

Shopping in the new neighborhood was primarily a woman's task and offered her the opportunity to shepherd the family through a cultural transition. In almost all ethnic groups, husband and children turned over their earnings to mother in order for her to pay the bills. Mothers, then, consumed in behalf of their households. As studies of the installment buying practices of working-class families show, the major role in decision-making and managing payments fell to the woman, who stretched the monthly budget to cover the costs of new curtains, a piano, a sewing machine, or a sofa.[96]

Mothers passed on to their daughters both cultural traditions and a model of adaptability within an untraditional environment. When working mother and daughter had little time to prepare marriage linens, mother invented compromises without letting the tradition die. A Russian immigrant girl recounted,

[For my trousseau], here is what happened. Mothers of that era have the peddlers. The peddler would come in the house. She would take six sheets, tablecloths, pay out fifty cents a week. You bought everything on payment. So when I got married, I got six sheets, some pillowcases, tablecloths.[97]

Figure 13.7
"The Window Side of Miss K's Parlour at Lynn, Mass." c. 1903. From *The Woman Who Toils: Being the Experiences of Two Gentlewomen as Factory Girls* by Mrs. John Van Worst and Marie Van Vorst (New York: Doubleday, Page & Company, 1903).

Women also adapted traditional marriage customs in order to meet the great expenses and desires of their daughters in establishing new homes. The Slavic wedding custom of paying to dance with the bride, originally intended to cover the cost of the wedding, in America was expected to include the costs of furnishing a home as well.[98] The next generation of wives thus went into marriage equipped with a material culture and set of values inherited from the meeting of two worlds.

While workers brought distinctive cultural heritages to bear on the furnishing of their urban-American homes, much less variety in material preferences resulted than one might have expected. Common pre-industrial small town experience, limits to the preferred and affordable merchandise available for purchase, and mixed ethnic worker communities seem to have encouraged a surprisingly consistent American working-class material ethos that was distinct from that of the middle class. The speed with which a particular working-class family forged a material transition to industrial life depended on numerous factors, among them the intent and length of the family's stay in urban America, and prior financial resources, and economic and social experience. Those who had previously encountered middle-class homes carried a mental model that may have influenced their furnishing choices once they achieved a degree of prosperity. Furthermore, an individual's commercial sophistication surely affected material adjustment.

At one extreme, immigrant Chicago stockyard worker Antanas Kaztauskis attributed many of his adjustment problems in America to his inexperience with money. He recalled the significance of a scene in his parents' log house in Lithuania when he first considered emigration. His "old mother sat near the wide fireplace, working her brown spinning wheel, with which she made cloth for our shirts and coats and pants," and his old father was having his boots repaired by an itinerant shoemaker. When the shoemaker urged the couple to send their son to America, his mother cried out, "Leave us alone—You leave us! We need no money—we trade our things for the things we need at the store—we have all we need—leave us alone!"[99] When Antanas arrived in Chicago, he met more experienced Lithuanians at his boarding house who echoed his mother's warning: "What you need is money."[100] For Antanas, the next four years were a trial of learning to live in this peculiar new world.

At the other extreme, Marcus Eli Ravage boarded with Russian relatives—former merchants—upon his arrival in New York who within a short three months had created a tenement flat that epitomized the transitional ideal.

During the day my relatives kept up the interesting fiction of an apartment with specialized divisions. Here was the parlor with its sofa and mirror and American rocking-chairs, then came the dining room with another sofa called a lounge, a round table, and innumerable chairs; then the kitchen with its luxurious fittings in porcelain and metal; then the young ladies' room, in which there was a bureau covered with quantities of odoriferous bottles and powder-boxes and other mysteries; and, last of all, Mrs. Segal's and the children's room. I remember how overwhelmed I was with this impressive luxury when I arrived. But between nine and ten o'clock in the evening this imposing structure suddenly crumbled away in the most amazing fashion. The apartment suddenly became a camp. The sofas opened up and revealed their true character. The bureau lengthened out shamelessly, careless of its daylight pretensions. Even the wash-tubs, it turned out, were a miserable sham. The carved dining-room chairs arranged themselves into rows that faced each other like dancers in a cotillion.

. . . The two young ladies' room was not, I learned, a young ladies' room at all; it was a female dormitory. The sofa in the parlor alone held four sleepers, of whom I was one. . . . I counted no fewer than nine male inmates in that parlor alone one night. . . . The pretended children's room was occupied by a man and his family of four, whom he had recently brought over, although he, with ambitions for a camp of his own, did not remain long.[101]

Ravage's relatives' ability to create this model transitional flat likely was related to their skills and tastes as Old World storekeepers; they probably arrived with a little surplus cash as well.

Once workers achieved a certain basic level of economic stability, their homes began to reflect this distinctive material ethos. While working-class people at the time may not have viewed their choices in reified terms, their set of preferences seems not arbitrary but a recurrent, symbolic pattern; not a simple emulation of middle-class Victorian standards with a time lag due to delayed prosperity, but rather a creative compromise forged in making a transition between two very different social and economic worlds. This working-class ethos of material values, inspired by rural values and reinforced within the urban neighborhood, departed in almost every way from esthetics favored by the middle class and promoted by the domestic reformers. Ironically, while middle-class people viewed the appearance of working-class homes as unsanitary, tasteless, and un-American, workers in fact felt that their new material world represented acculturation to American urban ways. Through the purchase of mass-produced objects, they struggled to come to terms with this industrial society.

Material acculturation occurred as an individual or family made peace between traditional and New World needs. While many workers must have realized their home decor differed from the styles promoted by the middle class, they still felt they had adapted to their new environment and had advanced far beyond their former conditions. While the middle-class person and reformer could not see it, the working-class homes steeped in comfort and covers stood as a symbol of being at home in industrial America.

At the turn of the century, the homes of both the middle class and the working class reflected the transitions in their respective social experience. On the one hand, middle-class people rejected Victorian decor for a simpler, more "American" esthetic, which they tried to impose on workers. On the other hand, the working class found in the ornate Victorian furnishing style an appropriate transition to industrial life. The "Victorian solution" was not an inevitable stage working people had to pass through, but a circumstance of need finding an available product. Furniture in the Victorian style persisted even as the Colonial Revival and Arts and Crafts dominated middle-class tastes. The old style well suited workers' rural-based material values, while satisfying their desire to adapt to mass produced goods, just as it had for the middle class several generations earlier. The contrast in middle-class and working-class tastes in this period suggests that working-class culture indeed had an integrity of its own.

Many studies of immigration have implied that people eventually were fully acculturated. Research in domestic interiors, however, suggests that vestiges of traditions may have survived in the home and that the decor of ethnic Americans may have remained distinctive. For example, Phyllis Williams's description of second-generation Italian homes in New York during the 1930s, Herbert Gans's investigation of second generation Italian homes in Boston during the 1950s and Carla Bianco's depiction of second- and third-generation Italian homes in Roseto, Pennsylvania, during the mid-1960s all illustrate the extent to which the transitional material ethos was still more significant for many Italians than emulation of contemporary middle-class standards.[102]

Of course, these interiors remained distinctive not just in ethnic terms but in class ones as well. This study has begun to explore the way that immigrant cultures transformed into a working-class culture and stood apart from middle-class values. In studying working-class material life in the 1950s and 1960s, Lee Rainwater and David Coplovitz have discovered similar patterns in working-class domestic values: a preference for plush and new furnishings over used ones; a taste for modern products, such as appliances; the valuing of the interior over the exterior appearance of the house; and a common conception of home as a private haven for the working-class family.[103] While these sociologists do not attempt to explain the historical development of material choices, connections to workers' homes in the 1885–1915 period are striking and suggest the need for further investigation of the intervening period.

The decades discussed in this essay, when waves of new workers were integrated into an expanding industrial society, may have served as the formative stage for the development of a working-class culture. We have seen how the transitional interior created by workers during this period, as they adjusted to twentieth-century American life, satisfied some ambivalence toward the urban, industrial world. Within this material compromise, traditional cultural values and new consumer benefits could coexist. If workers' homes throughout the twentieth century continued to reflect the attributes of this initial transition, as the studies of Rainwater, Coplovitz, Williams, Gans, and Bianco tentatively suggest, we may have evidence that contradictions still lie at the core of the American working-class identity. Workers may have reified and passed down this transitional style, or a contradictory attitude toward industrial society may continue to inform their domestic selections. In either case, working-class material values have emerged through both resistance and adaptation to the social environment and have remained distinct from those of the middle class. The chief legacy of this contradiction may be a worker population that on the one hand boasts a unique and discernible material culture and on the other hand does not identify itself forthrightly as a working class.

NOTES

1. See Lee Rainwater, *Workingman's Wife: Her Personality, World and Life Style* (New York: Oceana Publications, Inc., 1959); Lee Rainwater, "Fear and the House as Haven in the Lower Class," *Journal of the American Institute of Planners* 32 (January 1966), 23–31; Dennis Chapman, *The Home and Social Status* (London: Routledge and Kegan Paul; New York: Grove Press, 1955); Marc Fried, *The World of the Urban Working Class* (Cambridge: Harvard University Press, 1973); Michael Young and Peter Willmott, *The Symmetrical Family: A Study of Work and Leisure in the London Region* (London: Routlege and Kegan Paul, 1973).

2. Robert J. Lifton, "Woman as Knower," in Lifton, ed., *The Woman in America* (Boston: Beacon Press, 1971), pp. 27–51.

3. All historians who study "the working class" struggle with how to define it. While I am convinced that the experience of class is complex, I will adopt a simple definition for the purposes of this chapter and use "working class" to refer to skilled and unskilled workers. This chapter will explore the extent to which people in the manual trades developed a distinctive material culture.

4. Herbert Gutman, *Work, Culture and Society in Industrializing America* (New York: Vintage Books, 1977), pp. 3–78.

5. Siegfried Gideon, *Mechanization Takes Command: A Contribution to Anonymous History* (New York: W.W. Norton and Co., 1969), p. 365.

6. John Ruskin, "Of Queen's Gardens," *Sesame and Lilies* (London: Smith, Elder, 1865; New York: Metropolitan Publishing Co., 1871), quoted in Gwendolyn Wright, "Making the Model Home: Domestic Architecture and Cultural Conflict in Chicago, 1873–1913" (Ph.D. diss., University of California, Berkeley, 1978), p. 21.

7. Gideon, *Mechanization*, p. 384.

8. See Sam Bass Warner, Jr., *Streetcar Suburbs: The Process of Growth in Boston, 1870–1900* (Cambridge, Mass.: Harvard University Press, 1962) and photographs of newly developed areas in almost every town and city in America during this period.

9. William B. Rhoads, *The Colonial Revival* (New York: Garland Publishing, Inc., 1977).

10. Barbara Ehrenreich and Deirdre English, "The Manufacture of Housework," *Socialist Revolution* 26 (October-December 1975), 5–40.

11. C. Chester Lane, "Hingham Arts and Crafts," in Rhoads, *Colonial Revival*, p. 367. Even though American Arts and Crafts designers like Stickley were inspired by William Morris's English Arts and Crafts Movement, their debt to this source did not receive much attention in America. Stickley conveniently equated the American colonial experience with the medieval heritage being revived by the British.

12. Rhoads, *Colonial Revival*, p. 416.

13. Ibid., p. 207.

14. Ibid., p. 517.

15. Ibid., p. 524; see also Barbara Solomon, *Ancestors and Immigrants* (Cambridge, Mass.: Harvard University Press, 1956) on the restrictionist ideology of these Colonial Revival patrons.

16. Rhoads, *Colonial Revival*, p. 390.

17. *The Craftsman Magazine* (July 1903) in Rhoads, *Colonial Revival*, p. 285; also pp. 412, 832.

18. Gustav Stickley, "Als Ik Kan: 'Made in America' " in Rhoads, *Colonial Revival*, p. 488.

19. Mabel Kittredge, *Housekeeping Notes* (Boston: Whitcomb and Barrows, 1911), pp. 1–13.

20. College Settlements Association, *Annual Report 1902* (New York, 1902), 37.

21. Sophonsiba Breckinridge, *New Homes for Old* (New York: Harper and Brothers, 1921), p. 259.

22. Jane Addams, Letter to Sarah Alice Addams Haldeman, 13 September 1889. Courtesy of Jane Addams Paper Project, Hull House, Chicago, Illinois.

23. Esther Barrows, *Neighbors All: A Settlement Notebook* (Boston: Houghton, Mifflin, 1929), p. 37.

24. Roy Lubove, *The Progressives and the Slums: Tenement House Reform in New York City, 1890–1917* (Pittsburgh: University of Pittsburgh Press, 1962), p. 163.

25. Tamara Hareven and Randolph Langenbach, *Amoskeag: Life and Work in an American Factory City* (New York: Pantheon Books, 1978), p. 22.

26. Gerd Korman, *Industrialization, Immigrants and Americanization* (Madison: University of Wisconsin Press, 1967), p. 88.

27. See Maxine Seller, "The Education of the Immigrant Woman, 1900 to 1935," *Journal of Urban History* 4 (May 1978), 307–30; John Daniels, *Americanization via the Neighborhood* (New York: Harper and Brothers, 1920), pp. 174–222; Breckinridge, *New Homes*, pp. 280–98.

28. See Graham Taylor, *Satellite Cities* (New York: D. Appleton, 1915; New York: Arno Press, 1970); E.R.L. Gould, *The Housing of the Working People* (Washington: Government Printing Office, 1895); Robert Paine, "Housing Conditions in Boston," *Annals of the American Academy of Political and Social Science* 20, pp. 121–36; Morris Knowles, *Industrial Housing* (New York: McGraw Hill Book Company, Inc., 1920); Breckinridge, *New Homes*.

29. See Seller, "Education of the Immigrant Woman;" Daniels, *Americanization via the Neighborhood*.

30. Viriginia Yans-McLaughlin, *Family and Community: Italian Immigrants in Buffalo 1880–1930* (Ithaca: Cornell University Press, 1977), p. 134.

31. Ibid., p. 148.

32. See Seller, "Education of the Immigrant Woman."

33. See Lee Meriwether, *The Tramp at Home* (New York: Harper and Brothers, 1889), p. 66, for discussion of working girls' attitudes about being domestic servants.

34. Herbert Gans, *The Urban Villagers: Group and Class in the Life of Italian Americans* (New York: The Free Press, 1962), pp. 152–53.

35. Elizabeth Hasonovitz, *One of Them* (Boston: Houghton, Mifflin, 1918), p. 228.

36. Jane E. Robbins, M.D., "The First Year at the College Settlement," *The Survey* 27 (24 February 1912), 1801.

37. Barrows, *Neighbors*, pp. 7–8.

38. Ibid., pp. 40–41.

39. Here and elsewhere in this chapter, "material values" refers to preferences in the selection and arrangement of objects of material culture.

40. See Stephan Thernstrom and Peter R. Knights, "Men in Motion: Some Data and Speculations about Urban Population Mobility in Nineteenth Century America," *Journal of Interdisciplinary History* (Autumn 1970), 7–35; Humbert S. Nelli, *Italians in Chicago, 1880–1930* (New York: Oxford University Press, 1970), p. 25; Madelon Powers, "Faces Along the Bar: The Saloon in Working-class Life, 1890–1920," (manuscript, Dept. of History, University of California, Berkeley, 1979). Powers has found that "neighborhood saloons" drew together mixed ethnic groups living in the same residential areas.

41. Rhoads, *Colonial Revival*, p. 716; Lubove, *Progressives*, pp. 23–24.

42. James Henretta, "The Study of Social Mobility," *Labor History* 18 (Spring 1977), 165–78.

43. Philip Cowen, *Memories of an American Jew* (New York: International Press, 1932), p. 231.

44. Se Moses Rischin, *The Promised City* (Cambridge, Mass.: Harvard University Press, 1962), p. 22; Eli Ginzberg and Hyman Berman, eds., *The American Worker in the Twentieth Century: A History through Autobiographies* (New York: The Free Press, 1963), p. 12.

45. John Briggs, *An Italian Passage: Italians in Three American Cities, 1890–1930* (New Haven: Yale University Press, 1978), pp. 11, 272.

46. Pascal D'Angelo, *Son of Italy* (New York: Macmillan, 1924), p. 50.

47. David Riesman, *The Lonely Crowd: A Study of the Changing American Character* (New Haven: Yale University Press, 1950), pp. 40, 17–18, quoted in James Henretta, "Families and Farms: Mentalité in Pre-Industrial America," *William and Mary Quarterly* 35 (January 1978), p. 30.

48. Phyllis Williams, *South Italian Folkways in Europe and America* (New Haven: Yale University Press, 1938), p. 50.

49. Peter Roberts, *The Anthracite Coal Communities* (New York: Macmillan, 1904), p. 43.

50. See Stephan Thernstrom, *Poverty and Progress: Social Mobility in a Nineteenth Century City* (New York: Atheneum, 1971), pp. 136–37, 155–56; John Modell, "Patterns of Consumption, Acculturation, and Family Income Strategies in Late Nineteenth Century America," in *Family and Population in Nineteenth-Century America*, ed. Tamara Hareven and Maris Vinovskis (Princeton: Princeton University Press, 1978), pp. 206–40; Yans-McLaughlin, *Family and Community*, pp. 47–48, 175–77, for sacrifices made toward buying a house.

51. Edith Abbott and Sophonisba Breckinridge, *The Tenements of Chicago, 1908–1935* (Chicago: University of Chicago Press, 1936), pp. 263–64.

52. D'Angelo, *Son of Italy*, p. 5.

53. See Sydelle Kramer and Jenny Masur, eds., *Jewish Grandmothers* (Boston: Beacon Press, 1976); Mary Antin, *Promised Land* (Boston: Houghton, Mifflin, 1912; Sentry Edition, 1969), p. 195.

54. Donna Gabaccia, "Housing and Household Work in Sicily and New York, 1890–1910," (manuscript, Dept. of History, University of Michigan, Ann Arbor, n.d.), p. 18.

55. Antin, *Promised Land*, p. 337.

56. Knowles, *Industrial Housing*, p. 295.

57. Mario Puzo, *The Fortunate Pilgrim* (New York: Atheneum, 1965), p. 144.

58. Donald Cole, *Immigrant City: Lawrence, Massachusetts, 1845–1921* (Chapel Hill: University of North Carolina Press, 1963), p. 107.

59. Robert Woods, *The City Wilderness* (Boston: Houghton, Mifflin, 1898; New York: Arno Press, 1970), p. 102.

60. Margaret Byington, *Homestead: The Households of a Mill Town* (New York: Russell Sage Foundation, 1910), p. 55.

61. Thomas Bell, *Out of This Furnace* (Boston: Little, Brown, 1941), p. 62.

62. See Rose Cohen, *Out of the Shadow* (New York, 1918), pp. 196–97, quoted in Judith E. Smith, "Our Own Kind: Family and Community Networks in Providence," *Radical History Review* 17 (Spring 1978), 113; William Elsing, "Life in New York

Tenement Houses,'' in Robert Woods, *Poor in Great Cities* (New York: Charles Scribner's Sons, 1895), p. 50.

63. Byington, *Homestead*, p. 56.

64. Williams, *South Italian Folkways*, p. 17; Yans-McLaughlin, *Family and Community*, p. 223; Nelli, *Italians in Chicago*, p. 6.

65. Gaylord S. White, "With the Traveling Tuberculosis Exhibition," *The Survey* 16 (23 June 1906), 382.

66. Inventory Research at Old Sturbridge Village on western Massachusetts homes, 1790–1840, revealed a similar pattern: carpets and curtains were rare and precious. Research Dept., Old Sturbridge Village, Sturbridge, Massachusetts.

67. Carla Bianco, *The Two Rosetos* (Bloomington: Indiana University Press, 1974), p. 14; Williams, *South Italian Folkways*, p. 43.

68. Antin, *Promised Land*, p. 274 (emphasis is mine).

69. Robert Roberts, *The Classic Slum* (London: Penguin Books, 1971), p. 33.

70. Taylor, *Satellite Cities*, p. 194.

71. Barrows, *Neighbors*, p. 70.

72. *Reports of the President's Homes Commission* (Washington: Government Printing Office, 1909), p. 117.

73. Byington, *Homestead*, in Ginzberg, *American Worker*, p. 46.

74. Cole, *Immigrant City*, p. 107.

75. See Thomas Wheeler, ed., *The Immigrant Experience* (New York: Dial Press, 1971; London: Penguin Books, 1977), pp. 20, 155; Cowen, *Memories*, p. 233.

76. Antin, *Promised Land*, p. 164.

77. Williams, *South Italian Folkways*, p. 86.

78. Hasonovitz, *One of Them*, p. 6.

79. Williams, *South Italian Folkways*, p. 42.

80. Bianco, *Two Rosetos*, p. 124.

81. Kenneth L. Ames, "Grand Rapids Furniture at the Time of the Centennial," *Winterthur Portfolio* 10 (1975), p. 42.

82. Mary Buell Sayles, "Housing and Social Conditions in a Slavic Neighborhood," *Charities* 13 (3 December 1904), 258.

83. Breckinridge, *New Homes*, p. 135.

84. Lawrence Veiller, "A New Idea in Social Work," *Charities and The Commons* 20 (1 August 1908), 563.

85. Charles Weller, *Neglected Neighbors* (Philadelphia: John C. Winston Co., 1909), p. 19.

86. Ibid., p. 22.

87. Behrman, Samuel, *The Worcester Account* (New York: Random House, 1965), p. 226.

88. *West Side Studies* (New York: Russell Sage Foundation, 1914), pp. 100–101.

89. Bianco, *Two Rosetos*, p. 89.

90. Douglas Sladen and Norma Latimer, *Queer Things about Sicily* (London: Anthony Treherne, 1905), p. 85.

91. Williams, *South Italian Folkways*, pp. 42–43.

92. Ibid., p. 47.

93. See Williams, *South Italian Folkways*; Cowen, *Memories*; Wheeler, *Immigrant Experience*; also Jacob Riis photographs of Castle Garden and Lewis Hine photographs of Ellis Island.

94. Marie Ets, *Rosa* (Minneapolis: University of Minnesota Press, 1970), p. 161.

95. Henry Roth, *Call It Sleep* (New York: Cooper Square Publ., 1934; reprint New York: Avon Books, 1965), pp. 172, 187.

96. Byington, *Homestead*, p. 60. She interviewed women about their attitudes toward installment buying and discovered that in Homestead the most common purchases on installment were pianos, sewing machines, and couches, with poor families buying everything this way, including blankets, curtains, and clothing; Louise Moore, *Wage-Earner's Budgets* (New York: Henry Holt and Company, 1907), p. 146. She found sewing machines and pianos to be the most common purchases on installment among her lower New York City population sample. She noted with dismay, however, that there seemed to be an increase in "the extravagant tendency to purchase elaborate parlor furniture 'on time!' "

97. Kramer, *Jewish Grandmothers*, p. 100; see also Haraven, *Amoskeag*, p. 289, for French-Canadian version.

98. Alice G. Magarzyk, "The Bohemians in Chicago," *Charities* 17 (3 December 1906), 206–10; see Williams, *South Italian Folkways*, p. 101, for compromises in traditional Italian weddings.

99. Antanas Kaztauskis, "From Lithuania to the Chicago Stockyards: An Autobiography," *The Independent* 57 (4 August 1904), 241.

100. Ibid., p. 245.

101. Marcus Eli Ravage, *An American in the Making* (New York: Harper and Brothers, 1917; New York: Dover Publications, 1971), pp. 72–74.

102. Williams, *South Italian Folkways*, p. 50; Gans, *Urban Villagers*, Bianco, *Two Rosetos*.

103. Rainwater, *Workingman's Wife*; Rainwater, "House as Haven"; David Coplovitz, "The Problems of Blue-Collar Consumers," in *Blue Collar World: Studies of the American Worker*, ed. Arthur B. Shostak and William Gomberg (Englewood Cliffs, N.J.: Prentice-Hall, 1964), pp. 110–20.

Part III

ACCULTURATION TWICE: RETURN MIGRATION

Return migration is a subject long neglected by statisticians and historians.[1] Immigration was the movement that caught the eye. The visual impression was supported ideologically. People went to unlimited opportunities or at least superior opportunities in near or far-off industrially expanding centers. The glamor, the wages, the recreational and educational facilities of the metropolitan centers continually attracted manpower from the periphery. So the story goes. The empirically correct essence is that jobs were more easily available and that wages were relatively higher in the industrializing areas of the Atlantic world. If the customary division into a European and an American side is analyzed it appears that wages were not necessarily higher in the United States,[2] nor were there great differences in social or horizontal mobility between economically comparable areas.[3] Therefore it is not surprising that a considerable percentage of migrants returned.

The extent of remigration is not precisely known. The U.S. Bureau of Immigration began to count "passenger arrivals and departures" only in 1908—and the "passenger" category "excluded travel over international land borders," so that Mexicans and Canadians were not counted. Since the passenger-immigrant distinction has not been held constant over the years, these statistics are even more difficult to use than other immigration records.[4] A table compiled from several government sources by Charles A. Price gives remigration figures from 1899 to 1952. He lists arrivals, departures, net migration gain or loss, and percentage of departures compared to arrivals. His figures are summarized here:

Period	Arrivals	Departures	Net Immigration	% Departures
1899-1924	17,636,083	6,095,019	11,541,064	34.6
1925-1943	2,294,943	914,605	1,480,388	38.2
1944-1952	1,396,923	169,351	1,227,572	12.1
Totals	21,427,949	7,178,975	14,248,974	33.5

From 1899 to 1952 one third of all immigrants returned or moved on. In the depression decade, 1931–1940, a net loss of 85,000 was registered.[5] One of the best-known photographs of migrants, Alfred Stieglitz' "The Steerage" shows— and this is a fact which is almost unknown—return migrants.

Given the state of research the following essays can provide only a first approach. Lars-Göran Tedebrand demonstrates the possibility of investigating Swedish return migration in detail by using parish registers. He also reviews some of the literature in the field. He concludes that most of the return migrants "had not changed their social position during their time in America." Similarly, Ingrid Semmingsen in her study of Norwegian migration emphasized the conservative character of return: Migrants went back to agriculture in an attempt to preserve their original way of life. Scholars of remigration to Southern (agricultural) Italy are divided in their opinions. Some stress the reinforcing of a traditional way of life, the return to the land, while others discern a modernizing aspect as a result of innovations in living standards and farming methods.[6]

Both Keijo Virtanen in his analysis of Finnish return and Frances Kraljic in her essay on repatriated Croats concentrate on the acculturation process in the society of origin. The society had changed and the migrants' attitudes and expectations had changed, too. Return did not simply mean going back to customs internalized since childhood after a sojourn abroad. It meant a further acculturation, adjustment on the one hand and implantation of new patterns on the other. Given the limitations of their sources both authors are cautious about generalizations. Jonathan D. Sarna lays to rest the myth that conditions for Jewish migrants were so bad in the Old World that hardly any of them returned.

This section contains no essays on return migration by industrial workers who remained in industry at both ends of their voyage. Workers are considerably more difficult to trace after return than property-owning peasants. While the prevailing opinion about return to farming areas has been that migrants wanted to improve their position in the middle class, frequently in the lower middle class, this interpretation cannot simply be transferred to migrants returning as workers. The hypotheses need testing. International mobility of workers does not necessarily imply a rise in status either within the working class or an aspiration to rise into the middle class. It may lead to an abatement of class consciousness or at least of class organization because the migrants involved never stay long enough to organize. The opposite hypothesis may also be proposed. International mobility may increase working class consciousness as workers experience similar conditions of exploitation wherever they go. Return migrants may have an innovative impact on the shop floor. During their stay abroad they learn new technologies and acquire new skills. If they acquire new forms of class consciousness or organizational skills, they may be regarded as troublemakers by management and be isolated. (This, of course, is similar to the argument that American returnees in villages either formed separate rather than fully integrated groups or that they were in fact shunned by the village establishment as Saloutos argued.) Migrant workers' experience abroad may also have bearings on their relationships with other workers after return to the original culture. They may be considered outsiders because of their new ideas, but they may also take the place of leaders because of their broad experience. Finally, the question of interaction between the formation of class consciousness and national consciousness has to be raised. As yet the state of the discipline permits no answers to these questions.

NOTES

1. For a review essay on studies published up to 1980, see Dirk Hoerder, "Immigration and the Working Class: The Remigration Factor," *International Labor and Working Class History*, 21 (Spring 1982), 28–41. The most important additions since then include the Finnish return migration (see Keijo Vitanen's chapter in this volume); the Finnish return migration to the Soviet Union (Reino Kero, "The Canadian Finns in Soviet Karelia in the 1930s," in M. G. Karni, ed., *The Finnish Diaspora*, 2 vols. (Toronto, 1981), vol. 1, pp. 203–13, based on a dissertation), and Jewish return (see Jonathan D. Sarna's chapter in this volume).

2. See, for example, Peter R. Shergold, *Working Class Life: The "American Standard" in Comparative Perspective, 1899–1913* (Pittsburgh, 1982).

3. Hartmut Kaelble, *Historical Research on Social Mobility. Western Europe and the USA in the Nineteenth and Twentieth Centuries* (New York, 1981).

4. *Historical Statistics of the United States. Colonial Times to 1970*, 2 vols. (Washington, D.C. 1975), series C 296–301, "passenger arrivals and departures 1908 to 1970."

5. Stephan Thernstrom and Ann Orlov, eds., *Harvard Encyclopedia of American Ethnic Groups* (Cambridge, Mass., 1980), pp. 476, 1036–37. See also Bernard Axelrod, "Historical Studies of Emigration from the United States," *International Migration Review*, 6 (1972), 32–49.

6. A related question concerns the benefits that not the individual but the country of origin ("donating country") receives from the aggregate of the migrant workers' earnings and new skills. While the debate still rages among historians, an authoritative study of present-day return migration of European "guest workers" by the supra-national Organization for Economic Co-operation and Development concludes "None [of the researchers] was able to quote any really conclusive instance in which the returning labour was used in a manner at all conducive to development. In no way do the returning emigrants help to further their country's economic growth, whether by the use of their savings they have accumulated abroad or the experience they have acquired." *OECD-Observer*, 47 (1970), 11, quoted in Klaus-Peter Dietzel, "Die Rolle der rückkehrenden Arbeiter in der Entwicklungsstrategie des westdeutschen Imperialismus," *Das Argument*, 68 (1971), 764–81. It seems that labor migration is basically economic aid given by economically backward countries to industrializing or at present highly industrialized countries, which helps to cement their own backwardness.

REMIGRATION FROM AMERICA TO SWEDEN

14

Lars-Göran Tedebrand

In the spring of 1903, the twenty-year-old Halvar Olsson, son of a small free-holder in the province of Jämtland in northern Sweden, left his home-parish and emigrated from the Norwegian harbor of Trondheim to Minnesota. He returned to Sweden already in 1905. During his two-year stay in America, he worked as a farmhand, woodsman, and railway- and warehouseworker in Duluth, where he earned 1 dollar and 75 cents a day. He has told us this in his handwritten memoirs from the nineteen-fifties, a touching document from the hard life of the working people in Sweden one or two generations ago.

Halvar Olsson's stay in America was only a short experience in his life. This experience he shared with thousands of young Swedish workers and sons of farmers. According to official statistics, 981,017 Swedes emigrated to the United States and 178,251 persons remigrated to Sweden between 1875 and 1930. This means that remigration during this period totalled 18.2 percent of emigration. The stream of returning emigrants reached all delivering countries of emigration, and it was therefore a well-known fact that emigration did not always lead to permanent settlement and assimilation. Even the American naturalization statistics showed the varying degree of assimilation among different ethnic groups. Not until 1908 can we establish a certain comparative perspective on the territorial distribution of remigration. In that year the American statistics begin to provide direct reports of registered remigration by way of American ports. Between 1908 and 1931, a total of 4,077,263 persons returned from the United States to European and Asian countries. Among non-European nationalities Chinese and Japanese exhibit a high remigration frequency. This is hardly surprising, considering the formulation of American immigration policy and the psychological attitudes toward immigrants of these nationalities. Table 14.1 shows remigration statistics for the most represented European nationalities and folk groups.[1]

In proportion to emigration, remigration was strongest among Southern and Southeastern European immigrants. Italians and Greeks in particular reveal a

This essay was first published in H. Runblom and H. Norman, eds., *From Sweden to America* (Uppsala and Minneapolis, 1976), pp. 201–28. It is reprinted in slightly revised form by permission of the author and the Historika Institutionen vid Uppsala Universitet. For a map of Sweden with district ("län") boundaries see Figure 2.1 in this volume.

high return frequency. The high figures of remigration among nationalities which made up the so-called "new generation of immigrants" are partially due to the fact that around 1900 emigrants rarely settled in farming areas but rather in large cities and industrial regions—i.e. in labor markets which were the first victims of economic recession. However, this is only part of the picture. Of greater significance is probably the fact that mass emigration during the early 1900s contained contingents of transatlantic labor migrants. These particular migrations were part of an established pattern and, among other things, explain the exceptionally strong remigration to poor sections of southern Italy. Italian farm workers and farmers' sons who returned home as "Americani" after spending some time on the American labor market, resemble large numbers of their countrymen, the celebrated *golondrinas* (the swallows), who left for Latin America during the harvest season. The substantially repetitive element in Italian emigration is also shown by the fact that 10 percent of Italian immigrants in 1904 had already been in the United States before.[2]

The rise of an Atlantic labor market must be set in a larger context, where the expansion of American industry and the late industrialization of certain European countries comprise the major components of the explaining pattern. International manpower mobility was a well-known phenomenon in Europe both prior to World War I and during the 1920s and 1930s, and it only reflected the varying developmental stages of different regions. The absolute figures of labor migrants are amazingly high. As early as 1886 a quarter of a million Italians were working in France, which was the most important center of international labor migration. In 1931 no less than 900,000 Italians, 500,000 Poles, 330,000 Spaniards, and 300,000 Belgians resided in France. From this international "visiting worker perspective" we must see a great deal of remigration from North America.

Table 14.1
Remigration from the United States to Europe, 1903–1931. Distributed according to Nationalities and Folk Groups

Nationality	Number	Nationality	Number
Italians	1 240 884	Hungarians	156 019
Poles	339 428	Slovaks	132 763
Englishmen	208 081	Scandinavians	125 308
Greeks	197 088	Croatians-Slovenes	118 129
Germans	161 342	Russians	115 188

Source Annual Report of the Commissioner General of Immigration, Fiscal Year Ended June 30, 1931, U.S. Department of Labor. Washington, 1931.

STATUS OF RESEARCH

Frank Thistlethwaite has rightly characterized this interesting research field as "the further face of the moon."[3] A glance at the international research situation hardly contests this statement. Despite the extent of remigration international research on the topic is conspicuously meagre: most countries totally lack such statistics or only have deficient material. Studies of Norwegian, Irish, Italian, and Greek remigration, for example, are based on census reports, fragmentary statistics, and interviews. It is true that such research has made a few interesting structural observations and presented findings regarding the capital investments of returning migrants and the effects of remigration on receiving countries. However, the quantitative sources are so weak, and the methods of measurement sometimes so unfortunate, that the results are both contradictory and problematic in terms of generalized evaluations. Several examples can illustrate this point. Censuses taken in Norway in 1910 and thereafter required information on returning Norwegian Americans. In an irreproachable study the Norwegian historian, Ingrid Semmingsen, has worked with remigration statistics in the 1910 Census. She found that 40 percent of these individuals had been employed in American industry and mining enterprises, whereas only 10 percent had been farmers. After return to Norway these figures were reversed: 40 percent were farmers and only 11 percent worked in factories and mines.[4] The transition among returning emigrants from industrial to agricultural occupations shows that the directional movement of Norwegian re-immigration broke with the migrational tendencies in Norwegian society, at least during the pre-World War I period.

The Greek-American historian, Theodore Saloutos, has found an entirely different connection between returning emigrants and social trends.[5] Saloutos maintains that the urban life of remigrants in the United States dictated their choice of residence after their return to their native country. Although some remigrants returned to rural villages, the majority settled in cities such as Athens, Saloniki, and Pireus. In other words, the directional movement of Greek remigration would not only diverge from the Norwegian pattern but also—and more surprisingly— from the Italian.[6]

Another example of this somewhat confusing research situation can be mentioned. With regard to the 1920s historians have made a clear connection between remigration and the radicalization of the Norwegian labor movement. On the other hand, the Italian researcher, F. P. Cerase, maintains that return migration played a conservational role in Italian society. G.R. Gilkey, however, reaches a different conclusion: the returning "Americani" established new attitudes towards the traditional fabric of society in their native country.[7]

Return migration can, of course, have changed character over time. Moreover, it is rather obvious that its effects on receiving countries varied in proportion to its intensity and the stages of development in these countries. However, it is difficult to free oneself from the suspicion that these differences of opinion among researchers can largely be explained by the confusing array of source materials at their disposal.

The relationship between return migration and the Americanization process—that is, the technical and cultural impulses from America to Europe—is a complicated and important research topic. However, as long as we know so little about the structure and function of remigration, its effects on receiving countries must be considered an ancillary assignment. The major deficiency here is the inability of research to conduct systematic, statistical and demographic analysis of return migration from North America. In contrast to his international colleagues, the Swedish researcher of return migration has access to source material suitable for this purpose. Immigration was systematically recorded by parish priests in appropriate registers. Moreover, beginning in 1875 priests were instructed to transfer these reports to special immigrant lists in the *Summariska folkmängdsredogörelser* (Condensed Population Reports), which were submitted annually to the Central Bureau of Statistics in Stockholm.[8] These lists contained the immigrants' names, occupations, years of birth, and countries of emigration. From this year published records of Swedish population statistics contain aggregated immigration data based on this central source series.

Several theoretical and methodological considerations are appropriate before we describe remigration to Sweden from North America.

RETURN MIGRATION AS A COUNTER-STREAM

Return migration from North America is not an isolated phenomenon in migration history. As early as 1885 the English statistician Ravenstein pointed out that every stream of migration gives rise to a compensating counter-stream.[9] Counter-balanced streams of movement always appear in connection with internal and external migration. Two Swedish examples can suffice as an illustration here. During the course of industrialization after 1860 hundreds of thousands of people migrated from agricultural districts to urbanizing areas. However, this population drain occurred in stages and over a long period of time. The annual net shifts of population between the countryside and densely populated areas were rarely dramatic: nearly an equal amount of persons migrated in the opposite direction. Unemployment, assimilation difficulties, and other psychological factors forced many persons to return to the agrarian environment. Therefore, the direct return migration is very conspicuous with regard to internal population turnover. A study has shown, for example, that around 40 percent of the migrants who left a number of typically forested parishes in western Sweden during the period 1930–1944 returned to the parishes of out-migration.[10] This counter-balance effect assumed even greater importance in the context of external migration. The substantial immigration to Sweden from neighboring Scandinavian countries during the latter part of the 1800s was balanced by a nearly equal amount of movement in the opposite direction.[11] What distinguishes Swedish emigration to North America in this context is the relatively weak counter-movement and the highly substantial net population loss as compared with other countries.

It is, of course, unsatisfactory to regard return migration from North America as a mechanical counter-stream to emigration. Remigration as a self-perpetuating phenomenon can never be accepted as an historical explanation. The fact that we have called attention to obvious strains of labor migrants in the context of return migration demonstrates our accustomed objection to such a mechanical perspective.

A theoretical outline (Figure 14.1) can prove useful in discussing the stages of remigration. The arrows do not symbolize any exact chronological sequence but merely theoretical changes in trends. Two components are included as explaining variables: 1) differences in levels of economic development between the United States and Sweden; and 2) changes in the structure of emigration. New pioneer settlements, railroad construction, and industrial expansion in the United States up to 1890 should have had a sharply repressive effect on return migration. In this phase return to Sweden occurs at a relatively slow pace. It is not until the American industrial recessions of the 1890s and the acceleration of Swedish industrialization during the same decade that we can expect a strong intensification of return migration. Since mass emigration from Sweden had already culminated by this time it is likely that return migration also culminates at a rapid pace but retains a high level of intensity after 1900 as a result of increased numbers of labor migrants among emigrant contingents. In other words, the regression phase should be more evenly structured than in other types of growth processes. Improved communications and strong "America traditions" in certain areas can also have counteracted the regressive curve of return mi-

Figure 14.1
Background Factors for the Rise of Return Migration

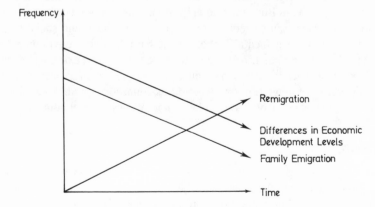

gration. The economic equalization between delivering and receiving countries of migration was most extreme during the international depression of the early 1930s. There is reason to assume that at this point return migration was even stronger in volume than emigration.

As mentioned above, we also need to emphasize the significance of emigration structure for the growth in volume of return migration. We cannot *a priori* expect any sizable degree of return migration during the early phase of Swedish emigration, which was dominated by family movements and concentrated on areas of colonization in the United States. In other words, the counterbalancing features of early Scandinavian emigration should have been far weaker than those of the early waves of emigration from Southern and Southeastern Europe. However, as emigration made the transition from family to individual movements the labor migrant element was automatically amplified in Swedish emigration. Another important fact is that individual emigration, more so than family emigration, was directed to areas that were sensitive to economic market fluctuations. Other factors as well can, over time, have amplified these counterbalancing features of transatlantic migration. After 1900 agrarian emigration from Sweden rises again. There is reason to assume that this phase of emigration contained substantial numbers of individuals who, for social and psychological reasons, preferred movement to America to proletarization in Swedish cities and industrial districts. Moreover, there is much to indicate that the repetitive element is amplified during the late phase of transatlantic migration.

Although it is possible to list general economic and structural causes of this remigration, the majority of returning emigrants made their decision on the basis of rational considerations. It seems reasonable to work with two major motives for return migration. Some emigrants can have regarded a certain period of residence in America as an interesting alternative to unfavorable labor market conditions in Sweden and can therefore have originally intended to return. One can expect a certain regulated phase shift between high emigration and high return migration. Yet, for various reasons many emigrants may never have been able to fulfill their original intentions of returning but remained in America for the rest of their lives. But return migration can also be seen as a process of rejection from American society. For various psychological and social reasons some emigrants never gained a foothold in the hard American environment and were forced to return to their native countries. Naturally, it is extremely difficult to distinguish between these two individual causes of return migration. However, detailed studies of remigration structure and its connections with American economic recessions can enable us to isolate some of these causal contexts.

METHOD

The Swedish source material allows us both to pose and answer a whole set of questions. What was the relationship between the volumes of emigration and return migration, and how did this relationship change over time? What impact did American economic recessions have on the intensity of remigration? What was the relationship between the regional distribution of return migration and major social transformations—that is, industrialization and urbanization? Was return migration strongest to rural areas or was it primarily an urban and industrial phenomenon? In other words, was return migration positively or negatively correlated with social trends? Once these central issues have been approached with the aid of aggregated data, we can focus attention on individuals and study the relationship between places of emigration and return migration, the duration of residence in America, the structure of remigration, as well as the distribution and change of return frequency among different emigrant cohorts.

A convenient way of answering these questions is to conduct a "three-stage" analysis. Structures and contexts which can be established on the national level are tested and diversified by a gradual narrowing of interest to local and individual studies. A first stage involves processing mass data from official national and län (administrative district) statistics, as they apply to the relationship between the frequencies of emigration and remigration and between urban emigration and remigration. In this way we can shed light on the relationship of remigration to general migration tendencies in Swedish society. In a second stage we intensify the regional analysis by establishing connections between re-immigration to a large number of rural districts and their social and economic structures. Väster-norrlands län in northern Sweden was selected for this intensive study. There are two main reasons for this regional limitation. First, emigration from Northern Sweden did not accelerate in intensity until the 1890s—that is, during a period when a sharp rise of remigration began to countervail emigration. Second, Väs-ternorrland comprises regions which in economic and social respects are clearly distinct from each other: this stems from the explosive expansion of the saw mill industry during the latter part of the 1800s. In a third stage of analysis we determine return frequency for a large number of emigrant cohorts. The Sundsvall district, which has Europe's and perhaps the world's largest compact area of timber industries, has been selected for this detailed analysis. Chronologically the study encompasses the period 1875–1913, but certain lines are extended up to 1930, which marks the end of mass emigration from Sweden.[12]

REMIGRATION

Frequency and Course of Development

The natural point of departure for a time-series analysis of remigration to Sweden from America is the relationship between return migration and emigration. Table 14.2 presents decade statistics of emigration from Sweden to the United States and remigration from the United States to Sweden during the period 1881–1930. Included are percentage figures of remigration in relationship to emigration. A graphic picture of remigration frequency in per mille of the average population during the period 1880–1913 is presented in Figure 14.2,

Table 14.2

Emigration and Remigration, Sweden and the United States, 1881–1930

Years	Emigration	Remigration	Remigration in per cent of emigration
1881–1890	324 285	18 766	5.8
1891–1900	200 524	47 138	23.5
1901–1910	219 249	44 029	20.1
1911–1920	8¹ 537	37 153	45.6
1921–1930	91 932	27 474	29.9
Total	917 527	174 560	19.0

Sources Bidrag till Sveriges officiella statistik, Serie A; Sveriges officiella statistik, Ut- och invandring.

Figure 14.2

Total Immigration to Sweden, Remigration from the United States, and Immigration Minus Remigration from the United States in Per Mille of the Median Swedish Population, 1875–1913

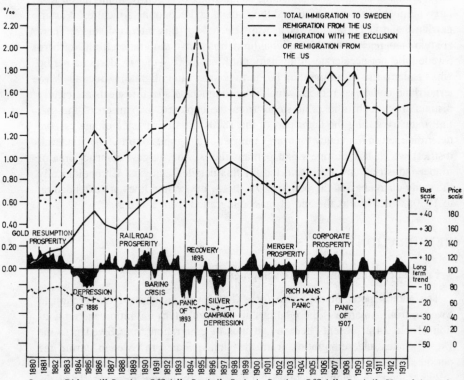

Sources Bidrag till Sveriges Officiella Statistik, Serie A; Sveriges Officiella Statistik, Ut- och invandring; J. A. Estey (1956), p. 20; L.-G. Tedebrand (1972), p. 225.

where comparisons have also been made with total immigration to Sweden and immigration from countries outside North America. The graph curve of American business cycles has also been charted directly above the bottom line in Figure 14.2.

The countervailing features of this transatlantic movement are still rather weak during the 1880s, and there is nothing to indicate that they might have been stronger during the early phase of mass emigration. The weak countermovements during the initial emigration decades were typical of Scandinavian emigration but may also have applied, for example, to German emigration, which never appears to have had any substantial amount of labor migrants.[13]

As shown by Figure 14.2, the trend of remigration is already increasing during the 1880s. Return frequency reaches a peak in 1893–1895: this comes as no surprise, considering the American economic recession at this time and the structural changes in Swedish emigration. This is followed by a falling trend up to 1902, when re-immigration rises once again to reach a new peak in 1908. The rate of returning subsequently remains high.

Since remigration is dependent upon the strength of the preceding emigration flow, we cannot observe any mathematically regulated growth of remigration volume over time. However, the heavily counterbalancing features in this late phase of mass emigration are visible. At the same time it is evident that remigration to Sweden never reaches the frequencies established by the ''new'' immigrant nationalities.

Prior to World War I remigration frequency never exceeds 1.5 per mille (in 1894) and is never less than 0.1 per mille (in 1879). During years of particularly high frequency returning migration nearly equalled emigration—as, for example, in 1894 and 1898, when remigration volume amounts to over 70 percent of emigration volume. Remigration exceeds emigration for the first time in 1918, as a result of the special conditions which prevailed during the war years. However, as was assumed previously, it is not until 1930 that remigration definitely surpasses emigration.

The rise of remigration occurs in obvious stages. The first occurs in 1882–1885, following the heavy wave of emigration in 1880–1882; the second in 1888–1892, following the prominent emigration of 1887–1888; and the third in 1892–1895, following the high emigration of 1892 and 1893. Remigration also increases after the heavy emigration of 1902 and 1903. As indicated earlier, the successive rise of remigration frequency reflects the fact that prominent years of emigration recruit large numbers of returning immigrants, partially independent of American economic developments. For example, remigration frequency rises in 1887–1890 despite economic prosperity in the United States during that period. In other words, there is a phase-shift connection between high levels of emigration and remigration, where the time interval is primarily explained by the length of migrants' stay in America.

On the other hand, the oscillations in the graph curve of return immigration are mainly due to American economic conditions. A comparison between remigration fluctuations and American business cycles reveals a very close inter-relation. American recessions triggered remigration, whereby Swedish immigrants were effectively removed from the American labor market. Remigration increased, for example, at the outset of American recessions in 1884, 1893–1894, 1904, and 1908. An extremely heavy wave of return immigrants occurred in 1894, when over 7,000 Swedish Americans returned home. In the fall of 1893 the American economy suffered its greatest crisis of the century, and the nearly 40,000 Swedes who emigrated that year met with wide-scale unemployment on the American labor market.

In contrast to the course of remigration, the curve of immigration to Sweden from countries outside of North America reveals a relatively even development. The oscillations here are to be seen primarily as a result of cooperative economic trends in Sweden and the other Scandinavian countries. Moreover, the curve of total immigration to Sweden is distinctly profiled by the curve of re-immigration, with its characteristically ascending oscillations.

This survey of Swedish emigration and remigration on the national level has shown that the countervailing features of early family emigration were relatively weak. Furthermore, an increase of emigration consistently leads to an increase of return migration after a certain length of time, greatly independent of conditions on the American labor market. The oscillations in the curve of remigration can be directly correlated with the alienating effects of American recessions on immigrant manpower. Due to improved economic conditions in Sweden mass emigration culminated before the turn of the century, and as a result return migration rapidly enters a saturation phase. However, an increased amount of labor migrants in this late phase of mass emigration helped to stabilize return frequency at a rather high level. Yet, remigration to Sweden never assumed the same proportions as it did to countries representing the so-called new generation of American immigrants. Finally, the economic equalization between delivering and receiving countries led to a situation during the final phase of mass emigration where remigration surpasses emigration.

Regional Distribution of Return Migration

Table 14.3 charts Sweden's population exchange with the United States for the period 1875–1913, as distributed by Swedish län and the city of Stockholm. It also shows remigration in percent of emigration, the population growth of each län, and their share of the national totals of emigration and remigration. In relationship to emigration, return migration is weakest to heavily forested län in Northern Sweden and strongest to agricultural län in Southern and Western Sweden. The relatively low level of remigration to Northern Sweden is due to two factors: first, the prominent pattern of family emigration among saw mill workers and farmers in this area even after 1900; second, the economic stagnation in the sawmill industry after 1890. Generally speaking, then, there is an obvious connection between the strength of remigration and the regional phase shift of family emigration.

Naturally, the län which assumed a larger share of the nation's remigration statistics compared with emigration occupy the greatest interest in this context. Table 14.3 shows that agrarian län with high emigration figures—for example, Kalmar, Gotlands, Älvsborgs, and Hallands län—had a substantially higher share of remigration than emigration. During the peak year of remigration in 1894 the last three län had an even greater percentage of remigration than emigration.

Return migration amounted to 15 percent of emigration for the nation as a whole from 1875–1913. However, the corresponding figures for the above län were 17 percent, 26 percent, 21 percent, and 19 percent respectively. In other words, remigration was strongest to agrarian län with a relatively slow pace of

Table 14.3
Population Exchange of Swedish Län and the City of Stockholm with the United States, 1875–1913

Area	Emigra-tion	Remigra-tion	Remigr. in % of Emigr.	Emigr. in % of Nat. Tot.	Remigr. in % of Nat. Tot	Popula-tion Growth
Stockholm	42 631	7 606	17.8	5.0	6.0	+146.5
Stockholms län	8 486	1 636	19.3	1.0	1.3	+62.6
Uppsala län ·	5 409	585	10.8	0.6	0.5	+24.9
Södermanlands län	10 333	1 731	16.8	1.2	1.4	+29.3
Östergötlands län	53 445	5 879	11.0	6.3	4.6	+12.7
Jönköpings län	52 797	6 218	11.8	6.2	4.9	+14.9
Kronobergs län	42 047	5 215	12.4	4.9	4.1	-5.0
Kalmar län	61 085	10 322	16.9	7.2	8.1	-4.9
Gotlands län	10 451	2 698	25.8	1.2	2.1	+1.4
Blekinge län	25 104	4 475	17.8	2.9	3.5	+13.8
Kristianstads län	44 016	7 232	16.4	5.2	5.7	+1.6
Malmöhus län	52 061	7 616	14.6	6.1	6.0	+40.6
Hallands län	44 130	9 131	20.7	5.2	7.2	+11.4
Göteborgs o. Bohus län	38 364	8 261	21.5	4.5	6.5	+62.1
Älvsborgs län	66 765	12 380	18.5	7.8	9.7	+1.9
Skaraborgs län	48 344	6 191	12.8	5.7	4.9	-4.8
Värmlands län	71 379	10 259	14.4	8.4	8.1	-2.6
Örebro län	32 514	4 381	13.5	3.8	3.4	+17.7
Västmanlands län	10 688	1 357	12.7	1.3	1.1	+29.6
Kopparbergs län	32 716	3 849	11.8	3.8	3.0	+27.6
Gävleborgs län	30 641	3 061	10.0	3.6	2.4	+57.8
Västernorrlands län	28 635	2 520	8.8	3.4	2.0	+70.8
Jämtlands län	17 129	1 434	8.4	2.0	1.1	+60.2
Västerbottens län	10 468	1 355	12.9	1.2	1.1	+69.4
Norrbottens län	13 706	2 027	14.8	1.6	1.6	+102.6

Source: Bidrag till Sveriges officiella statistik, Serie A; Sveriges officiella statistik, Ut- och invandring.

industrialization. Since this concentration does not decrease over time, it falls well in line with our prior assumption of a strong labor migrant strain in late agrarian emigration. Another immediate factor here is the significance of a long tradition of energetic ''commuting'' to America from farming districts in Southern and Western Sweden. External migration losses are somewhat reduced in the agrarian län if consideration is given to total emigration statistics—i.e. emigration minus remigration.

The lack of co-variation between the regional strength of remigration and the general migrational tendencies in Sweden during the industrialization period can be seen in the relationship between regional population growth and remigration frequency. The population growth of Sweden as a whole from 1875–1913 amounted to 29.0 percent. Of the nine län that assumed a greater share of national remigration than emigration, six have a population growth which is substantially under the national average. During this period Kalmar län, with its large amount of returning emigrants, suffered a population loss of 5 percent, the second largest in the nation after Kronobergs län. On the other hand, population growth in Älvsborgs and Gotlands län was limited to 2 percent and 1 percent respectively. In other words, there is no positive connection between population increase and remigration frequency on the level of Swedish län.

Urban Emigration and Remigration

During the decades up to World War I agrarian Sweden was successively broken down by industrialization and urbanization. The urban share of the population rose from 15 percent in 1880 to 26 percent in 1913. This process continued during the 1920s, and in 1930, 33 percent of the Swedish population lived in cities. As a means of illustrating the relationship of remigration to urbanization, a comparison will be made between the growth of Swedish cities and the strength of urban remigration. Table 14.4 shows the percentage of urban residents in the total population and the cities' share of emigration and remigration for the periods 1881–1910 and 1921–1930. All figures are expressed as a five-year median.

With the exception of the five-year periods 1891–1895, 1921–1925, and 1926–1930 the cities' share of remigration is somewhat larger than their share of emigration. However, during the remaining five-year periods there are rarely any pronounced differences in the strength of urban emigration and urban remigration. The sole exception is the period 1881–1885 which, on the other hand, was generally characterized by rather weak remigration. On the whole, it is striking that return to urban areas did not intensify during years of high return migration. In other words, there is no positive correlation between the general course of urbanization and the directional movement of remigration. Urban remigration was only significant during the initial phase. During the period of mass remigration, beginning in the late 1880s, the cities' share of returning migrants only exceeds their share of emigrants by a very small margin. Despite the prevailing patterns of urbanization, there is no rise in the amount of remigration to urban areas. Table 14.4 clearly shows that even up to 1930 the cities were incapable of attracting a share of returning emigrants which corresponded to their share of the total Swedish population. These findings indicate that the proportion of urban and industrial workers among returning emigrants cannot have been as great as prior research has been led to believe.

The above analysis, based on aggregated national statistics, has demonstrated that the regional distribution and directional movement of remigration diverged in essential respects from the transformative tendencies in Swedish society. In this context remigration to Sweden seems to possess tangible similarities with, for example, remigration to Norway but diverges from the pattern in Greece.

The Remigration Frequency of Rural Districts

The above results relative to the directional movement of remigration can be examined and reinforced by a study of returning migration to Västernorrland.[14] Figure 14.3 shows remigration in percent of emigration to Västernorrland's 63 rural parishes. All parishes in this län have been divided into 4 main groups in order to relate remigration frequency in greater detail to social structure and industrialization level: 1) industrial parishes; 2) rural-mixed parishes; 3) agricultural parishes; and 4) corporation parishes. The term rural-mixed parishes refers to areas with a certain degree of industrialization, whereas corporation parishes represent areas in which the lumber industry had acquired more than one-third of farm and forest acreage by 1900. Table 14.5 shows remigration in percent of emigration among rural regions of Västernorrland for the period 1875–1913.

Table 14.4
Urban Share of the Swedish Population Compared to Urban Share of Emigration and Remigration between Sweden and the United States, 1881–1930

Year	Total population	Urban share of Emigration	Remigration
1881–1885	16.3	14.0	21.8
1886–1890	18.1	17.9	20.6
1891–1895	19.4	22.7	19.1
1896–1900	20.9	20.3	24.1
1901–1905	22.3	20.2	21.4
1906–1910	24.3	21.1	21.6
1921–1925	30.3	27.3	24.8
1926–1930	31.8	30.6	30.6

Source: Bidrag till Sveriges officiella statistik, Serie A; Sveriges officiella statistik, Ut- och in-vandring; Historisk statistik för Sverige, Vol. I, Table A:4.

In Västernorrland as a whole remigration totalled 9 percent of emigration. Remigration was substantially stronger to agricultural parishes than other parishes. Remigration to some agricultural parishes totalled substantially more than ⅕ of emigration. Remigration to industrial parishes lay under the average for Västernorrland, whereas that of rural-mixed parishes equalled the average. It is not surprising that corporation parishes have the lowest figures of remigration; in these areas the proletarization process was wide-spread among former landowning farmers. Remigration to certain outlying corporation parishes amounted to only 3 percent of emigration.

In sum, the results of the national and regional analyses of remigration with regard to its geographical distribution confirm each other. Remigration is clearly concentrated in agrarian areas. In other words, remigration is strongest in areas which made the swiftest transition from family to individual emigration and had the greatest amount of labor migrants among emigrant contingents. Therefore, in certain emigrant districts where a phase shift occurred—as, for example, in the above corporation parishes—remigration was still remarkably weak after the turn of the century.

Residence in America: A Step in an Urbanization Process?

A central issue is whether returning Swedish Americans remigrated to their home districts or to other areas in Sweden. Similarly, to what extent did residence in America constitute a step in an urbanization or industrialization process among individuals? The agrarian orientation of remigration and its lack of correlation with social trends would indicate that such was not the case. However, on Figure 14.3 a large number of individual studies can help to illustrate this complex of problems. The diagram indicates the percent of returning principal persons (over 15 years of age) who settled in their parishes of emigration in relationship to all persons returning to Västernorrland during the period 1875–1913.

Figure 14.3 clearly shows that remigrants from America moved in a static direction toward parishes of emigration. Around 80 percent of Västernorrland's Swedish Americans returned to parishes of emigration. In other words, remigration reveals a remarkably "conservative" pattern. The most striking feature

Table 14.5
Västernorrland: Emigration and Remigration

Parish	Emigration	Remigration	Remigration in % of emigration
Industrial	14 188	1 204	8.5
Rural-Mixed	3 482	306	8.8
Agricultural	1 680	213	12.7
Corporation	6 840	512	7.5

Source Summariska folkmängdsredogörelser, The Central Bureau of Statistics, Stockholm.

is that industrial parishes did not attract more remigrants from other regions of emigration than agricultural parishes. While 790 (or 84 percent) of the 946 principal persons who returned to industrial parishes in Västernorrland originally emigrated from these areas, the corresponding figures for agricultural parishes were 136 (or 78 percent) of a total of 175 returning emigrants. Nearly 90 percent of those who returned to the wide-scale sawmill district around Sundsvall had

Figure 14.3
Remigrants from North America to Västernorrland, 1875–1913

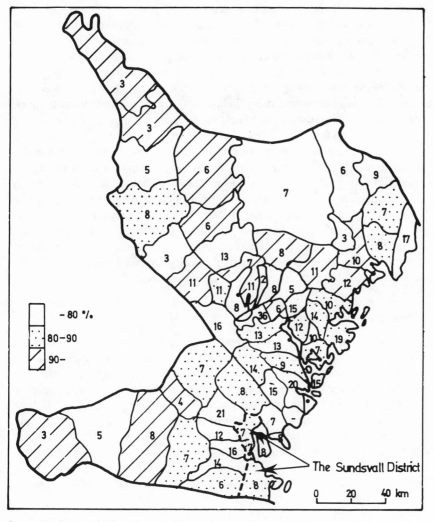

Source Registers of Migration, Parish Registers of Catechetical Examinations, and Parish Record Books from Church Archives in Västernorrlands län; Condensed Population Reports, The Central Bureau of Statistics, Stockholm; L.-G. Tedebrand (1972), pp. 236, 239.

originally emigrated from the area. These figures even indicate a certain return movement to agrarian regions by persons who had migrated to Swedish industrial parishes prior to emigration. All things considered, these results must be interpreted as follows: at the time of their remigration to Sweden, Swedish Americans did not settle in more urbanized areas than those from which they originally emigrated. In other words, cities and industrial parishes did not make sizable population gains at the expense of agricultural parishes in connection with return migration. This, of course, does not exclude the possibility that occasional returning emigrants did not settle in their old home districts or areas of emigration. However, as a rule this has not happened.

The "conservative" pattern of return migration is of substantial interest from the standpoint of migration psychology. Though not generally the case in migration contexts, it does appear that factors of social psychology can explain remigration. It is tempting to draw comparisons between returning emigrants' ties with their home districts and seasonal labor migrations within Sweden to extensive farming areas and rising industrial districts. A parallel can be made to the "rural-industrial barrier" which has been demonstrated in several local studies of internal migration in Sweden during the early phase of industrialization.[15] All of these phenomena symbolize the resistance of numerous agrarian groups to a permanent change of social and physical environment during the process of industrialization. A period of stay in America may have held far greater attraction for many farmers' sons than the proletarization process in Swedish cities and industrial areas. In many cases the "subjective" distance to America may have been shortened by a long tradition of emigration among agrarian groups. This interpretation provides a natural explanation for the strength of agrarian remigration and the surprisingly weak numbers of urban and industrial workers involved in the transatlantic migration of Swedish manpower.

Remigration Frequency

The functional nature of remigration can be illustrated in more detail by an analysis of its frequential distribution and change among different emigrant cohorts. The Sundsvall saw-mill district is suitable for this special analysis. It must be said at the outset that individual motives for the decision to remigrate are definitely hard to establish and usually defy meaningful analysis. Church records sometimes disclose very personal reasons behind the decision to remigrate. For example, four persons who returned to the Sundsvall district died only one or two months after their arrival, and in one case the cause of death was tuberculosis. Three women were reported to have suffered severe mental disturbances shortly after their return, and one of them was admitted to a regional hospital for care.[16]

Tabulatory material enables us to isolate more general tendencies. Table 14.6 shows the percent of returning emigrants prior to 1913 in each emigrant age cohort (men and women over 15 years of age) from the Sundsvall district during

Table 14.6
Remigration Frequency Prior to 1913 among Emigrant Men and Women over 15 Years of Age from the Sundsvall District, 1875–1909

Year	Male emigrants	Male remi-grants	Remigra-tion frequency %	Emigrant women	Female remi-grants	Remigration frequency %
1875	1	–	–	1	–	–
1876	2	–	–	1	–	–
1877	–	–	–	–	–	–
1878	1	–	–	1	–	–
1879	103	2	1.9	64	–	–
1880	96	6	6.3	91	3	3.3
1881	134	5	3.7	104	1	1.0
1882	109	8	7.3	88	2	2.2
1883	41	1	2.4	38	2	5.3
1884	22	1	4.5	18	1	5.6
1885	22	3	13.6	16	1	6.3
1886	18	–	–	13	–	–
1887	120	9	7.5	46	–	–
1888	105	9	8.6	77	3	3.9
1889	30	4	13.3	26	–	–
1890	40	4	12.5	21	1	4.8
1891	230	17	7.4	108	4	3.7
1892	365	47	12.9	235	20	8.5
1893	374	53	14.2	252	15	6.0
1894	39	9	23.1	87	3	3.6
1895	32	4	12.5	55	2	3.8
1896	24	4	16.7	41	1	2.6
1897	5	1	20.0	22	3	15.8
1898	20	–	–	27	1	3.7
1899	30	3	10.3	59	5	8.9
1900	36	2	5.6	72	9	13.0
1901	104	10	10.0	66	6	9.1
1902	305	29	9.5	203	15	7.4
1903	226	20	9.0	176	14	8.2
1904	62	5	8.1	90	8	9.8
1905	107	4	4.2	82	–	–
1906	175	15	8.6	107	9	9.1
1907	127	12	9.4	112	11	9.8
1908	42	2	5.4	52	3	6.5
1909	159	14	8.8	90	4	4.6
Total	3 304	305	9.2	2 541	147	5.8

the period 1875–1913. As indicated above, we cannot expect to see any mathematically regulated growth of remigration frequency. Hypothetically speaking, the following factors may have been significant for the fluctuations of this frequency. Large emigrant populations, especially after 1890 when family emigration began to decline, contained many labor migrants for whom the journey to America was only a temporary alternative to unfavorable prospects on the Swedish labor market. The American recessions promoted remigration by alienating immigrant manpower, and female remigration rose over time as a result of increased emigration by unmarried women after the turn of the century.

Few emigrants who came to America before the middle of the 1880s returned to Sweden (Table 14.6). The expansion of the American economy during this period, together with the strong element of family emigration among sawmill workers, had a curbing effect on remigration. However, a powerful increase of return migration can be observed among those emigrants who confronted the American depression in 1885. Major interest here is directed to the return frequency among large emigrant contingents from the Sundsvall district in 1892 and 1893, which met with the American economic crisis in the fall of 1893. The frequency of remigration among male emigrants in 1892–1894 varies between 13 and 23 percent as against 9 percent for the entire study period. Even the few male emigrants who confronted the depression in 1896–1897 show a high frequency of return. After 1900 we can observe a relatively high frequency of remigration among the large, male emigrant populations of 1901–1903. On the other hand, the frequency declines among those who immigrated to America during favorable economic cycles in 1905–1906.

The frequency of remigration among women reveals less correlation with fluctuations in American business cycles than the frequency among men. This is particularly evident in 1893 and 1894 and is definitely related to the fact that women were employed in branches which were less sensitive to economic fluctuations. Large numbers of them worked in private homes. However, their frequency of remigration grew gradually. Of those who emigrated during the period 1880–1889, men accounted for a 7 percent frequency of return and women 3 percent. From 1890 to 1899 the sexual composition of remigration frequency was 12 percent for men and 6 percent for women, whereas from 1900–1909 the frequency of women was not appreciably lower than that of men—that is, 7.5 percent as opposed to 8 percent. In other words, there was a strong phase shift of remigration by women as compared with that by men. This reflects the chronological phase shift of emigration by unmarried women in relationship to emigration by unmarried men.

The functional nature of remigration can be further illuminated if we expand this study to include the distribution of remigration frequency among different emigrant age groups. The statistical section of this study is omitted here.[17] Male emigrants aged 35–44 years have the strongest frequency of return. Only during the strong family emigration of the 1880s do these age groups show any weak return frequency. A particularly high frequency is noted among middle-aged males who came to America during peak years of emigration. Of those aged 35–39 and 40–44 years who emigrated in 1892, 1893, and 1902—that is, during years of severe economic recession in the sawmill industry—remigration accounted for respective figures of 17 percent, 10 percent, and 19 percent; and 15 percent, 18 percent, and 22 percent.

The fluctuations of remigration frequency among employed middle-aged males are instructive examples of the way in which periods of high unemployment in Sweden forced some married workers to seek temporary employment in America. One should also note that the assimilation capacity of middle-aged men may have been less than that of younger males. However, this factor does not explain the short-term fluctuations of remigration frequency among middle-aged workers.

The remigration frequency of middle-aged female emigrants was strikingly low. Most of them emigrated with their families, and therefore their share of what can be called the transatlantic labor migration of middle-aged men is eliminated.

A measurement of remigration frequency among older emigrants appears of little value due to the low absolute figures recorded for these groups. However, it is clear that older emigrants who were retired did not return to Sweden. It is likely that such persons came to America in order to join their children who had emigrated at an earlier date.

This analysis of remigration frequency among different emigrant age cohorts has been limited to one sawmill district in Sweden. However, it is probable that the results can be generalized. Due to the family character of Swedish emigration the frequency of remigration was low among men and women up until the middle of the 1880s. During the period of mass remigration in the 1890s the frequency among male emigrants was strikingly prominent, especially with regard to middle-aged cohorts. The migrant labor character of emigration was amplified during economic recessions in Sweden. This led to a tangible rise of remigration frequency among middle-aged male cohorts. The effects of American business recessions also heightened this frequency by alienating immigrant manpower from the American labor market. Remigration frequency among females increased after 1900. Older emigrants, finally, had a low frequency of return.

The Demographic Structure of Remigration

We should naturally expect that the migrant labor strain in remigration led to an even stronger overrepresentation of men among remigrants as compared to emigrants. Remigration to Sweden from America was, in fact, a clearly male phenomenon. Table 14.7 shows the sex distribution of adults (children under 15 years of age are omitted) in the population exchange between Sweden and the United States for 3 ten-year periods. The proportion of married migrants of both sexes is also indicated.

During the 1880s, 3 out of every 4 returning emigrants were men. Although this male dominance later declined, men still accounted for 64% of adult returning emigrants during the 1920s. The increased remigration of women was not, of course, due to a weakened frequency of return by migrant labor. Rather, it should be connected with short-range evaluations of employment prospects which had become more commmon among female emigrants.

The relatively high percentage of married persons among returning emigrants may come as some surprise. We can, in fact, illustrate the mechanisms of remigration by focusing special attention on the civil status of returning males. The Sundsvall district can exemplify this situation: 124 (or 74%) of the 168 married men who returned to this district from 1875 to 1913 emigrated and remigrated without their families. The percent of married men who returned on their own culminated from 1890 to 1894. The distribution of civil status among returning emigrants can thus also shed interesting light on the migrant labor strain in remigration.

In light of the principal interpretation of remigration outlined above, we should not expect any dramatic differences in the age distribution of emigrants and returning migrants. Table 14.8 presents a comparison between the age structure of emigrants and remigrants during the decade 1891–1900.[18]

Remigrants represented able-bodied age groups to a very strong degree. The type of ''pensioner-immigrant'' common to the 1960s and 1970s was very rare during the period of mass remigration. The major difference between these two populations is a rather prominent shift of gravity toward older age groups among remigrants. Remigrants aged 15–19 are particularly few in number, 3.1% as opposed to 23.8% for the same age group among emigrants.

The Length of Stay in America

The age distribution of returning Swedish Americans did not diverge dramatically from that of emigrants. This is due to the short amount of time which most remigrants had spent in America. The longest period spent in America by males was 24 years and by females 21 years. However, these are both extreme

Table 14.7
Emigration and Remigration by Sex

	Emigrants				Returning emigrants			
	Men %	Married %	Women %	Married %	Men %	Married %	Women %	Married %
1881–1890	57.6	21.7	42.4	24.5	74.2	30.0	25.8	42.6
1891–1900	52.7	17.9	47.3	16.3	65.5	33.6	34.5	34.4
1921–1930	65.8	15.7	34.2	24.9	64.0	27.7	36.0	38.9

cases. Most remigrants returned to Sweden after only a few years overseas. If we regard returning migration as a stage in a transatlantic labor migration, then we can expect to find overseas stays of relatively short duration for the majority of remigrants. Table 14.9 charts stays in America among male principal persons who returned to Västernorrland from 1880–1913. These statistics do not include returning migrants who settled in parishes other than those from which they originally emigrated. However, there is no reason to assume that this category of individuals would have diverged from the rest in terms of length of stay in America.

In most cases remigration occurred only one or two years after emigration. Not less than 71.7% of these remigrants stayed in America 4 years or less, and only 6.1% stayed more than 10 years. The reason for the low percentage of long-term stays in America is somewhat obvious. Long periods of stay ought to have led to substantial social integration in America and increased resistance to remigration.

Few stays of medium duration (5–9 years) are recorded among the strong wave of remigrants from 1890–1894. This is probably due to the fact that those who emigrated in the middle or late 1880s managed to become integrated in American society and resistant to the idea of returning before the depression of 1893–1894.

There are indications that the length of stay in America was socially selective. Over 40% of the remigrants to some agricultural parishes in Västernorrland stayed for periods of 5–9 years in America. A number of studies have also shown that many farmers' sons bought farms in Sweden with money saved in America.

Improvements in communications or reductions in travel costs do not explain

Table 14.8
The Age Structure of Swedish Overseas Migration, 1891–1900

Ages	Emigrants		Remigrants	
	Number	%	Number	%
0–14	29 578	14.5	6 851	14.2
15–19	48 603	23.8	1 504	3.1
20–24	56 940	27.8	6 754	14.0
25–29	27 628	13.5	9 774	20.3
30–34	15 246	7.5	8 833	18.4
35–39	9 056	4.4	5 588	11.6
40–44	5 248	2.6	3 317	6.9
45–49	3 411	1.7	1 929	4.0
50–	8 733	4.3	3 571	7.4
Total	204 513	100.0	48 121	100.0

Source: Bidrag till Sveriges officiella statistik, Serie A.

the long-term changes and short-term fluctuations affecting lengths of stay in America. This is demonstrated, for example, by the fact that extremely short periods of stay show no tendency to rise over time. Of decisive importance for the distribution of short periods of stay was the situation on the American labor market and its character of a temporary alternative to unfavorable employment prospects in Sweden. Peak years of emigration primarily recruit remigrants with short periods of stay in America. During the peak emigration years of 1890–1894 and 1900–1904 remigrants who spent one year in America amounted to 51.8% and 47.6% respectively, as opposed to 29.5% for the entire 1880–1913 period. The clearest examples of labor migrants are doubtlessly to be found among those who spent only a few years in America. Generally speaking, the short periods of stay in America highlight the specific character of remigration as an integrated part of an Atlantic labor market. Moreover, there is much to indicate that the repetitive element in this transatlantic migration was largely concentrated on remigrants with short periods of stay in America. All things considered, this "commuting" element comprised a substantial share of late transatlantic migration. Not less than 10.6% of those who emigrated as passengers on the Swedish American Line in 1922–1923 had been in America previously.[19]

The short periods of stay in America contributed to the rather consistent pattern of movement by migrants returning to original districts of emigration. For most remigrants a period of stay in America was not a step in a process of social adjustment. A special study of remigration to the city of Halmstad, on Sweden's West coast, can illustrate this point. Of those who returned to Halmstad from

Table 14.9
Lengths of Stay in America for Male Principal Persons Who Emigrated from
Västernorrland to North America and Remigrated, 1880–1913

Length of stay in years	1880 –84	1885 –89	1890 –94	1895 –99	1900 –04	1905 –09	1910 –13	1880 –1913
1	6	20	86	10	80	75	76	352
2	8	7	42	32	13	54	43	199
3	5	9	13	41	10	45	39	162
4	2	6	8	35	2	52	30	135
5–9	2	17	11	67	44	65	66	272
10–14	–	–	6	10	16	8	12	52
15–19	2	1	–	1	3	5	4	16
20–24	–	–	–	–	–	1	4	5
Total	25	60	166	196	168	305	273	1 193

Sources: Registers of Migration, Parish Registers of Catechetical Examinations, Parish Record Books, Parish Church Archives in the Sundsvall District. Summariska folkmängdsreogörelser, The Central Bureau of Statistics, Stockholm.

1870–1899, 93 percent had not changed their social position during their time in America.[20] This finding falls well in line with the strikingly static and "conservative" character of remigration to Sweden from North America.

This chapter began with Halvar Olsson, and finally we come back to him. In many respects he was representative of the returning Swedish-Americans. He came back after only two years in America, and he was young when he returned. The age structure of the return migrants resembled very much the age distribution of emigrants, men and women in their prime working-age. However, up to 1920 the group of return migrants was clearly dominated by men. The main reason why the age distribution of the returning Swedish-Americans diverged so little from the emigrants is the short time that most remigrants had spent in America. This tendency also emphasizes the role of migration across the Atlantic as part of the formation of an international labor market. The short periods of stay in America contributed to the rather consistent pattern of movement by migrants returning to original districts of emigration. For most remigrants a period of stay in America was not a step in a process of social adjustment. When Halvar Olsson returned to his home parish in Jämtland in 1905 he was also in this final respect typical of the majority of the returning Swedish-Americans. They had seen the prairies and cities of America, but they had never succeeded in dissolving their ties to the Swedish soil and culture.

NOTES

1. The American statistics apply to the fiscal year beginning July 1 and ending June 30.

2. Robert F. Foerster, *Italian Emigration of Our Times* (Cambridge, Mass., 1919), p. 36.

3. Frank Thistlethwaite, "Migration from Europe Overseas in the Nineteenth and Twentieth Centuries," in *Rapports* vol. V, XIe Congrès International des Sciences Historiques (Uppsala, 1960), p. 40.

4. Ingrid Semmingsen, *Veien mot Vest. Utvandringen fra Norge til Amerika, 1865–1915* [The way west, emigration from Norway to America], 2 vols. (Oslo, 1950), 2:460ff.

5. Theodore Saloutos, *They Remember America. The Story of the Repatriated Greek-Americans* (Berkeley and Los Angeles, 1956), passim.

6. F. P. Cerase, "A Study of Italian Migrants Returning from the USA," in *International Migration Review* (1967), no. 3, pp. 67ff.

7. G. R. Gilkey, "The United States and Italy. Migration and Repatriation," in F. D. Scott, ed., *World Migration in Modern Times*, (New Jersey, 1968), pp. 44ff.

8. See Lars-Göran Tedebrand "Sources for the History of Swedish Emigration," in Harald Runblom and Hans Norman, eds., *From Sweden to America. A History of the Migration* (Uppsala, 1976).

9. E. G. Ravenstein, "The Laws of Migration," in *Journal of the Royal Statistical Society* 48, Part 2, p. 199.

10. Jan Wallander, *Flykten från skogsbygden. En undersökning i Klarälvsdalen* [The flight from the forest districts. A study of the Klarälven valley] (Stockholm, 1948), p. 140.

11. Gustav Sundbärg, "Bidrag till utvandringsfrågan fran befolkningsstatistik syn-

punkt" [Contributions to the issue of emigration from the standpoint of population statistics] in *Uppsala Universitets Årsskrift* (1885 and 1886), 37ff; Lars-Göran Tedebrand, *Västernorrland och Nordamerika 1875–1913. Utvandring och återinvandring* [Emigration from Västernorrland County to North America and reimmigration to Västernorrland County] (Uppsala, 1972), pp. 259ff.

12. This discussion is primarily based on Tedebrand *Västernorrland och Nordamerika*, pp. 222-58. Remigration to Sweden has also been treated briefly by H. Nelson, *Emigrationsutredningen*, Bilaga VIII, pp. 77ff; Eric De Geer, "Emigrationen i Västsverige i slutet av 1800-talet" [Emigration from Western Sweden at the end of the 1800s] (Ymer, 1959) p. 215; Birgitta Odén, "Emigration från Norden till Nordamerika under 1800-talet. Aktuella forskningsuppgifter" [Emigration from Scandinavia to North America during the 1800s. Current tasks of research] in *Historisk tidskrift* (1963), 270f.; Lars Ljungmark, *Den stora utvandringen. Svensk emigration till USA 1840–1925* [The great emigration. Swedish emigration to the U.S. 1840–1925] (Stockholm, 1965), pp. 176f.; Sten Carlsson, "Från familjeutvandring till ensamutvandring. En utvecklingslinje i den svenska emigrationens historia" [From family emigration to individual emigration. A line of development in the history of Swedish emigration] in *Emigrationer. En Bok till Vilhelm Moberg 20.8.1968* (Stockholm, 1968), pp. 103ff.; and in more detail by Bo Kronborg and Thomas Nilsson, *Stadsflyttare. Industrialisering, migration och social mobilitet med utgångspunkt fran Halmstad, 1870–1910* [Urban migrants. Industrialization, migration and social mobility on the basis of Halmstad, 1870–1910] (Uppsala 1975), pp. 144ff.

13. Peter Marschalck, *Deutsche Überseewanderung im 19. Jahrhundert. Ein Beitrag zur soziologischen Theorie der Bevölkerung* (Stuttgart, 1973), p. 95. [Editor's note: This view has been refuted by recent research. From 1879 to 1914 about two million Germans arrived as workers.]

14. The analysis of return migration to Västernorrland includes the small numbers of immigrants from Canada.

15. See, for example, Björn Rondahl, *Emigration, folkomflyttning och säsongarbete i ett sågverksdistrikt i södra Hälsingland 1865–1910. Söderala kommun med särskild hänsyn till Ljusne industrisamhälle* [Emigration, internal migration and migrant labor movements in a sawmill district in Southern Hälsingland 1865–1910] (Uppsala, 1972), p. 259.

16. The relationship between physical health and changes in workers' physical environment during the course of industrialization constitutes an interesting and important research topic.

17. This study is based on Table 66 in Tedebrand, *Västernorrland och Nordamerika*, p. 249.

18. The table includes the relatively moderate exchange of population with other overseas countries besides the United States and Canada.

19. *Sociala Meddelanden*, vol. 3 (1924), 173.

20. Bo Kronborg and Thomas Nilsson, *Stadsflyttare*, p. 158.

FINNISH MIGRANTS (1860–1930) IN THE OVERSEAS RETURN MIGRATION MOVEMENT

15

Keijo Virtanen

From the point of view of an overall study of overseas migration, research on return migration must concern itself with four phases: life in the country of origin, emigration, life in the host country, and return. Return may lead to a new departure, and so on, but one day the circle comes to an end, either in the host country or in the country of origin (see Figure 15.1).[1] The point of departure for a study of return migration is the statement by the British statistician E. G. Ravenstein in 1885 that every current of migration movement occasions a compensatory counter-current.[2] The central aim of the present essay is to analyze the return migration of the Finns, taking into account the dichotomy between emigrants (emigrating between the 1860s and 1930) who returned and those who did not. At the same time the Finnish overseas return migration will be placed in a wider international context.

So far European research into overseas migration has paid very little attention to the counter-current, that is, return migration. The reason is not so much the failure to recognize the relevance of its investigation as the absence of comprehensive statistics and other material corresponding to that available for emigration. The Finns form one of the rare nationalities for which thorough research is possible. The sources, however, are made up of a large number of different pieces that have to be fitted together. While emigration is a mass phenomenon, the collection of evidence has to be carried out at the level of the individual, due to the absence of comprehensive and reliable material. A number of sample areas are therefore needed, but they must be complemented by recourse to other research material, plenty of which is available.[3]

Finnish migration has to be analyzed in the international context. The division into the "old" and "new" migration originated in the report of the Dillingham Commission's investigation of immigration into the United States, which was published in 1911. The "new" immigrants, who came from Eastern and Southern Europe, began to arrive in the 1880s and mainly worked in the cities. Virtually all of them were men. In addition, they were regarded as temporary labor in the host country, which would subsequently return to its country of origin.[4] Indeed, both the background factors and the actual conditions of migration had radically changed by the end of the nineteenth century, when the Finnish migration began

Figure 15.1
The Phases of Overseas Migration as a Continuous Circle: The Theoretical Scope of the Present Investigation

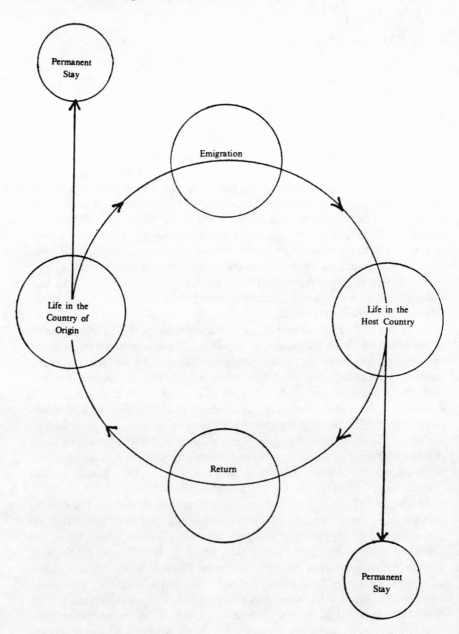

to reach its peak. The host country—in the main, the United States—had become a rapidly expanding industrial society, and this affected not only the "new" migration countries, but equally those of the "old" migration, whose migration continued into the twentieth century.

The clear majority of Finnish migrants did in fact consider themselves temporary labor. They left for economic reasons, wishing to earn as much as possible and then return home. One emigrant of 1922, when questioned in Florida in 1968 about his intention to return at the moment of emigration commented: "I should think everyone intends to." Another stated that he had intended to remain abroad until he had a "pocketful of money." Very few—according to the interviews carried out for this research—intended to leave their home country for ever, even though it "pushed" so many people overseas.

After all, the original cause of this mass movement of people was the "push": a radical change in the traditional basis of society. The population increased at an unprecedented rate in Europe during the nineteenth century as industrialization proceeded; with the rising standard of living, and improvements in medicine, the birthrate rose and mortality declined.[5] The increase in population became so rapid that the economy could not keep pace with it, leading in Finland as elsewhere in Europe to the emergence of a "relative surplus population," which the economy could not adequately support.

This relative surplus population had become a problem in Finland even in the 1840s. In the transitional period between 1815 and 1875 the main increase in population occurred in rural areas, leading to population pressure, since the range of economic opportunities did not expand accordingly. This was further reinforced by the one-sidedness of the country's economy, for in the 1860s about 85 percent of the Finnish population was still engaged in agriculture.[6] An increasing proportion of the rural population was non-self-supporting, since the number of farms did not increase as fast as the potential number of farmers. The proportion of landless population steadily increased toward the end of the nineteenth century, and its opportunities for supporting itself deteriorated.[7] As a result of this development, Finnish society in the nineteenth century was not in fact so stable as to rule out migration even at the beginning of the century; internal migration was actually greater at the beginning of the century than at the end. This was mainly due to the fact that emigration abroad was very low; those who wanted to move saw no other alternative than to move inside the country. The increase in emigration partially explains the reduction in internal migration toward the end of the century. Once emigration to North America had gained momentum, self-perpetuating factors came into play: factors such as family ties, with different members of the family emigrating at various times; or the migration tradition in a given area, with emigration gradually becoming a collective form of behavior or social norm.[8]

The emigration from Finland to overseas countries took on the nature of a mass movement at a later date (in the 1870s) than that from many central

European and Scandinavian countries; but it was in full swing when the "new" immigration began to reach North America.[9] The beginnings of the emigration from Finland thus fall somewhere in the middle of the European development.

The analysis of the Finnish return migration and its comparison with the movements from the Scandinavian countries reveals considerable similarities. The Finnish return rate among those emigrating between 1860 and 1930 (about 380,000 emigrants) was about one-fifth, which is on the same scale as in Sweden and Denmark.[10] The situation was quite different in countries such as Italy and Greece, which were typical "new" migration countries, where a large proportion of the migrants returned home, perhaps subsequently to commute overseas to work again.[11] But return migration to Britain was also very high.[12] The division into "old" and "new" migration countries by reference to the return rate or to the impermanent nature of the migration cannot be sustained in the Finnish and British cases.

Figure 15.2 presents a typology of the central factors that influence the dichotomy between the settlement overseas or permanent return to Finland. First, the analysis of the factors connected strictly with the area of origin shows that only just over 10 percent of the Finnish emigrants originated from towns; and they were even less strongly represented in the return migration, since the urban return rate was only around 5 to 10 percent of those emigrating. This is partly due to emigrants who first moved from the surrounding countryside to a town before moving on overseas. In many cases these migrants would return to the countryside directly. The return rate to Swedish towns was also lower than to the country as a whole.[13]

Second, regional variations were strikingly visible in the Finnish return migration, as was also the case in other countries. The return to areas of high emigration in southern Ostrobothnia and northern Satakunta was somewhat higher than average, while that to the areas of extremely high emigration in central Ostrobothnia, was approximately the same as the national level, that is, around one-fifth of the emigrants. It was also around 20 percent of those emigrating in the tenant farming areas of southern Finland. In eastern and northern Finland, however, the return rate was distinctly lower than for the country as a whole. These variations in the return rate are due to considerable differences in the socio-economic and demographic structure both of the emigration and of the population in general between one part of the country and another. Farmers and tenant farmers returned relatively more frequently than their children, and the latter in turn more frequently than members of the landless population. Farmers and tenant farmers usually returned permanently, whereas their children often migrated more than once, due to their lack of a sure livelihood in Finland.

Third, a general finding is that the older the migrant was at emigration, the more likely he or she was subsequently to return to Finland, with the exception of those over fifty at emigration, whose return rate was low. Their motives were connected with economic factors to a lesser degree than those of the younger groups. Fourth, the return rate for men was relatively much higher than that for the women: 75 to 85 percent of the migrants permanently returning to Finland were men. Fifth, married male emigrants normally returned after a few years to rejoin their families. Others sent tickets to their families in Finland and started a new life abroad. This family emigration reduced the probability of return considerably. As a whole, however, the permanent return rate for married em-

Figure 15.2

Factors Influencing the Probability of Settlement or Return

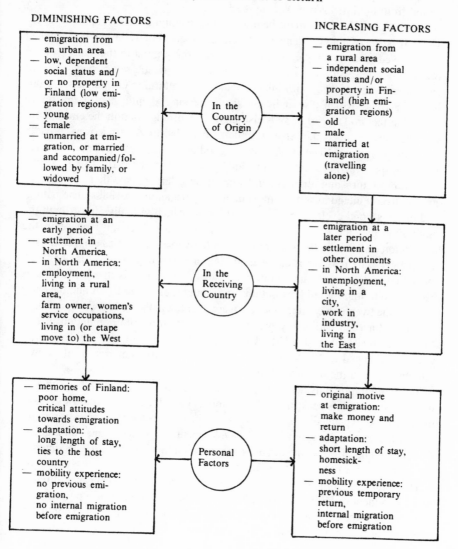

DIMINISHING FACTORS

INCREASING FACTORS

— emigration from an urban area
— low, dependent social status and/ or no property in Finland (low emigration regions)
— young
— female
— unmarried at emigration, or married and accompanied/followed by family, or widowed

In the Country of Origin

— emigration from a rural area
— independent social status and/or property in Finland (high emigration regions)
— old
— male
— married at emigration (travelling alone)

— emigration at an early period
— settlement in North America.
— in North America: employment, living in a rural area, farm owner, women's service occupations, living in (or etape move to) the West

In the Receiving Country

— emigration at a later period
— settlement in other continents
— in North America: unemployment, living in a city, work in industry, living in the East

— memories of Finland: poor home, critical attitudes towards emigration
— adaptation: long length of stay, ties to the host country
— mobility experience: no previous emigration, no internal migration before emigration

Personal Factors

— original motive at emigration: make money and return
— adaptation: short length of stay, homesickness
— mobility experience: previous temporary return, internal migration before emigration

igrants was much higher than that for the unmarried. Nearly half of those returning permanently to Finland were married, while this had only been the case with a quarter of the emigrants.

Turning the focus onto the receiving areas, the first point to make is that—in relative numbers—the later the person emigrated, the more probable was his return. Although the Finnish emigration began later than that from the Scandinavian countries, the peaks in the return migration occurred in approximately the same periods, if the following three phases, detectable in both the emigration and the return, are kept in mind: the period before 1893, 1893–1914, and the period from the First World War up to 1930.

The first phase lasted from the beginnings of the emigration until approximately 1893. It is impossible to identify the year precisely, but 1893 has been picked out in Sweden, for example, as an important turning point in the history of the return migration. Similarly, in Norway and Denmark the return began to rise steeply from the 1890s.[14] In Finland statistics on returning emigrants were initiated in 1894, which also indicates the increasing significance of the return migration factor. The early 1890s also marked a turning point in the emigration. By this decade the conquest and settlement of North America was, broadly speaking, completed. The availability of good and cheap farmland was decreasing. Transport facilities also significantly improved in the early 1890s. At the same time, return migration began to occur on a larger scale then, since emigration from Finland as a mass movement only began in the 1880s. The natural end of the second cycle is the First World War, which virtually cut off both the emigration and the return migration for many years. The third phase in the emigration ended in 1930, when emigration to overseas countries stopped almost completely. The reason for this was the international depression, together with the actual curtailment of immigration to Canada. Prior to this, the United States had started to impose mild restrictions on immigration in the 1890s and the early years of the twentieth century. Quotas were adopted in the 1920s. First, in 1921, the quota for each nationality was fixed at 3 percent of the population of that nationality recorded in the 1910 United States Census. In 1924 the reference year was changed to 1890, in order to further limit the immigration of "new" immigrants, and the quota was cut to 2 percent.

Return migration only achieved real significance in the second of these phases, in which it passed its peak in absolute numbers in all the Nordic countries. These trends can be explained to a large extent by the rapid industrial expansion in the United States and the technological development of transport and communications. It should also be noted that the immigration quotas of the 1920s deterred immigration, but not return migration.

The main flow of the Finnish overseas emigration (98-99 percent) was directed to the continent of North America, that is, to the United States (83 percent) and Canada (16 percent). It was not until the 1920s that other countries and continents began to attract more attention from emigrants, but this migration remained exceptional.[15] The return rate from Australia, for example, was extremely high. Approximately 50 percent returned permanently. The main reason for this was that Australia was a second-choice country of destination; secondly, there emerged hardly any of the supportive Finnish communities that emigrants could turn to in many parts of North America. The Australian immigrants also took up work that was not binding in nature. They worked in mining, as farm laborers, and on the docks. For the same reasons, even higher return rates occurred among the Finnish emigrants to South America and South Africa. The countries and continents of small immigration were thus unable to attract or retain immigrants to the same extent as North America. The hypothesis that increasing distance had a diminishing effect on the return migration rate is not borne out when the Finnish emigrations to North America and other countries are compared.[16]

With reference to the United States and Canada alone, periods of economic depression increased the return migration. A letter from a Finn in Bessemer, Michigan, to his brother in Finland, written in 1907 when the Finnish return migration was at its height and when the United States economy was undergoing a financial crisis, illustrates the hardships of migrant life:[17]

Hello Brother Kusti from Bessemer and many greetings.

I have been all right and I hope the same to you. The Flambo camp stopped running in the middle of November. I spent one week going from camp to camp but could not find work. All the camps were full of men. There were not enough beds and I had to sleep on the floor. I went to one camp on Saturday evening and I was planning to stay there over the weekend. But next morning I had to start walking to another camp again to get there before dark. And when I could not find work, I drove to Bessemer. So now I lie here at Lehtonen's. I am not sure whether I can find work before Christmas. I was planning to come to see you for Christmas but it is so cold that I will leave it until next summer. . . .

Jussi Mikola left for Finland on November 26. I am going to stay here until Christmas. After Christmas—if the camps start running again—I have to work for two or three months to get money for boarding. Because at the moment I just lie in bed and spend.[18]

On the other hand, the Finnish return migration was not as closely connected with economic cycles as emigration, since personal motives played a more important role in the decision to return than in the original decision to emigrate. The return did not constitute to the same extent a mass phenomenon as emigration.

The first jobs obtained by the men were typically in mining, forestry, or in a factory, while women mainly worked in service occupations. The motivation of the women to return was reduced by this work, which provided more favorable conditions for learning the new customs and language than did the men's occupations. The men's employment was relatively more sensitive to economic fluctuations in the host country. This further explains the relatively lower return rate for women than for men. However, the Finnish return was not as dependent on economic cycles as that of the countries in southern Europe; unlike the typical "new" migrants, Finnish immigrants did not usually work in large gangs in the cities as the Italians[19] and the Greeks did.[20]

Apart from mining and forest labor, the occupation most followed by the Finns was agriculture, the "right" form of livelihood for the "old" migrants, according to the Dillingham Commission. With the passage of time, many men began to establish farms, though often on very infertile land; the best land had already been taken by other ethnic groups by the end of the nineteenth century. In any case, farming had the effect of binding the immigrant to his adopted country. The general tendency of Finnish immigrants to settle in the countryside or small towns and their eagerness to set up farms of their own must have been a particularly strong factor reducing the probability of their return. However, we are not able to give any exact figures for the number of Finnish immigrant farmers in relation to workers. For example, many immigrants worked in the mines and had farms at the same time.

The Finnish immigrants in the United States spread over the States along the northern border from the Atlantic seaboard to the Pacific coast. In Canada they were concentrated in Ontario and British Columbia. The return rate appears to have been highest in the eastern States and Provinces. It declined the further west Finns worked and settled. One reason for this was a form of stage migration. When an immigrant began to search for a new place to live farther west, this usually meant the gradual abandonment of the idea of returning. Thus the hypothesis that the return migration rate falls with increasing distance is relevant in North America.[21] It represents a more significant geographical factor in the return than does the distribution of migrants between the United States and Canada. Thus the horizontal (east-west) factor was more important than the vertical (United States-Canada) factor in determining the probability of return.

Finally, we need to analyze the strictly personal factors influencing the decision of migrants to return or not (see Figure 15.2); these take on greater significance in the return since this did not have the same mass features as the emigration. The predominant motive for emigration, both in Finland and in many other countries, was the search for better earnings leading to an improved standard of living and a subsequent return home. Consequently, over half of the Finnish migrants who returned did so within five years of emigration. Studies of migrants from other countries, both of the "old" and "new" migrations, have revealed similar patterns.[22] A counterweight to the idea of returning was the overall situation in the country of origin, that is, economic conditions at emigration and critical attitudes toward emigration in the home country.[23]

The achievement of their objectives, however, was not the only motive for migrants to return, since adversities might also send them back. The most common cause mentioned by the migrants themselves was homesickness, arising from a failure to adapt to the host country, and this was at its strongest soon after arrival. These are typical expressions: "Longing for the old country brought me back to where I was born'' (a returnee of 1938), or ''I felt homesick the whole time'' (a returnee of 1933). The following description by an immigrant of her arrival in Canada in 1922 illustrates difficulties of adjustment due to the structure of the ethnic community itself rather than the host society:

Let me tell you a bit what sort of impression you got when you arrived in Canada as an immigrant from Finland. We lived for six months in Niegara Falls [*sic*]. And my husband, he was working for the Hydro, for the Electricity. And for the Public Works in Kapperliff (Copper Cliff). The Finnish-Canadians, those who'd gone there earlier, were nasty to newcomers, that much sometimes, that people sometimes got done in. Sort of by accident. They hated Finns, because they suspected they were what they called Butchers [a reference to the reprisals in the Finnish Civil War in 1918]. It was only the Communists who went on like that. So we decided to get out of there, and we went to Vindsor [*sic*], and then on to Detroit. There were lots of communists in Detroit too, but they didn't insist on a party card, like they did in Niegara. There was a Finnish parish in Detroit, with a church and everything. But you know, the life that the Finns led there, it was pretty boring. Work, that was what they talked about all the time . . . whenever the men got together, the first question was always, what shift're you on? And conversation was mostly, just about work. . . . [24]

The longer the lapse of time since the migrant's arrival in the new country, the less likely became his or her return to the home country. With the passage of the years came increasing familiarity with the life in the new country. The following extract describes this aspect:

Well at that time [in the 1920s] life in Canata [*sic*] was very difficult for the Finns cause the Finns who'd emigrated didn't know any English so they couldn't complain to the Canadian authorities . . . Well in the end the Canadian authorities did something about it and life changed for the better. There was a Finnish Society set up and everyone supposed to belong to it. It wasn't anything to do with parties but you weren't allowed to be a communist. . . . [25]

Not only did the culture of the host country cause difficulties of adaptation for the immigrants, but, as these extracts indicate, there were also tensions operating within the ethnic groups that aroused controversy. The Finnish immigrants were very active in political radicalism. In the 1920s about 40 percent of the members of the American Communist Party consisted of Finns. It also has been estimated that about 25 percent of the Finnish immigrants were socialists or communists in the United States and Canada.[26]

But these tensions were probably not of great significance in relation to the return; on the contrary, with the growth of the numbers of Finns in a particular area, conditions were likely to become more pleasant. It is a well-known fact that different groups tended to settle in the same areas: Finns in the little towns and in the countryside of northern Michigan and Minnesota; Italians in the big cities of the eastern parts of the United States; and so on. In these communities immigrants founded all kinds of organizations and joined in other group activities. For adaptation and assimilation these had a double meaning. On the one hand, these group activities eased the cultural shock that the immigrant faced after arrival. The immigrant roots were in completely different living conditions. The Finn, for example, came from the rural communities and from rural occupations; he was generally uneducated; his greatest asset was his physical strength. Immigrant communities helped him to get used to the new surroundings and to the new situation. But on the other hand, these communities were an obstacle to complete assimilation. The immigrant was isolated, and his ability to create new contacts was severely limited because of language difficulties. But over the years and decades as the immigrants became used to their new home, the desire to return to the old country faded; thus most Finns in America remained immigrants for the rest of their lives.

However, differing political ideologies and the resulting tensions between immigrants did cause a movement from North America to the Soviet Union in the 1920s and 1930s. The first phase of this migration took place in the early 1920s, when a certain number of Finnish-Americans set out to join in building the "Republic of Work." The main activities of the Finns were aimed at strengthening the economy of Soviet Karelia by the establishment of cooperatives. This project was started in 1922, and about one hundred Finnish-Americans took part, but it did not last for very long, since in December 1922 the Soviet government began to impose restrictions on foreign labor entering the country; and within a few years of the Finns' arrival most of them had returned to America, or, in a few cases, to Finland.[27] In the early 1920s there was also recruitment of Americans to work in other parts of Soviet Russia. For six years, starting in 1922, a number of them moved to the Kuzbas colony in Siberia, and Finns made up the largest ethnic grouping there. The majority of the members ultimately returned to the United States, though others moved to Karelia, the Urals, or the Caucasus.[28] There was also an entirely Finnish–American venture, the Sower's Commune, a farming cooperative established in southern Russia in 1922. There was rapid turnover among its members, but it continued with a strength of about one hundred members up to 1927; subsequently it began to change, for in 1932 it was reported to comprise as many as sixteen different nationalities. There is no further information about it after the middle of that decade, and it has been suggested that it may have been the victim of a purge.[29]

Emigration of Finns from North America to the Soviet Union only began on a large scale in the 1930s. During the depression it emerged as a serious alternative to return to Finland among members of the Finnish-American labor movement.[30] Difficulties of employment on the one hand, and expectations regarding conditions in the Soviet Union on the other, are given as the main reasons for this migration by one former migrant, for example, who returned from the Soviet Union to settle in Kauhajoki, Finland, as late as 1956. She had emigrated from Finland to Canada in 1928 and in 1933 moved with her husband to the Soviet

Union. Estimates of the overall numbers involved in this migration vary, but it seems certain that about six to eight thousand took part.[31]

Only some of those who did not settle permanently in the Soviet Union returned to Finland; others returned to America. It has been calculated that of those Finnish-Canadians who moved there from the area around Sudbury, Ontario, about one-fifth returned to Canada (mainly to the Sudbury area). Since this figure is based on a total of only seventy-eight departures, the findings cannot be considered as more than illustrative.[32] Another estimate, on the basis of the questionnaires, is that about half came back, either to the United States, Canada, or Finland.[33]

The analysis of the return migration does not include answering the question as to how many migrants would have returned if they had had the opportunity. However, from the point of view of the processes involved in deciding whether to return or not, this is of interest. While it is impossible to obtain any exact information, some indications are available. Migrants who were unable to afford the journey home were entitled to receive a repatriation grant from the United States government during the early 1930s. The conditions were that the migrant must have arrived in the country legally and that he or she must not have been in the country for longer than three years.[34] There are no data available on how many actually applied for this assistance. We do know—on the basis of the estimate made by the shipping companies—that about 10 percent of those returning had been so unsuccessful abroad that their families in Finland had to send them the money for the return ticket.[35] In the early 1970s there were still old Finnish lumberjacks living in the ''hotels'' in Duluth, Minnesota. They had stayed in these dilapidated farmer boarding houses for decades with no real contacts with the world outside, not even the Finnish community. We may presume that many of them would have returned to Finland during the depression years of the 1930s if they had had money for the return ticket.

While homesickness or similar reasons drove many of the migrants back to Finland, their intention in the majority of cases was, clearly, to settle permanently there. But return did not necessarily mean that the migrants would be happy back in Finland either. During their years of absence, changes had taken place in their home area, as also in the migrants themselves, sometimes creating insuperable tensions. About 10 percent of all the Finnish migrants made two or more journeys overseas in the period up to 1930; but relatively more of those who made at least two trips returned permanently to Finland than of those who had emigrated only once. An emigrant who revisited Finland and attempted to readjust to Finnish conditions without succeeding and therefore decided to re-emigrate was, nevertheless, more drawn to his or her old home area even at a later stage than those emigrants who only made a single journey. Similarly, those who had already moved at least once inside Finland before emigrating overseas were more likely to return than those who had lived all their lives in one place before emigrating. The former group were more used to moving, so that the return was also easier for them. On the other hand, the differences in the return rate between these groups are not large.

The immigrants in North America were, however, aware of the possible problems that might await them in the old country. Concrete evidence of this is to be found in plans for return in large groups, which envisaged settlement in an area entirely occupied by return migrants. One of the central figures in this project was an immigrant named Antero Havela who wrote a longish article on this topic in 1932 in the newspaper *Lännen Suometar* (*Western Finn*), published in Astoria, Oregon. Referring to the current depression in the United States, he concluded with the question, "What is our future in this country?" His solution was a mass movement back to Finland, to establish a lakeside community settlement somewhere near the cities of Helsinki, Turku, or Tampere. He believed that virtually all emigrants suffered to a considerable degree from homesickness and that organized return should therefore be pursued. A community of only Finnish-Americans would help the returning migrants to readapt to Finnish society more successfully.[36] Plans for common settlements of returnees were still being discussed in several places at the time of the Second World War, but they were never realized.[37]

These examples illustrate that many different problems had to be faced in connection with return and that efforts were made to solve these in advance. One such effort was the foundation in 1933 in Helsinki of the *Amerikan Suomalainen Seura* (Society of American Finns), whose aims included "to be a point of contact for Finns in America, and to provide assistance to members in difficulties; to provide guidance and support in the achievement of goals of material and intellectual progress . . . ." This society ceased its activities very soon, however, as did the *Suomen Ulkomaankävijäin Seura* (Finnish Overseas Travellers' Association), founded in 1934, which had only thirty-eight members two years later.

After all, the returning migrants had a relatively good chance of readjusting to life back home, primarily due to the fact that in most cases they had only been abroad for a few years. The majority also tended to be fairly well off when they returned; and since they often invested their savings either in farming or some other form of real estate, this too was likely to strengthen their ties with the area they had settled in and to lead to the abandonment of any ideas of reemigration overseas.

The returning migrants brought new influences back with them, which they tried to put into practice in Finland. But since the numbers returning to Finland were so small, this impact is not as clearly indentifiable as, for instance, in southern Europe, where the economic significance of the return migration was considerable.[38] One Finnish returnee of 1928 stated:

In a town [urban] society there wasn't much chance for unskilled emigrants to have much effect on the life of the town. I'm sure that returning emigrants—despite their hardworkingness and the bit of money they had—were on the receiving end.[39]

In Finland, too, the most easily recognizable impact of the returning migrants was in the economy, and in rural areas in the regions of high emigration this could even be quite striking. The following comment was made by a return migrant to Alahärmä, a rural commune in Ostrobothnia, in 1928:

When the emigrants had come back home to Alahärmä, and probably in other places as well, they enriched the economy, because there had been especially many men from this district who emigrated, and when they came back they repaired their buildings and farms in general. Some of them bought themselves a farm, and others bought extra land.[40]

This then was the situation in areas (particularly in Ostrobothnia) where the emigration had been so great that the return was locally significant even in absolute terms.

The returning migrants also wished to use the "mental capital" they had acquired abroad. Table 15.1 collates the answers of returned migrants to the questionnaire about what benefits other than economic ones they themselves considered they had acquired from emigrating:[41]

Table 15.1
Benefits, Other than Economic, Acquired from Migrating

Benefit	No. of Persons	Percent of Total
Broadening one's view of the world, new experience, seeing the world, etc.	421	67.9
Acquiring language skills	136	21.9
Learning a trade	34	5.5
Appreciating life in Finland	14	2.3
Meeting a spouse	10	1.6
Memories	5	0.8%
TOTAL	620	100.0

The majority of those returning migrants who answered this question thus referred to the broadening of their view of the world. A typical opinion was this: "Views broadened, practical experience, learned to live." The time spent abroad was "the best high school you could hope for."

Their access to local influence depended on the attitude in their home area to the various kinds of new ideas they held. Intellectual, political and moral ideas were more likely to encounter an emotional reception than economic influence, depending on the attitudes and value judgments of the people involved. For example, the local population's own views on political matters determined whether the influences brought with them by the migrants were seen positively or negatively. But, as one respondent commented, the returnees tended to be quite active in high emigration regions:

You see, the men who'd come back from America usually got elected to various kinds of jobs in local government and politics. Many of them . . . were active in the Agrarian Party. Some supported socialist ideas. I suppose it was only the most adventurous and active people who went off and emigrated in the first place.[42]

This impression is accurate, for the Finnish-Americans have been shown to have brought about an increase in rural radicalism in Finland; in the towns, on the other hand, socialist ideas were mainly home-grown. In Munsala, Otto Anderson and some other migrants who had returned from the United States founded the local Social Democratic Association as early as 1911, and in the 1919 elections following the Finnish Civil War, he was elected to the Finnish parliament (*Eduskunta*) as a Swedish-speaking Social Democrat.[43] Between the achievement of Finnish independent in 1917 and 1933, there were at least fifteen members of the *Eduskunta* who had been migrants in North America. Several of the socialists had studied at the Finnish-American institution, the Work People's College, in Duluth, Minnesota.[44]

The radicalizing influence of the returning migrants is particularly visible in rural Ostrobothnia. This is not difficult to explain, since the Finnish-American labor movement was exceptionally active in the first two decades of this century, and the return migration included people who had become radicalized abroad and who actively attempted to spread their ideas in their native area. Parliamentary activity in the *Eduskunta* increased the possibilities of influence considerably.

A comment by another returning migrant stressed the problems of readjustment to social life:

At that time [in the 1920s] moral life in Ganada [*sic*] was much cruder than in Finland, and the kind of language used about morality, too. Emigrants who came back had to be careful not to talk too crudely. People used to talk very soberly in those days round Härmä.[45]

It has been shown that the returning migrants had an impact on religious life and the Church in Finland. The spread of the Free Churches, in particular, and the introduction of legislation ensuring liberty of religion, has been attributed partly to the migration. This led the official Lutheran Church to adopt a critical attitude toward the emigration as a whole.[46] A concrete example of the religious impact of the returning migrants was the foundation in Kristinestad in 1882 of the first Methodist congregation in Finland.[47]

In general, however, the returning migrants do not appear to have caused much irritation in the surrounding community; with the exception of the high emigration areas, there were simply too few returning migrants for their impact to be identifiable. One writer, in 1910, recognized both good influences (e.g., broadening the view of the world and becoming familiar with voluntary activities) and bad ones (e.g., contempt for Finnish conditions and the women "dressing up").[48] Another returnee of 1932 stressed the limitations of the new experience:

Those American or Canadian emigrants who were working in the forests, or other kinds of casual work, had very limited opportunities to participate in social, political, or cultural activities, so I don't think they had anything to offer in these fields. They might have new ideas to do with the economy, though. I don't think there were any big differences in morality.[49]

This comment, somewhat pointedly stated, underlines the results derived from our analysis of return migration. Only in high emigration areas in Ostrobothnia did the returning migrants succeed in creating a recognizable impression on society in other fields as well as in that of the economy. There the rural economy received a stimulus, and the returning migrants were active in local affairs. Outside the high emigration areas the intellectual impact of the migrants in most fields remained insignificant, and the same also appears to apply to nations where the return migration occurred on a much larger scale than in Finland. Those who had never been away were not willing to modify their thinking, with the result that the ex-migrants had to adjust and in the course of time abandon many of their ideas.

In terms of the return migration in a wider context, the balance of Finnish overseas migration was definitely negative, for Finland only regained 75,000 of the 380,000 persons who had emigrated overseas prior to 1930. The final balance in a "new" migration country such as Italy was quite different, where the economy visibly prospered from the busy movement back and forth between Italy and the overseas countries and from the capital brought back by those returning.

The analysis also demonstrates that the Finnish migrants cannot be classified as part of the "new" migration; rather, in its main features the Finnish migration showed extensive similarities to that from the Nordic countries and differed radically from the overseas migration movement in southern European countries, which was essentially a temporary phenomenon, a form of intercontinental commuting to work. The application of the terms "old" and "new" migration as such in this context is thus rendered rather questionable, since the "counter-current" shows the division to be inadequate. This investigation of the settlement or return of the Finnish overseas migrants may offer comparative material when recent migrations are studied.[50] These migrations are caused by similar factors and pass through similar stages, even though the chronological and geographical context is different.

NOTES

1. The present chapter is based on the extensive research material I collected for my monograph entitled *Settlement or Return: Finnish Emigrants (1860–1930) in the Inter-*

national Overseas Return Migration Movement (Forssa, 1979). The quantitative analysis derives mainly from the Finnish passport lists, passenger lists of the shipping companies, church records, and district court registrars' records. The qualitative aspect consists of interview questionnaires, personal recollections, memoirs, and so forth. The central research findings and typologies of this article are based on this book and this material unless otherwise stated. It should also be mentioned that the core of the study is taken from six sample areas in Finland (Lohtaja, Elimäki, Jokioinen, Leppävirta, Polvijärvi, and Kristinestad); all the emigrants and all the returns of each emigrant from these areas have been researched and analyzed.

2. E. G. Ravenstein, "The Laws of Migration," *Journal of the Royal Statistical Society* 48, Part 2 (June 1885), p. 199.

3. See note 1. Material used for this study includes records of the district court registrars, passport lists, national statistics, records of shipping companies, and local parish records. In 1969 questionnaires were sent to return migrants (7,000 sent, 1,200 returned). In 1968 questionnaires had been sent to 20,000 Finnish emigrants living abroad, of which more than 2,500 were completed. Furthermore the *Report of the Migration Committee* published in 1924 yields valuable information.

4. See Maldwyn Allen Jones, *American Immigration* (Chicago, 1960), pp. 177–80, 323.

5. Eino Jutikkala, *Uudenajan taloushistoria* [The economic history of the modern period] (Turku, 1953), pp. 403–8.

6. Pekka Haatanen, "Suhteellisen liikaväestön ongelma Suomen maataloudessa" (The problem of the surplus population in Finnish agriculture) (Master's thesis, University of Helsinki, 1965), pp. 1, 6, 13–16, 29.

7. Ibid., pp. 17, 20–21.

8. Holger Wester, *Innovationer i befolkningsrörligheten. En studie av spridningsförlopp i befolkningsrörligheten utgående från Petalax socken i Österbotten* [Innovations in population mobility] (Stockholm, 1977), pp. 73–78, 177–78, 186, 189–91.

9. Cf. Theodore Saloutos, *They Remember America: The Story of the Repatriated Greek-Americans* (Berkeley, 1956), pp. 1–2; Arnold Schrier, *Ireland and the American Emigration 1850–1900* (Minneapolis, 1958), pp. 9, 158–59.

10. Cf. Kristian Hvidt, *Flugten til Amerika. Eller drivkraefter i masseudvandringen fra Danmark 1868–1914* (Odense, 1971), pp. 327–28; Lars-Göran Tedebrand, *Västernorrland och Nordamerika 1875–1913. Utvandring och återinvandring* (Uppsala, 1972), p. 223.

11. Robert F. Foerster, *The Italian Emigration of Our Times* (Cambridge, Mass., 1924), p. 23; John S. Lindberg, *The Background of Swedish Emigration to the United States. An Economic and Sociological Study in the Dynamics of Migration* (Minneapolis, 1930), p. 252 footnote 2; Saloutos, *They Remember America*, pp. 29–30; Betty Boyd Caroli, *Italian Repatriation from the United States, 1900–1914* (New York, 1973), pp. 49–50.

12. *International Migrations. Volume I. Statistics*, ed. Walter F. Willcox (St. Albans, 1929), pp. 204–5; see also Caroli, *Italian Repatriation*, pp. 6–8.

13. Lars-Göran Tedebrand, "Remigration from America to Sweden," in Harald Runblom and Hans Norman, eds., *From Sweden to America. A History of the Migration* (Uppsala, 1976), pp. 215–16.

14. Lindberg, *The Background of Swedish Emigration*, p. 247 (Sweden); Ingrid Semmingsen, *Veien mot vest. Annen del. Utvandringen fra Norge 1865–1915* (Oslo, 1950), p. 460 (Norway); Hvidt, *Flugten til Amerika*, p. 326 (Denmark).

15. It is justified to estimate that of about 380,000 Finnish overseas emigrants before 1930 approximately 315,000 went to the United States, 60,000 to Canada, 2,000 to Australia, 1,000 to South America, and 1,000 to South Africa.

16. Sune Åkerman, "Theories and Methods of Migration Research," in Runblom and Norman, eds., *From Sweden to America*, p. 21.

17. The heaviest return migration years for the Finns were 1907 and 1908, partly because of the depression and partly because emigration to America had been very high since 1899.

18. The America letter collection at the University of Turku, signum (archival call number): TYYH/S/m/Satakunta/13/LAP/XI.

19. Foerster, *Italian Emigration*, p. 41; see also Caroli, *Italian Repatriation*, pp. 56–57.

20. Saloutos, *They Remember America*, p. 11.

21. Åkerman, "Theories and Methods," p. 21.

22. See Foerster, *Italian Emigration*, p. 35; Semmingsen, *Veien mot vest*, p. 460; Saloutos, *They Remember America*, p. 51; Anthony H. Richmond, *Post-War Immigrants in Canada* (Toronto, 1967), p. 231; Caroli, *Italian Repatriation*, p. 50; Tedebrand, "Re-migration," pp. 225–27.

23. See, for example, Matti Tarkkanen, *Siirtolaisuudesta* [On migration] (Mikkeli, 1902), pp. 25–26; Teo Snellman, *Ulkokansalaistoiminta ja siirtolaisten huolto* [Activities on behalf of the Finnish Migrants] Vol. I (Helsinki, 1929), p. 10.

24. The interview questionnaire collection at the University of Turku, signum: TYYH/S/1/7061.

25. The interview questionnaire collection at the University of Turku, signum: TYYH/S/1/7104.

26. See Auvo Kostiainen, *The Forging of Finnish-American Communism, 1917–1924. A Study in Ethnic Radicalism* (Turku, 1978), pp. 32, 138.

27. Ritva-Liisa Hovi, "Amerikansuomalaiset osuuskunnat Neuvosto-Karjalassa 1920-luvun alkupuolella amerikansuomalaisten ja neuvostokarjalaisten sanomalehtien valossa" ["American-Finnish Cooperative Societies in the Soviet Karelia at the Beginning of the 1920s"], in *Turun Historiallinen Arkisto XXIV* (Turku, 1971).

28. Bill McNitt, "Americans in Soviet Russia: The Kuzbas Experiment" (Seminar paper, University of Michigan, 1971), pp. 1, 9, 17-18.

29. Ritva-Liisa Hovi, "Amerikansuomalaisten maanviljelyskommuuni Etelä-Venäjällä" ["An Agricultural Co-operation of American Finns in South Russia"], in *Turun Historiallinen Arkisto XXV* (Vammala, 1971).

30. See, for example, manuscript memoirs of Frank Sainio, migrant returning to Finland (Dept. of History, University of Turku).

31. Yrjö Raivio, *Kanadan suomalaisten historia I* [History of the Finns in Canada I], (Vancouver, 1975), p. 487.

32. Interview with Yrjö Raivio (1974, author's notes).

33. Reino Kero, "Emigration of Finns from North America to Soviet Karelia in the Early 1930s," in Michael G. Karni, Matti E. Kaups, and Douglas J. Ollila, Jr., eds., *The Finnish Experience in the Western Great Lakes Region: New Perspectives* (Vammala, 1975), p. 220.

34. See *Industrialisti* [Industrialist] (newspaper), Duluth, 27 June 1931.

35. See Rafael Engelberg, *Suomi ja Amerikan suomalaiset. Keskinäinen yhteys ja sen rakentaminen* [Finland and the American Finns] (Helsinki, 1944), p. 382.

36. *Lännen Suometar [Western Finn]* (newspaper), Astoria, 19 July 1932.

37. Engelberg, *Suomi ja Amerikan suomalaiset*, pp. 381, 384–85, 388–90.

38. See Saloutos, *They Remember America*, pp. 117–21, 123–24, 130–31; Caroli, *Italian Repatriation*, pp.57–61, 93, 98–99.

39. The interview questionnaire collection at the University of Turku, signum: TYYH/ S/1/7149.

40. The interview questionnaire collection at the University of Turku, signum: TYYH/ S/1/7161.

41. The interview questionnaire collection at the University of Turku, signum: TYYH/ S/1/5001-6268.

42. The interview questionnaire collection at the University of Turku, signum: TYYH/ S/1/7313.

43. Georg Backlund, "De politiska återverkningarna," in *Emigrationen och dess bakgrund* ["The Political Influence of Migration," in *Emigration and Its Background*] (Ekenäs, 1971), pp. 91, 94–95.

44. Yrjö Leiwo, "Hakemisto," in *Politiikkaa ja merkkimiehiä* ["Index," in *Important Politicians*] (Helsinki, 1935).

45. The interview questionnaire collection at the University of Turku, signum: TYYH/ S/1/7161.

46. Bill Widén, "De religiösa återverkningarna ["The Religious Influence of Migration"] in *Emigrationen och dess bakgrund* (Ekenäs, 1971), pp. 87–89.

47. Walter Sjöblom, *Kristinestads historia [History of Kristinestad Town]* (Kristinestad, 1915), p. 286.

48. Yrjö Alanen, *Siirtolaisemme ja kotimaa. Siirtolaisuuden vaikutuksesta kansamme oloihin ja luonteeseen [Our Emigrants and the Home Country]* (Helsinki, 1910), pp. 54–60.

49. The interview questionnaire collection at the University of Turku, signum: TYYH/ S/1/7234.

50. Since the Second World War, there has been a large amount of emigration from Finland to Sweden, to a lesser extent also to Canada and Australia.

ROUND TRIP CROATIA, 1900–1914   **16**

Frances Kraljic

Much has been made of the distinction between "old" and "new" European immigrants to the United States when discussing repatriation. A closer examination shows the limitations of such generalizations. Repatriation, as well as permanent settlement has taken place among all national groups regardless of the geographic origins of the migrants or readily available means of transport. Croatian immigrants were not alone in their return movement; Italians, Greeks, Germans, Poles, and Britons also left the United States in large numbers.[1] This chapter seeks to assess some of the consequences of the broad repatriation movement of Croatians and to demonstrate that the return was a result of the attitude of the people and their economic experience in the homeland.

The greatest population movement between the United States and Europe occurred in the period 1900 to 1914. Statistics of various European countries (including Croatia) and the United States concur that these were the years of mass emigration and repatriation. The United States Census Report of 1910 noted that while there was an immigration of about 8.5 million between 1900 and 1910, the census showed only 5,088,084 persons in the United States in 1910, who had arrived after 1 January 1901. This justified an estimate of 5.25 million as the total number of persons who had arrived since the preceding census. The difference of about 3.25 million persons represented, the report noted, in large part immigrants who returned to their own country and, to a lesser extent, those who died between their arrival and the date of the enumeration.[2] As to other demographic characteristics of the immigrants, the 1910 United States Census summarized:

In the case of persons from all the countries of southern and eastern Europe from which recent immigration has largely been drawn there was a very marked excess of males. The number of males to 100 females in 1910 was 154.6 for persons born in Austria, 160.8 for persons born in Hungary, 190.6 for persons born in Italy, and 137.3 for persons born in Russia. There is much less disparity between the sexes in the case of the foreign-born from the leading countries of northwestern Europe. These differences accord with the well-known fact that the immigrants of the earlier days, who came mainly from northwestern Europe, came to a large extent in families and settled permanently in this country, while much of the immigration from southern and eastern Europe consists of single men and married men who have come only for a temporary stay and have left their families in their home countries.[3]

THE EXTENT AND CHARACTERISTICS OF CROATIAN REPATRIATION

About half a million Croatians went to "America"—to the United States—between 1900 and 1914, the peak years of the migration (Figure 16.1). Immigration records show that more than 50 percent of them chose to remain as permanent residents. Estimates of those Croatian migrants who chose of their own will to return to the homeland at least once range from 20 percent to 44 percent. In some instances Croatian migrants entered and left the United States several times before making a decision about a permanent residence. Immigration records indicate that approximately 12 percent of the Croatians entering the United States between 1900 and 1914 had lived here previously.

This essay primarily examines Croatian repatriation; that is, Croatians who returned voluntarily to the country of their birth from the United States between 1900 and 1914 and the consequences of an American residence upon those who returned.[4] Repatriation, as used in immigration history, means "to return voluntarily to the country of one's birth or prime allegiance." This study concentrates on the years 1900 to 1914 because it was only in 1899 that United States Immigration reports began to classify Slavic immigrants according to nationality. The migration of Croatians to the United States and back to Croatia tapered off in 1914 as World War I commenced. After the war, Croatia became part of the "Kingdom of the Serbs, Croats, and Slovenes." Migration never attained the proportions it had assumed prior to World War I. Repatriation, however, continued after 1914.

American immigration statistics for the years 1908 to 1914 indicate that over 100,000 Croatians departed from the United States at the same time that almost 232,000 Croatians entered the United States, amounting to a repatriation rate of

Figure 16.1.
Yugoslav Migration to the United States, 1899–1924

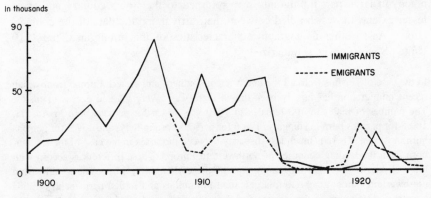

SOURCE: Branko Mita Colaković, <u>Yugoslav Migrations to America,</u> Figure 4-2 (San Francisco: R and E Research Associates, 1973), p. 45.

Table 16.1
Sex, Age, Literacy, Financial Condition, etc., of Immigrant Aliens Admitted, Fiscal Year Ending June 30, 1900 to 1914 by Peoples

Croatian and Slovenian

Year	Number Admitted	Sex Male	Sex Female	Age Under 14 Years	Age 14 to 44 Years	Age 45 Years and Over	Can Read but Cannot Write Male	Can Read but Cannot Write Female	Can Neither Read nor Write Male	Can Neither Read nor Write Female	Money $30 or Over	Money Less Than $30	Total Amount of Money Shown	Passage Paid Self	Passage Paid Relative	Passage Paid Other Than Self or Relative	Going to Join Relative	Going to Join Friend	Going to Join Neither Relative nor Friend	Have Been in U.S. Before
1900	17,184	14,934	2,250	667	15,819	698	25		6,149		1,791	13,406	214,987							1,693
1901	17,928	15,492	2,436	745	16,576	607	41		6,773		1,832	14,897	232,185							1,683
1902	30,233	27,097	3,136	989	27,870	1,374	33		12,322		2,308	26,012	336,673							1,889
1903	32,907	29,222	3,685	1,111	30,457	1,339	75		11,104		2,554	27,318	407,117							1,869
1904	21,242	17,644	3,598	1,225	19,314	703	50		7,170		686 $50*	18,682	321,200							1,540
1905	35,104	30,253	4,851	1,383	32,470	1,251	87		12,788		1,221	31,710	539,337							7,068
1906	44,272	38,287	5,985	1,674	41,653	945	76		16,941		964	38,313	582,503							5,595
1907	47,826	40,538	7,288	1,694	45,167	965	65		16,721		982	42,329	635,687							2,501
1908	20,472	15,476	4,996	1,567	18,321	584	11	7	4,459	1,199	743	16,819	307,360	16,921	3,432	119	12,592	6,874	1,006	1,416
1909	20,181	15,710	4,471	1,258	18,169	754	9	18	4,470	940	1,026	17,129	311,186	17,160	2,927	94	12,611	7,084	486	
1910	39,562	32,947	6,615	1,855	36,438	1,269	23	10	11,104	1,525	1,503	34,455	371,332	35,926	3,501	135	28,576	10,303	683	
1911	18,982	13,466	5,516	1,587	16,889	506	19	2	3,347	1,132	1,106	15,252	463,780	15,589	3,278	115	14,457	4,142	383	
1912	24,366	17,383	6,983	2,063	21,660	643	5	5	4,545	1,591	1,334	19,828	607,850	19,347	4,886	133	17,531	6,431	404	
1913	42,499	31,590	10,909	3,422	37,362	1,715	24	11	6,679	2,368	2,661	34,883	1,066,699	34,898	7,434	167	28,310	12,973	1,216	
1914	37,284	26,877	10,407	3,511	31,701	2,072	11	7	5,549	2,307	2,578	28,525	1,084,631	29,392	7,706	186	26,596	9,790	898	

Table 16.1—Continued

Dalmatians, Bosnians and Herzegovinians

Year	Number Admitted	Sex		Age			Literacy				Money			By Whom Passage Paid			Going to Join			Repeated Emigration
		Male	Female	Under 14 Years	14 to 44 Years	45 Years and Over	Can Read but Cannot Write — Male	Can Read but Cannot Write — Female	Can Neither Read nor Write — Male	Can Neither Read nor Write — Female	$30 or Over	Less Than $30	Total Amount of Money Shown	Self	Relative	Other Than Self or Relative	Relative	Friend	Neither Relative nor Friend	Have Been in U.S. Before
1900	675	637	38	37	613	25	2		210		183	215	14,187							
1901	732	630	102	40	664	28	—	—	202		164	273	14,560							
1902	1,004	895	109	45	895	64	—	—	343		218	487	18,855							
1903	1,736	1,544	192	33	1,625	78	1	—	405		280	1,024	26,056							
1904	2,036	1,094	132	47	1,913	76	1	—	707		$50* 161	1,757	46,392							
1905	2,639	2,489	150	62	2,450	127	5	—	985		200	2,315	55,575							
1906	4,568	4,346	222	77	4,398	93	8	—	1,980		231	4,107	86,724							
1907	7,393	7,061	332	109	7,075	209	6	—	3,612		353	6,449	141,696							
1908	3,747	3,379	368	115	3,568	64	2	1	1,474	138	192	3,228	66,398	3,535	199	13	1,960	1,435	352	1,416
1909	1,888	1,617	271	80	1,737	71	2	—	549	83	188	1,492	42,206	1,696	190	2	1,444	382	62	
1910	4,911	4,453	458	173	4,594	144	3	—	1,696	168	279	3,962	111,285	4,507	394	10	3,553	1,175	183	
1911	4,400	3,809	591	175	4,127	98	—	—	1,599	198	336	3,525	122,495	3,917	474	9	3,114	1,143	143	
1912	3,672	3,152	520	130	3,466	76	3	—	1,247	170	295	2,878	100,288	3,231	415	26	2,496	1,023	153	
1913	4,520	3,938	582	159	4,168	193	6	1	1,851	208	334	3,770	128,967	4,046	448	26	2,816	1,542	162	
1914	5,149	4,437	712	206	4,722	221	4	—	2,134	228	327	4,440	149,368	4,578	545	26	3,345	1,661	143	

Source: U.S. Commissioner General of Immigration, Annual Reports, 1910–1914 (Washington, 1900–1914).

Note: *Figure changed to $50 or more rather than $30 for earlier years.

Table 16.2
Occupations of Migrants

		Professional	Skilled	Farm Laborers	Farmers	Common Laborers	Servants	No Occupation[a]	Miscellaneous	Total
Occupations of Immigrants to the United States, by Peoples, 1899–1909										
Croatian and Slovenian	Number	228	13,952	80,167	4,290	146,278	17,558	32,825	683	295,981
	Percent	.1	4.7	27.1	1.4	49.4	5.9	11.1	.2	100
Dalmatian, Bosnian, Herzegovinian	Number	31	2,523	7,178	569	12,837	668	2,799	180	26,785
	Percent	.1	9.4	26.8	2.1	47.9	2.5	10.4	.7	100
Occupations of Emigrant Aliens Departing from the United States during the Fiscal 1908, 1909 and 1910, by Peoples										
Croatian and Slovenian	Number	42	7,821	808	887	30,169	792	3,546	350	44,415
	Percent	.1	17.6	1.8	2.0	67.9	1.8	8.0	.8	100
Dalmatian, Bosnian, Herzegovinian	Number	3	198	43	36	1,493	24	147	49	1,993
	Percent	.1	9.9	2.2	1.8	74.9	1.2	7.4	2.5	100

Source: U.S. Immigration Commission, 1907–1910, *Reports of the Immigration Commission*, 41 vols. (Washington, 1911), vol. 4, pp. 27–28, 47.

[a] Comprises mainly women and children.

Table 16.3
Sex, Age, and Length of Residence in the United States of Emigrant Aliens Departed, 1908–1914

Croatian-Slovenian

Year	Number Departed	Sex		Age			Continuous Residence in United States					
		Male	Female	Under 14 Yrs.	14 to 44 Yrs.	45 Yrs. & Over	Not Over 5 Yrs.	5 to 10 Yrs.	10 to 15 Yrs.	15 to 20 Yrs.	Over 20 Yrs.	Unknown
1908	28,589	26,753	1,836	422	26,086	2,081	23,058	5,187	202	101	41	—
1909	9,014	7,861	1,153	287	8,078	616	7,781	1,111	42	28	19	—
1910	7,133	6,110	1,023	281	6,281	571	5,746	987	66	18	18	288
1911	13,735	12,245	1,490	316	12,159	1,260	10,479	2,230	124	37	18	847
1912	13,963	12,529	1,434	256	12,211	1,496	8,832	3,975	442	59	24	631
1913	10,209	9,098	1,111	146	8,868	1,195	6,144	2,788	319	24	30	904
1914	14,440	12,790	1,650	224	12,521	1,695	9,976	3,563	627	26	50	198

Dalmatian, Bosnian, Herzegovinian

Year	Number Departed	Sex		Age			Continuous Residence in United States					
		Male	Female	Under 14 Yrs.	14 to 44 Yrs.	45 Yrs. & Over	Not Over 5 Yrs.	5 to 10 Yrs.	10 to 15 Yrs.	15 to 20 Yrs.	Over 20 Yrs.	Unknown
1908	1,046	999	47	21	934	91	847	183	4	7	5	—
1909	515	477	38	15	462	38	439	65	7	1	3	—
1910	432	410	22	9	388	35	366	60	2	3	1	—
1911	935	873	62	21	819	95	765	155	10	3	2	—
1912	927	893	34	7	823	97	653	253	18	1	1	1
1913	849	824	25	5	775	69	590	240	16	1	2	—
1914	878	847	31	7	775	96	563	282	25	4	4	—

Source: U.S. Commissioner General of Immigration, Annual Reports, 1908–1914.

44 percent.[5] Croatian immigration statistics for a longer period, 1900 to 1913, support a lower 20 percent repatriation rate.[6] Due to a lack of precise statistics, rigorous accuracy is not possible, but from a comparison of available statistics from both the United States and Croatia, it appears that from 33 to 40 percent of the Croatian immigrants who entered the United States between 1900 and 1914 returned home at least once. Repatriation figures amount to 165,000 to 200,000.[7]

The repatriation rate suggests that temporary emigration was a solution to political, social, or economic problems facing Croatians in these years. It is difficult to determine the issues prompting emigration and repatriation and the consequences for the individual and his own country. Since emigrants acted for their own benefit, the consequence of migration and return are more apparent for the individual involved than for the larger group or for Croatia itself.

The repatriate's lack of awareness of the more general consequence of his travels back to Croatia stems largely from his minimal formal education, from purely personal motivation for migration, and from the difficult political status of Croatia and Croatians before 1914. The historical background of those who considered themselves Croatians was so diverse and complex prior to World War I and to the establishment of the "Kingdom of Serbs, Croats, and Slovenes" in 1918 that it is difficult to discern reactions to emigration and repatriation by the several governments and elites in the homeland. The Croatians fell under the jurisdiction of different national regimes—Austrians, Hungarians, and Turks. As a consequence of the history and politics of the region and the people, many uncertainties exist with regard to motivation for emigration and repatriation, the benefits derived from repatriation, and the actual classification of Croatian repatriates according to nationality.

U.S. Immigration statistics recorded Croatian immigrants separately on a geographic basis. The use of geography and government as the basis for ethnic classification tends to confuse the migratory movement in this case. Slovenians are a specific national group, whereas Croatians, Dalmatians, Bosnians, and Herzegovinians all have the same national origin. Dalmatians, for example, are coastal Croatians, but they were classified separately by American immigration authorities because they were governed by Austria instead of Hungary. (See Tables 16.1-16.3.)[8] Note that the Yugoslav peoples, that is the South Slav peoples, consist of the Slovenes, the Croats, the Serbs, the Macedonians and the Bulgarians, of which the first three and part of the Macedonians are living in Yugoslavia.

THE POLITICAL, ECONOMIC, AND SOCIAL REASONS FOR REPATRIATION

Immigration data point toward economic motives for the two-way migration across the Atlantic. The sex, age, literacy, and occupations of the immigrants suggest the employment/work motive underlying the migration.[9] Several economists have attempted to link declining economic conditions in the United States with repatriation. Harry Jerome, Simon Kuznets, and Ernest Rubin all agree that immigration to the United States increased in times of prosperity and decreased in depression: Conversely, departures increased in times of depression and fell off in times of prosperity.[10]

Kuznets and Rubin pointed out that the incoming immigrants, many of whom were young unmarried men or men who had left their families at home increased the labor force proportionally more than the population as a whole. Immigration contributed about one-seventh to the total growth in population between 1870 and 1910 and about one-fifth to the growth in the labor force in the same period.[11]

Jerome noted that the arrival of hundreds of thousands of workers each year, especially during an upswing in business, resulted in a surplus of workers that affected the economy through decreased labor cost. Repatriation, Jerome argued, sometimes mitigated the effects of cyclical variation in unemployment by withdrawing large numbers from the labor force. As a safety valve it was imperfect, since some time necessarily elapsed between the decreased need for labor and the departure of workers. Since both countries involved often underwent similar business fluctuations at the same time, Jerome argued that migration could not serve the interests of both.[12]

In labeling the Yugoslav migrations to the United States prior to World War I as labor migrations (since most of the migrants intended to remain in the United States only temporarily), Branko Colaković concurs with the economic interpretation of repatriation. He compares this early migration to the present labor migration of Yugoslavs to the cities of western Europe.[13] Colaković indicated a political motivation for return to the old country, when after 1918 the old dream of all south Slavs was realized in the foundation of Yugoslavia, with victorious Serbia as the core of the new state.[14] Those who decided to settle permanently in America did so because of lost connections with the home country during the war. Military recruitment and the danger of travel were responsible for the break in the leave-and-return pattern of Croatians.[15]

Emigration overseas had been an important safety valve for the agricultural population pressure since the early 1900s. Countless numbers of Croatians were either unemployed or their employment was insufficient to provide an adequate living. For them, temporary emigration was the answer.[16] Colaković, however, emphasizes that Yugoslavs did not need to emigrate permanently in order to survive; there was no absolute but merely a relative population surplus. While food may not have been as plentiful as in America, Yugoslavs "did not have a bad life at home."[17] Robert Foerster's study of Italian emigration supports Colaković's contention that emigration did not come primarily from the most poverty stricken regions but rather from regions where there was a possibility of saving enough money for the passage.[18]

The low numbers of women and children also point conclusively to the temporary character of primarily economically motivated migration. The data show that the Croatian repatriate, like the immigrant in these years, was generally male and between fourteen and forty-four years of age. He was a common laborer who had spent no more than five years in the United States and who in some

cases did not leave the United States permanently.[19] It was by no means uncommon to make repeated trips across the Atlantic. United States Immigration
Commission Reports, minutes of the Croatian Sabor (Diet), Croatian newspapers
in both the United States and Croatia, as well as private accounts all assert the
economic significance of migration. Statistics showing $64 million shipped to
Croatia by way of banks and post offices support this view.[20] The supplemental
amount of money entering Croatia by way of letters and the repatriates themselves
is a matter of conjecture but was not inconsiderable. Fiorello LaGuardia, United
States Consular Agent at Fiume, reported in 1904 that "Every mail brings
thousands of dollars to the banks of Hungary and Croatia for deposit."[21]

THE EFFECTS OF REPATRIATION ON CROATIANS AND THE HOMELAND

Governmental authorities of Austria-Hungary had a good idea of the importance and influence of its temporary emigrants. It was the emigrants' money
which to a large extent served to influence conditions in Croatia (Table 16.4).
Temporary sojourns to the United States were considered the solution to the
economic problems faced by the migrants in their homeland. Their remitted

Table 16.4
Croatian Emigrant Remittances from the United States by Way of Banks and Post Offices, 1900–1912

Year	Kronen	Dollars[a]
1900	2,000,000	$ 400,000
1901	2,800,000	560,000
1902	5,700,000	1,140,000
1903	9,000,000	1,800,000
1904	7,500,000	1,500,000
1905	18,000,000	3,600,000
1906	40,200,000	8,040,000
1907	50,700,000	10,140,000
1908	25,300,000	5,060,000
1909	30,600,000	6,120,000
1910	45,700,000	9,140,000
1911	38,200,000	7,640,000
1912	45,600,000	9,120,000
Total	321,300,000	$64,260,000

Source: Josip Lakatoš, *Narodna Statistika* (National Statistics) (Zagreb 1914), p. 64.
Note: [a]Based on equivalent 5 Kronen = $1.00.

savings improved their families' and regions' economic well-being, while their departure in itself improved the economic plight of those who remained at home. U.S. Immigration Commission reports indicated that farm wages and land values rose sharply in Croatia as a result of emigration.[22]

Edward Steiner noted that villages in Hungary, Russia, and Italy to which migrants returned even after a brief stay in the United States benefited from their repatriates. Better housing, sanitary improvements, and improved agriculture were results of the saved wages. "Business," he wrote "in not a few instances has been put upon an American basis, which means not only more efficiency, but strange as it may seem, more honesty; and the scale of living has risen wherever a large number of people has gone to and fro across the sea."[23] Ivan Čizmić, in his study, noted among the positive results of migration a general improvement in diet. Wherever repatriation took place, the consumption of meat increased.[24] Ivan Lupis-Vukić, a repatriate himself, attributed the existence of two of the biggest steamship companies to immigrant remittances from America.[25] Funds from America were also responsible for the vast housing construction projects witnessed by Louis Adamić in Split.[26]

United States Consul Slocum summed up the influence of Croatian migration in a statement to the Immigration Commission:

Some of the results locally from unrestricted emigration may be noted in the increased respect given the returned emigrant. The Hungarian or Croatian peasant having left the chrysalis state in America returns to Hungary a butterfly of the world. More practical results may be noted in Vrata, Croatia, where a whole street may be seen the houses fronting upon which were constructed with earnings of returned emigrants.

On the other hand, also in Vrata may be seen a factory for the manufacture of bentwood funiture, the management of which has been forced to import labor, as the youth of the locality otherwise capable of the work had sought their fortune in the United States. Other results of the emigration may be noted in the comfortable, if not luxurious surroundings of simple peasant families whose sons have emigrated, and, successful, have not forgotten the loved ones at home in far-off Hungary.[27]

As early as the turn of the century *Croatian* leaders in the Sabor (Diet) had drawn attention to the less advantageous consequences of emigration. But in 1903 the *Hungarian* government entered into a contract with the Cunard Steamship Company for the maintenance of a direct steamship line between Fiume (Rijeka) and New York, thus facilitating migration across the Atlantic. The Cunard Company agreed to run steamers every two weeks, and the Hungarian government guaranteed them fares for 30,000 passengers (100–150 kronen or $20.00–$30.00 per person) annually, whether or not that number actually traveled.[28]

In August of 1905 when Baron von Hengelmüller, the Austro-Hungarian Ambassador to the United States, arrived in New York on board the Cunard Line steamer "Caronia," he denied the report that Austria-Hungary carried on activities to encourage emigration to the United States. The ambassador said that a scarcity of unskilled labor in Austria-Hugary due to emigration created difficulties for farmers seeking help at harvest time. This situation resulted in increased wages for unskilled labor and wages were now practically as high as in the United States. There was no reason for laborers to leave their native land. The contract with Cunard had been made, according to the ambassador, because considerable emigration did exist, especially Russian emigrants passing through Austria-Hungary, and such an agreement was profitable to both Hungary and Cunard.

The purpose of the contract between Cunard and Hungary was mainly to increase the number of passengers carried by the line and to secure a class of emigrants who sooner or later would return home, and thus further add to the revenue of the transportation line and Hungary. Hungary hoped to advance Hungarian economic interests at the expense of German ones.

Historically, landlocked Hungary had sought an access to the sea. By way of the 1867 agreement with Austria, Hungary was to administer Croatia and thus gained access to the sea. Hungary desired to develop this access for its shipping and trade. The Cunard Steamship Company, a transoceanic company, was capable of handling the magnitude of emigration from Hungary to America, while the Adria Royal Hungarian Ocean Steamship Company, Ltd., a smaller domestic company, would act as Cunard's representative and deputy in emigration. The development of Fiume as a port city would bolster the economic development of all of Hungary.[29]

If the migrations from Hungary were temporary, Hungarian shipping interests would benefit, and the monetary advantages derived from repatriation would alleviate economic difficulties within Hungary. Politically, emigration might have lessened some nationality problems for Hungary. In Croatia-Slavonia some residents held the *Ban* (governor) of Croatia responsible for the mass migration from Croatia. They charged that the *Ban* was following the policy of Vienna and Budapest in promoting the emigration so as to diminish nationality problems within Croatia. As Croatians were leaving Croatia-Slavonia, Hungarians and Germans were settling in Croatia.[30] Some historians have claimed that between 1880 and 1914, when some 600,000 Croatians left the country, some 200,000 Hungarians settled in Croatia.[31] Čizmić writes that between 1900 and 1910, 43,000 foreigners, especially Hungarians and Germans, settled in Croatia-Slavonia, while only 37,000 Croatians returned. According to the data regarding the mother-language of emigrants and immigrants in Croatia, 85 percent of the emigrants were Croatian and Serbian, and 15 percent comprised all other groups. The immigrants to Croatia were 19 percent Croatian and Serbian and 81 percent foreign.[32] From a nationalistic viewpoint, emigration from Croatia-Slavonia was undesirable. According to Čizmić the exodus of Croatians and entrance of foreigners hindered Croatian patriotic attempts to free themselves from Vienna and Budapest.[33]

All Croatian areas (Croatia-Slavonia, Dalmatia, Bosnia, and Herzegovina) showed a population growth between 1900 and 1910 despite large-scale emigration. Josip Lakatoš, the compiler of official statistics for the Kingdom of

Croatia-Slavonia, attributed the continued growth in population in part to immigration into Croatian areas and in part to natural increase.[34] The population of Croatia-Slavonia numbered 2,186,410 in 1890, 2,416,304 in 1900, and 2,621,954 in 1910. In 1890 there were 68,794 Hungarians in Croatia-Slavonia or 3.15 percent of the total population; in 1900 the number had risen to 90,781 or 3.8 percent, and in 1910, 105,948 Hungarians made up 4.1 percent of the total population.[35]

Some Hungarian migrants to Croatia also show up in the emigration totals. For them Croatia was the first step of a migration in stages. As Lakatoš noted, they were not returning to Hungary but preferred to depart for America. However, three-quarters of the Hungarians remained in Croatia.[36]

Bosnia's and Herzegovina's emigrating population was also offset by immigration. While statistics were not available to support his position, Lakatoš claimed that as Croatians from Bosnia and Herzegovina emigrated to America, Moslems were entering the area so as to lessen the visible effect of emigration on the population statistics. For Dalmatia there was no known inward flow of persons. Dalmatian districts suffered annual population losses of an average of 5.36 percent between 1900 and 1910 due to emigration.[37] It is difficult to state with certainty that Hungary prompted immigration into Croatia-Slavonia of its own nationals to diminish the nationality problems of the area. The statistics do, however, support the contention that Hungarians were moving into Croatia in sizeable numbers.

These movements and the effect of emigration were discussed in the Croatian Sabor. Internal political confusion, opposing political factions, and animosity and bitterness that ran through Croatia's leadership prevented effective action. Members of the Sabor agreed on the magnitude of the problems caused by migration from Croatia, but in stormy sessions they could not agree on a common solution. Money from America, they charged, was causing moral and physical harm to Croatia and its people.

Representative Zagorac, in his April 1910 address before the Sabor, noted the population shift that had taken place in the district of Lika-Krbava as a result of emigration. Elderly people and women remained alone in the district. He charged that drunkenness prevailed in Lika-Krbava. Women were drinking champagne purchased from the millions of kronen transmitted annually from America. Zagorac argued that the economic advantages derived from emigrant remittances were far outweighed by moral and physical harm to Croatia.[38] To further prove his point, he told the story of a young man who over a twelve-year period had sent his savings of 30,000 kronen ($6,000) to his father to repair the home and land. Upon encountering a fellow countryman, the young man learned that his father had spent all his savings foolishly and had never repaired their house.[39] *Narodni List* (National Gazette) also wrote of the harm remittances from America were causing in Croatia.[40] According to the newspaper unfaithful wives and cruel parents and relatives were squandering the hard-earned savings of their husbands and sons.[41]

Lupis-Vukić noted the bad effects of emigration and repatriation upon family life in particular and the future of Croatia in general. As thousands of Croatians in the best years of their lives left Croatia annually, the inner strength of Croatia suffered. For a small nation such as Croatia, any loss of population, especially a loss of the pre-World War I migration magnitude, could be detrimental to the national interests of Croatia within the Austro-Hungarian Empire. Many young Croatians lost their lives in America, young widows were left behind in Croatia, while other emigrants returned as victims of accidents and illness.[42]

MIGRATION AND FAMILY LIFE

Temporary labor migration, more than the family migration of earlier periods, imposed severe strains on the lives of those who remained at home. Wives, children, and parents often adjusted to the situation in accordance with the value system of their specific traditional culture. Čizmić called attention to the social drawbacks of emigration when he raised the question of the "absent" father. Emigrant fathers did not partake in child-rearing and could not understand the problems encountered by the mother in her attempt to raise the children alone. The long periods of absence were felt upon return when it was difficult for the emigrant and his family to adjust to each other and a changed situation. A more serious social problem, Čizmić wrote, resulted from those men who abandoned their families to emigrate to America.[43]

Vera St. Erlich's study of Yugoslav village life sheds light upon the issue of family life, morality, and marital infidelity in Croatian regions of heavy emigration. Women whose husbands were away for long periods were referred to as "grass widows" or "white widows," widows who did not go into mourning. Marital faithfulness for these women could mean many years or a lifetime of sexual abstinence.[44]

"Grass widows" from different parts of Croatia reacted differently to their situation. St. Erlich concluded that the faithfulness and unfaithfulness of lonely women depended mainly "on the more or less rapid penetration of the money economy and on the stability of the life of a district as a whole."[45] Coastal Croatians, from the area of Dalmatia, emigrated in large numbers and stayed away for many years but their wives remained faithful despite the tolerant views of public opinion. The main points of St. Erlich's material indicated that "stability of family living and accepted standards either old or new, resulted in wives being faithful even under the arduous strain of long separation from husbands."[46] Croatia proper, on the other hand, held different views from those of the coast. The general view in Croatia was that one or two years alone was too hard for a woman.

The majority of women whose husbands spend a long time in America have illegitimate children with other young fellows, with widowers, and even with married men. There are cases here of from two to five children got illegitimately and in one case by more than one man. This is not taken to be a great evil. There are moreover cases of the husband's coming back from America and keeping both wife and children. [Ivanic district][47]

The former military district of Croatia, a district of heavy migration to America, was another area where women reacted more decisively than those on the coast. In this district the importance of love life was held to be self-explanatory and there had been an old marked tendency toward extramarital relations so that greater tolerance was shown to the extramarital activities of "grass widows."

Most husbands learn of a wife's unfaithfulness, but yet hold their tongues. Definitely most men, a phlegmatic breed, scarcely pay any attention, while the wives here are most often plucky and strong, so men are simply afraid to say anything in reproach, as they may get the worst of it. [Kordūn area, Dvor district][48]

Husbands returning from America to the former military district were known to accept wives with children born during their absence.

Coastal Croatia responded differently to adultery. "When a husband who is in America learns that his wife is unfaithful, he stops writing to her and sending her money. Frequently he does not return at all." (Isle of Krk)[49] Married men from the Littoral had extramarital relations only when away from their villages.

Husbands are faithful if they stay at home . . . but when they emigrate they live without abstinence, nor do their wives hold this against them. Such relations can hardly be called unfaithfulness. They are not greatly condemned by the peasants, though a woman will say to herself that he had better have brought those ten dinars home. [Isle of Krk][50]

The most common complaint was the lack of sympathy between the wife at home and the husband in the New World, often resulting from the very difficult experiences they had encountered in the meantime.

THE SOCIAL IMPACT OF THE REPATRIATES

The United States Immigration Commission report remarked regarding the emigrant:

He leaves his village, a simple peasant in his peasant dress, usually not only unable to read and write, but even not desiring to. Ingrained in him are the traditions of his obligations to the church and his superiors. Unresisting he has toiled from early morning until late at night for a wage insufficient even for his meager wants. Without money and totally unprepared for the complicated industrial life, he comes to the New World. His new environment soon brings about changes in this respect, and when he goes back to his old home he is a different man. He is more aggressive and self-assertive. His unaccustomed money gives him confidence and he is no longer willing to pay deference to his former superiors. Frequently, too, the church has lost the influence it had had with him. Moreover, if he has not learned to read and write himself, he has at least seen the value of that ability and is more anxious than before to send his children to school.[51]

The *Karlovački Glasnik* (Karlovac Voice) reported that the returned Croatian from America had become affected by gentleman's manners, and "although accustomed to hard work, he was upon his return no longer willing to plow the land and care for the vineyards.'' The returnee viewed his future at home as limited. Food was neither as good nor as plentiful in Croatia. The newspaper noted that before long many returnees yearned to go back to America.[52]

Prospective migrants could not solve or attempt to solve economic problems by political action. Croatia was part of the Austro-Hungarian Empire. Some Croatian lands were administered from Budapest and others from Vienna, while Croatia proper had some local autonomy. In this political chaos and factionalism, the emigrants viewed migration as a personal solution to their economic difficulties. To the emigrant America's greatest influence was economic. America was responsible for his savings and the property he had acquired. To those who remained in Croatia, the returnees or ''*Amerikanci*,'' may have been different in their dress, shaven mustaches, gold teeth, improved hygiene, use of some English words and habits, but the major difference was money.

Most people who lived between two countries experienced divided allegiance and discontent with both. The Greek repatriates, as Theodore Saloutos has written, could not help but compare Greece with the United States and soon found themselves dissatisfied with both. The Croatian repatriates, undoubtedly, encountered similar circumstances. The homeland could not give them jobs and America was not home.

The Croatian immigrant's participation in American life was limited to his direct needs. His life revolved around the boarding house, the saloon, the immigrant banker, and the priest—all his own folk. This has led some historians to conclude that the immigrant went back home with little idea of America save that it was a land of opportunity, a place to make money.[53] While the immigrant may not have assimiliated, he was influenced by America, and for some the influence was sufficient to cause the returning immigrant some difficulty in adjusting to the old country. It is difficult to measure dissatisfaction, if any, among repatriates in their homeland. Their employment conditions changed considerably as well as their daily lives. The returnees were disinclined to return to agricultural field work. Village life in Croatia was not the same as life in American industrial cities. Many may have preferred living in larger towns. Certain conveniences, such as running water, electricity, and bathrooms, were absent in Croatia.

A CASE STUDY OF MIGRATION

An interview with a Croatian repatriate may serve as an example of the life of an ordinary man. Mladen Marković (pseudonym) is a Croatian who traveled to and from the United States during these years.[54] He came to the United States from the Isle of Krk intent on staying only a few years. His twenty-six-day voyage in 1910 had cost approximately thirty dollars. He was fifteen years old with virtually no schooling when he arrived at Ellis Island with little more than the necessary twenty dollars and hope for a job. With the help of cousins he was outfitted in American attire and found a job as a deck boy on a coastal ship route between New York and Virginia for fifteen dollars a month. After two years of work Mladen returned to his homeland. Eight months later, his savings exhausted and with news of an approaching war, he returned to the United States. Austria-Hungary did not draft him because he was not yet 18 years of age. Mladen remained in the United States during the war years until 1920, when he returned home again to get married because "it was not good to marry here." Men who did so were looked down upon. He married a young woman from his village in 1921, and the following year they had a son. One and one-half years later their second son was born. Mladen had left his new family for a third trip to the United States before the birth of his second son in 1924. He wife, Anica, was well acquainted with the realities of a husband and father in America. Her own father had spent years in New York working on a barge with only intermittent trips home. When she was seven years old and just starting school, her mother accompanied her father on his return trip to America, and Anica was left in the care of a grandmother for three years.

After a six-year absence from his family, Mladen left his second job in the Steelton, Pennsylvania, mines for a visit home.[55] Six months later, in May of 1931, he was once again in the United States. The following January, while he was back in New York, his daughter was born. In a period of twenty years Mladen had made four round trips to Croatia.

During his years in the United States Mladen always lived in a boarding house. At first he roomed with a Croatian family in a tenement on Manhattan's Tenth Avenue between Nineteenth and Twentieth Streets for one dollar a month. His rent entitled him to a mattress while ashore and a place to keep his possessions while at sea. His savings were kept with a cousin, who also did his shopping for him. Very rarely did he go beyond Tenth Avenue to department stores or city points of interest. Even though he was living in one of the major cities of the world, Mladen's daily life revolved around the small community of Croatians living on Manhattan's West Side. His provincialism grew out of a need to stay close to other Croatians. Even when Mladen moved to another city in order to obtain a job, it was to another community of Croatians.

Mladen explained that his repeated transatlantic voyages were necessary because, although he intended to stay in the United States only briefly, he was never able to accumulate enough savings to permit him to remain in the homeland permanently. The temporary nature of his migration led him to jobs of meager position with limited opportunity for advancement. When he arrived in New York for the fourth time in 1931 he obtained his third job as a porter for the Horn & Hardart restaurant chain.

Qualities, such as high literacy and skilled craftsmanship, which would have helped in finding better jobs in America, were lacking among Croatian immigrants. Having arrived in the United States with meager funds, it was imperative that the Croatian immigrants secure a job quickly upon arrival and that they hold on to that job. Clearly, their ethnic background influenced their career mobility in the new country. Most Croatians were forced to work at the lowest levels of the job market: in factories, docks, and mines, where accidents and risks were high. Limited efforts went into labor union activities. Strikes were costly, and the Croatian immigrants were ill-disposed to them. Transiency was a further detriment to work experience. Farming, business, and petty enterprise, requiring investment and long-range goals, were ignored. The short-range goal was to accumulate as much savings as possible and send it back home. Higher status jobs were avoided, as they did not immediately pay off as well as day labor. Lupis-Vukić observed in 1910:

If our people would emigrate permanently, without the intention of returning, they could cultivate the soil in America and their life abroad would not be so difficult. But our people travel to America with the intention of earning some money and returning home. Because of this, they can never devote themselves to becoming independent farmers, the work they are accustomed to. . . . They are forced to look for work in large industrial and mining centers which are already overfilled with unskilled workers of other nationalities.[56]

While working, Mladen saved as much as possible, yet upon his return to Croatia it was quickly spent. Debts were repaid; the family house was renovated and refurbished. A parcel of land might be purchased. He attributed some of the need for repeated voyages to a desire to visit his family. Many emigrants' families, however, lived beyond their means and boasted of their sons' or husbands' success. They often insisted that the sons go to America again so that the family could keep up their new standard of living. Since a good portion of the funds traveled somewhat "publicly," the amounts remitted were common knowledge in the emigrant's village. For the emigrant himself and for his family, this was a means of informing the entire village of his success in America. The more one sent home to one's family, the more successful and prosperous the emigrant was believed to be. As a consequence, living conditions in the United States were kept to a minimum. It would appear that this type of recognition of financial success by one's fellow villagers may have made the journey and difficulties experienced in America seem worthwhile to the emigrant. The remittances and the recognition given to a "successful emigrant" certainly prompted others to seek recognition for themselves by way of a journey to America. The actual return of an emigrant with his new suit of clothing, appearance, manner, and money encouraged others to seek their fortunes in emigration.

The men who left Croatia for the United States were men of a simple, poor background. Their native region was unable to provide them with an adequate living. For a variety of personal reasons, largely economic, the men were taken with the desire to emigrate to America. This fascination with America was true not only of Croatians but applied throughout Europe. Emigration was a common phenomenon in nineteenth- and twentieth century Europe. Since it was a common occurrence, emigration was not as great an issue for the individual emigrant as has been perceived by historians. The emigration was to be temporary, and the emigrant did not completely break his ties with homeland, family, and friends. He was not a pioneer; previous generations of migrants had established precedents and patterns. For young males it was a sign of maturity and independence to be able to emigrate, make a "fortune," and return home prosperous. Emigrants from a particular Croatian village stayed together in the United States. Young men from a given village traveled together to America, worked and lived together with other Croatians. When any one of the emigrants wrote a letter home, the entire village knew how its sons were faring in America. If good fortune or mishap hit anyone, the emigrants looked to each other for support, and the homeland was kept in close touch with the state of affairs of its emigrant sons.

CONCLUSIONS

The return to Croatia of approximately 200,000 men between 1900 and 1914 after a temporary stay in the United States presumably had significant consequences for the emigrants, for their homeland, and for the United States. A temporary stay in the United States redirected the character and lives of many migrants. The American spirit, as some have suggested, may have changed the Croatians.

Emigration and contact with America through letters and visits insinuated the notion of change into the mind of the European peasant, and from this notion sometimes grew the ideas of social advancement, self-improvement, and progress, all preconditions of political and social democracy. Wherever such a movement got underway and gained impetus in the home country, it was influenced by emigration and contact with America. The impulses so transmitted had helped to widen horizons and had implanted the prestige of America in the mind of the common man.[57]

The remittances and the return of the emigrant with some money, regardless of the amount, made a vast impression on the masses, who did not have much money at all. The recognition given to the repatriates' economic improvement urged many others to view emigration as the possible solution to their difficulties. The large number of Croatians who actually applied for and were given passports to emigrate supports this view. The idea of emigration spread among more and more Croatians by way of the repatriate and his remittances. The repatriates' dress, their bank deposits, their ability to better feed and clothe their families, and their purchase of land sparked an emigration desire among their fellow villagers.

For the emigrant himself the acquisition of some money changed his life. The actual degree of change is difficult to perceive. In terms of tangible items, such as personal appearance, hygiene, housing, employment, habits, and clothing, change did, according to reported accounts, take place. While it is true that emigration disrupted and sometimes destroyed family life, most returning immigrants came back to join their families. Greater or more substantial changes, such as those of religious, social, or political beliefs—intangible items—are not as apparent. There are cases of more active political involvement and anti-religious attitudes by some repatriates, but it is not certain how typical these cases are, given the fact that most returned because they had achieved their set goals of personal economic improvement.

For Croatia the influence of the repatriate was also economic. Temporary emigration was a temporary solution to the economic difficulties of low wages, underemployment, and lack of arable land facing Croatia in the early twentieth century. The decline and loss in population resulting from emigration may have lessened the national strength of Croatia, but repatriation did not result in any grave transformation of the homeland. The remittances partially solved an unfavorable balance of trade and the transatlantic voyages of the repatriates helped certain shipping interests. Hungary perceived and articulated the benefits of temporary emigration. Croatia, while under Hungarian and Austrian jurisdiction, was unable to do so. The repatriates' influence upon Croatia, though largely unrecorded, was significant to their fellow countrymen and to themselves.

The numbers involved in the movement across the Atlantic between 1900 and 1914 were large because conditions and policies in America and Croatia made mass movements possible. As policies changed after World War I, Croatians, as well as other nationals, stopped repatriating at the same rate that they had earlier. After a brief period of high repatriation to the newly established home state, the repatriation figures declined because it was no longer as easy to reenter the United States.

Statistics regarding the post-World War I period indicate that the return movement continued, and in certain of these later years the returnees exceeded the number of arrivals, as was the case in 1919, 1920, 1922, 1924, 1925, and 1931 through 1933. Immediately after World War I a new and changed political situation in Croatia may have been responsible for the exodus of immigrants from the United States. The years of later repatriation appear to correspond to years of economic crisis in the United States. As immigrants experienced the unemployment of the depression years, many chose to return home.

For other Croatian immigrants the changing policy would encourage them to change their temporary residence into a permanent stay in the United States. Once the decision to remain in the United States had been made, the life of the immigrant changed. In 1910 it was reported that only 24 percent of Croatian immigrants owned their own homes, since their intention was to accumulate as much capital as possible and return home quickly.[58] Eleanor Ledbetter commented that at the time of World War I and afterward the tendency to buy property increased. Certain neighborhoods in Cleveland were reported to have as many as 50 percent Slavic property owners.[59] In addition to buying property, permanent immigrants were more likely to learn English and acquire citizenship.

By the 1920s, when this more permanent migratory movement was well noted, Croatia was part of the Kingdom of Serbs, Croats, and Slovenes (Yugoslavia). The new government could begin the task of repatriation, something Croatia under Hungary could not do alone. The kingdom's Ministry of Social Policy established a special department, Savez Organizacija Iseljenika, Oris (Emigrants Federation) for the very purpose of keeping the emigrant more firmly attached to the homeland. It printed manuals dealing with migration issues and published a monthly journal, *Novi Iseljnik* (New Emigrant). While emigration from the Kingdom was free and open, the department aimed to maintain control over the migration of the kingdom's people.[60] This new government was well aware of the decline in emigrant remittances and savings with permanent emigration and the subsequent effect of such a decline on the new country's balance of payments.[61] Before the establishment of the emigration department of the kingdom, little actual help was give to repatriates by the Hungarian government except in cases of extreme hardship.

NOTES

1. As respective representative examples, see: Robert F. Foerster, *The Italian Emigration of Our Times* (Cambridge, 1919); Theodore Saloutos, *They Remember America* (Berkeley, 1956), and *Expatriates and Repatriates, a Neglected Chapter in United States History* (Rock Island, Ill., 1972); Alfred Vagts, *Deutsch-Amerikanische Rückwanderung: Probleme—Phänomene—Statistik—Politik—Soziologie—Biographie* (Heidelberg, 1960); William I. Thomas and Florian Znaniecki, *The Polish Peasant in Europe and America*, 2 vols. (New York, 1958); Wilbur Stanley Shepperson, *Emigration and Disenchantment* (Norman, 1965).

2. U.S. Bureau of the Census, *Thirteenth Census of the United States Taken in the Year 1910: Abstract of the Census* (Washington, 1913), p. 190.

3. Ibid., p. 191.

4. For a more thorough study of Croatian repatriation between 1900 and 1914, see Frances Kraljic, *Croatian Migration to and from the United States, 1900–1914* (Palo Alto, Calif., 1978).

5. United States Commissioner General of Immigration, *Annual Reports*, 1908–1914.

6. Josip Lakatoš, *Narodna Statistika [National Statistics]* (Zagreb, 1914), p. 64.

7. *Annual Reports*, 1900–1914.

8. The term "Croatian" includes all immigrants who considered themselves Croatian, from whatever province, for example, Croatia-Slavonia, Dalmatia, Istria, and Bosnia-Herzegovina and those who spoke the Croatian language. Emily Greene Balch, *Our Slavic Fellow Citizens* (New York, 1910), p. 271.

9. *Annual Reports*, 1900–1914.

10. Harry Jerome, *Migration and Business Cycles* (New York, 1926), pp. 241–42; Simon Kuznets and Ernest Rubin, *Immigration and the Foreign Born* (New York, 1954), p. 5

11. Kuznets and Rubin, *Immigration*, p. 4.

12. Jerome, *Migration*; pp. 241–42.

13. Branko Mita Colaković, *Yugoslav Migrations to America* (San Francisco, 1973), p. 162.

14. Ibid.

15. Ibid., p. 74; Jovan N. Dunda, "Izgledi Naših Iseljeničkih Uštednji [Perspectives for Our Emigrants' Savings], *Ekonomist* 11–12 (November–December 1940), p. 426.

16. Jozo Tomasević, *Peasant, Politics and Economic Change in Yugoslavia* (Stanford, 1955), p. 119.

17. Colaković, *Yugoslav Migrations*, p. 163.

18. Foerster, *Italian Emigration*, p. 104.

19. *Annual Reports*, 1900–1914; United States Immigration Commission, 1907–1910, *Reports of the Immigration Commission*, 41 vols. (Washington, 1911), vol. 4.

20. Lakatoš, *Narodna Statistika*, p. 64.

21. United States Department of Commerce and Labor, *Special Consular Reports* (Washington, 1903–1905), vol. 30, p. 5.

22. *Reports of the Immigration Commission*, vol. 4, pp. 385–86.

23. Edward Steiner, *On the Trail of the Immigrant* (New York, 1906), p. 340. Other authors dispute this interpretation.

24. Ivan Čizmić, *Iseljeništvo i Suvremena Ekonomska Emigracija s Područja Karlovca* (Zagreb, 1973), p. 302.

25. Ivan Lupis-Vukić, *Medu Našim Narodom u Americi [Among our people in America]* (Split, 1929), pp. 70–71.

26. Louis Adamić, *The Native's Return* (New York, 1934), p. 171.

27. *Reports of the Immigration Commission*, vol. 4, p. 387.

28. Ibid., vol. 4, pp. 358–59.

29. Janko Ibler, *Hrvatska Politika [Croatian Politics]*, 2 vols. (Zagreb, 1914), vol. 2, pp. 42–43.

30. George Prpić, *The Croatian Immigrants in America* (New York, 1971), p. 95.

31. Ibid.; Tomasević, *Peasant*, p. 153.

32. Čizmić. *Iseljenistvo*, p. 284.

33. Ibid., p. 304.

34. Lakatoš, *Narodna Statistika*, p. 9.

35. Ibid., p. 40.

36. Ibid., p. 41.

37. Ibid., p. 64.

38. Croatia-Slavonia, Sabor, *Stenografički Zapisnici Sabora Kraljevinah Hrvatske, Slavonije i Dalmacije 1908–1913, [Stenographic Reports of the Diet of the Kingdom of Croatia, Slavonia and Dalmatia 1908–13]* (Zagreb, 1910), vol. 1, pp. 317–18.

39. Ibid., p. 319.

40. *Narodni List [People's Herald]*, 28 June 1914.

41. Čizmić, *Iseljeništvo*, 303; Fran Milobar, *Izabrana poglavlja iz narodnog gospodarstvo [Selected Articles on National Economics]*, 2 vols. (Zagreb, 1902–1903), vol. 1, p. 240.

42. Lupis-Vukić, *O Iseljavanju našega naroda i o Americi [About Emigration of Our People and About America]* (Zadar, 1910), pp. 7–8.

43. Čizmić, *Iseljeništvo*, pp. 301–3.

44. Vera St. Erlich, *Family in Transition* (Princeton, 1966), pp. 307–9.

45. Ibid., p. 312.

46. Ibid., p. 328.

47. Ibid., p. 312.

48. Ibid., p. 316.

49. Ibid., p. 329.

50. Ibid., p. 336.

51. *Reports of the Immigration Commission*, vol. 4, pp. 387–88.

52. Čizmić, *Iseljeništvo*, p. 301; *Karlovački Glasnik [Herald of Karbvci]*, 16 March 1901.

53. Edward Alsworth Ross, *The Old World in the New* (New York, 1914), p. 137.

54. Mladen Marković to author, March 1974.

55. For a detailed study on acculturation of Slavic steelworkers in Steelton, see John Bodnar, *Immigration and Industrialization—Ethnicity in an American Mill Town 1870–1940* (Pittsburgh, 1977).

56. Lupis-Vukić, *O Iseljavanju i o Americi*, p. 8.

57. Ingrid Semmingsen, "Emigration and the Image of America in Europe," in *Immigration and American History*, ed. Henry Steele Commager (Minneapolis, 1961), p. 54.

58. Prpić, *Croatian Immigrants*, p. 412.

59. Eleanor Ledbetter, *The Yugoslavs of Cleveland* (Cleveland, 1918), p. 22.

60. Prpić, *Croatian Immigrants*, p. 256.

61. Dunda, "Izgledi,"p. 425.

THE MYTH OF NO RETURN: JEWISH RETURN MIGRATION TO EASTERN EUROPE, 1881–1914

17

Jonathan D. Sarna

No myth stands higher in the pantheon of received American Jewish historical wisdom than the myth of no return:

The difference between the Jewish and the non-Jewish immigrants can be defined in the following general way; whereas the others, in the main, sought to improve their lot, the Jews frequently looked simply for a refuge. . . . Others could, if they so chose, go back to their old countries; for Jews there was generally no way back. Jews came here to stay. When they left their old countries, they burned all their bridges behind them. . . . [1]

In making this assertion, C. Bezalel Sherman merely echoed conclusions reached by a distinguished coterie of earlier scholars. Samuel Joseph, whose *Jewish Immigration to the United States from 1881-1910* remains a basic work, asserted that "Jewish immigration exhibits a quality of permanence and stability to so great a degree as to render this fact one of its distinguishing characteristics." Demographer Liebmann Hersch found that "the rate of repatriation (emigrants per 100 immigrants) is much lower for Jews than for any other people." Jacob Lestschinsky boldly declared that "Jewish immigrants arrived everywhere with the intent to settle permanently."[2]

Statistics seemingly support these sweeping conclusions. As Lestschinsky demonstrated, from 1908 to 1925, 1,018,878 Jews immigrated into the United States while a mere 52,585 departed, a return emigration rate of barely 5.2%. By contrast, the return migration rate of Italians in this period was 55.8%, and even that of the Germans was 15.3%.[3] More significant data on return migration comes from figures confined to the years before World War One, since later statistics were skewed by wartime conditions and subsequent restrictions.

While a slightly larger percentage of Jewish immigrants returned during this period, the rate is still remarkably low, both absolutely and comparatively. Revealingly, Jews overall were almost twice as likely to return to Austria-Hungary, where they were treated comparatively well, than to Russia, where they faced persecutions and privation. In 1912, a recession year, the return migration rate among Austro-Hungarian Jews hit 19.7 percent (10,757 immi-

This essay was first published in *American Jewish History* 71 (1981–82), 256–268. It is reprinted with permission of the author and the publisher.

grants; 2,121 returnees). The comparable rate for Russian Jews was only 7.6 percent (58,389 immigrants; 4,448 returnees).[4]

Unfortunately, government statistics provide no direct information about Jewish immigrants who returned to Europe before 1908. Conclusions about Jewish departure rates are thus based entirely on later figures, the assumption being that earlier ones followed the same pattern.[5] This assumption has never been tested. In fact, it is completely groundless.

Before 1900, nobody seems to have commented on the lack of Jewish returnees; to the contrary, reports declared that the number of those returning was large. The *Jewish Messenger* in 1888 decried the existence of "hundreds of dispirited people who are as eager to leave the country as a few years or months ago they were so hopeful in reaching it." The newspaper claimed that eight hundred Jews were demanding return, even if it meant their traveling back to Europe in cattle ships.[6] Annual reports of the United Hebrew Charities (U.H.C.) similarly stressed the immigrant desire to return. Dr. George M. Price, who reported on "the tremendous number of those returning to Russia" to readers of the Russian Jewish periodical *Voskhod*, calculated that 7,580 immigrants returned with the U.H.C.'s assistance just from 1882–1889.[7] As late as 1896, Julius Goldman, speaking as a trustee of the Baron de Hirsch Fund, reported to the Jewish Colonization Association in Paris that "Hundreds of these people have said and are continually saying that their condition is worse than it was in Russia, and it is the opinion of those who are acquainted with them that thousands would return to Russia if they had the means and dared to do so."[8]

Such impressionistic reports can, of course, often be misleading. With hundreds of thousands of Jews immigrating to America, evidence that a few hundred or

Table 17.1
Departure of Emigrants, 1908–1914
(fiscal years ending June 30, absolute figures in thousands)

	Non-Jewish	Jewish by Origin			
		Total	Tsarist Russia	Austria-Hungary	Romania	Other
Departures	1,947	46.8	28.1	11.3	0.7	6.7
% Distribution		100.0	60.0	24.2	1.5	14.3
Admissions (immigration)	6,053	656.5	471.4	96.1	15.7	73.3
Ratio of departures to admissions (%)	32.2	7.1	6.0	11.8	4.5	9.1

Source: Simon Kuznets, "Immigration of Russian Jews to the United States: Background and Structure," *Perspectives in American History,* IX (1975), p. 40.

even a few thousand of them returned would hardly blunt existing generalizations. Returning emigrants might have been more noisy than representative, and contemporaries could have been deceived. Both quantitative and qualitative evidence, however, militate against this conclusion.

One indicator of return migration comes from census figures. While not specifically enumerating Jews, they did include tallies of foreign born Russians, of whom Jews comprised better than sixty percent.[9] Resulting figures can only be suggestive, particularly since the accuracy of the census count itself is questionable. But the vast difference between "expected population" (Russian-borns counted in the previous census, minus those who died, plus the decade's Russian immigrants, minus those who died), and the enumerated population as tallied by censustakers does require notice. In 1890, the expected Russian-born population, assuming a mortality rate of 19 per thousand since 1880, equalled 230,429 (29,487 surviving Russians from 1880 + 200,942 surviving immigrants, 1881–1890). Census takers counted 182,644 Russian-borns. The difference—47,785—yields a return migration rate of 22.4 percent. Naturally, American-born children of immigrants, not being foreigners, do not enter into this calculation. Using the same procedure for the next decade, this time assuming an annual mortality of 18 per thousand, yields a return migration rate of 26.46 percent (152,307 surviving Russians from 1890 + 467,753 surviving immigrants, 1891–1900 = an expected population of 620,060, some 130,693 Russians more than were actually counted).[10] Neither 22.4 percent nor 26.46 percent can be considered true Jewish return migration rates, owing to the large number of questionable variables employed, but both figures suggest that return migration before 1900 was much higher than generally assumed, likely in the range of 15 to 20 percent. Elias Tcherikower's independent estimate of up to 29 percent Jewish departures during the extraordinary economic crisis of 1882 lends credence to these figures, as does an estimate that East European Jewish return migration from England, 1895–1902, stood at least as high as 15.3 percent.[11]

More powerful evidence of Jewish return migration can be found in written sources from the early years of massive East European immigration. In 1882, the Hebrew language newspaper, *Hamagid* (Lyck, Prussia), noting a growing stream of departures, exclaimed "this is what American immigration has finally come to!" The *Boston Hebrew Observer* reported that some seventy-five Boston Jews rushed down to the Commonwealth Alms House in Tewksbury merely on the rumor that the city's Provident Association would pay their way home. A good many other immigrants, Bernard Horwich remembered, remained in America only long enough to save up and head back. Rabbi Moses Weinberger's estimate of the immigrant situation in the 1880s thus seems to have been accurate. Some Jews came to America "only to make money with the thought later of returning." Others, especially intellectuals and teachers, had "trouble finding steady work [and] after a few years shuffling about as if in a world of desolation. . . . g[a]ve up and return[ed] shamefacedly to their homelands."[12]

Many immigrants, particularly in the 1880s, were aided in their efforts to return home. Charities provided one way tickets as an investment; those who departed would not become a burden on the community. While Secretary of the Hebrew Emigrant Aid Society Augustus A. Levey claimed that "In no instance is any adult returned, except [if] he has himself urgently requested it," and a United Hebrew Charities report insisted that "In no cases were [immigrants] urged to go," the choice offered probably was "return to Europe or fend for yourself." Leonard L. Cohen's description of how English Jewish charities treated immigrant mendicants likely applies to America as well:

He tells us he cannot succeed without charity. He has been here, say, nine months. We say "if you cannot succeed here, and as you had nothing to bring you here, you had better go back." He rather demurs the first time, but the second time he agrees and he goes.[13]

Immigrant-run organizations like Philadelphia's Association for the Protection of Jewish Immigrants may have treated East Europeans more respectfully, but their aim was the same. They sought to help immigrants who could not support themselves return to where they thought they would be happier. A typical letter provided by the Philadelphia Association carefully set out why individuals wanted to go back and why they were found worthy of assistance.

To Whom It May Concern:
This is to cerfify that Mr. B. Breitbart and wife have been assisted by this Association to reach Europe as they are unable to support themselves in this country on account of their advanced age.
They desire to reach their native country, Russia, where they have children to support them.

Respectfully,
per J. Ehrlich, Agent[14]

In the hindsight of Jewish history even such benign movements to return pauper immigrants find few defenders. We know what happened to East European Jews in the end. American Jews in the 1880's, however, considered the reasons behind Jewish and non-Jewish immigration to be pretty well the same. Persecutions aside, they considered the majority of East European Jewish immigrants to be disenchanted *luftmentschen* seeking gold in a land of opportunity. Available evidence partly supports this view. Early immigrants, unlike more frequently described later ones, were overwhelmingly young, single and male. Many arrived in New York brimming with unrealistic hopes, filled with misinformation, and lacking marketable skills. In numerous cases, family, friends, or organizations had covered the cost of their voyages, and in not a few, immigrants expected to be cared for upon their arrival. So reality came as a shock; for many newcomers, conditions in the New World proved far worse than those they had left behind. They were happy to return.[15]

The existence of Jewish return migration should occasion no surprise. Immigrants have been returning for as long as they have been migrating; indeed, according to demographic theory, "for every migration stream there is a corresponding counterstream flowing in the opposite direction."[16] Native ties do not break easily. Return migration from America should also occasion no surprise. Though the topic has only recently begun to be studied by historians, its importance has been recognized by economists and social scientists for years, which is precisely why they kept statistics. Push and pull factors clearly operated on both sides of the Atlantic, motivating people to move now one way, now the other. Ships departing America frequently carried just as many migrants as those that arrived.[17]

Yet Jewish departure from America does evoke surprise, for East European Jews were supposedly fleeing from persecution. From our perspective, the fact that they returned to the land of their affliction seems puzzling. Evidence from the period, however, suggests that contemporaries would not have been puzzled. The *Jewish Messenger*, for example, considered immigration in the 1880s "no question of persecution or involuntary exile . . . [but] the mere seeking of a new home by people who are not satisfied with their lives in their native place." Many disagreed with the *Messenger*, notably former American consul to Rumania, Benjamin F. Peixotto.[18] The existence of the debate, however, is what is significant. In the Russian case, it took the Kishinev pogrom of 1903 to make most people agree that the best solution for Jewish problems was immigration. Before then opinions divided, many thinking that pogroms would pass.[19] As a member of Berlin's Central German Committee for the Relief of Russian Jews admitted to American investigators, "One part of our committee, in accordance with Baron de Hirsch's ideas, wants to clear Russia of Jews altogether; the other to prevent people as much as possible from emigrating."[20] Among Jews in Russia the same debate took place: Jewish notables like Baron Horace Günzberg opposed emigration, Zionists and some Jewish newspapers favored it. Since Russian policies toward Jews fluctuated wildly, both sides in the debate could offer convincing arguments. As a result, even Jews who had fled from persecution could justify returning home, especially if they thought that conditions in Russia had changed.[21] Those who had not fled on account of persecution returned with still fewer qualms. However they justified their actions, returnees merely bolstered the arguments of those who claimed that conditions in Eastern Europe were not so bad after all.

No single factor accounts for all return migration: Jews left America for as many reasons as they came. Deportations, increasing in number after 1897, account for some migrations, but they form a separate subject.[22] Most departees returned of their own free will. Specific events—deaths, business failures, unpleasant encounters, or the like—sometimes occasioned return trips, but deeper causes—social, cultural, economic and political ones—usually lay behind them. From a structural perspective, return migration occurred when push and pull factors, operating in tandem and behind-the-scenes, convinced an immigrant that another arduous journey was in his interest, for he would be better off where he came from. The two factors that particularly affected Jewish migration rates were economic conditions in America and political conditions in Europe: slumps caused return migration rates to rise, pogroms led them to fall.[23] But broad underlying factors of this sort should not obscure other considerations that came into play. Ultimately, each return migrant returned for reasons of his or her own.

Many migrants planned to return temporarily just in order to visit their old home towns. Some had aged relatives whom they longed to see; others sought brides, there being a shortage of Jewish women in America; still others came home merely to show off, to demonstrate that they had somehow made good; and in a few cases immigrants returned home to study.[24] The government discouraged all such visits. To be naturalized, one had to have "lived in this country without returning to Europe at least five years continuously." Once naturalized, one's application for a passport could easily be denied.[25] Still, many return visits took place, and not a few turned out to be one-way visits. According to Russian statistics, 12,313 more United States citizens entered Russian territory from 1881 to 1914 than left. According to American government investigators, plenty of Jews living in Russia held United States passports, among the most famous being Cantor Pinchas Minkowsky of Odessa, formerly of New York. In the case of Jews, as in the case of non-Jews, tourists and returnees often proved difficult to distinguish from one another.[26]

Another group of Jewish return migrants might best be termed temporary immigrants, people who came to America intending someday to return to Europe. The hope that Mottel's neighbors expressed in a Sholom Aleichem story—that "we'd arrive in America safe and sound, make good business, earn a lot of money and then return home"—was the hope expressed by many immigrants, and at least some succeeded in achieving their goal. The immigration commissioners reported on one Bialystok native, Mr. Levy, who amassed $20,000 in the New World and returned home to found a factory. Philip Cowen, editor of the *American Hebrew*, quoted a Russian Jewish beggar as saying "I came here five years ago to gather money for a dowry for my daughter. Thanks to you and some of your good neighbors, I have two hundred and fifty dollars together, and now I will have a fine son-in-law, for he is waiting for me in Russia." More enterprising immigrants employed their knowledge of English and Russian to engage in commerce. In 1903, according to Alexander Hume Ford, there was "a Russian American Hebrew in each of the large Manchurian cities securing in Russia the cream of the contracts for American material used in Manchuria." Of course, not all who hoped to get rich and return succeeded in doing so. Morris Raphael Cohen's father intended to "save enough money by hard work in America to enable him to return and set up some business in Minsk," but never did. After several trips back and forth across the Atlantic, the Cohens settled in America for good. Others, particularly Austro-Hungarians, journeyed to and from America numerous times. They expressed with their feet the ambivalence—the tension between love of the Old World and allure of the New—that all immigrants felt. Jewish temporary immigrants sought the ultimate synthesis: an American life-style on European soil. They desired, as poet Mitchell Kaplan expressed it, to journey back home to Vladnick, "and live there with never a care." Whether or not they succeeded in achieving this utopia in the short term, they ultimately faced severe disappointment.[27]

Tourists and prosperous returnees might be considered successful emigrants. They often travelled home in style, as if to publicize the progress they had made since journeying in the opposite direction.[28] Most, however, were not nearly so fortunate. Return, in their case, was by steerage or cattle ship; it symbolized failure. No matter how they explained it away, the fact remained that their hopes had gone unrealized; their American dreams turned sour.

Inability to find work was a prime cause of return migration. Better to return home than to wander the streets of New York homeless and jobless. In many cases, however, it was less the absence of work than the absence of meaningful work that engendered dissatisfaction. Dr. M. Merkin, a chemist and well-rounded intellectual, arrived in America around 1884 from Latvia. Though he made a name for himself as a Social Democrat and incisive thinker, he had to wash dishes in a restaurant for a livelihood. Not surprisingly, he did not remain in the country for long. Many early immigrants, particularly Am Olam intellectuals, told similar stories. Some of those who did find work had trouble adjusting to the demands of American industry. "I had to work very hard in America, so I thought if I had to work so hard I could do better here and I came back," one returnee admitted. Others, especially those unmarried, complained of homesickness and *anomie*: "Ah, home, my beloved home. My heart is heavy for my parents whom I left behind."[29]

Complaints about the harshness of American life—the boom-bust cycle, the miserable working conditions, the loneliness, the insecurity—could not help but cast return migrants in a bad light. In effect, returnees admitted their own weakness; those more fit had stayed where they were, resolving to succeed whatever the odds. Complaints about American religious life, on the other hand, had precisely an opposite effect. The pious migrant could hold his head high: he had spurned the gold of America for the sake of an Orthodox Jewish life. In his own eyes he became a martyr rather than a failure. This, of course, is not to deny that religion influenced decisions to return. Those determined to observe traditional rituals in America, particularly the Sabbath and Jewish holidays, faced enormous hardships, unlike any most had known before. With good reason a returnee called America "a Godless land," where "Jews were losing their religion very rapidly." With similar good reason, a fictional account of "Vichne Devoshe's" disaffection and ultimate return from America concentrates on the country's impieties and heresies. The American way of life posed a significant challenge to traditional Judaism, and those committed to Jewish law certainly faced a harder time in the New World than most had in the Old.[30] But to claim that these people returned on account of religion only leaves too much unexplained; after all, some Americans did manage to lead fully Jewish lives. Return migration more likely resulted from a range of factors, religion being just one of them. Returnees lay particular stress on that one to evoke sympathy and save face.

A full listing of the causes behind Jewish return migration would have to include such diverse grounds as an inability to adapt to America's climate, a cultural aversion to indoor toilets, a patriotic urge to defend a native land in war, and most somber of all, an *agunah*'s desperate need to find her missing husband.[31] The specifics, however, merely underline a more general conclusion: that return migration serves as a mirror through which immigrant problems may be viewed. Just as immigration casts into bold relief the hardships faced by Jews in the Old World, so return migration portrays their miseries in the New. That more Jews immigrated than returned, and that quite a few returnees later re-immigrated leaves no doubt as to the final verdict on where conditions were worse and where the promise was greater. But some Jewish immigrants of an earlier day, blessed neither with prophecy nor historical hindsight, discovered that the life they remembered having lost meant more to them than the America they had gained. Particularly in the years before the Kishinev pogrom, numbers of them returned home.

Twentieth-century American Jews, as we have seen, ignored the phenomenon of return migration; indeed, they denied it was a phenomenon at all. In many cases they did so innocently; they simply reported what they thought the statistics said. Those who knew better, however, also kept return migration under wraps. During the years when America was in the midst of a prolonged debate over immigration restriction, discussion of return migration would have been impolitic. American Jews attempted to portray all Jewish immigrants as refugees to freedom, modern day pilgrims. They specifically—and accurately—sought to distinguish Jews from the much maligned transient immigrants "who have no intention of permanently changing their residence and whose only purpose in coming to America is temporarily to take advantage of greater wages paid for industrial labor in this country." Jewish immigrants, Louis Marshall insisted, "can not go back." To suggest in those days that some did go back or had done so in the past would have besmirched a carefully nurtured image, at considerable potential risk.[32]

So until our day return migration has remained a neglected aspect of American Jewish history.[33] Rather than analyzing its dimensions, rate, and impact, we glory in its supposed non-existence. This is not to say that the East European Jewish returnee experience parallels that of other groups, for in fact it differs markedly. The time has come, however, to examine these differences, understand them, and place them in context. We shall probably discover that almost as much can be learned from those who left America as from those who stayed.

NOTES

1. C. Bezalel Sherman, *The Jew Within American Society* (Detroit, 1961), pp. 55–60.

2. Samuel Joseph, *Jewish Immigration to the United States from 1881–1910* (New

York, 1914), p. 139; Liebmann Hersch, "International Migration of the Jews," in Walter F. Willcox, ed., *International Migrations* (New York, 1931), vol. 2, p. 478; Jacob Lestschinsky, "Jewish Migrations, 1840–1956," in Louis Finkelstein, ed., *The Jews* (New York, 1960), vol. 2, p. 1565. See also Uri D. Herscher and Stanley F. Chyet, *A Socialist Perspective on Jews, America and Immigration* (Cincinnati, 1980), p. 52; Salo W. Baron, *Steeled by Adversity* (Philadelphia, 1971), p. 280; and Peter I. Rose, "Introduction," in Rose, ed., *The Ghetto and Beyond* (New York, 1969), p. 7.

3. Lestschinsky, "Jewish Migrations," p. 1565. Kristian Hvidt, *Flight to America* (New York, 1975), p. 181, suggests that United States figures considerably underestimate the extent of return migration.

4. Figures calculated from Walter F. Willcox, *International Migrations* (New York, 1929), vol. 1, pp. 464, 480. On this important and little appreciated difference between Russian and Austro-Hungarian Jews, see Joseph, *Jewish Immigration*, pp. 135–37; Peter Wiernik, *History of the Jews in America* (New York, 1972), p. 282; Judd L. Teller, *Strangers and Natives* (New York, 1968), pp. 5–10; and more generally, Johann Chmelar, "The Austrian Emigration, 1900–1914," *Perspectives in American History* 7 (1973), 275–378.

5. Simon Kuznets, "Immigration of Russian Jews to the United States: Background and Structure," in *Perspectives in American History* 9 (1975), 47–48, assumes that return migration in early years was less than in the post-1908 period. No evidence supports this view.

6. *Jewish Messenger*, 14 September 1888, p. 4; 21 September 1888, p. 4.

7. George M. Price, "The Russian Jews in America," translated by Leo Shpall, *Publications of the American Jewish Historical Society* 48 (1958), 44–46; *Thirteenth Annual Report of the Board of Relief of the United Hebrew Charities of the City of New York* (New York, 1887), pp. 14–16, 31.

8. Julius Goldman to Jewish Colonization Association (6 October 1896), Baron de Hirsch Fund Papers, American Jewish Historical Society.

9. On the use of "Russian-origin" census data for Jewish statistics, see Elias Tcherikower, ed., *The Early Jewish Labor Movement in the United States*, translated and revised by Aaron Antonovsky (New York, 1961), pp. 363–65; Kuznets, "Immigration of Russian Jews," p. 41; and Erich Rosenthal, "The Equivalence of United States Census Data for Persons of Russian Stock or Descent with American Jews: An Evaluation," *Demography* 12 (May 1975), 275–90.

10. I have borrowed some of my procedures here from Simon Kuznets and Ernest Rubin, *Immigration and the Foreign Born*, National Bureau of Economic Research Occasional Paper #46 (New York, 1954).

11. Elias Tcherikower, ed., *Geshikhte fun der yidisher arbeterbavegung in di Fareynikte Shtatn* (New York, 1943) vol. 1, p. 245. British figures calculated from *Report of the Royal Commission on Alien Immigration with Minutes of Evidence and Appendix* (London, 1903), appendix, tables 5, 81; see evidence #15325 and 15515 for the estimate that each case of repatriation involved an average of three people.

12. *Hamagid* 26 (1 November 1882), 341; *Boston Hebrew Observer*, 23 November 1883, quoted in Jacob Neusner, "The Impact of Immigration and Philanthropy Upon the Boston Jewish Community (1880–1914)," *Publications of the American Jewish Historical Society* 46 (1956), 73–74; Bernard Horwich, *My First Eighty Years* (Chicago, 1939), p. 126; Moses Weinberger, *Jews and Judaism in New York* (in Hebrew) (New York, 1887), pp. 1, 18. For other references, see Isaac M. Fein, *The Making of an American*

Jewish Community (Philadelphia, 1971), p. 148; Israel Kasovich, *The Days of Our Years* (New York, 1929), pp. 179, 277–78; William M. Bolton, "William M. Bolton Looks Back: Extracts From An Oral History," in Barry Herman, ed., *Jews in New Haven* II (New Haven, 1979), p. 133; Marcus E. Ravage, *An American in the Making* (New York, 1971), p. 10; Myron Berman, ed., "My Recollections and Experiences of Richmond, Virginia, U.S.A., 1884–1892 by Joseph Joel," *Virginia Magazine of History and Biography* 87 (1980), 344, 356; *Report of the Commission of Immigration of the State of New York* (Albany, 1909), pp. 75–88, 221.

13. Augustus A. Levey to Hermann Makower (21 July 1882) quoted in Zosa Szajkowski, "The Attitude of American Jews to East European Jewish Immigration (1881–1893)," *Publications of the American Jewish Historical Society* 40 (March 1951), 242; *Thirteenth Annual Report of the Board of Relief of the United Hebrew Charities of the City of New York* (New York, 1887), p. 15; *Report of the Royal Commission on Alien Immigration*, Evidence #15650, 15770, 16442–43.

14. Association for the Protection of Jewish Immigrants Correspondence, Box 1355, p. 41, American Jewish Archives, Cincinnati, Ohio; Richard F. Address, "The Reaction of the Philadelphia Anglo-Jewish Press to the Russian Immigrant Community, 1882–1892," miscellaneous file, American Jewish Archives. For other evidence of return migration, see the papers of this association at the Philadelphia Jewish Archives Center, particularly the passage order books. I am grateful to Harold J. Kravitz for describing these papers to me; see also Steven W. Siegel, "Immigration Records at the Philadelphia Jewish Archives Center," *Toledot*, I (Summer 1977), 3.

15. Irving Howe, *World of Our Fathers* (New York, 1976), pp. 67–118; Elias Tcherikower, "Jewish Immigrants to the United States, 1881–1900," *Yivo Annual of Jewish Social Science*, VI (1951), 157–76; Tcherikower, ed., *Early Jewish Labor Movement*, pp. 56, 68, 71, 107, 115, 122, 125; Alexander Harkavy, "Chapters From My Life," translated and edited by Jonathan D. Sarna, *American Jewish Archives* 33 (April 1981), 35–52.

16. Donald Bogue, "Principles of Demography," p. 765 quoted in Robert Rhoades, *The Anthropology of Return Migration*, Papers in Anthropology #20 (Norman, Okla., 1979), p. 1.

17. Rhoades, *Anthropology of Return Migration* contains a full bibliography. Important recent studies include Betty B. Caroli, *Italian Repatriation from the United States* (New York, 1973), pp. 3–22; Lars-Göran Tedebrand, "Remigration from America to Sweden," in Harold Runblom and Hans Norman, editors, *From Sweden to America: A History of the Migration* (Minneapolis, 1976), pp. 201–27; Bernard Axelrod, "Historical Studies of Emigration from the United States," *International Migration Review* 6 (Spring 1972), 32–49; and Sune Åkerman, "From Stockholm to San Francisco: The Development of the Historical Studies of External Migrations," *Annales Academiae Regiae Scientarium Upsaliens* 19 (1975), 10, 19–24.

18. *Jewish Messenger*, 21 September 1888, p. 4; Benjamin F. Peixotto, "What Shall We Do With Our Immigrants?" *The American Hebrew*, 1 April 1887, pp. 114–15.

19. Zosa Szajkowski, "Paul Nathan, Lucien Wolf, Jacob H. Schiff and the Jewish Revolutionary Movements in Eastern Europe (1903–1917)," *Jewish Social Studies* 29 (January 1967), 3–26, 75–91; idem, "The Impact of the Russian Revolution of 1905 on American Jewish Life," *Yivo Annual of Jewish Social Science*, 17 (1978), 102–9; Philip E. Schoenberg, "The American Reaction to the Kishinev Pogrom of 1903," *American Jewish Historical Quarterly* 63 (March 1974), 262–83; I. Michael Aronson, "The At-

titudes of Russian Officials in the 1880s Toward Jewish Assimilation and Emigration," *Slavic Review* 34 (1975), 1–18.

20. *Letter From the Secretary of the Treasury Transmitting A Report of the Commissioners of Immigration....* (Washington, 1892), vol. 1, p. 28.

21. For example, Kasovich, *Days of Our Years*, p. 179.

22. Zosa Szajkowski, "Deportation of Jewish Immigrants and Returnees Before World War I," *American Jewish Historical Quarterly* 67 (June 1978), 291–306.

23. In addition to works cited above in note 17, see Julie DaVanzo, "Differences Between Return and Nonreturn Migration: An Econometric Analysis," *International Migration Review* 10 (Spring 1976), 13–27.

24. Alton Goldbloom, *Small Patients: The Autobiography of a Children's Doctor* (New York, 1959), pp. 45–65; Ravage, *An American in the Making*, pp. 3–26; Philip Cowen, *Memories of an American Jew* (New York, 1932), p. 240; Isaac Metzker, ed., *A Bintel Brief* (New York, 1971), p. 63; "Abraham Kaspe," *Universal Jewish Encyclopedia*, vol. 6, p. 331; and *Message from the President of the United States in Answer to the Resolution of the House of Representatives of August 20, 1890, Concerning the Enforcement of Proscriptive Edicts Against the Jews in Russia* (Washington, 1890), contain various accounts of return visits to Eastern Europe.

25. John F. Carr, *Guide to the United States for the Jewish Immigrant* (New York, 1913), p. 34; Reuben Fink, *How to Bring Relatives Into America and How to Travel Out of America* (in Yiddish), (New York, 1919), pp. 5–19.

26. Statistics calculated from Willcox, *International Migrations*, vol. 1, pp. 798–99; see also Cowen, *Memories of an American Jew*, p. 228; and Åkerman, "From Stockholm to San Francisco," pp. 20–21.

27. Sholom Aleichem, *The Adventures of Mottel the Cantor's Son*, translated by Tamara Kahana (New York, 1961), p. 76; Weinberger, *Jews and Judaism in New York*, pp. 26–27; *Letter from the Secretary of the Treasury Transmitting a Report of the Commissioners of Immigration*, p. 88; Cowen, *Memories of an American Jew*, pp. 88, 198; Alexander Hume Ford, "America's Debt to the Russian Jew," *Colliers Weekly* 31 (6 June 1903), 10; Morris Raphael Cohen, *A Dreamer's Journey* (Boston, 1949), pp. 23–24; Tcherikower, *Early Jewish Labor Movement in the United States*, pp. 121–22; Mitchell Kaplan, "Back Home," *Just Folks* (New York, 1927), pp. 49–52.

28. Edward Steiner, *On the Trail of the Immigrant* (New York, 1906), p. 360.

29. Melech Epstein, *Jewish Labor in U.S.A.* (New York, 1969), vol. 1, p. 139; Cowen, *Memories of an American Jew*, p. 249; Metzker, *Bintel Brief*, p. 114; cf. *Letter From the Secretary of the Treasury Transmitting a Report of the Commissioners of Immigration*, p. 28.

30. F. C. Gilbert, *From Judaism to Christianity* (Concord, 1916), p. 64; Oyzer Blaustein, *Vikhne Dvoshe fort tsurik fun Amerike* (Vilna, 1894). Other references to religious factors in return migration include Joseph Gillman, *The B'nai Khaim in America* (New York, 1969), p. 58; Aaron Rothkoff, "The American Sojourns of Ridbaz: Religious Problems Within the Immigrant Community," *American Jewish Historical Quarterly* 57 (1968), 557–72; Arthur A. Chiel, ed., "An Ethical Will," *American Jewish Historical Quarterly* 61 (March 1972), 230; Szajkowski, "The Attitude of American Jews," p. 243; and Alter F. Landesman, *Brownsville* (New York, 1971), pp. 74–76. J. D. Eisenstein, who faced similar pressures, remained in America; see Lloyd P. Gartner, "From New York to Miedzyrecz: Immigrant Letters of Judah David Eisenstein, 1878–1886," *American Jewish Historical Quarterly* 52 (1963), 239. Rabbis have traditionally had a high

rate of return; see Moses A. Shulvass, *From East to West* (Detroit, 1971), p. 17.

31. For climate, see *Letter from the Secretary of the Treasury Transmitting a Report of the Commissioners of Immigration*, p. 28. Regarding toilets, see Gillman, *B'nai Khaim in America*, p. 58; cf. Zane L. Miller, *Boss Cox's Cincinnati* (Chicago, 1968), p. 40; and Richard M. Dorson, *American Folklore* (Chicago, 1977), pp. 94–95. On patriotic returnees, see Metzker, *Bintel Brief*, p. 46; and Louis Greenberg, *The Jews in Russia* (New York, 1976), vol. 2, p. 100. On returning *agunot*, see Metzker, *Bintel Brief*, pp. 78–79; Szajkowski, "The Attitude of American Jews," p. 243.

32. Joseph, *Jewish Immigration*, p. 133; "Hearing on Immigration Bills," (pamphlet in Klau Library, Hebrew Union College, Cincinnati; evidently, Washington, 1910), p. 10; see Charles Reznikoff, ed., *Louis Marshall: Champion of Liberty* (Philadelphia, 1957), p. 140; and generally, Esther Panitz, "In Defense of the Jewish Immigrant (1891–1924)," *American Jewish Historical Quarterly* 55 (1965), 57–97.

33. The only studies to consider return migration at any length are Jacob Shatzky, "Polish Jews Emigrate from America" (in Yiddish), *Yivo Bleter* 20 (September 1942), 125–27; Irving A. Mandel, "The Attitude of the American Jewish Community Toward East-European Immigration, 1880–1890," (Rabbinic thesis, Hebrew Union College, 1947), pp. 60–61; and Szajkowski, "Deportation of Jewish Emigrants and Returnees before World War I."

AFTERWORD: WORKING CLASSES AND NATIONS

18

Eric J. Hobsbawm

If it is wrong to assume that workers have no country, it is equally misleading to assume that they have only one, and that we know what it is. We talk of the French, German or Italian working class, and in doing so we indicate, quite rightly, that much the most important forces defining any particular working class are those of the national economy of the state in which a worker lives, and the laws, institutions, practices and official culture of that state. An Irish labourer migrating to Boston, his brother who settled in Glasgow, and a third brother who went to Sydney would remain Irish, but become part of three very different working classes with different histories. At the same time, and as this example suggests, it is also wrong to assume that the members of such national working classes are or ever were homogeneous bodies of Frenchmen, Britons or Italians, or, even when they saw themselves as such, that they are not divided by other communal demarcations, or that they are *exclusively* identified with the state which defines their effective existence as a class and an organised movement. It is equally wrong to assume that such an identification is eternal and unchanging. These assumptions are based on the myths of modern nationalism, a nineteenth century invention. Though they are not entirely fictitious, they are not much more realistic than the opposite assumption that national or communal identity are irrelevant to the proletariat.

No doubt it is possible to discover countries in which the working class is nationally homogeneous in this sense—perhaps in Iceland, with its 250,000 inhabitants—but for practical purposes such cases may be neglected. All national working classes tend to be heterogeneous, and with multiple identifications, though for certain purposes and at certain times some may loom larger than others. An Indian shop-steward in Slough may see himself for one purpose as a member of the British working class (as distinct from his brother who remained in India), for another as a coloured person (as distinct from the whites), for another as an Indian (as distinct from the British or Pakistanis), for yet another as a Sikh (as distinct from Christians, Hindus or Muslims), as a Punjabi (as distinct from a Gujerati), probably also as someone from a particular area and

This essay was first published in *Saothar. Journal of the Irish Labour History Society* 8 (1982), 75–85, which is available from the Irish Labour History Society, Irish Congress of Trade Unions, 19 Raglan Road, Dublin 4. It is reprinted with permission of the author and the publisher.

village in the Punjab, and certainly as a member of a particular network of kinship. Of course some of these identifications, however important for everyday purposes (e.g., in arranging the marriage of sons and daughters), are politically rather subordinate.

Moreover, one identification does not exclude the others. The Andalusians, Basques and Catalans who fought Napoleon did so as Spaniards, without in the least losing the sense of the differences which separated them from each other. What is more, such identifications change over time, as well as with the context of action. Sicilian and Calabrian labourers went to America and became Americans, but in doing so they also came to see themselves—as they probably had not done before—as Italians who belonged, to some extent, not only to the old country but also to a nation whose members were scattered across the world from Argentina and Brazil to Australia. Conversely, workers who once saw themselves primarily as Belgians, in spite of talking two quite different and mutually incomprehensible languages, today identify themselves primarily as Flemings and French-speaking Walloons.

These multiple identifications give rise to something like a "national" problem within working classes only when they seriously get in each others' way. So far as one can tell there was no serious national problem before 1914 in the mines of South Wales where English immigrants, English- and Welsh-speaking Welshmen, a handful of Spaniards and doubtless a few other minorities worked together, joining the South Wales Miners Federation and supporting Labour. There was in the Ruhr, where a mass of immigrant Polish miners, separated from the Germans by language and from the free-thinking Social Democratic Party by Catholicism, showed a marked reluctance to support the party of their class. Again, to take the extreme case of the USA, where the working class consisted largely of immigrants incapable initially of understanding either the language of the country or of other groups of immigrants: their national and linguistic differences undoubtedly made the formation of a working class consciousness more difficult, though they did not entirely inhibit it, and certainly did not prevent the formation of a general political consciousness of the immigrant poor—the "ethnic Americans" who, much as they fought with each other, collectively formed the basis of the Democratic Party in the big cities. But they certainly created no major political problems for the country which officially welcomed them and was neutral about their religions. The very same people who in their home states—as Irishmen in the United Kingdom, as Poles in Russia and Germany, as Czechs in Austria—constituted a "national problem" which threatened the political unity or even the existence of these states, were of little more significance across the ocean than in the choice of candidates for municipal elections.

Indeed, the example of the Irish in Britain illustrates the same point. Most of them were both workers and, very consciously, Catholic and Irish. Until the twenty-six counties separated from the United Kingdom, most of them found a formula which combined national and class identification by supporting, or allying with, parties and movements which claimed to be in favour of both, or at any rate not hostile to both. (Few Irish Nationalist candidates stood in Britain, and outside the Scotland division of Liverpool, none was elected.) Unions with a strong Irish tinge—the National Union of Dock Labourers was commonly known as "the Irish union"—behaved much like other unions. No doubt this was facilitated by the fact that the movements which claimed to stand for "the people" or the working class—Liberals, Labour and Socialists—opposed the oppression of Ireland, joined in protests against it, and indeed supported the Irish Nationalist demand for Home Rule for a united Ireland. After Irish separation had been achieved, the bulk of the Catholic Irish in Britain, insofar as they organised and voted at all, undoubtedly gravitated to the parties of their class. Nor did the fact that they enjoyed dual political rights seem to create any major difficulties: even today Irishmen who vote Labour in Britain will not necessarily feel obliged to vote for a Labour or working class party when they return to the Republic of Ireland.

This relatively smooth integration is all the more striking when we recall that at the grassroots anti-Catholic and anti-Irish sentiments were powerful and sometimes savage in Britain—and by no means only in Liverpool and Glasgow. Moreover, in the case of Ulster or British Orange workers, Protestant identification unquestionably cut across both class and national identification. Nevertheless, for the majority group among the Irish, perhaps just because they were so evidently a majority, the double identification as Irish and (when in Britain) British workers, seems to have been relatively unproblematic.[1]

Thus practically all so-called national working classes consist of a jig-saw of heterogeneous groups. On the one hand, historical development has tended to weld these together into more or less nation-wide blocks, so that differences between Kerrymen and Tipperary men are subordinated to a general Irishness (except, perhaps, for purposes of sporting contests), or between Catholic and Lutheran Germans into a general German-ness (except for purposes of electoral identification). Such nation-wide "national consciousness" is historically recent, though some examples (perhaps "Englishness") date back rather longer. But on the other hand the mobility and the shifting of people in contemporary society, which may be essentially described as a world on the move, create new bonds and new frictions breaking up these blocks.

Thus mass migration into the mines of South Wales, mainly from England, created a strongly Welsh working class, but one which ceased to speak Welsh, thus intensifying the silent tensions between the English-speaking majority of the Welsh and the regionally concentrated and diminishing Welsh-speaking minority. A much smaller migration into North Wales—but one not absorbed into the fabric of the local social structure—has, as we know, produced considerable friction between the Welsh and the English in that region, and, in some parts, a transfer of political loyalties from the all-British Labour Party (inheritor of the all-British Liberal Party) to Plaid Cymru. Similarly, even without migration, changes in the economy, in society and in politics may disturb the established stable pattern of relations between different groups, with unpredictable and sometimes catastrophic results. We have seen this happen in recent years in Cyprus, where Greeks and Turks had long co-existed, and in the Lebanon, a notorious jig-saw puzzle of Maronite, Orthodox and variously Catholic Christians, Sunni and Shiite Muslims, Arabs, Armenians, Druzes and various others. Still, the major disturbances have almost certainly come from mass mobility, our economic and social transformations implying mass migration within and between states. Neither capitalist nor socialist industrialisation is conceivable without it. And this produces the special problem of "strangers" or "foreigners"—a problem already created in many regions by pre-capitalist patterns of settlement and colonisation. This clearly affects the working class very directly.

There are two aspects to the intermingling of different communities, of which the relation between "natives" and immigrants is a particularly clear example.

First, there is the fourfold pattern of the balance between the two. We may neglect case (a), a country without working class emigration or immigration as too rare to be significant. Case (b), a country with little emigration but significant immigration, is comparatively rare, though France might fit the bill. The French, while receiving masses of foreign workers since industrialisation, have never moved outside their frontiers themselves. Case (c) is rather more common: countries with little immigration but a good deal of emigration: in the nineteenth century Norway and the territory of the present Republic of Ireland were obvious examples. Case (d), which is probably the most common in industrial Europe, consists of countries with both substantial emigration and immigration—as in nineteenth-century Britain and Germany. Both immigration and emigration have a bearing on the history of national working classes for, as every Irishman knows, emigration does not snap the links between the exiles and the home country, not least in the history of its labour movement. Tranmael, the leader of the Norwegian labour movement during and after World War I, had been in the Industrial Workers of the World in the USA, whither the Norwegians migrated. Tom Mann migrated to Australia and returned to Britain. As for the Irish movement, its history is filled with returned emigrants: Davitt, Larkin, Connolly.

The second aspect concerns the complexity of the pattern of migration and the distribution of migrant groups. Emigrants from one state or national group may either flow in a single stream to one region and nowhere else, as the peasants from the Creuse in central France moved as building labourers to Paris, or they may fan out to produce a temporary or permanent diaspora which may be world-wide. Wherever there was hard-rock mining on the globe in the nineteenth century, groups of Cornishmen were to be found. The converse of this phenomenon is even more relevant for our purposes.

In some regions or countries, the game of "foreigners" has only two players: Poles and Germans in the Ruhr, Basques and Spaniards in the Basque country. More commonly the working class contains an immigrant sector composed of a variety of groups of "strangers" of different kinds, divided among themselves as well as separated from the natives, and in the extreme case the working class is predominantly composed of immigrants, as in the USA, Argentina and Brazil during the major period of mass migration before 1914. Yet, whether the number of players in the game is greater or smaller, the pattern which usually develops is one of occupational specialisation, or a sort of national stratification.

Thus in 1914 there were few mines in the Ruhr which did not have a majority of Polish miners, and even today everyone in Britain expects construction sites to be full of Irishmen. What tends to set one national or religious or racial group of workers against another, is not so much occupational specialisation in itself, as the tendency for one group to occupy, and seek to monopolise, the more highly skilled, better paid and more desirable jobs. Such divisions and stratifications occur even in nationally homogeneous working classes, but it is certain that they are enormously exacerbated when they coincide with divisions of language, colour, religion or nationality. Belfast is an unhappy and obvious case in point.

Yet communal differences alone have not prevented labour movements from organising workers successfully across such divisions. A powerful Social Democratic party in Vienna united Czech and German workers. Before 1914 the differences between Flemish and Walloon workers in Belgium were politically so insignificant that a standard work on socialism in Belgium by two leaders of the Labour party there did not bother to so much as mention the "Flemish question." Today, when all Belgian parties are linguistically divided, the motto "Workers of all Lands, Unite" incised in Flemish on the Labour Hall in Ghent, remains as a melancholy reminder of this lost unity. Highly unified working classes with a powerful class consciousness have been forged out of a mixture of natives and various immigrant groups, as in Argentina. Single working class movements have even been created, as in India, out of a conglomerate of mutually hostile and linguistically incomprehensible castes, language groups and religions. For that matter, even in Ulster men who feared for their lives from Catholic or Protestant proletarians outside the shipyard or dock gates were—and perhaps still are—prepared to act together inside them for purposes of industrial disputes. The historical as well as practical problem is to discover under what circumstances such class unity can come into being, work, or cease to work.

Three circumstances may be suggested, in which natural or communal divisions may fatally disrupt working classes. Such disruption may arise from the influence of nationalist or other political movements outside the working class; from rapid and major changes in the composition of that class (or more generally, in society) which established patterns cannot absorb; and from the attempt to maintain disproportionately favourable conditions by strict limitations of entry into the working class.

The last case is probably the least common, for while the tendency to form "labour aristocracies" is fairly general, blanket exclusion is rather uncommon, except on the grounds of colour and sex, two barriers which, because of their visibility, are very difficult to cross. Still, where such blanket exclusion operates or has operated, as in the White Australia policy, the Chinese Exclusion Laws in the USA and anti-black discrimination in South African industry, it has certainly come primarily from within the unusually favoured local working class, afraid of losing its exceptionally advantageous conditions. Where exclusion is totally successful, there is no split in the working class, since the excluded are kept out altogether. Where the favoured and the unprivileged co-exist, as in South Africa, in practice two parallel and perhaps mutually hostile working classes tend to develop. However, in capitalist and probably also socialist industrialisation it is rare for labour to be consistently so favoured or so strong as to impose permanent blanket exclusiveness. Consequently even labour movements based on the attempt to create congeries of labour aristocracies, as in mid-nineteenth century Britain, aimed at labour movements which were inclusive, that is they recognised that they ought ideally to achieve the organisation of all workers, and certainly of all who were likely to penetrate into the enclosure they reserved for their trade or occupation. Within such a comprehensive movement, the special advantages of labour aristocracy ought, of course, to be safeguarded.

Changes in the social composition of the working class may be divisive, insofar as they disturb established social patterns and allow rivalries within the class to be nationally or communally coloured, or class lines to coincide with national or communal lines. This has been the danger in regions like Catalonia and, even more, the Basque country, where industrial development leads to a mass influx of Spanish workers, slow to learn to speak Catalan and even slower to learn Basque, and rather despised by native Catalans or feared by native Basques. Nobody acquainted with the problems of the coloured minorities in Britain would want to underestimate the consequent sense of mutual hostility and even fear between different groups of workers. This is all the more dramatic, since traditionally organised labour movements have actively discouraged national, racial or religious prejudices. At the same time one may doubt whether these frictions, *by themselves*, are of decisive significance. It is chiefly when the state and its institutions are involved, as by demands for a linguistic monopoly, or for legal equality, or for autonomy or separatism, that they become explosive—as they unfortunately have in Ulster. In fact, traditionally national and regional minority groups in states, especially when composed of workers, have, other things being equal, tended to support the mass party on the progressive wing of the majority nation's politics as being the most likely to defend their minority interests. Even today American blacks and white ethnics, between whom no love is lost, both tend to vote for the Democratic Party, while in Britain Asian and West Indian workers tend to vote Labour in spite of the racialism of many white working class Labour voters.

However, the most powerful divisive forces, in the form of political parties and movements such as those inspired by nationalism, come from outside the working classes. Historically such movements have hardly ever originated within them, though they have often sought to appeal to them. They were divisive, not only because they naturally accentuated the linguistic, religious, physical and other distinctions between ''their'' sector of a heterogeneous working class and the rest, but also because their objects were by definition at odds with those of class consciousness. They sought to substitute the dividing line between "the nation" (including both its exploiters and exploited) and "the foreigners" (including all workers classifiable as such) for class lines. Moreover, in the early stages of nationalist movements, nationalists either took little interest in the issues which preoccupied workers as workers—organised or unorganised—or regarded the solution of such problems as conditional on the prior achievement of the nationalist objectives. The discovery that national and social liberation must go together, was not usually made by the pioneers of nationalist movements, which is why some of the most effective nationalist parties and organisations emerged out of socialist agitations e.g. the Polish Socialist party whose leader, Pilsudski, became the head of independent Poland after World War I, and labour Zionism, which became the real architect of Israel. Even when the discovery was made within nationalist movements, activists who gave too high a priority to social liberation were difficult to digest. The nationalist reputation of Michael Davitt has suffered accordingly.

Historically it has proved difficult to deny and prevent class consciousness, since it arises naturally and logically out of the proletarian condition, at least in the elementary form of "trade union consciousness," that is to say the recognition that workers as such need to organise collectively against employers in order to defend and improve their conditions as hired hands. Thus Catholic trade unions were formed not because most "social Catholics" at the end of the nineteenth century favoured them—they regarded them, in Albert de Mun's words, as "the specific organisation of the war of one group against another" and preferred mixed associations of employers and workers—but because the latter did not meet the trade union needs of Catholic workers. In France "social Catholics" accepted them, with more or less reluctance, between 1897 and 1912. Again, even in countries with strong national loyalties among workers, trade unionism tended to resist the fragmentation of unions along national lines. Czech workers certainly did not think of themselves as the same as German workers, but while they were inclined to vote for Czech political parties rather than non-Czech or all-Austrian ones, the pressure to split the Austrian trade union movement along national lines did not come from within the labour movement. It arose some time after the split into national sections of the Social Democratic Party had become effective, and was resisted more strongly by the All-Austrian unions. Indeed, even after the split had taken place, the majority of Czech unionists remained in the All-Austrian organisations, where, of course, they were entitled to form their own Czech branches and had their own Bohemian leadership. Similarly today, while the parties of the Left in Spain have split along national or regional lines, there has been no comparable tendency to divide the all-Spanish trade union movements. The reasons are obvious. The unity of all workers is an evident asset when they go on strike for economic reasons, and even though for other purposes they may think of themselves chiefly as Catholics or Protestants, black or white, Poles or Mexicans, it is advisable to put these distinctions aside for such purposes as asking for higher wages.

Nevertheless, it is equally clear that if class consciousness cannot be eliminated, it certainly neither excludes nor, usually, dominates national sentiments. The collapse of the Second International in 1914 into socialist parties and trade union movements most of which supported their belligerent governments, is familiar. What is less familiar, since the internationalism of labour historians has not insisted on it, is the strong current of chauvinism which is found in some politically radical working classes. Thomas Wright, the "Journeyman Engineer" who reported on the English working class of the 1860s, notes specifically that the older, radical and Chartist generation of workers combined a passionate distrust of all who were not workers with a John-Bullish patriotism. In itself, strong national sentiment may not be of great political consequence. English and French workers, who almost certainly did not like what they thought they knew about one anothers' country, have never since 1815 been expected to fight against their neighbours across the Channel. At times social-revolutionary or anti-war sentiment may override patriotism, as in the last years of World War I. Even at such times patriotism may not be negligible. It has been suggested that in France (unlike Britain) the growth of mass working-class support for the Russian Revolution was distinctly slow until it became clear it would not jeopardise the chances of victory in the West. A similar phenomenon may be observable in the Habsburg Empire. While the famous wave of anti-war strikes in January 1918, which began in the armanents works near Vienna, rapidly spread throughout the engineering factories of ethnic Austria and Hungary, it did *not* spread to the Czech areas of Bohemia. It has been suggested that anti-war mobilisation was inhibited here by the policy of the nationalist movement (by this time echoed among many Czech workers), which relied on an Allied victory for the achievement of its aim—the independence of what was shortly to become Czechoslovakia.

In certain circumstances the appeal of nationalism or patriotism to workers was likely to be particularly effective. One of these occurred when they could identify with an existing nation-state *as citizens* rather than mere passive subjects, that is, where their integration into the political and hegemonic system of their rulers was under way, not least through that major agent of conscious socialisation from above, a public system of elementary education. Class and private discontent did not prevent most English, French or German workers from seeing Britain, France and Germany as in some sense "their" country, as say, Austrian ones in 1914 did not (because there was no nation-state), or Italian workers and peasants did not, since few even spoke and even fewer could read Italian, and hardly any of them had enjoyed the right to vote for more than a year. Another occurred, where nationalist agitation, often building on memories of a former political state or autonomy, or organisations embodying the separateness of a nationality (e.g., the Catholicism of the dependent people as against the Protestantism or Orthodoxy of the ruling state) were in existence before an industrial working class developed. This was the case among people like the Irish, the Poles and the Czechs. However, as already suggested, what made national sentiments explosive and capable of destroying the cross-national unity of the working class was that they were intertwined with issues directly affecting the state and its institutions. Thus linguistic nationalism becomes explosive when language ceases to be merely a medium of communication between people, but one language or dialect rather than another becomes "official"—for example, the language of law-courts, schools, and public notices.

All this implies that working-class consciousness, however inevitable and essential, is probably politically secondary to other kinds of consciousness. As we know, where it has come into conflict in our century with national, or religious, or racial consciousness, it has usually yielded and retreated. It is clear that, for certain limited purposes, working class consciousness and the labour movements it generates—at all events at the elementary "trade-unionist" level— are very strong indeed. They are not indestructible, for sheer force has frequently destroyed such movements, but even these are potentially permanent and revivable. We have recently seen such consciousness and such movements revive in the very different circumstances of two rapidly industrialising countries, Brazil and Poland. They may well be the decisive lever for major political changes, as looked likely in 1980–1981 in Poland. But historians must note that it is equally clear that working class consciousness alone co-exists with other forms of collective identification and neither eliminates nor replaces them. And, as Lenin rightly observed, while it will spontaneously and everywhere generate "trade unionist" practices and (where it is allowed to) organisations or other movements for corporate pressure and self-defence, it does not automatically generate mass parties with a socialist consciousness.

That such parties were generated almost as a matter of course during a certain historical period, mainly between the 1880s and the 1930s, is significant, but requires more historical explanation than it has generally received. These parties, or their lineal successors are still in being and often influential, but where they did not already exist, or the influence of socialists/communists was significant in Labour movements before World War II, hardly any such parties have merged out of the working classes since then, notably in the so-called Third World. This may have implications for traditional socialist expectations about the role of the working class and working class parties in bringing about socialism, which need not be discussed here.

What bearing has all this on the making of the Irish working class? The major fact which requires explanation, at least for outsiders, is why labour as an independent political force has in the past been relatively negligible in Ireland, compared with the countries of the United Kingdom. Neither in North nor South have class movements of the workers made a more than marginal political mark. This is not adequately explained by the lack, until recently, of much industrialisation in the twenty-six counties. It is certainly not explained by any lack of industrialisation in Ulster. Moreover, from the days when Dublin was a stronghold of trade societies to the period before World War I, when both Belfast and Dublin were the scene of some of the largest and most dramatic industrial disputes in the United Kingdom, Ireland has been familiar with labour battles. The most

obvious explanation is that—except at moments or for rather limited trade unionist purposes— the potential Irish constituency for such working class movements
have identified themselves in politics as Catholic nationalists or Protestant unionists rather than as "labour." It is difficult to think of any other country in western
Europe in which this has been so marked and persistent a characteristic of the
working class.

Without pushing the analogy too far, a comparison of Ireland with Belgium,
a more recently partitioned country and working class, may be instructive. As
north-east Ulster and the rest of Ireland followed their divergent economic evolution, so did Wallonia and Flanders. Wallonia industrialised heavily, while
Flanders, though containing a major port (Antwerp) and a significant industrial
centre (Ghent), remained predominantly agrarian and saw itself as underprivileged. As old-fashioned nineteenth century basic industries lost their firm footing
in Ulster and Wallonia, so Flanders and to some extent the Republic of Ireland,
have become more industrialised and prosperous; but not, like the old zones, as
part of the British or—*de facto*—the French industrial economies, but within a
European and transnational framework. As Catholics and Protestants are inseparable in Belfast, so Flemings and French-speakers are inseparable in Brussels.

Yet Belgium, though occupied from time to time, has long been independent
of its immediate neighbours (France and the Netherlands) and, since 1830, it
has been an independent state, whereas the connection with Britain clearly dominated Irish affairs throughout, and still dominates those of Ulster. In the Belgian
working class the two groups hardly mixed, since the language border is rather
clearly marked. Where they did mix, as in Brussels, the city grew slowly enough—
from say 6 percent of the population in the early nineteenth century to about 9
percent in 1911—for Flemish immigrants to be assimilated, as it seemed they
were willing to be, facing little real resistance. On the other hand Belfast grew
from very little to about a third of the population of the six counties during the
century, at first by a mass influx of Ulster Catholics which, around the middle
of the century, looked as though it might swamp the Protestants, later by a mass
growth of Ulster Protestants, which reduced the Catholics to a permanent and
embittered minority. By 1911 Belfast was disproportionately more Protestant
than the rest of the province, and Catholics were far more systematically excluded
from the city's skilled trades than they had been in 1870.

The Belgian labour movement grew up from the 1880s as a strong, single,
and unified body operating across language lines, and largely engaged, before
1914, in the struggle for universal male suffrage, which minimised internal
divergences within the working class. It was not seriously split linguistically
until after World War II. Not so in Ireland, where the official commitment to a
single all-Irish labour movement often concealed an essentially Catholic-nation-
alist orientation struggling against the trade union movement of skilled workers
who were quite content with the usual district autonomy within an all-UK organisation. Morever, the established dominance of the national issue (Home Rule
or independence from Britain) deprived Labour of a unifying issue of political
mobilisation, such as the fight for electoral democracy provided in Belgium.

The paradox of the Irish situation in the period when a major labour movement might have been expected to emerge—from the end of the 1880s to 1914, the era of "new unionism" and "labour unrest"— is that three factors converged to tie Catholic workers to Fenian nationalism. Mass nationalist mobilisation and Orange resistance equated political Irishness with Catholicism. The old craft unionism of skilled workers (concentrated in industrial Ulster) would in any case not have been much use to unskilled workers, but the increasingly systematic exclusion of Catholics from skilled Ulster trades intensified the tensions between the two sectors of the working class. Finally, the very radicalism, or even socialist and revolutionary convictions, of the "new" union leaders and organisers, who wanted to break with the caution and "reformism" of the old unions, had political implications in Ireland which it did not have in Britain; for in Ulster, at least, organised skilled workers were not only "old" unionists but also tended to be Orangemen. In short, both political mobilisation (National and Unionist) and the class mobilisation of hitherto unorganised and unorganisable workers, united to divide the working class. A labour movement which was both *political* and *industrial* and which united Protestant and Catholic, Orange and Green, skilled and unskilled, became impossible. It would have been possible only if divisions between sections of workers had not coincided with divisions between Catholic and Protestant (which increasingly implied between Green and Orange), as they did in Belfast, the test of any united Irish labour movement. In any case, such a movement would have been possible only by overlooking the separation from Britain, that is, by regarding the issues around which Irish politics revolved as irrelevant to Labour as such. It is not impossible to conceive of this, but the prospect hardly seemed realistic between 1880 and 1921. The most that could be expected of a political labour movement neutral as between Orange and Green, but many of whose members were far from neutral as individuals, would have been a pressure group for the specific interests of trade unionists, or for legislation of specific interest to wage-workers: in fact something like an all-Irish Labour Representation Committee. Yet even in Britain itself, the Labour Representation Committee, though in theory operating outside the field of political dispute between Liberals and Conservatives, which was distinctly less impassioned than that between Nationalists and Unionists, actually had great difficulty until after World War I in emancipating itself from the political loyalties of so many organised workers to one of the two parties, and the suspicion of those who supported the other.

This, then, was the dilemma of Irish labour leaders. It was independent of their personal convictions. A case can be made for James Connolly's choice of the "Green" option, on the grounds that most Irishmen were Catholics, and that in any case the dour and respectable "old unionists" (and Unionists) of Protestant Belfast hardly looked like promising material for social revolution. Yet if the Catholic labouring masses seemed to offer better prospects for revolutionaries—after all, even Jim Larkin, who was not an Irish nationalist in the sense Connolly was or became, had his greatest triumphs among them—the Green option automatically excluded that united movement of all Irish workers of which Connolly dreamed. But Connolly's decision for an Irish labour movement which would not merely appeal essentially to Southerners and Catholics in practice, but was nationalist in aspiration, had even more serious consequences. It meant the subordination of southern Irish labour to nationalism. Marxist parties have sometimes succeeded in transforming their societies after taking the lead of movements of national liberation, but hardly ever, if at all, in competition with previously established and strong national movements under other leadership. In spite of Connolly's efforts and his leadership in 1916 it was the IRA and not the Citizens' Army which took over the green flag. Connolly lives on in official memory as a Fenian martyr rather than as a Marxist revolutionary. Perhaps this was inevitable. One cannot confidently say otherwise. Nevertheless it meant that a strong and independent political movement of labour developed neither in the North nor in the South, though it is possible that today the conditions for such a movement are better in the South, because partition is *de facto* no longer a significant issue in the Republic. In the North, as we know, it still is.

Does this mean that Ireland contained not one but two working classes or even, as some enthusiasts hold, not one but two nations? In the literal sense this is obviously not so. Catholics and Protestants in Ulster no more formed separate working classes in any economic or operational sense than they did on Clydeside. Such questions arise chiefly because it is often assumed, without much thought, that working classes, or any other large classes, do not "exist" except as monolithic blocks, as it is assumed that a nation is not "real" unless each member, living on its territory, who is not a certified foreigner or a defined "minority," is uniformly coloured right through with whatever is considered the accepted national dye. Today this is usually language, though the Irish have learned the hard way that this dye does not always take. In a few European countries and many more Afro-Asian ones it is still religion. Rightwing Americans think it is a set of conventional practices and beliefs, lacking which a person is "un-American." This is not so. The unity of classes and nations is defined by what they have in common as against other groups, and not by their internal homogeneity. There is no state which does not contain regional, sectional, or other differences among its population, and these are potentially disruptive, as the recent rise of separatist movements in western Europe proves. The only difference in principle between Ireland and Bavaria is that the Catholic-Protestant difference in Ireland has proved disruptive, whereas the attempt to prove that the Protestant minority in the northern part of Bavaria (Franconia) is oppressed by the Catholic majority is at present confined to a lunatic fringe of ultra-left ex-students. Similarly, all working classes contain internal conflicts, though usually they remain subordinate.

On the other hand the course of history can both merge and split societies and, therefore, the classes within them. It has divided Ireland. Given that there now exist separate political units and economies in North and South, it becomes impossible any longer to speak of a single Irish working class any more than a single Bengali or German working class, to name but two other partitioned nations. Separate states are powerful definers of economy and society. This does not mean that the two Irelands cease to have much in common, as have the two Germanies—not least kinfolk and culture. We may speculate about what might happen if both were united—given the widening divergences it is increasingly difficult to say ''re-united''—but in both cases the question is at present academic. To this extent history has up to the present led to the making of two Irish working classes.

Of these, the Ulster working class suffers particularly, indeed one is tempted to say uniquely, acute divisions. The only parallel one can readily think of is the Hindu-Moslem communal tension on the Indian subcontinent. For these reasons no general conclusions about working class and nation can be drawn from Ulster. Ireland remains resolutely unique in this respect. So, no doubt, does every other country or nation, once historians concentrate their attention sufficiently upon it. However, unfortunately the uniqueness of Irish historical development has manifested itself—so far— largely at the expense of the making of its working class and its labour movement.

NOTE

1. The problem of the Republican militants in Britain who saw or see themselves exclusively as anti-British Irish, as of the ''spoiled Catholic'' Irish, often on the most militant wing of British labour movements, would need to be considered separately. But, at least since the 1880s, this problem concerns numerically small minorities.

BIBLIOGRAPHIC ESSAY **19**

Dirk Hoerder

The number of publications on labor migration to individual European states and to the United States and Canada is legion. Hardly any, however, employ a comparative perspective. In many instances it is still necessary to go back to studies dating from the turn of the century, because they provide more detail – and occasionally more analysis – than recent studies. This bibliography is arranged alphabetically by country; titles referring to both the culture of origin and the receiving society have been listed under the latter with a cross-reference under the former. Migration before World War I has received special emphasis, though a number of studies include the interwar years. There are hardly any studies at all that compare present-day labor migration with that of the turn of the century, though the similarities are obvious. This is partly a reflection of the separation of scholarly disciplines as a result of which migration up to 1945 is the realm of historians, that since the fifties has been the realm of sociologists. One effort to bridge this gap was sponsored in the early fifties by UNESCO. French and Belgian sociologists with a penetrating historical perception studied immigration from both countries between the end of the nineteenth century and the early fifties. (See R. Clemens et al. and P. De Bie for Belgium, A. Girard et al. for France and the frame of reference for this project by W. D. Borrie.) Since it is impossible to provide a bibliography of present-day migration from south and southeastern Europe to the northern and western European countries, a single reference will have to do: Stephen Castles and Godula Kosack, *Immigrant Workers in Western Europe*, (London, 1973). Transatlantic migration is not represented in this bibliographic essay either, since it is well known and titles can be gleaned from any standard bibliography. Finally, return migration receives less attention than it deserves. This has been dealt with extensively by D. Hoerder, "Immigration and the Working Class: The Remigration Factor," *Int. Labor and Working Class History* 21 (Spring, 1982), 28–41.

GENERAL STUDIES

Two conference reports are of great importance to understand the contemporary approach to migration and the labor market, one on state intervention in labor migration, Paris 1889, and that on the international organization of the labor market, Budapest 1910. The standard statistical work on the international migrations, which in its accompanying essays presents most of the information still not digested by scholarly and public opinion is Willcox and Ferenczi (1929, 1931). Brinley Thomas began to use the concept of an Atlantic economy in 1954, but he has also received less than sufficient attention from historians geared to thinking in terms of the boundaries of national states.

Boissier, E. *De l'assimilation des étrangers* (Geneva, 1911).
Borrie, W. D. *The Cultural Integration of Immigrants* (Paris, 1952).
Congrès international de l'intervention des pouvoirs publics dans l'émigration et l'immigration, tenu à Paris, les 12, 13 et 14 août 1889 (Paris, 1890).
Conze, W. "Die Wirkungen der liberalen Agrarreformen auf die Volksordnung in Mitteleuropa im 19. Jahrhundert," *Vierteljahrschrift für Sozial- und Wirtschaftsgeschichte* 38 (1948–1951): 8ff.
Ferenczi, Imre, *Kontinentale Wanderung und die Annäherung der Völker. Ein geschichtlicher Überblick* (Jena, 1930).
Gonnard, René, *L'émigration européenne au XIXe siècle* (Paris, 1906).
Thomas, Brinley. *Economics of International Migration* (London, 1958).
———, *Migration and Economic Growth* (London, 1954).
Varlez, L., *Les migrations internationales et leur réglementation* (Geneva, 1929).
———, *Le rythme saisonnier des migrations humaines* (Geneva, 1928).
Verhandlungen der Budapester Konferenz betreffend Organisation des Arbeitsmarkts (7.- 8.10.1910) (Leipzig, 1911).
Weber-Kellermann, Ingeborg, *Erntebrauch in der ländlichen Arbeitswelt des 19. Jahrhunderts* (Marburg, 1965).
Willcox, Walter F., and Ferenczi, Imre, eds., *International Migrations*, 2 vols. (New York, 1929, 1931).

AUSTRIA

The complex patterns of migration in the Austro-Hungarian empire as a whole have received far too little attention. However, a number of studies, usually undertaken after the creation of nation-states out of the imperial conglomerate, do exist for specific ethnic groups and nationalities. Many of them are efforts to recapture a past that meant dispersion of sometimes considerable parts of an ethnic group across the empire, across Europe, and to North America. These studies are listed under the respective countries. Presently important research work is being done at the Österreichische Akademie der Wissenschaften, Kommission für Raumforschung by Josef Ehmer, Heinz Faßmann et al.

Brousek, Karl M., *Wien und seine Tschechen: Integration und Assimilation einer Minderheit im 20. Jahrhundert* (Vienna, 1980).
Caro, Leopold, *Auswanderung und Auswanderungspolitik in Österreich* (Leipzig, 1909).
Chmelar, Hans, *Höhepunkte der österreichischen Auswanderung. Die Auswanderung aus den im Reichsrat vertretenen Königreichen und Ländern in den Jahren 1905–1914* (Vienna, 1974).
Friedmann, Arthur, *Arbeitermangel und Auswanderung* (Vienna, 1907).

Glettler, Monika, *Pittsburgh-Wien-Budapest: Programm und Praxis der Nationalitäten-politik bei der Auswanderung der ungarischen Slowaken nach Amerika um 1900* (Vienna, 1980).

———, *Die Wiener Tschechen um 1900. Strukturanalyse einer nationalen Minderheit in einer Großstadt* (Munich, 1972).

BELGIUM

Belgium is one of the best studied countries as regards labor migration. The high rates of in- and out-migration to which internal migration has to be added provide a wealth of information. Belgian workers, agricultural as well as industrial, were sought after at the turn of the century because they were considered "racially superior" to workers from the East or South.

André, R., "Les migrations en Belgique," *La Géographie* (1968).

Battistini, M., *Esuli italiani in Belgio, 1815–1861* (Florence, 1968).

Braeckman, C., *Les étrangers en Belgique* (Brussels, 1973).

Chlepner, B. S., "L'étranger dans l'histoire économique de la Belgique," *Revue de l'Institut de Sociologie* (1931).

Clemens, René; Vosse-Smal, Gabrielle; and Minon, Paul; *L'assimilation culturelle des immigrants en Belgique. Italiens et Polonais dans la région liègeoise* (Liège, 1953).

De Bie, Pierre, "L'assimilation des ouvriers mineurs italiens et polonais en Belgique. Notes sur une Enquête," *Etudes européennes de Population* (Paris, 1954), pp. 337–41.

De Man, H., "Ein Jahrhundert belgische Wanderbewegungen," *Zeitschrift für Geopolitik* (1942).

Frost, J., *Belgische Wanderarbeiter* (Berlin, 1908).

Lechat, M., "Le mouvement étranger au Borinage," *Revue de l'Institut de Sociologie* (1950).

Lemoine, R. J., "Les étrangers et la formation du capitalisme en Belgique," *Revue d'Histoire économique et sociale* (1932).

Lentacker, F., SEE France.

Morsa, J., "L'immigration en Belgique (1890–1954)," *Population et famille* 9-10 (1966).

Schepens, Luc, "Emigration saisonnière et émigration définitive en Flandre occidentale au XIXe siècle," *Revue du Nord* (1974).

———, *Van Vlaskutser tot Franschman. Bijdrage tot de geschiedenis van de Westvlaamse plattelandsbevolking in de negentiende eeuw* (Bruges, 1973).

Vandervelde, Emil, "Die ländliche Auswanderung und die Arbeiterzüge in Belgien," *Neue Gesellschaft* II, H. 16 (1906), 186–87.

Virgili, F., SEE Germany.

BULGARIA

Migration from Bulgaria was both east- and westward. As these titles indicate, a considerable part of it was middle-class movement toward commercial centers or free land.

Bur, M., "Marchands balkaniques en Hongrie – XVIIIe siècle," in *Etudes balkaniques* 3 (Sofia, 1972).

Dergavin, N. S., "Les colonies des Bulgares en Russie," in *S.B.N.U.* (Sbornik za navodni umotvorenija i narodopis [Publications on Bulgarian ethnology and folk poetry]) 39 (Sofia, 1914).

Kossev, D.; Diculescu, VL; and Paskaleva, V., *Situation et Activité économique de l'émigration bulgare en Valachie au XIXe Siècle* (1965).

Spiezzo, A., "Die orthodoxen Handelsleute aus dem Balkan in der Slowakie," in *Balkan Studies*, vol. 9, no. 2 (Thessaloniki, 1968).

Velichi, C., *La contribution de l'émigration bulgare de Valachie à la renaissance politique et culturelle du peuple bulgare (1762–1850)* (Bucharest, 1970).

CZECHOSLOVAKIA

In Czechoslovakia research on emigration began early and achieved a first high point in the prolific publications of J. Auerhan. As in Poland and Yugoslavia, ethnographic approaches have provided important stimuli for historical studies.

Auerhan, Jan, *Čechoslováci v Jugoslávii, v Rumunsku, v Maďarsku a v Bulharsku* [The Czechoslovaks in Yugoslavia, Rumania, Hungary, and Bulgaria] (Prague, 1921).

———, *České osady na Volyni, na Krymu a na Kavkaze* [Czech settlements in Volhynia, the Crimea and Caucasia] (Prague, 1920).

———, *Československé jazykové menšiny v evropském zahraničí* [Czechoslovak ethnic minorities in foreign European countries] (Prague, 1935).

———, *Osady českých emigrantů v Prusku, Polsku a Rusku* [Settlements of Czech emigrants in Prussia, Poland, and Russia] (Prague, 1920).

Folprecht, Josef, "Čechové v Německu" [The Czechs in Germany], *Časopis Svobodné školy politických nauk* 4 (1931–1932), 39–43, 80–87.

Glettler, Monika, SEE Austria.

Hejret, Jan, *Vystěhovalecká otázka. Příspěvek k české a slovanské otázce* [The question of emigration: A contribution to the Czech and Slavonic questions] (Prague, 1909).

Hellich, Jan, "Vzpoura podruhů na panství podlěbradském roku 1791 za vystěhovalecké horečky" [A revolt of laborers on the estate of Poděbrady during the emigration fever of 1791], *Časopis pro dějiny venkova* 13 (1926), 120–25.

Heroldová, Iva, *Život a kultura českých exulantů z 18. století* [Life and culture of the Czech emigrants of the 18th century] (Prague, Ústav pro etnografii a folkloristiku ČSAV, 1971).

Kutnar, František, *Počátky hromadného vystěhovalectví z Čech v období Bachova absolutismu* [The beginning of mass emigration from Bohemia during the period of Bach's absolutist regime] (Prague, 1964).

Mastný, Vojtěch, "Statistika vystěhovalectví českého proletariátu do Spojených států" [Statistics of emigration of Czech proletariat to the United States], *Demografie* 4 (1962), 204–11.

Pitronová, Blanka, "Emigrace slezských poddaných do Uher v první polovině 19. století" [Emigration of Silesian subjects to Hungary during the first half of the 19th century], *Slezský sborník* 59 (1961), 174–88.

Šašek, Ivo, *Les migrations de la population intéressant le territoire de la Tchécoslovaquie actuelle (depuis le XVIIe siècle à nos jours)* (Geneva, 1935).

Sedláček, Jan, *Čechoslováci v Nizozemí, Belgii a Anglii* [The Czechoslovaks in the Netherlands, Belgium, and England] (Prague, 1937).
Šuffner, Roman, "O stěhování amerických Čechů na Amur" [Problem of emigration of American Czechs to the Amur], *Slovanský přehled* 44 (1958), 165–66.
Vyhlídal, Jan, *Čechové v Pruském Slezsku* [The Czechs in Prussian Silesia] (Prague, 1899, 3d ed., 1900).
Urban, R., *Čechoslováci v Rumunsku* [The Czechoslovaks in Rumania] (Prague, 1930).

DENMARK

Denmark imported little labor, except for Swedish and Polish agricultural workers. Its internal migration as antecedent to the emigration to North America has been analyzed by K. Hvidt.

Hvidt, Kristian, *Flugten til Amerika eller drivkraefter i massudvandringen fra Danmark 1868–1914* (Odense, 1971); rev. Engl. transl., *Flight to America. The Social Background of 300,000 Danish Emigrants* (New York, 1975).
Nellemann, George, *Polske Landarbejdere i Danmark og dere efterkommere 1893–1929* [Polish agricultural workers and their children] (Copenhagen, 1981).

FINLAND

Finland has produced a large amount of literature on Finnish migration to European countries, particularly Russia and Sweden. This work is being continued at the Migration Institute—Siirtolaisuusinstituutti— at the University of Turku. For information the comprehensive bibliography by Koivukangas and Toivonen should be consulted.

Karni, Michael G., ed., *Finnish Diaspora I: Canada, South America, Africa, Australia and Sweden* (Toronto, 1981).
———, *Finnish Diaspora II: United States* (Toronto, 1981).
Koivukangas, Olavi, and Toivonen, Simo, *Suomen Siirtolaisuuden ja Maassamuuton. Bibliografia* [A bibliography on Finnish emigration and internal migration] (Turku, 1978).

FRANCE

France, as the European immigration country par excellence, has received much scholarly attention. Several authors deal with economic aspects of immigration (Mauco, Mercier) and governmental policies (Frezouls). Even policy studies of the turn of the century retain interest, since many of the advocated reforms and concepts for acculturation have still not been implemented by today's European governments facing an immigrating rather than a rotating foreign labor force. The reactions of French workers and their organizations to in-migration in the early decades of this century has been examined by J. Delevsky, P. Gemähling, and M. Hollande. Long before economists seriously began to work with theories of segmented labor markets, K. Schirmacher provided an early understanding of the split labor market of Paris. Most immigrant groups have found their historians: Belgians (Lentacker), Italians (Girard/Stoetzel and Marcel-Rémond), Poles (Girard/Stoetzel, Janowska, Kaczmarek), Russians (Ledré). Attempts to turn voluntary labor migration into forced labor in wartime have been discussed by G. S. Cross. The different patterns of acculturation of ''old'' immigrants – Poles and Italians before World War Two – and ''new'' immigrants – the same nationalities plus members of the colonial populations – are the subject of research by Girard/Stoetzel. The extremely important internal migration in France has been surveyed in the monumental study by A. Chatelain (1976). Its implications for the migrants are probed in a perceptive and sympathetic essay by I. Bertaux-Wiame.

Bertaux-Wiame, Isabelle, ''The Life History Approach to the Study of Internal Migration: How Women and Men Came to Paris between the Wars,'' in Paul Thompson and Natasha Burchardt, eds., *Our Common History: The Transformation of Europe* (London and Atlantic Heights, NY, 1982), 186–200.

Bonnet, Jean-Charles, *Les pouvoirs publics français et l'immigration dans l'Entre-deux-guerres* (Lyon, 1976).

Chatelain, Abel, *Les migrations de la population* (Paris, 1963).

———, *Les migrants temporaires en France de 1800 à 1914*, 2 vols (Lille, 1976).

Chevalier, Louis, *Problèmes français de l'immigration* (Paris, 1947).

Cross, Gary S., ''Toward Social Peace and Prosperity: The Politics of Immigration in France during the Era of World War I,'' *French Historical Studies* 11 (Fall 1980), 610–32.

Delevsky, J., *Antagonismes sociaux et antagonismes prolétariens* (Paris, 1924).

Didion, Maurice, *Les salariés étrangers en France* (Paris, 1911).

Frezouls, P., *Les ouvriers étrangers en France devant les lois du travail et de la prévoyance sociale* (Montpellier, 1909).

Gemähling, Paul, *Travailleurs au rabais. La lutte syndicale contre les sous-concurrences ouvrières* (Paris, 1913).

Girard, Alain, and Stoetzel, Jean-François, *Français et immigrés*, 2 vols. (Paris, 1953–1954), vol 1: *L'attitude française, l'adaptation des Italiens et des Polonais*; vol 2: *Nouveaux documents sur l'adaptation. Algériens, Italiens, Polonais. Le service sociale d'aide aux émigrants*.

Hollande, Maurice, *La défense ouvrière contre le travail étranger* (Paris, 1912).

Janowska, Halina, *Polska emigracja zarobkowa we Francji* [Polish emigration to France in search of a living, 1919–1939] (Warsaw, 1964).

Kaczmarek, Czeslaw, *L'immigration polonaise en France* (Paris, 1929).

Ledré, *Les émigrés russes en France* (Paris, 1929).

Lentacker, F., *La frontière franco-belge. Etude géographique des effets d'une frontière internationale sur la vie de relations* (Lille, 1974).

———, ''Les ouvriers belges dans le département du Nord au milieu du XIXe siècle,'' *Revue du Nord* (January-March 1956).

———, ''La situation des travailleurs belges en France de 1871 à 1914,'' in *Les relations franco-belges de 1830 à 1934. Actes du Colloque de Metz, 15–16 novembre 1974.*

Lugand, Joseph, *L'immigration des ouvriers étrangers en France et les enseignements de la guerre* (Paris, 1919).

Marcel-Rémond, G., *L'immigration italienne dans le Sud-Ouest de la France* (Paris, 1928).

Mauco, Georges, *Les étrangers en France. Leur rôle dans l'activité économique* (Paris, 1932).

Mercier, Christian, *Les déracinés du capital. Immigration et accumulation* (Paris, 1977).

Pitié, Jean, *Exode rural et migrations intérieures en France: l'example de la Vienne et du Poitou-Charentes* (Poitiers, 1971).

Poussou, Jean-Pierre, "Les mouvements migratoires en France et à partir de la France de la fin du XVᵉ siècle au début du XIXᵉ siècle: approche pour une synthèse," *Annales de Démographie Historique* (Paris, 1970).

Ray, Joanny, *Les Marocains en France* (Paris, 1938).

Rodet, Yves, *L'immigration des travailleurs étrangers en France* (Paris, 1924).

Schirmacher, Käthe, *La spécialisation du travail par nationalité à Paris* (Paris, 1908).

GERMANY

Labor import to Germany has been studied by turn-of-the-century contemporaries, especially by A. Knoke and A. Sartorius von Waltershausen. The implications for the labor movement, particularly in connection with the international socialist conference in Stuttgart in 1907, have been assessed by M. Schippel. For the unions' attitudes, see also the weekly *Correspondenzblatt* of the German central trade union federation, Allgemeiner Deutscher Gewerkschaftsbund. A first survey was provided in the 1930s by F. Burgdörfer. Publications dating from the years 1933 to 1945 need not be consulted, as they served the ideology that a master race, "Herrenrasse," needed subhuman eastern workers. Since 1945 scholarship in the German Democratic Republic has concentrated on the continuities of labor importation from the period of industrialization through both wars to the present "guest worker" migration to West Germany. The most important research center is at the University of Rostock, with Lothar Elsner as its director. It publishes the series *Fremdarbeiterpolitik des Imperialismus*. Numerous scholars, Polish, East and West German, and United States, have dealt with the acculturation of Polish agricultural laborers and miners in the Ruhr district. Italian migrant workers have received less attention, Czechs none at all. Several studies deal with the ethnic heterogeneity of specific areas: Ruhr district (W. Brepohl), Berlin (H.-H. Liang), Silesia (L. Schofer). The best surveys by historians from the Federal Republic of Germany are those by K. Bade and D. Langewiesche.

Bade, Klaus J., "German Emigration to the United States and Continental Immigration to Germany in the Late Nineteenth and Early Twentieth Centuries," *Central European History* 13 (1980), 348–77.

———, ed., *Auswanderer—Wanderarbeiter—Gastarbeiter. Bevölkerung, Arbeitsmarkt* und *Wanderung in Deutschland seit der Mitte des 19!. Jahrhunderts* (Ostfildern, 1984).

Brepohl, Wilhelm, *Der Aufbau des Ruhrvolkes im Zuge der Ost-West-Wanderung. Beiträge zur deutschen Sozialgeschichte des 19. und 20. Jahrhunderts* (Recklinghausen, 1948).

Burgdörfer, Friedrich, "Die Wanderungen über die deutschen Reichsgrenzen im letzten Jahrhundert," in *Allgemeines Statistisches Archiv* 20 (1930).

Elsner, Lothar, "Sicherung und Ausbeutung ausländischer Arbeitskräfte. Ein Kriegsziel im 1. Weltkrieg," *Zeitschrift für Geschichtswissenschaft* 24 (1976), 530–46.

————, ed., *Fremdarbeiterpolitik des Imperialismus*, nos. 1–15 (Rostock, 1975–).

Gemmeke, F., "Polnische Schnitter im Hochstift Paderborn," *Die Warte* 37 (Paderborn, 1983).

Heinrich, Chr., "Saisonarbeiter im Blickfeld der Volkskunde," in Lothar Elsner, ed., *Fremdarbeiterpolitik des Imperialismus*, no. 7 (Rostock, 1980).

Janowska, Halina, "Polonia westfalsko-nadrénska w latach 1918–1939" [Polish emigration centres in Westphalia and Rhineland, 1918–1939], *Problemy Polonii Zagranicznej* 4 (1968).

Kleßmann, Christoph, *Polnische Bergarbeiter im Ruhrgebiet 1870–1945. Soziale Integration und nationale Subkultur einer Minderheit in der deutschen Industriegesellschaft* (Göttingen, 1978).

Knoke, Anton, *Ausländische Wanderarbeiter in Deutschland* (Leipzig, 1911).

Köllmann, Wolfgang, "Industrialisierung, Binnenwanderung und 'Soziale Frage'," *Vierteljahrschrift für Sozial- und Wirtschaftsgeschichte* 46 (1959), 60ff.

Kozlowski, J., "Zum Wirken der SPD und der PPS unter den polnischen Auswanderern in Deutschland bis 1914," in Lothar Elsner, ed., *Fremdarbeiterpolitik des Imperialismus*, no. 7 (Rostock, 1980).

Langewiesche, Dieter, "Wanderungsbewegungen in der Hochindustrialisierungsperiode. Regionale, interstädtische und innerstädtische Mobilität in Deutschland 1880–1914," *Vierteljahrschrift für Sozial- und Wirtschaftsgeschichte* 64 (1977), 1–40.

Langkau, Götz, "Die deutsche Sektion in Paris," *International Review of Social History* 17 (1972), 103–50.

Lehmann, J., "Bemerkungen zur Beschäftigung ausländischer Arbeitskräfte in Deutschland während der ersten Jahre der faschistischen Diktatur," in Lothar Elsner, ed., *Fremdarbeiterpolitik des Imperialismus*, no. 7 (Rostock, 1980).

Liang, Hsi-Huey, "Lower Class Immigrants in Wilhelmine Berlin," *Central European History* 3 (1970), 94–111.

Liman, St., "Polnische Wanderarbeiter in Dänemark um die Wende von 19. zum 20. Jahrhundert," in Lothar Elsner, ed., *Fremdarbeiterpolitik des Imperialismus*, no. 7 (Rostock, 1980).

Linde, Hans, "Die soziale Problematik der masurischen Agrargesellschaft und die masurische Einwanderung in das Emscherrevier," in H. U. Wehler, ed., *Moderne deutsche Sozialgeschichte* (Cologne, 1968), pp. 456–70.

Murphy, Richard C., "Polish Immigrants in Bottrop, 1891–1933. An Ethnic Minority in a German Industrial City" (Ph.D. diss., University of Iowa, 1977).

————, "Polnische Bergarbeiter im Ruhrgebiet: Das Beispiel Bottrop," in Hans Mommsen and Ulrich Borsdorf, eds., *Glück auf Kameraden. Die Bergarbeiter und ihre Organisationen in Deutschland* (Cologne, 1979), pp. 89–108.

Murzynowska, Krystyna, *Polskie wychodźstwo zarobkowe w Zagłebiu Ruhry 1880–1914* [Polish economic emigration in the Ruhr basin, 1880–1914] (Wroclaw, 1972) (German translation: Dortmund, 1979).

Nichtweiss, Johannes, *Die ausländischen Saisonarbeiter in der Landwirtschaft der östlichen und mittleren Gebiete des Deutschen Reiches* (Berlin, GDR, 1959).

Obermann, Karl, "Die Arbeitermigrationen in Deutschland im Prozeß der Industrialisierung und der Entstehung der Arbeiterklasse in der Zeit von der Gründung bis zur Auflösung des Deutschen Bundes (1815–1867)," *Jahrbuch für Wirtschaftsgeschichte I* (1972), 135–81.

Poniatawska, A., "Polnische Saisonarbeiter in Pommern bis 1914," in Lothar Elsner, ed., *Fremdarbeiterpolitik des Imperialismus*, no. 7 (Rostock, 1980).

Pönicke, Herbert, *Studien zur Wanderung sächsisch-thüringischer Handwerker in die baltischen Provinzen im 18. und 19. Jahrundert* (Hamburg, 1964).

Sartorius von Waltershausen, A., *Die italienischen Wanderarbeiter* (Leipzig, 1903).

Schippel, Max, "Die Konkurrenz der fremden Arbeitskräfte," *Sozialistische Monatshefte* 10, II (1906), 136–44.

Schofer, Lawrence, *The Formation of a Modern Labor Force: Upper Silesia, 1865–1914* (Berkeley, Calif., 1975; German translation, 1983).

Virgili, F., "Vlämische Wanderarbeiter in Deutschland," *Landwirtschaftliche Presse* (1908).

Wehler, Hans-Ulrich, "Die Polen im Ruhrgebiet bis 1918," in H-U. Wehler, ed., *Moderne deutsche Sozialgeschichte* (Cologne, 1968), pp. 437–55.

Werner, B., "Bemerkungen zum Einsatz ausländerischer Arbeiter in der deutschen Industrie von 1890 bis 1914," in Lothar Elsner, ed., *Fremdarbeiterpolitik des Imperialismus*, no. 7 (Rostock, 1980).

Zunkel, F., "Die ausländischen Arbeiter in der deutschen Kriegswirtschaftspolitik des 1. Weltkriegs," in G. A. Ritter, ed., *Entstehung und Wandel der modernen Gesellschaft* (Berlin, 1970)., pp. 280–311.

GREAT BRITAIN

Though Great Britain attracted a limited number of German and East European workers during the nineteenth century, most studies deal with internal migration, especially that from Scotland and Wales, and with Irish and Jewish immigration. The works cited here are not concerned with immigration from the Commonwealth countries after the Second World War.

Barber, Sarah, "Irish Migrant Agricultural Labourers in Nineteenth Century Lincolnshire," *Saothar. Journal of the Irish Labour History Society* 8 (1982), 10–23.

Buckman, J., "The Economic and Social History of Alien Immigration to Leeds, 1880–1914" (Ph.D. thesis, University of Strathclyde, 1968).

Cairncross, A. K., "Trends in Internal Migration, 1841–1911," *Transactions. Manchester Statistical Society* (1939), 105th Session, 21–29.

Campbell, P. C., *Chinese Coolie Emigration to Countries within the British Empire* (London, 1923).

Collins, E. J., "Migrant Labour in British Agriculture in the Nineteenth Century," *Economic History Review* ser. 2, vol. 29 (1976), 38–59.

Darby, H. C., "The Movement of Population to and from Cambridgeshire between 1851 and 1861," *Geographical Journal* 101, no. 3 (1943), 118–25.

Fishman, William J., *East End Jewish Radicals, 1875–1914* (London, 1975).

Friedlander, D., and R. J. Roshier, "A Study of Internal Migration in England and Wales. Part I," *Population Studies* 19, no. 3 (1966), 239–79.

Gainer, Bernard, *The Alien Invasion. The Origins of the Alien Act of 1905* (London, 1972).

Garrard, John A., *The English and Immigration, 1880–1910* (London, 1971).

Gartner, Lloyd P., *The Jewish Immigrant in England, 1870–1914* (1960; 2d ed.: London, 1973).

Gilley, Sheridan, "English Attitudes to the Irish in England, 1789–1900," in Colin Holmes, ed., *Immigrants and Minorities in British Society* (London, 1978).

Halpern, Georg, *Die jüdischen Arbeiter in London* (Stuttgart, 1903).

Handley, James E., *The Irish in Modern Scotland* (Cork, 1947).

———, *The Irish in Scotland* (Cork, 1943).

———, *The Navvy in Scotland* (Cork, 1970).

Hechter, M., *Internal Colonialism. The Celtic Fringe in British National Development, 1536–1966* (London, 1975).

Holmes, Colin, ed., *Immigrants and Minorities in British Society* (London, 1978).

Jackson, John Archer, *The Irish in Britain* (London, 1963).

Jones, Eric L., "The Agricultural Labor Market in England, 1793–1892," *Economic History Review* 17 (1964–1965), 322–38.

Kellenbenz, Hermann, "German Immigrants in England," in Colin Holmes, ed., *Immigrants and Minorities in British Society* (London, 1978).

Kerr, B. M., "Irish Seasonal Migration to Great Britain 1800–1838," *Irish Historical Studies* 3 (September 1943).

Landa, M. J., *The Alien Problem and Its Remedy* (London, 1911).

Lawton, R., "Irish Immigration to England and Wales in the Mid-Nineteenth Century," *Irish Geography* 4 (1) (1959), 35–54.

———, "Recent Trends in Population and Housing in England and Wales," *Sociological Review* 11 (3) (1963), 303–21.

Lees, Lynn Hollen, *Exiles of Erin. Irish Migrants in Victorian London* (Manchester, 1979).

Little, Kenneth, *Negroes in Britain: A Study of Racial Relations in English Society* (London, 1947, 1972).

MacDonald, D. F., *Scotland's Shifting Population, 1770–1850* (Glasgow, 1937).

O'Higgins, Rachel, "The Irish Influence on the Chartist Movement," *Past and Present* 20 (November 1961).

Redford, Arthur, and Chaloner, W. H., *Labour Migration in England 1800–1850* (London, 1926; 2d rev. ed., Manchester, 1964).

Roth, Cecil, *A History of the Jews in England* (Oxford, 1941).

Shannon, H. A., "Migration and the Growth of London, 1841–1891," *Economic History Review* 5 (1935), 79–85.

Snell, Harry, *The Foreigner in England* (London, 1904).

Walvin, James, *Black and White: The Negro in English Society 1555–1945* (London, 1973).

Welch, Ruth, *Migration Research and Migration in Britain* (Birmingham, 1970).
White, Jerry, *Rothschild Buildings: Life in an East End Tenement Block 1887–1920* (London, 1980).
Zubrzycki, Jerzy, *Polish Immigrants in Britain. A Study of Adjustment* (The Hague, 1956).

GREECE

Migration from Greece to other European countries remained a middle-class phenomenon before the 1960s. As in the case of its neighbor to the north, Bulgaria, a considerable proportion of migration from Greece to North America followed the pattern of a swift rise into the lower middle class.

Enepekides, P., *Griechische Handelsgesellschaften und Kaufleute in Wien* (Thessaloniki, 1959).

HUNGARY

Emigration from Hungary to other parts of the Austro-Hungarian empire or to other European countries has received little attention. The recent study by J. Puskás explains reasons for emigration in considerable detail.

Braun, Marcus, *Immigration Abuses. Glimpses of Hungary and Hungarians* (New York, 1906; new edition, 1972).
Budai, Barna, "A Pool szerződés és a kivándorlás" [The pool contract and emigration], in *Magyar Gazdák Szemléje* [Hungarian Farmers' Review] 1 (1911).
Puskás, Julianna, *From Hungary to the United States (1880–1914)* (Budapest, 1982).
A magyar szent korona országainak kivándorlása és visszavándorlása 1899–1913 [Emigration and remigration in the countries of the Hungarian sacred crown] (Magyar Statisztikai Központi Hivatal, Magyar Statisztikai Közlemének [Hungarian Statistical Publications], New Series 67).
Rácz, István, *A paraszti migráció és politikai megítélése Magyarországon 1849–1914* [Peasant migration and its political assessment in Hungary, 1849–1914] (Budapest, 1980).
Tonelli, Sándor, "Utazás a magyar kivándorlókkal" [Travelling with the Hungarian emigrants], in *Közgazdasági Szemle* (1908), 431.

IRELAND

Migration from Ireland to Great Britain has been studied in detail. The books by J. A. Jackson and L. H. Lees are of particular importance.

Barber, Sarah, SEE Great Britain.
Collins, E. J. T., SEE Great Britain.
Gilley, Sheridan, SEE Great Britain.
Jackson, John Archer, SEE Great Britain.
Lees, Lynn Hollen, SEE Great Britain.

ITALY

The study of migration from Italy produced important works up to the Great Depression: R. Sandron and R. F. Foerster on the whole of migration, A. Sartorius von Waltershausen on Italians in Germany, and a number of studies dealing with Italian workers in Switzerland and France jointly with other in-migrating ethnic groups. The acculturation in France and Belgium up to the first years after World War II was dealt with by R. Clemens, A. Girard, and J.-F. Stoetzel in the early fifties. Recently two broad surveys have helped to make the history of the migration more accessible, Z. Ciuffoletti et al. have published a documentary history; G. Rosoli, the director of the Centro Studi Emigrazione in Rome, has edited a well-documented anthology of essays on Italian emigration since 1876.

Amman, Hektor, SEE Switzerland.
Ascolani, A. and Birindelli, A. M., *Introduzione bibliografica ai problemi delle migrazioni* (Rome, 1971).
Assante, Franca, *Il movimento migratorio italiano dall' unità nazionale ai giorni nostri* (Naples, 1976).
Avagliano, Lucio, *L'emigrazione italiana. Testi e documenti* (Naples, 1976).
Bertelli, L.; Corragnani, G.; and Rosoli, G. F.; eds., *Migrazioni. Catalogo della biblioteca del Centro Studi emigrazione* (Rome, 1972).
Boscardin, Lucio, SEE Switzerland.
Ciuffoletti, Zeffiro, and Degl'Innocenti, Maurizio, eds., *L'emigrazione nella storia d'Italia 1868–1975* (Florence, 1978).
Clemens, René, SEE Belgium.
De Michelis, G., SEE Switzerland.
Foerster, Robert F., *The Italian Emigration of Our Times* (Cambridge, Mass., 1919).
Girard, Alain, and Stoetzel, Jean-François, SEE France.
Habicht, Hans-Martin, SEE Switzerland.
Lorenz, J., SEE Switzerland.
Manzotti, F., *La polemica sull'emigrazione nell'Italia unita* (Città di Castello, 2nd edition, 1968).
Michels, Roberto, SEE Switzerland.
Ministeri Affari Esteri, ed. V. Briani, *Emigrazione e lavoro italiano all'estero. Elementi per un repertorio bibliografico generale* (Rome, 1967).
Rosoli, Gianfausto, ed., *Un secolo di emigrazione italiana, 1876–1976* (Rome, 1978).
Sandron, R., *L'emigrazione italiana. Legislazione, statistiche, accordi internationali, organie servizi statali* (Rome, 1927).
Sartorius von Waltershausen, A., SEE Germany.

NORWAY

Since migration from Norway to other European countries was negligible, no studies of importance exist. The standard work on Norwegian emigration remains that by I. Semmingsen.

Semmingsen, Ingrid, *Veien mot Vest. Utvandringen fra Norge til Amerika, 1825–1865* [The way west. Emigration from Norway to America, 1825–1865] (Oslo, 1941).

POLAND

In recent years emigration from Poland has received much attention. The classic study is, of course, that of W. I. Thomas and F. Znaniecki published in 1927. The concept of a Polish diaspora all over the world, called "Polonia," has given rise to important research, partly concentrated at the Instytut Badań Polonijnych, the Polonia Research Institute, at the Jagiellonian University in Cracow (H. Kubiak, A. Brôzek, G. Babiński et al.). The best survey available is C. Bobińska and A. Pilch, eds., 1975. Numerous Polish and East and West German authors as well as one U.S. scholar have dealt with the acculturation of Polish workers in Germany. Migration to France has been analyzed by Polish and French authors. Because of the small numbers involved, migration to Denmark has only recently been studied.

Bobińska, Celina, and Galos, Adam, "Poland: Land of Mass Migration (19th and 20th Centuries)," in *Poland at the 14th International Congress of Historical Sciences in San Francisco, 1975* (Wroclaw, 1975), pp. 169–209; reprinted in *Les migrations internationales* (Paris, 1980), pp. 467–502.

———, and Pilch, Andrej, eds., *Employment-Seeking Emigrations of the Poles Worldwide in the 19th and 20th Centuries* (Cracow, 1975).

Borowski, Stanislaw, "Emigration from the Polish Territories under German Rule 1815–1914," in *Studia Historiae Oeconomicae* 2 (1967).

Brożek, Andrzej, "Grundzüge der Bevölkerungswanderungen im ehemaligen preußischen Osten im 20. Jahrhundert bis 1944–45" [Outline of population migration in the former Prussian East in the 20th century until 1944–45], in *Tradition und Neubeginn* (Cologne, 1975), pp. 355–66.

———, *Ostflucht na Slasku* ["Ostflucht" in Silesia] (Katowice, 1966).

———, *Robotnicy spoza zaboru pruskiego w przemyśle na Górnym Slasku (1870–1914)* [Workers from outside the Polish territories under German rule in Upper Silesian industry (1870–1914)] (Wroclaw, 1966).

Clemens, René, SEE Belgium.

De Bie, Pierre, SEE Belgium.

Drewniak, Bogustaw, *Emigracja z Pomorza Zachodniego (1816–1914)* [Emigration from Western Pomerania 1816–1914] (Posnan, 1966).

———, *Robotnicy sezonowi na Pomorzu Zachodnim* (1890–1918) [Seasonal workers in Western Pomerania, 1890–1918] (Posnan, 1959).

Gemmeke, F., SEE Germany.

Girard, Alain, and Stoetzel, Jean-François, SEE France.

Janowska, Halina, SEE France and Germany.

Kaczmarek, Czeslaw, SEE France.

Kleßmann, Christoph, SEE Germany.

Lorenz, J., SEE Switzerland.

Murphy, Richard C., SEE Germany.

Murzynowska, Krystyna, SEE Germany.

Nellemann, George, SEE Denmark.

Nichtweiß, J., SEE Germany.

Spustek, Irena, *Polacy w Piotrogrodzie 1914–1917* [Poles in Petrograd, 1914–1917] (Warsaw, 1961).

Thomas, William I., and Znaniecki, Florian, *The Polish Peasant in Europe and America*, 2 vols. (New York, 1927).
Wehler, Hans U., SEE Germany.
Zubrzycki, Jerzy, "Emigration from Poland in the Nineteenth and Twentieth Centuries," in *Population Studies* 1, no. 3 (1953).
————, *Polish Immigrants in Britain* (The Hague, 1956).

RUMANIA

Rumanian migration was of little importance in Europe, and therefore few scholars have devoted interest to it.

Constantinescu, Miron, "La migration des Roumains vers les deux Amériques," in *Les Migrations Internationales de la Fin du XVIIIe Siècle à nos Jours* (Paris, 1980).
Fremde Landarbeiter in Rumänien (Vienna, 1907).
Metes, Stefan, "Emigrari românesti din Transilvania în secole XIII-XX," in *Cercetari de demografie istorica* (Bucarest, 1971).
Morariu, Tiberiu, *Emigrari maramuresene în Transilvania* (Sibiu, 1944).

RUSSIA

Scholarship on migration in Russia, into and out of it, is difficult to assess. Studies on the settlement of the South Russian Plains and Siberia by G. Demko and D. W. Treadgold do not concern labor migration. The early immigration was one of entrepreneurs and artisans. The formation of the Russian working class is dealt with by B. A. Anderson, R. Johnson, and A. G. Rashin. Labor migration from Russia to European metropolitan centers concerned mainly Jews who fled the pogroms to settle in Paris and London. Migration from the Russian empire is, of course, only to a limited extent ethnic Russian migration. Much of it consisted of the members of the numerous ethnic groups that belonged to the empire.

Anderson, Barbara A., *Internal Migration during Modernization in late Nineteenth-Century Russia* (Princeton, N.J., 1980).
Demko, G., *The Russian Colonization of Kazakhstan, 1896–1916* (Bloomington, 1969).
Heller, Otto, *Sibirien: ein anderes Amerika* (Berlin, 1930).
Iatsounski, V.-K., "Le rôle des migrations et de l'accroissement naturel dans la colonisation des nouvelles régions de la Russie," *Annales de Démographie Historique* (1970), 302–8.
Johnson, R., "Peasant Migration and the Russian Working Class: Moscow at the End of the Nineteenth Century," *Slavic Review* 35, no. 4, (1976), 652–64.
Johnson, Robert E., *Peasant and Proletarian: The Working Class of Moscow in the Late Nineteenth Century* (New Brunswick, N.J., 1979).
Leasure, J. W., and Lewis, R. A., "Internal Migration in Russia in the Late Nineteenth Century," *Slavic Review* 27, no. 3 (1968), 375–94.

Rashin, A. G., *Formirovanie Promishlennogo Proletariata v Rossi* [Formation of the industrial proletariat in Russia] (Moscow, 1940).

Treadgold, Donald W., *The Great Siberian Migration. Government and Peasant in Resettlement from Emancipation to the First World War* (Princeton, NJ, 1957).

Von Laue, T., "Russian Peasants in the Factory," *Journal of Economic History* 21, no. 1 (1961), 261–80.

SWEDEN

Swedish migration is probably the best studied in the world since the beginning of the Uppsala Migration Research Project in the early 1960s at the University of Uppsala. Its results concerning North America have been summarized in a collective work edited by Harald Runblom and Hans Norman, *From Sweden to America. A History of the Migration* (Minneapolis and Uppsala, 1976). Most of the studies listed here dealing with migration in Scandinavia and to other parts of Europe have been undertaken in connection with this project.

Åkerman, Sune, "Internal Migration, Industrialization and Urbanisation (1895–1930): A Summary of the Västmanland Study," in *Scandinavian Economic History Review* 23 (1975), 149–58.

———, "Intern befolkningsomflyttning och emigration" [Internal migration and emigration], in *Emigrationen fra Norden indtil 1. Verdenskrig. Rapporter til det Nordiske historikermøde i København 1971* (Copenhagen, 1971).

———, "Rural and Urban Immigration," in *The Scandinavian Economic History Review* 1 (1972), 95–101.

———; Cassel, Per Gunnar; and Johansson, Egil, "Background Variables of Population Mobility: An Attempt at Automatic Interaction Detector Analysis. A Preliminary Research Report," in *The Scandinavian Economic History Review* 1 (1974), 32–60.

Beckman, E., *I tjenst hos främlingar, Svenska utvandrare i Norra Tyskland* [On employment in a foreign country. Swedish emigrants in Northern Germany] (Stockholm, 1885).

Carlsson, Sten, "Emigrationen från Småland och Öland 1861–1930. Social och regional fördelning" [Emigration from Småland and Öland. Social and regional distribution], in *Historielärarnas förenings årsskrift* (1966–1967), 41–63.

Eriksson, Ingrid, and Rogers, John, "Mobility in an Agrarian Community. Practical and Methodological Considerations," in *Aristocrats, Farmers, Proletarians. Essays in Swedish Demographic History* (Uppsala, 1973).

Hannerberg, D.; Hägerstrand, T.; and Odeving, B.; eds., *Migration in Sweden* (Lund, 1957).

Kronborg, Bo, and Nilsson, Thomas, *Stadsflyttare. Industrialisering migration och social mobilitet med utgångspunkt från Halmstad, 1870–1910* [Urban migrants. Industrialization, migration and social mobility on the basis of Halmstad, 1870–1910] (Uppsala, 1975).

Lindberg, John S., *The Background of Swedish Emigration to the United States. An Economic and Sociological Study in the Dynamics of Migration* (Minneapolis, 1930).

Littmarck, R., *Mälardalens nomader* [The nomads of the Lake Mälar valley] (Uppsala, 1930).

Martinius, Sture, *Befolkningsrörlighet under industrialismens inledningsskede i Sverige* [Population mobility in Sweden during the initial phase of industrialism] (Göteborg, 1967).

Moore, J., *Cityward Migration. Swedish Data* (Chicago, 1938).

Nilsson, Runo B. A., "Rallareliv" [The life of railway construction workers] (Diss., Uppsala, 1982).

Norberg, Anders, and Åkerman, Sune, "Migration and The Building of Families. Studies on the Rise of the Lumber Industry in Sweden" in *Aristocrats, Farmers, Proletarians. Essays in Swedish Demographic History* (Uppsala, 1973).

Rondahl, Björn, *Emigration, folkomflyttning och säsongarbete i ett sågvenksdistrikt i södra Hälsingland 1865–1910. Söderala kommun med särskild hänsyn till Ljusne industrisamhälle* [Emigration, internal migration and migrant labor movements in a sawmill district in southern Hälsingland 1865–1910] (Uppsala, 1972).

Rosander, G., *Herrarbete. Dalfolkets säsongvisa arbetsvandringar i jämförande belysning* [Work for masters. Seasonal labor migration from Dalarna in comparative perspective] (Uppsala, 1967).

Willerslev, R., "Netto vandringen fra Sverige til Danmark 1850–1910. En komparativ undersøgelse," *Scandia* 45 (1979), 83–106.

Wirén, Agnes, *Uppbrott från örtagård. Utvandring från Blekinge under begynnelseskedet till och med år 1870* [The initial phase of emigration from Blekinge län up to 1870] (Lund, 1975).

SWITZERLAND

Switzerland, with the highest percentage of foreign workers in Europe throughout the history of labor migration, has been studied in detail. Acculturation of Italians has received special emphasis. The awareness that foreigners were there to stay has served as a scholarly impetus. But the recurrent waves of anti-alien sentiment also have given rise to studies measuring integration and outlining policies to achieve that goal.

Addor, Georges, *De l'assimilation des étrangers en Suisse* (Zürich, 1913).

Amman, Hektor, *Die Italiener in der Schweiz* (Basle, 1917).

Boscardin, Lucio, "Die italienische Einwanderung in die Schweiz mit besonderer Berücksichtigung der Jahre 1946–1959" (Diss., Basle, 1962).

De Michelis, G., *L'emigrazione italiana nella Svizzera* (Rome, 1903).

Habicht, Hans-Martin, *Probleme der italienischen Fremdarbeiter im Kanton St. Gallen vor dem Ersten Weltkrieg* (Zürich, 1977).

Hagmann, Hermann-Michel, *Les travailleurs étrangers. Chance et tourment de la Suisse* (Lausanne, 1966).

Lorenz, J., *Polnische Arbeiter in der Schweiz* (Zürich, 1910).

———, *Zur Italienerfrage in der Schweiz* (Zürich, 1907).

Michels, Roberto, *Le colonie italiane in Svizzera durante la guerra* (Rome, 1922).

Perrenoud, Alfred, "Les migrations en Suisse sous l'Ancien Régime: quelques problèmes," *Annales de démographie historique* (1970), 251–59.

Raymond-Duchesal, Claire, *Les étrangers en Suisse* (Geneva, 1929).

YUGOSLAVIA

Immigration to the areas of the Yugoslav peoples has received scholarly attention because it coincided with the export of capital into that region before World War I. Emigration at that time was mainly to North America, partly to other sections of the Austro-Hungarian empire. Several research centers specialize in the study of migration before 1945. Among these are the Matica Iseljenika Srbije in Belgrade (Serbia), the Matica Iseljenika Hrvatske and the Zavod za Migracije i Narodnosti in Zagreb (Croatia), and several institutions in Ljubljana (Slovenia). The Center for Migration Studies in Zagreb and the Center for Regional Studies in Belgrade are more concerned with present-day migration to Northern European countries since the 1950s, return migration, and the underlying economic causes.

Cvijic, Jovan, *La Péninsule Balkanique. Géographie Humaine* (Paris, 1918).

Ekmecic, Milorad, "The International and Intercontinental Migration Movements from the Yugoslav Lands from the End of the XVIIIth Century till 1941," in *Les migrations internationales de la fin du XVIIIᵉ siècle à nos jours* (Paris, 1980).

Lenoch, Ivo, *Suedslaviens ueberseeische Auswanderung* (Split, 1928).

Rosambert, André, *Les Colonies Lorraines du Banat Yougoslave* (Nancy, 1931).

———, *Emigrations et implantations occidentales en Europe Sudorientale* (Nancy, 1952).

INDEX

ABOUT THE CONTRIBUTORS

Klaus J. Bade is Professor of Modern History at the University of Osnabrück, West Germany. He held a John F. Kennedy Memorial Research Fellowship at Harvard University in 1976–1977 and has directed several research projects on modern German economic and social history as well as on the history of the German colonial empire 1884–1914/18. He has published books on German imperialism and more recently on migration in Germany: *Vom Auswanderungsland zum Einwanderungsland? Deutschland 1880 bis 1980.* (Berlin, 1983); (ed.), *Auswanderer–Wanderarbeiter–Gastarbeiter: Revölkerung, Arbeitsmarkt und Wanderung in Deutschland seit der Mitte des 19. Jahrhunderts*, 2 vols., (Ostfildern, 1984).

Lizabeth Cohen is completing a Ph.D. at the University of California, Berkeley. Her dissertation is a social history of working-class Chicago during the 1920s and the Great Depression. She has worked at a number of history museums on projects interpreting material culture.

Lothar Elsner is Professor of General History at the University of Rostock, German Democratic Republic. He specializes in the international labor movement. His numerous publications on twentieth-century history concentrate on migration, employment of foreign workers, and policies on foreign workers developed by West European governments. He is general editor of the seminal series *Fremdarbeiterpolitik des Imperialismus* and is completing a study of governmental attitudes toward foreign workers in Germany since 1890.

Heinz Faßmann is a scholar at the Austrian Academy of Sciences. He teaches empirical methods in social sciences at the University of Vienna. He attended a post-graduate seminar at the Ford Institute and in 1983 received the Camillo-Sitte Prize awarded jointly by the Technical University of Vienna and the Austrian Department of Science and Research. His work on labor migration to Vienna has been completed and a book about guest workers in Austria was published in 1984.

Monika Glettler has held several fellowships for archival research in Austria, Czechoslovakia, and Hungary. She was Visiting Associate Professor at Columbia University, New York, in 1980–1981. In 1977 she was awarded a prize by the Theodor-Körner-Stiftungsfonds in Vienna for her book *Sokol und Arbeiterturnvereine der Wiener Tschechen bis 1914* and in 1981 she received the Anton-Gindely-Preis in Vienna for her books *Die Wiener Tschechen um 1900* and *Pittsburg–Wien–Budapest. Programm und Praxis bei der Auswanderung der ungarischen Slovaken nach Amerika um 1900.* She teaches at the University of Munich.

Nancy L. Green (Ph.D., University of Chicago, 1980) teaches migration studies and French history at the Ecole des Hautes Etudes en Sciences Sociales in Paris and

Stanford University in Tours. She has recently completed a book on Jewish immigrant workers in Paris, 1881–1914.

Eric J. Hobsbawm was educated at Vienna, Berlin, London, and Cambridge, where he was a Fellow of King's College from 1945 to 1955. Until his retirement, he was Professor of History at Birkbeck College, University of London. He has also been visiting professor at Stanford and MIT. His main publications include *Primitive Rebels* (1959), *The Age of Revolution* (1962), *Labouring Men* (1964), and, with George Rudé, *Captain Swing* (1969), and *Industry and Empire* (1968).

Dirk Hoerder teaches North American social history at the Univesity of Bremen, West Germany. He has specialized in the common people during the era of the American Revolution and in international labor migration from the 1870s to the 1930s. His publications include *Crowd Action in Revolutionary Massachusetts, 1765–1780* (New York, 1977) and *American Labor and Immigration History: Recent European Research* (Urbana, Ill., 1983).

Christoph Kleßmann is Professor of Contemporary History at the University of Bielefeld, West Germany. His main subjects are Polish and German history. He has paid particular attention to the acculturation of Polish workers in the Ruhr district. One of his recent publications is a history of Germany, 1945–1955, *Die doppelte Staatsgründung* (Göttingen, 1982).

Frances Kraljic teaches American history at the City University of New York, and Kingsborough Community College, Brooklyn, New York. She participated in the Fulbright Conference on Ethnicity in Dubrovnik, Yugoslavia, and has received grants from IREX and the Immigration History Research Center, Minnesota. She currently holds a National Endowment for the Humanities Fellowship in the History and Humanities Program at the CUNY Graduate Center.

Robert Lewis Mikkelsen is presently a Secondary School Lecturer in Harstad, Norway. He studied at the University of Wisconsin, Madison, and at the University of Oslo. In 1981 he served as the Norwegian representative at the American Studies Curriculum Project held in Washington, D.C. He lectured in American Civilization at the University of Tromsø, Norway, during the academic year 1982–1983. Mr. Mikkelsen was cooperating language specialist for Norwegian-language labor periodicals in the United States and Canada within the "Labor Newspapers Preservation Project" coordinated at the University of Bremen from 1979 to 1983.

Hans Norman, a member of the Uppsala Migration Research Project, has studied migration patterns, social mobility, and demographic structures in an emigration area, Örebro County, and an immigrant destination, Worcester, Mass. Together with Harald Ronblom he prepared the *Nordisk Emigrationsatlas* [Nordic emigration atlas], 2 vols. (Gärle, 1980).

Claudius H. Riegler (Ph.D., University of Erlangen-Nürnberg, 1982) is now doing research on the implementation of environmental policies at the International Institute for Comparative Social Research, Science Center, West Berlin. He teaches language to first- and second-generation German immigrant children in Sweden and organizes education programs at Öja Course Center in Southern Sweden, where he lives. He is author of a book on labor migration from Sweden to Germany, 1868–1914, and coauthor of *The Immigrants' Swedish History*, both published in 1984.

Gianfausto Rosoli, who is at the Centro Studi Emigrazione Roma (CSER), is director of the quarterly *Studi Emigrazione* and author of many essays and research projects on Italian migration for national and international institutions including the Foreign Ministry, the National Council for Research, UNESCO and ILO. He has edited *Un secolo di emigrazione italiana: 1876–1976* (Rome, CSER, 1978) and coauthored, with P. Cannistraro, *Emigrazione Chiesa e fascismo. Lo scioglimento dell' Opera Bonomelli (1922–1928)* (Rome, 1979).

Harald Runblom has specialized in Swedish migration to Latin America and to Canada. He is editor, with H. Norman, of *From Sweden to America. A History of the Migration. A Collective Work of the Uppsala Migration Research Project* (Minneapolis and Uppsals, 1976).

Jonathan D. Sarna is Assistant Professor of American Jewish History at the Cincinnati campus of Hebrew Union College. He is the author of *Jacksonian Jew: The Two Worlds of Mordecai Noah* (New York, 1981) and of numerous articles.

William H. Sewell (Ph.D., University of California, Berkeley, 1971) teaches history and sociology at the University of Arizona. He has published *Work and Revolution in France: The Language of Labor from the Old Regime to 1848* (Cambridge, Mass., 1980). A book on social structure, migration, and social mobility in nineteenth-century Marseille is forthcoming from Cambridge University Press in 1984.

Lars-Göran Tedebrand has been lecturing at the Department of History, Uppsala University, since 1969 and was appointed to the Swedish Humanistic-Social Science Research Council Professorship in Historical Demography at the University of Umeå in 1982. He has dealt with migrational processes and social change during the industrialization of the lumber areas in northern Sweden, with emphasis on emigration to the United States and Canada. His publications include *Västernorrland och Nordamerika 1875–1913. Utvandring och återinvandring* [Emigration from Västernorrland County to North America and re-immigration] (Uppsala, 1972) and Selånger. En sockens historia [Selånger. A history of a parish] (1983).

Keijo Virtanen is the Acting Professor of History of Civilization and teaches general history at the University of Turku. He is closely connected with the University of Turku migration research project and is the director of a new project on the impact of American culture in Finland. He has studied and researched extensively in the United States and Canada. His publications concentrate on migration history, American cultural history, and Finnish socialist and communist movements.